THE A+ EXAMS GUIDE
Second Edition

Preparation Guide for the CompTIA Essentials,
220–602, 220–603, and 220–604 Exams

CHRISTOPHER A. CRAYTON

TECHNICAL EDITOR BRIAN CULP

Charles River Media
A part of Course Technology, Cengage Learning

COURSE TECHNOLOGY
CENGAGE Learning™

Australia • Brazil • Japan • Korea • Mexico • Singapore • Spain • United Kingdom • United States

COURSE TECHNOLOGY
CENGAGE Learning™

**Publisher and General Manager,
Course Technology PTR:** Stacy L. Hiquet

Associate Director of Marketing: Sarah Panella

Manager of Editorial Services: Heather Talbot

Marketing Manager: Mark Hughes

Acquisitions Editor: Jennifer Blaney

Project Editor: Dan Foster, Scribe Tribe

Technical Reviewer: Brian Culp

CRM Editorial Services Coordinator: Erin Johnson

Copy Editor: Julie McNamee

Interior Layout Tech: Judith Littlefield

Cover Designer: Tyler Creative Services

Indexer: Jerilyn Sproston

Proofreader: Julie Grady

For product information and technology assistance, contact us at
Cengage Learning Customer & Sales Support, 1-800-354-9706

For permission to use material from this text or product, submit all requests online at **cengage.com/permissions**
Further permissions questions can be emailed to
permissionrequest@cengage.com

Library of Congress Control Number: 2007939360
ISBN-13: 978-1-58450-566-2
ISBN-10: 1-58450-566-4

Course Technology
25 Thomson Place
Boston, MA 02210
USA

Cengage Learning is a leading provider of customized learning solutions with office locations around the globe, including Singapore, the United Kingdom, Australia, Mexico, Brazil, and Japan. Locate your local office at: **international.cengage.com/region**

Cengage Learning products are represented in Canada by Nelson Education, Ltd.

For your lifelong learning solutions, visit **courseptr.com**
Visit our corporate website at **cengage.com**

Printed in the United States of America
1 2 3 4 5 6 7 11 10 09 08

Dedicated to all my students and all certification exam test takers who have the courage to change their lives by achieving certification success!

To Nancy and Ken Crayton, Amanda, Theo and Gizmo, Scott Barr, Hoss, David Howard, Carol and Brodie Howard, Alex Butakow and Keiser College, Laura and Nelson Baranes, Linda and Mike Davis, Chip Plyer, Rickey Johnson, Ron Lindsey, Jon Richmond—thank you for your love, guidance, support, and friendship.

This book is also dedicated to all computer book technical authors and teachers I have learned from over the years, including Ron Gilster, William Stanek, Brian Culp, Jean Andrews, Ed Tittle, and Pawan K. Bhardwa.

Contents

Acknowledgments

First and foremost, I would like to thank Jennifer Blaney from Charles River Media publishing for her support and patience throughout this project. Jen has worked with me for several years now and has been very supportive since I first put pen to paper and wrote *A+ Adaptive Exams* in 2002.

A sincere thank you to Charles River Media publishing for their support and dedication to the second edition of this book. Their fine work brought the first edition of my book to "Best Selling" status, and it is greatly appreciated.

Thank you to the chief technical editor of this book, Brian Culp. Brian is one of my favorite authors. It has been a privilege and an honor to have him involved with this project.

A very special thank you to Bala Swaminathan, director of Education and Training at CompTIA, for his continued support of my writings and the CompTIA approval rating.

About the Author

Chris Crayton is a technical consultant, security consultant, and trainer. Formerly, he worked as a networking instructor at Keiser College (2001 Teacher of the Year); as a network administrator for Protocol, an electronic customer relationship management (eCRM) company; and at Eastman Kodak Headquarters as a computer and network specialist. Chris has authored several print and online books, including *Microsoft Windows Vista 70–620 Exam Guide Short Cut* (O'Reilly, 2007), *CompTIA A+ Essentials 220–601 Exam Guide Short Cut* (O'Reilly, 2007), *A+ Adaptive Exams* (Charles River Media, 2002), *The A+ Exams Guide, The A+ Certification and PC Repair Handbook* (Charles River Media, 2005), and *The Security+ Exam Guide* (Charles River Media, 2003). He has also recently co-authored the *CompTIA Security+ Study Guide & DVD Training System, Second Edition* (Syngress, 2007). Chris is also a technical editor/reviewer for several major publishing companies, including Thomson, Pearson, Charles River Media, Wiley, Que, O'Reilly, Syngress, and Apress. He holds MCSE, MCP+I, A+, and Network+ certifications.

1

The CompTIA A+®
Certification Exams

In This Chapter

- The CompTIA A+ Certification Exams and 2006 Exam Objectives
- Registering for the A+ Tests
- Test Site Requirements and a Little Advice
- How Computerized Testing Works
- Your State of Mind
- Useful Tools, Tips, and Study Techniques
- Book Structure and Sample Review Questions

Welcome to the second edition of the very best available tool to help you prepare for and pass the current A+ Certification exams! This book is based on the best selling A+ Exams Guide and has been totally updated to include all of the domains and objectives for the newly released CompTIA A+ exams.

In the next several pages, you will learn the importance of A+ certification and how it can affect your career and personal computing goals. You will learn why you should use this particular book to prepare for the current A+ exams and future certification exams. You will gain insight into the process of scheduling an exam and what to expect when you get to the test site.

If you are interested in gainful employment in the technology industry, you should be certified. The majority of businesses today require applicants to provide proof of certification as a way to show that you are qualified for a selected technical position. If you are applying for a position as a PC technician, network administrator, systems engineer, software engineer, developer, or programmer, A+ certification is normally a minimum requirement or at least a start. If you are already employed and want to enhance your technical job opportunities, as well as your income, A+ certification is for you. Many businesses today require their entire IT staff to be A+ certified. CompTIA states the following regarding the latest A+ exams: "CompTIA A+ certification validates the latest skills needed by today's computer support professionals. It is an international, vendor-neutral certification recognized by major hardware and software vendors, distributors, and resellers. CompTIA A+ confirms a technician's ability to perform tasks such as installation, configuration, diagnosing, preventive maintenance, and basic networking. The exams also cover domains such as security, safety and environmental issues, and communication and professionalism."

THE COMPTIA A+ CERTIFICATION EXAMS AND 2006 EXAM OBJECTIVES

CompTIA has recently updated its A+ exams. To receive the A+ certification credentials, you must pass the A+ Essentials exam (220-601) and one of these exams: 220-602 (IT Technician), 220-603 (Remote Support Technician), or 220-604 (Depot Technician). For your convenience, all of the objectives for each of these exams are provided in this chapter.

Note that CompTIA recommends at least 500 hours of hands-on lab or field experience before taking these tests. We recommend an A+-based training class, six months of hands-on (real world) experience, and the mastering of all questions included in this book and its accompanying CD-ROM.

The CompTIA domains, objectives, concepts, and modules are public knowledge, and are provided in PDF (Portable Document Format) for download at the following CompTIA Web site: *http://certification.comptia.org/a/*.

A+ ESSENTIALS EXAM OBJECTIVES

The CompTIA A+ Essentials exam tests your knowledge of basic computer hardware and operating systems. Questions on the actual exam test your knowledge and skills in installing, upgrading, repairing, configuring, troubleshooting, diagnosing, and optimizing computer systems. The exam also tests your knowledge regarding networks, security, safety, environmental issues, and soft skills (customer service). This exam is meant as a benchmark for entry-level computer service technicians. Table 1.1 shows the A+ Essential domains and their percentage covered on the exam. Following that is the complete list of CompTIA A+ Objectives.

TABLE 1.1   A+ Essentials (220-601) Domains and Percentage of Examination

Domain	Examination Percentage
1.0 Personal Computer Components	21%
2.0 Laptop and Portable Devices	11%
3.0 Operating Systems	21%
4.0 Printers and Scanners	9%
5.0 Networks	12%
6.0 Security	11%
7.0 Safety and Environmental Issues	10%
8.0 Communication and Professionalism	5%
Total	100%

1.0 PERSONAL COMPUTER COMPONENTS

1.1 Identify the Fundamental Principles of Using Personal Computers

- Identify the names, purposes, and characteristics of storage devices:
  - FDD
  - HDD
  - CD/DVD/RW (e.g., drive speeds, media types)
  - Removable storage (e.g., tape drive; solid state, such as thumb drive, flash, and SD cards; USB; external CD-RW; hard drive)
- Identify the names, purposes, and characteristics of motherboards:
  - Form Factor (e.g., ATX/BTX, micro ATX/NLX)
  - Components:
    - Integrated I/Os (e.g., sound, video, USB, serial, IEEE 1394/FireWire, parallel, NIC, modem)
    - Memory slots (e.g., RIMM, DIMM)
    - Processor sockets
    - External cache memory
    - Bus architecture
    - Bus slots (e.g., PCI, AGP, PCIe, AMR, CNR)
    - EIDE/PATA
    - SATA
    - SCSI Technology
    - Chipsets
    - BIOS/CMOS/Firmware
    - Riser card/daughterboard

- Identify the names, purposes, and characteristics of power supplies, for example, AC adapter, ATX, proprietary, voltage.
- Identify the names, purposes, and characteristics of processors/CPUs:
  - CPU chips (e.g., AMD, Intel)
  - CPU technologies:
    - Hyperthreading
    - Dual core
    - Throttling
    - Micro code (MMX)
    - Overclocking
    - Cache
    - VRM
    - Speed (real versus actual)
    - 32 bit versus 64 bit
- Identify the names, purposes, and characteristics of memory:
  - Types of memory (e.g., DRAM, SRAM, SDRAM, DDR/DDR2, RAMBUS)
  - Operational characteristics:
    - Memory chips (8, 16, 32)
    - Parity versus nonparity
    - ECC versus non-ECC
    - Single-sided versus double-sided
- Identify the names, purposes, and characteristics of display devices, for example, projectors, CRT, and LCD:
  - Connector types (e.g., VGA, DVI/HDMi, S-Video, Component/RGB)
  - Settings (e.g., V-hold, refresh rate, resolution)
- Identify the names, purposes, and characteristics of input devices, for example, mouse, keyboard, bar code reader, multimedia (e.g., web and digital cameras, MIDI, microphones), biometric devices, and touch screen.
- Identify the names, purposes, and characteristics of adapter cards:
  - Video, including PCI/PCIe and AGP
  - Multimedia
  - I/O (SCSI, serial, USB, parallel)
  - Communications, including network and modem
- Identify the names, purposes, and characteristics of ports and cables, for example, USB 1.1 and 2.0, parallel, serial, IEEE 1394/FireWire, RJ45 and RJ11, PS2/Mini-DIN, centronics (e.g., mini, 36), and multimedia (e.g., 1/8 connector, MIDI Coaxial, SPDIF).
- Identify the names, purposes, and characteristics of cooling systems, for example, heat sinks, CPU and case fans, liquid cooling systems, and thermal compound.

1.2 Install, Configure, Optimize, and Upgrade Personal Computer Components

- Add, remove, and configure internal and external storage devices:
  - Drive preparation of internal storage devices, including format/filesystems and imaging technology
- Install display devices.
- Add, remove, and configure basic input and multimedia devices.

1.3 Identify Tools, Diagnostic Procedures, and Troubleshooting Techniques for Personal Computer Components

- Recognize the basic aspects of troubleshooting theory:
  - Perform backups before making changes.
  - Assess a problem systematically, and divide large problems into smaller components to be analyzed individually.
  - Verify even the obvious, determine whether the problem is something simple, and make no assumptions.
  - Research ideas and establish priorities.
  - Document findings, actions, and outcomes.
- Identify and apply basic diagnostic procedures and troubleshooting techniques:
  - Identify the problem, including questioning the user and identifying user changes to computer.
  - Analyze the problem, including potential causes, and make an initial determination of software and/or hardware problems.
  - Test related components, including inspection, connections, hardware/software configurations, and device manager, and consult vendor documentation.
  - Evaluate results and take additional steps if needed, such as consultation, use of alternate resources, and manuals.
  - Document activities and outcomes.
- Recognize and isolate issues with display, power, basic input devices, storage, memory, thermal, and POST errors (e.g., BIOS, hardware).
- Apply basic troubleshooting techniques to check for problems (e.g., thermal issues; error codes; power; connections, including cables and/or pins; compatibility; functionality; software/drivers) with components:
  - Motherboards
  - Power supply
  - Processors/CPUs
  - Memory
  - Display devices
  - Input devices
  - Adapter cards

■ Recognize the names, purposes, characteristics, and appropriate application of tools, for example, BIOS, self-test, hard drive self-test, and software diagnostics test.

1.4 Perform Preventive Maintenance on Personal Computer Components

■ Identify and apply basic aspects of preventive maintenance theory:
  • Visual/audio inspection
  • Driver/firmware updates
  • Scheduling preventive maintenance
  • Use of appropriate repair tools and cleaning materials
  • Ensuring proper environment
■ Identify and apply common preventive maintenance techniques for devices such as input devices and batteries.

2.0 LAPTOPS AND PORTABLE DEVICES

2.1 Identify the Fundamental Principles of Using Laptops and Portable Devices

■ Identify names, purposes, and characteristics of laptop-specific items:
  • Form factors, such as memory and hard drives
  • Peripherals (e.g., docking station, port replicator, media/accessory bay)
  • Expansion slots (e.g., PCMCIA I, II, and III; card; express bus)
  • Ports (e.g., mini PCI slot)
  • Communication connections (e.g., Bluetooth, infrared, cellular WAN, Ethernet)
  • Power and electrical input devices (e.g., autoswitching and fixed-input power supplies, batteries)
  • LCD technologies (e.g., active and passive matrix; resolution, such as XGA, SXGA+, UXGA, WUXGA; contrast ratio; native resolution)
  • Input devices (e.g., stylus/digitizer, function (Fn) keys, and pointing devices such as touch pad, point stick/track point)
■ Identify and distinguish between mobile and desktop motherboards and processors, including throttling, power management, and WiFi.

2.2 Install, Configure, Optimize, and Upgrade Laptops and Portable Devices

■ Configure power management:
  • Identify the features of BIOS-ACPI.
  • Identify the difference between suspend, hibernate, and standby.
■ Demonstrate safe removal of laptop-specific hardware, such as peripherals, hot-swappable devices, and nonhot-swappable devices

2.3 Identify Tools, Basic Diagnostic Procedures, and Troubleshooting Techniques for Laptops and Portable Devices

■ Use procedures and techniques to diagnose power conditions, video, keyboard, pointer and wireless card issues:
- Verify AC power (e.g., LEDs, swap AC adapter).
- Verify DC power.
- Remove unneeded peripherals.
- Plug in external monitor.
- Toggle Fn keys.
- Check LCD cutoff switch.
- Verify backlight functionality and pixilation.
- Stylus issues (e.g., digitizer problems).
- Unique laptop keypad issues.
- Antenna wires.

2.4 Perform Preventive Maintenance on Laptops and Portable Devices

■ Identify and apply common preventive maintenance techniques for laptops and portable devices, for example, cooling devices; hardware and video cleaning materials; operating environments, including temperature and air quality; storage; transportation; and shipping.

3.0 Operating Systems

Unless otherwise noted, operating systems include Microsoft Windows 2000, XP Professional, XP Home, and Media Center.

NOTE

3.1 Identify the Fundamentals of Using Operating Systems

■ Identify differences among operating systems (e.g., Mac, Windows, Linux) and describe operating system revision levels, including GUI, system requirements, and application and hardware compatibility.
■ Identify names, purposes, and characteristics of the primary operating system components, including the registry, virtual memory, and the filesystem.
■ Describe features of operating system interfaces:
- Windows Explorer
- My Computer
- Control Panel
- Command prompt
- My Network Places

- Taskbar/systray
- Start menu
■ Identify the names, locations, purposes, and characteristics of operating system files:
- BOOT.INI
- NTLDR
- NTDETECT.COM
- NTBOOTDD.SYS
- Registry data files
■ Identify concepts and procedures for creating, viewing, and managing disks, directories, and files in operating systems:
- Disks (e.g., active, primary, extended, and logical partitions)
- Filesystems (e.g., FAT 32, NTFS)
- Directory structures (e.g., create folders, navigate directory structures)
- Files (e.g., creation, extensions, attributes, permissions)

3.2 Install, Configure, Optimize, and Upgrade Operating Systems

References to upgrading from Windows 95 and NT may be made.

■ Identify procedures for installing operating systems, including the following:
- Verification of hardware compatibility and minimum requirements
- Installation methods (e.g., boot media such as CD, floppy, or USB; network installation; drive imaging)
- Operating system installation options (e.g., attended/unattended, filesystem type, network configuration)
- Disk preparation order (e.g., start installation, partition and format drive)
- Device driver configuration (e.g., install and upload device drivers)
- Verification of installation
■ Identify procedures for upgrading operating systems, including the following:
- Upgrade considerations (e.g., hardware, application and/or network compatibility)
- Implementation (e.g., backup data, install additional Windows components)
■ Install/add a device, including loading and adding device drivers and required software:
- Determining whether permissions are adequate for performing the task
- Installing device drivers (e.g., automated and/or manual search and installation of device drivers)
- Using unsigned drivers (e.g., driver signing)
- Verifying installation of the driver (e.g., device manager and functionality)

■ Identify procedures and utilities used to optimize operating systems, for example, virtual memory, hard drives, temporary files, service, startup, and applications.

3.3 Identify Tools, Diagnostic Procedures, and Troubleshooting Techniques for Operating Systems

■ Identify basic boot sequences, methods, and utilities for recovering operating systems:
  • Boot methods (e.g., safe mode, recovery console, boot to restore point)
  • Automated System Recovery (ASR) (e.g., Emergency Repair Disk [ERD])
■ Identify and apply diagnostic procedures and troubleshooting techniques:
  • Identify the problem by questioning the user and identifying user changes to the computer.
  • Analyze the problem, including potential causes and the initial determination of software and/or hardware problems.
  • Test related components, including connections, hardware/software configurations, and device manager, and consult vendor documentation.
  • Evaluate results, and take additional steps if needed, such as consultation, alternate resources, and manuals.
  • Document activities and outcomes.
■ Recognize and resolve common operational issues, such as bluescreen, system lock-up, input/output device, application install, start or load, and Windows-specific printing problems (e.g., print spool stalled, incorrect/incompatible driver for print).
■ Explain common error messages and codes:
  • Boot (e.g., invalid boot disk, inaccessible boot drive, missing NTLDR)
  • Startup (e.g., device/service failed to start, device/program in registry not found)
  • Event Viewer
  • Registry
  • Windows reporting
■ Identify the names, locations, purposes, and characteristics of operating system utilities:
  • Disk management tools (e.g., DEFRAG, NTBACKUP, CHKDSK, Format)
  • System management tools (e.g., device and task manager, MSCONFIG.EXE)
  • File management tools (e.g., Windows Explorer, ATTRIB.EXE)

3.4 Perform Preventive Maintenance on Operating Systems

■ Describe common utilities for performing preventive maintenance on operating systems, for example, software and Windows updates (e.g., service packs), scheduled backups/restore, and restore points.

4.0 PRINTERS AND SCANNERS

4.1 Identify the Fundamental Principles of Using Printers and Scanners

■ Identify differences between types of printer and scanner technologies (e.g., laser, inkjet, thermal, solid ink, impact).

■ Identify names, purposes, and characteristics of printer and scanner components (e.g., memory, driver, firmware) and consumables (e.g., toner, ink cartridge, paper).

■ Identify the names, purposes, and characteristics of interfaces used by printers and scanners, including port and cable types:
  - Parallel
  - Network (e.g., NIC, print servers)
  - USB
  - Serial
  - IEEE 1394/FireWire
  - Wireless (e.g., Bluetooth, 802.11, infrared)
  - SCSI

4.2 Identify Basic Concepts of Installing, Configuring, Optimizing, and Upgrading Printers and Scanners

■ Install and configure printers/scanners:
  - Power and connect the device using the local or network port.
  - Install and update the device driver, and calibrate the device.
  - Configure options and default settings.
  - Print a test page.

■ Optimize printer performance, for example, printer settings such as tray switching, print spool settings, device calibration, media types, and paper orientation.

4.3 Identify Tools, Basic Diagnostic Procedures, and Troubleshooting Techniques for Printers and Scanners

■ Gather information about printer/scanner problems:
  - Identify symptom.
  - Review device error codes, computer error messages, and history (e.g., event log, user reports).
  - Print or scan a test page.
  - Use appropriate generic or vendor-specific diagnostic tools, including Web-based utilities.

- Review and analyze collected data:
  - Establish probable causes.
  - Review service documentation.
  - Review knowledge base, and define and isolate the problem (e.g., software versus hardware, driver, connectivity, printer).
- Identify solutions to identified printer/scanner problems:
  - Define specific cause, and apply the fix.
  - Replace consumables as needed.
  - Verify functionality, and get user acceptance of the problem fix.

5.0 Networks

5.1 Identify the Fundamental Principles of Networks

- Describe basic networking concepts:
  - Addressing
  - Bandwidth
  - Status indicators
  - Protocols (e.g., TCP/IP, including IP; classful subnet; IPX/SPX, including NWLINK; NETBEUI/NETBIOS)
  - Full-duplex, half-duplex
  - Cabling (e.g., twisted pair, coaxial cable, fiber optic, RS-232, USB, IEEE 1394/FireWire)
  - Networking models, including peer-to-peer and client/server
- Identify names, purposes, and characteristics of the common network cables:
  - Plenum/PVC
  - UTP (e.g., CAT3, CAT5/5e, CAT6)
  - STP
  - Fiber (e.g., single-mode and multimode)
- Identify names, purposes, and characteristics of network connectors (e.g., RJ45 and RJ11, ST/SC/LC, MT-RJ).
- Identify names, purposes, and characteristics (e.g., definition, speed, connections) of technologies for establishing connectivity:
  - LAN/WAN
  - ISDN
  - Broadband (e.g., DSL, cable, satellite)
  - Dial-up
  - Wireless (all 802.11)
  - Infrared
  - Bluetooth

- Cellular
- VoIP

5.2 Install, Configure, Optimize, and Upgrade Networks

- Install and configure network cards (physical address).
- Install, identify, and obtain wired and wireless connections.

5.3 Identify Tools, Diagnostic Procedures, and Troubleshooting Techniques for Networks

- Explain status indicators, for example, speed, connection, activity lights, and wireless signal strength.

6.0 SECURITY

6.1 Identify the Fundamental Principles of Security

- Identify names, purposes, and characteristics of hardware and software security:
  - Hardware deconstruction/recycling
  - Smart cards/biometrics (e.g., key fobs, cards, chips, scans)
  - Authentication technologies (e.g., user name, password, biometrics, smart cards)
  - Malicious software protection (e.g., viruses, Trojans, worms, spam, spyware, adware, grayware)
  - Software firewalls
  - Filesystem security (e.g., FAT32, NTFS)
- Identify names, purposes, and characteristics of wireless security:
  - Wireless encryption (e.g., WEP.x, WPA.x) and client configuration
  - Access points (e.g., disable DHCP/use static IP, change SSID from default, disable SSID broadcast, MAC filtering, change default username and password, update firmware, firewall)
- Identify names, purposes, and characteristics of data and physical security:
  - Data access (basic local security policy)
  - Encryption technologies
  - Backups
  - Data migration
  - Data/remnant removal
  - Password management
  - Locking workstation (e.g., hardware, operating system)

■ Describe importance and process of incidence reporting.

■ Recognize and respond appropriately to social engineering situations.

6.2 Install, Configure, Upgrade and Optimize Security

■ Install, configure, upgrade, and optimize hardware, software, and data security:
  - BIOS
  - Smart cards
  - Authentication technologies
  - Malicious software protection
  - Data access (basic local security policy)
  - Backup procedures and access to backups
  - Data migration
  - Data/remnant removal

6.3 Identify Tool, Diagnostic Procedures, and Troubleshooting Techniques for Security

■ Diagnose and troubleshoot hardware, software, and data security issues:
  - BIOS
  - Smart cards, biometrics
  - Authentication technologies
  - Malicious software
  - Filesystem (e.g., FAT32, NTFS)
  - Data access (e.g., basic local security policy)
  - Backup
  - Data migration

6.4 Perform Preventive Maintenance for Computer Security

■ Implement software security preventive maintenance techniques, such as installing service packs and patches and training users about malicious software prevention technologies.

7.0 SAFETY AND ENVIRONMENTAL ISSUES

7.1 Describe the Aspects and Importance of Safety and Environmental Issues

■ Identify potential safety hazards and take preventive action.

■ Use Material Safety Data Sheets (MSDS) or equivalent documentation and appropriate equipment documentation.

■ Use appropriate repair tools.

■ Describe methods to handle environmental and human (e.g., electrical, chemical, physical) accidents, including incident reporting.

7.2 Identify Potential Hazards, and Implement Proper Safety Procedures, Including ESD Precautions and Procedures, Safe Work Environment, and Equipment Handling

7.3 Identify Proper Disposal Procedures for Batteries, Display Devices, and Chemical Solvents and Cans

8.0 COMMUNICATION AND PROFESSIONALISM

8.1 Use Good Communication Skills, Including Listening and Tact/Discretion, When Communicating with Customers and Colleagues

■ Use clear, concise, and direct statements.
■ Allow the customer to complete statements, and avoid interrupting.
■ Clarify customer statements by asking pertinent questions.
■ Avoid using jargon, abbreviations, and acronyms.
■ Listen to customers.

8.2 Use Job-Related Professional Behavior, Including Notation of Privacy, Confidentiality, and Respect for the Customer and the Customer's Property

■ Behavior:
  • Maintain a positive attitude and tone of voice.
  • Avoid arguing with customers or becoming defensive.
  • Do not minimize customers' problems.
  • Avoid being judgmental or insulting, or calling the customer names.
  • Avoid distractions or interruptions when talking with customers.
■ Property:
  • Telephone, laptop, desktop computer, printer, monitor, and so on.

220-602 IT TECHNICIAN EXAM OBJECTIVES

The CompTIA A+ 220-602 IT Technician Exam is meant for those who work or intend to work in mobile, technical environments with a lot of customer or client interaction. Examples of these jobs include: Enterprise Technician, IT Administrator, Field Service Technician, or PC Technician.

It is a good idea to have already passed the A+ Essentials exam before taking this exam. In fact, CompTIA highly recommends it. If you have already taken and passed the A+ Essentials exam, and you pass this exam, you will be awarded the CompTIA A+ certification with the IT Technician designation. Table 1.2 shows the 220-602 exam domains and the percentage of the examination directed toward each domain. Notice that the domains are the same as the Essentials exam. However, the percentage of the examination directed at each domain differs. Following Table 1.2, you will see a detailed list of 220-602 exam objectives.

TABLE 1.2   IT Technician (220-602) Domains and Percentage of Examination

Domain	Percentage of Examination
1.0 Personal Computer Components	18%
2.0 Laptop and Portable Devices	9%
3.0 Operating Systems	20%
4.0 Printers and Scanners	14%
5.0 Networks	11%
6.0 Security	8%
7.0 Safety and Environmental Issues	5%
8.0 Communication and Professionalism	15%
Total	100%

1.0 PERSONAL COMPUTER COMPONENTS

1.1 Install, Configure, Optimize, and Upgrade Personal Computer Components

■ Add, remove, and configure personal computer components, including selection and installation of appropriate components:
  - Storage devices
  - Motherboards
  - Power supplies
  - Processors/CPUs
  - Memory
  - Display devices
  - Input devices (e.g., basic, specialty, multimedia)
  - Adapter cards
  - Cooling systems

1.2 Identify Tools, Diagnostic Procedures, and Troubleshooting Techniques for Personal Computer Components

- Identify and apply basic diagnostic procedures and troubleshooting techniques:
  - Isolate and identify the problem using visual and audible inspection of components and minimum configuration.
- Recognize and isolate issues with peripherals, multimedia, specialty input devices, internal and external storage, and CPUs.
- Identify the steps used to troubleshoot components (e.g., check proper seating, installation, appropriate components, settings, and current driver):
  - Power supply
  - Processors/CPUs and motherboards
  - Memory
  - Adapter cards
  - Display and input devices
- Recognize names, purposes, characteristics, and appropriate application of tools:
  - Multimeter
  - Antistatic pad and wrist strap
  - Specialty hardware/tools
  - Loop-back plugs
  - Cleaning products (e.g., vacuum, cleaning pads)

1.3 Perform Preventive Maintenance of Personal Computer Components

- Identify and apply common preventive maintenance techniques for personal computer components:
  - Display devices (e.g., cleaning, ventilation)
  - Power devices (e.g., appropriate source, such as power strip, surge protector, ventilation and cooling)
  - Input devices (e.g., covers)
  - Storage devices (e.g., software tools, such as Disk Defragmenter and cleaning of optics and tape heads)
  - Thermally sensitive devices, such as motherboards, CPUs, adapter cards, memory (e.g., cleaning, air flow)

2.0 LAPTOPS AND PORTABLE DEVICES

2.1 Identify Fundamental Principles of Using Laptops and Portable Devices

- Identify appropriate applications for laptop-specific communication connections, such as Bluetooth, infrared, cellular WAN, and Ethernet.

- Identify appropriate laptop-specific power and electrical input devices, and determine how amperage and voltage can affect performance.
- Identify the major components of the LCD, including inverter, screen, and video card.

2.2 Install, Configure, Optimize, and Upgrade Laptops and Portable Devices

- Describe removal of laptop-specific hardware such as peripherals, hot-swappable, and nonhot-swappable devices.
- Describe how video sharing affects memory upgrades.

2.3 Use Tools, Diagnostic Procedures, and Troubleshooting Techniques for Laptops and Portable Devices

- Use procedures and techniques to diagnose power conditions, and video, keyboard, pointer, and wireless card issues:
  - Verify AC power (e.g., LEDs, swap AC adapter).
  - Verify DC power.
  - Remove unneeded peripherals.
  - Plug in external monitor.
  - Toggle Fn keys.
  - Check LCD cutoff switch.
  - Verify backlight functionality and pixilation.
  - Stylus issues (e.g., digitizer problems).
  - Unique laptop keypad issues.
  - Antenna wires.

3.0 OPERATING SYSTEMS

NOTE

Unless otherwise noted, operating systems include Microsoft Windows 2000, XP Professional, XP Home, and Media Center.

3.1 Identify the Fundamental Principles of Operating Systems

- Use command-line functions and utilities to manage operating systems, including proper syntax and switches:
  - CMD
  - HELP
  - DIR
  - ATTRIB
  - EDIT

- COPY
- XCOPY
- FORMAT
- IPCONFIG
- PING
- MD/CD/RD
■ Identify concepts and procedures for creating, viewing, and managing disks, directories, and files on operating systems:
  - Disks (e.g., active, primary, extended, and logical partitions and filesystems, including FAT32, NTFS)
  - Directory structures (e.g., create folders, navigate directory structures)
  - Files (e.g., creation, attributes, permissions)
■ Locate and use operating system utilities and available switches:
  - Disk management tools (e.g., DEFRAG, NTBACKUP, CHKDSK, Format)
  - System management tools
    ■ Device and Task Manager
    ■ MSCONFIG.EXE
    ■ REGEDIT.EXE
    ■ REGEDT32.EXE
    ■ CMD
    ■ Event Viewer
    ■ System Restore
    ■ Remote Desktop
  - File management tools (e.g., Windows EXPLORER, ATTRIB.EXE)

3.2 Install, Configure, Optimize, and Upgrade Operating Systems

NOTE

References to upgrading from Windows 95 and NT may be made.

■ Identify procedures and utilities used to optimize operating systems:
  - Virtual memory
  - Hard drives (e.g., disk defragmentation)
  - Temporary files
  - Services
  - Startup
  - Application

3.3 Identify Tools, Diagnostic Procedures, and Troubleshooting Techniques for Operating Systems

■ Demonstrate the ability to recover operating systems (e.g., boot methods, recovery console, ASR, ERD).

- Recognize and resolve common operational problems:
  - Windows-specific printing problems (e.g., print spool stalled, incorrect/incompatible driver form print)
  - Autorestart errors
  - Bluescreen error
  - System lock-up
  - Device drivers failure (input/output devices)
  - Application install, start, or load failure
- Recognize and resolve common error messages and codes:
  - Boot (e.g., invalid boot disk, inaccessible boot drive, missing NTLDR)
  - Startup (e.g., device/service failed to start, device/program in registry not found)
  - Event Viewer
  - Registry
  - Windows reporting
- Use diagnostic utilities and tools to resolve operational problems:
  - Bootable media
  - Startup modes (e.g., safe mode, safe mode with command prompt or networking, step-by-step/single-step mode)
  - Documentation resources (e.g., user/installation manuals, Internet/Web-based, training materials)
  - Task and Device Manager
  - Event Viewer
  - `MSCONFIG` command
  - Recover CD/recovery partition
  - Remote Desktop Connection and Assistance
  - System File Checker (SFC)

3.4 Perform Preventive Maintenance for Operating Systems

- Demonstrate the ability to perform preventive maintenance on operating systems, including software and Windows updates (e.g., service packs), scheduled backups/restore, and restore points.

4.0 PRINTERS AND SCANNERS

4.1 Identify the Fundamental Principles of Using Printers and Scanners

- Describe processes used by printers and scanners, including laser, ink dispersion, thermal, solid ink, and impact printers and scanners.

4.2 Install, Configure, Optimize, and Upgrade Printers and Scanners

■ Install and configure printers/scanners:
   • Power and connect the device using local or network ports.
   • Install and update the device driver, and calibrate the device.
   • Configure options and default settings.
   • Install and configure print drivers (e.g., PCL™, PostScript™, GDI).
   • Validate compatibility with the operating system and applications.
   • Educate users about basic functionality.
■ Install and configure printer upgrades, including memory and firmware.
■ Optimize scanner performance, including resolution, file format, and default settings.

4.3 Identify Tools and Diagnostic Procedures to Troubleshooting Printers and Scanners

■ Gather information about printer/scanner problems.
■ Review and analyze collected data.
■ Isolate and resolve identified printer/scanner problems, including defining the cause, applying the fix, and verifying the functionality.
■ Identify appropriate tools used for troubleshooting and repairing printer/scanner problems:
   • Multimeter
   • Screwdrivers
   • Cleaning solutions
   • Extension magnet
   • Test patterns

4.4 Perform Preventive Maintenance of Printers and Scanners

■ Perform scheduled maintenance according to vendor guidelines (e.g., install maintenance kits, reset page counts).
■ Ensure a suitable environment.
■ Use recommended supplies.

5.0 NETWORKS

5.1 Identify the Fundamental Principles or Networks

■ Identify names, purposes, and characteristics of basic network protocols and terminologies:

- ISP
- TCP/IP (e.g., gateway, subnet mask, DNS, WINS, static and automatic address assignment)
- IPX/SPX (NWLink)
- NETBEUI/NETBIOS
- SMTP
- IMAP
- HTML
- HTTP
- HTTPS
- SSL
- Telnet
- FTP
- DNS
- Identify names, purposes, and characteristics of technologies for establishing connectivity:
  - Dial-up networking
  - Broadband (e.g., DSL, cable, satellite)
  - ISDN networking
  - Wireless (all 802.11)
  - LAN/WAN
  - Infrared
  - Bluetooth
  - Cellular
  - VoIP

5.2 Install, Configure, Optimize, and Upgrade Networks

- Install and configure browsers:
  - Enable/disable script support.
  - Configure proxy and security settings.
- Establish network connectivity:
  - Install and configure network cards.
  - Obtain a connection.
  - Configure client options (e.g., Microsoft, Novell) and network options (e.g., domain, workgroup, tree).
  - Configure network options.
- Demonstrate the ability to share network resources:
  - Models
  - Configure permissions
  - Capacities/limitations for sharing for each operating system

5.3 Use Tools and Diagnostic Procedures to Troubleshoot Network Problems

- Identify names, purposes, and characteristics of tools:
  - Command-line tools (e.g., IPCONFIG.EXE, PING.EXE, TRACERT.EXE, NSLOOKUP.EXE)
  - Cable testing device
- Diagnose and troubleshoot basic network issues:
  - Driver/network interface
  - Protocol configuration
  - TCP/IP (e.g., gateway, subnet mask, DNS, WINS, static and automatic address assignment)
  - IPX/SPX (NWLink)
  - Permissions
  - Firewall configuration
  - Electrical interference

5.4 Perform Preventive Maintenance of Networks, Including Securing and Protecting Network Cabling

6.0 SECURITY

6.1 Identify the Fundamentals and Principles of Security

- Identify the purposes and characteristics of access control:
  - Access to operating system (e.g., accounts such as user, admin, and guest; groups; permission actions; types; and levels) components and restricted spaces
- Identify the purposes and characteristics of auditing and event logging.

6.2 Install, Configure, Upgrade and Optimize Security

- Install and configure software, wireless, and data security:
  - Authentication technologies
  - Software firewalls
  - Auditing and event logging (enable/disable only)
  - Wireless client configuration
  - Unused wireless connections
  - Data access (e.g., permissions, basic local security policy)
  - Filesystems (converting from FAT32 to NTFS only)

6.3 Identify Tools, Diagnostic Procedures, and Troubleshooting Techniques for Security

- Diagnose and troubleshoot software and data security issues:
  - Software firewall issues
  - Wireless client configuration issues
  - Data access issues (e.g., permissions, security policies)
  - Encryption and encryption technology issues

6.4 Perform Preventive Maintenance for Security

- Recognize social engineering, and address social engineering situations.

7.0 SAFETY AND ENVIRONMENTAL ISSUES

7.1 Identify Potential Hazards and Proper Safety Procedures, Including Power Supply, Display Devices, and Environment (e.g., Trip, Liquid, Situational, Atmospheric Hazards, High-Voltage Equipment, and Moving Equipment)

8.0 COMMUNICATION AND PROFESSIONALISM

8.1 Use Good Communication Skills, Including Listening and Tact/Discretion, When Communicating with Customers and Colleagues

- Use clear, concise, and direct statements.
- Allow the customer to complete statements, and avoid interrupting.
- Clarify customer statements by asking pertinent questions.
- Avoid using jargon, abbreviations, and acronyms.
- Listen to customers.

8.2 Use Job-Related Professional Behavior, Including Notation of Privacy, Confidentiality, and Respect for the Customer and the Customer's Property

- Behavior:
  - Maintain a positive attitude and tone of voice.
  - Avoid arguing with customers and becoming defensive.
  - Do not minimize customers' problems.
  - Avoid being judgmental or insulting or calling the customer names.
  - Avoid distractions or interruptions when talking with customers.
- Property:
  - Telephone, laptop, desktop computer, printer, monitor, and so on.

220-603 REMOTE SUPPORT TECHNICIAN OBJECTIVES

The CompTIA A+ 220-603 Remote Support Technician exam is meant for those who work in remote environments with a concentration on client interaction, client training, and operating system and connectivity issues. Examples of Remote Support Technician job titles include Remote Technician, Help Desk Technician, and Call Center Technician.

It is advisable to have already passed the CompTIA A+ Essentials examination before taking this exam. Those who pass both CompTIA A+ Essentials and exam 220-603 will receive CompTIA A+ certification with the Remote Support Technician designation. As with the previously mentioned exams, the domains concentrations remain the same, however, the percentage of examination questions focusing on each domain differs. Table 1.3 displays the 220-603 domains and percentage of the examination directed toward each domain. Following Table 1.3 is a complete list of the 220-603 objectives.

TABLE 1.3 Remote Support Technician (220-603) Domains and Percentage of Examination

Domain	Percentage of Examination
1.0 Personal Computer Components	15%
2.0 Operating Systems	29%
3.0 Printers and Scanners	10%
4.0 Networks	11%
5.0 Security	15%
6.0 Communication and Professionalism	20%
Total	100%

1.0 PERSONAL COMPUTER COMPONENTS

1.1 Install, Configure, Optimize, and Upgrade Personal Computer Components
- Add, remove, and configure display devices, input devices, and adapter cards, including basic input and multimedia devices.

1.2 Identify Tools, Diagnostic Procedures, and Troubleshooting Techniques for Personal Computer Components

■ Identify and apply basic diagnostic procedures and troubleshooting techniques:
  - Identify and analyze the problem/potential problem.
  - Test related components, and evaluate the results.
  - Identify additional steps to be taken if/when necessary.
  - Document activities and outcomes.
■ Recognize and isolate issues with display, peripheral, multimedia, specialty input device, and storage.
■ Apply steps in troubleshooting techniques to identify problems (e.g., physical environment, functionality, and software/driver settings) with components, including display, input devices, and adapter cards.

1.3 Perform Preventive Maintenance on Personal Computer Components

■ Identify and apply common preventive maintenance techniques for storage devices:
  - Software tools (e.g., Disk Defragmenter, Check Disk)
  - Cleaning (e.g., optics, tape heads)

2.0 OPERATING SYSTEMS

NOTE

Unless otherwise noted, operating systems include Microsoft Windows 2000, XP Professional, XP Home, and Media Center.

2.1 Identify the Fundamental Principles of Using Operating Systems

■ Use command-line functions and utilities to manage Windows 2000, XP Professional, and XP Home, including proper syntax and switches:
  - CMD
  - HELP
  - DIR
  - ATTRIB
  - EDIT
  - COPY
  - XCOPY
  - FORMAT
  - IPCONFIG
  - PING
  - MD/CD/ RD

- Identify concepts and procedures for creating, viewing, and managing disks, directories, and files in Windows 2000, XP Professional, and XP Home:
  - Disks (e.g., active, primary, extended, and logical partitions)
  - Filesystems (e.g., FAT 32, NTFS)
  - Directory structures (e.g., create folders, navigate directory structures)
  - Files (e.g., creation, extensions, attributes, permissions)
- Locate and use Windows 2000, XP Professional, and XP Home utilities and available switches:
  - Disk Management Tools (e.g., DEFRAG, NTBACKUP, CHKDSK, Format)
  - System Management Tools
    - Device and Task Manager
    - MSCONFIG.EXE
    - REGEDIT.EXE
    - REGEDIT32.EXE
    - CMD
    - Event Viewer
    - System Restore
    - Remote Desktop
  - File Management Tool (e.g., Windows Explorer, ATTRIB.EXE)

2.2 Install, Configure, Optimize, and Upgrade Operating Systems

- Identify procedures and utilities used to optimize the performance of Windows 2000, XP Professional, and XP Home:
  - Virtual memory
  - Hard drives (e.g., disk defragmentation)
  - Temporary files
  - Services
  - Startup
  - Applications

2.3 Identify Tools, Diagnostic Procedures, and Troubleshooting Techniques for Operating Systems

- Recognize and resolve common operational problems:
  - Windows-specific printing problems (e.g., print spooler stalled, incorrect/incompatible driver form print)
  - Autorestart errors
  - Bluescreen error
  - System lock-up
  - Device drivers failure (input/output devices)
  - Application install, start, or load failure

- Recognize and resolve common error messages and codes:
  - Boot (e.g., invalid boot disk, inaccessible boot device, missing NTLDR)
  - Startup (e.g., device/service has failed to start, device/program references in registry not found)
  - Event viewer
  - Registry
  - Windows
- Use diagnostic utilities and tools to resolve operational problems:
  - Bootable media
  - Startup modes (e.g., safe mode, safe mode with command prompt or networking, step-by-step/single-step mode)
  - Documentation resources (e.g., user/installation manuals, Internet/Web-based, training materials)
  - Task and Device Manager
  - Event Viewer
  - MSCONFIG command
  - Recovery CD/Recovery partition
  - Remote Desktop Connection and Assistance
  - System File Checker (SFC)

2.4 Perform Preventive Maintenance for Operating Systems

- Perform preventive maintenance on Windows 2000, XP Professional, and XP Home, including software and Windows updates (e.g., service packs).

3.0 PRINTERS AND SCANNERS

3.1 Identify the Fundamental Principles of Using Printers and Scanners

- Describe processes used by printers and scanners, including laser, ink dispersion, impact, solid ink, and thermal printers.

3.2 Install, Configure, Optimize, and Upgrade Printers and Scanners

- Install and configure printers and scanners:
  - Power and connect the device using network or local ports.
  - Install/update the device driver, and calibrate the device.
  - Configure options and default settings.
  - Install and configure print drivers (e.g., PCL, PostScript, and GDI).
  - Validate compatibility with OS and applications.
  - Educate users about basic functionality.

- Optimize scanner performance, for example, resolution, file format, and default settings.

3.3 Identify Tools, Diagnostic Procedures, and Troubleshooting Techniques for Printers and Scanners

- Gather information required to troubleshoot printer/scanner problems.
- Troubleshoot a print failure (e.g., lack of paper, clear queue, restart print spooler, recycle power on printer, inspect for jams, check for visual indicators).

4.0 NETWORKS

4.1 Identify the Fundamental Principles of Networks

- Identify names, purposes, and characteristics of the basic network protocols and terminologies:
  - ISP
  - TCP/IP (e.g., Gateway, Subnet mask, DNS, WINS, static and automatic address assignment)
  - IPX/SPX (NWLink)
  - NETBEUI/NETBIOS
  - SMTP
  - IMAP
  - HTML
  - HTTP
  - HTTPS
  - SSL
  - Telnet
  - FTP
  - DNS
- Identify names, purposes, and characteristics of technologies for establishing connectivity:
  - Dial-up networking
  - Broadband (e.g., DSL, cable, satellite)
  - ISDN networking
  - Wireless
  - LAN/WAN

4.2 Install, Configure, Optimize, and Upgrade Networks

- Establish network connectivity, and share network resources.

4.3 Identify Tools, Diagnostic Procedures, and Troubleshooting Techniques for Networks

■ Identify the names, purposes, and characteristics of command-line tools:
  - IPCONFIG.EXE
  - PING.EXE
  - TRACERT.EXE
  - NSLOOKUP.EXE
■ Diagnose and troubleshoot basic network issues:
  - Driver/network interface
  - Protocol configuration:
    ■ TCP/IP (e.g., Gateway, Subnet mask, DNS, WINS, static and automatic address assignment)
    ■ IPX/SPX (NWLink)
  - Permissions
  - Firewall configuration
  - Electrical interference

5.0 SECURITY

5.1 Identify the Fundamental Principles of Security

■ Identify the names, purposes, and characteristics of access control and permissions:
  - Accounts, including user, admin, and guest
  - Groups
  - Permission levels, types (e.g., filesystems, shared), and actions (e.g., read, write, change, execute)

5.2 Install, Configure, Optimize, and Upgrade Security

■ Install and configure hardware, software, wireless, and data security:
  - Smart card readers
  - Key fobs
  - Biometric devices
  - Authentication technologies
  - Software firewalls
  - Auditing and event logging (enable/disable only)
  - Wireless client configuration
  - Unused wireless connections
  - Data access (e.g., permissions, security policies)
  - Encryption and encryption technologies

5.3 Identify Tools, Diagnostic Procedures, and Troubleshooting Techniques for Security Issues

- Diagnose and troubleshoot software and data security issues:
  - Software firewall issues
  - Wireless client configuration issues
  - Data access issues (e.g., permissions, security policies)
  - Encryption and encryption technology issues

5.4 Perform Preventive Maintenance for Security

- Recognize social engineering, and address social engineering situations.

6.0 COMMUNICATION AND PROFESSIONALISM

6.1 Use Good Communication Skills, Including Listening and Tact/Discretion, When Communicating with Customers and Colleagues

- Use clear, concise, and direct statements.
- Allow the customer to complete statements, and avoid interrupting.
- Clarify customer statements by asking pertinent questions.
- Avoid using jargon, abbreviations, and acronyms.
- Listen to customers.

6.2 Use Job-Related Professional Behavior, Including Notation of Privacy, Confidentiality, and Respect for the Customer and the Customer's Property

- Behavior:
  - Maintain a positive attitude and tone of voice.
  - Avoid arguing with customers or becoming defensive.
  - Do not minimize customers' problems.
  - Avoid being judgmental or insulting or calling the customer names.
  - Avoid distractions or interruptions when talking with customers.
- Property:
  - Telephone, laptop, desktop computer, printer, monitor, and so on.

220-604 DEPOT TECHNICIAN OBJECTIVES

The CompTIA A+ 220-604 Depot Technician examination is primarily meant for those who work or are preparing to work in the area of hardware. This exam is meant for such job roles as Depot Technician, Hardware Technician, or Bench Technician.

As with the 220-602 and 220-603 exams, CompTIA highly recommends that you pass the A+ Essentials examination before taking this exam. Candidates who pass both CompTIA A+ Essentials and exam 220-604 will become A+ certified with the Depot Technician designation. Table 1.4 displays the 220-604 exam objectives as well as the percentage of questions that the exam will target toward each domain. Following Table 1.4 is the complete list of 220-604 exam objectives.

TABLE 1.4   Depot Technician (220-604) Domains and Percentage of Examination

Domain	Percentage of Examination
1.0 Personal Computer Components	45%
2.0 Laptop and Portable Devices	20%
3.0 Printers and Scanners	20%
4.0 Security	5%
5.0 Safety and Environmental Issues	10%
Total	100%

1.0 PERSONAL COMPUTER COMPONENTS

1.1 Install, Configure, Optimize, and Upgrade Personal Computer Components

■ Add, remove, and configure internal storage devices, motherboards, power supplies, processors/CPUs, memory, and adapter cards, including the following:
  • Drive preparation
  • Jumper configuration
  • Storage device power and cabling
  • Selection and installation of appropriate motherboard
  • BIOS set-up and configuration
  • Selection and installation of appropriate CPU
  • Selection and installation of appropriate memory
  • Installation of adapter cards, including hardware and software/drivers
  • Configuration and optimization of adapter cards, including adjusting hardware settings and obtaining network card connections
■ Add, remove, and configure systems.

1.2 Identify Tools, Diagnostic Procedures, and Troubleshooting Techniques for Personal Computer Components

- Identify and apply diagnostic procedures and troubleshooting techniques:
  - Identify and isolate the problem using visual and audible inspection of components and minimum configuration.
- Identify the steps used to troubleshoot components (e.g., check proper seating, installation, appropriate component, settings, current driver):
  - Power supply
  - Processors/CPUs and motherboards
  - Memory
  - Adapter cards
- Recognize names, purposes, characteristics, and appropriate application of tools:
  - Multimeter
  - Antistatic pad and wrist strap
  - Specialty hardware/tools
  - Loop-back plugs
  - Cleaning products (e.g., vacuum, cleaning pads)

1.3 Perform Preventive Maintenance of Personal Computer Components

- Identify and apply common preventive maintenance techniques:
  - Thermally sensitive devices (e.g., motherboards, CPUs, adapter cards, memory):
    - Cleaning
    - Air flow (e.g., slot covers, cable routing)
  - Adapter cards (e.g., driver/firmware updates)

2.0 LAPTOP AND PORTABLE DEVICES

2.1 Identify the Fundamental Principles of Using Laptops and Portable Devices

- Identify appropriate applications for laptop-specific communication connections:
  - Bluetooth
  - Infrared devices
  - Cellular WAN
  - Ethernet
- Identify appropriate laptop-specific power and electrical input devices:
  - Output performance requirements for amperage and voltage
  - Identify the major components of the LCD (e.g., inverter, screen, video card)

2.2 Install, Configure, Optimize, and Upgrade Laptops and Portable Devices

■ Demonstrate the safe removal of laptop-specific hardware, including peripherals, hot-swappable, and nonhot-swappable devices.

■ Identify the affect of video sharing on memory upgrades.

2.3 Identify Tools, Diagnostic Procedures, and Troubleshooting Techniques for Laptops and Portable Devices

■ Use procedures and techniques to diagnose power conditions, video issues, keyboard and pointer issues, and wireless card issues:
  - Verify AC power (e.g., LEDs, swap AC adapter).
  - Verify DC power.
  - Remove unneeded peripherals.
  - Plug in external monitor.
  - Toggle Fn keys.
  - Check LCD cutoff switch.
  - Verify backlight functionality and pixilation.
  - Stylus issues (e.g., digitizer problems)
  - Unique laptop keypad issues
  - Antenna wires

3.0 Printers and Scanners

3.1 Identify the Fundamental Principles of Using Printers and Scanners

■ Describe the processes used by printers and scanners, including laser, inkjet, thermal, solid ink, and impact printers.

3.2 Install, Configure, Optimize, and Upgrade Printers and Scanners

■ Identify the steps used in the installation and configuration processes for printers and scanners:
  - Power and connect the device using network or local ports.
  - Install and update the device driver.
  - Calibrate the device.
  - Configure options and default settings.
  - Print a test page.
■ Install and configure printer/scanner upgrades, including memory and firmware.

3.3 Identify Tools, Diagnostic Methods, and Troubleshooting Procedures for Printers and Scanners

- Gather data about printer/scanner problems.
- Review and analyze data collected about printer/scanner problems.
- Implement solutions to solve identified printer/scanner problems.
- Identify appropriate tools used for troubleshooting and repairing printer/scanner problems:
  - Multimeter
  - Screwdrivers
  - Cleaning solutions
  - Extension magnet
  - Test patterns

3.4 Perform Preventive Maintenance of Printer and Scanner Problems

- Perform scheduled maintenance according to vendor guidelines (e.g., install maintenance kits, reset page counts)
- Ensure a suitable environment
- Use recommended supplies

4.0 SECURITY

4.1 Identify the Names, Purposes, and Characteristics of Physical Security Devices and Processes

- Control access to PCs, servers, laptops, and restricted spaces:
  - Hardware
  - Operating systems

4.2 Install Hardware Security

- Smart card readers
- Key fobs
- Biometric devices

5.0 SAFETY AND ENVIRONMENTAL ISSUES

5.1 Identify Potential Hazards and Proper Safety Procedures, Including Power Supply, Display Devices, and Environment (e.g., Trip, Liquid, Situational, Atmospheric Hazards, High-Voltage Equipment, and Moving Equipment).

REGISTERING FOR THE A+ TESTS

This book has you and your certification status in mind. You (the exam candidate) must reduce the stress levels involved with preparing and scheduling for the tests to focus your energy on your goal: getting A+ certified. The *A+ Exams Guide Second Edition* is the best resource available to help you achieve that goal. The paragraphs that follow contain valuable information that will help alleviate the stress of scheduling your exam.

In the United States and Canada, there are two companies to register with to take the A+ certification tests (as well as other certification tests such as Microsoft certification exams): Pearson VUE and Prometric. You can register online or call either company. To register with Pearson VUE, visit *www.pearsonvue.com/comptia/*. To register with Prometric, visit *www.prometric.com/CompTIA/default.*

Oh, and here's probably your best registration resource of all: www.comptia. org. From the CompTIA homepage, there's a handy link called "Exam Prices and Registration." Click there, and you're given a page where you can start the registration process with either testing company. Just select your country and state and you're on your way. You are required to register at least 12 hours before you take the test. If you decide to cancel after registering, you must call 12 hours before your scheduled test time to cancel, or you will forfeit your money. Your best bet is to pick a target date for taking the tests, give yourself at least 30 days to study this book, and answer all questions correctly on the included test-preparation CD-ROM. Register

ON THE CD

at least 3 days ahead of the date and time you want to sit for the exams. Ask the registration person for the nearest test center location.

Currently, the cost of each test is $158 (U.S.). You do not get your money back if you fail. That's around $316 to get A+ certified (not including this book)—so don't fail! You can take each test separately or take them together. For example, you could register and take the A+ Essentials exam and IT Technician exam back to back. For complete CompTIA exam pricing by country, visit *www.comptia.org/ certification/general_information/test_pricing.asp?type=certification.*

If you pass one test, you will get credit for that test only. You must pass two tests to become A+ certified. One of these tests must be the A+ Essentials. The second exam will be one of the "Technician" titles as previously discussed. A passing grade is needed on both exams, of course, but it is not necessary to take all four exams to become A+ Certified.

In other words, if you pass one test (Essentials exam) and fail the other (IT Technician exam), you must re-register for the test you failed and pass it to complete the certification objectives. If you pass two tests, you are instantly A+ certified. A welcome kit will be sent to you within four to six weeks, depending on shipping and other factors.

You need to have the following information ready before you register:

- Your name, company name, and your mailing address.
- The exam name and number you want to take, for example, A+ Essentials 220-601, 220-602, 220-603, or 220-604.
- Your method of payment. For quick registration and getting the testing date and time slot that fits your schedule, pay with a valid credit card. Other forms of payment must be received by the registration center before the tests can be scheduled.

TEST SITE REQUIREMENTS AND A LITTLE ADVICE

You should arrive at the test site one hour before your exam. Take a little time to get comfortable with the surroundings at the test site, sign in at the registration desk, and study any charts and details that you feel are your weak points. Depending on the schedule of tests at the test site, you can generally take care of the paperwork, find a quiet area to do some last-minute cramming, and then go take the tests. If no one is scheduled before you, it may be possible to take the tests before your scheduled time. You will be asked to provide two forms of identification at the testing site. A valid driver's license and a credit card are sufficient. One form of identification must be a photo ID. When you are ready to enter the testing room, you will be given a blank sheet of paper and a marker or pencil. You cannot take any other books or notes with you. Cell phones are usually not allowed. If you are taking two A+ exams together, you will be allowed a quick break after the first one.

After you have signed in at the testing center, a testing coordinator will direct you to a computer that will have your test ready to go. You may be required to enter a security ID before you start the test. This ID is normally your social security number. The testing coordinator will inform you of any special procedures for the particular testing center.

The CompTIA Certification Program has been changed recently to produce a more valuable and desired certification. This book is up to date with the current exams. For more information about the CompTIA A+ Certification Program and other CompTIA certifications, visit the CompTIA Web site at *www.comptia.org. certification.*

HOW COMPUTERIZED TESTING WORKS

The majority of computerized certification tests offered today are given in either conventional or adaptive format. Because you are studying A+, which is considered an entry-level certification, this will likely be one of your first computerized testing experiences. For that reason, it's important that you understand the basics regarding each of these testing techniques. It's kind of like having a home field advantage if you fully understand how the test (your opponent) "thinks" and "reacts." As a general rule, you should always educate yourself on the particular testing format in which the tests you choose to take will be presented. Next, we will discuss the basics of conventional and adaptive testing.

CONVENTIONAL TESTING

A conventional computerized test is fixed in length with a set number of questions that you must answer in a certain amount of time. You will often find conventional tests referred to as fixed length, traditional, or linear.

All of the current A+ Certification tests are in conventional format. You will be allotted 90 minutes to complete each exam. The A+ Essentials exam currently contains 100 questions with a passing score of 675. The IT Technician, Remote Support Technician, and Depot Technician exams each contain 90 questions with a minimum passing score of 700. You must answer all questions in order to finish each exam. A timer in the upper-right corner of the test screen displays the amount of time you have remaining to complete the test.

Again, you will be required to answer all multiple-choice questions. Be careful—some questions require more than one answer. If there are circles next to your choices, you must choose only one answer. However, if you see squares next to your choices, you will have the option to select one or more answers. Read the questions carefully; they usually say, "Choose Two" or "Choose Three." If a question asks you to "Choose Two" and you select only one answer, the test will prompt you to choose two before you can proceed. The same is true for "Choose Three," and so on.

Some questions require you to click a graphic radio button to display a diagram or image. Be careful when viewing graphics; some are notorious for being unclear. Make sure you know what you are selecting on the images. You'll probably be asked to select the correct answer or best choice from the displayed diagram or image. Some diagrams require you to select or identify several choices. You will be allowed to refer back to the diagram to make your selections. This is a good place to use scratch paper to keep your thoughts straight.

As with most conventional exams, you will have the option to "mark" a question for later review. In other words, you can review previously answered questions by going back.

You will encounter many situational questions on these new exams. To be more specific, you will be presented with a problem situation. You will have to choose which troubleshooting method or approach is best to resolve that particular situation. Some of the more difficult questions may ask in what order certain steps should be taken to isolate and ultimately resolve a problem.

When you have finished the last question on the test, your final score will be tabulated, and your test results will be instantly presented to you. You will know then and there whether you have passed or failed the test.

ADAPTIVE TESTING

Many certification exams are given in Computerized Adaptive Testing (CAT) format. Traditionally, CompTIA releases its new exams in conventional testing format and then eventually converts them to adaptive format. As stated earlier in this chapter, the current exams are in conventional format. But again, it's better for you to have a clear understanding early in your test-taking career of how adaptive tests work. You will likely encounter them again after you have passed A+. For that reason, the following information on adaptive testing is provided.

The adaptive testing software engine evaluates your most recently answered question. If you answered the question correctly, the next question is generated from a group of more difficult questions, until the testing software is satisfied that you have met the required level of knowledge on that subject matter. If you answered the question incorrectly, a less difficult question is generated. This process continues as the testing engine accurately keeps track of your knowledge level. Picture a graph running behind the scenes, keeping track of your answers. The more questions you answer correctly, the higher above the passing line you move. The more you answer incorrectly, the farther you fall below the passing line. If you are approaching question number 20 (on a typical 30-question adaptive exam), and you have answered most of the questions correctly, the testing software will determine that you know the subject matter and may end the test. However, if you are answering the questions inconsistently and riding the pass/fail line on the graph, you may be required to answer up to 30 questions until the software determines whether you pass or fail.

If it all sounds a bit complex, it is. Bear in mind, however, the adaptive test's secondary purpose: to keep exam candidates from seeing as many exam questions as possible. Unlike the case with a conventional test where everyone gets the same questions, with an adaptive exam it's likely that two exam candidates would see two entirely different sets of questions. This (in theory) renders "brain dumps" and other test question-specific information less useful, as memorizing the answer to one question won't be of any help if another question appears on the exam. I'll share more of my thoughts on "brain dumps" in just a bit. At any rate, that's why adaptive exams exist.

YOUR STATE OF MIND

It is important to focus when studying for and taking a certification test. Make sure that you give yourself time daily to study this book and its accompanying practice test CD-ROM without any distraction. It is not a good practice to study when you are tired and unable to retain the required information. You should be well rested and in a good frame of mind when you take these tests. Don't stay up all night before taking the exams trying to cram 15 years of technical information into your head.

Confidence, along with good study habits, plays a very big role in this process and increases your chances of success. When preparing to take a certification exam, not only should you prepare to pass, but you should also prepare to score as close to 100% as possible.

The A+ exams are usually the first certification tests taken by people interested in the information technology (IT) industry. Make sure this is a positive experience to set the stage for your future certification testing goals. Learn to develop good study habits early on in your certification career. This book is based on information, tools, and techniques that have spring boarded thousands of students and professionals to A+ certification success and beyond. Many of the people who have used these study techniques to master A+ have gone on to successfully take and pass such certification exams as CompTIA's Network+, Server+, and Security+; and Microsoft's MCSA (Microsoft Certified Systems Administrator) and MCSE (Microsoft Certified Systems Engineer).

USEFUL TOOLS, TIPS, AND STUDY TECHNIQUES

Many test takers prepare for certification exams by focusing only on certain areas of subject matter they assume will be on the exam. This is a huge mistake. The current A+ exams cover a broad range of information. To increase your chances of passing, you must spread your focus of study across all identified areas of content in this book, based on the domains specified by CompTIA.

It seems that most certification preparation guides are geared toward have you figure out some sort of magical strategy to answer questions correctly and ultimately pass the tests. Anyone who has come before you and passed these exams will tell you that it's really quite simple. Prepare yourself well with proper study, and choose the right answer to each question on the exam.

The book you are holding in your hands will help you become A+ certified. Read the entire book twice. It has been crafted with your certification success in mind.

ON THE CD

The practice tests included on the CD-ROM are very accurate and are good simulations of the real tests. Take the practice tests repeatedly until you score 100% every time. When you take a test, whether it is a practice test or a real test, read each question carefully, and go with your initial choice. Try not to read too much into the questions. Certification developers are great at making the wrong answers look good. They include key words in the questions to confuse you. The longer you sit there staring at the screen, the more likely you are to pick the wrong answer. Here is another useful tip: do not worry about the questions you have already answered. If you are not sure of a particular question you have answered, mark it for later review when you have answered all questions. Only focus on the questions in front of you, and try not to think of anything else. Learn to prepare yourself well, and always remember that the difference between pass and fail can be one question.

Test takers who have gone before you post "brain dumps" on many Internet sites. These are usually questions that they remember seeing on the test. Be very careful if you study these postings—many of them contain incorrect answers and information. These brain dumps may be helpful by identifying certain topics or material that may show up the test, but you should really know the material.

If you study this book, take the suggestions, and do the groundwork, you should do very well on the real tests.

BOOK STRUCTURE AND SAMPLE REVIEW QUESTIONS

Unlike many other books that try to separate the study chapters by exam name and number, this book prepares you for all four of the A+ exams by subject matter topic. If you paid close attention to the previously listed exam objectives for all four exams, you noticed that all of the exams contain the same basic core objectives. The only real difference is that each exam specifies a different percentage toward each subject matter. For example, the A+ Essential exam specifies a 5% examination percentage toward Communication and Professionalism and 9% of the examination percentage toward Printers and Scanners, whereas the IT Technician specifies a 15% examination percentage toward Communication and Professionalism and 14% of the examination percentage toward Printers and Scanners. CompTIA has basically just created four different exams with a different amount of questions focusing on each of its domains depending on the exam. Study this entire book and take the practice exams on the included CD-ROM and you will be prepared for all four exams.

You may also notice that this book includes chapters that contain information regarding Windows Me and Windows NT. These operating systems are not specified in the CompTIA 2006 Objectives. However, the technology contained in these operating systems is covered! These operating systems are still very much in place in the real business world and in homes, so you better be familiar with them as a savvy technician. So be forewarned. The exams are going to drill you with the technology and terms associated with these operating systems.

Several chapters in this book contain a "References" section at the very end of the chapter. These sections contain specific Web site addresses that have been picked out of the chapter to help you expand your knowledge of a particular subject. Use these Web site references to optimize your success rate on the real exams.

You will notice Note icons throughout the book. These Note icons are used to warn you of important information that has been identified as a specific CompTIA Objective identified on a current exam. In other words, information throughout the book that is targeted by a Note icon is likely to be on the exam.

At the end of each chapter in this book, you will be able to test your knowledge by answering several chapter content-related review questions. You may see questions relative to earlier chapters as you move forward. This design is in place to help you build on your skill sets as you move through the book. Use a piece of paper to cover the answers provided underneath the questions (don't cheat). If you do not understand the question or the answer, you may have to go back and do some review work. Pay very close attention; you may see similar questions on the actual tests.

Notice the circles next to your choices in questions 1 and 2. You will select one answer.

1. **You are starting up your PC. The floppy diskette drive light stays on. What is most likely the problem?**
   - ○ A.   The floppy drive is defective.
   - ○ B.   The data cable is defective.
   - ○ C.   The data cable is on backwards.
   - ○ D.   The CMOS battery is bad.

   Correct Answer = C

2. **You want to improve hard disk access time in Windows 9.X. Which utility should you use?**
   - ○ A.   Task Manager
   - ○ B.   System Monitor
   - ○ C.   Control Panel
   - ○ D.   Disk Defragmenter

   Correct Answer = D

   Notice the squares next to your choices in questions 3 and 4. You will select one or more answers.

3. **Which of the following represent types of video RAM? (Choose 3)**
   - □ A.   SGRAM
   - □ B.   VRAM
   - □ C.   MRAM
   - □ D.   WRAM

   Correct Answers = A, B, and D

4. **To help ensure that PS/2 mice and keyboards are connected properly to a system, the ports on the back of a system are color coded. What colors identify the PS/2 mouse and keyboard ports? (Choose 2)**
   - ☐ A. Black
   - ☐ B. Yellow
   - ☐ C. Green
   - ☐ D. Purple

   Correct Answers = C and D

CHAPTER SUMMARY

Chapter 1 introduced you to the CompTIA A+ certification tests and testing formats, which included conventional and adaptive testing. It provided you with a breakdown of the test structure and what you should expect to see from the start of the test to the finish. You were introduced to the exact CompTIA A+ domain objectives, concepts, and modules from which your knowledge will be tested. You learned useful tips and study techniques that you should develop early on in your certification test preparation days (and nights) to save you time, money, and disappointment in the long run. Finally, you were introduced to review questions and their format. The best practice and preparation for any certification exam includes a combination of confidence and practice with relative practice questions.

Great lengths have been taken in this chapter to answer as many of your questions as possible regarding A+ certification preparation in general. If you have more general questions regarding A+ certification, visit the CompTIA Web site at certification.comptia.org .

REFERENCES

http://certification.comptia.org/a/. The CompTIA A+ Certification 2006 Exam Objectives can be downloaded in PDF format from this Web site.

www.pearsonvue.com/comptia/. You can easily register for your A+, as well other certification exams, at this Pearson VUE Web site.

www.prometric.com/CompTIA/default.htm. You can easily register for your A+, as well other certification exams, at this Thompson/Prometric Web site.

www.comptia.org/. The CompTIA home page.

www.comptia.org/certification/general_information/test_pricing.asp?type=certification. You can find CompTIA's exam pricing schedules listed by country at this Web site.

2 Motherboards, Power, BIOS, and Expansion Buses

In This Chapter

- Motherboards and Form Factors
- Slots and Sockets
- Electricity and the Power Supply
- Preventive Maintenance and Safety
- CMOS, BIOS, and Plug and Play (PnP)
- POST and Error Codes
- Expansion Bus Architecture
- North and South Bridges
- PCMCIA (PC Cards)

MOTHERBOARDS AND FORM FACTORS

The *motherboard*, sometimes referred to as the planar or system board, is the central part of a computer that brings together all devices attached to the computer. The main components on the motherboard are the CPU (central processing unit) and CPU chipset, the expansion bus, I/O (input/output) interface, disk drive controllers, and random access memory (RAM). The motherboard's main function is to distribute power and data to all devices attached to it.

Motherboards have different form factors. *Form factor* simply describes the physical size and layout of the motherboard, its power supply, connected components (such as memory and expansion bus components), and even the computer case itself. Several form factors and their features are described next.

ADVANCED TECHNOLOGY (AT) AND BABY AT

Until 1997, the advanced technology (AT) and baby AT form factors were the most popular types of motherboards on the market. The main difference between the two is the width of the motherboards themselves. The AT motherboard is 12" × 13". The baby AT is 9" × 10". See Figure 2.1 for the baby AT and its components.

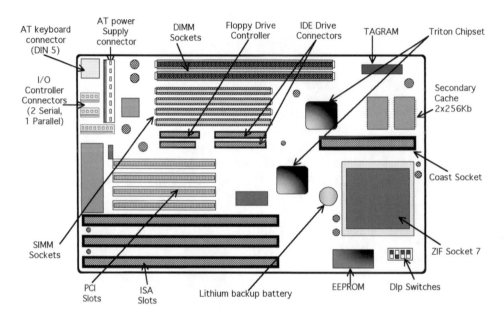

FIGURE 2.1 Baby AT (socket 7) motherboard and components.

The AT and baby AT form factors placed the processor and memory socket locations toward the front of the motherboard. Very long expansion cards were designed to extend over them, which made removing the processor difficult. You had to take the expansion cards out first to remove the processor or to get to the memory. Note that an AT power supply gives an output of 12V and 5V to the motherboard. Additional regulators are needed on the motherboard if 3.3V cards (peripheral component interconnect, or PCI) or processors are used.

This design was acceptable when clearance and cooling were not an issue. With the advent of faster Pentium-class processors that required more cooling and memory sockets that extended off the motherboard, a better design of motherboard was needed.

Study the motherboard diagrams very closely. The A+ exams may show you a similar graphic representation that requires you to identify individual motherboard components. In fact, count on it!

LPX

In 1987, Western Digital introduced the Low Profile Extensions (LPX) motherboard form factor to meet the need for a slimmer desktop. This goal was accomplished based on the implementation of a riser card that extended from the motherboard and allowed expansion cards to be installed parallel to the motherboard.

NLX

As the need for more expansion slots and easier access to components increased, the LPX form factor was redesigned by Intel and named the NLX (InteLex) form factor. The NLX form factor moved the riser card from the center of the mother-board to the outside edge.

ATX

The ATX form factor was developed to solve the problems associated with the baby AT form factor design (see Figure 2.2 and Figure 2.3). This new design had many advantages that affected not only the motherboard but also the system unit and power supply. The dimensions of the ATX form factor are 12" × 9.6". A mini ATX is typically 11.2" × 8.2".

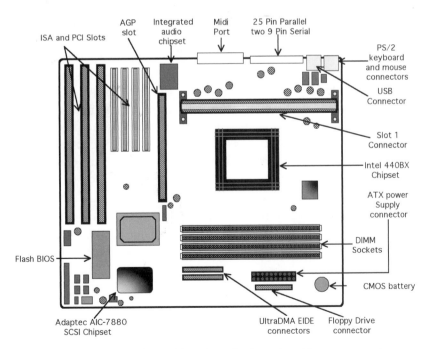

FIGURE 2.2   Drawing of ATX (Slot 1) motherboard and its components.

FIGURE 2.3 Photo of ATX motherboard and its components.

The ATX design provides the following advantages.

Integrated I/O port connection: Baby AT motherboards have cables connecting them to the physical serial and parallel ports mounted on the system unit. With the ATX form factor, this connection is integrated into the motherboard. The ATX form factor uses a 20-pin plastic power supply connector, called a *keyed connector,* which can be plugged into the motherboard in one direction only.

Integrated PS/2 mouse connector: ATX motherboards have PS/2 mouse ports integrated into the motherboard. Most baby AT motherboards do not have a PS/2 mouse port. Older style AT motherboards required a serial mouse. (The serial interface is covered in Chapter 8.) For the exam, remember that the mouse on the PS/2 system is color coded with a green connector. The keyboard on a PS/2 system uses a purple color-coded connector.

Easier access to components: The ATX motherboard was designed with functionality and accessibility in mind. It provides much easier access to components than the baby AT form factor and offers more room in general for additional components.

Improved power supply connection: The new ATX form factor incorporated a single 20-pin connector in place of a pair of 6-pin connectors used on the baby AT motherboard.

Support for 3.3V: The ATX motherboard supports 3.3V power from the ATX power supply. This voltage is used by most newer processors.

"Soft switch" power support: The ATX power supply uses a signal from the motherboard to turn itself off. This feature enables you to use the power management utilities offered with newer operating systems to shut down a computer, as opposed to physically turning it off with the power button.

Better airflow: With the ATX form factor, the processor is moved closer to the power supply, providing it with better air circulation and cooling. For proper air circulation, it is also important to replace any slot covers on the back of a computer that may be missing as a result of removed expansion cards.

Some very important facts to remember for the exam include the following:

- Most AT-style motherboards use a 5-pin DIN (Deutsches Institut für Normung) keyboard connector.
- The ATX motherboard uses the smaller 6-pin mini DIN keyboard connector, which is more commonly referred to as a *PS/2 connector.*
- The keyboard PS/2 connector is identical to the mouse PS/2 connector.
- Motherboards use *jumpers* to configure or adjust certain onboard settings such as the motherboard's clock speed, which is measured in megahertz (MHz). Older motherboards used dual in-line package (DIP) switches to perform this function.

MicroATX

The MicroATX form factor was developed to meet the need for a smaller and less expensive motherboard. The MicroATX design offers all the functionality of the traditional ATX and is also backward compatible with ATX. The MicroATX, with a maximum size of 244 mm × 244 mm, form factor also uses the same power connectors, uses a similar mounting pin structure, and supports the same chipsets as its predecessor. Compared to ATX, which usually has five slots, most MicroATX motherboard form factors have only three slots for PCI or PCI Express expansion slots to conserve on space. To further educate yourself with this technology, the following First International Computer, Inc. Web site offers some useful information: *www.fic.com.tw/support/motherboard/faq.aspx?type=microatx#qid470.*

FlexATX

Intel's FlexATX was derived from the MicroATX motherboard form factor standard. It is the smallest ATX form factor and is interchangeable with MicroATX and standard ATX chassis. To meet the FlexATX standard, a motherboard can be no larger than 9.0" × 7.5" (229 × 191 mm).

The FlexATX allows for ATX cost and performance benefits while allowing manufacturers to design a wide variety of smaller form factors such as LCD–based computing devices or all-in-one systems (think of Apple's iMac desktop system as one such example).

BTX

Developed by Intel, the BTX (Balanced Technology Extended) form factor was created to alleviate some of the heat-related problems and restraints caused by newer graphics card, processors, heat sinks, and other components. The BTX motherboard specification features a lower profile than the ATX form factor, and a more efficient thermal design that allows for a straighter air flow and a better overall structural design, which allows components to be located closer together to reduce latency. Although this is the newest form factor, it is likely that the 2006 A+ Exams will have you identify components on the more prevalent ATX form factor.

SLOTS AND SOCKETS

A CPU or processor can be installed on the motherboard in two major ways: socket design and slot design. The socket design is square and made for a pin grid array (PGA) or a staggered pin grid array (SPGA) chip package. The socket is made up of many tiny holes that correspond to pins on the bottom side of the CPU. This socket is known as a zero insertion force (ZIF) socket. Socket design is also referred to as flat architecture (see Table 2.1).

TABLE 2.1 Major Sockets, Slots, and the CPUs They Support

Socket or Slot	CPU
Socket 7	Pentium (75 MHz), MMX, X86, Cyrix MLL, AMD K-5, K-6
Socket 8	Pentium Pro
Socket 370	Pentium III PGA, Celeron PGA
Socket 423	Pentium 4 (423-pin Willamette), Pentium Northwood, Celeron Willamette
Socket 478	Second-generation Pentium 4 (478-pin Northwood), Willamette, Celeron Family (478-pin Northwood)
Socket 479	Pentium M, Celeron M, based on the Banias and Dothan cores
Socket 603 and 604	Intel Xeon processors based on Northwood and Willamette P4 cores

→

Socket or Slot	CPU
Socket A	AMD Athlon PGA, AMD Duron, AMD Athlon XP, and Sempron
Socket M	Intel Processors based on Yonah core
Socket 754	Low-end AMD Athlon 64 and Sempron processors that have single-channel memory support
Socket T\LGA 775	Pentium 4 and Celeron, based on Northwood, Prescott, Conroe, Kentsfield, and Cedar Mill cores
Socket 939	AMD Athlon 64, AMD Athlon 64 FX, AMD Athlon 64 X2, and AMD Opteron processors that have dual-channel memory support
Socket 940	AMD Opteron and first AMD Athlon FX processors
Socket AM2	Sempron, AMD Athlon 64, AMD Athlon 64 X2, AMD Athlon 64 FX, and AMD Opteron
Socket F	AMD Opteron and higher-end AMD Athlon 64 FX
Slot 1	Pentium II, Pentium III SEC, and Celeron SEP
Slot A	AMD Athlon SEC
Slot 2	Pentium II Xeon, Pentium III Xeon

Slot technology is implemented when a CPU that is already attached to an integrated circuit (IC) board is plugged into a slot on the motherboard. This slot is typically known as slot 1. Slot technology is pretty much the standard today. Variations of slot and socket technologies are designed to support specific CPUs (see Table 2.2).

TABLE 2.2   Details of Major Slots and Sockets

Socket 7	321 pinholes (19 x 19) SPGA ZIF socket
Socket 8	387 pinholes (24 x 26) MSPGA ZIF socket
Socket A	453 pinholes (19 x 19) SPGA ZIF socket
Slot 1	242 leads, SEC slot
Slot A	242 leads, SEC slot
Slot 2	330 leads, SEC slot
Socket 423	423 pinholes PPGA
Socket 478	478 pinholes PPGA FC-PGA2

Pay close attention to the tables mentioned here. The 2006 A+ Exams are sure to test your knowledge regarding the newer slots, sockets, and CPUs. Know them well. Covering all the processors available today is beyond the scope of this book. For more information regarding processors and the sockets or slots they use, visit http://en.wikipedia.org/wiki/List_of_microprocessors.

ELECTRICITY AND THE POWER SUPPLY

The flow of electrons is known as electricity. When electricity flows in only one direction, it is called *direct current* (DC). When electricity flows in two directions or in a bidirectional fashion, it is called *alternating current* (AC). To understand the flow of electricity through a computer system and troubleshoot electrical issues in a computer system, you should be familiar with the following electrical terms:

Current: *Current* is the amount of electricity moving across a wire. Current is measured in milliamperes or amperes (amps).

Resistance: *Resistance* is a measure of how much an object resists or holds back the flow of current. When electrical resistance is increased, the amount of current is decreased. Resistance is measured in ohms.

Voltage: *Voltage* is a measure of the pressure on electrons as they are being pushed through a medium. Voltage is measured in volts.

Wattage: *Wattage* is the amount of work that electrical current is capable of performing. Wattage is measured in watts. You should be very concerned about wattage and its effects when changing or repairing a power supply. A common practice is to simply replace a power supply that is defective.

The main function of your computer's power supply is to convert AC to DC. Current that enters the power supply from an electrical outlet in the wall is typically at 110V or 115V AC.

The power supply converts AC to the +5V, –5V, +12V, or –12V DC current that the motherboard and its components require.

A useful tool to test power (voltage) coming from the power supply and going to the motherboard is a digital multimeter. The wires that extend from the typical power supply have different colors, and each represents a different voltage: red = +5V, white = –5V, yellow = +12V, and blue= –12V.

Older motherboard form factors (such as AT) accept the P8 and P9 Molex-type connectors from the power supply. These connectors plug into the motherboard side by side. When plugging the P8 and P9 connectors into the AT motherboard, you must remember to keep the black ground wires next to each other. If you don't, you may cause electrical damage to the board. The ATX form factor introduced a single "keyed" power connector that eliminated the risk of plugging the P8 and P9 connectors into the wrong power sockets on the motherboard. See Figure 2.4 for P8 and P9 power connectors. Also see Figure 2.5 for a standard AT motherboard AT power connection and Figure 2.6 for an ATX motherboard power connector.

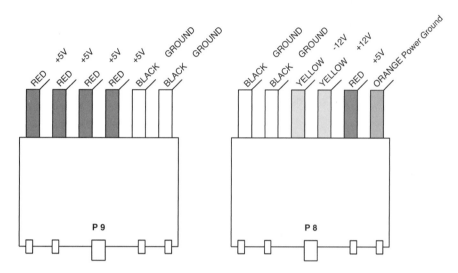

FIGURE 2.4   P8 and P9 power supply connector wiring.

FIGURE 2.5   AT power connector.

FIGURE 2.6 ATX power connector.

If you are troubleshooting a "dead" computer, first verify that electricity is coming from the AC wall outlet. Next, use a digital multimeter to measure the voltage going from the power supply to the motherboard. There are fuses in a computer system that can also be tested with a multimeter. A good fuse measures a resistance of 0 ohms. If the fuse is bad, the multimeter registers a resistance of infinity ohms. If your system continuously reboots on its own, it may not be receiving enough power from the power supply.

UNINTERRUPTIBLE POWER SUPPLY

To protect your computer and data, your computer should be connected to an uninterruptible power supply (UPS), otherwise known as a battery backup. If it is not connected to a UPS, your computer may be subject to a power surge. If your computer screen is flickering, you may be experiencing simple power sag. The UPS (if properly maintained) provides power to the computer in the event of a power failure; it is not meant to be a long-term power-providing solution.

The three types of UPS are online, standby, and line-interactive. In an online UPS, the battery is contained in a circuit. In a standby UPS, the battery is not contained in the circuit. A line-interactive UPS has the best characteristics of the online and standby UPSs.

A laser printer should never be plugged into a UPS. A laser printer draws a large amount of electricity, so it should be placed on its own electrical circuit separate from the system unit and other electrical devices.

SURGE SUPPRESSORS

A surge suppressor is a device used to protect electronic equipment, such as computer systems, printers, modems, and monitors, from transient voltage or "spikes" that occur in the flow of electricity. In North America, the average or "effective" AC power voltage is around 110V to 120V. Spikes, which can be caused by lightning or other electrical conditions, can cause electrical surges of hundreds or even thousands of volts. A surge suppressor or "protector" can stop AC voltage from going above or below a certain amount of voltage. A typical surge protector has several outlets that equipment can be plugged into, a main power switch, and a three-pronged plug that plugs into a power outlet.

PREVENTIVE MAINTENANCE AND SAFETY

An important acronym to be familiar with is *electrostatic discharge* (ESD). ESD is a phenomenon that occurs when electricity builds up (usually in a person's body) and is passed on to the computer and its components. ESD can cause serious damage to your computer and components. You should always wear a protective ESD wrist strap, which contains a resistor, when handling the components inside the system unit. Expansion cards, such as a network interface card (NIC) or video adapter card, have onboard memory and ROM chips that can be damaged by ESD. Always wear a protective wrist strap when installing these components. Never use a piece of wire to ground yourself if you are using an ESD wrist strap. Instead, use a grounded ESD mat to absorb and discharge. In addition, you should never wear an ESD wrist strap when working on a monitor. A monitor can store high levels of voltage (about 15,000 V), which can cause serious bodily harm when interacting with a resistor in an ESD strap. Warm and dry environments are a breeding ground for static electricity buildup. Place any spare electronic components, such as motherboards, hard drives, memory modules, and processors, in a reusable ESD protective bag and store them in a cool and dry environment. When cleaning the inside of your computer, be sure to use a special-purpose vacuum designed not to create ESD.

Use the following guidelines for keeping your system clean:

ROM media: Dip media in a diluted cleaning solution, and let air-dry.

Inside of computer: Spray with a can of condensed air. Use a small brush for the system unit itself.

Airflow: Use two internal fans to keep the air cool and circulated inside your system. This prevents too much dust from settling between components.

Circuit boards: Clean with a contact cleaning solution.

Electromagnetic interference (EMI): This is caused when electrical wires are placed too close to each other or when the wires cross each other. This can cause havoc with computer signals traveling down a wire.

Another consideration in an electronic environment is fire safety. You should have a plan in case of fire and have the proper equipment available and ready to use. To extinguish an electrical fire, use a type C or multipurpose-type ABC extinguisher. In an environment with a built-in preventive sprinkler system, consider having protective plastic drop cloths available to cover your most important computer systems. If a fire-detection sprinkler system is in place and fire is detected, you may lose electronic assets to water damage.

You should be familiar with four types of handheld fire extinguishers:

- **APW (Air Pressurized Water):** An APW fire extinguisher is a large silver handheld extinguisher that is filled with a combination of air and water. It should never be used to put out a chemical or electrical fire. This is an older type of extinguisher that is used primarily to take the heat element away from a fire.
- **Dry Chemical (ABC and BC):** These types of handheld extinguishers are very effective at putting out various types of fire. Dry chemical extinguishers smother a fire with a phosphorous chemical that separates the oxygen and fuel within a fire. ABC type extinguishers can be used to put out chemical, electrical, or normal wood burning or paper fires. You can identify whether the extinguisher is an "ABC" or a "BC" extinguisher by the pictures and labels on the extinguisher itself. Never use a "BC" extinguisher on a fire classified as "A." Class "BC" fires are electrical and chemical only. Class "A" fires are normal paper/wood burning fires. Simply put, educate yourself on the type of extinguishers available at your facility. Chances are, you have "ABC" type fire extinguishers proliferated around your building.

Computer-related electrical fires should be extinguished with an extinguisher that is rated for class "C" fires. For the exam, if your server or workstation is on fire, use a Class "BC" or "C" extinguisher.

- **Carbon Dioxide (CO2):** These types of extinguishers use carbon dioxide gas to remove or displace the oxygen in a burning fire. They can easily be identified by a hard black "horn" or spout used to spray the chemical. Carbon dioxide handheld fire extinguishers are designed to put out "BC" type fires.
- **Halon:** Halon extinguishers are filled with a gas instead of a chemical powder. This gas is more effective at putting out "ABC" type fires than an "ABC" type extinguisher. Besides providing better fire suppression than the previously mentioned extinguisher types, a Halon extinguisher will not ruin whatever you have just saved from fire destruction. The chemicals in an "ABC" type extinguisher will ruin electrical wires, computers, or anything else you use them on. Although Halon works well at putting out fires, Halon extinguishers are banned in many places. It has been scientifically proven that Halon gas depletes the ozone and is considered very dangerous to humans. A good substitute for

Halon is FM-200. FM-200 is a widely accepted, chemically based fire suppressor that extinguishes fire by cooling or removing the heat from the flames.

MATERIAL SAFETY DATA SHEET (MSDS)

A Material Safety Data Sheet (MSDS) is a document created and posted for workers and emergency personnel or officials that specifies a set of guidelines regarding the proper handling, transporting, storing, and disposing of a hazardous substance or chemical. Most MSDSs also contain information regarding first aid treatment should exposure to danger occur. They are usually prominently displayed for easy reference in areas where a danger exists. If an emergency occurs, such as exposure to a toxic chemical, the proper actions can be taken to treat the situation based on the information posted on the MSDS. Failure for a company or organization to create and post MSDSs in required (hazardous) areas might result in serious consequences to a business such as a fine or loss of business license.

The exam will likely question your basic knowledge of MSDSs. Make sure you know what they are and what they are used for.

NOTE

COMPLEMENTARY METAL OXIDE SEMICONDUCTOR (CMOS)

CMOS is a battery-backed bank of flash memory chips on the motherboard. The information and settings stored in CMOS can be *flashed,* meaning that they can be changed. The information stored in the CMOS is read by the system BIOS on startup. A lithium battery on the motherboard provides power to hold the CMOS system settings when the computer is off. If the CMOS battery begins to lose some of its battery charge, a CMOS checksum error may appear when the computer starts up. If the battery loses its charge completely, chances are that some or all of your system settings will be lost, including date and time, hard drive settings, and system password. Knowing that the system settings will be lost if the CMOS battery loses its charge or is removed from the motherboard can prove useful. If the user has forgotten the password to enter the system setup, you can remove the CMOS battery, wait about three minutes, and then put the battery back into the motherboard. This process clears the system settings, including the setup password that is locking you out. After clearing the CMOS settings and reentering setup, you should first check to see if the system date and time are correct. Second, check the major hard drive settings for accuracy, including heads, sectors, and cylinders. Another way to clear settings is to shorten the CMOS jumper on the motherboard. In other words, locate the CMOS jumper on the motherboard, and close or "short" the circuit with a plastic jumper. Consult the motherboard manufacturer's instructions for the location of the CMOS jumper and instructions for this process.

You can modify your system setting by pressing F2 or Delete during system booting. This selection depends on what type of BIOS is installed on your computer. Here are some settings that you can change in system setup: system setup password, system date and time, boot sequence, parallel port settings, com/serial ports, hard drive type and size, memory, floppy drive, and plug-and-play options.

If the user plans to upgrade the CPU chip, the CMOS chip may have to be changed or upgraded as well. In addition, if a CMOS checksum error ever appears during the system startup, the BIOS may need upgrading.

THE SYSTEM BASIC INPUT/OUTPUT SERVICES

The system basic input/output service (BIOS) is made up of a group of tiny programs that control input and output services to devices internal to the computer. The BIOS itself is usually stored on a read-only memory (ROM) chip that is usually soldered onto the motherboard. Newer BIOSs come in the form of *flash ROM*, which is ROM that can be changed. The major manufacturers of BIOS are Phoenix, Award, and AMI. You may have seen one of their names flash by on the computer screen as the BIOS carries out instructions during boot. From time to time, a user may want to upgrade, or flash, the current version of BIOS with software updates from the manufacturer. You should know the make and model of the motherboard for BIOS updates and document system configuration settings before upgrading the BIOS.

When a computer is booted, instructions are first available to the system from the ROM BIOS. The main functions of the BIOS are to carry out boot operations and to act as an intermediary among peripheral devices, software applications, and operating systems. One such boot operation, by the way, is to give the user the opportunity to edit CMOS settings by pressing a key like <Delete> or <F2>. As mentioned earlier, the BIOS is permanently stored on ROM chips. The next section describes some types of BIOS chips

Programmable Read-Only Memory (PROM) Chips

Programmable ROM (PROM) is a BIOS chip that cannot be changed. Data can only be stored on it once. A device known as a ROM burner is used to record information into the chip. If the PROM chip goes bad or loses its information, there is no way to reprogram it. The user has no choice but to get another chip from the manufacturer.

Erasable Programmable Read-Only Memory (EPROM) Chips

Erasable PROM (EPROM) BIOS chips look almost identical to PROM chips, with the exception of a little window that is used to shine an ultraviolet light through to erase their contents. This was great for upgrading the BIOS if you had a tool to erase the chip's contents.

Many BIOS chips in the past were EPROM chips. They were easily identified on the motherboard by the shiny label on the top of the chip that usually contained the manufacturer's name and version of the chip.

Electronically Erasable Programmable Read-Only Memory (EEPROM)

By applying a higher voltage to one of the pins on the EEPROM chip, the program on the chip is erased. A new program or set of instructions can then be electronically written to the chip. EEPROM is also known as flash ROM and is the most common type of ROM memory in use on motherboards today.

PLUG AND PLAY (PNP)

Plug and play (PnP) was introduced with Windows 95 to autodetect devices that were connected to the computer. This worked well if the devices were PnP compliant. Unfortunately, not all devices met or meet this standard and must be configured manually. Three requirements must be met to meet the industry standard definition for PnP: PnP hardware, PnP BIOS, and PnP operating system.

A PnP BIOS can autodetect devices connected to the computer and automatically assign resources to them. If a new PnP device is added to a system, the BIOS checks an ESCD database (a running list of active system resources assigned) stored on the CMOS chip to see what resources are unavailable and can be assigned to the new device. In modern computers, the PnP settings are configured in the BIOS under the Advanced Settings option. Legacy or non-PnP devices are normally configured first; PnP devices are configured next. The following operating systems are considered PnP compliant: Windows 9.X, Windows Me, Windows 2000, Windows XP, and Windows Vista. For an operating system to use PnP features and recognize new devices, the PnP option in the system BIOS settings must be enabled.

POWER-ON SELF-TEST (POST) AND ERROR CODES

The power-on self-test (POST) is a self-diagnostic program that runs a test on RAM, I/O devices, and the CPU on system startup. The POST is stored in the ROM BIOS and requires at least a processor, memory, and video adapter to complete its diagnostic tests. The POST recognizes errors related to BIOS configuration settings and I/O connectivity, such as a stuck keyboard. Be forewarned: you may be asked to identify errors that the POST might not recognize. Table 2.3 lists some examples of POST numeric error codes that you may encounter while using a computer. You may also encounter one or two POST numeric error code questions on the test.

TABLE 2.3   Common Post Error Codes

1XX	System board error
201	Memory error
301	Keyboard error
5XX	Monitor error
601	Floppy drive/adapter error
1101	Serial card error
1701	Hard drive controller error

Sounds, or beep codes, are also associated with POST operations and system startup to alert you in the event of an error. Most BIOS manufacturers, such as IBM, Phoenix, and Award, provide their own distinct set of beep codes. A list of IBM's common beep codes is provided in Table 2.4. The test will likely focus on numeric error codes. If you are interested in learning more about beep codes specific to BIOS manufacturers that are not listed, you should consult that manufacturer's Web site.

TABLE 2.4   Common IBM Beep Codes

Beep Description	Error Associated with Beep
No beep	Motherboard or power failure
1 short beep	All POST operations completed successfully
2 short beeps	POST error
1 long beep, 1 short beep	Motherboard error
1 long beep, 2 short beeps	Video adapter failed
1 long beep, 3 short beeps	Video adapter error
3 long beeps	Keyboard failure

EXPANSION BUS ARCHITECTURE

Electronic signals need a medium on which to travel on from one location to another. The motherboard is really a circuit board composed of little electronic data paths that allow all those 0s and 1s to travel from one location to another. These little "highways" are known as the motherboard's bus or I/O bus. The motherboard's I/O bus leads to expansion buses. The expansion buses are narrow slots on the motherboard, developed with different architectures that accept integrated circuit boards, otherwise known as cards. These circuit boards, or cards, can be used to communicate with devices such as monitors, printers, modems, and CD devices.

There are different buses for memory, processors, addresses, and expansion slots. Each of these buses may have different bus widths or number data paths associated with their architecture. In simple terms, if you are looking at an older motherboard that will only accept 8 bits of information at a time, and you have a 16-bit processor to connect to that motherboard, a bottleneck will occur. The motherboard cannot use the full 16 bits of information from the processor.

Table 2.5 lists the most popular expansion slots. An important note for the test: most modern motherboards use AGP, PCI, and industry standard architecture (ISA) slots.

TABLE 2.5   Popular Expansion Slots

Bus/Slot	Bits	Comments
ISA	8 or 16 bits	Operates 8 or 8.33 MHz
EISA	32 bits	Supports PnP and bus mastering; ISA slot compatible
VL-Bus	32 bits	Supports bus mastering; compatible with ISA
MCA	16 or 32 bits	Supports PnP and bus mastering; older proprietary architecture
PCI	32 bits	Supports PnP, bus mastering, and burst mode; uses a host bridge to communicate with other expansion slots
PCI-2	64 bits	Supports PnP, bus mastering; PCI slot compatible
PCI-X	64 bits	Supports PnP, bus mastering; PCI slot compatible; replaced by PCI-e
PCI-e	8 Gbps (x32)	Supports PnP; replaces most PCI, PCI-X, and AGP
AGP	32 or 64 bits	Designed for accelerated graphics and video processing

PCI 32-BIT/64-BIT

PCI is by far the most commonly used bus standard for most NICs, sound cards, and modems today. PCI is an expansion bus technology that was created by Intel. The PCI bus is designed to sync up with the clock speed of the system's CPU. There are two main PCI bus implementations: PCI 32-bit bus and PCI 64-bit bus. Most of the motherboards on the market today implement a PCI 32-bit bus that runs at 33 MHz. The PCI 32-bus is able to access up to 4 GB of memory, largely to support the speeds and data throughput of its Pentium-class processors. Prior to the PCI expansion bus, PCs used the much larger (and slower) EISA and VLB expansion slots.

A PCI 64-bit bus runs at clock speeds of 33 MHz and 66 MHz and has a throughput rate of up to 133 MBps. It uses double 32-bit PCI cycles called Dual Address Cycles (DAC), which allows a 64-bit PCI bus to access up to 17 billion gigabytes of memory space. This means a PCI 64-bit running at 66-MHz speed offers greater bandwidth and throughput, which in turn provides better performance for such technologies as Ethernet, graphics, and much more. PCI technology is designed to transmit data at 32 bits at a time with a 124-pin connection and 64 bits at a time using a 188-pin connection.

PCI-X

Developed by HP, IBM, and Compaq, PCI-X was created to replace generic PCI. PCI-X, based on the PCI standard, doubles the data bus throughput rate, resulting in a doubling of the transfer rate. In other words, it is twice as fast as PCI. PCI-X is backward compatible with PCI. PCI and PCI-X cards can be intermixed, but you should remember for the exam that the speed is limited to the speed of the slowest card on the bus. PCI-X technology has quickly been replaced by PCI-e, which is discussed next.

PCI-e

The PCI-e (PCI Express) is a serial computer expansion card interface that is a much faster technology intended to replace slower PCI, PCI-X, and AGP interfaces. PCI-e uses serial links called *lanes*. The first version or specification of PCI-e is called PCI-e 1.1, which supports x1, x2, x4, x8, x16, and x32 lanes. Each of these "lanes" can carry 250 MBps in each direction, making it a dual simplex link that is able to transmit and receive signals over a single lane at the same time. It is stated that PCI-e has a maximum transfer rate of 16 GBps. The second specification of PCI-e was slated to come out January of 2007 and is called PCI-e 2.0. PCI-e doubles the data rate of each lane from 250 MBps to 500 MBps and is backward compatible with PCI-e 1.1. For the exam, you should note that PCI Express is not compatible with the PCI bus. Although the PCI-e physical cards have roughly the same dimensions, the PCI-e connectors and voltages differ from the PCI standard.

MINI PCI

Mini PCI is a PCI bus version especially made for laptops. Mini PCI is a standard for attaching peripheral devices to a laptop computer motherboard and is an adaptation and smaller version of the PCI bus. Mini PCI supports bus mastering and DMA. They use a 32-bit, 33-MHz bus. The three Mini PCI form factors are Type I, Type II, and Type III cards. The Type I and Type II form factors use a 100-pin stacking connector. The Type III form factor uses a 124-pin edge connector.

ACCELERATED GRAPHICS PORT (AGP)

The Accelerated Graphics Port (AGP) specification was designed to offer a faster and clearer display of graphical images such as 3D images and video at a time where the PCI expansion bus offered essentially the only other option. PCI simply couldn't keep up with the graphics cards of its day.

The AGP specification, which was developed by Intel, is based on PCI technology. However, unlike PCI, AGP works on its own point-to-point dedicated channel and allows a graphic's controller to directly access a computer system'sRAM to provide the faster production of images to the monitor. AGP technology uses memory dynamically. What does that mean? When the memory is not being used by AGP for such things as rendering, texturing, alpha blending, z-buffering, or the general production of images, it is restored to the operating system for other purposes.

AGP 2x, 4x, and 8x

AGP technology comes in several specifications. To the end consumer or user, these specifications are better known as acceleration speeds. In simpler terms, you can purchase an AGP video card at various rates of acceleration. The higher the acceleration rate, the better the card.

You should be aware of two main Intel specifications for AGP:

AGP Specification revision 2.0: This specification defines interfaces supporting AGP 1x and 2x.

AGP Specification 3.0: This specification defines AGP 4x and 8x technology. With AGP 8x, it is possible to deliver more than 2.1 GB. This specification was developed to handle the graphics-bandwidth-hungry applications of today and the near future, although when the future arrived, a newer, faster bus specification arrived as well in the form of PCI-e. As of this writing, today's fastest graphics cards operate over the PCI-e bus.

For the exams, you should remember that there are variations of the AGP slot: AGP 1x (66 MHz/Maximum data rate of 266 MBps), AGP 2x (133 MHz/Maximum data rate of 533 MBps), AGP 4x (266 MHz/Maximum data rate of 1,066 MBps), and AGP 8x (533 MHz/Maximum data rate of 2,133 MBps).

UNIVERSAL SERIAL BUS (USB)

Universal serial bus (USB) is a fairly new serial bus PnP architecture that uses the PCI bus to communicate between the CPU and memory. USB 1.0 offers speeds up to 12 Mbps, and USB 2.0 offers speeds up to 480 Mbps. USB allows the user to attach many low-speed devices to a computer without the need for an expansion card. Devices such as mice, keyboards, printers, and CD-ROMs have been designed with their own built-in controllers that accept the USB standard. You can connect up to 127 peripheral devices to a system with the use of one USB port. In other words, let's say you want to connect a USB keyboard and a USB mouse to your system. These two USB devices together only require one system resource interrupt request (IRQ).

For the exam, make sure you are able to identify USB ports if presented with a picture of a motherboard or system unit. Also remember that USB 1.1 supports speeds up to 12 Mbps, and USB 2.0 offers speeds up to 480 Mbps. USB supports up to 127 devices and is used as a high-speed interface to attach peripheral devices such as cameras, printers, and scanners to a computer system. If you require more information regarding USB, the following HowStuffWorks Web site does a great job of explaining how USB ports work: *http://computer.howstuffworks.com/usb3.htm.*

RISER CARDS

As computer systems have evolved and the great need for more internal system unit space has increased, PCI riser cards have become a welcomed solution in the battle for motherboard extension and overall space savings inside a computer system. When a riser card is plugged into a motherboard, it forms a right angle with the motherboard as opposed to lying flat above the motherboard. This allows for more technology to be plugged into the motherboard and provides more space overall. PCI riser cards also provide additional slots for both 64-bit and 32-bit adapter cards.

Riser cards also allow for faster production of new technologies. For example, developers and manufacturers of technologies have had to go through a lengthy certification process in the past to get their technologies certified for "on the motherboard integration." Riser cards allow for technologies to be developed faster by placing them above the motherboard on a riser card. You'll see a perfect example of this when we discuss the Audio Modem Riser (AMR) slots a bit later.

Many types of riser cards are available on the market today. Some of the most popular include riser cards for memory modules such as DIMM, RIMM, and SODIMM (memory modules are discussed in Chapter 4). There are other popular riser cards, such as the Slot1 Riser Cards that are used for Pentium II processors and the Slot2 riser cards that are used for XEON processors (processors are discussed in more detail in Chapter 3). There are also riser cards for other technologies such as audio, modem, local area network (LAN), and USB. If you look closely at the CompTIA A+ 2006 Objectives, you will notice that Audio Modem Riser (AMR) and Communication Network Riser (CNR) are targeted. For that very reason, we will discuss them next.

AUDIO MODEM RISER (AMR)

Intel created the Audio Modem Riser (AMR) specification. This specification for motherboard architecture allows analog I/O functions to be separate from the motherboard by placing them on a riser card that contains a codec (compressor/decompressor) chip. Separating analog I/O functions from the motherboard allows designers to develop newer and better technology faster without having to go through the grueling and time-consuming certification process for motherboard manufacturer approval and integration. Another extremely important benefit to this riser card technology is the high quality of audio that can be produced as a result of this process.

The Audio Modem Riser technology has been superseded, however, by motherboard-embedded audio and networking components. Communication Network Riser (CNR)

The Communication and Network Riser (CNR) is an Intel created standard that applies to riser cards. A CNR card is an ATX-compatible PCI riser card that offers logic support for such technologies as audio, modem, LAN, and USB. The idea is to allow developers to better integrate and compact this technology into a smaller, more scaleable hardware device that makes better use of motherboard resources and system unit space.

NOTE

The following Adex Electronics, Inc. Web site provides a superb display and explanation of various riser cards: www.adexelec.com/riser.htm.

The following reference is available on the Web in PDF format: www.formfactors.org/developer/specs/atx/ATX_Spec_V1_0.pdf. It explains many technical details associated with the ATX form factor riser card specification. Pay special attention to the PCI Slot assignments on ATX form factor boards with ATX riser support.

Both AMR and CNR technologies have been identified as targets for the CompTIA 2006 Objectives exam. Make sure you know what they are.

NORTH AND SOUTH BRIDGES

PCI architecture is based on the concept of *bridging*. A PCI bus has a north bridge and a south bridge. The north bridge communicates with the CPU and is used to send signals to devices that run at higher speeds such as memory, AGP, CPU, or PCI-e. The south bridge communicates with a super I/O chip and is used to send signals to slower devices, such as ISA slots, COM, and LPT ports.

PCMCIA (PC Cards)

This section is designed to get you up to speed with the most popular laptop computer expansion card technologies. The two major expansion card technologies for laptop systems that are targeted by CompTIA 2006 Objectives are PCMCIA (PC Cards), which can be either a 16- or 32-bitexpansion card technology, and Mini PCI, which is a 32-bit bus technology.

In the early 1990s the Personal Computer Memory Card International Association (PCMCIA) standard was developed for laptop computer expansion cards. This 16-bit standard is offered in the form of three various card types that all use the same type of 68-pin connector. The major differences among the three card types are their size and function. The three types of PC cards that you need to be familiar with for the exam are as follows:

- Type I is 3.3 mm thick and is typically used for memory such as RAM, OTP, Flash memory, or SRAM cards.
- Type II is 5 mm thick and is used for modems, TV, and NIC cards.
- Type III is 10.5mm thick and is used for hard drives.

Mini PCI

The need for faster connection speeds and overall throughput spawned the need for a faster/wider bus that would support newer technologies such as wireless and bandwidth hungry media adapters. Thus, the Mini PCI form factor was born. Inspired by the PCI special interest group (SIG), the Mini PCI is a 32-bit 33 MHz technology that is based on the PCI form factor, which is found in most modern desktops. Keep in mind that the Mini PCI cards are internal cards or "modules" that are typically installed by the laptop or system manufacturer. Mini PCI comes in three different form factors. The main differences in these form factors are the way in which they connect to the system board and other I/O connectors. Following are the three types of Mini PCI form factors:

Type I: This card form factor connects via a twisted-pair cable to the phone (RJ11) or network (RJ45) connectors inside a laptop or system. It connects to the system board with a 100-pin stacking connector. This card can be positioned somewhat away from the edge of the system board or docking station chassis because the RJ45 or RJ11 jacks do not reside on the card.

Type II: Based on their design, Type II cards must be located at the edge of the system board or docking station chassis to connect the card's built-in RJ11 or RJ45 I/O connectors directly to the mounted external RJ11 and RJ45 ports.

Like the Type I Mini PCI form factor, Type II connects to the system board with a 100-pin stacking connector.

Type III: Type III cards have the flexibility of connecting to external I/O (RJ11 and RJ45) ports via the same cable connection type as that used with a Type I card. They differ from Type I and Type II Mini PCI cards in the way they connect to the system board. Type III uses a 124-pin card-edge connector that is similar to the connector used by small outline, dual in-line memory modules (SODIMMs) to connect to the system board. Type III Mini PCI cards have a lower profile, which allows manufactures to create smaller laptops.

CHAPTER SUMMARY

In this chapter, you were introduced to motherboards and their form factors, slots and sockets, expansion board architectures, power, POST, BIOS, and other important information. On the exams, be prepared to list the major motherboard components by form factor, answer basic power-related troubleshooting questions, and know whether slot or socket technology is implemented. Many questions on the current A+ tests are likely to be related to topics that were discussed in this chapter. Throughout this book, you may also find that some of the review questions and answers are not discussed word for word in the chapter they represent. Your ability to research may be tested a little and that is what makes an excellent technician! Good luck.

REVIEW QUESTIONS

1. **You are at a customer site and receive complaints that an important server computer freezes when booting up and displays an error code of 301. What should you check?**

   ○ A. Keyboard
   ○ B. Floppy drive cable
   ○ C. Properly seated memory
   ○ D. Hard drive

   Correct Answer = A

   If the POST detects an issue on boot up, it will display a numeric code. A numeric code of 301 indicates a keyboard-related issue. This is a very common issue and typically just requires the keyboard connector to be reseated into the keyboard port on the back of the system. For the exams, remember that 201 is a memory error, 601 is a floppy drive error, and 1701 is a hard drive controller error. Know your codes for use in the field and on the exams!

2. **Your computer will not start. There are no lights whatsoever. What would you do first to troubleshoot this problem?**
   - ○ A. Buy a new hard drive
   - ○ B. Change the CMOS battery
   - ○ C. Test the Power supply
   - ○ D. Verify AC wall outlet has power

   Correct Answer = D

   If you are troubleshooting a "dead" computer, first verify that there is electricity coming from the AC wall outlet.

3. **Which of the following devices are compatible with an AGP slot?**
   - ☐ A. Type II PC card
   - ☐ B. Parallel port
   - ☐ C. Serial port
   - ☐ D. Video card

   Correct Answer = D

   The AGP slot was designed for accelerated graphics and video processing.

4. **You have replaced a bad CMOS battery. What should you check next?**
   - ○ A. COM port settings
   - ○ B. Hard drive settings
   - ○ C. Date and time
   - ○ D. BIOS version

   Correct Answer = C

   After clearing the CMOS settings and reentering setup, you should first check to see if the system date and time are correct.

5. **You have experienced a floppy drive failure. What error code will your POST most likely display?**
   - ○ A. 301
   - ○ B. 161
   - ○ C. 601
   - ○ D. 1701

   Correct Answer = C

   Table 2.3 identifies common POST error codes. Error code 601 identifies a Floppy Drive/Adapter Error.

6. **A computer is continuously rebooting on its own. What is most likely the problem?**
    ○ A.   There is a ghost in the machine.
    ○ B.   The CMOS battery is losing its charge.
    ○ C.   You are experiencing ESD.
    ○ D.   The system is not getting enough power.

    Correct Answer = D

    If your system continuously reboots on its own, it may not be receiving enough power from the power supply.

7. **You cannot remember your password to get into the system settings on boot up. How can you address this? (Choose Two)**
    ☐ A.   Remove the CMOS Battery.
    ☐ B.   Use a multimeter.
    ☐ C.   "Short" the CMOS jumper.
    ☐ D.   Press Ctrl+Alt+Del.

    Correct Answers = A and C

    Removing the CMOS battery or "shorting" the CMOS jumper will clear the CMOS settings, which include a previously stored password. This will allow you to reenter CMOS and change the system settings.

8. **Label all of the components specified on the diagram in Figure 2.7.**

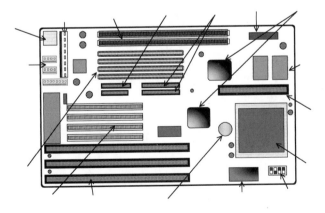

Figure 2.7   Baby AT motherboard.

Answers: See Figure 2.1.

9. **Label all of the components specified on the diagram in Figure 2.8.**

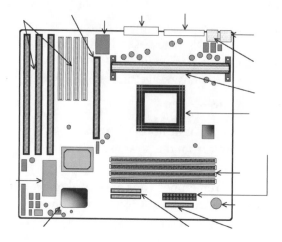

Figure 2.8 ATX motherboard.

Answers: See Figure 2.2.

10. **What information is usually found in a MSDS? (Choose Four)**
    - ☐ A. Microsoft systems development software
    - ☐ B. Disposal instructions
    - ☐ C. First aid instructions
    - ☐ D. Hazardous material handing information
    - ☐ E. Transportation instructions

    Correct Answers = B, C, D, and E

    Material Safety Data Sheets (MSDS) contain information regarding the proper handling, disposal, and transportation of hazardous material. They also contain first aid instructions should an emergency or exposure to a hazard occur.

11. **Which of the following is an ATX-compatible PCI riser card that offers logic support for such technologies as audio, modem, LAN, and USB?**
    - ○ A. SODIMM riser card
    - ○ B. Scalable Logic Card Interpreter (SLCI)
    - ○ C. Communication Network Riser (CNR) card
    - ○ D. All of the above
    - ○ E. None of the above

    Correct Answer = C

The Communication and Network Riser (CNR) is an Intel created standard that applies to riser cards. A CNR card is an ATX-compatible PCI riser card that offers logic support for such technologies as audio, modem, LAN, and USB.

12. **Which Intel standard allows analog I/O functions to be separate from the motherboard?**

    ○ A. SLCI
    ○ B. NLX
    ○ C. AMR
    ○ D. Soft switch
    ○ E. None of the above

    Correct Answer = C

    This Audio Modem Riser (AMR) specification for motherboard architecture allows analog I/O functions to be separate from the motherboard by placing them on a riser card that contains a codec chip. Intel developed the AMR standard.

13. **Of the following devices, which is used to protect electronic equipment from transient voltage or "spikes"?**

    ○ A. Multimeter
    ○ B. Surge suppressor
    ○ C. Integrated I/O port
    ○ D. AC compressor/decompressor
    ○ E. None of the above

    Correct Answer = B

    A surge suppressor is a device used to protect electronic equipment, such as computer systems, printers, modems, and monitors, from transient voltage or "spikes" that occur in the flow of electricity.

14. **An educated remote user calls you and states that he needs you to send a replacement modem card for his laptop computer. What type of PCM-CIA card will you send?**

    ○ A. Type I
    ○ B. Type II
    ○ C. Type III
    ○ D. Type IX
    ○ E. None of the above

Correct Answer = B

Type II PCMCIA cards are used for NICs or modems and are 5mm thick.

15. **You company's main server computer is on fire! What type extinguisher should you use?**

    ○ A. Type I
    ○ B. Type II
    ○ C. Class "A" rated
    ○ D. Class "C" rated
    ○ E. All of the above

    Correct Answer = D

    Computer-related electrical fires should be extinguished with an extinguisher that is rated for class "C" fires.

16. **Which type of Mini PCI card must be located at the edge of the system board or docking station chassis to connect the card's built-in RJ11 or RJ45 I/O connectors directly to the mounted external RJ11 and RJ45 ports?**

    ○ A. Type I
    ○ B. Type II
    ○ C. Type III
    ○ D. Type IX
    ○ E. None of the above

    Correct Answer = B

    Based on their design, Type II cards must be located at the edge of the system board or docking station chassis to connect the card's built-in RJ11 or RJ45 I/O connectors directly to the mounted external RJ11 and RJ45 ports.

17. **Which motherboard chipset is used for handling faster communications for components such as memory, CPU, AGP, or PCI-e?**

    ○ A. South bridge
    ○ B. West bridge
    ○ C. East bridge
    ○ D. North bridge
    ○ E. None of the above

    Correct Answer = D

    The north bridge communicates with the CPU and is used to send signals to devices that run at higher speeds such as memory, AGP, CPU, or PCI-e.

The south bridge communicates with a super I/O chip and is used to send signals to slower devices, such as ISA slots, COM, and LPT ports. The east and west bridges do not exist and are incorrect answers.

18. **What is the maximum data throughput of an AGP 8x slot?**

    ○ A.   133 MBps
    ○ B.   266 MBps
    ○ C.   533 MBps
    ○ D.   2133 MBps
    ○ E.   None of the above

    Correct Answer = D

    Once again, for the exams, you should remember the AGP specification variations: AGP 1x (66 MHz/Maximum data rate of 266 MBps), AGP 2x (133 MHz/Maximum data rate of 533 MBps), AGP 4x (266 MHz/Maximum data rate of 1,066 MBps), and AGP 8x (533 MHz/Maximum data rate of 2,133 MBps).

19. **You are tasked with upgrading 200 client systems at XYZ Company to use the USB 2.0 interface. What speed does the USB 2.0 standard support?**

    ○ A.   1 GB
    ○ B.   460 MBps
    ○ C.   480 MBps
    ○ D.   840 MBps
    ○ E.   None of the above

    Correct Answer = C

    USB is a fairly new serial bus PnP architecture that uses the PCI bus to communicate between the CPU and memory. USB 1.0 offers speeds up to 12 Mbps, and USB 2.0 offers speeds up to 480 Mbps. All other answers are incorrect.

20. **You have upgraded several components in the main file server at XYZ Company. You are concerned about power and want to see if the server can handle the new components. Which tool would you use to test the power in the recently upgraded file server?**

    ○ A.   Loopback plug
    ○ B.   Digital multimeter
    ○ C.   Loopback adapter
    ○ D.   None of the above

Correct Answer = B

The power supply converts AC to the +5V, –5V, +12V, or –12V DC current that the motherboard and its components require. A useful tool to test power (voltage) coming from the power supply and going to the motherboard and components is a digital multimeter. A loopback plug or loopback adapter is used to test the operation of data ports and connections.

REFERENCES

www.fic.com.tw/support/motherboard/faq.aspx?type=microatx#qid470. This First International Computer Inc. Web site offers some useful information regarding the MicroATX motherboard form factor.

http://en.wikipedia.org/wiki/List_of_microprocessors. The Wikipedia site has an excellent description of the major processors and the slots or sockets they use.

http://computer.howstuffworks.com/usb3.htm. This HowStuffWorks Web site provides great information regarding USB technology and USB ports.

www.adexelec.com/riser.htm. This Adex Electronics, Inc. Web site provides a superb display and explanation of various riser cards.

www.formfactors.org/developer/specs/atx/ATX_Spec_V1_0.pdf. This desktop form factor's Web site provides an excellent education on motherboard form factors in general and, in this case, an excellent explanation of the ATX form factor specification for riser cards.

3 Processors and Cache

In This Chapter

CPU DEFINED

The CPU, also known as the microprocessor, is the core or central intelligence of a computer system. The CPU accepts data input, processes the data, and carries out instructions. The CPU handles logical and mathematical functions. It is important to have as fast a CPU as possible for quick calculation and manipulation of data. A fast CPU is essential to many of the latest applications and operating systems, which simply won't run on processors released two or three years ago. The speed of the CPU (measured in megahertz) and the motherboard (clock speed) determine the amount of time it takes to complete a desired function or task.

A motherboard and its components (including the CPU) are always in danger from ESD. As mentioned in Chapter 2, ESD can damage the circuitry on a motherboard and destroy a CPU. Although upgrading a processor is rare (and may involve upgrading the entire motherboard as well), CompTIA recommends that you always transport components in an antistatic ESD-protective bag, and wear a protective ESD wrist strap when upgrading a CPU.

The new A+ exams will likely test your knowledge of newer microprocessors; their motherboard speeds; the slot or socket technology they are associated with; Levels 1, 2, and 3 caches; and basic processor troubleshooting.

CLOCK AND BUS SPEEDS

The motherboard contains an oscillating system crystal, or oscillator. This built-in timer or clock controls the speed at which the CPU can transfer information to and from memory and communicate with peripheral devices. Clock speed is normally expressed in megahertz (MHz). For example, if you have a 550 MHz Pentium III processor, the clock speed is 550 MHz. One MHz is equal to 1 million cycles per second of the oscillating clock. The clock speed on the motherboard can be configured with little plastic jumpers located on the motherboard itself. Most motherboards are designed to run at multiple clock speeds. It is important to set the CPU and other motherboard components to run at the maximum clock speed of the motherboard; the wrong settings can result in an overheated processor. Also, if a processor fan on top of your processor is being used for cooling purposes, you should occasionally verify that it is working properly. If it has failed, the system may lock up, and the processor may suffer irreversible damage due to overheating.

Looking at a motherboard, you can see little pathways that lead from component to component. These pathways are actually tiny copper wires that carry information from place to place. These wires make up the system bus. Bus speed is measured by the width of the bus. The width of the bus is calculated by the number of bits of information the bus can move at a given time. The actual speed of the bus is calculated in terms of megahertz. Typical bus widths are 16, 32, and 64 bits. Most systems today have 64-bit wide buses that run at 100 MHz. Newer chipsets on the market run at 133 MHz.

THE EXTERNAL DATA BUS

The external data bus is made up of tiny wires integrated into the motherboard that the CPU uses as a means to communicate with peripheral devices.

THE ADDRESS BUS

The CPU uses the address bus, which is also made up of tiny wires integrated into the motherboard, to access areas of memory by the Memory Controller Chip (MCC). The address bus keeps track of locations in memory called memory addresses. The number of memory addresses in a system is based on the size, or "width," of the address bus.

CACHE LEVELS 1, 2, AND 3

The processing and calculation of information takes place inside the processor itself. When the processor needs quick, predetermined information, it relies on cached memory. *Cached memory* is a special set of memory chips that are internal or external to the processor itself. Cached memory is physically closer to the CPU than RAM and is therefore much faster. Cache memory is designed for quick access by the processor.

Level 1 cache, otherwise known as internal or primary cache, is internal to the processor. It is not part of any other memory and is not restricted by the system clock. Level 1 cache is fast memory that the CPU uses first for quick storage and calculation. Unfortunately, Level 1 cache is not very large in storage capacity. Its storage capability ranges from 8 KB to 64 KB. Level 2 cache, otherwise known as external or secondary cache, is external to the processor. It is slower than Level 1 cache but can provide more than 512 KB of storage space. Performance gains are mostly realized from the storage capacity of the Level 2 cache.

Technology advances again! Recently, manufacturers such as Intel have developed technology that brings an additional 1 MB (1024 KB) Level 3 (L3) cache onto the CPU chip. This Level 3 cache addition has dramatically increased the speed at which a processor or dual processors can access stored information. This in turn provides better processor support for overall application access speed and system support.

To educate yourself further on cache, processors, and other newer components, you should check out the specifications listed at the following Intel Web site: *http://program.intel.com/SHARED/products/servers/index.htm.*

You will be tested on cache Levels 1, 2, and 3. Make sure you know their differences.

CHIPSETS AND CONTROLLERS

CPUs are generally faster than the devices they communicate with. So that smooth communication can take place between CPUs and peripheral devices, interfaces known as chipsets have been developed to handle this transition or *buffering* of information. Early computers used separate chips to control the transition of data for specific tasks. Some of the early chips and notable controller interfaces include the following:

The bus controller chip: Handles or "supervises" the flow of information on the different motherboard buses.

The Direct Memory Address (DMA) controller: The DMA controller allows devices to use addressed memory without interacting with the CPU.

Math coprocessor: Supervises the flow of information between the math coprocessor and the CPU.

SUPER I/O CONTROLLER

The super I/O controller was a great advancement that combined the functions of older, separate controller chips into one *smart chip*. The super I/O controller chip became a welcomed standard. Some of the major functions controlled by the super I/O include control of serial port Universal Asynchronous Receiver/Transceiver (UART), control and support for floppy disk and tape drives, and control functions related to parallel ports and their enhanced capabilities.

CHIPSET CONTROLLERS (BUILT-IN)

Chipsets are designed to support specific devices, motherboards, CPUs, and computers that they will control. Following are several built-in devices and controllers included with common chipsets:

Enhanced Integrated Drive Electronics (EIDE) controller: The EIDE (or IDE) controller is used to communicate and support devices such as hard disk drives, floppy disk drives, CD-ROMs, and other storage devices. Most computers today have chipset support for two EIDE onboard controllers.

Memory controller: The memory controller controls the flow of data in and out of memory. Devices that need access to the system memory or RAM must first pass through this controller.

PCI bridge: As mentioned in Chapter 2, PCI bridging, or north and south bridge, is used to connect the PCI interface on the motherboard with older devices, such as ISA.

DMA controller: This manages the availability and support for ISA and AT Attachment (ATA) devices. (ATA is a set of rules or specifications that apply to the IDE controller. Both are described in Chapter 7.)

SCSI adapters, network interface cards, and sound cards: All of these use DMA channels to move data in and out of system memory without assistance from a CPU. This controller provides the ability for the previously mentioned devices to access the system memory. SCSI adapters are discussed in Chapter 8.

Real-Time Clock (RTC): Controller support is provided for the RTC. The RTC controls system date and time.

PS/2 mouse: This controller provides a direct interface between the PS/2 mouse and the processor.

Keyboard controller: Controls functions between the keyboard and the CPU.

IRDA (Infrared Data Association) controller: Infrared controller packaged with most laptop computers.

RISC Versus CISC

Th two important terms apply to the programming and instruction sets of chipsets: Reduced Instruction Set Computer (RISC) and Complex Instruction Set Computing (CISC).

RISC is a technology used in high-end computing systems that uses a limited number of instructions and fewer transistors than CISC. The result is a less expensive chipset. Most Sun computing systems incorporate RISC technology.

Most conventional computing systems use CISC. CISC architecture is capable of supporting many more instructions than RISC. Pentium systems use CISC technology.

SEC and SEP

In Chapter 2, you became familiar with slot and socket technology. *Slot technology* integrates the processor onto a circuit board or IC board. The circuit board is then plugged into a motherboard slot. The actual edge of the circuit board that is plugged into the motherboard comes in two forms: Single Edge Connector (SEC) or Single Edge Processor (SEP). Many modern processors, including the Celeron, AMD Athlon, Pentium II, Pentium III, and Pentium IV, use either SEC or SEP packaging and employ slot technology. Intel's SEC design contains both a CPU and a Level 2 cache. Modern processors like the Core 2 Duo use PGA, which is described next.

PGA and SPGA

Socket technology typically uses a ZIF socket on the motherboard that awaits a processor with many tiny pins extending from the bottom side of the square processor. The configuration of these pins is called a PGA package. A second design of the PGA standard is SPGA, in which the tiny pins underneath the processor are staggered, thereby allowing the processor to be smaller.

Processors and Modes

In 1978, the Intel 8086 processor was introduced. Recently, many of the processors on the market have been based on the characteristics of the 8086 processor. Several modes and advancements in early processors designed to maintain backward compatibility with the original 8086 processor are worth mentioning.

REAL MODE

Provided by the 8086 (XT) processor, real-mode processing offers the processor access to the limited memory space or environment of 1 MB (1024 KB of memory addresses). Real mode uses a 16-bit data path and has a direct access path to RAM.

PROTECTED MODE

Introduced with the 80286 processor, protected mode allows the processor to access memory above 1 MB (1024 KB) and up to 16 MB. Protected mode allows programs to use a 32-bit data path.

VIRTUAL REAL (PROTECTED) MODE

Introduced with the 80386 processor, virtual real (protected) mode allows multiple programs to run at the same time in their own protected separate memory addresses or Virtual Machines (VMs). If one of these programs or VMs fails, the other programs are not affected.

386DX

Made of CMOS material, the 386DX provides 32-bit processing power and can run in virtual real mode. A 386 operates at +5V, is capable of addressing up to 4 GB of memory, and has an internal cache. The clock speeds for 386DX range from 16 MHz to 33 MHz.

386SX

Released in 1988, the 386SX is a scaled-down version of the 386DX. It has a smaller, 16-bit external bus and a 24-bit memory address bus that addresses 16 MB of RAM. This makes the 386SX less expensive than the 386DX. It was available from 16 MHz to 33 MHz.

386SL

In 1990, the 386SL was introduced to meet the demand for a smaller processor with lower power consumption. This need came from the desire for laptop computing systems that required smaller components. The 386SL is basically the 386SX designed for laptops and their power management capabilities. The 386SL was offered with a 25 MHz clock speed.

486DX

The 486DX featured 32-bit internal and external memory address buses. It offered internal Level 1 cache at 8 KB. This processor introduced burst mode memory and had a coprocessor or Floating-Point Unit (FPU) integrated into the CPU chip.

486SX

The 486SX is a scaled-down version of the 486DX processor. The math coprocessor was disabled by the manufacturer and sold as a lower-cost alternative to the DX model.

486DX2

The 486DX2 was designed to run at double the speed (with the exception of the external bus) of its predecessor, the 486DX. The 486DX2 processor operates at +3.3V.

AMD 5X86 (K5)

The AMD K5 was offered as a 75 MHz to 133 MHz processor, released by AMD. It was produced to be competitive with early Pentium CPUs. The K5offered 50, 60, and 66 bus speeds, and an internal (primary) cache of 24 KB. The AMD K5 uses Socket 7 technology. The K5 has a Level 1 cache of 24 KB.

CYRIX 5X86

Cyrix 5X86 is a Socket 7-type CPU released to compete with early Pentiums.

THE EARLY PENTIUMS (60 MHz TO 200 MHz)

The first Pentium processor, which became known as the classic Pentium I, was offered in 1992, and it was backward compatible with previous Intel processors. The early Pentiums operated with a data bus of 64 bits, an address bus of 32 bits, and a memory bus of 64 bits. It offered 16 KB of Level 1 cache. The Pentium I introduced the single-cycle instruction technology known as dual pipelining.

PENTIUM PRO

The Pentium Pro offered onboard Level 1 cache at 16 KB and Level 2 cache at 256 KB, 512 KB, or 1 MB, which answered the need for large amounts of cached memory. It introduced the concept of quad pipelining and dynamic processing. The Pentium Pro worked well for a program-intensive workstation or server. Unfortunately, it did not handle 16-bit (DOS) application code well.

AMD K6

The K6 was developed as competition for the Pentium Pro. Speeds available were 166 MHz, 200 MHz, 233 MHz, 266 MHz, and a Super Socket 7 version designed to run at 100 MHz motherboard bus speed and higher clock speeds. The AMD K6 has an internal cache size of 64 KB.

Cyrix 6X86MX

To compete with the Pentiums, AMD and Cyrix developed a Processor Rating (PR) system designed to match up equivalent competitor clock speeds. The Cyrix 6x86MX processors ranged from PR-166 to PR-366. The 6x86 had an external bus speed of 75 MHz.

Celeron

Introduced as a lower-end Pentium II, the Intel Celeron processor came to the market to answer the need for less-expensive chips that could keep pace with the Pentiums. Depending on its version, the Celeron could be purchased in PII- or PIII-comparable speeds. Celeron packages came in PGA or FC-PGA format and required a 66 MHz motherboard. The Celeron is compatible with Multimedia Extensions (MMX). It has a Level 1 cache of 32 KB.

In May of 2002, Intel introduced a new Celeron based on the same technologies used to produce the Willamette Pentium 4. This Socket 478 processor came in speeds of 1.7 GHz and 1.8 GHz, offered 128KB of L2 cache (as opposed to the Pentium 4's 256 KB), ran at 1.75V, and had a 400 MHz front side bus (100 MHz quad pumped effective at 400 MHz). In November of 2002, Intel would release a newer, updated Celeron model based on the Pentium 4 Northwood Core. It was offered as a 2.0 GHz product (Socket 478) running at 1.5V, with 128 KB of L2 cache, and a 400 MHz front side bus (100 MHz quad pumped effective at 400 MHz).

Xeon

The Xeon processor succeeded the Pentium Pro. It was meant to be a server computer processor, primarily because of its choices of Level 2 cache, which was available at 512 KB, 1 MB, or 2 MB. Xeon was also noted for its capability to support up to eight processors in one computer and up to 64 GB of memory.

Pentium II

The Pentium II processor is available in 233 MHz, 266 MHz, 300 MHz, 333 MHz, 350 MHz, 400 MHz, and 450 MHz clock speeds. This processor is designed to take full advantage of MMX technology. MMX introduced new hardware technology processing that is integrated into the system for better calculation and acceleration of multimedia. The Pentium II provides a larger pipeline cache size than its predecessor, the Pentium I. It has a Level 1 cache of 32 KB and a Level 2 cache of 512 KB. The Pentium II uses Slot 1 technology. In Table 3.1, you can see a comparison of Pentium II processor speeds to their corresponding motherboard clock speeds.

TABLE 3.1   Pentium II Processor and Motherboard Speed Comparison

Pentium II Processor Speed	Motherboard
233 MHz	66 MHz
266 MHz	66 MHz
300 MHz	66 MHz
333 MHz	66 MHz
350 MHz	100 MHz
400 MHz	100 MHz
450 MHz	100 MHz

PENTIUM III

Pentium III offers 32 KB of Level 1 cache and fully supports Level 2 cache at 512 KB. It is offered with clock speeds that range from 450 MHz to 1.4 GHz. It is available in a second-generation SEC package known as SECC2. Remember, the Pentium III uses both Slot 1 and Socket 370 technologies.

AMD ATHLON AND DURON

A processor available through AMD is the AMD 1 GHz Athlon processor, which replaces the AMD K-6 series. Athlon is available in both Slot A and Socket A formats and boasts a 200 MHz to 400 MHz Alpha EV-6 bus.

The AMD Duron, released to the public in 2000, was meant to be the Celeron's major competitor. The AMD Duron was developed for the mid-range workstation market. The Duron processor clock speeds range from 600 MHz through 1.3 GHz. The Duron used either Slot A or Socket A technology, has the Level 2 cache internal to the processor (unlike the Athlon, which has the Level 2 cache external to the processor), and is rated at a motherboard speed of 100 MHz.

ATHLON XP

The Athlon XP was introduced in November of 2001 by AMD as a follow-up to the very successful Athlon line of processors. Athlon XPs range in speed from 1.33 GHz to 2.167 GHz, but you won't find them listed anywhere with those clock speeds. AMD decided, in an interesting public relations move, to rename the processors according to how they compared to previous Athlon processors. For example, an Athlon 1500+ (clocked at 1.3 GHz) is comparable with the previous Athlon model clocked at 1.5 GHz (had they gone over 1.4 GHz with the classic

Athlon). The difference in performance was attributed to "Quantispeed Architecture," which (in simplified terms) means that the processor is handling more operations per clock cycle—not new technology, just a catchy new name.

The original XPs, based on the Palomino core, came clocked at 1.33 GHz (XP 1500+) through 1.60 GHz (XP 1900+). These processors were soon replaced with a processor revision dubbed the Thoroughbred, which reduced the core size using the 0.13-micron process. The advantage to the revised line with the smaller core was that lower core voltages could be used for lower clocked processors. Voltage requirements scaled with processor speed, so a 1.47 GHz (1700+) would only require 1.50V, whereas the higher-clocked processor at, say, 1.80 GHz (2200+) required 1.65V. (Lower voltage consumption rates meant less heat, which made it more attractive to consumers at large.) Both Thoroughbred and Palomino Athlon XPs used a 266 MHz front side bus (133 MHz double data rate effective at 266 MHz), with 256 KB of L2 cache. *All* of the processors in the Athlon XP line use Socket A technology, with DDR-SDRAM memory options in chipsets as the memory configuration of choice.

Only recently has the XP line of processors again been revised. The newly released Barton core boasts not only a larger L2 cache (512 KB) but also a faster front side bus, effectively at 333 MHz. Bartons are currently being offered in variable speeds, all the way up to 2.167 GHz (Athlon XP 3000+).

Pentium 4

Originally introduced on July 2, 2001, the Pentium 4 ranges in speed from 1.3 GHz to 3.20 GHz. It is important to realize, however, that the Pentium 4 has undergone some serious changes throughout its life span.

When the Pentium 4 was introduced in mid-2001, it was available as a Socket 423 and (in later processor models) Socket 478 processor. Dubbed the Willamette, it came with a 400 MHz (100 MHz quad pumped effectively 400 MHz) front side bus and 256 KB of L2 cache. In this form, it was available in speeds that ranged from 1.3 GHz to 2.0 GHz. These processors were only used with costly RDRAM (Rambus) and generally were regarded as "fast but too expensive."

In early 2002, however, the current iteration of the Pentium 4 was introduced: the Northwood. The Northwood is based solely on Socket 478 technology and out of the gate offered 512 KB L2 cache. The extra 256 KB of L2 cache offered a 10% performance increase for similarly clocked processors (as there was an overlap of processor speeds between the Willamette and the Northwood). Also, the physical size of the silicon core had been reduced from 217 mm^2 to 146 mm^2. The decrease in core size also benefits the new Northwood in terms of voltage requirements, as the requirement dropped from 1.75V (for Willamette) to 1.5V. With these processors came the several different chipsets supporting several different memory types, from SDRAM, DDR SDRAM, and, of course, the original RDRAM.

The Northwood core, itself, has undergone changes since its inception. The 533 MHz (133 MHz quad pumped effective at 533 MHz) front side bus versions of the processor were released in May of 2002. And only just recently, the 800 MHz (200 MHz quad pumped effective at 800 MHz) front side bus version has been released.

The test is likely to present you with questions that test your knowledge of processor/motherboard compatibility and speed. For example, you should know that early Pentiums, such as the 75 MHz Pentium, were designed to run at a 66 MHz motherboard bus speed. The original Pentium through the Pentium II 333 MHz processors were designed to run at a 66 MHz motherboard bus speed. The Pentium II 350 MHz through the Pentium III series processors are intended to run at a 100 MHz motherboard bus speed.

You should remember for the exams that the Pentium 4 introduced Hyperthreading, which is Intel's trademark for the implementation of the simultaneous multithreading technology on the Pentium 4 serious of microprocessors.

ITANIUM AND ITANIUM II

The first Itanium microprocessor chip was released by Intel in 2001 and has since been superseded by the Itanium 2 Chip, which currently has a code name of Montecito. The Itanium family of Itaniums is based on Intel's 64-bit architecture that was formally known as IA-64. The Itanium series was released to meet the need for processing power of hungry servers and high-end computing systems. For Itanium and Itanium II processor speeds, cache, pins, and supporting packaging, refer to Table 3.2.

INTEL PENTIUM DUAL CORE

Although it's likely that this will not be on the most current A+ Exams, it is important for you as aspiring computer help desk support, technicians, and network administrators to be familiar with the newly released Intel Pentium Dual Core series of processors. Released in laptop computers in early 2007, the first Dual Core Pentiums were released and based on one of three architectures: the 32-bit Pentium M, *Yonah,* or 64-bit Core *Allendale* cores. Ultimately, they would target both mobile and desktop systems. Also in June of 2007, Intel released the Pentium E2140 and E216 processors with support for Intel 64 extensions. These are based on the 64-bit Allendale core.

Table 3.2 displays the most commonly tested CPU information on the current A+ Exams. Although basic CPU slots and sockets were covered in Chapter 2, a more detailed slots and sockets comparison chart is provided (see Table 3.3) now that you are more up to speed with processors.

TABLE 3.2 CPU Chips Comparison and Characteristics

Processor	Speed (MHz)	Heat Sinks	Cooling Fans	Cache	Packaging	Pins
8088	5-8	No	No	No	DIP	40
80286	6 10 12	No	No	No	LLC PGA PLCC	68
80386SX	16–33	No	No	No	PGA	100
80386DX	16–33	No	No	No	PGA	100
80486SX	16–33	No	Yes on 33 MHz	0–256 KB	PGA	100
80486DX	25–50	No	Yes on 33 MHz	0–256 KB	PGA SQFP	168 208
Pentium	60–166	Yes	Yes	256–512 KB	PGA	296
Pentium Pro	233–266	Yes	Yes	256 KB–1 MB	PGA	387
Pentium II	233–500	Yes	Yes	512 KB	SEC	242
Pentium III	450 MHz–1.13 GHz	Yes	Yes	256–512 KB	SEC/PGA	242/370
Pentium IV	1.30 MHz–3.20 GHz	Yes	Yes	256–512 KB	PGA	423/478
Itanium	733–833 MHz	Yes	Yes	96 KB	PAC	418
Itanium II	900 MHz–1.0 GHz	Yes	Yes	256 KB	OLGA	611

TABLE 3.3 Sockets/Slots, Pins, and the Processors They Support

Socket	Pins	Processor
Socket 4	237 PGA	Pentium 60/66, Pentium Overdrive
Socket 5	320 PGA	Pentium 75-133, Pentium Overdrive
Socket 7	321 PGA	Pentium 75-200, Pentium Overdrive
Socket 8	387 PGA	Pentium Pro
Slot 1	242 SEC/SEPP	Pentium II, Pentium III, Celeron
Slot 2	330 SECC-2	Xeon
Super Socket 7	321 PGA	Pentium MMX, Pentium Pro, AMD K6-2, K6-2+, K6-3, K6-3+
Socket 370	370 PGA	Celeron, Pentium III, Cyrix III
Socket 418	418 PAC	Itanium

→

Socket	Pins	Processor
Socket 423	423 PGA	Pentium IV
Socket 478	478 PGA	Pentium IV
Socket 603	603 PGA	Pentium IV-based Xeon, Xeon MP
Socket 611	611 OLGA	Itanium II
Socket 940	micro-PGA	AMD Opteron
Socket A	462 PGA	AMD Athlon, Athlon XP, Duron
Slot A	242 Slot A	AMD Athlon

Covering every available microprocessor by every manufacturer is beyond the scope of this book. For more information and a detailed list of microprocessors please visit *http://en.wikipedia.org/wiki/List_of_microprocessors*.

CPU OVERCLOCKING AND THROTTLING

CPU overclocking is a process of tweaking the CPU's clock rate to achieve a higher rate than it was originally intended for.

The CPUs clock rate is measured in Hertz, which is the basic measurement used to calculate cycles per second. The clock rate for a typical CPU can be adjusted in the computer's BIOS settings. Other computer components such as graphics cards and memory can also have their clock rates adjusted. Computer enthusiasts and scientists tweak clock rates ultimately to test and achieve higher rates of performance. Many people will buy low-end computer components at low prices with the intent of raising their clock rates to speed up processing and stretch the limits further than originally intended by the manufacturer.

The benefits to achieving higher clock speeds are obvious. As stated, components can be purchased cheaper and their performance raised to that of the more expensive components. Processing performance for applications, graphics, and games can also be increased. However, inherent dangers are associated with improper overclocking. If you improperly overclock and do not follow certain specifications or benchmarks, components can be in danger of overheating. For example, one of the most common problems associated with overclocking is a failed processor fan that cannot support cooling the processor running at the higher rate of speed. This can result in a failing processor that in turn can cause a system to freeze and or reboot continuously. System stability and performance is never guaranteed with overclocking. With that said, you should always follow the manufacturer's warnings and guidance when attempting to overclock.

CPU throttling is a method used to lower the clock frequency of a CPU, thus reducing the amount of power used to operate a system. If proper methods are implemented to lower the CPU clock frequency, the result is reduced voltage to the power supply, more efficient speeds, prolonged battery usage, a cooler and quieter running system, and overall better system performance. Intel uses a technology called SpeedStep in its laptop CPU line of products. AMD uses a technology called Cool'n'Quiet in desktops and servers and a CPU throttling technology called PowerNow! in its laptop systems.

COOLING FANS AND HEAT SINKS

All the components inside the system unit can generate heat. This heat can be very dangerous to your processor. The processor is one of the main heat-generating components inside the system unit. When a system is on for a while, the processor, expansion cards, and memory chips heat up. When the system is turned off, these components cool down. Such continual changes in temperature can result in expansion and contraction of the mentioned components. Over time, these components can work their way out of their sockets and slots. This phenomenon is known as *thermal card* or *chip creep*. It is very important to maintain proper temperatures in the system unit to protect the components.

Most computers today incorporate the use of processor cooling fans and heat sinks to maintain a temperature between 90°F and 110°F. The cooling fan usually sits on top of the processor, drawing heat from it and pushing the heat out and away from the motherboard, where it can be drawn out of the system unit by the power supply fan. Some CPUs need more than a cooling fan. In these cases, a heat sink can be placed between the processor and the cooling fan to assist with the extraction of heat from the processor.

LIQUID COOLING

Liquid cooling is used to super-cool processors far past the limits of standard heat sink/fan combinations. Many different types of liquid cooling apparatuses are available, but most work under the same basic premise: they cool water with a radiator, pump that water over the CPU to absorb heat, and then pump the water back to the radiator to recool and dissipate that heat.

All liquid cooling devices have the same basic parts: a radiator (with fan to help dissipate heat from the radiator), tubing, a water reservoir, a water block (which acts as a sort of heat sink for the processor) that water flows through (this is where the heat transfer takes place), and a pump. To understand liquid cooling devices, refer to the diagram in Figure 3.1.

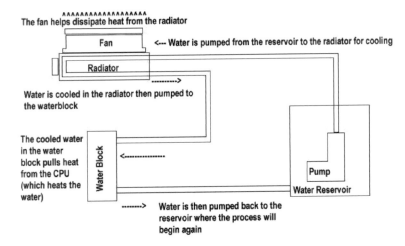

FIGURE 3.1   Processor liquid cooling process.

Although water can be used, many other substances that are more thermally conductive are being used in different types of systems. At the very least, even in the case of a system using only water, distilled water (only pure H_2O) is used in combination with a coolant substance that helps reduce algae and mineral deposits.

Liquid cooling systems are primarily used by people seeking to overclock their processors past stock operating speeds. Liquid cooling systems require a great deal of setup and maintenance to ensure that there is no leakage, which could be devastating to the hardware. Routine cleanings and water/coolant changes are necessary to avoid mineral and algae buildup, and constant monitoring of system temperatures is necessary to ensure that water is being properly pumped and cooled throughout the system. Although only CPU cooling has been discussed, several variations facilitate the cooling of other devices (e.g., video card GPU/memory and system memory).

THERMAL COMPOUNDS

A thermal compound is defined as a semifluidic grease that conducts heat several times more efficiently than air. Why is this important? To the naked eye, the mating surfaces of a heat sink and CPU are smooth and flat; however, on a microscopic level, they are anything but smooth, with peaks and valleys on both surfaces. In fact, when the two surfaces are mated, less than 1% of the surface of each entity (the peaks on both the heat sink and CPU) touches the other surface. The result is a great deal of air left between the processor and the heat sink. Air is an extremely poor thermal conductor, and the end result is a CPU that runs hot (causing damage). Thermal compound is used to fill the space between the mating surfaces and help transfer heat from the CPU to the heat sink. Figure 3.2 shows a thermal pad that goes on the bottom of the heat sink. Also Figure 3.3 shows a four-part installation of a processor, fan, and heat sink.

FIGURE 3.2   The thermal pad goes on the bottom of the heat sink.

FIGURE 3.3   Installation of a processor, fan, and heat sink.

VRM (Voltage Regulator Module)

A VRM (Voltage Regulator Module) is a motherboard-installable module that regulates the electrical voltage that is fed to the system's microprocessor. Most motherboards today have a built-in voltage regulator or a VRM. Its function is to protect the processor by detecting and correcting any changes in voltage. Various processors require different amount of voltage for basic I/O functions and core operations, and the VRM's job is to detect this voltage amount. It then supplies a constant voltage to the processor. If you are considering upgrading your processor, you must consult both the processor and motherboard manufacturers' instructions regarding the specific voltage requirements for your new processor's core and I/O functions. You may need to add a VRM, depending on the voltage requirement of your new processor.

It is likely that the A+ exams will expect you to know that a VRM is a motherboard-installable module that regulates the electrical voltage that is fed to the system's microprocessor.

Chapter Summary

As you have learned in this chapter, the CPU is the core of a computing system. Supporting components and technology that enhance its features surround the CPU. Bus architecture and cache play a major role in the overall performance of a processor. In this chapter, you were guided through a general history of the processor, from the early 8086 to the new Pentium 4 processors. As you have seen, competition has clearly kept the manufacturers continually striving to make a better, faster, more affordable CPU.

As mentioned earlier in this chapter, the new A+ exams are likely to focus on newer processors and bus speeds. You will probably be tested on basic processor troubleshooting and maintenance. Let's get serious and focus: your future as a skilled technician may depend on it. Imagine that you just paid $158 to take the next practice test. One wrong question, and you lose your money and your shot at getting certified.

REVIEW QUESTIONS

1. **Which of the following are valid AMD processors? (Choose Two)**

    ☐ A. Athlon
    ☐ B. Celeron
    ☐ C. K6
    ☐ D. K9

    Correct Answers = A and C

    The AMD Athlon and the AMD K6 are valid AMD processors. Intel developed the Celeron processor. K9 is used as a description for police dogs.

2. **Which of the following processors runs at a 66 MHz motherboard speed?**

    ○ A. Pentium III 500
    ○ B. Pentium IV
    ○ C. Pentium II 300
    ○ D. 80386

    Correct Answer = C

    The Intel Pentium II 300 runs at a 66 MHz motherboard speed. See Table 3.1 for a Pentium II processor and motherboard speed comparison.

3. **Which of the following processors runs at a 100 MHz motherboard speed?**

    ○ A. Pentium III 500
    ○ B. XT
    ○ C. Pentium I
    ○ D. 80386

    Correct Answer = A

    The Pentium II 350 MHz through the Pentium III series processors are intended to run at a 100 MHz motherboard bus speed.

4. **Your processor fan has malfunctioned. What result might you expect? (Choose Two)**

    ☐ A. Serial port errors
    ☐ B. Processor damage
    ☐ C. 601 POST error
    ☐ D. System halts

    Correct Answers = B and D

If your processor fan has failed or malfunctioned, your system may lock up or "halt," and your processor may suffer irreversible damage due to over-heating.

5. **The AMD Duron processor was developed with what type of workstation in mind?**

   ○ A. Low end
   ○ B. Midrange
   ○ C. High end
   ○ D. MSCDEX

   Correct Answer = B

   The AMD Duron processor was developed for midrange workstations.

6. **What should you always put your processor and other components in when storing or transporting?**

   ○ A. An EMI bag
   ○ B. An FDISK bag
   ○ C. A grocery bag
   ○ D. An antistatic ESD bag

   Correct Answer = D

   An antistatic ESD bag will protect your processor as well as other electronic computer components from electrostatic discharge.

7. **You are considering upgrading your processor. What must you also consider for this upgrade?**

   ○ A. An NLM
   ○ B. A permanent swap file
   ○ C. An MPV
   ○ D. A VRM
   ○ E. Your jealous friend's feelings
   ○ F. None of the above

   Correct Answer = D

   If you are considering upgrading your processor, you must consult both the processor and motherboard manufacturer's instructions regarding the specific voltage requirements for your new processor's core and I/O functions. You may need to add a VRM depending upon the voltage requirement of your new processor.

8. **To provide faster access to memory and provide better overall application and system support, CPU manufacturers have added this to newer processors. What is it?**
   - ○ A. ESD protection
   - ○ B. VLM
   - ○ C. L6 cache
   - ○ D. L3 cache
   - ○ E. Seal of approval
   - ○ F. None of the above

   Correct Answer = D

   The L3 cache addition to newer processors has dramatically increased the speed at which a processor, or dual processors, can access stored information. This in turn provides better processor support for overall application access speed and system support.

9. **Which of the following processor lines have products that use Socket 478 technology? (Choose Two)**
   - ☐ A. Pentium 4 (Northwood)
   - ☐ B. Celeron
   - ☐ C. Duron
   - ☐ D. Pentium 3

   Correct Answer = A and B

   Both Pentium 4 and Celeron's latest incarnation use Socket 478. The Duron uses both Socket A and Slot A technology, and the Pentium 3 uses either Slot 1 or Socket 370 technology.

10. **The first series of Pentium 4 processors had how much L2 cache?**
    - ○ A. 128 KB
    - ○ B. 256 KB
    - ○ C. 512 KB
    - ○ D. The first model of Pentium 4 had no L2 cache

    Correct Answer = B

    The first Pentium 4's were enabled with 256 K of L2 cache, which has since been updated to 512 KB.

11. **Which of these are necessary in a liquid cooling system? (Choose Two)**
    - ☐ A.   Radiator/fan
    - ☐ B.   Heat sink fan combination for processor
    - ☐ C.   Water block
    - ☐ D.   Water filter

    Correct Answer = A and C

    A liquid cooling system requires a radiator (with fan to help dissipate heat from the radiator), tubing, a water reservoir, and a water block (which acts as a sort of heat sink for the processor, that water flows through a radiator/fan and a water block. The water block as the primary cooling device replaces a heat sink fan combination for the CPU in a liquid cooling setup. Although a water filter sounds good in theory, the water/coolant must be changed out routinely to avoid algae/mineral deposits.

12. **You have recently overclocked your boss's computer to achieve faster rates of performance and possibly result in a big raise for you. Unfortunately, her computer is now freezing and rebooting constantly. Which of the following is most likely the cause of this problem?**
    - ○ A.   Failed memory
    - ○ B.   Failed hard drive
    - ○ C.   Failed graphics card
    - ○ D.   Failed CPU fan and CPU

    Correct Answer = D

    One of the most common problems associated with overclocking is a failed processor fan that cannot support cooling the processor running at the higher rate of speed. This can result in a failing processor, which in turn can cause a system to freeze and or reboot continuously.

13. **Which processor introduced the concept of Hyperthreading?**
    - ○ A.   Pentium Dual Core
    - ○ B.   Pentium 4
    - ○ C.   Pentium 3
    - ○ D.   Itanium

    Correct Answer = B

You should remember for the exams that the Pentium 4 introduced Hyperthreading, which is Intel's trademark for the implementation of the simultaneous multithreading technology on the Pentium 4 series of microprocessors.

14. **The Itanium II uses which socket and runs at which speeds? (Choose Two)**
    ☐ A. Socket 611
    ☐ B. 900 MHz-1.0 GHz
    ☐ C. Socket 478
    ☐ D. 1.30 MHz-3.20 GHz

    Correct Answer = A and B

    If you got this one right, you are a top-notch student and are most likely ready for any of the A+ exam! The Itanium II uses Socket 611 and has speeds between 900 MHz and 1.0 GHz. The Pentium IV uses Socket 478 and has speeds of 1.30-3.20 GHz. Refer to Table 3.2 and Table 3.3.

15. **Which of the following are used for computer system cooling purposes?**
    ○ A. Thermal compounds
    ○ B. CPU fans
    ○ C. Heat sinks
    ○ D. Motherboard form factors
    ○ E. All of the above

    Correct Answer = E

    You can't get this one wrong! All of the choices are used to for computer system cooling.

REFERENCES

http://program.intel.com/SHARED/products/servers/index.htm. This Intel Web site can be used as an excellent resource on the latest specifications for server and workstation components.

http://en.wikipedia.org/wiki/List_of_microprocessors. The Wikipedia site has an excellent listing of microprocessors.

4 Understanding Memory

MEMORY DEFINED

Memory is where the computer temporarily stores electronic instructions and data. Computing systems have different types of memory, which produce different results. For example, when a processor needs to store and retrieve information quickly to carry out a specified function or calculation, it stores and retrieves data from cache memory that is internal to the processor. If access to information isn't needed as quickly, the data or instructions may be stored in RAM (main memory). Memory is simply storage for the data and instructions that are processed by the system's CPU. The physical medium that stores these instructions can vary in location and speed.

There are many different types of physical and logical memory to suit specific operational needs. The memory types addressed in this chapter are those you need to be familiar with to successfully prepare for the CompTIA A+ exams.

RANDOM ACCESS MEMORY (RAM)

RAM, also known as primary storage or main memory, is where the CPU and applications store information and instructions for future use. RAM is considered volatile memory. Volatile memory loses all its stored information when it is disconnected from its power source. In other words, when you turn off the computer, you lose all the information stored in RAM. For example, if you are entering data into a document and suddenly experience loss of power to the system, you will lose the information you have entered into the document unless it has been saved to a permanent storage location, such as the hard disk, CD-ROM, Zip disk, or floppy disk.

The CPU uses unique locations of RAM, called memory addresses, to store information. Memory addresses vary in size depending on how much RAM is available in the system.

RAM Speed

RAM access speed is measured in nanoseconds (ns, or billionths of a second). Older computers operated with RAM access speeds that ranged from 80 ns to 120 ns. Today, it is common to find RAM access speeds of 50 ns and faster. Memory speeds can vary greatly, depending on the type of memory being used. In fact, memory such as Synchronous Dynamic Random Access Memory (SDRAM) is measured in megahertz, not nanoseconds. You can determine the access speed of memory by looking at the last printed number on most DRAM chips; for example, BAC4G302H-05 means the access speed is 50 ns. An important consideration when installing new memory in a system is to match the speed of the memory to the speed of the motherboard's bus.

For the test, it is important to remember that the RAM speed is faster in nanoseconds as the number decreases—that is, 6 ns is faster than 10 ns.

NOTE

RAM Size

The smallest unit of information measured in a computer system is a bit. A bit is represented in electronic computer terms as a (binary) 0 or 1. There are 8 bits in 1 byte. (See Chapter 5 for more information on binary conversion.)

RAM size and storage capacity are measured in multiples of bytes known as megabytes, gigabytes, and terabytes. Table 4.1 will assist you with RAM units of measure.

Some important considerations when purchasing memory or a new computer are what type of memory and how much memory is required. Specific types of memory serve different functions (memory types are discussed later in this chapter). For most

TABLE 4.1   RAM Units and Sizes

Unit Measured	Size of Unit
Bit	Binary digit equal to 0 or 1
Byte	8 bits
Kilobyte	1024 bytes
Megabyte	1,048,576 bytes
Gigabyte	1,073,741,824 bytes
Terabyte	1,099,511,627,776 bytes

modern day home and office workstations, 1 to 2 GB's of RAM should be sufficient to support most of today's memory-hungry applications. High-end server computers require more memory to process, calculate, and serve applications to workstations. Server computers today generally have at least 4 GB to 8 GB of RAM installed.

MEMORY TYPES AND CHARACTERISTICS

Many forms of memory have been available since the first computer was introduced. Table 4.2 provides a quick reference to the conceptual aspects of memory that you should be aware of before taking the A+ tests.

TABLE 4.2   Memory Concepts

Memory type	Packaging	Volatile	Nonvolatile
Main DRAM	DIP	X	
Main SDRAM	DIMM	X	
Main DDRAM	DIMM	X	
Main RDRAM	RIMM	X	
Main VRAM	Adapter	X	
Cache Level 1	IC Card	X	
Cache Level 2	IC Card	X	
Cache Level 3	IC Card	X	
ROM BIOS	Chip		X
Virtual memory	Swap file on hard drive		X

READ-ONLY MEMORY

You should recall from Chapter 2 that ROM contains small programs installed at the factory. ROM is installed on the motherboard and on some types of expansion boards. ROM chips contain the system BIOS, whose main function is to carry out boot operations by communicating with I/O devices and programs.

DYNAMIC RANDOM ACCESS MEMORY (DRAM)

DRAM is the most common type of memory in use by modern CPUs today and is considered affordable. DRAM is volatile memory that will lose all its stored information if it is disconnected from the power source. A DRAM chip is made up of little storage units called cells. Each cell contains a capacitor. A capacitor is an electronic device that can hold an electrical charge that can be positive or negative. If the charge is positive, the capacitor registers a binary digit value of 1. If the charge is negative, the capacitor registers a binary digit value of 0. The capacitors in DRAM must be electronically refreshed continuously to hold their information. DRAM is considered a very slow type of memory, with speeds of approximately 50 ns. Originally, DRAM chips were mounted on the motherboard using dual inline packages (DIPs). DIPs are long chips with flimsy pins that are very difficult to install on the motherboard. DIPs tended to heat up quickly due to thermal cycling and often caused the DRAM chips to creep out of their sockets. This creeping effect is known as chip creep. Today, DRAM chips are soldered onto integrated circuit boards that are inserted into the motherboard more securely.

STATIC RANDOM ACCESS MEMORY

SRAM or static RAM is memory that also holds data as long as there is power available to the chip. Power is provided to the SRAM chip by the system battery. SRAM does not require the use of capacitors and does not need to be constantly refreshed, as does DRAM. Instead, SRAM uses a flip-flop method of regenerating its contents by means of transistors.

Through the use of its own internal clock, SRAM is synchronized with the motherboard's bus speed, thereby helping SRAM achieve higher speeds than DRAM.

Level 2 memory cache (fast memory frequently accessed by the processor) is stored on SRAM chips. SRAM typically comes in sizes of 128 MB to 4 GB and is more expensive than DRAM.

POPULAR DRAM ADVANCES AND TECHNOLOGIES

Many technological improvements have been made to DRAM to create a faster type of memory. The following sections describe some of these improvements.

Fast Page Mode (FPM) DRAM

FPM DRAM is faster than DRAM but is relatively slow compared to other enhancements. With FPM, the memory controller knows ahead of time to look in the pages of addressed memory after the CPU's read or write requests. This reduces the amount of time the memory controller has to wait to take instructions from the CPU and read from or write to memory. FPM DRAM is not suitable for motherboard bus speeds greater than 60 MHz.

Extended Data Output (EDO) DRAM

EDO DRAM was the first memory introduced with the capability to hold several pieces of information at a time without having to be refreshed. In other words, if the CPU needs to access the same information several times, the information can wait in EDO memory until the CPU is through accessing it. The information does not have to be continuously reloaded or reregistered into memory. EDO was intended to run with Pentium systems rated between 60 MHz and 75 MHz.

EDO is faster than FPM memory. EDO memory was advertised to increase system performance by 60%. True benchmarks of EDO showed a 10% to 15% increase in performance.

Burst EDO (BEDO) DRAM

Burst EDO memory is a form of EDO DRAM that can process multiple (up to four) memory addresses at a time in small bursts. Burst EDO did not have great success because it could not retain its synchronization with the processor for long periods.

Synchronous Dynamic Random Access Memory (SDRAM)

SDRAM is similar to DRAM, except that it uses an internal clock to synchronize input and output operations with the CPU. The synchronization between the memory and CPU results in enhanced performance. SDRAM uses burst mode (automatic retrieval of data before it is requested) for read and write operations. SDRAM sends data in high-speed bursts by using burst mode. SDRAM speed is not measured in nanoseconds; instead, it is measured in megahertz.

Double Data Rate SDRAM (DDR SDRAM)

DDR SDRAM dramatically increases memory throughput by allowing data to be transferred on both the rising and falling edges of the system clock as opposed to just the rising edge. What does this mean in English? Data throughput is (approximately) doubled on a memory chip that implements DDR SDRAM technology. DDR SDRAM is very effective for laptop computer systems because it draws less power. It is also sometimes referred to as SDRAM II. DDR SDRAM can be easily purchased in 128 MB, 256 MB, and 512 MB increments. DDR SDRAM has a bus clock speed of 100 MHz and a transfer of data rate equal to 200 MHz. It comes packaged on a 184-pin DIMM.

DDR2 SDRAM

DDR2 SDRAM was released in 2003 at two initial speeds of 200 MHz (referred to as PC2-3200) and 266 MHz (PC2-4200). DDR2 transfers data at twice the speed of standard DDR and comes in a 240-pin memory module as apposed to the DDR, which comes in a 184-pin memory module. DDR2 is not backward compatible with DDR.

MDDR

MDDR, also called Mobile DDR SDRAM, is memory used in mobile devices such as PDAs, cell phones, and music players. MDDR RAM uses a lower voltage of 1.8V, which allows a lower power consumption.

RDRAM (Rambus) DRAM

Rambus RDRAM is proprietary memory from Rambus, Inc. RDRAM improves on memory latency by transferring data in and out of memory at about 600 MHz. RDRAM can achieve this speed by synchronizing directly with the memory bus instead of the motherboard bus. Rambus memory uses a narrow bus width and comes on proprietary memory modules called RIMMs. Rambus RDRAM is being used in conjunction with the newer Pentium 4s offered by Intel.

VIDEO MEMORY

The need for high-speed graphics acceleration, higher resolution, and faster video refresh rates has spawned a growing need for better engineered video memory. For the A+ tests, you need to be familiar with the following types of video memory.

Video Random Access Memory (VRAM)

A computer screen is made up of many tiny dots called pixels. The bit depth is the number of bits assigned through VRAM to each pixel. The more VRAM that can be assigned to each pixel, the greater the bit depth will be. This results in better resolution and color scale. The larger the monitor, the more pixels there are to fill, which creates a greater need for video memory.

VRAM is memory specifically designed for video. VRAM acts as a buffer between the CPU and the monitor. It is designed with two access paths (or dual ports), which provide separate passages to the same area of memory or memory address. This means that two devices can access VRAM at the same time. With this design, the video adapter chip, known as RAMDAC (RAM Digital-Analog Converter), can convert the digital signals to analog to be displayed on the screen, and at the same time, the video controller (processor) can bring more data into VRAM. VRAM does not need to be refreshed as often as DRAM.

Windows Random Access Memory (WRAM)

Do not be confused—WRAM does not mean Microsoft Windows memory. WRAM is similar to VRAM, with the exception that WRAM makes better use of the dual ports available through VRAM. WRAM can take advantage of more memory address storage space, resulting in better color depth and video resolution (1600 $\times$ 1200). WRAM is faster than VRAM.

Synchronous Graphics RAM (SGRAM)

SGRAM is a form of DRAM that uses a single port. SGRAM uses its own program instructions, called masked write and block write commands, to provide better throughput for graphic-intensive applications. SGRAM is synchronized with the CPU clock speed and can support up to 100 MHz. If you ever receive a nonmaskable interrupt error, you are probably experiencing defective RAM or SGRAM.

GDDR3 and GDDR4 (Graphics Double Data Rate 3 and Graphics Double Data Rate 4)

GDDR3 and GDDR4 are graphics card memory specifications developed by ATI Technologies. These types of memory target mainly game consoles such as PlayStation and Xbox 360. You need to know specifically that they are used for graphics memory, but it's unlikely that you will be tested on their finer points, such as GDDR3 transfers 4 bits of data per pin in two clock cycles.

CACHED MEMORY

As mentioned in Chapter 3, the processor uses cached memory for very fast access to information. Level 1 cache is considered primary cache and is internal or built-in to the processor itself. Level 2 cache is secondary cache that is external to the processor. Level 3 cache adds 1 MB (1024 KB) on to the CPU chip. With memory caching, a memory cache controller anticipates (about 90% correctly) what the processor is going to require from memory. This method eliminates the processor's constant need to access the slower DRAM.

VIRTUAL MEMORY (SWAP FILE)

Today's popular operating systems are typically configured with a predetermined amount of hard drive space set aside to act as a memory buffer area for main memory (RAM). This area of hard drive space is referred to as *virtual memory*, *swap file*, or *page file*. (The different names refer to the same area of hard drive space.) Data is temporarily moved, or *swapped* between memory and the hard drive. Moving data out of main memory and placing it into a swap file frees up valuable space in main memory for other purposes. The swap file size can vary depending on the amount of free space available on the hard drive. You can manually configure the swap file size or let the operating system take care of its configuration.

If you are running an application that uses up all of the current RAM, the extra memory needed to run the application can be provided automatically from virtual memory. This memory area is managed differently from main memory. As you may recall, data is stored in memory addresses within RAM. These addresses are known as *real memory addresses*. With virtual memory, the operating system logically divides the set-aside hard drive space into memory pages that contain virtual memory addresses. These virtual memory pages can typically hold more memory addresses than RAM can. The process by which these virtual memory addresses are converted into real memory is called *memory mapping*. For virtual memory to be used, the operating system must be able to run in protected mode. DOS was only able to run in real mode. Microsoft Windows 3.x introduced 386 enhanced mode, which paved the way for virtual memory utilization.

For the exams, if you get an operating system message stating that you are low on virtual memory, the best two options are to increase the operating system paging file or add more RAM.

MEMORY PACKAGING

We have discussed memory types and how they function. Now we will focus on how memory is packaged together and attached to the motherboard.

A DRAM chip is considered one unit or a single chip. When several DRAM chips are soldered onto a circuit board, a bank of chips is formed. The combination of DRAM chips soldered onto the circuit board makes up a memory module or memory package. The memory modules are inserted into the motherboard to form rows of memory banks. There are several types of memory modules, each of which has its own characteristics and design.

Pay very close attention to the packaging methods discussed in this chapter. The A+ exams are very likely to test your knowledge on memory modules, including SIMMs, DIMMs, RIMMs, SODIMMs, and MicroDIMMs. You will likely be shown a graphic and asked to describe the memory module being displayed. You should remember the following bulleted items for common memory packaging design and see Table 4.3 for a quick reference on memory modules.

- 72-pin DIMM is used for FPM and EDO DRAM.
- 72-pin SODIMM is used for FPM DRAM and EDO DRAM.
- 44-pin SODIMM is used for SDR SDRAM.
- 168-pin DIMM is used for SDR SDRAM.
- 184-pin DIMM is used for DDR SDRAM.
- 200-pin SO-DIMM is used for DDR SDRAM and DDR2 SDRAM.
- 240-pin DIMM is used for DDR2 SDRAM.

TABLE 4.3   Memory Module Quick Reference

Module Type	Number of Pins	Memory Bus Width
SIMM	30 pins	8 bits
SIMM	72 pins	32 bits
DIMM	168 pins	64 bits
RIMM	184 pins	16 bits (or 2 bytes wide)
SODIMM	72 pins	32 bits
SODIMM	144 pins	64 bits
MicroDIMM	144 pins	64 bits

GOLD AND TIN EDGE CONNECTORS

SIMMs and DIMMs both have edge connecters (or leads) that are pushed into the motherboard's memory slots. These edge connectors come in two distinct forms: tin (silver colored) and gold colored. There is not much of a difference between the two forms, but the color of the connector must match the color of the inside of the motherboard's memory slot. The inside of the motherboard's memory slot is either gold or tin. In short, match the gold-edged SIMM or DIMM connector to the gold memory slot on the motherboard. Match the tin (silver-colored) edge connector to the silver-colored memory slot on the motherboard. The two different metal forms have different chemical compositions; a mismatch in color may result in corrosion and eventually cause the system to fail or become unbootable.

SINGLE INLINE MEMORY MODULE (SIMM)

A SIMM is a memory module that has either a 30-pin or 72-pin edge connector that inserts into the motherboard memory sockets at a 45° angle. A 30-pin SIMM (see Figure 4.1) has DRAM chips soldered onto one side of its circuit board. Older, 30-pin SIMMs used FPM technology and generally came in sizes of 256 KB to 4 MB, with an 8-bit memory bus width. The newer 72-pin SIMMs use EDO technology and come in sizes ranging from 1 MB to 128 MB, with a 32-bit bus width. A 72-pin SIMM (see Figure 4.2) can have DRAM chips soldered on one or both sides of the circuit board. As you learned earlier in this chapter, memory speed is measured in nanoseconds. Most SIMMs run at 60 ns, 70 ns, or 80 ns.

FIGURE 4.1   A 30-pin SIMM.

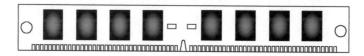

FIGURE 4.2   A 72-pin SIMM.

DUAL INLINE MEMORY MODULE (DIMM)

Systems that provided 64-bit or wider memory buses opened the door for the DIMM. Most modern computers provide memory slots on the motherboard that support the 168-pin DIMM (see Figure 4.3). A DIMM is larger than a SIMM and has an additional set of leads that make it impossible to install the DIMM improperly. DIMMs come in different voltages (3.3V and 5.0V) and are available in buffered or unbuffered form. When purchasing new DIMMs, you should consult the motherboard manufacturer's guide.

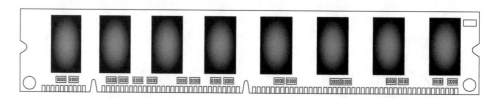

FIGURE 4.3   A 168-pin DIMM.

SMALL-OUTLINE DUAL INLINE MEMORY MODULE (SODIMM)

A SODIMM is a smaller DIMM that was specifically designed for laptop computers. There are two major types of SODIMMs. They come on a module that has 72 pins with a transfer rate of 32 bits or a module with 144 pins at a transfer rate of 64 bits (see Figure 4.4).

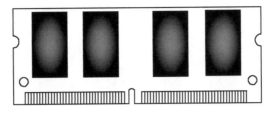

FIGURE 4.4   A SODIMM.

The following Crucial Technologies Web site has a great PDF document that explains how to properly install a SODIMM in a laptop computer system: http://images.crucial.com/pdf/sodimm_install.pdf.

MICRO DUAL INLINE MEMORY MODULE (MICRODIMM)

MicroDIMMs are memory modules that are often used in subnotebook computers. They have 144 pins and provide a 64-bit data path (see Figure 4.5).

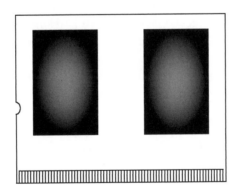

FIGURE 4.5   A MicroDIMM.

The following TransmetaZone Web site provides a great demonstration regarding the installation of a 128 MB, 144-pin MicroDIMM: www.transmetazone.com/articleview.cfm?articleid=1195&page=4.

RAMBUS INLINE MEMORY MODULE (RIMM)

Trademarked by Kingston Technology Corp., a RIMM is a memory module that uses RDRAM chips. A RIMM uses a special circle-like technology that rotates data in a unidirectional, looped system between the RIMM modules and special blank memory banks called continuity RIMMs (C-RIMMs) that must be placed between RIMMs. This looping system eliminated the bottleneck that resulted from DRAM and its bidirectional bus, which caused data to wait before being sent down a row of memory modules. A RIMM is physically smaller than a DIMM and uses a different pin configuration. Noticeably, a RIMM uses a 184-pin connector (see Figure 4.6).

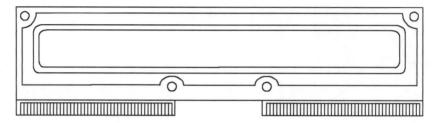

FIGURE 4.6 A RIMM.

Installing SIMMs, DIMMs, and RIMMs

There was a time when installing memory modules into a computer could be very painful on your fingers. Older motherboards did not have the clip and spring features supported by today's motherboard memory slots, which allow the memory modules to be easily pushed into place.

Here are the basic steps for installing SIMMs, DIMMs, and RIMMs into your computer:

1. Unplug the power to the computer.
2. Remove the system unit case cover.
3. Make sure you are wearing an ESD wrist strap.
4. Identify the SIMM or DIMM slots.
5. With both hands, line up the SIMM, DIMM, or RIMM with the open motherboard memory slot.
6. Push firmly on both sides of the SIMM, DIMM, or RIMM until it is seated in the slot. (SIMMs should be inserted into the motherboard at a 45° angle.)
7. Replace the system unit case.
8. Take off your ESD wrist strap.
9. Plug the power cord back into the computer, and turn the computer on.

In newer computers, you will see that the new memory has been added when the POST runs its memory count. Your memory will be automatically configured. In older systems, you may have to make changes to your memory settings in the system BIOS configuration utility before the new memory is recognized.

When installing or adding memory to a memory bank, you should avoid mixing different types of memory modules together. You can mix different speeds of memory within the same memory bank. However, the speed of the slowest module within a bank of RAM will become the speed used by the system. Remember the following when installing memory:

- SIMMs should be installed in increments of two or four memory modules per memory bank.
- DIMMs can be installed in units of one (one module) per memory bank.
- RIMMs should be installed in pairs and be the same size, type, and speed. If you fail to match paired memory modules, your system may not boot, or you may receive a POST error.

The exam will likely present you with a graphic display of a memory module and ask you to identify it by name. You should know what all the memory modules mentioned in this chapter physically look like, or there is a good chance you will find yourself counting pins on the test display screen!

COMPACTFLASH

CompactFlash is a type of memory card that depends on flash memory. CompactFlash is commonly used in devices such as PDAs, pocket PCs, and digital cameras. They are smaller than a regular PC card and can be easily used with a special adapter in Type I and Type II PC card slots.

CompactFlash technology has also become very popular in the wireless world. In fact, 11 Mbps wireless CompactFlash network cards are available everywhere, and connecting your PDA, pocket PC, or other devices to a network is now easy and hassle-free.

MEMORY PARITY AND ECC

The integrity of memory and its contents are crucial to the successful operation of a computing system. Two logical diagnostic memory tools serve as a system of checks and balances for the contents of DRAM: parity and error correction code, or Error Checking and Correction (ECC).

PARITY

As you may recall, there are 8 bits in 1 byte. Parity checking adds another bit, called a parity bit (ninth bit), to each byte of information that is stored in memory to verify its integrity. In other words, an even or odd parity bit is added to every byte of information (8 bits). The parity bit for each byte of information is made to force all bits or units to have either an odd or even number of bits. Later, when the byte of information is needed, the computer checks to verify the even or odd state of the byte; if it does not match its original assignment of even or odd parity, a memory parity error occurs, and the system may halt. Some parity errors may show up on the computer screen if the parity check fails. A parity error 1 indicates that the parity error or check has failed on the motherboard. A parity error 2 indicates that the error has most likely occurred on a memory expansion board. Parity is a tool used only to detect errors in memory—parity does not fix memory problems.

Calculating the number of parity bits associated with memory is fairly simple. If 1 parity bit is assigned to every byte (8 bits) of data, you can calculate that 16 bits have 2 parity bits, 32 bits have 4 parity bits, and 64 bits have 8 parity checking bits.

Less expensive memory modules are available that provide fake parity. Fake parity does not provide a valid test of data stored in memory; it simply fools the system into believing that any results from memory are acceptable.

Another way of manufacturing a less expensive memory module or chip is to disable parity altogether.

Inexpensive or used memory is often to blame for parity errors and General Protection Faults (GPFs). Generally, GPFs occur when more than one application or program attempts to access or write to an area of memory already assigned to another application.

ERROR CORRECTION CODE OR ERROR CHECKING AND CORRECTION

ECC works in conjunction with the memory controller to not only detect errors found in data as it passes out of memory but also to fix single-bit errors with its built-in logic. ECC adds a special bit to data, called an error correction code bit, which is decoded by the memory controller for accuracy.

Some SDRAM chips support ECC. DIMMs (which normally have eight chips on a circuit board) that have a ninth chip show the presence of ECC. You can look in the BIOS configuration to see if ECC is enabled. ECC is worth the extra expense because of its reliability.

LOGICAL MEMORY

Chances are that the current A+ exams will not test you on the use of logical memory, as did previous tests. The current exams are likely to test your knowledge of loading device drivers and configuration files that support more current operating systems. However, newer operating systems must remain backward compatible to support older applications, so you should understand the concepts of logical memory.

Operating systems and software divide areas of memory into logical sections in which applications and programs can run. Many operating systems, such as Windows NT, Windows 9.x, Windows 2000, Windows Me, and Windows XP, automatically divide and maintain logical memory areas. Older operating systems, such as DOS, PC DOS, and Windows 3.x, required manual configuration of logical memory areas by skilled technicians who were very familiar with the configurations of DOS and logical memory management software tools.

Logical memory is divided into four basic divisions, as shown in Table 4.4.

TABLE 4.4   Logical Memory Divisions

Memory Area	Memory Description
Conventional memory	The first 640 KB of system memory addresses are used to load and run device drivers, programs, and applications. This is also referred to as lower memory area.
Upper memory area (UMA)	The first 384 KB of memory above conventional memory are used for device drivers, video RAM, and ROM BIOS. This is also referred to as expanded or reserved memory.
High memory area (HMA)	The first 64 KB of extended memory, minus 16 bytes, provide "real-mode" support to operating system.
Extended memory (XMS)	All memory addresses above 1 MB and up to 4 GB is used primarily for programs and applications.

CONVENTIONAL MEMORY

In the early days of personal computing, the original PC and software developers created 640 KB of addressable memory space and named it *conventional memory*. At the time, it was assumed that 640 KB would be more than enough memory to store the entire operating system, software device drivers, and applications. This amount of memory was acceptable in the early 1980s, when operating systems were small, and applications ran one at a time. As time progressed, the need for addressable memory space increased greatly. Today's computing systems require very large amounts of memory for operating systems, Graphical User Interfaces (GUIs), and multitasking applications.

Upper Memory Area (UMA)

The UMA, also referred to as reserved memory, is the first 384 KB of memory addresses directly above conventional memory. The first section of upper memory addresses is reserved for video RAM and ROM. The top section of memory addresses in upper memory is reserved for the system BIOS. (You may have heard the term *shadowing* before. In computer terms, shadowing refers to moving ROM BIOS information into the reserved area of memory.) BIOS programs for expansion boards other than video are located or "mapped" to the memory addresses between video RAM and the system BIOS. Table 4.5 lists the areas in reserved memory with associated computer hexadecimal memory addresses. Unused memory addresses in upper memory are referred to as Upper Memory Blocks (UMBs).

TABLE 4.5   Reserved (Upper) Memory Map

Reserved Memory Area	Assigned Memory Address Range (Hexadecimal)
System BIOS	F000–FFFFF
Optional BIOS area	C8000–EFFFF
Video BIOS	C0000–C7FFF
Color text	B8000–BFFFF
Mono text	B0000–B7FFF
VGA/EGA	A0000–AFFFF

As applications grew more sophisticated, the need for more conventional memory space increased. To meet this demand, developers redesigned the UMA into expanded memory. Special DOS memory-management programs and device drivers, such as EMM386.exe, Memmaker, and Himem.sys, were developed to move device drivers out of conventional memory and into expanded memory, freeing up space for the operating system and applications.

- EMM386.EXE uses Limulation (conversion of extended memory to expanded memory) to open access to the UMBs. This makes it possible to load programs and device drivers into memory using the AUTOEXEC.BAT and CONFIG.SYS files of DOS.
- Memmaker was introduced with DOS 6.0. This utility allows you to free up conventional memory by loading device drivers and terminate-and-stay-resident programs (TSRs) into UMBs.

■   Himem.sys is a memory device driver that also opens the HMA and directs programs to memory addresses in extended memory. Himem.sys must be loaded in the config.sys file for access to extended memory.

High Memory Area (HMA)

The HMA is the first 64 KB of extended memory minus 16 bytes. This area of memory is controlled by Himem.sys and is the only area of extended memory available to a processor running in real mode.

Extended Memory (XMS)

Extended memory includes all addressable memory above the reserved memory (above 1 MB) and up to 4 GB. You must have at least a 286 processor to take advantage of extended memory.

If you are interested in learning more about logical memory and its divisions, you may find the following PCGuide.com Web site informative: www.pcguide.com/ref/ram/logic-c.html.

NOTE

Chapter Summary

This chapter introduced you to computer memory types and characteristics. At this point, you should be able to physically identify the types of RAM packages discussed. You should also be able to describe the three main types of video memory, have a basic understanding of memory error detection and correction, and have conceptual knowledge of logical memory. For the exam, you should focus on valid memory acronyms and physical RAM packages. The following review questions will help you familiarize yourself further with these concepts.

Review Questions

1. **Which of the following are valid types of memory modules used in a computer? (Choose Three)**

   ☐ A. ZIMM

   ☐ B. SwapSIM

   ☐ C. RIMM

   ☐ D. DIMM

   ☐ E. ZDRIMM

   ☐ F. SIMM

Correct Answers = C, D, and F

RIMM, DIMM, and SIMM are valid memory modules.

2. **Of the following types of RAM, which is the fastest?**
   ○ A. Page Fault RAM
   ○ B. FPM DRAM
   ○ C. EDO RAM
   ○ D. Swap File RAM

   Correct Answer = C

   EDO is faster than FPM memory. Page Fault RAM and Swap File RAM are fictional names.

3. **Which type of memory is internal to the processor?**
   ○ A. Level 1 cache
   ○ B. Bus RAM
   ○ C. BEDO RAM
   ○ D. EDO RAM
   ○ E. Parity with ECC

   Correct Answer = A

   Level 1 cache is considered primary cache and is internal or built-in to the processor itself.

4. **Which type of memory uses burst mode to send data?**
   ○ A. CD-RW RAM
   ○ B. SDRAM
   ○ C. High-speed RAM
   ○ D. Coast RAM

   Correct Answer = B

   SDRAM uses burst mode (automatic retrieval of data before it is requested) for read and write operations. SDRAM sends data in high-speed bursts by using burst mode.

5. **What type of memory module is displayed in Figure 4.7?**

FIGURE 4.7   A memory module.

- ○ A. 168-pin DIMM
- ○ B. 72-pin SIMM
- ○ C. RIMM
- ○ D. 30-pin SIMM

Correct Answer = D

6. **What type of memory module is displayed in Figure 4.8?**

FIGURE 4.8   A memory module.

- ○ A. 168-pin DIMM
- ○ B. 72-pin SIMM
- ○ C. RIMM
- ○ D. 30-pin SIMM

Correct Answer = B

7. **What type of memory module is displayed in Figure 4.9?**

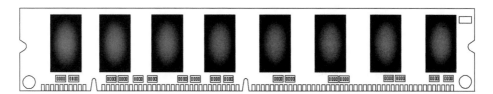

FIGURE 4.9   A memory module.

○ A. 30-pin SIMM
○ B. 72-pin SIMM
○ C. SGRAM
○ D. 168-pin DIMM

Correct Answer = D

8. **How many DIMMS are required per memory bank on a motherboard?**

○ A. 2
○ B. 1
○ C. 1,073,741,824
○ D. 8

Correct Answer = B

DIMMS can be installed in units of 1 (one module) per memory bank. In other words, you can install one DIMM on a motherboard if you so choose.

9. **Which of the following statements is not true?**

○ A. A kilobyte is equal to 1,024 bytes
○ B. A megabyte is equal to 1,048,576 bytes
○ C. A gigabyte is equal to 1,073,741,824 bytes
○ D. All of the above statements are true

Correct Answer = D

All statements are true. Reference Table 4.1 for details.

10. **Which of the following memory modules are specifically designed for laptop computers?**

○ A. FSO RAM
○ B. SOSORIMM
○ C. SODIMM
○ D. SDIMM
○ E. None of the above

Correct Answer = C

A SODIMM is a smaller DIMM specifically designed for laptop computers. There are two major types of SODIMMS. They come on a module that is 72 pins with a transfer rate of 32 bits or a module with 144 pins at a transfer rate of 64 bits.

11. **What would a technician use WRAM for?**

   ○ A. Video
   ○ B. Audio
   ○ C. Windows memory
   ○ D. L3 cache acceleration
   ○ E. None of the above

   Correct Answer = A

   WRAM is used for video.

12. **What type of memory module is displayed in Figure 4.10?**

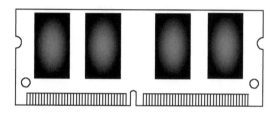

   FIGURE 4.10   A memory module.

   ○ A. 30-pin SIMM
   ○ B. SODIMM
   ○ C. SGRAM
   ○ D. 168-pin DIMM

   Correct Answer = B

13. **What type of memory module is displayed in Figure 4.11?**

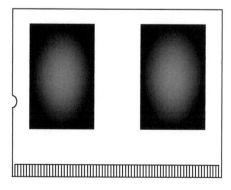

   FIGURE 4.11   A memory module.

   ○ A. 30-pin SIMM
   ○ B. SODIMM
   ○ C. MicroDIMM
   ○ D. 168-pin DIMM

Correct Answer = C

14. **What type of memory module is displayed in Figure 4.12?**

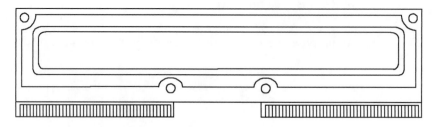

FIGURE 4.12 A memory module.

   ○ A. 30-pin SIMM
   ○ B. MicroDIMM
   ○ C. SGRAM
   ○ D. RIMM

Correct Answer = D

15. **Which of the following describe DDR2? (Choose Two)**
   □ A. Not backward compatible with DDR
   □ B. Packaged in a 240-pin memory module
   □ C. Is backward compatible with DDR
   □ D. Mainly used in game consoles such as PlayStation and Xbox 360
   □ E. Memory used in mobile devices such as PDAs, cell phones, and music players

Correct Answers = A and B

DDR2 memory modules are not backward compatible with DDR, and DDR2 memory modules are commonly packaged in a 240-pin memory module. GDDR3 and GDDR4 are graphics card memory specifications developed by ATI Technologies. These types of memory target mainly game consoles such as PlayStations and Xbox 360. MDDR, also called Mobile DDR SDRAM, is memory used in mobile devices such as PDAs, cell phones, and music players.

16. **What is being installed in Figure 4.13?**

FIGURE 4.13   A memory module.

○ A.   30-pin SIMM
○ B.   SODIMM
○ C.   168-pin DIMM
○ D.   RIMM

Correct Answer = B.

A SODIMM is being installed in a notebook computer.

17. **You have been asked by a client to upgrade the memory in several company laptop systems. Which of the following are valid types of memory that may be options for the laptops? (Choose Four)**

☐ A.   160-pin SODIMM
☐ B.   100-pn SODIMM
☐ C.   144-pin SODIMM
☐ D.   200-pin SODIMM
☐ E.   72-pin SODIMM

Correct answers = B, C, D, and E

SODIMMS come in packaging of 72-, 100-, 144- or 200-pins.

18. **What is wrong with the memory installation being conducted in Figure 4.14?**

FIGURE 4.14 A memory module.

- ○ A. The technician is trying to install a SIMM in a DIMM slot.
- ○ B. The technician is not using two hands to seat the memory stick.
- ○ C. The indentations are not properly matched up with the notches.
- ○ D. The technician should be using rubber gloves to avoid ESD.

Correct Answer = B

Two hands are not being used to properly install the memory stick. When installing memory in a computer system, you should always use two hands and press firmly down on both sides of the memory stick for it to be properly seated. All other choices are invalid.

19. **You need to upgrade the memory in several client computer systems using 240-pin memory modules. What type of memory will you be installing?**

- ○ A. SIMMs
- ○ B. Virtual memory
- ○ C. DIMMs
- ○ D. None of the above

Correct Answer = C

You will be installing DIMMS. Remember, 240-pin DIMMS are used for DDR2 SDRAM. SIMMs are older memory types that came in 30-pin and 72-pin packages.

20. **You receive a call from a client stating that a system is low on virtual memory. What two options should you consider to rectify this issue? (Choose Two)**

☐ A.   Increase the size of the paging file.

☐ B.   Tell the customer not to run more than one program at a time.

☐ C.   Add more RAM to the system.

☐ D.   Add more Video RAM to the system.

Correct Answers = A and C

If you ever receive a warning that a system is low on virtual memory, you should increase the size of the paging file or simply add more RAM to the system.

REFERENCES

http://images.crucial.com/pdf/sodimm_install.pdf. This Crucial Technologies Web site has a great PDF document that explains how to properly install a SODIMM in a laptop computer system.

www.transmetazone.com/articleview.cfm?articleid=1195&page=4. This Transmeta-Zone Web site shows you how to install a 144-pin MicroDIMM into a laptop computer.

www.pcguide.com/ref/ram/logic-c.html. This PC Guide Web site provides some very interesting details regarding logical memory.

5 System Resources and Input Devices

In This Chapter

BINARY

Humans use a base 10 numbering system. Computers operate using a base 2 numbering system called binary. Binary works well with computers because there are only two values, or digits, that a computer recognizes: 0 and 1.

As you may recall from Chapter 4, the smallest unit of measure in a computer is a negative or positive electrical charge held in a cell within a capacitor. Hard drives must store data without a constant electrical charge, and so do optical media. If an electrical charge is negative, a 0 digit is represented. If the charge is positive, a 1 is represented. A 0 or a 1 represents a single bit. (There are 8 bits (combinations of 0s and 1s) in 1 byte. In human terms, a computer uses 1 byte of information to determine a single character, symbol, space, number, or letter. A group of bytes together form a word.

There are two ways to convert a binary number to a decimal number, or a decimal number to binary. The simplest way is to use a scientific calculator. The default software calculator installed by most versions of Windows is handy for this task. Click Start > Programs > Accessories > Calculator, and change the view to scientific. Enter a number in decimal, and click the Bin radio button; the decimal number will be converted to binary. Click the Dec radio button to convert the binary number back to a decimal number. The Windows calculator can also be used to convert decimal numbers to hexadecimal format. (Hexadecimal notation is discussed later in this chapter.) Use the Hex radio button for this purpose.

Manually converting a binary number to decimal is a little more difficult. Figure 5.1 represents an 8-bit byte, 00101101. The top row of numbers in the figure represents base 2 increments (increasing powers of 2, from right to left). To convert the binary number 00101101 to a decimal number, simply multiply the 0s and 1s by their corresponding power of 2. Add the eight results together, and you have the decimal equivalent to 00101101. You can replace the binary number 00101101 in Figure 5.1 with any combination of bits to calculate a different binary number's decimal equivalent. See Table 5.1 for examples of other binary numbers and their decimal equivalents.

TABLE 5.1 Binary Numbers and Their Decimal Equivalents

Binary Number	Decimal Equivalent
00000000	0
00000001	1
00000010	2
00000011	3
00000100	4
00001010	10

Use Figure 5.1 to calculate the decimal equivalent of 00101101 by multiplying the 0s and 1s by their corresponding power of 2.

$$0 \times 128 = 0$$
$$0 \times 64 = 0$$
$$1 \times 32 = 32$$
$$0 \times 16 = 0$$
$$1 \times 8 = 8$$
$$1 \times 4 = 4$$
$$0 \times 2 = 0$$
$$1 \times 1 = 1$$

128	64	32	16	8	4	2	1
0	0	1	0	1	1	0	1

Figure 5.1 8-bit byte and Base 2 increments.

Add the eight results together:

$0 + 0 + 32 + 0 + 8 + 4 + 0 + 1 = 45$ (the decimal equivalent of 00101101)

HEXADECIMAL

Hexadecimal is a base 16 numbering system associated with memory and other addresses in a computer. The hexadecimal numbering system consists of the following 16 numbers and letters: 0, 1, 2, 3, 4, 5, 6, 7, 8, 9, and A, B, C, D, E, and F. The letter A represents a decimal equivalent of 10, B = 11, C = 12, D = 13, E = 14, and F = 15. Hexadecimal numbers use an *h* suffix to identify the address as a hexadecimal number—for example, 10*h*. Hexadecimal is easier to read because it is based on groups of four bits (known as *nybbles*), unlike binary, which uses groups of eight bits.

Table 5.2 displays decimal, binary, and hexadecimal equivalents.

TABLE 5.2   Decimal, Binary, and Hexadecimal Equivalents

Decimal	Binary	Hexadecimal
0	0000	0
1	0001	1
2	0010	2
3	0011	3
4	0100	4
5	0101	5
6	0110	6
7	0111	7
8	1000	8
9	1001	9
10	1011	B
12	1100	C
13	1101	D
14	1110	E
15	1111	F

OVERVIEW OF SYSTEM RESOURCES

Many devices inside or attached to a computer system require communication with the system's processor and memory to send and receive data and instructions. The three built-in mechanisms that allow this communication to take place are interrupt requests (IRQs), Direct Memory Access (DMA) channels, and I/Os.

INTERRUPT REQUESTS

An *IRQ* is a wire incorporated into the motherboard's bus that is used by a device, such as a printer or a keyboard, as a mechanism to capture the attention of the CPU for a request of service.

The default IRQ assignment for a standard 101-key keyboard is IRQ 1. When you enter data using the keyboard, you are requesting the CPU to stop what it is doing and take notice of your request to input data. Your request is sent to the CPU by using IRQ 1.

There are 16 IRQ assignments in a computer system. (Refer to Table 5.3 for typical system default IRQ settings.) Early computers had 8 IRQs. As the need for more devices increased, another 8 IRQs(a byte's worth) were added.

TABLE 5.3 Typical System Default IRQ Assignments

IRQ	Device Assigned
0	System timer
1	Standard 101/102 keyboard
2	Interrupt controller (cascaded to IRQ 9)
3	COM2 and COM4 (serial ports 2 and 4)
4	COM1 and COM3 (serial ports 1 and 3)
5	LPT2 (extra printer or sound card)
6	Floppy drive controller
7	LPT1 (parallel port)
8	Real-Time Clock (RTC)
9	Cascaded to IRQ 2
10	Available (advanced audio)
11	Available (SCSI or VGA card)
12	PS/2 mouse
13	Math coprocessor
14	Primary hard drive controller (IDE)
15	Secondary hard drive controller

For the exam, remember that the system reserves IRQ 2 to connect the two sets of eight IRQs. In other words, IRQ 2 is "cascaded" to IRQ 9, which provides the usage of IRQs 9 through 15. Of the 15 IRQs available, 10 are used for I/O devices, and 5 are reserved for system devices.

An IRQ is assigned to every port, slot, and device on the motherboard. The IRQ assignments are typically handled by the system BIOS settings on start-up. Some expansion cards and peripheral devices (usually legacy, non-PnP devices) are configured manually through the use of jumpers on the motherboard or on the device. A network interface card (NIC), for example, may allow you to change the memory address and IRQ settings with the use of plastic jumpers on the card. Note that an IRQ can only be assigned to one active device at a time. Multiple devices can be assigned to the same IRQ. If two devices attempt to use the same IRQ at the same time, an IRQ conflict may occur. IRQ conflicts typically occur when new devices, such as sound cards, modems, and NICs, are added to a system with their manufacturer's default settings. For example, suppose a sound card is installed that is assigned to IRQ 5. Then you install a NIC that has a preassigned manufacturer's setting of IRQ 5. You reboot the system and notice that the new NIC is not recognized or won't function. Chances are that the sound card is currently using IRQ 5, and a conflict has occurred. You will have to manually assign the NIC to an open IRQ.

To check for any device conflicts on a system (assuming use of Windows 2000), click Start > Settings > Control Panel > System > Hardware > Device Manager. If you see a yellow diamond containing a black exclamation point, you have a device conflict.

IRQ 14 is reserved for the primary IDE or ATA controller (hard drive controller). Two devices can be attached to the primary IDE controller. The first device is the *master*, or primary hard drive. The second device attached to your primary IDE/ATA controller is the *slave*, or secondary device. This secondary device is typically another hard drive, CD-ROM, DVD-ROM, or DVD-R. If you wanted to add a third and fourth drive, you would need to use the secondary IDE controller and IRQ 15, which also allow two more devices to be attached. Refer to Figure 5.2 for a typical Windows 2000 display of IRQ assignments.

The old A+ Hardware core exam asked simple IRQ questions such as, "What is IRQ 2 used for?" The current A+ exams will likely have you resolve at least one basic IRQ conflict. The review questions at the end of this chapter will help you sharpen your IRQ conflict-resolution skills.

DIRECT MEMORY ACCESS CHANNELS (DMAs)

DMA is a memory controller with a straight path to memory. DMA channels, unlike IRQs, allow DMA devices to access memory directly, without interrupting the CPU. This allows the CPU to carry out more important functions and the DMA devices themselves to process requests faster.

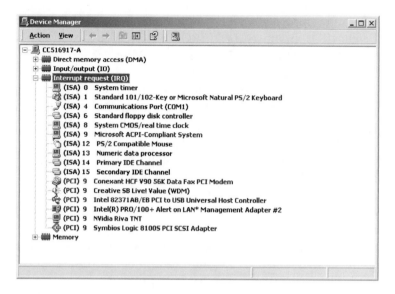

FIGURE 5.2   Windows 2000 display of IRQ settings.

DMA controller chips are integrated into the motherboard and control the DMA channels. DMA devices, such as ISA (non-PnP) cards and IDE/ATA controller interfaces, have access to DMA services. DMA does not support PCI or AGP technology.

Early computing systems, such as the AT-class computer, provided only one DMA controller with only four DMA channels, which supported 8-bit and 16-bit cards. Today's computers are equipped with two DMA controllers and eight DMA channels, DMA 0 to DMA 7. Table 5.4 shows standard DMA channel device assignments. See Figure 5.3 for a Windows 2000 display of DMA channels. You need to be familiar with DMA channel assignments 2 and 4 for the test. You may also be asked to identify which DMA channels are available by default for use with peripheral devices.

As with IRQs, there can only be one active device using a DMA channel at a time. If more than one device attempts to access a DMA channel already in use, a DMA conflict will occur.

Different forms of DMA technology are available. Third-party DMA is the original implementation of the DMA. The DMA controller chip resides on the motherboard and is designed for supporting ISA devices. Newer, first-party DMA is very popular. With first-party DMA, the DMA controller resides on the peripheral device. This allows the peripheral to actually take control of the system bus to handle the transfer of data in and out of memory. This process is referred to as *bus mastering*. Newer DMA modes are available, such as ultra DMA, offering even faster transfer rates of data.

TABLE 5.4   DMA Channel Device Assignments

DMA Channel	Device Attached
0	Available
1	Available
2	Floppy drive (possible tape drive)
3	Available
4	Second DMA controller (cascades to DMA channels 0–3)
5	Available
6	Available
7	Available

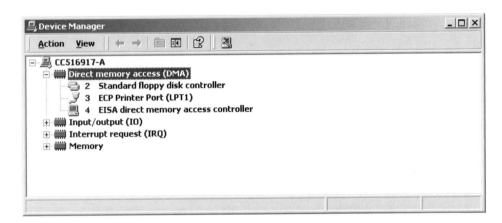

FIGURE 5.3   Windows 2000 Direct Memory Access (DMA) assignments.

INPUT/OUTPUT ADDRESSES (I/Os)

To be recognized by an operating system and programs, input and output devices attached to a computer system require unique identifications in memory. These unique identifications are called memory addresses. They are also referred to as I/O addresses and I/O port addresses.

You may encounter memory address questions on the exam. In a question such as "Which address does a particular device use?," the address in question is the memory address. Table 5.5 identifies memory address assignments.

Devices attached to the motherboard perform I/O operations by accepting instructions sent to them by operating systems and programs. The instruction sets are

TABLE 5.5 Base Memory Address Assignments

Memory Address	Device
00F0	Math coprocessor
060h	Keyboard controller
170h	Secondary IDE hard drive controller
1F0h	Primary IDE hard drive controller
220h	Sound card
300h	NIC
330h	SCSI adapter
3F2h	Floppy drive controller
3F8h	COM1
2F8h	COM2
3E8h	COM3
2E8h	COM4
378h	LPT1
278h	LPT2
C000–C7FFF	Video adapter (memory address)

first sent to preassigned unique memory addresses or memory address ranges that represent each attached device. Devices require different amounts of memory for processing. The size of memory allocated to a device's memory address can vary. The average device in a system uses 4, 8, or 32 bytes of memory address space. A video card, which requires significant amounts of memory to process output, may need more memory space assigned to its I/O address than a mouse would. The bus architecture of a device is the determining factor for the amount of memory space allocated to it.

Many memory addresses are available in a typical computer system. However, an I/O memory address conflict may occur if a device attempts to use the same memory address space already assigned to another device. It is possible to change a device's I/O address by a process called *memory-mapped I/O*. After a device is mapped to a legitimate I/O address, the CPU can recognize it.

INPUT DEFINED

Input is anything that goes into a computer in the form of data, graphics, commands, or sounds. Devices used to place or feed information into a computer, such as a keyboard or a mouse, are called input devices. Many devices can serve as both input and output devices, including hard disks, floppy disks, and writable CD-ROMs. The main input devices used today and addressed on the CompTIA A+ exams are described in the following sections.

KEYBOARDS

The keyboard is one of the most widely used peripheral input devices. As you know, users manually enter characters, numbers, punctuation, and symbols that represent data and commands into a computer system via the keyboard. Keyboards are available in many different forms, shapes, and sizes. Most are manufactured to meet the English standard computer keyboard layout known as QWERTY. QWERTY is the first line of character keys on the top left side of the keyboard. The keyboard keys are laid out into three main groups: alphanumeric, punctuation, and special function keys. You can configure a keyboard's settings through the use of the keyboard applet in most Windows-based operating systems.

There are actually three types of keyboards: the original PC keyboard with 84 keys, the AT-style keyboard (which also has 84 keys), and the enhanced keyboard with 101 keys. The main differences between the three designs are the layout and placement of the special function keys. Today's keyboards are designed with interchangeable connectors that allow them to be used with different systems. A 6-pin mini-din (PS/2) connector is most commonly used today to connect a keyboard to a computer. (See Chapter 8 for more on keyboard connectors.)

Keyboard Technologies

The two main keyboard technologies are switch technology, which is mechanical, and capacitive technology, which is nonmechanical. Each technology has its own specific design and usefulness.

Switch Technology

When you enter data using a keyboard, you are actually pushing on a keycap that is attached to a key switch. The key switch closes a circuit, which creates a signal. This electronic signal is converted to a digital scan code by the keyboard's processor and is manipulated until it is finally readable by an application in American Standard Code for Information Interchange (ASCII) format.

There are two contact key switches worth mentioning:

Foam element and foil key switch: This key switch is a combination of stem, foam element, foil, and spring. When a key is pressed, the stem pushes on the foam, foil, and spring combination, which eventually touches copper contacts on the keyboard's circuit board to create a signal. The spring pushes the stem back up to its original position and awaits the next keystroke.

Rubber dome key switch: This key switch technology uses a rounded rubber dome with carbon material on its underside. When a key cap is pressed, a stem pushes on the rubber dome, which in turn pushes the carbon material onto the circuit board, thus completing the circuit.

Capacitive Technology

Capacitive technology, the nonmechanical keyboard technology, uses a switch housing that contains two conductive plates and a stem. When a key is pressed, the stem pushes the top plate toward the bottom plate, causing a change in capacitance within the switch housing. The keyboard controller recognizes the change in capacitance, and a signal is created.

Keyboard Troubleshooting and Maintenance

Keyboards are considered Field-Replaceable Units (FRUs). FRUs are computer parts or components that a technician can easily replace while troubleshooting computer systems in a work area or on a job site. The best way to fix a broken or defective keyboard is to replace it. Keyboards are inexpensive components. Like a computer monitor, it can cost more to have a keyboard repaired than replaced.

The keyboard is connected to a port that is connected to the motherboard. If you think you have a bad keyboard, you should verify that the problem exists with the keyboard itself and not with the motherboard. Follow these simple steps to verify if your keyboard is bad.

1. Turn the computer off.
2. Carefully unplug the keyboard connector from the back of the system.
3. Plug a known working keyboard with a similar keyboard connector into the system.
4. Turn the computer on.

If the known working keyboard is functional, the original keyboard or its connector is bad. If the known working keyboard is not functional, you most likely have a motherboard-related issue.

Keyboard problems are rare. Common keyboard issues are typically related to stuck keys or loose keyboard connectors and are most likely detected by the POST at system boot with a 301 error (refer to POST error codes in Chapter 2).

Keeping a keyboard in good working order requires regular cleaning. To clean a keyboard, follow these basic steps.

1. Turn the computer off.
2. Carefully unplug the keyboard connector from the back of the system.

3. Turn the keyboard upside down, and shake it until any foreign material is dislodged.
4. Use a can of compressed air to spray out dust and other particles.
5. Use a very dilute combination of soap and water applied with a nonabrasive cloth to remove stains from the keycaps. Alternatively, soak the keyboard in distilled, demineralized water.
6. Carefully plug the keyboard back into the system. (Verify that the keyboard is completely dry before doing so.)
7. Turn the computer on.

If a keyboard has been subjected to a major soda, coffee, or other chemical spill, you can rinse it off with water or run it through the rinse cycle in a dishwasher (no-heat cycle; this is recommended only for mechanical keyboards, not capacitive). For best results, replace the keyboard.

For the exams, you should also note the following bulleted items regarding keyboards and remember the important keyboard commands displayed in Table 5.6.

■ Keyboards come in the 101- and 102-style varieties and are input devices.
■ Newer keyboard use a 6-pin mini DIN connector.
■ Older style AT keyboards use a 5-pin DIN connector.
■ Keyboards should never be connected or disconnected while the power to the system is on. This can result in an ESD that can damage the keyboard and the motherboard of the system.
■ Laptop computers use an 84-key compact keyboard.

TABLE 5.6   Important Keyboard Commands and Their Functions

Keyboard Commands	Function
/E	Launches Explorer
/F	Launches Find Files or Folders
/F1	Starts Help
/M	Minimizes all windows
/Tab	Scrolls through open taskbar items

MICE AND POINTING DEVICES

The PC mouse was developed as an ergonomic device that allows its user to select data and menus, and adjust the location of an insertion point (cursor). The invention of the GUI, such as Windows, spawned the demand for the mouse. Today, if you notice a computer without a mouse attached, it probably has a touch-screen video display for inputting data and selecting menus. Figure 5.4 shows an assortment of input and pointing devices. Many types of mice are available today. The main types of mice you should be familiar with for the exam are as follows:

Mechanical: This is a common type of mouse in use. A mechanical mouse contains a hard rubber ball, wheels, and sensors. When the mouse unit is moved, the rubber ball moves in the same direction, which makes the wheels supporting the ball spin. The mouse's built-in sensors detect the movement of the wheels. The sensors send the detected signal to the computer. If your mouse pointer does not respond correctly as you move about the screen, you may need to inspect the rubber ball inside the mouse unit for foreign particles. Figure 5.5 shows the bottom of a ball mouse.

Optical: There are no moving parts inside the optical mouse. This type of mouse uses an optical system with a sensor to calculate the x and y coordinates of the screen's cursor.

Optomechanical: This is a combination of the mechanical and optical mouse. A rubber ball is used in conjunction with a photo-interrupter disk. Light-emitting diodes are used to detect mouse movements.

FIGURE 5.4 Input and pointing device assortment.

FIGURE 5.5 Opening the bottom of a ball mouse.

Serial Mouse

Almost every computer has at least one serial (COM) port. A serial mouse's female DB-9 connector attaches to the computer's male DB-9 (9-pin) serial port. (See Chapter 8 for more information on connectors.) Before connecting a serial mouse to a serial port, you should check your BIOS configuration settings to verify that a COM port is available for the serial mouse to use. Remember, IRQs are assigned to COM ports. If the COM port you want to use has already been assigned to a modem, the serial mouse may not work.

A serial mouse can be connected to a PS/2 mouse port with a serial-to-mini DIN adapter.

PS/2 Mouse

The *PS/2* mouse is a PnP device that uses IRQ 12 by default. This default IRQ assignment frees up a COM port that was previously needed to support a serial mouse.

It is important that you do not unplug a PS/2 mouse when the system is turned on. Unplugging an "active" mouse can cause damage to your system and your mouse.

USB Mouse

A *universal serial bus (USB)* mouse is a hot-swappable PnP device, which means it can be plugged into an already powered-up system and is automatically detected by the operating system. With most new operating systems, the USB mouse drivers (software used to support the mouse) are automatically installed.

Trackballs

A *trackball* is a mouse with a plastic ball housed on its topside that uses less desk space than a traditional mouse. A thumb or finger is used to maneuver the ball. Trackballs use optomechanical technology and are connected to a system with a PS/2 or USB connection.

Infrared Wireless Mouse

The wireless mouse uses infrared (IR) technology. A beam of infrared light goes from a receiver, which gets its power from a serial or PS/2 port, to the mouse. There must be a clear path from the mouse to the receiver for the mouse to work properly. This is called line-of-site infrared technology.

Touchpads

A *touchpad* is a small pad that is sensitive to the touch. It is used as a pointing device with most laptop computers. You direct the mouse pointer on your computer screen by sliding your finger across a square or rectangular pad. You can start programs and select objects by tapping on the pad. A touchpad does everything a mouse can do and eliminates the need for a mouse-tail (wire).

Joysticks

Joysticks are used mostly for computer games and Computer-Aided Design (CAD) programs. A joystick is a pointing device that is attached to a sound or video card's Musical Instrument Digital Interface (MIDI) port, also known as a game port. The exam might ask you to identify the MIDI (game) port on a sound card. Do not confuse this port with a 15-pin video connection (see Chapter 8 for information on connectors). Like a mouse, a joystick can move the screen pointer in all directions.

Stylus and Digitizer

A *stylus* is a handheld pen-shaped device that is commonly used as a pointing or writing instrument to input text and interact with a computer. A stylus, which uses an electronic tip or head instead of ink, is used to input text or small pictures into computer devices such as PDAs (Personal Data Assistants) or touch screens. PDAs and touch screens typically use a digitized electronic tablet to accept responses from a stylus.

You use the stylus and tap or write on a digitizer. A *digitizer* is a device that converts analog signals (of or from photos, images, and even audio) into digital representations of the original analog signal that a computer can understand. In human terms, the device converts the position of a point on a surface into a digital data equivalent or data image. One of the main problems associated with the stylus and the digitizer (the part of the screen that recognizes the stylus tap) is that dirt and dust particles can get wedged under the screen frame causing unrecognized taps from the stylus.

Touch Screen

A touch screen is a computer display device that reacts to human touch. It can be classified as both an input and output device because it "inputs" signals through a controller to a processor and then "outputs" or "presents" information through a display screen. Touch screens are most often used in such places as kiosks, restaurants, and in some training facilities where the use of a pointing device such as a mouse or a keyboard might prove cumbersome or awkward. Touch screens are typically connected to computer systems through external USB or serial ports.

Three different types of touch screen technology are used today:

Surface wave: This touch screen technology is by far the most advanced. It uses ultrasonic waves that run across the touch screen. When a particular area of the touch screen is pushed with a finger or touched with a pointing device, such as a stylus, that area is "absorbed," and a signal representing that area is sent to a controller. One drawback to this technology is that it is highly sensitive to outside conditions, such as inclement weather.

Resistive: This technology uses a metallic layer that is electrically conductive and resistive. When an area on the screen is touched with a finger or stylus, a change occurs in the electrical current present within that area. This electrical change is registered, and an event is passed to the controller for further processing. Resistive technology touch screens are much more affordable than surface wave touch screens, and they are not affected by normal outside weather conditions, such as water. The drawbacks are that resistive displays are substantially less clear to the sight than surface wave or capacitive technology.

Capacitive: Capacitive technology employs a screen that is covered with a substance or material that stores electrical charges. Electrical sensors (circuits) are located at the corners of the screen. These sensors recognize when an area on the screen has been touched by human contact. They in turn gather the electrical charges registered and forward the collected information to a controller for processing. Capacitive technology provides a good deal of clarity. It is not affected by normal outside conditions, such as dust and weather.

MODEMS

The current A+ exams are likely to target your knowledge of analog dial-up modem commands and troubleshooting customer-related modem issues.

Many types of modems are available on the market today, including cable, wireless, cell phones access cards, Digital Subscriber Line (DSL), and analog dial-up modems. For the purpose of the A+ Depot Technician exam, we will focus on analog dial-up modems.

Modem is an acronym for modulate demodulate. A computer sends data from the CPU to a modem in digital format. The modem (modulator) converts digital data to analog format, which can be sent over a Plain Old Telephone Service (POTS) line. When the analog signal reaches the receiving modem, it is converted back to digital format, which can be understood by the receiving computer.

Typical 56 Kbps analog modems are connected to a system internally or externally. An internal modem is inserted into an expansion slot on the motherboard. An external modem is connected to an RS-232c standard serial port with a 9-pin or 25-pin modem cable, or a USB port with a USB cable connector. After an analog modem has been connected to the computer system, either internally or externally, it can then be connected to a traditional phone jack with an RJ11 connector.

As discussed earlier in this chapter, a computer works with data in units of 8 bits, called a byte. A serial port transmits data only 1 bit at a time. A Universal Asynchronous Receiver Transmitter (UART) chip is used to break down incoming bytes into bits that can be transmitted serially (1 bit at a time) out of the serial port. There are three types of UART chips:

8250: The first UART chip is used in XT and AT computers and has a 1-byte buffer.

16450: Introduced in the AT with a 2-byte buffer.

16550A: Introduced with the 486 computers and is common in Pentiums. This chip uses 16-byte, First-In First-Out (FIFO) buffering.

A modem, like any other device attached to a computer, requires a software driver in order to be recognized by the operating system. If a modem software driver is outdated, the user may experience intermittent problems with the connection to the Internet or another modem. Another consideration is that if your dial-up connection to the Internet is unusually slow or unstable, you should first contact your local phone company and have them clear the noise on the phone line.

You can test the ability of an analog modem to send and receive signals properly with an analog loop-back adapter or a loop-back plug.

AT MODEM COMMANDS

The Hayes Microcomputer Products Company developed some of the earliest modems. Many modems are compatible with the modem standards set forth by Hayes (*Hayes compatible*). Hayes developed a set of modem commands that can be used to control modems manually. Today, the control and configuration of modems is generally handled by the operating system. Table 5.7 identifies some of the basic Hayes-compatible AT modem commands that you should be familiar with for the A+ exams.

TABLE 5.7 AT Modem Commands

AT Command	Command Action
ATA or A0	Answer call
ATD or ATDT	Dial the number specified
ATE	Echo (show) command on screen
ATH and ATH0	Hang up or disconnect modem
ATZ	Reset the modem
XON/XOFF	Modem flow control

MODEM FLOW CONTROL (HANDSHAKING)

When using dial-up communications, it is typical for a sending device to deliver data faster than a receiving device can accept it. *Flow control*, or *handshaking*, is a verification process that two communication devices use to verify that proper communication is taking place. Several flow-control protocols are available to assist with the smooth transmission of data from a Data Terminal Equipment (DTE) device, such as a serial port, to a Data Communication Equipment (DCE) device, such as a modem, and vice versa. These protocols are as follows.

XON/XOFF: This software flow control mixes control characters in with the data to perform handshaking between devices. When the receiving device's buffer is full, it sends a request, or XOFF message, to the sending device. When the buffer on the receiving device is ready to accept more data, an XON message is sent to the sending device, and transmission resumes. This is a commonly used type of flow control, although it does have a high margin of error.

RTS/CTS (Request To Send/Clear To Send): A dependable, commonly used form of hardware flow control between a computer and a modem, the RTS signal represents a computer, and the CTS signal represents a modem. If a computer is not ready to receive data, it drops its RTS signal. Its attached modem in turn drops its CTS signal and refuses to accept incoming data. When the computer is ready to receive data, it raises its RTS signal, which in turn raises its attached modem's CTS signal, and data acknowledgment can resume.

XMODEM: An error-checking method used to verify that data is not corrupted or lost; XMODEM sends data in 128-byte blocks.

YMODEM: Data is sent in 1024-byte blocks over a dial-up connection. The YMODEM error-checking protocol is faster than XMODEM and is less reliable than ZMODEM.

ZMODEM: This method also sends data in 1024-byte blocks. The ZMODEM protocol is faster than XMODEM. ZMODEM can resume or restart a file transfer at the point it previously failed.

SCANNERS

A *scanner* is an input device that captures analog images in the form of text, photographs, or drawings and converts them to digital information (0s and 1s) that can be recognized by a computer system supporting scanner software. A scanner uses a sensor to capture the reflection of light from a desired object to create a digitized image. Scanner software or supporting applications can be used to modify the digital image to suit the needs of the user. Finally, the image can be duplicated, printed, saved as a file, or sent as an e-mail attachment.

Optical scanners and digital cameras use Charge-Coupled Devices (CCDs) to sense variations in light reflected off an image. These tiny CCDs are lined up in rows or arrays.

A CCD represents a pixel. A pixel (picture element) is an area in a graphic image. Computer monitors, for example, are split into sections that are represented by millions of pixels. The more pixels there are to an area, the sharper the graphic image or monitor resolution. Scanner resolution is measured in optical dots per inch (dpi). In simple terms, a CCD in a scanner represents one dot on a graphic image. The more CCDs there are per area in a scanner, the sharper the final image will be.

Scanners are available in various forms and offer different delivery methods:

Flatbed scanner: The most common type of scanner; larger flatbed scanners that bind documents together are often seen in business environments. With a flatbed scanner, a document or image is placed on a flat glass surface. A light source and an array of sensors (CCDs) pass below the document.

Single sheet-fed scanner: Smaller, single-feed flatbed scanners can be purchased at reasonable prices for home use. This type of scanner uses a set of rollers to feed the image to be scanned past the light source and sensors. This is not a useful scanner for large amounts of information to be scanned.

Handheld scanner: A handheld scanner is a flexible device that allows you to scan stationary objects or images. It is also a useful tool for gathering inventory information; for example, a bar code scanner can be used to gather stock information at a grocery store or warehouse.

Just like any other hardware device, a scanner needs a software driver to communicate with a computer system or network. Today, most scanners use a very common driver known as TWAIN (Technology Without An Interesting Name). The TWAIN driver interprets the data between the programs used to scan and communicate with the actual scanner itself. This common driver allows the program or application to easily communicate with the scanner without having to know all the details about the scanner.

There are several ways to interface a scanner to your computer system, including parallel, SCSI, and USB connections. These types of connectors are discussed in detail in Chapter 8.

SOUND CARDS

A sound card can act as an input or output device. It combines all the technology needed to convert audio signals to digital and digital signals to audio, through the use of Digital-to-Analog Converters (DACs) and Analog-to-Digital Converters (ADCs).

A sound card can be integrated into the motherboard, or it can be an expansion card that is connected to the motherboard through a PCI or ISA expansion slot. As is the case with every peripheral device attached to the motherboard, a sound card requires the use of system resources, such as an IRQ, a DMA channel, and an I/O address. PCI sound cards are fairly easy to install. If the system has a PnP operating system and BIOS, you just install the card into an open PCI slot, and the BIOS takes care of the system resources and configuration for you. The majority of ISA sound cards on the market are preconfigured with a set of onboard jumpers that specify the use of IRQ 5. This can cause an IRQ conflict if you already have an LPT2 (a second printer port) or another device, such as a NIC, already configured to use IRQ 5. Some sound cards use special software drivers that are installed into system files, such as DOS's AUTOEXEC.BAT and CONFIG.SYS. These system files run when the computer is started and tell the operating system to recognize that there are sound-related devices attached to the computer.

Most sounds cards are connected to a CD-ROM by a wire known as a CD audio cable that comes standard with a CD-ROM device. This allows the sound card to act as an input device between your CD-ROM and the computer system. If you are using your CD-ROM as a music device, and no sound is coming from your PC speaker or attached sound system speakers, you should verify that the wire is connected between the sound card and the CD-ROM.

Sound cards are a combination of components that allow audio to be manipulated and transferred in and out of a computer system. Following are some of the important components that make up a sound card:

- An *ADC*, which is a circuit used to convert infinite analog wave signals in the form of human voice, music, or camera, to digital signals (0s and 1s) that can be understood, manipulated, and stored by a computer system.
- A *DAC* is a circuit used to convert stored digital data back to infinite analog wave signals that are outputted to audio devices, such as a microphone or speakers.
- *Analog inputs* are sound cards designed with input jacks that accept low-level voltage input from devices such as musical instruments, CD players, and microphones.

- *Analog outputs* are designed to support sound card output to speakers. There are normally two analog outputs found on a sound card. For novices, this is where you plug in your PC speakers.
- A *MIDI/game port* is a sound card port that provides support for a joystick (external game device attachment). It also provides support for musical instruments and synthesizers. The MIDI/game port is often mistaken for a video card connector on the back of a computer. It is possible that on the exams you will see a graphic of a sound card, and you may be asked to identify the joystick/MIDI port or speaker output jacks.
- Many newer sound cards have a *synthesizer chip* built onto the sound card. This chip is used to support external MIDI devices and uses a technology known as wave-table synthesis.

DIGITAL CAMERAS

Digital cameras have taken the world by storm. They are considered an input device used to capture images that can be downloaded to a computer system. Once downloaded, the digital images can be fine-tuned and manipulated with graphical software applications to suit the needs of the end user. The final result can then be stored, e-mailed, or printed.

Like scanners, most digital cameras use CCDs to capture images. Most digital cameras are connected to a computer system using a USB port or serial port that is IEEE 1394 compliant. They can also use infrared technology to download images to a system. Most digital cameras have two ways in which to store images: internal storage, which typically has to be erased after a maximum number of images have been taken; or removable or "external" storage, which is comparable to conventional camera film. Following are the four most popular technologies employed for storing images externally:

- PC cards
- CompactFlash
- SSFDC (Solid State Floppy Disk Card)
- Miniature card

Digital cameras have become so popular these days that operating systems such as Windows Me, Windows 2000, and Windows XP all have Control Panel applets called "Scanners and Cameras," which can be used to easily add, configure, and troubleshoot these devices. Windows Vista even includes an application called Windows Photo Gallery that lets users easily import and manage digital pictures (it's available as a free download for Windows XP users), and Mac users have long enjoyed the iPhotos program's many capabilities.

The following digital camera resource page Web site provides a wealth of information regarding new digital camera technology products and reviews: *www.dcresource.com/*

PDAs (Personal Data Assistants)

A PDA is a small, mobile, handheld computing device that includes features such as fax, phone, networking, and Internet. Most PDAs in use today can accept input through the use of a stylus (mentioned earlier in this chapter), a small keyboard, and possibly voice input through voice recognition technologies. A very interesting development for PDAs was the implementation of the Graffiti handwriting recognition system. This allows the user to write text to the operating system directly through the PDA's display screen with a stylus. The information written on the display screen is actually converted from input to text. The text can then be manipulated, stored, or e-mailed.

The most popular operating systems installed on most PDAs today are Microsoft Windows CE, PalmOS, and EPOC.

Synchronization

After data is inputted into a PDA system, it is often necessary to transfer or synchronize this data to a desktop computer system, laptop, or another PDA on a regular basis. Most PDAs come with a cradle that conveniently connects to a desktop with a serial (most commonly USB) cable. When the PDA is in the cradle, information can be transmitted or synced to the desktop system. Most cradles also provide power recharge capabilities while the PDA rests in the cradle. Data can be transferred through the serial connection from the PDA to a connected system and vice versa. In simple terms, the PDA's cradle is to a PDA what a docking station is to a laptop computer. (Docking stations will be discussed later in this chapter.) The most common methods used today to transfer information from one PDA to another PDA are through IR/IRDA (Infrared/Infrared Data Association) or Bluetooth (wireless specification standard). It is very important to note that PDAs can easily connect with each other, home computers, business systems, and phones using today's popular wireless standards, such as Bluetooth. Infrared and wireless connectivity will be explained in greater detail in Chapter 8.

The A+ exams are likely to question you on how data is transferred from PDA to desktop and from PDA to PDA.

Technological advances, which allow most PDAs to do everything that a regular desktop can do, have made PDAs a must-have in today's hectic mobile e-business world. You can use a PDA to remotely work with such things as databases, spreadsheets, documents, e-mail, games, and calendars.

LAPTOPS

A laptop is a battery- or AC-powered mobile computer system that typically weighs between two and five pounds. Its compactness makes it ideal for mobile users who are on the go and need to work or access data, whether in or out of the office. Great strides have been made over the past few years to improve the effectiveness and ease of using laptop systems. Technological improvements regarding such things as battery power, docking stations, port replicators, wireless accessibility, USB, form factors, and overall general size have contributed to the growth in laptop use.

There are many ways to connect to peripheral devices from laptops. Although these technologies will be further discussed in the chapters to come, it is very important for the exams that you recognize them in this section. Some of the more traditional ways to connect a laptop or a system to a printer, scanner, or other device include parallel, serial, USB, and FireWire connections. However, it has become even more popular to connect to these devices through wireless technologies such as the Bluetooth wireless standard. The Bluetooth standard has also become popular for connecting keyboards, mice, and many other devices to computing systems. This welcome standard eliminated the need for multiple wires and cords and offers the user more freedom and flexibility. Bluetooth uses a short-range radio signal to create a point-to-point link that operates from 2.4 to 2.48 GHz. It is especially useful for laptops.

If a laptop is plugged into a power outlet and abruptly shuts down after the laptop is unplugged from the outlet, it is a sure sign that the laptop battery is no longer holding a charge and should be replaced.

Laptops use PCMCIA cards for additional computer-related components such as memory, NIC cards, modems, and hard drives. The three main PCMCIA card types are Type 1, which are 3.3 mm thick and used for memory; Type II, which are 5.0 mm thick used for NIC cards, modems, and other peripherals; and Type III, which are 10.5 mm thick and used for hard disk drives.

DOCKING STATIONS

A *docking station* is basically a housing or frame that allows a laptop computer to act as a desktop system when it is inserted or "plugged in" to the docking station. Docking stations contain electronic interfaces that allow laptops to connect with peripheral devices, such as monitors and printers. Docking stations allow the flexibility of using larger keyboards and monitors when a laptop is inserted into a docking station. They are typically equipped with bays and slots for extra storage media and additional expansion cards.

A laptop system has its own configuration or "personality." To be more descriptive, it has its own set of configuration software services as well as hardware device drivers for such things as video and networking. This is called a *hardware profile.* Most operating systems installed on laptop systems today allow the use of hardware profiles. When most operating systems are installed, a default hardware profile is created. A separated hardware profile can be set up and used for drivers loaded when a laptop is docked in a docking station. If more than one hardware profile is present on a laptop system, the user is prompted to choose the profile they want to use. The choices are usually "docked" or "undocked" profile. You can rename these profiles from within the operating system to anything you want—for example, "At Work" or "At Home."

One of the most common mistakes made by laptop users is choosing the wrong hardware profile when a system is booted. If you choose a docked profile when the laptop is undocked, or vice versa, it is likely that the wrong device drivers will be loaded for video, mouse, keyboard, network, printing, or sound. Make sure you pick the right profile. Rebooting and selecting the proper hardware profile can quickly resolve issues resulting from this common mistake.

PORT REPLICATORS

A *port replicator* replicates laptop ports. It is basically a docking station without slots for storage or extra expansion card usability. Similar to docking stations, port replicators provide things such as parallel and serial ports. When a laptop is attached to a port replicator, easy access can be accomplished to stationary devices such as large monitors, printers, joysticks, MIDI devices, and full-size keyboards. Note that there are no real industry standards for docking stations and port replicators. These devices are usually proprietary to a particular laptop manufacturer. In other words, when you purchase a particular laptop computer, you will have to buy the docking station or port replicator made by the laptop's manufacturer.

BATTERIES AND POWER

Charging and keeping charged the batteries that keep today's portable electronic devices alive has become a very popular topic, and CompTIA will no doubt target this topic on the A+ exams. Several types of rechargeable chemical batteries are available today, and each has its own characteristics. You do not have to focus on the detailed science of batteries. However, you do need to be able to identify the following battery types that CompTIA has included in their 2006 objectives:

NiCad (Nickel-Cadmium)

NiCad batteries are rechargeable batteries that lose their strength after only a few hours of use. Earlier NiCad batteries suffered from a phenomenon known as memory effect. If these battery types were recharged before most of their power was used up, they would lose their ability to become fully charged.

NiMH (Nickel Metal Hydride)

A *NiMH battery* is a rechargeable battery that was designed to provide long-lasting power and overall battery savings for such devices as energy-hungry PDAs and digital cameras. NiMH batteries are considered inexpensive at around $2.50 a battery. NiMH batteries do not suffer from the phenomenon of memory effect, as did early NiCad batteries, and they can store up to 50% more power. The average AAA NiMH battery has a standard rating of 1.2V. Traditional alkaline batteries carry a rating of 1.5V.

Lithium Ion

A *lithium ion battery* contains lithium derived from chemicals. Lithium is the lightest metal available and is ideal for electrochemical potential. Lithium rechargeable batteries offer twice the power life of NiCad.

Lithium batteries are the most commonly used battery types for mobile systems. They are lightweight, safe, efficient, and do not suffer from memory effect. They are, of course, more expensive than the previously mentioned battery types.

Fuel Cell

The *fuel cell* was the latest and greatest power invention introduced in the struggle to efficiently deliver more power to laptops and mobile systems. A fuel cell produces hydrogen that is converted from methanol or alcohol. It was proposed that fuel cell technology would replace the popular lithium ion batteries that are used in most laptops today. Fuel cells can last up to 10 hours and may eliminate the need for rechargeable batteries.

CHAPTER SUMMARY

In this chapter, you learned how a computer converts digital information to a readable format that humans can understand. This chapter also addressed important input devices and the system resources they use to communicate with the computer's main components. To be a proficient computer technician, it is essential that you are aware of how computer resources work together. So that you can properly install, upgrade, diagnose, and troubleshoot a system, it is imperative that you understand IRQs, DMA channels, and base I/O memory addresses. It is a safe bet that the A+ exams are going to focus on these areas.

REVIEW QUESTIONS

1. **What is the default address used by the primary IDE controller?**

   ○ A. C000-C7FFF
   ○ B. 1F0h
   ○ C. 378h
   ○ D. 3F8h

   Correct Answer = B

   C000-C7FFF is used for the video adapter memory address. 378h is the memory address reserved for LPT1. 3F8h is the memory address reserved for COM1.

2. **What is the default address used by the secondary IDE controller?**

   ○ A. 170h
   ○ B. 1F0h
   ○ C. 378h
   ○ D. 3F8h

   Correct Answer = A

   1F0h is the memory address reserved for the primary IDE controller. 3F8h is the memory address reserved for COM1. 378h is the memory address reserved for LPT1.

3. **What is he default I/O address for COM2?**

   ○ A. 170h
   ○ B. 1F0h
   ○ C. 378h
   ○ D. 2F8h

   Correct Answer = D

   170h is reserved for the secondary IDE controller. 1F0h is the memory address reserved for the primary IDE controller. 378h is the memory address reserved for LPT1.

4. **The floppy drive controller uses which DMA channel?**

   ○ A. 1
   ○ B. 2
   ○ C. 4
   ○ D. 7

   Correct Answer = B

   DMA channel 2 is used for a floppy drive or a possible tape drive unit. DMA channels 1 and 7 are available. DMA channel 4 is used for the second DMA controller (cascades to DMA channels 0-3).

5. **How many devices can you attach (chain) to a single IDE controller or channel?**

   ○ A. 1
   ○ B. 2
   ○ C. 4
   ○ D. 127

   Correct Answer = B

   Two devices can be attached to a single IDE controller. For example, the first device attached to the primary IDE controller would be your master or primary hard drive. The second device attached to your primary IDE/ATA controller is your slave or secondary device.

6. **Which IRQ is reserved for the system timer?**

   ○ A. 0
   ○ B. 1
   ○ C. 2
   ○ D. 9

Correct Answer = A

IRQ 1 is reserved for a standard 101/102 keyboard. IRQ 2 is an interrupt controller (cascaded to IRQ 9). IRQ 9 is cascaded to IRQ 2.

7. **Which of the following are valid touch screen technologies? (Choose Three)**
   - ☐ A. Capacitive
   - ☐ B. Conducive
   - ☐ C. Resistive
   - ☐ D. Surface wave
   - ☐ E. Switch
   - ☐ F. All are valid touch screen technologies.

   Correct Answers = A, C, and D

   Common touch screen technologies include capacitive, resistive, and surface wave technologies.

8. **What is the most common way to transfer information between two PDAs?**
   - ○ A. IR
   - ○ B. USB
   - ○ C. SCSI
   - ○ D. LPT
   - ○ E. RS232
   - ○ F. IEEE 1284
   - ○ G. None of the above

   Correct Answer = A

   The most common methods used today to transfer information from one PDA to another PDA are through IR (Infrared)/IrDA (Infrared Data Association) or Bluetooth (Wireless specification standard).

9. **Which of the following ports are most often used when connecting a digital camera to a computer system (choose two)?**
   - ☐ A. SCSI Port
   - ☐ B. Port 25
   - ☐ C. USB Port
   - ☐ D. Parallel Port
   - ☐ E. IEEE 1394 compliant Port
   - ☐ F. Port 1099

Correct Answers = C and E

Most digital cameras are connected to a computer system using a USB port or serial port that is IEEE 1394 compliant.

10. **A laptop user using a docking station at work calls you and states that he cannot connect to the network and his LCD screen is "all messed up." What is most likely the problem?**
    - ○ A. The NIC card's video driver is corrupt.
    - ○ B. The wrong user profile is in use.
    - ○ C. The wrong hardware profile is in use.
    - ○ D. The network is malfunctioning.
    - ○ E. The ports on the laptop are not IEEE 1284 compliant.
    - ○ F. None of the above

    Correct Answer = C

    One of the most common mistakes made by laptop users is choosing the wrong hardware profile when a system is booted. If you choose a docked profile when the laptop is undocked or vice versa, it is likely that the wrong device drivers will be loaded for video, mouse, keyboard, network, printing, or sound.

11. **Which of the following devices is similar to a docking station with the exception that it doesn't provide extra slots for storage and expansion cards?**
    - ○ A. Port replicator
    - ○ B. Port sniffer
    - ○ C. Hardware profile
    - ○ D. AC/DC converter
    - ○ E. None of the above

    Correct Answer = A

    A port replicator is similar to a docking station except it does not have slots for storage or expansion cards.

12. **Which of the following battery types suffer from the phenomenon known as memory effect?**
    - ○ A. Lithium ion
    - ○ B. NiMH
    - ○ C. NiCad
    - ○ D. Copper tip
    - ○ E. Silver bunny battery
    - ○ F. All of the above

Correct Answer = C

Earlier NiCad batteries suffered from a phenomenon known as memory effect. For example, if these battery types are recharged before most of their power is used up, they will lose their capability to become fully charged.

13. **Which of the following produces hydrogen that is converted from methanol or alcohol and was intended to replace the lithium ion battery?**
    - ○ A. Lithium ion
    - ○ B. NiMH
    - ○ C. NiCad
    - ○ D. Copper tip
    - ○ E. Fuel cell
    - ○ F. None of the above

Correct Answer = E

A fuel cell produces hydrogen that is converted from methanol or alcohol. It was proposed that fuel cell would replace the popular lithium ion batteries used in most laptops computer systems. It lasts up to 10 hours without a need to recharge.

14. **Your client wants you to purchase a laptop for him that has the longest battery life. Which of the following offers the longest battery life?**
    - ○ A. Lithium Ion
    - ○ B. NiMH
    - ○ C. NiCad (Nickel-cadmium)
    - ○ D. Copper tip
    - ○ E. Duracell
    - ○ F. Nickel-Metal-Hydride

Correct Answer = A

In a nutshell, the battery of choice for most laptops is Li-Ion or Lithium Ion. Lithium Ions do not suffer from memory effects, are light, and have a long battery life.

15. **Your client plugs his laptop into a wall outlet while at work and unplugs it while on the road. The client is now experiencing problems. When he unplugs the laptop it immediately shuts down. What is most likely the problem?**

    ○ A. The laptop battery needs replacing.
    ○ B. The laptop hard drive is failing.
    ○ C. The laptop is improperly configured to always shut down when unplugged.
    ○ D. There is a short between the battery and the motherboard.

    Correct Answer = A

    If a laptop is plugged into a power outlet and abruptly shuts down after the laptop is unplugged from the outlet, it is a sure sign that the laptop battery is no longer holding a charge and should be replaced.

16. **You have been asked to upgrade memory, modems, NICs, and hard drives for your client's roaming sales force. What types of PCMCIA expansion cards will you need to consider?**

    □ A. Type IV
    □ B. Type I
    □ C. Type V
    □ D. Type II
    □ E. Type III

    Correct Answers = B, D, and E

    For NICs, modems, and hard drives, the three main PCMCIA card types are Type 1, which are 3.3 mm thick and used for memory; Type II, which are 5.0 mm thick and used for NIC cards, modems, and other peripherals; and Type III, which are 10.5 mm thick and used for hard disk drives.

17. **You have been asked to by the senior administrator to update the drivers in several scanners around your building. Which type of software driver should you be familiar with before attempting this specific task?**

    ○ A. Printer
    ○ B. Huckleberry
    ○ C. Printer and FAX
    ○ D. TWAIN

    Correct Answer = D

Today, most scanners use a very common driver known as TWAIN. The TWAIN driver interprets the data between the programs used to scan and communicate with the actual scanner itself.

18. **A client calls and states that users in a remote location are tired of all the cables and wires required to connect to printers and various other peripherals around the office. Which of the following technologies could you offer the client as a possible solution to resolve this issue?**

    ○ A. FireWire
    ○ B. IEEE 1394
    ○ C. Bluetooth
    ○ D. WUSB 2.0

    Correct Answer = C

    The Bluetooth wireless standard has become popular to connect keyboards, mice, printers, and many other devices to a computing system. This welcome standard eliminates the need for multiple wires and chords and offers the user more freedom and flexibility. Choice B. IEEE 1394 is FireWire and uses a wire.

19. **You are connecting your customer's peripheral devices to all laptop systems. While working on the installation, one of your customers asks you "at what frequencies do Bluetooth devices operate?" What do you say?**

    ○ A. 1.4 to 3.46 GHz
    ○ B. 2.4 to 2.48 GHz
    ○ C. 4.26 to 4.34 GHz
    ○ D. None of the above

    Correct Answer = B

    The Bluetooth wireless standard has become popular to connect keyboards, mice, printers, and many other devices to a computing system. Bluetooth devices operate at 2.4 to 2.48 GHz.

20. **Which of the following is a device that converts analog signals into digital representations of the original analog signal?**

    ○ A. A stylus
    ○ B. A port replicator
    ○ C. A digitizer
    ○ D. None of the above

Correct Answer = C

A digitizer is a device that converts analog signals (of or from photos, images, and even audio) into digital representations of the original analog signal that a computer can understand. In human terms, the device converts the position of a point on a surface into a digital data equivalent or data image. A stylus is a handheld pen-shaped device that is commonly used as a pointing or writing instrument to input text and interact with a computer. You use the stylus and tap or write on a digitizer. A port replicator replicates laptop ports. It is basically a docking station without slots for storage or extra expansion card usability.

REFERENCES:

www.dcresource.com/. This digital camera resource page provides a wealth of information regarding new digital camera technology products and reviews.

6 Basic Output Devices

In This Chapter

OUTPUT TYPES AND DEVICES

Output is defined as data or information that is sent out of a computer system, program, or device. Output can take many forms, including electronic characters, numbers, symbols, signals, sounds, paper, and/or graphics.

Output is generally categorized into two main types: transient and final. *Transient output* is temporary output that is produced in the form of electronic signals or data moving from one location to the next, to be used for only a short period. An example of transient output is an electronic request from one device to another to carry out a specific function, such as an operating system sending a request or message to a printer to print. The request to print is temporary. Transient output can be in the form of information stored in RAM or a temporary swap file on a hard drive. It exists to serve a temporary purpose. In other words, transient output is output that is not stored or saved.

Final output is more permanent. It is data or information that can be saved, recorded, or physically held on to. Some examples of final output are printed reports, images displayed on a video display monitor, sound from computer speakers, or files stored in a permanent location, such as a hard drive, floppy disk, writable CD-ROM, or DVD.

An output device is any machine or peripheral device that is capable of producing information from binary data that it receives from the CPU. Typical output devices are printers, plotters, video displays, computer speakers, and synthesizers. To list all the various output devices available on the market is beyond the scope of this book. However, this chapter will prepare you well for the A+ exams topics that relate to output devices and their functions.

VIDEO DISPLAY DEVICES

The computer monitor is by far the most common computer output device in use today. It is the window to the electronic world. Think about it: How many people around the world are staring at a computer screen at this very moment?

A computer monitor is a vehicle by which information that has been processed is presented to the end user. The components involved in producing a final image from a computer system are a video adapter (or video card) and a monitor. The computer monitor has had many names since its inception. In the early (DOS) days of computing, the monitor was called a console, or CON for short. It has also been called a CRT, which is an acronym for Cathode Ray Tube.

Computer monitors are categorized into two main groups: CRTs and Liquid Crystal Displays (LCDs).

 A computer monitor uses a DB-15 pin-style male connector to attach to the 15-pin female connector on the back of a computer. If one of these pins is bent or broken, the display screen may flicker, turn many strange colors, or show nothing at all. In addition, it is essential to know that most of today's video adapters contain their own BIOS chip, which interacts between the video card and the system processor.

CATHODE RAY TUBE (CRT)

A CRT is based on the same technology used in a television set. An electronic beam is directed by a glass vacuum tube that uses an electron gun to the back of a glass screen that has a phosphorus coating. When the beam of electrons hits the phosphorus material, moving from the top of the slightly curved glass to the bottom, the phosphors combine to form pixels, and visible light representing a viewable image is displayed.

The two types of CRTs are monochrome (single color plus background) and color (multiple colors). A monochrome monitor uses two colors—a solid color (usually black or grayscale) that represents the background, and amber, green, or white for the foreground. A single beam from the electron gun illuminates the foreground area with a single color.

Color monitors use three electron gun beams to represent each of the three colors of light from the basic primary colors of Red, Green, and Blue (RGB). These are the primary colors from which all other colors are derived. As a side note: Solid colors are derived from the three primary colors to form the colors Cyan, Magenta, and Yellow (CMY). If you look at a typical desktop color printer's ink cartridge, you will see the CMY solid colors. The combination of the three electron beams projected from the electron gun form a triangular representation of the three primary colors. This is called a triad picture element, or pixel (see Figure 6.1). The final image displayed on the CRT screen is a combination of many pixels with different intensities. The more pixels or dots that can be grouped together, the greater the color depth (i.e., number of possible colors).

Here are a couple of important CRT terms that you should be familiar with:

Shadow mask: A thin metal sheet that the electron gun beams must pass through. The shadow mask ensures that the electron beam hits the correct phosphor.

Degauss: A method used to remove any magnetic fields that may cause the shadow mask to become magnetized. For example, placing a magnetic speaker too close to a CRT can cause the visual image to become distorted. Degauss normally runs when you turn your monitor on. Most modern CRTs have a manual degauss button.

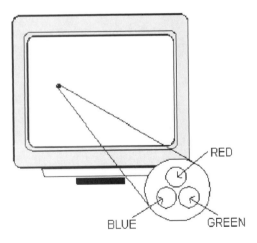

FIGURE 6.1 Representation of a triad pixel element.

DOT PITCH, RESOLUTION, AND COLOR DEPTH

A pixel is basically a dot on a CRT or LCD display. As previously stated, the more pixels that can be grouped together, the more defined the final image will be. *Dot pitch*, which is measured in millimeters (mm), is the distance between pixels. For example, a 0.28 dot pitch measurement means that the pixels are 0.28mm apart from each other on the display. When purchasing a monitor, it is important to get as low a dot pitch measurement as possible for a clear, well-defined image. Popular dot pitch measurements are 0.31mm, 0.28mm, 0.27mm, 0.26mm, and 0.25mm.

Resolution is the total number of pixels that can be displayed on a screen at one time. To calculate resolution, you multiply the number of pixels per horizontal row by the number of vertical rows of pixels. For example, standard VGA resolution is 640 × 480, which equates to 307,200 pixels. Color depth is the total amount of pixels that a screen or monitor can display. To be more specific, the total number of bits used to represent a pixel stored in video memory is referred to as *color depth*. Commonly used color depths are 32 bit, 24 bit, 16 bit, and 8 bit. Early computing systems used 8-bit color. Each pixel uses 1 byte of video memory. Each pixel can exist as one of 256 colors. The software that creates the image using either 18 bits, 24 bits, or 32 bits per pixel defines these colors; therefore, 256 colors can be displayed on the monitor, selected from a palette of 262,144 or 16,777,216 colors. Table 6.1 shows video color depths.

Pixel per inch (PPI) is used to measure computer display resolution. PPI is also referred to as dots per inch (DPI). PPI or DPI can also be used to describe display resolution for scanner images as well as digital camera images.

TABLE 6.1 Video Color Depths

Color Name	Available Colors	Color Depth (Measured in Bits)
Monochrome	2	1
VGA	16	4
256 (colors)	256	8
High color	65,536	16
LCD color	262,144	18
True color	16,777,216	24
True color	4,294,967,296	32

You will not have to do pixel calculations on the A+ exams. You may be required to know video adapter types and their resolutions. Table 6.2 shows an overview of video adapters and their corresponding resolutions.

TABLE 6.2   Video Standards and Resolutions

Video Adapter	Resolutions
MDA	720 × 350
CGA	320 × 200
	640 × 200
EGA	640 × 350
VGA	640 × 480
	320 × 200
SVGA	800 × 600
	1024 × 7680
	1280 × 1024
	1600 × 1200
XGA	1024 × 768
WXGA	1280 × 800
WXGA+	1440 × 900
SXGA+	1400 × 1050
UXGA	Ultra VGA
	1600 × 1200

REFRESH RATES

The tiny phosphors inside a CRT lose their illumination very quickly. They must be refreshed many times per second so that the image displayed on the screen does not fade or flicker. The electron gun inside the CRT must redraw the image continuously to keep the phosphors active. This process is called a CRT's *refresh rate.*

A CRT's refresh rate is measured in Hertz. The higher the number of Hertz (Hz), the faster the CRT's refresh rate. Common video refresh rates run from 60 Hz all the way through 120 Hz (depending on the quality of the monitor). An 80-Hz refresh rate, for example, means that a screen will be redrawn, or "refreshed," 80 times per second. Something else to remember is that the higher the resolution, the fewer Hertz options you will have to choose from. (Typically, at 1600 × 1200, you are limited to only 7580 Hz; whereas at 1280 × 1024, you might have an option to go as high, as say, 100 Hz.)

Have you ever been watching television and noticed that when a monitor is displayed, you can se a horizontal line traveling vertically? That's because typically, a television's refresh rate (around 30 Hz) is significantly lower than a standard PC monitor's refresh rate. If the monitor is set even at the bare minimum 60 Hz, the television would only be displaying the screen half as fast as the monitor. The result is that a horizontal line is drawn (that typically runs from bottom to top) because the television can't keep up with the monitor. The higher the refresh rate is set on the monitor, the faster the horizontal line will travel. Monitor refresh rate is something that will definitely have an impact on your PC experience (especially as time passes). Most people find that 60 Hz is far too low a refresh rate, and it can even cause some people to experience headaches after prolonged use of a monitor at that setting. Most people who work on computers for extended periods of time tend to use 75 Hz because it is easier on the eyes.

Don't set your refresh rate (in an operating system's display panel settings) faster than the recommended refresh rate stated by the monitor's manufacturer because this may cause your monitor to go blank.

NOTE

Two scan rates are used to determine the ultimate speed of the refresh rate. The horizontal scan rate is the speed at which the phosphors are refreshed from left to right. The vertical scan rate is the speed at which the entire screen is refreshed.

Interlacing is a refresh process in which every other row of pixels (even or odd) is refreshed by the electron gun to increase monitor resolution. The electron gun refreshes the odd number of rows in a display and then returns to refresh the even rows. Although interlacing helps to increase resolution, it also causes the display to jitter or flicker.

Noninterlacing occurs when every row of pixels is refreshed consecutively. This reduces jitter and screen flicker and generally provides for a better viewing experience. When purchasing a monitor, it is a good idea to buy a noninterlaced display.

High resolution requires video memory (VRAM). The higher you set your display resolution and the more colors you choose to support, the more VRAM your system will require. The A+ tests may ask you to identify the amount of memory needed to support a particular resolution with a defined number of colors.

For example, how much memory is needed to support a resolution of 1024 × 768 using 24-bit, true color? The answer is 4 MB. Table 6.3 provides the answer to this question, along with other video resolutions and VRAM requirements.

TABLE 6.3   Video Resolution and VRAM Requirements

Video Resolution	8 Bits 256 Colors	16 Bits 65,000 Colors	24-Bit True Color 16.7 Million Colors
640 × 480	512 KB	1 MB	1 MB
800 × 600	512 KB	1 MB	2 MB
1024 × 768	1 MB	2 MB	4 MB
1280 × 1024	2 MB	4 MB	6 MB
1600 × 1200	4 MB	8 MB	8 MB

You can also use the following mathematical formula to assist you with calculating VRAM requirements:

Memory requirement = horizontal pixels × vertical pixels × color depth

VIDEO DISPLAY STANDARDS

The very first video adapter was an MDA (Monochrome Display Adapter). MDA has a resolution of 720 × 350 pixels and is capable of supporting text but not graphics or color. CGA (Color Graphics Adapter) and EGA (Enhanced Graphics Adapter) were the early display standards for monitors. CGA was capable of producing just two colors with a resolution of 640 × 200. EGA could produce 16 colors with a resolution of 640 × 350. These video technologies were used in the early- and mid-1980s. If you worked for extended periods using these technologies in the 1980s, your eyesight might be the worse for it now.

VIDEO GRAPHICS ARRAY (VGA)

VGA is the standard for all graphic devices, such as monitors and video cards. It has a resolution of 640 × 480 with a color depth of 16 colors, or 320 × 200 with 256 colors. VGA uses analog signals, as opposed to the digital signals used by its predecessors, CGA and EGA. The original implementation of the VGA standard introduced the following video subsystem standards to assist with processing and ultimately produce a better image:

Frame buffer: The frame buffer is a memory buffer used to store data before it is displayed. The amount of information stored before it is sent to the display is called a *frame.*

Graphics command language: With VGA, the CPU manages all the work of producing an image. The graphics command language introduced a set of simple commands that alleviated some of the CPU's video-related tasks.

CRT controller: The CRT controller produces signals that control and reset the electron guns inside the monitor.

Sequencer: The sequencer is basically a timer on the video adapter. It loads display addresses into memory and operates with a 16-bit internal counter.

Serializer: The serializer is used to serialize data held in video memory before it is sent to an attribute controller.

Attribute controller: This houses a color template that determines the *value,* or color, of a pixel.

Display memory: This bank of 256 KB DRAM separated into four 64 KB color planes stores screen-displayed information.

Graphics controller: The graphics controller carries out logical functions and calculations on data being placed in display memory.

VGA introduced many advantages, including these subsystems. Unfortunately, it didn't use resources fast enough to support the demands of GUIs and applications that were hungry for new standards. VGA circuitry is directly tied to the processor. It relies on the processor to do most of its work, which takes a toll on the processor's performance.

8514/A

IBM standard 8514/A was introduced at the same time as the VGA standard. It provided three new graphics modes that enabled higher resolution and color and was well suited for IBM's proprietary Micro Channel Bus. The 8514/A standard provided some processing capabilities. It supported a resolution of 1024 × 768 and 256 colors in graphics mode.

EXTENDED GRAPHICS ADAPTER

Extended Graphics Adapter (XGA) cards were introduced in later IBM PS/2 model computers. The XGA adapters use either 512 KB or 1MB of VRAM and are capable of bus mastering using IBM's Micro Channel Architecture (MCA). Using 1 MB of VRAM, XGA supports a graphics resolution of 1024 × 768 and 256 colors, or 640 × 480 using high color (16 bits). This standard was followed by SXGA (Super Extended Graphics Adapter, capable of 1280 × 1024), UXGA (Ultra Extended Graphics Adapter, capable of 1600 × 1200), and WUXGA (Widescreen Ultra eXtended Graphics Array). WUXGA is a wide-screen version of UXGA and has a display resolution of 1920 × 1200 pixels with a 16:10 screen aspect ratio. It's compatible with HDTV, which uses a 1920 × 1080 image at a 16:9 ratio.

SUPER VGA AND ULTRA VGA

Technically, SVGA and Ultra VGA (UVGA) are not distinct video standards; they are words that describe a video card's capability to achieve higher resolution and colors. Manufacturers of SVGA and UVGA video cards each provide their own sets of instructions and software drivers to maximize the performance of the cards they produce. A group of graphic and video card manufacturers known as the Video Electronics Standards Association (VESA) has standardized video rules. SVGA was originally developed by VESA as competition to IBM's proprietary 8514/A and XGA technologies. (XGA was introduced by IBM in 1990 as a replacement for their old 8514/A video standard, capable of displaying 640 × 480 to 1024 × 768.) All varieties of SVGA support a palette of 16 million colors. The basic SVGA resolutions are 800 × 600, 1024 × 768, 1280 × 1024, and 1600 × 1200.

S-Video

S-Video is an analog video interface standard that carries video data as two separate signals: brightness and color. It is unlike `composite` video, which carries the whole set of signals in one signal. S-Video is most commonly used in TVs, DVD players, game consoles, video recorders, TV receivers, and DVRs. In fact, most TV-out connectors on graphics cards are S-Video. S-Video carries high-bandwidth at `480i` or `576i` video resolution. S-Video uses a four-pin Mini-DIN connector that uses a 75-ohm termination.

DVI (Digital Visual Interface)

Digital Visual Interface (DVI) is a video interface technology that maximizes the visual quality of digital displays such as flat panel LCD computer `displays` and digital projectors. DVI carries uncompressed digital video data to a display. It is mostly compatible with the High-Definition Multimedia Interface (HDMI) standard in digital mode (DVI-D). DVI offers a maximum screen resolution at 60 Hz of 1854 × 1483 pixels (standard 1.25 ratio) or 2212 × 1243 (wide-screen 1.77 ratio). For more information regarding DVI resolution and connectors, visit *http://en.wikipedia.org/wiki/Dvi*.

HDMI

HDMI is a digital audio/video interface standard capable of transmitting totally uncompressed streams. HDMI provides an interface between any digital audio/video source device such as a DVD player, `PC`, game console, and a compatible digital audio and/or video monitor such as a digital television (DTV). HDMI has replaced older analog technologies such as S-Video, composite, and VGA. Traditional HDMI supports a maximum pixel clock rate interface of 165 MHz at 60 Hz or WUXGA (1920 × 1200). The new Version 1.3 of HDMI supports 340 MHz and provides support for WQXGA (2560 × 1600). There are several versions of HDMI, however, it is not likely that you will have to know these for the exams. For more information regarding HDMI resolution and connectors, visit *http://en.wikipedia.org/wiki/Hdmi*.

MONITOR SHAPES AND SIZES

Today, monitors are available in many shapes, sizes, and colors. Monitor size is calculated in inches. Popular monitors are available in the following sizes: 15, 17, 19, and 21 inches. The size of a monitor screen is measured diagonally from the bottom-right corner to the top-left corner; this is known as the monitor's *nominal size*. The actual viewable size of the display is typically at least an inch smaller than the advertised nominal size of the monitor. For example, a 19-inch monitor (nominal size) actually has a viewable size area of less than 18 inches. A 17-inch monitor has a viewable display area of 15.6 inches. The monitor's *bezel*, which is the black plastic boundary that supports and surrounds the edge of the glass screen, reduces the viewable size of the display area.

Smaller monitors (generally 15 inches and smaller) have trouble displaying higher resolutions because they cannot support very small pixels. Typically, monitors that are 15 inches or smaller can only display up to 1024 × 768, 17-inch monitors can display up to 1280 × 1024, and 19-inch and larger monitors can display 1600 × 1200. A larger monitor that supports smaller pixels is handy for higher resolution settings and fitting in more icons on the desktop. If you increase the resolution settings in the Windows 2000 Display Properties window, the icons on the desktop become smaller (see Figure 6.2).

NOTE

If you change your monitor's resolution, video card drivers, or NIC drivers, and then cannot reenter the Windows GUI, you can enter the operating system by using Safe Mode. Safe Mode loads only the drivers needed to enter the operating system for troubleshooting purposes. Higher resolution changes and other drivers are not loaded when you enter Safe Mode.

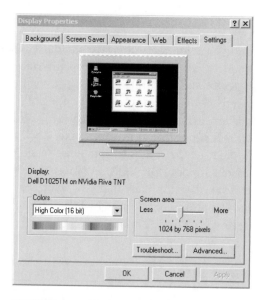

FIGURE 6.2 Windows 2000 Display Properties window.

Graphics

Two technical drawing methods are used to draw an image on a video screen: raster graphics and vector graphics.

Raster graphics: Raster images are digital images that are created from a grid of x (horizontal) and y (vertical) coordinates. The x and y coordinates represent the locations of pixels on a display screen. Raster is the most common method used to produce an image. Some of the more common types of raster formats are JPEG, BMP, and TIFF images. These raster image types are produced from software graphics applications such as Microsoft Paint. Most monitors and printers produce information in raster format and are considered raster output devices.

Vector graphics: Vector graphics programs produce a sharper image than raster. Vector is based on mathematical equations that define where and how an image is to be drawn or sized on a display. Vector graphics programs, such as Corel Draw, Microsoft Visio, and Adobe Illustrator, are used to create scalable, detailed drawings. Two- and three-dimensional graphic animations are created using vector graphics technology and software.

Liquid Crystal Display (LCD)

Liquid Crystal Display (LCD) is a flat-panel display technology that is used in most laptop computers. LCD technology can also be used for other display devices, such as car radio displays, clocks, desktop computers, and any other display devices that can take advantage of flat-panel technology. The biggest advantages of LCD flat screens are that they reduce physical space requirements, they are lightweight and portable, and they require less energy to operate. (Laptop LCDs are powered by low-voltage DC.) Traditional CRTs take up more desktop space than LCDs and require more energy to operate. With an LCD, what you see is basically what you get. Unlike CRTs, in which the nominal size is less than the described measurement of the monitor, the measurement of an LCD screen is accurate.

LCD technology uses two panels of a polarizing substance, with a liquid crystal solution between the two panels. An electric charge is sent through the crystals, causing them to form a shield from light. The crystals either allow or disallow the passage of light and eventually form an image.

Different types of LCDs serve different purposes and provide various levels of display quality. Some of the more common types are listed here:

Passive matrix LCD: A passive matrix display uses LCD elements, electrical current, and a grid of wires to control the passage of light. It has a fixed resolution of pixels.

Active matrix LCD: This LCD type is based on Thin Film Transistor (TFT) technology. It constantly refreshes each pixel, providing a consistently sharp image. This technology provides better visual quality than passive matrix and is more expensive.

Dual scan: With dual scan, the LCD screen is divided in two. Each half of the screen is refreshed separately. This process increases the resolution rate but decrease the brightness (contrast) level of the LCD.

Caution should be taken when cleaning LCD screens. Soaps and other products are not recommended because they often damage the screen. The best way to clean a screen or LCD is by spraying water on a lint free cloth and gently wiping the surface of the screen.

MONITOR POWER MANAGEMENT

A monitor uses a tremendous amount of AC. The Environmental Protection Agency (EPA) came up with a program and a set of standards, known as Energy Star, to reduce the amount of energy used by monitors and PC-related equipment. To see if a monitor is Energy Star compliant, click Start > Settings > Control Panel > Display > Screen Saver. If the monitor is compliant, you will see the Energy Star logo and "Energy saving features of monitor" (see Figure 6.3).

FIGURE 6.3 Windows Energy Star Compliance logo.

IMPORTANT MONITOR/VIDEO-RELATED INFORMATION AND TEST TIPS

The following important monitor/video-related information and test tips are included to give you an extra boost in the exam room. Pay close attention here; this information may help you in the field as well:

- Using a video resolution of 800 × 600 is equivalent to using SVGA video mode.
- Video cards are most often designed for AGP slots.
- If your monitor goes blank after changing your video resolution from say 640 × 480 (16 Colors) to 800 × 600 (16-bit high color), your refresh rate has probably been set too fast for your monitor to handle.
- The amount of time required for CRT's electron beam to draw or "paint" a screen is called the refresh rate.
- 4 MB of VRAM is required to display 1024 × 768 at 24-bit color.
- If you have a monitor that is displaying abnormal, odd colors such as green or orange, there is a high probability that your monitor is either defective or you have a bad or bent pin on your monitor's cable connector.
- WRAM is used for and on many video cards today.
- If you can't see entire pages displayed on your monitor when browsing the Internet, the first thing you should do is adjust your video resolution settings.
- Always unplug the power from your system when installing video cards.
- For a system's POST (power-on self-test) to complete at boot up, it must recognize video support.
- If you change your monitor's refresh rate and nothing will display on your monitor, the first step you should take is to restart the computer and enter Safe Mode. Safe Mode loads the basic video drivers and settings, which allows you to troubleshoot.
- A VGA connector has 15 pins.
- If a signal to an Energy Star Compliant monitor does not vary or change, it can change or "switch" to a lower power status.

PRINTERS

A printer is an output device that accepts information from a computing system and produces output, usually text and graphics, to the end user in paper form. Many printing devices and printing technologies are available today. For the purpose of studying for the exam and its printer troubleshooting questions, we will focus on the current printer port standards, dot matrix, inkjet, and laser printer technologies.

Printers can be categorized into groups based on the way they apply an image or text to a consumable product, such as paper. The three most popular printer groups are impact printers, thermal ink printers, and laser printers.

Impact printers: Impact printers include dot matrix and daisy wheel printers. They typically use a print head, which can get very hot, with pins to strike against an ink ribbon to create a character, number, or symbol. They are very noisy and are considered old-fashioned technology. Their main purpose in today's world is for printing multipart, carbon-copy forms.

Thermal ink printers: Thermal ink printers include the very popular inkjet and bubble-jet printers. Small nozzles are used to disperse ink onto paper to form an image. These printers are considered affordable and are commonly used in households across the world.

Laser printers: Laser printers use an electrophotographic process (EP) to place an image on paper. This more-expensive technology is well worth the price for the speed at which it can print, as well as the quality it can produce. Laser printer speed is measured by the number of Pages Per Minute (PPM) that the printer can produce. Laser printers can be found in most business environments.

PARALLEL PORT STANDARDS

Printers can be connected to a computer using several methods as well as special connectors. (Connectors are discussed in detail in Chapter 8.) Currently, the fastest available connection for a printer is realized through a USB connection. Older printers were and still are connected to a computer system's DB-9 male serial port connector, which is capable of transmitting only 1 bit of information at a time in a half-duplex manner (i.e., it cannot send and receive information at the same time).

Today, most printers are connected to a computer system using a Data Bus (DB) 25-pin male connector that inserts into a DB 25-pin female connector on the back of the system. This is known as an LPT/parallel port connection (or LPT1). Parallel transmission of data is bidirectional, meaning that the parallel port can communicate with the CPU during transmission. Parallel communication transfer rates are 8 bits at a time. The opposite end of the DB 25-pin male connector cable is connected to a printer with a Centronics 36-pin connector.

The Institute of Electrical and Electronics Engineers (IEEE) has developed a set of parallel port communication standards that control the flow of data between computer systems and print devices. These standards (protocols) are known as IEEE 1284.

Questions on the test may refer to printer cables and the IEEE standard they represent. Remember that the IEEE 1284 is a standard for parallel communication and printer cables.

There are five modes (IEEE standards) of parallel communication that you need to know for the test. Keep in mind that bidirectional is considered a standard.

Compatibility mode: This is an obsolete, unidirectional, parallel communication, forward-only mode implemented with the original 36-pin Centronics connector.

Nibble mode: Also obsolete, nibble mode is used to reverse the communication between a printer and a host by two 4-bit pieces of information at a time. Nibble mode complements compatibility mode and is also considered bidirectional.

Byte mode (SPP): Byte mode is a very common mode of parallel reverse communication that sends 8 bits of information at a time, side by side. Picture a typical parallel cable with eight separate "highways" next to each other. One bit of information travels down each "highway" at the same time.

Extended Capabilities Port (ECP) mode: ECP mode is the fastest form of bidirectional printer-to-host, parallel port transmission standard available. It uses both forward and reverse transmission techniques and sends data 8-bit wide at a time. ECP also supports handshaking and compression.

Enhanced Parallel Port (EPP) mode: EPP mode is similar to ECP in its capability to support forward and reverse communication and 8-bit-wide transmission of data. EPP does not support handshaking.

PRINT QUEUES AND THE SPOOLER SERVICE

Before a print request is sent to a physical printer, it is typically held temporarily in a print queue (buffer) in the operating system. If you send multiple print jobs to a printer, they wait in the print queue until the previous print job completes. If a print job errors out or gets stalled in the print queue, all jobs waiting to print in the queue will not print until the stalled or "hung" print job is deleted or canceled. Figure 6.4 shows a Windows print queue display with print jobs waiting to print. Most current operating systems run a system service known as the spooler service. The *spooler service* controls the print queue. If simply canceling or deleting the stalled print job does not allow waiting print jobs to print, you may have to stop and start the spooler service.

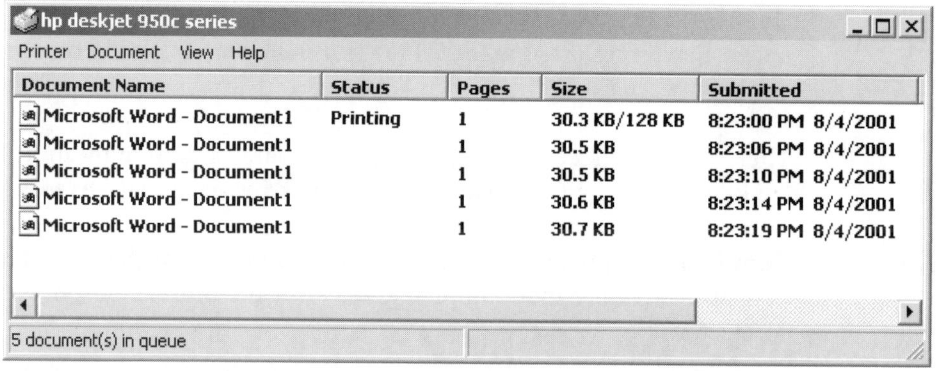

```
hp deskjet 950c series                                              _ □ ×
Printer  Document  View  Help
```

Document Name	Status	Pages	Size	Submitted
Microsoft Word - Document1	Printing	1	30.3 KB/128 KB	8:23:00 PM 8/4/2001
Microsoft Word - Document1		1	30.5 KB	8:23:06 PM 8/4/2001
Microsoft Word - Document1		1	30.5 KB	8:23:10 PM 8/4/2001
Microsoft Word - Document1		1	30.6 KB	8:23:14 PM 8/4/2001
Microsoft Word - Document1		1	30.7 KB	8:23:19 PM 8/4/2001

```
5 document(s) in queue
```

FIGURE 6.4   Windows print queue with print jobs waiting to print.

DOT MATRIX AND INKJET PRINTERS

A *dot matrix* printer is a form of impact printer whose technology closely resembles that of a typewriter. They have survived based on their capability to print multiple-part forms and because of their paper-feeding capabilities. Dot matrix printers are commonly found in stores, doctors' offices, banks, and any other location where multiple-part paper forms and receipts are needed.

Dot matrix printers contain their own print buffer. This buffer is a storage location for the information to be printed after it is sent from the CPU. After the information has been sent to the dot matrix print buffer, the printer's processor calculates the best approach to printing the lines and characters needed and makes adjustments to the paper feeders if necessary.

The dot matrix printer has a magnetic print head that contains either 9 or 24 pins. A 24-pin print head is used to print letter-quality pages. A 9-pin print head is used for draft quality. Each of the pins on the print head has its own solenoid, spring, and coil. A dot matrix printer uses a series of dots per inch (dpi) to form an image, symbol, character, or number. When the printer processor receives enough information from the print buffer to begin printing, a signal is sent to the magnetic print head. A combination of events takes place, and the pins attached to the print head hit an ink ribbon, which is held in place by a platen, that is between the pins and the paper. After the pin has applied its dot, it is pulled back, and the next pin applies its dot. This process repeats until a character is complete. All of this happens very quickly. The friction caused by the constant movement of the print head can make it get extremely hot. When working on a dot matrix printer, never touch the print head until it has time to cool down. Dot matrix printer speeds are measured in printed characters per second (cps). Characters-per-second speeds differ based on print quality and manufacturer. Dot matrix printers are capable of up to 500 cps.

Dot matrix printers use either a pressure roller or tractor-feed method of pulling continuous-form paper through the printer one line at a time. The continuous use of a dot matrix printer without proper maintenance can cause the tractor-feed rollers and platen to become misaligned. This commonly results in ink fading as it is applied from left to right or uneven lines of output across the paper. Lack of proper maintenance can also result in constant paper jams. Use a can of compressed air regularly to spray out any loose particles around the tractor rollers. Rubber-cleaning solutions should be used to clean the tractor belts and rollers.

Inkjet printers are very popular and are used in many homes and small businesses. Inkjet technology is typically faster than dot matrix but not as fast as the average laser printer. Its main benefits are its affordability and ease of maintenance compared to laser printer technology.

Inkjet printers use a type of print head that houses many tiny nozzles, sometimes referred to as jets. These jets spray or drop fast-drying ink into a condensed area to form the tiny dots that make up a character. A thermal resistor actually heats up the ink until it expands and is eventually forced out of the print nozzle in the form of a bubble or droplet. The ink bubble is then sprayed or dropped onto paper. The ink droplets can tend to smear or splatter when they hit the paper, which causes the dot created on the paper to become somewhat distorted. To refine this process, the thermal resistor bubble-creation process was replaced with piezoelectric crystal. The piezoelectric process uses crystals that react to electric charge. When charged, a crystal draws or pulls ink from an ink storage unit held above the crystal. In simple terms, the piezoelectric process can cut or refine the exact amount of ink needed to refine the dot placed on paper. This reduces the smudging effect of traditional inkjet technology and provides better printer resolution. In fact, this process allows resolutions greater than 1440 dpi.

Inkjet printers accept paper one sheet at a time. This process, called *single-sheet form feed*, involves pulling paper into the printer with rollers. The paper is aligned under a print mechanism that moves across the paper to apply an image.

If sheets of paper connected into one long sheet are placed in printer guides with plastic teeth, the printer is said to be a continuous form-feed printer. Inkjet printers use single-sheet form-feed technology. Dot matrix printers use the continuous form-feed process.

LASER PRINTERS

The previous A+ Core Hardware Service Technician exams bombarded the examinee with questions relating to the minute details of the stages of the laser printing electrophotographic process (EP). The current exam may also address some of these details. It is very important that you understand this process and its intricacies, as well as the laser printer paper-feeding process. Equally important, however, is to focus your study on printer troubleshooting and maintenance in general. The current A+ exams test laser printer questions seem to be headed in the direction of the overall use of the technology. For example, you may know that a uniform charge of –600V is applied to the laser printer's photosensitive drum by the primary corona wire during the conditioning phase of the EP process, but that knowledge will not help you on the test if you can't answer a question asking you how to dispose of a toner cartridge properly.

A *laser* printer is a popular type of nonimpact printer that is capable of producing resolutions of 1400 dpi or greater, with a usual minimum requirement of 600 dpi. Laser printers use technology similar to that of photocopiers.

A laser printer also puts many dots on paper that eventually form an image. Unlike the previously mentioned printing technologies, however, the laser printing process uses plastic toner particles that bond to an electrophotosensitive drum to create an image. These toner particles are actually a combination of organic material, plastic, and iron. A toner cartridge houses the powder toner and is inserted into the laser printer itself. A used toner cartridge should be sent back to the toner cartridge manufacturer for proper disposal or possible refilling. Note for the exam that the toner, paper, and disposable ribbons are considered printer-consumable items. If laser-printed output begins to appear wavy or inconsistent, the problem may be an empty or malfunctioning toner cartridge.

The laser printing process begins after you send a document or image from your computer to the laser printer. After the image is accepted by the laser printer, a laser beam and a mirror are used to write an electrostatic representation of the image to a photosensitive drum. The electronically charged drum then rolls through the toner, which adheres to the drum to form an image. At this stage of the process, a sheet of paper is fed into the printer, where it receives an electrostatic charge. The paper is then rolled over to the drum, and the toner image is transferred to the paper. In the next process, the toner is heated and fused to the paper. The final output is directed out of the printer, and the printer awaits the next document or image. This process is repeated every time a page of information is sent to the printer.

PRINTER QUALITY TYPES

Printer quality type standards refer to the quality of the printed dots produced, mainly by dot matrix printers. Printer quality types can also apply to other printing technologies, such as laser printing. You should be familiar with the following printer type qualities for the A+ exams.

Letter Quality (LQ): LQ is the standard for printing today; it is the best quality type available and requires a device that can support a minimum of 300 dpi. LQ produces characters that are crisp and clear. There are no noticeable spaces between the dots printed on the paper. LQ is used mostly in higher-end dot matrix and laser printers.

Near Letter Quality (NLQ): Dot matrix and inkjet printers that produce output at 150 dpi use NLQ. The dots that make up a character, number, or symbol are printed over twice, which gives them a better look than draft quality. Unfortunately, the tiny printed dots are still somewhat noticeable.

Draft quality: Draft output is a very low-grade print quality. All the dots that make up a printed image are noticeable.

RASTER IMAGE PROCESSING

A *raster* is a rectangular area or grid of the monitor's display area used for images or for the mathematically created vector drawing processes. The size of the raster area depends on the resolution of the display area. Monitors use autosizing to calculate the raster grid size of a display area. A *Raster Image Processor* (RIP) is used to translate complicated raster images and vector drawings sent to a laser printer. The RIP requires memory to store large images before they are processed. If there is not enough memory in the printer to support the image to be stored, you will likely get a "Memory Overflow" error message. Resolution Enhancement Technology (RET) allows a printer to print raster images at a higher resolution than the printer is technically capable of. RET uses a combination of technologies to fill in the spaces between dots on an image for better visual quality. Decreasing the printer's resolution and decreasing the RET can also help to reduce the frequency of "Memory Overflow" error messages.

LASER TECHNOLOGIES

Laser printer manufacturers use different laser printing technologies and processes to attain the same result of producing a high-quality image on final output. For the A+ exams, we are focusing on the electrophotographic (EP) process. There are three important laser-printing processes that you should be familiar with:

LCD process: The LCD process technology replaces the laser used in the EP process with an LCD panel or grid to write an image to the photosensitive drum.

Light-Emitting Diode (LED) process: LEDs are used in this technology in place of a laser beam to provide a light source to the photosensitive drum.

Electrophotographic process (EP): EP is by far the most common printing process in use today. A laser beam, mirror, toner, and EP drum are used to produce a final image.

THE EP LASER PRINTING PROCESS

The stages of the EP laser printing process that you need to be familiar with for the A+ exams are listed next. Figure 6.5 shows a diagram of the EP laser printing process.

Cleaning: The EP drum must be cleaned, erased, and desensitized of any electronic charge it may have as a result of a previous process. A rubber blade is used to remove any toner or particles from the drum. The used toner is disposed of into a cleaning unit or bucket. A fluorescent lamp is used to remove any electronic charge retained by the EP drum from a previous process. This preparation stage is vital; the drum must be properly prepared to produce a sharp image.

Conditioning: At this point, the EP drum cannot hold an image; it needs to be conditioned to do so. This is accomplished with a charge of −600V applied to the EP drum by the primary corona wire. The charge is evenly distributed across the entire drum, creating an electronic field. This process enables the drum to become photoconductive and prepares it for the writing phase.

Writing: At this stage of the process, the printer's laser beam writing unit and a series of mirrors are used to draw tiny dots on the EP drum, which represent the final image to be produced. The area of the drum that the laser beam comes in contact with loses some of its negative charge (by approximately −100V) and becomes relatively more positive (the charge is still considered negative, just not as negative as the areas not hit by the laser beam). When the laser beam has finished creating the image on the relatively positive EP drum, the printer's controller starts the paper sheet-feed process by pulling a sheet of paper into the printer. The paper stands ready at the printer's registration rollers until the controller directs it farther into the printer.

NOTE

Paper-feed rollers have sensors to control the proper flow of paper out of the paper tray. It is a common occurrence to receive a "paper jam" error on the printer LED display—but on investigation, you find that there is no paper in the tray. Chances are that there is a particle of foreign matter in the way, or the sensor is dirty. While troubleshooting, always check the paper-feed sensors first in this situation.

Developing: At this point in the process, the EP drum is ready to accept toner on the areas or dots that have a more positive charge. The toner cartridge houses a toner-developing roller that is magnetized and constantly turning. The magnetized roller attracts the toner particles located near it and dispenses the toner to the positively charged areas (dots) on the rotating EP drum. The EP drum now has a "picture," or mirror duplicate of the image, to be placed on the paper.

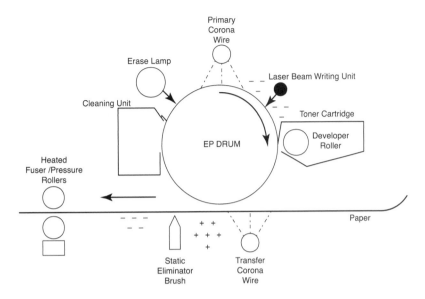

FIGURE 6.5   The EP laser printing process.

Transferring: It's time to get the image, drawn in toner, from the EP drum to the paper. Keep in mind that the toner is being held on the EP drum with a relative negative charge. At this point, the paper has been pulled into the printer. The paper passes by the transfer corona wire, or in some printers a transfer roller, where it receives a highly positive charge on its back side. The paper then passes under the negatively charged EP drum, and the toner is transferred onto the highly charged paper. A static charge eliminator, otherwise known as an eliminator comb, is used to keep the paper from wrapping itself around the EP drum.

Fusing: The toner must now be fused, or bonded, onto the paper. A fuser assembly, which is a quartz heating lamp inside a roller tube, is situated above a rubber roller pressure assembly. The paper and its toner are fed between the two devices. The toner is heated (melted) by the fuser assembly and pressed onto the paper permanently by the pressure rollers. Note that there is a built-in temperature sensor on the heated rollers. If the temperature during this process rises above 180°F, the sensor will shut down the printer. The most likely internal component of a laser print that can cause harm in the form of burns to a technician or user is the fuser. The fuser gets very hot when it heats up to melt toner onto paper. Remember this point for the exams.

Silicon oil is used to lubricate the fusing rollers during the fusing process to keep the paper from sticking to the rollers.

NOTE

End of cycle: A cleaning pad is used to remove excess toner and residue from the heated rollers. The paper containing the final image is rolled out of the printer.

The Wikipedia Web site has an excellent description of laser printers and scanners. It is definitely worth your time to visit *http://en.wikipedia.org/wiki/ Laser_printer.*

INK DISPERSION

Dispersion can be defined as the act of dispersing, which means to separate, distribute, or scatter in different directions. Most printer inks are made up of a combination of ingredients, including pigments, resins, solvents, and varnishes. For a printed document or photo to be clear and precise, the printer ink pigments must be dispersed free of lumps and other particles, in a smooth and even manner. Scientifically speaking, ink dispersion has to do with the ink manufacturing and production processes involved with how pigments are separated or broken down from other material. For the A+ exams, note that if ink is improperly dispersed, or if there is a problem with an ink dispersion nozzle (used with most inkjet printers), printing may become faded or unclear.

DYE SUBLIMATION

Dye sublimation technology and dye sublimation printers have brought clear, crisp, photo-quality printing home. With a dye sublimation printer, a heat-sensitive print head moves over a ribbon of transparent film that contains heat-activated inks or sections that represent the four primary printing colors of Cyan, Magenta, Yellow, and Black. (CMYK). These solid inks are vaporized and sublimate (adsorb) onto special polymer-coated gloss paper.

Here some important highlights regarding dye sublimation:

- Produces smooth, clear prints, making digital pictures look very realistic
- Final print is less susceptible to fading over time
- Offers very fast printing
- More expensive than inkjet printers
- Uses special "gloss" paper

In conclusion, the process of dye sublimation produces a smooth, photographic-quality image.

Dye sublimation technology and dye sublimation printers have become very popular with the heavy use of digital cameras today. CompTIA recognizes this and will most likely ask you about this technology on the exam.

NOTE

PRINT, COPY, FAX, AND SCAN

In the past, the average home or small office required separate devices for such tasks as printing, copying, faxing, and scanning. This required enormous amounts of desk/office space, as well as a high cost of ownership and maintenance. Enter the MFD (Multifunction Device)! An MFD is a device that combines the functionality of a printer, a copier, a scanner, and a fax machine into one unit. An MFD has only one warranty, so you don't need a separate warranty for each of your devices. An MFD is usually connected to a computer system with one cable (usually parallel or USB) and possibly an RJ11 patch for a phone line. An MFD typically requires only one power cord. A networked MFD is typically connected to a switch or router and can be accessed by many users if set up to do so. Most MFDs come with easily installed software packages that allow you set up all of the MFD's software drivers and functions with minutes. The popularity of MFDs has pretty much flattened the market for single, stand-alone devices. The most popular versions of MFDs offer inkjet or laser jet technology.

MFDs have been identified by CompTIA as part of the 2006 A+ objectives. Make sure you are familiar with these combination devices that are used to print, copy, fax, and scan.

NOTE

FINISHERS (STAPLING, ETC.)

Most high-end printers allow the use of optional units called multifunction finishers. A *multifunction finisher* is simply a printer-attachable unit that allows some or all of the following options and features:

- Ability to stack multiple sheets of letter- or ledger-size paper
- Ability to offset multiple print jobs
- Ability to stack sheets into booklets
- Ability to staple sheets of letter- or ledger-size paper
- Ability to fold single pages
- Ability to saddle stitch and fold booklets

Most finishers have interfaces that are proprietary to the printer manufacturer, meaning they are not interchangeable between printers. The jamming of staples or paper causes the majority of problems that occur with most finishers. Every manufacturer has its own set of procedures for dealing with these jams. You should follow the finisher's manufacturer instructions for finisher-related jams.

IMPORTANT PRINTER INFORMATION AND TEST TIPS

The following printer-related information and test tips are included to ensure that you are well prepared for the many printer-focused questions that may come your way on the real exam:

- A dot matrix's printer pins strike or "hit" paper to create a final image.
- In the laser printing process, if the printer drum has an image on it, but the printer is just printing blank pages, there is most likely a transfer corona failure or problem.
- If you experience printed lines of miscellaneous characters, text, or code followed by blank sheets of paper after installing a new printer, it is likely that you have installed the wrong printer driver, or you have a loose printer cable.
- With inkjet printing, ink is sprayed onto the paper with a nozzle.
- Such things as ribbons and paper are considered to be printer consumables.
- By no means should a laser printer ever be plugged into a UPS.
- Centronix, DB25, and USB represent possible printer connections.
- Humidity, worn rollers or bad feeder separator pads, and bad media are all very common causes for more than one sheet of paper being fed into a printer at a time.
- Laser printers have ozone filters that are used to protect the environment. It is very important that a laser printer's ozone filter be vacuumed or replaced during routine printer maintenance.
- If you send a print job to a printer and nothing is printed at all except blank pages, verify that your toner cartridge is not empty and is in good condition. You should also verify that you have removed the manufacturer's tape from the toner cartridge if it is new.
- Ribbon tension that is too high can lead to smudges.
- Inconsistent or missing characters may be the result of broken pin heads.
- If the tops of characters are missing, the print head may be misaligned with the platen and may need reseating.
- If a cartridge is causing problems, replace the entire cartridge.
- Laser printers use Page Description Language (PDL) to print one page at a time.
- USB 2.0 provides the greatest throughput for printers. It has a maximum speed of 480 Mbps and supports up to a total of 127 devices. The first USB specification had transmission speeds up to 12 Mbps.
- IEEE 1394, also known as FireWire, is also used for many printer connections. FireWire supports a maximum speed of 400 Mbps and supports up to 63 devices.
- If a printer is ever printing garbled text or characters, it is likely that the print driver is incorrect or has become corrupt.

CAD/CAM

CAD/CAM (Computer-Aided Design/Computer-Aided Manufacturing) is a specialized program or graphics software package that works in conjunction with specialized hardware to help architects and manufacturers create and design such things as computers, buildings, and office layouts. CAD/CAM helps with the designing of special-purpose machines for automation. With CAD/CAM, a designer can create, view, and change 2D and 3D drawings. The CAD software allows the designer to zoom in, select, and modify particular parts of a design.

Several years ago, CAD required specially built computer systems. Today, CAD/CAM software packages are designed to run on multipurpose/multifunctional workstations and servers. The software does, however, have minimum and recommended system requirements, and you should review the manufacturer's recommendations when installing these packages.

To be useful and effective, CAD/CAM programs also depend on specialized input and output devices, such as high-end computer monitors, specialized printers, plotters, digitized tablets, and light pens.

For the A+ exams, you do not have to demonstrate that you can create automation equipment using CAD/CAM. What is important is that you understand that CAD/CAM is very graphics intensive and requires as much computer horsepower as you can get your hands on to use it effectively.

CHAPTER SUMMARY

This chapter introduced some of the most common types of output devices in use today. You should pay close attention to monitor types and their associated resolutions, colors, and technologies. At this point, you should also have a good understanding of dot matrix and laser printing technology, including the EP laser printing process. If you have trouble answering the review questions at the end of this chapter, go back and read the chapter again. To pass the A+ exams, you must master questions very similar to these questions relating to output devices.

REVIEW QUESTIONS

1. **A video adapter resolution of 800 × 600 represents which video standard?**
   - A. CGA
   - B. VGA
   - C. SVGA
   - D. Monochrome

Correct Answer = C

As displayed in Table 6.2, a resolution of 800 × 600 is supported by SVGA. CGA supports 320 × 200 and 640 × 200. VGA supports 640 × 480 and 320 × 200. Monochrome supports 720 × 350.

2. **You should not use this while working on a monitor. However, you should use this when installing a video adapter card. What is it?**
   ○ A. An electron gun
   ○ B. Antiphosphorous beam
   ○ C. A multimeter
   ○ D. An ESD wrist strap

Correct Answer = D

You should never wear an ESD wrist strap while working with the components inside of a monitor. An electronic reaction may occur that can be deadly. You should however wear a protective wrist strap while installing adapter cards in your system to protect them from ESD. An electron gun is used in a monitor to direct an electronic beam to the back of a glass screen that has a phosphorous coating. A multimeter is a device used to measure wattage.

3. **Which of the following are printer consumable items? (Choose Three)**
   ☐ A. Platen
   ☐ B. Print buffer
   ☐ C. Toner cartridges
   ☐ D. Printer drivers
   ☐ E. Printer paper
   ☐ F. Printer ribbons

Correct Answers = C, E, and F

Toner cartridges, paper, and disposable ribbons are considered printer consumable items.

4. **Several users have been trying to print reports to a networked printer. The users complain that their reports are not printing. What would you do to solve this issue?**
   ○ A. Press the reset button on the printer.
   ○ B. Go into Safe Mode, and remove the print driver.
   ○ C. Realign the platen.
   ○ D. Delete the reports from the printer queue (buffer). Then, stop and start the print spooler service.

Correct Answer = D

With a networked printer, print jobs are typically queued in a printer buffer that is managed by the print spooler service. If print jobs are not printing to a networked printer, this process will clear the print queue and allow print jobs to be resubmitted and printed.

5. **Your printed output appears to be fading from left to right. What is causing this problem?**
   - ○ A.   The printer ribbon is old.
   - ○ B.   Your print driver is outdated.
   - ○ C.   The platen is out of alignment.
   - ○ D.   The print head is wearing out.

   Correct Answer = C

   A misaligned platen commonly results in a faded level of ink application to the paper as it is applied from left to right or may result in uneven lines of output across the paper.

6. **A laser printer is producing inconsistent, wavy output. What is a very common cause associated with this problem?**
   - ○ A.   The rollers are broken.
   - ○ B.   The fuser is damaged.
   - ○ C.   The platen is out of alignment.
   - ○ D.   The toner cartridge is empty.

   Correct Answer = D

   If your laser printed output begins to appear wavy or inconsistent in print, you may have an empty or malfunctioning toner cartridge.

7. **Of the following choices, which uses a heat-sensitive print head that moves over a ribbon of transparent colored film?**
   - ○ A.   Color impact
   - ○ B.   Dye sublimation
   - ○ C.   Laser transformation
   - ○ D.   Ink dispersion

   Correct Answer = B

   With a dye sublimation printer, a heat-sensitive print head moves over a ribbon of transparent film that contains heat-activated inks.

8. **Dye sublimation uses a heat-sensitive ribbon or film that is made up of the primary printing colors. What are the four primary printing colors?**

   ○ A. Magenta, Black, Yellow, and Blue
   ○ B. Yellow, Blue, Black, and Red
   ○ C. Cyan, Magenta, Yellow, and Black
   ○ D. Red, White, Blue, and Magenta

   Correct Answer = C

   With a dye sublimation printer, a heat-sensitive print head moves over a ribbon of transparent film that contains heat-activated inks or sections that represent the four primary printing colors of Cyan, Magenta, Yellow, and Black (CMYK).

9. **Which of the following is considered the newest and fastest form of connectivity for printers?**

   ○ A. Serial
   ○ B. USB
   ○ C. Parallel
   ○ D. ECP
   ○ E. ECC

   Correct Answer = B

   Currently, the fastest available connection for a printer is realized through USB technology and a USB connection.

10. **What should you check first if a printer has no paper, but there is an error code on a printer LED that states there is a paper jam?**

    ○ A. Paper-feed sensors
    ○ B. USB port
    ○ C. Drum
    ○ D. Platen
    ○ E. Ink cartridge

    Correct Answer = A

    Paper-feed rollers have sensors to control the proper flow of paper out of the paper tray. It is a common occurrence to receive a "paper jam" error on the printer LED display but on investigation, you find that there is no paper in the tray.

11. **What acronym describes a multifunction device that is used to print, scan, copy, and fax?**

    ○ A.   CMYK
    ○ B.   NLD
    ○ C.   CMY
    ○ D.   NLQ
    ○ E.   MFD

    Correct Answer = E

    An MFD is a device that combines functionality of a printer, a copier, a scanner and a fax machine into one unit.

12. **Which of the following are common features of a multifunctional finisher?**

    ○ A.   Ability to stack multiple sheets of letter or ledger-sized paper
    ○ B.   Ability to fold single pages
    ○ C.   Ability to stack sheets into booklets
    ○ D.   Ability to staple sheets of letter or ledger-sized paper
    ○ E.   All of the above

    Correct Answer = E

    All of the items listed are common features of a multifunctional finisher.

13. **What is the smallest monitor (in terms of size) that can be used to display 1600 × 1200?**

    ○ A.   15-inch CRT
    ○ B.   17-inch CRT
    ○ C.   19-inch CRT
    ○ D.   17-inch LCD

    Correct Answer = C

    The 15-inch CRT can typically only display up to 1024 × 768, and the 17-inch CRT and LCD can only do 1280 × 1024 (just because the screen is a true 17-inch screen, you are still limited to 1280 × 1024).

14. **Which one of these statements is true? (Assuming that the refresh rate listed is the max the monitor could handle at the given resolution).**

    ○ A. A 15-inch monitor, running at 1024 × 768 at a refresh rate of 65 Hz, is capable of displaying 1280 × 1024 at 60 Hz.

    ○ B. A 17-inch monitor that can handle 1280 × 1024 at 80 Hz is more than likely capable of handling 1024 × 768 at approx. 95-100 Hz.

    ○ C. A 19-inch monitor that displays 1024 × 768 at 80Hz is more than likely capable of handling 1600 × 1200 at 85 Hz.

    ○ D. None of the above.

    ○ E. All of the above.

Correct Answer = B

A 15-inch monitor is not capable of 1280 × 1024 (smallest monitor capable of 1280 × 1024 is 17-inch). The 19-inch monitor running 1024 × 768 at 80 Hz could probably display 1600 × 1200 . . . but not at a higher refresh rate than running at 1024 × 768!

15. **What is the best way to clean a screen or LCD?**

    ○ A. Water and nonabrasive soap

    ○ B. Windex and a lint free paper towels

    ○ C. Water added to a lint free cloth

    ○ D. All of the above

Correct Answer = C

Caution should be taken when cleaning LCD screens. Soaps and other products are not recommended because they often damage the screen. The best way to clean a screen or LCD is by spraying water on a lint free cloth and gently wiping the surface of the screen. All other choices are incorrect and will damage your screen or LCD.

16. **Which of the following are video interface standards? (Choose Three)**

    ☐ A. S-Video

    ☐ B. DVI

    ☐ C. HDMI

    ☐ D. DIVA

    ☐ E. Video-R

    ☐ F. Printer ribbons

Correct Answers = A, B, and C

S-Video is an analog video interface standard that carries video data as two separate signals: brightness and color. It is unlike composite video that carries the whole set of signals in one signal. Digital Visual Interface (DVI) is a video interface technology that maximizes the visual quality of digital displays such as flat panel LCD computer displays and digital projectors. The High-Definition Multimedia Interface (HDMI) is a digital audio/video interface standard capable of transmitting totally uncompressed streams.

17. **Which of the following are parallel printer modes? (Choose 3)**

   ☐ A. DMA
   ☐ B. STP
   ☐ C. ECP
   ☐ D. IEEE 1394
   ☐ E. EPP
   ☐ F. Bidirectional

   Correct Answers = C, E, and F

   You can change parallel printing modes in systems BIOS. The parallel printer modes standards include unidirectional ports, bidirectional ports, enhanced parallel ports (EPP) and enhanced capability ports (ECP). You should remember for the exams that EPP and ECP ports are the fastest of the four parallel transmission modes.

18. **Which internal component of a laser printer is most likely to cause harm?**

   ○ A. Fuser
   ○ B. Primary corona
   ○ C. Roller assembly
   ○ D. Drum

   Correct Answer = A

   Caution should be taken when working on the inside of a laser printer. The most likely internal component of a laser printer that can cause harm in the form of burns to a technician or user is the fuser. The fuser gets very hot when it heats up to melt toner onto paper. You should remember this point for the exams.

19. **A customer has swapped good working printers around in the office with other coworkers. They all have different operating systems, and now everyone's printer is printing garbled characters. The customer could really use your newly acquired A+ skills at this time. What most likely happed?**

   ○ A. The customer's printer infected all of the other printers with a print virus.
   ○ B. The wrong print drivers have been installed.
   ○ C. The platens are misaligned.
   ○ D. The drums are all damaged from the moves.

   Correct Answer = B

   If the A+ exams tell you that a printer is printing garbled text, remember the printer drivers are likely incorrect or corrupt. That is most likely the cause of the problem in this example. The fact that the users have different operating systems is also a key to this solution. Use your head on these questions and on the real exams! All other choices are not likely and incorrect.

20. **Your boss wants you to buy a laptop with the very best resolution possible. Which of the following options offers the highest resolution?**

   ○ A. VGA
   ○ B. WXGA+
   ○ C. SXGA+
   ○ D. UXGA

   Correct Answer = D

   Of these choices, UXGA offer the greatest screen resolution of 1600 × 1200. VGA offers 640 × 480. WXGA+ offers a 1440 × 900 resolution. SXGA+ offers 1400 × 1050 resolution.

REFERENCES

http://en.wikipedia.org/wiki/Laser_printer. The Wikipedia Web site offers a great description of laser printers and scanners. This one is definitely worth your time!

http://en.wikipedia.org/wiki/Dvi. The Wikipedia Web site that gives a great explanation of DVI resolution and connectors.

http://en.wikipedia.org/wiki/Hdmi. This Wikipedia Web site describes HDMI technology in detail. It has great information regarding HDMI versions, resolution, and connectors.

7 Storage Devices and Interfaces

In This Chapter

- The Floppy Drive
- The Hard Drive
- Drive Controllers and Interfaces
- Device Installation, Configuration, and Troubleshooting
- RAID (Redundant Array of Independent Disks)
- Optical Storage Devices
- SuperDisks and Zip Drives
- Thumb Drives, Flash Drives, and SD Cards
- Backup Tapes and Backup Types

In Chapter 4, we discussed RAM, which is temporary or primary storage. In this chapter, we discuss forms of permanent or secondary storage devices, such as hard drives, floppy drives, Zip drives, tape devices, and optical storage. Permanent storage devices are sometimes referred to as mass storage or auxiliary storage devices. We also explore the interfaces and technologies used to connect storage devices to a computing system. Some of the more common interfaces are IDE/ATA, Serial ATA (SATA), and SCSI.

The exams are likely to test your knowledge of the proper methods of configuring, connecting, and troubleshooting storage. The past A+ Core Hardware exam focused heavily on storage devices. The current exams will probably concentrate on your ability to install and configure multiple hard drives, and it will dwell on the details of SCSI configurations and priorities. Pay close attention to the topics discussed in this chapter; knowledge of these topics may determine whether you pass or fail the exams.

THE FLOPPY DRIVE

A *floppy drive* is an internal device that reads or writes information to and from magnetic floppy disks and communicates with the system's CPU. The floppy drive is typically mounted into an available drive bay inside the system unit. A floppy drive adapter kit may be necessary if you are installing a floppy drive unit into a large drive bay. Older computing systems used 5.25-inch floppy drives that required a larger bay. Some computing systems today come with a standard 3.5-inch floppy drive installed. Similar to a hard drive, a floppy disk stores information on magnetic media. A hard drive's storage medium is called a platter. A floppy drive's storage medium is called a floppy disk. The major advantage of a floppy disk is that it is portable. You can store files on a floppy disk and take it wherever you go. The major disadvantages of floppy disks are that they are slow to access and cannot store as much information as a hard disk.

A floppy disk must receive both a low-level format and a high-level format before it can be considered useful.

A *low-level format* prepares the floppy disk with an organized structure by creating sectors, tracks, and clusters on the floppy disk. A *high-level format* prepares the floppy disk with a File Allocation Table (FAT) and adds a root directory to it. You can format a floppy from a DOS command prompt or through the use of an operating system GUI, such as Windows. Preformatted floppy disks can be purchased just about anywhere computer supplies are sold.

To format a floppy disk from a DOS prompt, simply place the disk in the floppy drive "A," and type "format a:". A low-level format as well as a high-level format will be carried out on the disk. When the format process is complete, the floppy will be ready to have files saved to it. (See "The Hard Drive" later in this chapter for more information on the formatting process.)

There are two basic forms of floppy disk media available:

5.25-inch: This style of floppy disk was popular in the1980s. The 5.25-inch floppy came with two common data storage capacities: 360 KB and 1.2 MB. The 5.25-inch floppy disk used a 5.25-inch floppy drive that is now considered obsolete.

3.5-inch: This floppy drive is found in some computers today. The 3.5-inch floppy disk can store 720 KB (double density) or 1.44 MB (high density) of data.

FLOPPY DRIVE COMPONENTS

A floppy drive's components are similar to that of a hard drive. The read/write (R/W) heads read and write data onto the floppy media and work in tandem with an erase tunnel mechanism to erase information if requested by the floppy drive's controller. The head actuator, sometimes referred to as a stepping motor, is controlled by the floppy disk controller; it moves the drive's R/W heads in and out of place. A spindle motor, driven by a belt system, makes the floppy disk spin or rotate at the desired speed. The speed at which the floppy disk spins is measured in revolutions per minute. A floppy drive uses a circuit board, also known as a logic board, which controls all of the floppy drive's components and communicates with the computer system. Finally, there are two floppy drive connectors. One is used to connect the floppy drive to the system's power supply, and the other is used to connect the floppy drive to the motherboard's floppy drive controller.

FLOPPY DRIVE CONFIGURATION AND TROUBLESHOOTING

A floppy drive is connected to a floppy drive controller on the motherboard with a data cable. The data cable has a red stripe that runs down its right side. The red stripe represents pin 1 on the data cable. When plugging the data cable connector into the floppy drive controller on the motherboard, you must match pin 1 on the data cable connector to pin 1 on the controller. The same is true when connecting the other end of the data cable to the floppy drive itself. If you plug the floppy drive's data cable in backwards, the LED light on the front of the floppy drive unit will stay lit, and you will not be able to access the floppy drive.

A computer system reserves certain letter designations for its components. The active partition on hard drive 0 gets assigned drive letter C by default. The letters A and B are reserved by the system for assignment to the floppy drives. A typical 3.5-inch floppy drive is attached to the far end of a ribbon data cable (after the twist in the ribbon cable) and gets the letter A assignment. If you have a second floppy drive, such as a 5.25-inch floppy drive, it should be attached to the middle connector on the floppy data cable, and it gets the letter B assignment.

Over time, floppy drives and floppy disks can get dirty and warped. This can cause them to fail mechanically or render them incapable of data storage and retrieval. If you attempt to access your floppy drive and receive an error message such as "Drive A is not ready, Abort, Retry or Fail," either your floppy disk is bad, or your floppy drive needs cleaning and/or maintenance.

There are times when you may need to boot up your computer with a bootable floppy disk installed in the A drive. This is frequently done for troubleshooting purposes, maintenance, or operating system installation. If you are unable to boot from your bootable floppy disk, check your boot sequence settings in the BIOS configuration and verify that your system is set to boot from the A drive before the C or D drive. Otherwise, the system will not look for your bootable floppy at start-up.

One of the most common mistakes people make is to leave a nonbootable floppy disk in a floppy drive when restarting the system. This can cause the error message "Nonsystem disk or disk error; replace and strike any key to continue." Ejecting the nonbootable floppy from the drive and pressing any key on your keyboard will bypass this error message, and your system will continue to load. (By the way, there is no such thing as an "any" key.)

Exchanging floppy disks with others and using them in your system without proper virus protection poses a serious virus threat to your computer. The two most common sources of virus attack come from floppy disks and the Internet. Always scan your floppy media for viruses.

The procedure that follows outlines the proper installation steps of installing a floppy drive:

1. Disconnect power to the computer system.
2. Insert the floppy drive into an available floppy drive bay.
3. Screw in the two screws.
4. Plug the floppy cable into the drive and into the mainboard (FD1 interface) while being aware of the pin 1 position.
5. Connect the floppy to the last connector on the cable. This will make the floppy drive the "A drive." Plugging it in to the connector toward the middle of the cable will make it the "B drive."
6. Connect one of the available power supply power connectors to the drive.

THE HARD DRIVE

Many names have been associated with the hard drive since its inception. It has been called the hard disk, the fixed disk, Direct Access Storage Device (DASD), and the C drive. For the purposes of our A+ exams study focus, we will use the terminologies *hard drive* and *hard disk*.

The hard drive is a component attached to a computer system unit in a fixed manner. It is usually installed in a drive bay that is inaccessible from the front of the system unit. When purchasing a computer, it is important to consider a system unit that has enough drive bays available to support multiple hard drives. You may want to expand your storage capabilities in the future.

The hard drive is used as a mass storage device for data and programs. The hard drive is made up of metal platters, a spindle motor, an actuator arm, and a set of R/W heads. Hard drive space is measured in kilobytes, megabytes, and gigabytes.

Today's hard drives generally have a storage capacity between 100 GB and 250 GB, and rotation speeds between 5200 and 7400 rpm (revolutions per minute). See Figure 7.1 for a standard PC EIDE hard drive

FIGURE 7.1   A standard EIDE hard drive.

For data to be stored, organized, and retrieved from a hard drive in a timely, organized fashion, the hard drive's media (platters) must be divided into separate tracks, sectors, cylinders, and clusters. The sizes of these separations are collectively known as a hard drive's geometry.

As mentioned earlier, a hard drive's components are similar to a floppy drive's. Following are some of the main components and organizational units that make up a hard drive:

Platter: A hard drive has many platters. A platter is a circular, magnetized disk that holds information and programs. The platters that make up a hard drive are stacked on top of each other with head actuators and R/W heads between them. Platters can store information on both sides.

Landing zone: Older hard drives used the landing zone as a place to position the R/W heads of a hard drive when they were not in use. The landing zone is an area of the hard disk that does not have data stored. The landing zone is now obsolete.

Read/write (R/W) heads: Hard drives and floppy drives have R/W heads that read and write data to the hard drive's platters. Most hard drives have two heads for each platter. One head is used to read and write data to the top of the platter, the other is used to read from and write to the bottom side of the platter. Six platters (or magnetic disks) have a total of 12 heads.

If you hear a grinding noise coming from inside your computer, your R/W heads may be "crashing" onto the hard drive's platter. This will most likely result in a hard drive failure.

Tracks: A hard drive platter is divided into many tracks. Picture a horse-racing track with separate lanes all lined up next to each other, forming a circle. The platter is the entire race track. The tracks are separate lanes running parallel to each other in a circle. The tracks are numbered consecutively for organizational purposes. The first track is track 0 and is located closest to the outside edge of the platter. Floppy disks also have tracks. The average floppy has 80 tracks.

Sectors: The smallest measurable area on a hard drive is a sector. A sector can hold a maximum of 512 bytes of information. A sector is a section of a track. Picture the race track again. A single lane is broken down into smaller units called sectors. A platter on a typical hard drive contains approximately 63 sectors per track (this number can vary depending on your system's BIOS settings). Figure 7.2 illustrates the single side of a platter and identifies a sector within a track. A group of sectors is called a cluster.

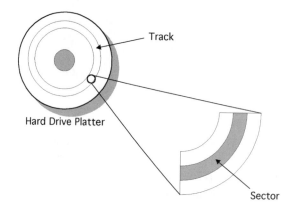

FIGURE 7.2 A single side of a platter sector and track.

Cylinders: Cylinders are a logical grouping of similarly numbered tracks on all the platters combined. For example, if you have 6 platters, you would have a total of 12 surfaces, or sides. Each side of the platter would have its own track 4. Remember, the tracks are numbered starting with track 0 from the outside edge of the platter. If you combine the 4 tracks on the 12 surfaces, you will have a logical cylinder 28. Typical BIOS configuration settings allow for a total of 1,024 cylinders.

When your computer is powered on, the system BIOS looks for the boot sector, or Master Boot Record (MBR), on a hard drive for operating system load instructions. The boot sector is assigned to head 0, cylinder 0, track 0, and sector 0 on the first platter of a hard drive. If your boot sector becomes damaged or corrupted, you will most likely receive a "Bad or missing operating system" error message. This is a really good time to be happy about the daily backups you have been performing on your system. You may need to restore data back to the hard drive after you repartition and reformat the damaged disk. Read on for more information about partitioning and formatting. See Figure 7.3 for an example BIOS setup program displaying hard drive information.

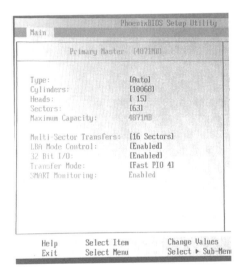

FIGURE 7.3   A BIOS setup program displaying hard drive information.

For the exams, remember that access time is a measurement of the average time that it takes the drives R/W heads to access data on the hard drive. The seek time is the amount of time it takes for the drives head to move between the cylinders and land on a certain track. The data transfer rates are measured in megabytes per second (MBps) where data is transferred between the drive and the computer system.

HARD DRIVE PARTITIONING AND FORMATTING

Two primary methods are used to prepare hard drives for supporting operating systems and applications: partitioning and formatting. Without being partitioned and formatted with an organized, logical file structure, a hard drive would be nothing more than a large metal paperweight. You must apply the following processes to a hard drive for it to be useful.

Partitioning

A hard drive normally receives a low-level format and is partitioned at the factory. If you receive or purchase a hard drive without a preinstalled operating system, you will need to partition and format the drive yourself.

Partitioning is the process of dividing one physical hard drive into separate areas of storage. In other words, you can create several logical hard drives out of one physical hard drive. This is useful for storing files, installing multiple operating systems, and supporting multiple file system structures, such as FAT32 and NTFS (NT File System). Two partition types can be created on a hard drive: primary partitions and extended partitions:

> **Primary partitions:** A primary partition is a partition that contains an active, bootable operating system, such as DOS or Windows. It is the partition that provides the system files necessary to boot into the operating system. A hard drive can be divided into four primary partitions, but only one of the four primary partitions can be set as the active partition. The active partition is specifically designated as the boot partition. It contains the MBR. The system BIOS looks to the active partition for boot-up commands. This partition is always labeled "C:".

> **Extended partitions:** Extended partitions can be separated into units called logical partitions. There can be up to 23 logical partitions on a single hard drive. Each logical partition receives a different alphabetic assignment, such as D, E, or F. These partitions are used mostly for file and applications storage. Any partition other than the primary partition is considered an extended partition.

DOS, Windows 3.x, and the early versions of Windows 95 are FAT16 operating systems, and they will allow you to create only a single partition size up to 2 GB. If you want to use more than 2GB of hard drive space with these operating systems, you need to create multiple partitions of 2 GB. If you want to use more than 2 GB for a single partition on a single hard drive, you need to use a newer operating system that supports FAT32 or NTFS. Windows 98, Windows 2000, and Microsoft Me allow you to create a single partition of up to 4 TB (terabytes).

FDISK

FDISK is a common DOS utility program that enables the partitioning of a hard drive. FDISK is located on a DOS bootable disk and is run from the command prompt.

To use FDISK, simply enter "FDISK" at a command prompt. If your hard drive is larger than 512 MB, a menu appears that asks if you would like to enable large disk support. You have the option of replying "Y" for yes or "N" for no. Pressing "Y" accepts the default of yes, and you are presented with the FDISK Options menu. At the FDISK Options menu, you can create one large partition for the whole hard drive. However, if you plan on dividing your hard drive into primary and extended partitions, you need to use options 1, 2, and 3 to partition the disk accordingly. If you create more than one primary partition, you need to set one of them as the active, bootable partition. After creating partitions with FDISK and formatting partitions for operating systems and files, you can always use FDISK again to create new partitions. The FDISK Options menu has an option for displaying partition information, which can be a useful tool to assist you with making the right partition choices to suit your needs.

You can also purchase third-party partitioning programs that allow you to partition a hard drive through the use of a GUI.

NOTE

For the test, you can use FDISK to divide a hard drive into three primary partitions and one extended partition. The extended partition can be divided into 23 logical partitions. If you are installing a new hard drive and receive an "Invalid Media Type" error message after booting the computer, you can use the FDISK utility to repartition the drive and set the active partition. If you run FDISK after installing a large hard drive, and the entire space available on the new drive is not recognized, chances are your BIOS did not recognize the hard drive changes or was not updated before you ran FDISK.

Note that FDISK has an undocumented switch called /MBR. This switch causes FDISK to write the MBR to the hard disk without altering partition table information. If you use the command FDISK /MBR, you will replace a systems boot loader with a generic boot loader. This is typically done if the originally installed system boot loader has become corrupted. Many viruses are written to infect a system's MBR. Running the FDISK /MBR switch will also help remove these MBR infector viruses.

Formatting

Before an operating system or application can be installed on a partitioned hard drive, the drive must be formatted. Formatting is a two-level process that prepares a partition on a hard drive to accept an operating system, along with files and programs.

Two levels of formatting are implemented before the operating system is installed:

Low-level format: A low-level format is usually done at the factory before the hard drive is shipped. A low-level format is a type of physical formatting process that erases all information and prepares the hard drive for a logical structure. This type of format also looks for bad areas on the drive and marks them so that they are not used as potential storage locations. A low-level format creates tracks and sectors on the hard drive platters and determines what type of disk controller will be able to access the hard drive; the controller may be IDE/ATA, EIDE, or SCSI. A low-level format takes place before the hard disk is partitioned.

High-level format: High-level formatting is often referred to as "formatting a hard drive." A high-level format creates a FAT and root directory on the hard drive. This is the process that actually prepares the drive for an operating system. The FAT is a logical structure that keeps track of which sectors certain files are stored in on the hard drive. The FAT can identify good and bad sectors on a hard drive. When you install a newer operating system or upgrade your current operating system to a newer version, the formatting process is normally done for you automatically. A high-level format takes place after the hard drive has been partitioned.

FORMAT.COM is a DOS utility program that is also run from the DOS command prompt. The FORMAT command will allow you to format the hard drive in preparation for an operating system. You can also format the hard drive from within an operating system, such as Windows, if the operating system supports FORMAT.

From a DOS command prompt, type "FORMAT D:". You can replace "D:" in this example with the letter of any drive you want to format.

ScanDisk and Defrag

Over time, the constant use of your hard drive can cause the sectors to get worn out or damaged. Utility programs such as ScanDisk, Norton Utilities, and Check It are available to help you identify bad sectors on a hard drive. If you are developing bad sectors on your hard drive, it is a good idea to run ScanDisk and select the Thorough option in the ScanDisk settings options. This runs a complete scan of your hard drive and attempts to fix any bad sectors it finds.

When files are written to a hard drive, they are not stored in contiguous order (one file written directly after another file). Files are stored in a noncontiguous order (anywhere there are available blocks of space). After a while, this can cause the clusters on your drive to become fragmented. It takes time for the CPU to request a file from the hard drive, and it takes even more time if the files are not in any order. Windows offers a built-in utility program called Disk Defragmenter that will help put clusters of files into a contiguous, structured order. Running Disk Defragmenter, or Defrag, can increase the disk access time and the overall performance of your system. If a customer complains that his system is getting slower over time, running the Defrag utility will most likely assist you with restoring the customer's disk access time. Note that Windows 9.x, Me, 2000, XP, and Vista offer a built-in defragmenter utility. Windows NT does not. This is discussed in more detail in later chapters of this book.

DRIVE CONTROLLERS AND INTERFACES

A hard drive uses its own internal controller board and processor to manage the interaction of R/W operations. The controller board also provides support for interfaces such as IDE/ATA (Parallel ATA), EIDE, SATA, and SCSI.

Before we continue with interface specifications, it is important for you to understand the basic connectors located on a typical hard drive (see Figure 7.4). Two main connectors and a set of jumpers are usually located at the rear of the hard drive. The first connector is a five-pin power connector that receives 5V and 12V DC power from the system's power supply. The 5V power is the "dangerous power" used by the hard drive's circuit board. If the 5V power fluctuates, your hard drive's circuit board and components may be in danger. The 12V power is used to power the hard drive's motor and actuator heads. The second connector is an IDE 40-pin data connector or an SCSI connector. This connector is used to transmit and receive information and instructions from the computer's processor.

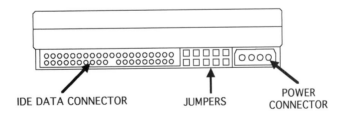

FIGURE 7.4 A hard drive with built-in connectors.

Plastic jumpers are used with IDE interfaces to set the configuration of the hard drive as either a master or a slave drive, along with the use of a data cable that supports multiple or shared interfaces. SCSI devices use plastic jumper blocks to uniquely identify SCSI drives or controller cards.

A hard drive communicates with a computer system through the use of an interface. Several communication transfer interfaces and standards ensure that a hard drive will be compatible with a system's motherboard and processor. These standards are in place to assist manufacturers with a common set of electronic rules for interfaces.

ST506 INTERFACE

Now obsolete, the ST506 was the first standard interface developed in 1980 by Seagate Technologies (ST). This interface required the installer to modify the CMOS configuration manually, provide a low-level format, partition the drive manually, and finally, provide a high-level format. This standard was universally accepted based on its capability to attach to a standard interface data cable.

ESDI INTERFACE

Introduced in 1983, the Enhanced System Device Interface (ESDI) standard for hard drives was the first interface standard to have a controller actually reside on the hard drive itself. It required a compatible ESDI controller installed on the motherboard. ESDI technology was several times faster than ST506 and was much more expensive as a result.

IDE/ATA INTERFACE (PARALLEL ATA)

The IDE/ATA (Parallel ATA) is still currently the most widely accepted interface standard. The IDE is an interface controller built into the hard drive. ATA, now also called PATA (Parallel ATA) is actually a set of rules or specifications that apply to the IDE controller. The ATA standard is a 16-bit, parallel connection. ATA allows you to have a master drive (drive 0) and a slave drive (drive 1). ATA also provides a way for multiple hard drives to communicate with the same system bus. If your motherboard does not have an IDE/ATA interface, or your system only has one IDE controller, you can purchase an IDE add-on expansion card, such as a PCI card that supports this technology. This will allow you to have up to four devices.

One of the major advantages of IDE is that it can provide sector translation. This allows you to change the drive's properties in CMOS configuration settings. It also allows computer systems to recognize hard drives larger than 528 MB by using Logical Block Addressing (LBA) support. LBA is considered a type of IDE transaction. You can enable LBA support, if available, in your BIOS configurations settings for your hard drive.

There are two common transfer methods or protocols used to communicate information between memory and an IDE/ATA hard drive controller:

Programmable Input/Output (PIO): PIO is a standard whereby the transfer of information between memory and the drive is controlled by the system's processor. PIO is measured in megabytes per second. Most versions of IDE/ATA can use PIO modes 0 and 1. Table 7.1 shows PIO modes and transfer rates per second. IORDY is a CMOS configuration that controls the speed of a disk head as it moves across a platter. IORDY is used with PIO modes 3 and 4.

Direct Memory Access (DMA): All IDE/ATA hard drives support DMA. As mentioned in Chapter 5, DMA is used to transfer information from memory directly to a peripheral, such as a hard drive, without interrupting the processor.

TABLE 7.1   PIO Modes and Transfer Rates Per Second

PIO Mode	Transfer Rate Per Second	Standard
0	3.3 MB	ATA
1	5.2 MB	ATA
2	8.3 MB	ATA
3	11.1 MB	ATA-2
4	16.7 MB	ATA-2/ATA-3

Several improvements have been made to the original implementation of the ATA standard interface. These improvements allow more devices to be attached to an ATA interface and increase the speed at which data can pass between an ATA interface and a device. Some of the ATA standards that you should be familiar with are listed here:

ATA: Traditional ATA, also known as IDE, provides support for up to two hard drives per controller. ATA has a 16-bit interface and uses PIO modes 0, 1, and 2.

ATA-2: ATA-2 provided support for LBA (drives larger than 504 MB) and is sometimes referred to as Fast ATA. ATA-2 provides support for PIO modes 3 and 4. ATA-2 is basically the same technology as EIDE (discussed in the next section). It is an improvement on the original IDE/ATA standard that allows for up to four devices to be connected to one motherboard interface controller, for a total of eight devices in a typical system.

ATA-3: ATA-3 is the latest revision to the ATA standard. ATA-3 features enhanced security, better power management, support for PIO mode 4, and a new feature called *Self-Monitoring Analysis and Report Technology* (SMART), which will warn you of certain failures.

Ultra-ATA: Known as Ultra-DMA, ATA-33, or UDMA/-33, Ultra-ATA provides support for multiword DMA mode 3 running at 33 Mbps. The technology assists with keeping the CPU synchronized with faster hard drives.

Ultra-ATA/66: ATA/66 is an ATA version that doubles the traditional ATA throughput to 66 Mbps. An ATA/66 data cable is different from an ATA/33 cable. You can differentiate the two by the number of wires in each data cable.

Ultra-ATA/100: ATA/100 is an ATA implementation that improves upon the bottlenecks caused by the ATA/66 version of ATA. The most significant difference between ATA/100 and ATA/66 is in the increased transfer rate and error-checking capabilities included with ATA/100. ATA/100 has a clock period of 20 ns and a data transfer rate of 100 Mbps. For a system to run in Ultra-ATA/100 mode, the following requirements must be met:

- You must have an Ultra-ATA/100-capable system board and BIOS.
- You must use an Ultra-ATA-capable 40-pin, 80-conductor cable.
- You must use an operating system that can handle DMA transfers. Windows 95 (OSR2), Windows 98, Windows Me, Windows 2000, Windows XP and Vista are all capable of this.
- You must have an Ultra-ATA/100-compatible device, such as an ATA/100 hard drive.

Ultra ATA/133: As hard drive manufacturers continue to develop faster drives, the need for faster throughput between the host system and the hard drive is needed. To satisfy the bottleneck caused by the ATA/100, the faster ATA/133 was developed. ATA/133 has a clock period of 15 ns and a data transfer rate of 133 Mbps. Here are some features to remember regarding Ultra-ATA/133:

- ATA/133 maintains backward compatibility with ATA/100, ATA/66, and ATA/33.
- ATA/133 uses an 80-conductor cable with a 40-pin connector.
- The ATA/133 solution addresses large hard drive accessibility issues, and ATA/133 allows the use of hard drives larger than 137.4 GB.

EIDE (Similar to ATA-2) Interface

Enhanced IDE (EIDE) technology is the same technology as IDE/ATA; however, it improves on the original IDE standards by allowing ATA drives to use PIO modes 3 and 4. An EIDE interface can support up to four drives on the same interface, including CD-ROMs and tape drive units. EIDE uses Advanced Technology Attachment Packet Interface (ATAPI) standards to allow a controller to communicate with CD-ROM and tape drive devices.

Serial ATA (SATA)

Just about everything in the computer electronics world eventually evolves into something smaller, faster, and more efficient. This includes the standards for ATA. The Serial ATA (SATA) specification is a serial link point-to-point disk-interface connection standard that was developed by the Serial ATA Working Group to overcome some of the limitations of the earlier mentioned ATA (parallel) specifications. S-ATA is a point-to-point connection that uses a special SATA serial cable, which makes use of a minimum of four wires for sending and receiving data. Figure 7.5 displays a SATA cable and connector. Serial is faster than parallel. The clock rate of the original SATA (unofficially SATA1) was a whopping 1.5 GHz (150 Mbps). Soon after, the SATA 3.0 Gbps standard was released and is backward compatible with SATA1. At current time, the SATA 6.0 standard is being implemented, although the SATA 3.0 standard meets transfer rates of hard drives and other devices.

FIGURE 7.5 A SATA cable.

Following are some very important points to remember regarding the new SATA specification:

- It uses a minimum of four wires with pairs for transmitting and receiving.
- It is a point-to-point connection.
- It has a maximum cable length of 3 feet.
- The increased (3-foot) cable allows the use of external SATA compatible drives (drive arrays).
- It will eliminate the need for master/slave jumper settings in the future.
- Compatible devices are hot swappable.
- Most newer computer systems support a maximum of two S-ATA connections.
- SATAs connect through PCI adapters or chips.
- SATA uses a seven-pin connector that is much more compact than a traditional ATA connector.
- The SATA controller is typically located on the motherboard or implemented as an add-in RAID card.

- With better pin efficiency, SATA uses only 4 signal pins; parallel ATA uses 26 signal pins.
- SATA, which has lower voltage than parallel ATA, reduces input signaling voltages to approximately 250 millivolts, whereas parallel ATA signaling voltages can reach as high as 5V.

Serial ATA (SATA) has been identified as a CompTIA 2006 Objective. The A+ exams will likely ask you to identify SATA connections on a motherboard. Pay close attention to Figure 7.6. Be familiar with this figure for the exam!

FIGURE 7.6   SATA motherboard connections.

Make sure that you are familiar with the important points mentioned in this section. It is very likely that you will run across them in the exam room. The Serial ATA Working Group page is also quite informative at *www.serialata.org/*.

SCSI INTERFACE

If you need more than four devices and want the fastest throughput available for storage devices, then you need an SCSI chain. An *SCSI chain* is a group of SCSI devices attached together with a centralized SCSI controller that requires only one IRQ for the entire chain of devices. SCSI is not technically defined as an interface; it is really an I/O bus in itself.

SCSI technology supports peripheral devices such as hard drives, hard disk arrays, tape units, and CD-ROMs.

If you want to attach a tape drive unit to an SCSI interface, you must enable INT 13h support on the SCSI controller card.

SCSI devices have unique SCSI ID numbers associated with them. These ID numbers are typically set with a jumper block on the SCSI device that includes three switches. Each switch setting represents a series of binary numbers that sets a unique ID for each device. Each number represents the device's position on the SCSI chain; these numbers are 0 through 7 for an SCSI-1 chain. The highest ID that can be assigned on a three-jumper SCSI-1 device is 7. A typical SCSI-1 chain can have up to eight devices (numbered 0 to 7) attached to it. An SCSI controller card is considered a device and uses SCSI ID number 7. That leaves seven SCSI IDs (0 to 6) available for peripheral devices.

A SCSI controller card, otherwise known as an SCSI adapter card, can be plugged into any available PCI, VESA Local (VL-Bus), EISA, or ISA expansion slot.

SCSI priorities are applied from the highest ID number on the SCSI chain to the lowest number. For example, on an SCSI-1 chain, the controller with the unique SCSI ID of 7 has the highest priority. The priority decreases as you move down the SCSI chain to device 0. The same is true for the more popular SCSI-2 chain, which allows for 16 devices numbered 0 to 15. Device 15 would have the highest priority on the chain; device 0 would have the lowest priority.

An SCSI chain must be terminated at both ends. Most SCSI devices come with a built-in terminator (*terminator* is another word for *resistor*). A terminator absorbs a signal so that the signal is not sent back to where it came from, causing a signal collision to occur. If you have an SCSI chain with a hard drive and a CD-ROM, you will need to terminate both ends of the SCSI chain for proper signal transmission to occur. In this case, you would terminate the SCSI hard drive and the SCSI CD-ROM.

There have been several improvements made to SCSI technology since its original implementation. The following list stresses the important facts in reference to SCSI advances:

SCSI-1: The original implementation of SCSI technology, SCSI-1, implements an 8-bit data bus and supports 4 Mbps data transmission rates. It requires a host adapter and can support up to seven other devices. SCSI-1 uses a 25-pin DB connector.

SCSI-2: Similar to SCSI-1, except that SCSI-2 uses a 50-pin Centronics connector, SCSI-2 is the most common implementation of SCSI. It supports up to 16 devices, including the controller card. SCSI-2 introduced the concepts of bus mastering and command queuing to SCSI. These improvements increased transfer rates and allowed SCSI devices to handle multiple instruction sets.

SCSI-3: Also referred to as Fast/Wide SCSI, SCSI-3 is a combination of SCSI specifications. SCSI-3 uses a 16-bit bus and supports data transfer rates to 40 Mbps. SCSI-3 includes three subsets that are known as SCSI parallel interface or SPI specifications. These specifications are SPI-1 (Ultra-SCSI), SPI-2 (Ultra 2 SCSI), and SPI-3 (Ultra 3 SCSI). Each specification adds to the functionality and throughput capabilities of SCSI-3. For the A+ test, 16-bit Fast/Wide SCSI is the most common implementation of SCSI.

SCSI TERMINATION

Both ends of an SCSI bus must be terminated. The use of terminators prevents a signal from becoming distorted and prevents reflection that can cause severe data errors. There are two distinct types of SCSI termination used for a single-ended SCSI bus. They are known as active termination and passive termination.

- *Active termination* uses a voltage regulator to control the impedance at both ends of an SCSI bus. More stable than passive termination, active termination actually maintains a certain amount of impedance. Active termination was developed for a Fast SCSI-2 bus.
- *Passive termination* uses a terminating resistor at the end of an SCSI bus to reduce the amount of reflection. It does not regulate power between a device and a controller; instead, it converts power (usually +5V) to an expected level of impedance. The main purpose of leveling out impedance is to prevent these reflections. This impedance level is typically close to that of the impedance level for the SCSI cable being used. Passive termination was designed for SCSI-1 or SCSI-2 and is less popular than active termination.

If you are interested in learning more details regarding SCSI and SCSI termination, visit the STA (SCSI Trade Association) Web site at:*www.scsita.org/aboutscsi/ SCSI_Termination_Tutorial.html#top.*

NOTE

SCSI offers better transfer rates that SATA and offers support for more devices per channel. Remember, SCSI offers 7 or 15 devices on each channel. Unless using a port multiplier, SATA only offers one device (drive) per channel.

HIGH VOLTAGE DIFFERENTIAL (HVD)

The original SCSI standard for SCSI interfaces was named single-ended (SE) SCSI, or SCSI-1. This specification for SCSI devices, which used a 50-pin connector, proved very susceptible to noise and did not offer long SCSI cable lengths. The HVD SCSI specification was introduced to overcome the noise and short cable length issues present in the original (SE) SCSI specification.

HVD is a method by which an SCSI interface places data signals on an SCSI cable. HVD SCSI interfaces use dual lines for each SCSI data signal. HVD SCSI is less susceptible to noise than SE and has a maximum cable length of 25 meters (approximately 82 feet). HVD SCSI interfaces can provide 20 Mbps data transfer rates for narrow SCSI devices and 40 Mbps transfers for wide SCSI. HVD SCSI uses +5V logic and terminators that run on 5V DC power.

LOW VOLTAGE DIFFERENTIAL (LVD)

LVD is the newer data transmission standard for SCSI devices. LVD uses much less power than HVD and is less expensive. It is backward compatible with earlier single-ended SCSI (SCSI-1 and SCSI-2) and can automatically sense which type of SCSI you have. In other words, when your device is first powered up, LVD can distinguish whether your SCSI device is LVD compatible or single-ended. This autosensing LVD feature is called *multimode operation*. LVD devices standards are defined (fall under) the Ultra 2 SCSI/SCSI-3 standards.

Here are some of the benefits included with the LVD standard:

- LVD uses 3.3V or 1.5V, which replaces the standard +5V used by HVD devices. Do not mix LVD and HVD on SCSI cable (BUS) because they are not electronically compatible, and damage to your LVD-compatible device may result.
- LVD uses a dual wire system (uses two wires for each signal) and filters noise more effectively than HVD.
- The reduction in noise reflections allows for higher transmission rates, which in turn allows for the use of longer data cables. In simple terms, the data signals can travel farther.

HVD and LVD SCSI transmission standards are directly in line with the new A+ Exam Objectives. Make sure you can identify their differences for the exam. Pay particular attention to the benefits of using LVD.

Serial SCSI

The original SCSI standards were actually called Parallel SCSI. Recently, the advent of four variations of SCSI have been developed: SSA, FC-AL, FireWire, and Serial

Attached SCSI (SAS). These versions of SCSI have advantages over the original implementations of SCSI. Primarily, they provide better data transfer rates and support hot swapping. However, this new technology comes at a price. Currently, Serial SCSI devices are more expensive than their parallel predecessor.

DEVICE INSTALLATION, CONFIGURATION, AND TROUBLESHOOTING

A typical IDE/ATA interface supports two devices per motherboard controller. Most systems today have two separate motherboard controllers, allowing for a total of four devices to be attached. An EIDE interface can support up to four devices per controller, for a total of eight devices. EIDE is the same as ATA-2. ATA-2 is an improvement on IDE/ATA that also allows for up to four devices per controller, which equates to eight total devices.

For the purposes of the current A+ exams, we will focus on the traditional IDE/ATA standard interface that allows for two devices to be attached to each of the two motherboard controllers. This allows us to have a total of four devices—for example, two hard drives, a CD-ROM, and a tape drive unit.

IDE hard drives, CD-ROMs, floppy drives, and other storage devices have jumper settings that determine the role they will play on an IDE interface. A *jumper* is a plastic and metal clip that is placed on two or more pins. These pins protrude from a device or a motherboard to close a circuit. With these jumpers, you can set the hard drive to be a master or slave drive, or choose cable-select settings.

If you want to specify a certain connector on an IDE data cable, set your jumpers for cable select.

NOTE

A motherboard typically has a built-in primary and secondary controller (interface). A ribbon cable with a red stripe that represents pin 1 connects the hard drive and an optional device, such as a second hard drive or CD-ROM, to the motherboard's primary IDE controller. Your primary master hard drive should be attached to the connector at the far end of the ribbon cable. When connecting the data cable to the hard drive, make sure that you match pin 1 on the adapter to pin 1 on the hard drive. The slave device should be connected to the middle connector. And finally, attach the other end of the data cable to the motherboard's controller, verifying again that pin 1 on the cable matches pin 1 on the controller. The secondary controller can be used to connect two more devices to the motherboard. If you are only using the primary controller to connect devices, you can disable the secondary controller in the BIOS to free up IRQ 15 for other peripheral devices. The first device attached to the secondary controller is known as the secondary master. The second device attached is called the secondary slave.

If you install a second device to an IDE interface, such as a hard drive, and the operating system is PnP, the operating system will automatically assign a letter designation to the new device.

If you are installing two new hard drives on the same IDE channel, you need to configure one to be the master drive and one to be the slave drive. If you reboot, and the slave drive is not recognized by the system BIOS, you should test the slave drive by configuring it to be the master drive, removing the original master, and rebooting the system. This will tell you if you have an incompatible or bad drive.

If you notice that a hard drive's LED light indicator is constantly lit or pulsing, this is a sign that you need to install more memory.

Following are the basic steps to installing a hard drive:

1. Unplug the power cord that is connected to the back of the computer. Put on your antistatic wrist protector.
2. Remove the screws or clips that attach the computer's case to the system unit itself.
3. Determine whether the hard drive will be installed as a master or a slave device and make the necessary jumper changes on both drives to reflect your decision.
4. Plug one end of the data cable into the hard drive. Ensure that pin 1 on the data cable matches pin 1 on the drive. Plug the center connector into the slave drive if required. Plug the other end of the ribbon cable into the motherboard, also matching pin 1 of the cable to pin 1 on the motherboard's controller.
5. Connect an available system power connector into the hard drive's power socket. Do the same for the slave drive if using a slave drive.
6. Anchor the hard drive or drives into an open drive bay with screws.
7. Replace the system unit's cover. Take your wrist strap off. Plug the computer's power cord back into the system. Power the computer on.
8. If the CMOS hard drive settings are set to autodetect, the hard drive or drives should be detected for you. If not, you will have to manually set the drive's geometry, including the number of cylinders, sectors, and heads, in the CMOS settings.
9. Partition and format the drive or drives if no operating system is present.

RAID (REDUNDANT ARRAY OF INDEPENDENT DISKS)

Although the A+ exams are not likely to nail you with high-level questions regarding the various types of RAID (Redundant Array of Independent Disks) implementations, you need to understand the basic implementations of RAID. Besides, anyone pursuing a career in the computing industry needs to understand fault-tolerance basics and RAID.

RAID is one of the most popular means of providing fault-tolerant systems in use today. Through a process known as disk or "data" striping, RAID divides data into separate units and distributes the data across two or more hard disks. There are many variations of RAID available, but the most popular are the following:

RAID level 0: This level of RAID is not considered fault tolerant. It spreads data in blocks across multiple disks but provides no data redundancy. This level of RAID only produces better performance. If one disk fails with this configuration, all data is lost.

RAID level 1: This level is also known as "disk mirroring." With RAID level 1, all data is duplicated or written to a second hard disk. If one of the disks fails, the information is still available on the second disk. This level of RAID is fault tolerant, although its performance is not rated as well as RAID level 5.

RAID level 3: This level also spreads data units across several disks, but it also uses a dedicated disk for parity information, which is used for error-correction purposes. In simple terms, it provides a basic level of fault tolerance.

RAID level 5: This level provides excellent fault tolerance and good performance. It stores parity information across all disks in the disk array and provides concurrent disk reads and writes. It is the most popular RAID implementation.

With all that being said about RAID, it is important that you know that RAID requires fast controllers/interfaces to be effective. All that reading and writing to multiple hard disks can quickly hamper a workstation's or server's capability to properly store and process data.

OPTICAL STORAGE DEVICES

Optical storage devices and the usefulness of optical storage media, such as the Compact Disc Read-Only-Memory (CD-ROM), Compact Disc Recordable (CD-R), Compact Disc Rewritable (CD-RW), and Digital Versatile Disk (DVD), have taken the computer industry by storm. Optical media were originally intended as a replacement for recordable cassette tapes in the music industry; but as we know, optical media offer many advantages to the data storage world and have put the once beloved 1.44 MB floppy disk to shame. Although optical storage devices have a much slower access time than hard drive technologies, they offer many benefits. We can store books, music, pictures, and files on optical storage media. We can watch movies with DVD technology. The possibilities are almost endless, at least until the next form of storage media comes around.

CD-ROM

A CD-ROM is an optical storage disc capable of storing large amounts of data. A typical CD-ROM can hold 600 MB to 800 MB of information. This is equal to the storage capacity of about 700 1.44 MB floppy disks. CD-ROMs are well suited for storing graphics files, movies, and music. A CD-ROM is typically written to, or burned, once with information provided by the manufacturers of the CD-ROM. Optical media such as CD-ROMs have information burned into them by a laser beam. Actually, the term *burned* is used quite loosely here. For information to be written to a CD-ROM, the actual process involves changing the reflective proper-ties of an organic dye that covers a CD-ROM by using a laser. The data can only be written to a disc one time. Reading the data on a CD-ROM requires the use of a CD-ROM device or player.

CD-ROM players and writers can be installed internally or connected externally to a computer system. Most computers today come with an internal CD-ROM player installed. An internal CD-ROM device is typically installed as a slave device on either the primary or secondary IDE controller. An external CD-ROM device is con-nected to an SCSI, parallel, or USB port.

MSCDEX.EXE (Microsoft CD-ROM Extension) is a file that contains a 16-bit software driver, which enables older operating systems, such as DOS and Windows 3.x, to interact with and control CD-ROM players. MSCDEX was later replaced in Windows 95 by the 32-bit CD-ROM File System (CDFS), which offered better performance.

CD-R

A CD-R is an optical form of media that allows information to be written to the CD-ROM one time and read many times by the end user. It is sometimes referred to as Write-Once, Read-Many (WORM). To create CD-ROMs using CD-R technology, you need a CD-R drive and a CD-R software program installed in your system.

CD-R technology is excellent for storing personal data and providing data backup capabilities. When purchasing such a unit and software, make sure that it has the capabilities for multisession recording. This is the ability to add files to a section of the CD-ROM that has not yet been written to. CD-R technology has become more affordable and is now commonplace.

CD-RW

CD-RW is the most popular CD technology at the present time. A CD-RW disc, with the use of a CD-ROM writing device, allows you to write information to the entire disk many times (approximately 25 times). CD-RW disks are more expensive than CD-R but are well worth the price for the capabilities they offer. CD-RW technology will most likely be replaced by DVD technology as DVD storage advances become more affordable.

DVD

DVD is the optical player and storage technology of choice. It has the capability to store up to 17 GB of data, which is many times that of a CD-ROM, and can support several full-length motion pictures on one disc. DVD uses Motion Pictures Expert Group (MPEG) compression standards to provide its tremendous storage capabilities. Another great feature of DVD technology is that it is backward compatible with CD-R and CD-RW. This means that DVD drives can read CD-ROMs that you have created with CD-R or CD-RW technology.

Several types of DVD technology are available today:

DVD-ROM: This is the DVD drive installed in your computer.

DVD-R: Similar to CD-R technology, the DVD-R disc can record, or be written to, one time. It is capable of recording up to 3.95 GB of information.

DVD-RW: With this DVD-based technology, this disc can be written to many times and can store data on either side of the disc.

DVD-RAM: Similar to CD-RW, a DVD-RAM disc can be written to many times (approximately 100,000 times). However, a double-sided DVD-RAM can store up to 9.4 GB, dwarfing the storage capacity of CD-RW and DVD-RW. DVD-RAM drives are most often backward compatible and can read most variations of both CD and DVD technologies.

TEST-RELATED TIPS FOR OPTICAL DEVICES

If a CD or DVD unit has become inoperative, and you need to open the tray that holds the CD or DVD media, you can insert a pin or paper clip into the tiny hole on the front of the unit. This forces it to open the tray.

If you have inserted a music CD into your CD device, and no sound is coming from the PC or connected stereo speakers, verify that the audio cable is connected to an installed sound card.

If you install a new CD-ROM, CD-RW, or DVD device into a computer, and it doesn't work after the installation, the first troubleshooting step should be to verify that the jumper settings on the device are configured properly.

SuperDisks and Zip Drives

SuperDisks and Zip drives are used to store substantial amounts of information, which can help you free up hard disk space. They are excellent portable storage alternatives when you need more storage capability than a 1.44 MB floppy can provide.

The average SuperDisk can store 120 MB of data, while remaining compatible with the average 1.44 MB floppy disk. SuperDrive technology supports IDE, PCM-CIA, USB, and parallel connectivity.

Zip disks resemble floppy disks but are about twice as thick. Zip disks can store either 100 MB or 250 MB, which is convenient for storing graphics or any other large files or programs for archival purposes, as well as for exchanging large amounts of information. Zip drive technology supports a parallel or SCSI connection. The Zip drive can be external or internal to the system unit.

Thumb Drives, Flash Drives, and SD cards

USB thumb drives (flash drives) are typically small, lightweight, portable, rewriteable flash-type drives that currently come in 32 MB to 64 GB storage capacities. They are the most popular portable backup and transfer devices today. USB thumb drives offer several advantages over other portable storage devices such as floppy disks. They are smaller and faster, hold more data, and are more dependable. Most operating systems such as Windows, Linux, and MAC OS come with built-in support for these devices as well. Operating systems such as Windows Vista take full advantage of USB flash drive technology. In fact, Windows Vista ReadyBoost uses USB flash to act as system memory.

A Secure Digital (SD) card is a flash-type memory card used in portable devices such as PDAs, digital cameras, cell phones, and GPS units. Most modern SD cards are available in storage capacities that range from 8 MBs to 8 GBs.

Backups Tapes and Backup Types

Creating a copy of your critical files, programs, and configured operating systems is critical to the life of your business (and your job) in the event of hardware or software malfunction or other disaster.

Removable storage media such as floppy disk, Zip disk, optical disk, tape cartridge, CD-ROM, DVD, or removable hard drives can be used in combination with software to backup your data to and store that data offsite in case of a disaster or emergency. The type of storage media you use will depend on the amount of information you need to back up and the speed at which you need the backup to process.

Many types of backup software packages are available on the market that allow you to carry out various backup types and functions. Two of the most popular are ARCServe by Computer Associates and Backup Exec by Veritas. Most operating systems available today come with their own internal backup programs. For example, most versions of Windows come with Microsoft Backup. Unix and Linux operating systems offer the tar (tape archive) command.

BACKUP TYPES

The backup type and plan you implement depends on the amount of data you have to back up and the frequency at which the data changes. In other words, if the majority of your files, folders, and other data change consistently throughout the day, you may want to consider a full backup on a daily basis. However, if the majority of your data does not change quite so often, you may want to consider a one-time weekly full backup and a daily incremental or differential backup.

GFS (Grandfather-Father-Son) backup strategy is the name that is often used to describe a backup strategy that includes a daily, weekly, and monthly backup. With this type of backup system, the daily backup is considered the son, the weekly full backup is the father, and the last full backup of the month is considered the grandfather. This backup strategy is based on seven backups a week. A full backup is run once a week and an incremental or differential backup is run on the other days.

Make sure you are familiar with GFS for this exam.

NOTE

Whether you choose a daily incremental or a daily differential backup, it mainly depends on how much media you have available and how fast you want to be able to restore the data.

A+, Network+, Security+, and countless other certification exams often focus on what type of backup method to use for the "easiest" or "fastest" restore in a given situation. Do not miss the easy questions! A GFS backup strategy using a daily differential backup provides the "easiest" and "fastest" restore! Be careful on the exam. Some questions may be provided to you with very minimal information and leave you wondering how they can ask such questions. Try to keep focus on the overall concept CompTIA is targeting.

NOTE

Files and folders that reside in most popular operating systems have four basic attributes assigned to them: read-only, hidden, system, and archive. When a file or folder has been added, written to, or changed, the archive bit changes. Backup system software uses the properties of this archive bit to determine whether or not the file or folder should be backed up based on this "flagged" archive bit. Keep this in mind as you study the following basic backup types that you will need to know for the exam:

Full: This backup type includes all folders, directories, files, and programs that reside on a system or disk. A full backup resets all archive bits regardless of their status. It is not typically productive to run a full backup every business day unless you have an incredible amount of backup storage space or a very small business with few systems.

Incremental: With this type of backup, only files that have changed or have been added since the last full or incremental backup are backed up. The archive bit is cleared or "reset." If you have a large amount of daily information to back up, you should consider a backup plan that includes one weekly full backup and a daily incremental backup. Remember, if you need to do a restore with this plan, you will need to use your weekly full backup tape and every incremental tape created since the last full backup for a proper restore. In simple terms, an incremental backup job will run faster than a differential, but it will take longer to restore.

Differential: This backup type does not clear the archive bit (or set it to off). A differential restore is simply restoring the last full backup tape followed by the most recent differential backup tape. In simple terms, a differential backup job will take longer than an incremental to back up, but it will do a restore much faster than an incremental.

Copy: A copy is simply a backup of files, folders, and directories that are copied to another location, whether it is a network share, tape, or hard drive.

CHAPTER SUMMARY

This chapter covered very important material in relation to the current A+ exams and its heavy focus on storage devices and their interfaces. We covered the installation, configuration, and troubleshooting of the major storage devices and their components. To be a proficient computer technician, you need hands-on practice installing and troubleshooting storage devices and computer-related equipment.

REVIEW QUESTIONS

1. **A technician installs a 2 GB hard drive and proceeds to run the FDISK utility. FDISK only shows a 540 MB hard drive. What action did not take place?**

   ○ A. FDISK will only recognize 540 MB by default.
   ○ B. The version of FDISK was not updated.
   ○ C. The BIOS was never updated.
   ○ D. The technician should have run Defrag.

   Correct Answer = C

   When installing a new hard drive, it is important to verify that your hard drive settings have been updated in the system BIOS settings. If your BIOS settings for your hard drive are set to AUTO (autodetect), the full capacity of your hard drive should be recognized.

2. **What is the maximum number of devices, not including the SCSI controller card, that can be attached to a fast-wide SCSI-2 bus?**

   ○ A. 1
   ○ B. 7
   ○ C. 10
   ○ D. 15

   Correct Answer = D

   A fast-wide SCSI-2 bus can support 15 devices not including the SCSI controller card. SCSI-1 can support 7 devices.

3. **Which numbers display the SCSI priorities for devices on a SCSI chain from lowest to highest?**

   ○ A. 1-8
   ○ B. 7-1
   ○ C. 0-15
   ○ D. 2-14

   Correct Answer = C

   On a SCSI-1 chain, the controller with the unique SCSI ID of 7 has the highest priority. The priority decreases until you move down the SCSI chain to device 0. The same is true for the more popular SCSI 2 chain, which allows for 16 devices numbered 0-15. Device 15 would have the highest priority on the chain; device 0 would have the lowest priority. The answer to this question is 0-15.

4. **Your computer made a grinding noise and then the screen goes blank. What is the most probable cause?**

    ○ A. The R/W heads crashed onto the hard drive's platter.
    ○ B. A virus caused your resolution to exceed itself.
    ○ C. Your computer went into Hibernation Mode.
    ○ D. You installed your hard drive cable backwards resulting in a crash.

    Correct Answer = A

    If you hear a grinding noise coming from inside your computer, your R/W heads may be "crashing" onto the hard drive's platter. This will most likely result in a hard drive failure.

5. **You have noticed that your system is running slower over time, and you also notice several bad sectors. What two utilities would you run to rectify this situation?**

    ○ A. FDISK and FORMAT from the command prompt.
    ○ B. COMMAND.COM and Defrag.
    ○ C. Create 23 logical partitions and make one active.
    ○ D. ScanDisk with the Thorough option and Defrag.

    Correct Answer = D

    If you are developing bad sectors on your hard drive, it is a good idea to run ScanDisk and select the Thorough option in the ScanDisk settings options. Running Defrag will place the files stored on your hard drive in contiguous order resulting in better file access performance.

6. **You want to add a second IDE hard drive to your system. You only have one IDE controller on your motherboard. The controller is already connected to a hard drive and a CD-ROM. What would you do?**

    ○ A   Install an IDE add-on card.
    ○ B. Use a hard drive on the network.
    ○ C. Unplug the CD-ROM, and attach the second hard drive when you want to use it.
    ○ D. Connect the second hard drive to a floppy drive controller.

    Correct Answer = A

If your motherboard does not have an IDE/ATA interface, or your system only has one IDE controller, you can purchase an IDE add-on expansion card, such as a PCI card that supports this technology. This will allow you to have up to four devices.

7. **You install a 5.25-inch floppy drive. When you power the computer on, the floppy drive light stays on. Where did you go wrong?**
   - ○ A. You plugged the floppy drive cable in backwards.
   - ○ B. You have an incompatible slave drive configuration.
   - ○ C. You dislodged the onboard video card.
   - ○ D. You didn't update the BIOS.

   Correct Answer = A

   If you plug the floppy drive's data cable in backwards, the LED light on the front of the floppy drive unit will stay lit, and you will not be able to access the floppy drive.

8. **You power your computer on and receive a "Bad or missing operating system" message. What is most likely the cause of this message?**
   - ○ A. Your memory is corrupt.
   - ○ B. You have an incompatible slave drive configuration.
   - ○ C. You have a missing or corrupt boot sector.
   - ○ D. Your SCSI controller card has a priority of 15.

   Correct Answer = C

   If your boot sector becomes damaged or corrupt, you will most likely receive a "Bad or missing operating system" error message.

9. **A SCSI adapter card can be used with which available expansion slots? (Choose 3)**
   - ☐ A. PCI
   - ☐ B. VL-Bus
   - ☐ C. EISA
   - ☐ D. USB
   - ☐ E. AGP

   Correct Answers = A, B, and C

   A SCSI adapter card can be plugged into any available PCI, VESA local (VL-Bus), EISA, or ISA expansion slots.

10. **A technician installs a brand new hard drive and attempts to format the drive. Unfortunately, the technician receives a message stating, "Invalid media type." What should the technician do?**

    ○ A.   Purchase another brand new hard drive
    ○ B.   Schedule ScanDisk and reboot
    ○ C.   Run Defrag.
    ○ D.   Run antivirus software immediately.
    ○ E.   Use the FDISK utility.

    Correct Answer = E

    If you are installing a new hard drive and receive an "Invalid media type" error message after booting the computer, you will need to use the FDISK utility to repartition the drive and set the active partition.

11. **Which of the following hard drive settings are stored in CMOS?**

    ○ A.   RMA, HDD, LBA
    ○ B.   Manufacturer, ship date, RMA
    ○ C.   Cylinders, heads, and sectors
    ○ D.   Jumper settings, HDD backup
    ○ E.   HDD, LVD, and HVD
    ○ F.   All of the above

    Correct Answer = C

    If the CMOS hard drive settings are set to auto-detect, the hard drive or drives should be detected for you. If not, you will have to manually set the drive's geometry, including the number of cylinders, sectors, and heads in the CMOS settings.

12. **This serial standard is faster than parallel ATA. It is a hot-swappable, point-to-point standard that offers a maximum cable length of 3 feet. What is the standard being described?**

    ○ A.   USB-ATA
    ○ B.   Fast/Wide-ATA
    ○ C.   ESDI
    ○ D.   SATA
    ○ E.   Ultra-ATA
    ○ F.   None of the above

    Correct Answer = D

The Serial ATA (SATA) specification is a serial link point-to-point disk-interface connection standard that was developed by the Serial ATA Working Group to overcome some of the limitations of ATA (parallel) specifications. SATA is a point-to-point connection that uses a special SATA serial cable.

13. **What type of connector does Serial ATA use?**
    - ○ A. 26-pin
    - ○ B. 40-pin
    - ○ C. 7-pin
    - ○ D. 15-pin
    - ○ E. No pins
    - ○ F. None of the above

    Correct Answer = C

    SATA uses a 7-pin connector that is much more compact than a traditional ATA connector.

14. **What do you need to run in Ultra ATA/100 mode?**
    - ○ A. An operating system that can handle DMA transfers
    - ○ B. An Ultra ATA-capable 40 pin, 80-conductor cable
    - ○ C. An Ultra ATA/100-compatible device
    - ○ D. An Ultra ATA/100-capable system board and BIOS
    - ○ E. All of the above
    - ○ F. None of the above

    Correct Answer = E

    For a system to run in Ultra ATA /100 mode, you need an Ultra ATA/100-capable system board and BIOS; an Ultra ATA-capable 40 pin, 80-conductor cable; and an operating system that can handle DMA transfers. Windows 95 (OSR2), 98, Windows Me, Windows 2000, Windows XP and Vista are all capable of this.

15. **Low Voltage Differential (LVD) is the new data transmission standard for SCSI devices. Which of the following choices describe LVD?**
    - ○ A. LVD uses 3.3V or 1.5V, which replaces the standard +5V.
    - ○ B. LVD uses a dual wire system and filters noise more effectively.
    - ○ C. LVD allows for the use of longer data cables.
    - ○ D. LVD's autosensing feature is called multimode operation.
    - ○ E. All of the above

Correct Answer = E

LVD uses 3.3V or 1.5V, which replaces the standard +5V used by HVD. LVD uses a dual wire system (uses two wires for each signal) and filters noise more effectively than HVD. Data signals can travel farther allowing for the use of longer data cables. LVD's autosensing feature called multi-mode operation, can distinguish whether your SCSI device is LVD compatible or single-ended.

16. **What does active termination use to control the impedance of a data signal at both ends of a SCSI bus?**
    ○ A. Voltage regulator
    ○ B. MSCDEX
    ○ C. Terminating resistor
    ○ D. Seven-pin connector
    ○ E. A dongle

    Correct Answer = A

    Active termination uses a voltage regulator to control the impedance at both ends of a SCSI bus. More stable than passive termination, active termination actually maintains a certain amount of impedance.

17. **What does passive termination use at the end of a SCSI bus to reduce reflection?**
    ○ A. Voltage regulator
    ○ B. Voltmeter
    ○ C. Terminating resistor
    ○ D. Voltage resistor
    ○ E. Terminating regulator

    Correct Answer = C

    Passive termination uses a terminating resistor at the end of a SCSI bus to reduce the amount of reflection.

18. **What was the original standard for SCSI interfaces called?**
    ○ A. GOSCSI
    ○ B. SE
    ○ C. HVD
    ○ D. LVD
    ○ E. Differential

Correct Answer = B

The original SCSI standard for SCSI interfaces was named single ended (SE) SCSI. This specification for SCSI devices proved very susceptible to noise and did not offer long SCSI cable lengths.

19. **Which RAID level provides the best level of fault tolerance and performance?**

    ○ A.   RAID 32
    ○ B.   RAID 0
    ○ C.   RAID 1
    ○ D.   RAID 5
    ○ E.   None of the above

    Correct Answer = D

    RAID level 5 places parity information across all disks in an array. It provides the best combination of fault tolerance and performance of the popular RAID implementations.

20. **You are upgrading a system with two new hard drives. One is 120 GB, and the other is 200 GB. You want the 200 GB drive to be the master, and you want both drives on the same IDE channel. How do you configure the master/slave settings on an IDE bus channel?**

    ○ A.   IDE bus settings in the CMOS
    ○ B.   IDE bus setting in the BIOS
    ○ C.   Hard drive jumpers on the motherboard
    ○ D.   Jumper settings on the hard drives
    ○ E.   None of the above

    Correct Answer = D

    Hard drive master/slave configurations are determined by the jumper settings on the hard drives. There can only be two IDE devices attached to one IDE bus. That is why most systems have two IDE controllers so that up to four IDE devices can be attached to a system. For more IDE devices, you could purchase an IDE expansion board. All other answers are incorrect. If you were tricked by this question, you are not ready to take the exams!

21. **You are a certified A+ Technician. Your apprentice, who states he has the A+ credentials, has just installed two drives on a secondary IDE controller channel. Unfortunately, when the system boots, neither of the drives are recognized. What would do first to solve this problem? (Choose 2)**

    ☐ A.   Check your apprentice's A+ credentials.
    ☐ B.   Check the master\slave configuration settings on both of the drives.
    ☐ C.   Check the IDE cables.
    ☐ D.   Check the boot.ini settings in the OS.
    ☐ E.   Check the CMOS settings.

    Correct Answers = B and C

    Although it would be a good idea at this point for future reference, checking your apprentice's A+ credentials with CompTIA will not resolve this issue. If hard drives are not recognized after an installation, the master\slave configurations settings are more than likely misconfigured on the drive or drives, or there is a problem with the physical IDE cable.

22. **You are upgrading a system that currently has four IDE devices. A DVD drive and three hard drives. You want to add three more IDE hard drives to the system for RAID purposes. How many IDE controllers will be required to support all of the IDE devices you need in this system?**

    ○ A.   2
    ○ B.   4
    ○ C.   7
    ○ D.   5
    ○ E.   None of the above

    Correct Answer = B

    As mentioned earlier, most systems have two IDE controllers so that up to four IDE devices can be attached to a system. In this case, you would need to get an IDE expansion card to increase the number of IDE controllers. Because one controller can support two devices, you would need four controllers to support the seven IDE devices total you want installed.

23. **Four users at your administrative office have been given USB removable hard drives to back up and secure their important data. They all have fairly new systems and use multiple USB devices such as mice and keyboards. You need to implement a solution to support the new USB hard drives the users have been given. What should you do?**

   ○ A. Get a USB hub (self-powered), and attach the USB removable drives to it.
   ○ B. Get a bus-USB hub, and attach the USB drives to it.
   ○ C. Tell the users to back up their data on their local "C" drives.
   ○ D. None of the above

   Correct Answer = A

   You should get a USB hub (self-powered) and attach the USB removable drives to it. USB hard drives typically use more power than is available through a bus-powered USB hub and telling the users to back up their data on their local "C" drives will not provide a good solution if their "C" drives fail!

REFERENCES

www.serialata.org/. This site is the home of the Serial ATA Working Group. Serial ATA interface standards information is available at this site.

www.scsita.org/aboutscsi/SCSI_Termination_Tutorial.html#top. This SCSI Trade Association Web site has an easy-to-understand paper regarding SCSI and SCSI termination.

8

Cables, Connectors, and Ports

In This Chapter

- External Ports
- Asynchronous and Synchronous Transmission
- Parallel Ports and Connectors
- Serial Ports and Connectors
- Keyboard and Mouse Connectors
- Video Connectors
- USB Connections
- FireWire (IEEE 1394)
- SCSI Connectors
- Networking Connectors and Cables
- Wireless Connectivity

Computing systems and other electronic devices use cables, connectors, and ports as a means to connect to and communicate with other devices. A cable is used to connect two devices. On each end of a cable is a connector; connectors are characterized as male or female. A cable's male connector plugs into a female port, which may reside on a computer system or peripheral device. A female connector is connected to a male port, which may also be located on a system or peripheral device. Ports can be classified as internal or external to a system. Internal ports reside inside the system unit and connect components and devices directly to the motherboard. External ports are an extension of the motherboard or a peripheral device's circuit board that protrudes from the system or device. A port on the back of a system unit is often referred to as a connector. It is important for the purposes of the test that you realize the term *port* can be used interchangeably with the term *connector*. As you go through this chapter, you will be introduced to some of the finer details related to cables and connectors. It is important to keep in mind that the exam will focus on the DB 25-pin and 36-pin Centronics D-shell parallel connector, 9-pin serial (COM) connector, DB 15-pin video connector, game/MIDI port connector, and 50-pin SCSI cable connector.

EXTERNAL PORTS

On the back of a computer system, you will find ports that are an extension of the motherboard's form factor. You may find port extensions for devices such as NICs, AGP cards, modems, or sound cards. The expansion cards that these ports are attached to are inserted into the motherboard's form factor. Most motherboards today are based on the ATX form factor, as described in Chapter 2, and include external connections for a parallel port, two serial ports, USB or FireWire (IEEE 1394) ports, a game controller port with microphone and speaker jacks, and a video port. Figure 8.1 shows the external ports associated with the ATX form factor. Pay special attention to the keyboard and mouse PS/2 connectors; the exam may focus on your ability to identify these in a graphic.

The central focus of this chapter is these ports and the connectors associated with them. Before we continue with the fine details of ports and connectors, you need to understand the transmission methods that many devices are capable of using.

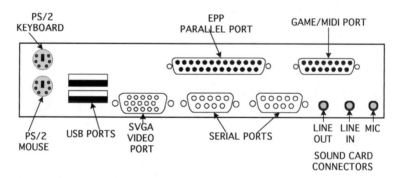

FIGURE 8.1 ATX form factor and external ports.

ASYNCHRONOUS AND SYNCHRONOUS TRANSMISSION

Most peripheral devices, such as printers, scanners, and modems, use *asynchronous* transmission methods. With asynchronous transmission, data is not synchronized. Unlike synchronous transmission, data is not sent as a steady stream in a predetermined fashion. Instead, a start bit and a stop bit are placed between each piece, or "packet" of information. Asynchronous transmission methods are typically used for devices attached to parallel or serial ports.

Unlike asynchronous transmissions, synchronous transmissions are steady streams of data that are predetermined by a clock or counter. The CPU communicates with internal devices synchronously, basing the transmission of data and instructions on its own internal clock.

TRANSMISSION MODES

When two devices connect to each other, they establish and use a transmission mode. The transmission mode established between the two devices depends on the technology and configuration of the devices. Three general transmission modes are available that determine whether the transmission of data between two devices will occur only one way, one way at a time, or both ways at the same time. These transmission modes are simplex, half-duplex, and full-duplex.

Simplex: The simplex form of data transmission goes only one way; data or information can be transmitted in only one direction. A radio and speakers are examples of devices that use simplex communication.

Half-duplex: With half-duplex data transmission, data can be transmitted in both directions but can only be transmitted in one direction at a time. An example of this transmission method is a walkie-talkie: both parties can speak, but only one party can speak at a time.

If two devices are set up so that they cannot send and receive data at the same time, they are using half-duplex data transmission.

Full-duplex: In full-duplex transmission, or simultaneous transmission, data or voice can be transmitted and received at exactly the same time. Human speech during a regular phone conversation is an example of full-duplex transmission that doesn't work well. Two parties can speak at the same time, although they might not understand each other.

PARALLEL PORTS AND CONNECTORS

A parallel port, otherwise referred to as LPT1 or LPT2, is an external interface associated with the IEEE 1284 standard that is used to connect a computer to peripheral devices such as printers, CD-ROM players, scanners, or tape unit devices. Figure 8.1 shows a standard parallel port on the back of a system unit. A parallel port uses parallel transmission methods to transmit or send data one byte at a time to a peripheral device. A parallel cable has eight internal wires, and each wire is capable of sending 1 bit of information at a time. (Remember, there are 8 bits in 1 byte.) Information is transmitted 8 bits across all at once, for a total of 1 byte, in only one direction at a time using parallel transmission.

It is important to note for the exams that parallel transmission methods are faster than serial transmissions. Serial transmission methods will be discussed shortly.

A parallel port on the back of a computer system is a female DB-25 connector that accepts a DB 25-pin male connector on one end of a parallel cable. The other end of a parallel cable has a 36-pin male Centronics D-shell connector that connects to a Centronics connector located on the back of a printer or device. Figure 8.2 shows the connectors on both ends of a typical parallel printer cable. Printer and scanner Centronics connectors typically use two clips to secure the connector to the port located on the back of the device. In addition, it is important to note that a parallel cable can also be used to connect or network two computers together.

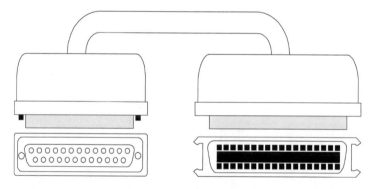

FIGURE 8.2   A parallel printer cable.

To ensure that the signals traveling down a parallel wire do not become distorted, the length of a parallel cable should not exceed 10 feet. Remember for the exams that parallel transmission occurs 1 byte at a time.

The newest addition to the IEEE 1284 standard for bidirectional communications and printing is the Type C-Mini 36-pin parallel connector. Also known as Half Pitch Centronics36 connectors, these compact-size parallel connectors are often used with laptops and some newer printers. The Type C-Mini 36-pin parallel connector also provides support for Enhanced Parallel Port (EPP) applications.

The Type C-Mini 36-pin connector has been identified as one of the A+ 2006 Objective additions. Make sure that you are aware that this is an IEEE 1284 Mini 36-pin parallel connector with clip latches, which provides support for EPP applications.

In concluding our discussion of parallel cables and connectors, there are three types of parallel connections that you should be familiar with:

Type A: A DB-25 male or female connector that uses thumbscrews.

Type B: The standard Centronics 36-pin ribbon connector plug.

Type C: The Mini 36-pin Centronics connector plug with clip latches.

The following RAM Electronics Industries, Inc. Web site offers some very good images of the three main parallel connector types as well as many of the other connectors mentioned in this chapter: *www.ramelectronics.net/html/connecters.html.*

SERIAL PORTS AND CONNECTORS

Older computers typically came equipped with one or two RS232C-compliant serial ports that are also located on the back of a computer system. (Refer to Figure 8.1 for a standard serial port.) A serial port transmits data 1 bit at a time. To transmit a byte (8 bits) serially, 8 separate bits are transmitted one at a time, one after another. For example, try to picture pouring eight marbles into a funnel all at the same time. Only one of the marbles can exit the funnel at a time. All the other marbles will follow the first marble until the funnel is empty. Serial transmission is much slower than any of the parallel transmission techniques.

An operating system identifies serial ports in the BIOS setup program and references the serial ports as COM ports. The first serial port is referenced as COM1, the second serial port is referenced as COM2, and so on for COM3 and COM4.

Serial ports can come in the form of a DB 9-pin or older style DB 25-pin male connector. Most systems today have one DB 9-pin (male) serial port that is used for a serial mouse or a communications device, such as a modem.

Two basic serial cables are available that are used to connect a device to a serial port. The most common serial cable in use today has a DB 9-pin female adapter on one end of the cable that plugs into the DB 9-pin male serial port on the system unit. The other end of the cable has a DB 25-pin male connector, which is connected to a DB 25-pin female connector on the external device. An older-style serial cable is the DB 25-pin female to DB 25-pin male, which can connect two devices that have DB 25-pin serial ports. Yes, serial cables can network two computers together, but you should expect very slow transmission rates. Regardless of which serial cable is in use, the maximum length of a serial cable should not exceed 25 feet. Figure 8.3 displays the pin array configurations for male and female DB 9-pin and DB 25-pin serial connectors.

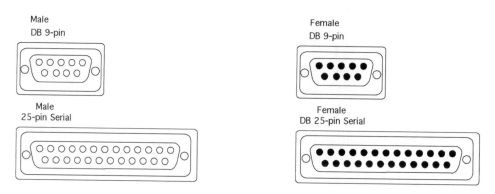

FIGURE 8.3   Male and female DB 9-pin and DB 25-pin serial connectors.

KEYBOARD AND MOUSE CONNECTORS

Three main types of connectors are used for keyboards and mice: the 5-pin Deutsche Industrie Norm (DIN) connector, the 6-pin Mini-DIN (PS/2) connector, and the USB mouse and keyboard connector. Modern ATX form factor motherboards use PS/2 connectors for both the mouse and the keyboard. Older AT systems typically used a 5-pin DIN connector for the keyboard and a serial mouse. Figure 8.4 shows a 5-pin DIN and a 6-pin Mini-DIN (PS/2) connector.

The 5-pin DIN keyboard connector was used in AT- and XT-class computers for a keyboard connection. It is much larger than a 6-pin mini-DIN connector and requires its own 5-pin port. The more popular 6-pin Mini-DIN, otherwise known as a PS/2 connector, is the standard connector in use today for mice and keyboards. Nearly all systems today support PS/2 connections for mice and keyboards. Refer to Figure 8.1 for PS/2 mouse and keyboard ports on the back of a system using the ATX form factor.

Newer systems support USB mice and keyboard connections, which are very easy to install, support, and use. USB connectors will be discussed shortly.

Older systems use a serial port DB-9 connector for what is commonly referred to as a bus mouse. A bus mouse requires the use of a free COM port and IRQ.

FIGURE 8.4   A 5-pin DIN and 6-pin Mini-DIN connector.

Following are some very important facts to remember about mice and keyboards for the exams. The most important feature to look for when replacing a mouse or keyboard is the connector associated with the device.

- A PS/2 mouse and an ATX-style keyboard connector look identical. It is easy to make the mistake of plugging the keyboard connector into the mouse port, or vice versa.

You should only connect a PS/2 mouse or keyboard to a system unit if the system is powered off. If the system is on when you make a keyboard or mouse swap, it is possible that the mouse or keyboard may not be recognized.

NOTE

- USB mice and keyboards can be replaced, or "hot-swapped" while a system is running.

VIDEO CONNECTORS

All computer monitors have at least one thing in common: they all connect to a female DB 15-pin port on the back of a computer system. (Figure 8.1 shows a standard female DB 15-pin video port on the back of a system unit.) The DB 15-pin port may be attached directly to the motherboard, or it may be located on a video expansion card.

The female DB 15-pin port has three rows of five pinholes that accept a male DB 15-pin connector, which is attached to the end of the monitor's cable. Each of the 15 pins on the monitor's DB-15 connector has a different pin assignment that carries out a specified video function related to power, color, or refresh rate. Many monitor-related problems can occur if one of these pins gets bent or broken. You must take great care when connecting a DB 15-pin connector to a DB 15-pin port on the back of your system. Table 8.1 displays the functionality of each of the 15 pins on a DB 15-pin video connector.

The A+ exams are likely to present you with a question or diagram that tests your knowledge of the difference between a DB 15-pin video connector and a game/MIDI port, otherwise known as a joystick/MIDI port on a sound card. (See Figure 8.1 for the location of a game/MIDI port on a system unit.)

Remember for the exam that a female DB 15-pin video port has three rows of five pinholes. A joystick/MIDI port on a sound card has two rows of pinholes: one row of eight pinholes and one row of seven pinholes.

NOTE

TABLE 8.1 Individual Pin Assignments for a DB 15-Pin Video Connector

Pin Number	Video Function
1	Red video
2	Green video
3	Blue video
4	Monitor identification 2
5	Ground pin/unused
6	Red video return
7	Green video return
8	Blue video return
9	Unused
10	Ground
11	Monitor identification 0
12	Monitor identification 1
13	Horizontal synchronization
14	Vertical synchronization
15	Unused

USB CONNECTIONS

As mentioned in Chapter 2, USB is a fairly new technology that supports mice, keyboards, scanners, printers, and digital cameras. USB is an external serial bus that supports both low-speed and high-speed devices, and it offers data transfer rates of up to 12 Mbps. Some of the advantages that USB technology has to offer are listed here:

- USB can support up to 127 devices with the use of one system resource.
- USB is PnP compliant; USB devices are automatically recognized and configured by the operating system.
- USB supports hot plugging.
- The cables and connectors that are used to attach USB devices to a system are standardized.

USB devices can be hot-swapped while an operating system is up and running. This means that you can attach or detach a USB mouse or keyboard when a computer is powered on.

The exam will likely display several adapter images. Be prepared to identify a USB connector.

NOTE

Two types of USB connectors are in use today. Type A USB connectors have one of their connectors permanently attached to a device, such as a keyboard or a mouse. Type B USB connectors are totally detachable from both a device and a port. Figure 8.5 displays a typical Type A USB connector. Type A connectors look like a rectangle, and Type B connectors look like a rounded square. You can't plug a Type A connector into a Type B port and vice versa.

FIGURE 8.5   A typical type A USB connector.

One end of a Type A connector is actually built into the peripheral device. The other end of a Type A connector connects to a Type A port located on a host or USB hub. A Type A connector is flat and rectangular. Type B USB connectors are square and plug into a Type B USB port on both the device and the host. Refer to Figure 8.1 for the location of USB ports on a system unit.

USB 2.0

The newest version of USB is called USB 2.0. USB 2.0 is sometimes referred to as Hi-Speed USB and supports transmission rates of up to 480 Mbps. It is fully backward compatible with the previous version of USB (USB 1.1). In a nutshell, USB 2.0 uses the same exact connector cables and ports as the first version of USB. This USB specification was developed to meet the bandwidth-hungry needs of new devices and their technologies.

Here are some USB tips for the exam:

- The newest type of serial bus architecture is USB.
- A USB port can supply power for most USB devices.
- Digital devices such as cameras most often use USB ports.
- USB supports hot plugging of devices such as mice and keyboards. You can connect or disconnect them when a computer system is powered up.
- Windows 95 requires special drivers and operating system "supplements" before it will recognize USB devices.
- One system resource (IRQ) will support up to 127 USB devices.

The exam will ensure that you know that USB is RS232 compliant. In plain English (and on the CompTIA exam), this means that USB, RS232, and serial connections are all basically the same thing. For example, you might see something similar to this: "What is a very popular connection method for camcorders or digital cameras?" The possible choice of answers may include USB, RS232, or serial connection. You'd better choose them all!

FireWire (IEEE 1394)

FireWire is associated with Apple's original implementation of the IEEE standard 1394. The IEEE 1394 standard references high-speed serial transmissions of up to 400 Mbps (in version 1394a) and 800 Mbps (in version 1394b). FireWire is PnP compatible and hot-swappable; it also allows up to 63 devices to be connected to one port. A PnP system uses the process known as "enumeration" to assign an address and autodetect any FireWire-connected devices.

A FireWire connector is somewhat similar in shape to a USB connector. The main difference is that a FireWire connector is larger and squarer than a typical USB connector. Figure 8.6 displays a FireWire connector.

FireWire technology and other forms of the IEEE 1394 standard are expected to replace most serial and parallel connections in the future. For now, the IEEE 1394 standard is well suited for devices that require high speeds and large real-time throughput, such as video equipment. IEEE 1394 supports data transfer rates of 100 Mbps to 800 Mbps.

NOTE

The A+ exams may ask, "Which technology is faster, IEEE 1394 or USB?" Make sure that you are prepared to identify technologies by their IEEE association. You may know all there is to know about connecting devices together, but if you can't identify technologies and standards, you will not be able to pass the exams.

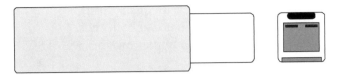

FIGURE 8.6   A FireWire connector.

If you want to learn more regarding FireWire, the following HowStuffWorks, Inc. Web site offers a superb explanation of FireWire basics: *http://computer. howstuffworks.com/firewire1.htm.*

SCSI CONNECTORS

As mentioned in Chapter 7, SCSI interfaces can be attached internally or externally to a computer system. For example, a SCSI hard drive can be attached to an internal SCSI controller on the motherboard. A device such as a SCSI printer or SCSI CD-ROM can be connected to an external SCSI controller card that extends out of the back of a computer. The devices that attach to SCSI controller cards have SCSI interfaces built onto them. There are internal and external SCSI connectors that reflect the SCSI standard being implemented on the device or controller. The most common SCSI interface connectors in use today are 50-pin and 68-pin SCSI internal and external SCSI connectors, as well as the 80-pin internal SCSI SCA connector. Devices such as printers and CD-ROMs use a SCSI 50-pin or 68-pin cable and connectors. SCSI SCA 80-pin connectors are used for hot-swappable hard drives, most commonly with internal RAID (Redundant Array of Independent Disks, or Redundant Array of Inexpensive Disks) configurations. The SCA SCSI adapter card includes a built-in power connection to support its special voltage requirements. Figure 8.7 shows the basic SCSI connectors and SCSI pin configurations. Remember, the exam will most likely focus on the 50-pin or 68-pin SCSI cable.

SCSI technology offers the fastest available printing capabilities.

NOTE

Here are several useful tips to remember about SCSI technology and interfaces:

- Most SCSI cables are 50-pin.
- SCSI Wide refers to a 68-pin parallel interface cable.
- SCSI-3 is considered ultra-wide and can support up to 16 devices, including the controller card.
- SCSI-3 is backward compatible with previous forms of SCSI technology.

- Each SCSI device must have a unique SCSI ID.
- A SCSI chain must be terminated at both ends.
- You cannot network two computers together with a SCSI cable.

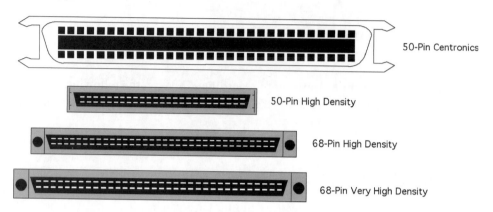

FIGURE 8.7   Basic SCSI connectors and their pin configurations.

NETWORKING CONNECTORS AND CABLES

More than 2,500 types of cable are used for connecting computers and peripherals. The majority of computers today still use some type of wire or cable to transmit data from one system to another. There are three main types of network cables in use that you need to be familiar with for the exams: coaxial, twisted pair (TP), and fiber optic. Each of these cable types has characteristics that set it apart from the others, such as cost, distance limitations, data transfer methods, data transfer rates, and installation methods used. The exam will focus on your ability to identify which technology is used by a certain cable category and which cable medium should be used to connect two or more specific devices.

COAXIAL CABLE

Coaxial cable is a type of copper cabling that is often used for Ethernet LAN and cable TV connections. The two common types of coaxial cable, thicknet and thinett, are described next.

Thicknet

Thicknet coaxial cable, also known as 10Base5, is approximately half an inch thick; it is a heavy type of cable with a copper core, which was used with early mainframe computers and early networks. Thicknet coaxial still exists, but it is very limited in its ability to achieve the high data transfer rates that are needed to support today's bandwidth-hungry computers and applications.

Thicknet coaxial cable has the ability to carry 10 Mb (megabits) of data a total distance of 500 meters, or approximately 1,500 feet. Thus, the naming convention scheme of 10Base5 has been established for coaxial cable. In other words, 10Base5 means that 10 Mb of information can travel over a baseband medium, or base, a total of 500 meters (the naming convention drops the last two zeros): $5 \times 100 = 1,500$ feet; the true measurement is closer to 1,640 feet.

Thicknet coaxial cable was and sometimes still is used as a backbone connection that connects to a small thinnet cable by use of a vampire tap and an Attachment Unit Interface (AUI) connector.

Thinnet

Thinnet coaxial cable, also known as 10Base2, is approximately a quarter-inch thick. It is a thinner, more flexible type of coaxial cable that is usually connected directly to a NIC with a BNC or BNC T-connector. Figure 8.8 displays a BNC and BNC T-connector. Thinnet is much easier to install and work with than thicknet, but thinnet only carries a data signal the distance of 185 meters, or approximately 607 feet.

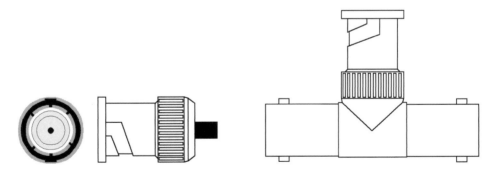

FIGURE 8.8   A BNC and BNC T-connector.

Both thicknet and thinnet coaxial can make up a network referred to as a bus network. (Bus networks are described in Chapter 9.) A bus network must be terminated at both ends of a cable, or the bus network will fail. Thus, thicknet and thinnet both require terminators at both cable ends.

TWISTED-PAIR CABLE

Twisted-pair (TP) cable arose from the need to replace the distance and other limitations associated with coaxial-type cable. TP is referred to as 10BaseT. Once again, the 10 refers to the transmission rate of data, Base refers to a baseband media type, and the T refers to the twisted pair, or wiring twists in the cable itself.

There are two types of TP wiring: Shielded Twisted Pair (STP) and Unshielded Twisted Pair (UTP).

Shielded Twisted Pair

STP is basically the same type of wire as UTP, with the exception that STP uses a woven copper braided shielding and foil wrapping that protect the twisted wire pairs from outside interference, such as Electromagnetic Interference (EMI). This shielding makes an STP wire less susceptible to cross-talk from other wires. STP is more expensive than UTP, based on its extra protection and capability to transmit a data signal over a greater distance than UTP.

Unshielded Twisted Pair

UTP is also a 10 Mbps baseband cable. UTP, generally referred to as 10BaseT, is the most common type of Ethernet cable in use today and is found mostly in what is called a star typology network. (Star typology networks are discussed in detail in Chapter 9.) UTP in its simplest form is two insulated copper wires that can carry a data signal 100 meters, or approximately 328 feet.

To keep wiring standards uniform, there are 7 categories of UTP wiring, as specified by the Electronics Industries Association (EIA) and the Telecommunications Industries Association (TIA):

Category 1 (CAT1): CAT1 is the original implementation of UTP used for telephone cable. It is capable of transmitting voice but not data. This type of phone wire was installed before the mid-1980s.

Category 2 (CAT2): CAT2 is a UTP cable type made up of four twisted pairs of wires. It supports transmission rates up to 4 Mbps.

Category 3 (CAT3): CAT3 can transmit data up to 10 Mbps. It has four twisted pairs that are twisted three times per foot.

Category 4 (CAT4): CAT4 cable is capable of data transmissions up to 16 Mbps. It has four twisted pairs of wire.

Category 5 (CAT5): CAT5 cable is capable of data transmission rates of up to 100 Mbps. It is also made of four twisted pairs of wire. CAT5 UTP is also referred to as 100BaseT or 100BaseTX. It carries a data signal 100 meters, or approximately 328 feet.

Category 5e (CAT5e): Otherwise known as "Enhanced" CAT 5 cable, CAT5e is capable of data transmission rates of up to 350 Mbps. Like CAT5, CAT5e can carry a data signal up to 100 meters, or 328 feet, without a bridge or other form of amplification. Also like CAT5, CAT5e is made of four twisted pairs of wire. The difference here is that CAT5e was created to support high-speed gigabit Ethernet devices and technology, such as ATM (Asynchronous Transfer Mode). CAT5e has better performance and resistance, and suffers less from attenuation than traditional CAT5.

- CAT5 and CAT5e both have 100-ohm impedance and are terminated with RJ45 connectors.
- CAT5e is backward compatible with traditional CAT5.
- CAT5e is built using a 24-gauge conducting wire.
- The "enhanced" electrical technology built into CAT5e makes it possible for CAT5e cable to support additional bandwidth needed for such technology as gigabit Ethernet.

Category 6 (CAT6): The CAT6 cabling standard is rated up to 550 Mbps or 1000Mbps.

- CAT6 cabling is built using 23-gauge conductor wire.
- CAT6 has a better performance rating than CAT5e and suffers less from cross-talk and noise.
- CAT6 is more expensive to install and support than CAT5 or CAT5e.

CAT5 UTP is the most popular UTP cable in use today and will most likely be the focus of UTP category questions on the exams. However, CAT5e and CAT6 are newer specifications, and are identified as 2006 A+ Objectives. Be prepared to answer basic CAT5e and CAT6 questions, as well.

To keep you sharp for the exam, here are the updated IEEE standard requirements for UTP cabling:

10BaseT: IEEE standard for requirements of sending data at 10 Mbps over UTP cable.

100BaseT: IEEE standard for requirements of sending data at 100 Mbps over UTP cable.

1000BaseT (also known as gigabit Ethernet): IEEE standard for requirements of sending data at 1,000 Mbps over UTP cable.

Twisted-Pair Connectors

There are two types of UTP connectors you need to know about for the test: RJ11 connectors and RJ45 connectors.

An RJ11 phone connector was used for early categories of UTP to connect a modem to a typical phone jack, or your phone to a phone jack. In technical circles, an RJ11 wire is a simple phone wire that houses four wires or connections. See Figure 8.9 for an RJ11 connector.

An RJ45 connector is the most common type of TP data cable connector in use. It houses eight wire traces. The RJ45 connector on one end of a TP wire plugs into a NIC that is installed into a system. The RJ45 connector on the other end of the TP cable plugs into a network hub, router, or RJ45 wall jack. Figure 8.10 shows an RJ45 connector.

FIGURE 8.9 An RJ11 connector.

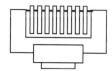

FIGURE 8.10 An RJ45 connector.

Crossover Cable

A crossover cable is a type of Ethernet TP cable that is commonly used to connect two computers in a peer-to-peer fashion. The crossover cable switches the transmit and receive lines of the cable, which allow two computers to communicate directly with each other without the use of a hub or router. If you want an inexpensive alternative to purchasing a hub, a crossover cable is the way to go to connect two computers.

A null modem cable can also be used as a crossover cable to network two computers. A null modem cable is a serial cable that is connected to the serial ports of two system units.

FIBER-OPTIC CABLE

Fiber-optic cable, otherwise known as 10BaseFL, is the network wire of choice. It is capable of extremely fast transmission rates over long distances, without interference.

A fiber-optic cable has a core that is composed of plastic or glass. A glass cladding or sheath covers the core. Finally, a Kevlar fiber jacket surrounds the entire wire. Data can be transmitted through a fiber-optic cable with a laser or LED at a rate of 2 GBps or higher. The data signal on a fiber-optic wire can travel up to a distance of 100 kilometers (about 60 miles), depending on which technology is being implemented with the fiber and if a repeater is used. Fiber-optic cables use special ST-, SC-, and LC-type form factor connectors to attach to NICs and fiber-optic ports. These connectors are precisely crafted and specially designed to suit fiber-optic cable connection requirements.

An LC (Lucent Connector) connector is a miniaturized version of the fiber-optic SC connector. It looks like the SC but is about half the size and has a 1.25 mm ferrule instead of 2.5 mm.

MT-RJ (Mechanical Transfer Registered Jack) is another type of fiber-optics connector. It supports full-duplex transmission and has a lower cost factor than ST- and SC-type fiber connectors. It has a latch like an RJ45 connector and is also much easier to install and terminate than ST- or SC-type connectors.

Fiber-optic cable needs great care and consideration when being installed. Specially trained, certified fiber installers are usually employed to carry out this task. Because of its high transmission speeds and specialized installation methods, fiber-optic technology is quite expensive.

Next we will discuss the two fiber-optic cable mode technologies that you will need to be familiar with for the exam.

Single-Mode (SM)

Single-mode (SM) fiber optic, also referred to as monomode fiber, is a fiber technology meant for very long distance data transmissions. With SM fiber, a laser is used to generate a single pulse of light, or "mode of light," into the fiber media. This light is used as a data transmission carrier for a very long distance. Photodiodes are used to receive the transmission sent over the fiber-optic media.

Multimode (MM)

Multimode fiber (MM) uses LEDs (Light Emitting Diodes) to generate signals of light into the core fibers for transmission over fiber media. This mode of fiber is designed to carry many light signal rays, or "modes," at the same time over a shorter distance than single mode. If the light rays, or "modes of light," have to travel too far with this mode, modal dispersion occurs, and transmission fails. The core of the fiber media used with MM is larger than with SM; thus, the accepting photodiodes have a much larger circumference.

Here are some key points to remember:

■ The core of SM fiber is much smaller than the core for MM type fiber.
■ SM fiber has greater distance and bandwidth capabilities than MM fiber.

- SM fiber is more expensive than MM fiber.
- Repairing breaks is much more difficult in SM fiber-optic media.
- MM fiber uses LEDs to generate signals of light.
- With SM fiber, a laser is used to generate a single pulse of light.
- Bridged media connectors (converters) are available, which enable Ethernet connections to be converted to fiber and fiber connections to be converted to Ethernet. MM fiber converters can support distances up to 2 Km. SM fiber converters support distances of up to 60 Km.

You should remember the key points regarding SM versus MM fiber for the exam. These two modes have been identified as CompTIA 2006 Objectives and are likely to appear on the exam.

Table 8.2 provides a comparison chart of the major networking cables described in this chapter.

TABLE 8.2 Cable Comparison Chart

Cable Type	Transmission Speed	Distance
10BaseT	10 Mbps	100 M/328 ft
10Base2	10 Mbps	185 M/607 ft
10Base5	10 Mbps	500 M/1,500 ft
100BaseT	100 Mbps	100 M/328 ft
Fiber optic	100 Mbps to 2 GBps	100 K/60 miles

IDC (INSULATION DISPLACEMENT CONNECTOR)

An insulation displacement connector (IDC) is used in various types of network termination media or connection equipment. An IDC removes the insulation on a cable or wire when a connection is made. It works by piercing, or "crimping" the insulation around the cable's wires with a special tool called an IDC wire crimper. This technique is used to push or force a single wire between two pieces of plastic, or "blades," which are part of a connector, such as an RJ45 patch. An IDC assists with the process of timely termination and makes for an effective and reliable connection.

S/PDIF CONNECTOR

S/PDIF (Sony/Philips Digital Interface Format) is a standard audio transfer file format or protocol used to carry digital signals between devices and stereo components. To be more specific, S/PDIF is used to connect the output of a DVD player to that of a home theater receiver that supports DTS (Digital Theater Systems) surround sound. S/PDIF specifications include 75-ohm coaxial or fiber cabling; an RCA, BNC, or TOSLINK connector; signal level of 0.5 to 1V; and maximum resolution of 20 bits (24 bit optional).

WIRELESS CONNECTIVITY

All those messy, dangling computer wires and connectors will soon be a thing of the past. Wireless technology has become very popular and affordable. In fact, you can set up a small wireless network at home for about $400. All you really need to set up a wireless network is a couple of transmitters, receivers, and a pair of wireless NICs. The operating system configuration for a wireless network is another story in itself.

There are two main forms of wireless technologies in use for connecting computers together: Radio Frequency (RF) and Infrared (IR).

RADIO FREQUENCY

Many computer peripheral devices today use RF technology. With RF, a wireless mouse, keyboard, or modem can communicate with a host system as long as the distance between the peripheral and host does not exceed a specified distance. RF devices use transmitters, receivers, or transceivers (or a combination of these devices) to communicate back and forth. A typical RF mouse or keyboard transmits data through a built-in transmitter to a waiting receiver, which is attached to a system unit through a PS/2 or serial connection. RF devices are designed to meet the IEEE 802.11 standards that apply to wireless networking.

INFRARED (IR)

Infrared (IR) transmission is a wireless form of transmission that also uses a transmitter and receiver. Instead of sending information with radio signals, however, IR uses a beam of light that is not visible to the human eye to transmit data between two devices. Line-of-sight is a very popular type of IR technology used to connect wireless devices, such as a mouse or keyboard, to a host system. The Infrared Data

Association (IRDA) is the organization that is responsible for IR transmission standards. IR technology has become very popular with laptop computers, PDAs, and digital cameras. With the infrared IRDA Standard 1.1, the maximum transmission rate is 4 Mbps with a data size of 2,048 bytes.

Following are some of the common uses available for IR transmission:

■ Messages can be sent between PDAs or between laptop computers.
■ Faxes can be sent from any device using IR technology.
■ Pictures or images from a digital camera can be sent to a desktop or laptop computer.
■ Letters or documents can be sent from a desktop or laptop computer to a printer.

The majority of IR transmissions occur between two computers or a single computer and an infrared-enabled device, such as a printer or PDA. The sending host or device uses an IR transmitter or "emitter," which sends pulses of IR light to the receiving host or device that accepts the pulses with an IR receiver. For the transmission of this signal to occur, there must be a direct line of sight between communicating systems or devices, as well as a protocol and a computer name resolution.

IR was originally designed for point-to-point bidirectional transmissions via an RS232C serial port. Today, most modern systems come equipped with an IRDA-standard port that can interface directly with an IR transmitter/receiver. IR connections can also be made through a parallel or USB port.

Keep in mind that IR is sometimes called the "one-to-one" technology. You can only send to or receive from one device at a time. In other words, while you are transmitting or receiving information between your desktop computer and your PDA, you cannot transmit or receive data from your laptop at the same time using IR.

Popular operating systems such as Windows 95/98/Me/NT/2000/XP/and Vista offer support for adding IR devices. Early versions of Windows 95 required a special IRDA software patch that could be downloaded from Microsoft.com to enable IR support. For your system to use IR, support must be enabled in your system's BIOS.

WIRELESS NETWORKING AND SECURITY

Wireless transmission is defined as the sending of signals over electromagnetic radio waves. Wireless networks have become very widespread. In many cases, wireless networks have replaced the need for tradition wiring. But in larger networks, wireless technology is typically used as an extension or addition to a wired network. Wireless networks offer the ability for computing in places that would be otherwise hard to reach with a wire or cable. The use of wireless technology has been widely accepted by the military, hospitals, businesses, cell-phone companies, Global Positioning System (GPS) customers, museums, and home users alike. The IEEE has developed standards for wireless technologies. These standards are a set of rules that provide a sort of instruction map of guidelines for technology developers to follow when creating new technologies or adding to existing technologies. The IEEE standards that apply to wireless networking are 802.11, 802.11a, 802.11b, and 802.11g. In its simplest of forms, a wireless network, or WLAN (Wireless Local Area Network), is displayed connected to a "wired" LAN in Figure 8.11. Basic wirelesses networks typically have a wireless client, an authentication server or host, and an access point.

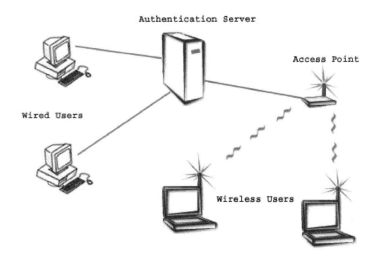

FIGURE 8.11   A basic wireless network.

The need to secure the use of wireless technologies and remote wireless user access has become paramount. Not too long ago, wireless connections were thought to be somewhat secure. Recently, these thoughts have changes, based on security holes found in the technology. Next we will discuss 802.1X standards and basic wireless protocols.

WiFi

WiFi is a wireless technology based on the IEEE 802.11 standards that is used for Internet and VoIP phones, games, and connectivity for televisions, DVD players, and digital cameras. WiFi devices can connect to the Internet when they are in the range of a wireless network connected to the Internet. A service set identifier (SSID) is a code used in WiFi wireless networks that is attached to all packets on the network identifing each packet as part of that wireless network. The SSID code can be up to 32 alphanumeric characters and is case sensitive. In a wireless network, all wireless devices must share the same SSID to communicate with each other. The client SSID on wireless networks are set either manually, by entering the SSID in the client's network settings, or automatically, by leaving the SSID blank or unspecified.

802.1X

The use and support of wireless networking, equipment, security, and protocols is on the rise. Although the fine details regarding 802.1X will most likely not be addressed on the exam, the following information will give you a very good understanding of wireless concepts.

802.1X is an IEEE standard for wireless connectivity that uses port-based access control. It falls under the influence of the initial IEEE standard 802.11 for WLANs. The IEEE and the standards that apply to networking technologies in general are explained in Chapter 9. In this chapter, we will discuss all of the IEEE 802.11 standards for wireless networking. The 802.1X standard is designed to provide a better framework that supports improved security for users of wireless networks by the implementation of centralized authentication. Standard 802.1X uses the Extensible Authentication Protocol (EAP), which enables the technology to work with wireless, Ethernet, and Token Ring networks.

With 802.1X authentication, a wireless client who wants to connect to and be authenticated on the network is called a *supplicant*. The supplicant must first request access from an access point, which is also known as an authenticator. If the access point detects the request for access from the supplicant, the access point will enable the supplicant's port and only let 802.1X traffic be transmitted. This allows the client to transmit a start-up message, known as an EAP start message; the supplicant's identity and credentials are then provided to the access point. The access point then transmits the information to an authentication server, which is typically a server that runs RADIUS (Remote Authentication Dial-In User Service). The authentication server can use various algorithms to eventually allow the user to be authenticated. After the server authenticates the validity of the user, it will transmit either an acceptance or rejection acknowledgement of the client's request to the access point. If the access point receives positive feedback from the RADIUS authentication server, the access point will enable or activate the supplicant's port for normal network traffic.

In simple terms, here is how 802.1X wireless authentication works. See Figure 8.12 for a visual regarding 802.1X authentication. To best understand this process, match the following descriptions with their corresponding numeric values in Figure 8.12:

1. A Start message is sent from the remote client to the access point, and the access point asks the client for identification.
2. The client sends its identity to the access point. The access point then transmits or forwards the client's identity to an authentication server.
3. The authentication server transmits an accept or reject message to the access point.
4. If the access point receives an accept message from the authentication server, the client's port activates, and the client is allowed to communicate with the server.

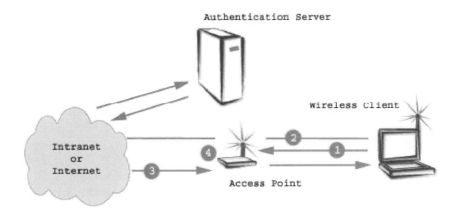

FIGURE 8.12 802.1X wireless authentication.

The 802.1X standard is fairly standard, and it is likely that CompTIA will target it extensively on the exam. Make sure you study Table 8.3 before taking the exam so that you are familiar with 802.11 protocols, frequencies, and ranges. You should be aware of the basic concepts. Microsoft does a great job explaining this technology. If you are interested in learning more about 802.1X, you may find the following site very informative: *www.microsoft.com/windowsxp/pro/techinfo/planning/wirelesslan/solutions.asp.*

WAP

WAP (Wireless Application Protocol) is a wireless standard that applies to wireless communication protocols and devices. There are several standards that are used by various wireless device service manufacturers. WAP is positioned to allow interoperability between them.

TABLE 8.3 802.11 Protocols, Frequencies, and Ranges

Protocol	Frequency	Throughput (Typ)	Data Rate (Max)	Range (Indoor)	Range (Outdoor)
802.11a	5.15-5.25/ 5.25-5.35/ 5.49-5.725/ 5.725-5.85 GHz	23 Mbps	54 Mbps	~35 meters	~75 meters
802.11b	2.4-2.5 GHz	4.5 Mbps	11 Mbps	~40 meters	~80 meters
802.11g	2.4-2.5 GHz	20 Mbps	54 Mbps	~40 meters	~90 meters
802.11n	5 GHz and/ or 2.4 GHz	74 Mbps	74 Mbps	~70 meters	NA

WAP has its own built-in security called WTLS (Wireless Transport Layer Security), which uses secure certificates and a client/server verification/authentication process.

WEP

WEP (Wired Equivalent Privacy) is a wireless security protocol specified under IEEE 802.11b. WEP is intended to provide a WLAN with a similar security level as the protection that can be found in traditional LANs. WEP attempts to secure the obvious security hole that exists between a wireless client and an access point by encrypting the data that is transmitted. After the data has been safely transmitted, conventional network security measures (e.g., VLANS, antivirus, tunneling, and authentication solutions) can be implemented for security purposes.

The exam is likely to ask you very basic questions relating to wireless networking; for example, What technology does WEP have to do with? Or, what does WAP do? For this exam, it is sufficient to know that they are wireless standards that apply to wireless communication protocols and devices.

WIRELESS ACCESS POINTS

Wireless access points are used in WLANs as central points of communication between wireless users. They are sometimes referred to as transceivers because they have the ability to transmit and receive RF signals. They are the "hub" of wireless networks. Access points can also serve as a connection point between wireless users and a wired LAN, as depicted in Figure 8.11.

Access points allow wireless users to roam in a generally predefined area called a *cell*. This cell is actually the area in which the RF signals can be successfully transmitted from the access point to the roaming, or wireless, user and back again. In a small business environment, this area is typically around 100 feet, depending upon many outside physical and electrical conditions. In many businesses today, it is very common to find multiple access points strategically positioned around the business environment. When mobile users move outside the transmission area of one particular cell, they enter another cell area without losing the RF signal to the entire WLAN. Much larger cell areas are used for broadcasting such things as cellular phone "wireless" radio waves. These cell areas can be as small as a city block or carry radio waves several hundred miles.

WIRELESS ANTENNAS

In wireless networking, an antenna is used to propagate, or radiate RF signals to wireless users and access points in a wireless network. There are various antennas for wireless networking, and each has its own physical characteristics and specialized features. The two main types of wireless antennas that we need to be concerned about are the following:

Directional antenna: A directional antenna can direct an RF signal farther than an omnidirectional antenna. It focuses its power in a single direction, which minimizes RF interference. Directional antennas are well suited for long-distance transmissions and work well for transmitting RF signals between buildings or other locations where a direct line of site can be established.

Omnidirectional antenna: An omnidirectional antenna transmits its signals in many different directions, usually in a 360° radius. They are ideal for homes, classrooms, or small businesses. A good 802.11b omnidirectional antenna will evenly blanket your WLAN. Most omnidirectional antennas are either snap-on or dipole antennas. A snap-on is typically connected to a radio card located within a mobile or portable access point. A dipole antenna, the simplest form of antenna, is a mobile antenna that connects to a radio card with a relatively short cable.

AD-HOC

If a wireless network is set up using a peer-to-peer mode where wireless stations communicate directly with each other without the use of an access point, the wireless network is said to be using ad-hoc mode. An ad-hoc mode is usually implemented for temporary wireless transmission purposes.

BLUETOOTH

Bluetooth is a wireless industrial specification standard for the exchange of information between devices such as laptops , PCs, printers, and mobile phones in personal area networks (PANs). Bluetooth uses short-range radio frequency and provides a secure communications protocol for short-range wireless networks. Bluetooth comes in three power classes and provides wireless transmission ranges of 1, 10, and 100 meters. If you need to set up a small wireless network with several peripherals, such as keyboards, mice and printers, bluetooth is a secure, cost-effective solution.

VoIP

VoIP (Voice over Internet Protocol) is a technology that uses special (VoIP) protocols and IP-based networks to route voice conversations over the Internet. Some of the challenges facing VoIP are available bandwidth, network latency, packet loss, jitter, security, and reliability. For the A+ Exams, it is important that you can identify VoIP. Setting up VoIP networks is beyond the scope of the current A+ Exams.

SITE SURVEYS

Before you install a wireless network solution into an existing building or between existing buildings (building to building), you should first have a professional site survey conducted by certified RF engineers. These engineers can properly recommend and assist you with an integration plan, as well as keep you in line with federal, state, and local regulations as they apply to wireless networks.

With traditional network installations, it is much easier to plan out a network topology and possibly foresee obstacles that will need to be addressed. However, with wireless networks that implement the use of radio transmission techniques, it is very difficult to plan for and determine how a network will react to the surrounding conditions. Obstacles such as asbestos-lined walls, trees, and other physical impediments can severely impact the effectiveness of wireless communication. The interference with other RF bands in busy airways can severely hamper your performance and ability to communicate between access points. Certified site survey technicians can detect potential interference between RF bands with a tool called a spectrum analyzer.

A good site survey should provide you with the most suitable wireless equipment options to integrate with your current topology and applications. It should also provide you with a wireless standard that is in line with your required transmission speeds and ultimately your budget.

If you are interested in getting a wireless network solution, the first step is to have a site survey performed.

NOTE

CHAPTER SUMMARY

This chapter introduced you to several of the many types of cables and connectors used to attach devices together. There are literally thousands of connectors, wire types, and media used to make connections and data transfer possible between devices. The Internet is a great tool to use if you are interested in finding out more details on the subject matter discussed in this chapter. By now, you should have a good basic understanding of cables and connectors. If you require more information and are hungry for more study material regarding cables and connectors, and for an all around great site for A+ study in general, visit MCSE Certification Resources at *www.mcmcse.com/comptia/aplus/notes/2003notes.shtml.*

REVIEW QUESTIONS

1. **Which of the following can connect or "network" two computers together? (Choose Three)**
   - ☐ A.   A 6-pin Mini-DIN
   - ☐ B.   A serial cable
   - ☐ C.   10Base2
   - ☐ D.   A parallel cable

   Correct Answers = B, C, and D

   You can connect two computers together with a serial cable, an Ethernet thinnet 10Base2 cable, or a parallel cable. A 6-pin Mini-DIN connector is used to connect a PS/2 mouse or keyboard to a computer.

2. **How does a parallel port transmit data to a device?**
   - ○ A.   1 bit at a time
   - ○ B.   1 byte at a time
   - ○ C.   Serially
   - ○ D.   By use of a parallelogram

   Correct Answer = B

   A parallel port uses parallel transmission methods to transmit or send data 1 byte at a time to a peripheral device. A serial port transmits data 1 bit at a time.

3. **If two devices cannot send and receive data and information simultaneously, they are using which form of data transmission?**

   ○ A. Full duplex
   ○ B. Quarter duplex
   ○ C. Half duplex
   ○ D. Half simplex

   Correct Answer = C

   With half duplex transmission, data can be transmitted in both directions but can only be transmitted in one direction at a time. Full duplex is simultaneous transmission where data or voice can be transmitted at exactly the same time.

4. **A parallel printer cable has a different connector on each end. Name the two types of connectors on a parallel printer cable. (Choose Two)**

   ☐ A. DB 25-pin male connector
   ☐ B. DB 9-pin connector
   ☐ C. An RS232c-compliant cable
   ☐ D. 36-pin Centronics connector

   Correct Answers = A and D

   A parallel port on the back of a computer system is a female DB 25 connector that accepts a DB 25-pin male connector on one end of a parallel cable. The other end of a parallel cable has a 36-pin male Centronics D-shell connector that connects to a Centronics connector located on the back of a printer or device. A DB 9-pin connection is used for connecting a modem or serial mouse to the back of a system. RS232C is a serial port standard.

5. **A connector that has two levels of 15 total pins is which type of cable?**

   ○ A. Monitor cable
   ○ B. Modem cable
   ○ C. Serial port
   ○ D. Game port

   Correct Answer = D

   A game or MIDI female port on the back of system has two levels of 15 total pins that accept a male connector with two levels of 15 total pins.

6. **Which is the fastest technology available for printers?**

   ○ A.   SCSI
   ○ B.   Parallel
   ○ C.   USB
   ○ D.   Serial

   Correct Answer = A

   The fastest technology available for printers today is SCSI.

7. **Which technology has the fastest data transfer rates?**

   ○ A.   IEEE 1394
   ○ B.   Parallel
   ○ C.   USB
   ○ D.   A fast crossover cable

   Correct Answer = A

   FireWire is much faster than USB or parallel; it supports data transfer rates of 100 Mbps to 400 Mbps.

8. **Name the minimum category cable type that can be used to support 100BaseT.**

   ○ A.   Category2
   ○ B.   Category3
   ○ C.   Catagory4
   ○ D.   Category5

   Correct Answer = D

   Category5 UTP supports 100BaseT or 100BaseTX. Category2, 3, and 4 cable types do not support 100baseT.

9. **Name the minimum category cable type that can be used to support 10BaseT.**

   ○ A.   Category3
   ○ B.   RJ11
   ○ C.   Catagory4
   ○ D.   Category5

   Correct Answer = A

The minimum cable type needed to support 10BaseT is Category3. An RJ11 phone connector is used for earlier categories of UTP to connect a modem to a typical phone jack or your phone to a phone jack.

10. **Which of the following is an IEEE standard for parallel type C?**

   ○ A. Standard Centronics 36-pin
   ○ B. Mini 36-pin Centronics connector
   ○ C. FireWire (IEEE 1394)
   ○ D. DB 25 male

   Correct Answer = B

   The newest addition to the IEEE-1284 standard for bidirectional communications and printing is the Type C-Mini 36-pin parallel connector.

11. **Which of the following are associated with parallel printer ports? (Choose three)**

   ☐ A. Bidirectional
   ☐ B. IEEE 1284
   ☐ C. EPP
   ☐ D. USB
   ☐ E. Omnidirectional

   Correct Answers = A, B, and C

   Parallel printer ports support bidirectional as well as Enhanced Parallel Port (EPP) application data transmissions. They are associated with the IEEE 1284 parallel standard that is used to connect a computer to peripheral devices such as printers.

12. **Which of the following IEEE standards addresses FireWire?**

   ○ A. IEEE 802.11
   ○ B. IEEE 1284
   ○ C. IEEE 1234
   ○ D. IEEE 1394
   ○ E. None of the above

   Correct Answer = D

   The IEEE 1394 standard references FireWire high-speed serial transmissions of up to 400 Mbps (in version 1394a) and 800 Mbps (in version 1394b). You must know the differences among IEEE 802.11, IEEE 1284, IEEE 1394, and RS232 for the real exam!

13. **What process will a PnP system use to detect connected FireWire-compatible devices?**

    ○ A. FireWire-N-Play
    ○ B. Enumeration
    ○ C. Collaboration
    ○ D. IRDA standard 1.1
    ○ E. None of the above

    Correct Answer = B

    FireWire is PnP-compatible and hot-swappable. It also allows up to 63 devices to be connected to one port. A PnP system uses enumeration to assign an address and autodetect any FireWire-connected devices.

14. **A NIC that supports SC or ST connections is an example of which type of technology?**

    ○ A. FireWire
    ○ B. Ethernet
    ○ C. Fiber optic
    ○ D. IR or IRDA
    ○ E. None of the above

    Correct Answer = C

    Fiber-optic cables use special ST- and SC-type connectors to attach to NICs and fiber-optic ports. These connectors are precisely crafted and specially designed to suit fiber-optic cable connection requirements.

15. **When a sending host or device uses a transmitter or "emitter" to send pulses of light to a receiving host or device, which technology is being implemented?**

    ○ A. FireWire
    ○ B. Ethernet
    ○ C. Fiber optic
    ○ D. IR
    ○ E. RF
    ○ F. None of the above

    Correct Answer = D

    The majority of infrared (IR) transmissions occur between two computers or a single computer and an infrared-enabled device such as a printer or a PDA. The sending host or device uses an IR transmitter or "emitter," which sends pulses of IR light to the receiving host or device, which accepts with an IR receiver.

16. **You want to use an IR keyboard with your new desktop system. What must be enabled for you to do this?**

    ○ A. Simplex transmission
    ○ B. COM4
    ○ C. ECC
    ○ D. IR support in your systems BIOS
    ○ E. None of the above

    Correct Answer = D

    For your system to use IR or IRDA (same thing), support must be enabled in your systems BIOS.

17. **What is considered the "hub" in a wireless network?**

    ○ A. Ad-hoc
    ○ B. Access point
    ○ C. WLAN
    ○ D. Receiver
    ○ E. None of the above

    Correct Answer = B

    Wireless access points are sometimes referred to as transceivers because they have the ability to transmit and receive RF signals. They are the "hub" of wireless networks.

18. **Your boss has asked you to implement a wireless network solution for your company. What is the first step you should take before implementing this solution?**

    ○ A. Site survey
    ○ B. Purchase access point and wireless NICs
    ○ C. Convert all Ethernet to fiber
    ○ D. Activate 128-bit encryption
    ○ E. None of the above

    Correct Answer = A

Before you install a wireless network solution into an existing building or between existing buildings (building to building), you should first have a professional site survey conducted by certified RF (Radio Frequency) engineers.

19. **Your boss has asked you to implement a fiber-optic solution for your corporate enterprise. You need a solution for fast data transmission over a very long distance. What fiber-optic solution will you recommend?**

    ○ A. Double-mode (DM)
    ○ B. Single-mode (SM)
    ○ C. Multimode (MM)
    ○ D. Multihomed (MH)

    Correct Answer = B

    SM fiber optic, also referred to as monomode fiber, is a fiber technology meant for very long distance data transmissions.

20. **What does multimode (MM) fiber use to generate signals of light rays or "modes"?**

    ○ A. Laser
    ○ B. Phaser
    ○ C. Core illuminator
    ○ D. LED
    ○ E. None of the above

    Correct Answer = D

    MM fiber uses LEDs to generate signals of light into the core fibers for transmission over fiber media. This mode of fiber is designed to carry many light signal rays or "modes" at the same time over a shorter distance than SM.

21. **Which category of UTP uses a 23-gauge conductor wire and is rated for speeds up to 550 MB or 1,000 MB?**

    ○ A. CAT5
    ○ B. CAT6
    ○ C. CAT5e
    ○ D. CAT4b
    ○ E. CAT6g

    Correct Answer = B

CAT6 cabling is built using 23-gauge conductor wire. The CAT6 cabling standard is rated up to 550 MB or 1000 MB.

22. **In Figure 8.13, which connector is being connected?**

FIGURE 8.13

○ A.   A CAT6 connector
○ B.   A standard RS232 connector
○ C.   A standard IEEE 1394 connector
○ D.   A DB 15-pin connector
○ E.   None of above

Correct Answer = D

The female DB 15-pin port has three rows of five pinholes that accept a male DB 15-pin connector, which is attached to the end of the monitor's cable.

23. **You are making a special length cable and need to attach RJ45 connectors. Which tool would you use?**

○ A.   Punchup tool
○ B.   Multimeter
○ C.   Wire crimper
○ D.   Loopback plug
○ E.   None of the above

Correct Answer = C

Wire crimpers are used to attach connectors such as RJ45 and RJ11 to cables. A punchup tool doesn't exist. A hardware loopback plug, also known as a loopback adapter, is a device used to redirect outgoing data signals back into the system. A multimeter is used to test electrical current in a system.

24. **Your boss just got a new laptop and wants everything wireless. This includes a mouse, keyboard, and printer. What technology would you consider for this setup?**

   ○ A. Bluetooth
   ○ B. Fiber optic
   ○ C. SCSI
   ○ D. Ethernet

   Correct Answer = A

   Bluetooth is definitely the way to go here. Bluetooth is a wireless technology standard that operates at 2.4 to 2.48 GHz with speeds up to 720 Kbps. Fiber optic, SCSI, and Ethernet are all valid technologies. However, they would not be the appropriate solution here.

25. **Which of the following is a code used in WiFi wireless networks that is attached to all packets on the network identifying each packet as part of that wireless network?**

   ○ A. Codeblue
   ○ B. Bluecode
   ○ C. SSID
   ○ D. SISD

   Correct Answer = C

   A service set identifier (SSID) is a code used in WiFi wireless networks that is attached to all packets on the network identifying each packet as part of that wireless network. The SSID code consists of 32 alphanumeric characters and is case sensitive. In a wireless network, all wireless devices must share the same SSID to communicate with each other.

REFERENCES

www.ramelectronics.net/html/connecters.html. This RAM Electronics Industries, Inc. Web site offers some very good images of the three main parallel connector types, as well as many of the other connectors mentioned in this chapter.

http://computer.howstuffworks.com/firewire1.htm. This HowStuffWorks, Inc. Web site offers a superb explanation of FireWire basics.

www.microsoft.com/windowsxp/pro/techinfo/planning/wirelesslan/solutions.asp. This Microsoft Web site explains wireless LAN technology in good detail.

www.mcmcse.com/comptia/aplus/notes/2003notes.shtml. This is the MCSE Resources site that has a great general A+ study guide.

9 Basic Networking

In This Chapter

- IEEE 802 Specifications
- OSI Reference Model
- Network Categories
- Network Topology
- Protocols
- Bridges, Routers, Switches, and Hubs
- Network Interface Cards
- The Internet and Viruses
- Cable, ISDN, DSL, and Satellite
- Firewalls
- VPN
- Troubleshooting and Basic Networking Test Tips

In Chapter 8, you were introduced to some of the important cables and connectors that are used to link computers and peripherals; many of the topics discussed were intended to prepare you for basic networking. In Chapter 9, we will focus on the various types of networks—the communication methods computers use to talk to each other—and some of the important hardware used in various network typologies. We will also focus on troubleshooting network-related connectivity issues, as well as harmful threats that may come in the form of an uneducated user or a computer virus.

It is very important for anyone studying networking architecture and concepts to be familiar with the IEEE 802 specifications for networking components and the Open Systems Interconnect (OSI) reference model, which provides a set of standards for computers to communicate with each other. These two topics are the foundation on which networks are based. However, it is unlikely that the A+ exams will tax you with detailed questions on these two topics. The IEEE 802 standards that you may need to know for the exam will be identified.

257

IEEE 802 Specifications

The IEEE is a technical organization that develops standards for local area networks (LANs) and wide area networks (WANs). The IEEE 802 project standards were developed in the 1970s as a set of specifications, or rules, that manufacturers and users can use as a sort of road map for understanding and developing networks and network-related devices. The IEEE specifications are associated with certain networking layers of the OSI networking model, which is discussed in this chapter.

Throughout this book, you have been introduced to many of the IEEE standards and the particular technologies to which they apply. For example, in Chapter 8, you were introduced to the IEEE standard 1394, which applies to high-speed serial transmission, as well as the IEEE 1284 standard, which applies to parallel transmission. Project 802 was developed to address standards for NICs, network cables, and WANs. There have been many additions and addendums to the IEEE 802 standards as technology has progressed.

The 13 categories of the 802 specifications and their associations are as follows:

802.2: The Logical Link Control (LLC) sublayer of the OSI networking model.

802.1: Internetworking.

802.3: Carrier Sense Multiple Access/Collision Detection (CSMA/CD) LANs (Ethernet).

802.4: Token bus LAN.

802.5: Token Ring LAN.

802.6: Metropolitan Area Network (MAN).

802.7: Broadband Technical Advisory Group.

802.8: Fiber Optic Technical Advisory Group.

802.9: Integrated voice and data networks.

802.10: Network Security Technical Advisory Group.

802.11: Wireless networking.

- 802.11a—Applies to 5 GHz wireless technology, commonly at 6 Mbps, 12 Mbps, or 24 Mbps transmission rates.
- 802.11b—Applies to 2.4 GHz wireless technology at 11 Mbps transmission rate.
- 802.11d—Enhancement to 802.11a and 802.11b, which allows for global roaming controlled at the Media Access Control (MAC) layer.
- 802.11g—Also applies to 2.4 GHz wireless technology range and offers wireless transmission rates up to 54 Mbps.
- **802.12**: Demand priority access LAN 100BaseVG, any LAN.

802.15: Wireless personal area networks. This communications specification was approved in 2002 by the IEEE for wireless personal area networks.

- ▪ 802.15.1—Bluetooth short range (10 m) wireless device technology for cordless mouse, keyboard, and hands-free headset at 2.4 GHz.

The three IEEE 802 standards that are most important for A+ study purposes are 802.3, which represents Ethernet; 802.5, which refers to Token Ring or token passing; and 802.11, which refers to wireless networking. Later in this chapter, we will discuss topologies, such as bus, star, mesh, and ring. It is important to remember that the 802.3 Ethernet standards apply to bus and star networks that use CSMA/CD access methods, whereas Token Ring topologies use token-passing methods to place a data signal on a wire.

As mentioned earlier, the IEEE 802 standards apply mostly to the physical aspects of networking components. For example, they have to do with how a NIC is connected to a network or what types of media transmission methods are used to carry a signal down a physical wire.

Just about every networking component manufactured today is designed to meet one of the previously mentioned IEEE standards. If you purchase a hub, cable/DSL router, NIC, or wireless network component, take a look at the specifications on the package or in the advertisement. You will see that the product was manufactured to meet one of the standards set forth by the IEEE.

For more information regarding the IEEE standards and updates to these standards, visit the IEEE home page located at *www.ieee.org/portal/index.jsp.*

OSI Reference Model

As networking became more popular, a well-organized, logical framework for connecting networks and developing applications was needed. In the late 1970s, the International Standards Organization (ISO) developed the OSI networking reference model.

The OSI reference model is a seven-layer logical approach to network communication that includes specifications for the actual hardware connection to the network at the bottom layers, and rules for applications and more complicated functions at the higher layers. Networking rules for communication, also known as *protocols*, exist at almost every layer of the OSI model. The more complicated the protocol, the higher up on the model it resides. Network transmission, security, session connection information, and hardware are each associated with a particular layer.

Picture yourself sitting at your computer, working on a Microsoft Word document. You are actually using functions that reside at the top layer of the OSI reference model, known as the application layer, or layer 7. You decide to attach the Word document to an e-mail message and send it to a co-worker. The message, or signal that you are sending, is directed from the application layer (layer 7) down to the physical layer (layer 1), where it is placed in converted format (0s and 1s) on a network medium, such as a wire, and transmitted to your co-worker. Your co-worker on the receiving end accepts the message through his or her physical layer (layer 1). The message is converted back to a readable format from 0s and 1s and is presented to your co-worker's application layer (layer 7).

Here are the seven layers of the OSI reference model, starting with layer 7.

7. **Application layer:** Applications, e-mail, FTP, user authentication, and any other major services that the end user directly interacts with are associated with this high-level layer. Network access and forms of error recovery are handled at this layer. High-level devices, such as gateways, are also present. Application-specific protocols, such as X.500, SMTP, SNMP, Telnet, and SMB, reside at this layer, as well as the presentation and session layers.

6. **Presentation layer:** Data on the sending computer is converted to a format that can be transmitted over media to another computer. On the receiving end, data is converted into a format that the end user or application layer can understand. Encryption and data translation occur at this level. The network redirector operates at this level as well.

5. **Session layer:** The session layer establishes, holds, and controls sessions or connections between two applications. It provides checkpoint and synchronization service between two communication sessions. Security is handled at this layer.

4. **Transport layer:** The transport layer's primary concern is flow control and data handling. Large forms of data are broken down into manageable packets that can be presented to the higher layers on the receiving end. The successful transmission of data is acknowledged at this layer. If the transfer of information is incomplete or interrupted, this layer is responsible for requesting the information to be retransmitted by the sending application or session. Transfer protocols such as TCP, NetBEUI, NWLink, and SPX reside at this layer.

3. **Network layer:** The network layer is responsible for the routing of information to the correct network, device, or computer. Logical names are converted to physical names at this layer. In other words, computer Internet Protocol (IP) addresses are converted to their Media Access Control (MAC) equivalents. Priority of connection and quality of service are also handled at this layer. A network router and switch reside at this layer, as do network protocols, such as IP and IPX.

2. **Data Link Layer:** Data frames received from the network layer are converted into bits (0s and 1s) at the data link layer in preparation for the physical layer. On the receiving end, bits are packaged together into frames that can be understood by the higher layers. Frame synchronization, flow control, and error handling are addressed at this level. The data link layer has two sublayers, known as the Logical Link Control (LLC) and MAC layers. The LLC sublayer is associated with IEEE standards 802.1 and 802.2 and is responsible for the implementation and placement of Service Access Points (SAPs). The MAC sublayer is associated with IEEE standards 802.3, 802.4, 802.5, and 802.12. The MAC sublayer communicates directly with a NIC. It is responsible for error-free communication between network interfaces. Devices called *bridges*, which segment network traffic, operate at this layer.

1. **Physical Layer:** The physical layer is the physical adapter or connection to the network wire or medium. It is where bit(s) streams of information are prepared to go across the network medium. Incoming bits of information are organized and prepared to move through the higher layers.

If you are interested in pursuing a career in networking, it is very important that you understand the theory behind the OSI reference model. You will also need a solid understanding of the OSI reference model and the IEEE specifications if you are interested in passing CompTIA's Network+ and Security+ certification examinations. However, that is another story altogether—or is it? This book has been designed as a springboard to your computer certification future. You will already have a great start toward CompTIA's Network+, Security+, and Server+ certification examinations when you complete this book.

If you are interested in viewing one of the very best charts available regarding the OSI Reference Model, visit the following Web site: *http://en.wikipedia.org/ wiki/Osi_model.*

NETWORK CATEGORIES

A *network* is defined as two or more computers attached to each other that share information. Networks can be formed to make up a LAN or a WAN. A LAN is a network that resides in one physical location, such as a building. It usually has a limited number of computers attached to it and is designated a certain scope or range of computer IP numeric addresses. A WAN is a larger network that usually combines two or more LANs together over a larger physical distance. For example, a business may have two LANs in different buildings or different cities. The two

LANs can be connected to form a WAN. A WAN typically has a larger range of computer IP addresses and is used to control communication between LANs. Access to a WAN is usually accomplished through use of a leased or dedicated T1 line, or a dial-up modem connection using ISDN, cable, or DSL.

There are two basic types of networks in use today: peer-to-peer and server-based. Each of the two network categories has its own set of built-in characteristics that differentiate it from the other.

PEER-TO-PEER NETWORKS

A *peer-to-peer network* is a small network, usually of 10 or fewer computer systems, connected without the use of a larger specialized server computer. In peer-to-peer networks, a workstation can function as both a client and a server computer. In other words, a single computer can share information or devices attached to it or act as its own entity to carry out day-to-day workstation functions.

A peer-to-peer network does not require a high-end server computer to provide login authentication or a highly trained staff to secure and administer network resources. A peer-to-peer network uses password-protected shares that use share-level security at the workstation level. The user of the workstation decides who will be able to read, write, execute, or delete files that exist. Windows 3.11/95/98/Me/NT/2000/XP/Vista, OSX, and Linux operating systems can all provide peer-to-peer capabilities.

Many small businesses and home enthusiasts implement peer-to-peer networks. They are a less expensive alternative to server-based networks that require a single or multiple server system and are fairly easy to maintain, as long as you remember all the passwords that may be associated with all the files, folders, and devices.

SERVER-BASED NETWORKS

A server-based network is typically implemented for networks that have more than 10 computers and that require quick access to services that specialized high-end servers can provide. A server-based network is designed to centralize the control and administration of network access (security) and resources. When a user logs on to a server-based network, a specialized server that controls network access authenticates the user by using user-level security. A network administrator or manager is typically empowered in a server-based network to control, monitor, and carry out the daily network maintenance associated with this type of network. Some examples of operating systems that can provide server-based functionality are Microsoft Windows NT Server, Windows 2000 Server, Windows Server 2003, Novell Netware, and Unix.

Server computers are designed to provide specific services to client computers. Some of the different types of server computers are listed in Table 9.1.

TABLE 9.1   Types of Network Server Computers

Server Type	Server Function
Authentication server	Centralized location of security accounts database used to allow users access to the network, for example, Windows NT Primary Domain Controller (PDC).
Database server	Houses the common database and is responsible for storage and management of data warehouse services— for example, Microsoft SQL Server.
Application server	Handles high-end operations to take load off of client computers. Application software is installed on a server. Client computers request services from the application server.
Print server	Handles all client-side requests for network printing. Manages network printers and print queues.
Communications server	Responsible for e-mail, fax, Internet access, and dial-up modem connections. Microsoft Exchange Server is an example of a communications server application.
Web server	Serves up Internet or intranet Web pages, for example, a server that runs Microsoft Internet Information Services (IIS) or Samba.

Network Redirector

The network redirector is software that is built into the code of a network operating system. The redirector intercepts requests made by the system's processor and decides whether the request should be forwarded to another system on the network or should remain local to the system. If a request is made from a client workstation for a particular instruction, such as printing to a network printer, the redirector grabs the request and sees that it is forwarded to the network so that print operations can commence.

Universal Naming Convention

A Universal Naming Convention (UNC) name is used to access a particular share on a particular workstation or server on a network. If you want to access a resource, such as a printer or folder that has been shared on the network, you can gain access to it by typing in the UNC name from the Start > Run option in Windows. A UNC name always follows the format *Servername\sharename*. For example, suppose you want to access a folder on the network named "Certified." The Certified folder resides on a server named "Bigserver." You would go to Start > Run and type in "\\Bigserver\Certified". If you have permissions to the Certified folder, you can have access to it.

NETWORK TOPOLOGY

A network's topology is the actual physical layout of the network. The topology of a network is based on factors such as the number of workstations and servers required, the communication methods that will be implemented, and the cables and specialized equipment that are available.

The three standard network topologies are bus, star, and ring. Be sure that you can identify the three main topologies and the cable type associated with each. The exams are likely to present you with a topology diagram similar to the three figures you will see in this chapter, or to ask which cable type is associated with each topology. For example, 10Base2 is associated with a bus topology network.

The three topologies and their associated characteristics form the framework from which most networks are based. All three topologies are described next.

BUS

An Ethernet bus topology, otherwise known as a linear bus, is a topology designed for a limited number of computers that are typically attached to a single wire, or trunk, in a straight line. As more workstations are added to a bus topology, performance decreases. Figure 9.1 displays a typical bus topology.

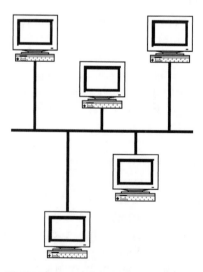

FIGURE 9.1   A bus topology network.

The main type of cable implemented in a bus topology network is 10Base2 (which was described more fully in Chapter 8). Devices called terminators must be placed on both ends of a bus network or wire to keep the data signal that is placed on the wire from bouncing back and forth, a phenomenon referred to as *signal bounce*. All computers on the bus listen for the data signals. If the signal is addressed to a particular workstation, the workstation accepts the signal. If the physical wire or connection that makes up the bus topology is damaged or breaks, the individual computers on the bus will still be able to operate independently but will not be able to accept data signals and communicate with other computers on the bus network.

Bus and star networks use CSMA/CD MAC methods to place a signal on a wire. CSMA/CD is an Ethernet error-detection method used to ensure proper data handling on a wire.

BNC (Bayonet Nut Connector) and BNC barrel connectors are used to attach a bus cable to a device or connect one piece of the bus cable to another. A device called a repeater is used to boost or regenerate the signals placed on a 10Base2 or bus network. Adding a repeater to a bus can extend the length of the entire bus network. For distances associated with a bus network, refer to Chapter 8 and 10Base2 distance capabilities.

STAR

A star topology physically looks like a star. Figure 9.2 shows a simple star topology network. A star topology uses a central device, which can be a hub, a router, or a switch. We will refer to a simple hub for the central connection point in a star network.

All devices in a star topology network are typically connected to a hub with twisted pair (TP), otherwise known as 10BaseT cable. A star topology network is known to require large amounts of cable for larger networks. The hub provides a central location at which the network can be managed and tested. If one computer fails on a star network, the other computers connected to the hub can still function and communicate with one another. If the hub fails, however, all communication between devices will cease.

RING

A ring topology network is best understood by picturing an actual circle of cable. Workstations and servers are all connected to the circle of cable. Each computer attached to the circle regenerates the data signal sent in the form of a token. The circling of the token to each of the servers and workstations on the ring is known as *token passing*. If the wire that makes up the ring is damaged, all network activity on the ring ceases. Keep in mind that IEEE 802.5 is a standard that applies to token-passing technology. Figure 9.3 displays a simple Token Ring topology.

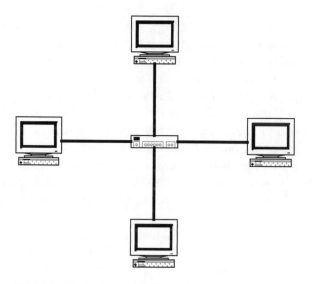

FIGURE 9.2 A star topology network.

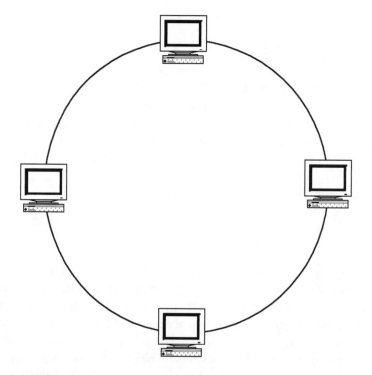

FIGURE 9.3 A ring topology network.

MESH

In a mesh topology network, all nodes (systems) are connected to each and every other node on the network (see Figure 9.4). If the connection from one node to another node fails, a different route can be taken to access other nodes on the mesh network. This redundancy makes a mesh network one of the most reliable topologies available. Mesh networks are classified into two types of topologies. The more expensive but more redundant full-mesh topology and the less expensive not as redundant partial mesh topology. Typically, a partial mesh topology is used as a backbone to connect full mesh topology networks together.

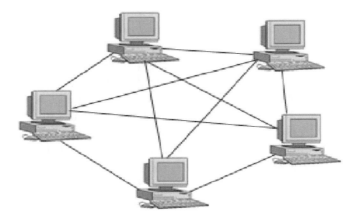

FIGURE 9.4   A mesh topology network.

PROTOCOLS

As mentioned earlier in this chapter, network protocols are a common language or set of rules that computers use to communicate with one another. Protocols come in packages known as protocol stacks. Individual protocols reside at each layer of the OSI reference model to carry out specified functions. If an exam tests you on protocols, it will most likely focus on the TCP/IP and IPX/SPX protocol stacks. There are many network protocols in use. We will focus on the protocols you need to know for the exams.

TCP/IP (IPv4)

Transmission Control Protocol/Internet Protocol (TCP/IP) is the most popular protocol in use today. It is the protocol of choice for the Internet. TCP/IP is commonly used with Ethernet, Token Ring, and Internet or network dial-up connections. Every computer on a TCP/IP network uses an IP address as a unique numeric identification. An IP address is a 32-bit numeric combination of 4 period-delimited octets, each of which can be a number from 0 to 255. An IP address can be up to 12 digits long.

An example of an IP address is 209.15.176.206. This IP address is associated with the domain name address that is provided by a domain name system (DNS) server of the publisher of this book, charlesrivermedia.com. From a DOS prompt, you can use the TCP/IP ping utility to test a connection to the Charles River Media, Inc. Web site. Try it. Using Windows 2000, navigate to the DOS prompt. At the DOS prompt, type "Ping charlesrivermedia.com." You should receive an associated IP address of the Web site as well as four echo replies.

Another popular TCP/IP utility is the tracert command. The tracert will tell the route you are using to establish a connection with a destination computer. In other words, it gives you all of the TCP/IP addresses and domain names of the computers you are using to reach your final destination. Try the tracert command from the DOS prompt. Type "tracert charlesrivermedia.com." You will receive the IP addresses and domain names of the computers you are hitting to get to the Charles River Media, Inc. Web site. The time it takes for your request to go from each destination's IP address is measured in units of time called *hops*. A subnet mask is used to specify which particular network a TCP/IP address belongs to.

You can check the IP configuration of your computer using two popular commands. If you are using Windows 95/98, type "winipcfg" at the DOS prompt. If you are using Windows NT/Me/2000/XP/Vista, type "ipconfig" or "ipconfig/all" at the DOS prompt. Your computer's IP address, subnet mask, and default gateway settings will be displayed. If you use Linux, you should use the command ifconfig to display similar results.

If your computer is unable to communicate with other computers on the network, and all the other computers are functioning correctly, you should first check your computer's IP address configuration settings. They may not be properly configured. If this is the case, your computer can only access itself.

TCP/IP address classes are divided into five distinct classes as defined by the InterNIC. The InterNIC is a consortium of businesses whose purpose is to manage certain services for Internet users and business. One of the primary services provided by the InterNIC is the management and assignment of TCP/IP address classes. The five classes of TCP/IP addresses provided by the InterNIC are listed here:

Class A: Used for large networks. Supports up to 16 million host systems on each of 127 networks.

Class B: Used for medium-sized networks. Supports up to 65,000 host systems on each of 16,000 networks.

Class C: Used for small- to mid-size networks. Supports up to 254 host systems on each of 2 million networks.

Class D: Used for multicast service only.

Class E: Used for experimental purposes only.

Address Classes A, B, and C each have their own set or block of reserved IP addresses that are specifically used for private internal networks. These IP addresses are not routable addresses and cannot be seen or accessed by default beyond the boundary of the local network on which they are used. The reserved addresses for Class A networks are 10.0.0.0 through 10.255.255.255. The reserved addresses for Class B networks are 172.16.0.0 through 172.31.255.255. The reserved addresses for Class C networks are 192.168.0.0 through 192.168.255.255.

The A+ exams just may ask you a question such as:

1. **Which of the following IP addresses is reserved for internal use and cannot be used on the Internet?**

   ○ A.   172.14.42.5
   ○ B.   172.42.42.5
   ○ C.   172.31.42.5
   ○ D.   172.52.42.5

The correct answer to this question is C: 172.31.42.5. Notice that all of the other choices do not fit into the range of privately reserved Class B. In other words, the IP address would have to fall between 172.16.0.0 and 172.31.255.255 to be considered private.

IPv6

The previous version of TCP/IP was IPv4. IPv4 has been around for years. However, as a result of millions of new networks and individual users, IPv4 has run out of available IP addresses. As a result, a new version of IP had to be developed. IPv6 is the newest version of IP. IPv6 uses a 128-bit addressing scheme and also uses a hex numbering scheme to avoid long IP addresses. Here is an example of the hex address format: 3FFE:B00:800:2::C. IPv6 is the latest version of IP. It is packaged with most newer operating systems and, in most cases, has replaced the earlier IPv4 based on its major improvements. IPv6 provides rules and support for the following types of addressing:

Unicast: Transmit rules for message sending from a single host to another single host.

Anycast: Rules for transmission from a single host to the nearest possible host from a grouping of hosts.

Multicast: Rules for transmission from a single host to an entire group of hosts.

The most important fact to remember regarding these two versions of IP is that IPv6 allows for IP addresses to be lengthened from the IPv4 limitation of 32 bits to 128 bits.

IPv6 also allows better authentication, privacy, and improved data delivery assurance.

IPX/SPX

Internetwork Packet Exchange/Sequenced Packet Exchange (IPX/SPX) is a protocol stack used in Novell networks that supports routing. There are several versions of Novell operating systems in use today. When connecting a system to a Novell network, it is often necessary to bind a specific frame type to your NIC for connection to various Novell operating system versions. Frame type specifications are beyond our study focus; just remember that if you are having trouble connecting to a Novell network, you should first verify that the proper frame type is bound to your NIC.

NetBIOS

NetBIOS (Network Basic Input/Output System) is a program or API (Application Programming Interface) that allows application programs on separate computers to recognize and talk to each other. NetBIOS operates at both the session and transport layers of the OSI reference model. Operating systems such as DOS and Windows use a message format called SMB (Server Message Block) to assist with the sharing of folders, files, devices, and other tasks/tools. NetBIOS relies on and uses the SMB format.

NetBIOS was originally created by IBM, and was later adopted and changed for use in operating systems that were created by Microsoft and Novell.

NetBIOS is not routable. This means that it, alone, does not allow communication between systems or programs that exist on separate networks (usually separated by routers). In other words, NetBIOS works well in LANs, not WANs. For WAN communication, you need TCP/IP.

NetBEUI

NetBEUI (NetBIOS Extended User Interface) is a nonroutable, small, efficient transport layer protocol meant for use in small networks with 1 to 200 workstations.

NetBEUI does not have the overhead associated with larger protocols and is very efficient for workgroups or peer-to-peer networks.

In a nutshell, if you have a small workgroup that includes operating systems such as Windows 95/98/Me/2000/XP/NT, installing NetBEUI will allow them to efficiently communicate with each other. According to Microsoft, the only configuration requirement needed for installing the NetBEUI protocol is a valid computer name.

NetBIOS and NetBEUI are specific CompTIA 2006 Upgrade Objectives. Know them well; it is likely that they will show up on the exams.

ADDRESS RESOLUTION PROTOCOL (ARP)

Address Resolution Protocol (ARP) is used to map an IP address at the network layer of the OSI model, to a physical hardware address at the MAC sublayer. ARP translates a logical, dynamic address (IP) into a physical, static address (MAC).

Packets that arrive at a gateway (typically a router) on a network are "resolved" by an ARP cache or "Table" and directed to the proper destination system or subnetwork based on this IP to MAC resolution technique.

Every NIC has a hard-coded hardware or 128 bit, nonchangeable MAC address programmed to it or "burned" to its PROM chip by the manufacturer. ARP resolves the computer system's IP address to this hardware address. On a typical Windows 2000 system, you can view your computer system's IP, MAC address, and local ARP cache by navigating to a command prompt and entering: "arp –a".

The following are the results of entering "arp –a" on a system:

Interface: 10.1.18.67 on Interface 0x1000003

Internet Address	Physical Address	Type
10.1.18.1	00-00-0c-07-ac-0d	Dynamic
10.1.18.77	00-d0-b7-4f-22-f2	Dynamic
10.1.18.137	00-10-5a-01-d1-2a	Dynamic
10.1.18.211	00-d0-b7-4f-55-1b	Dynamic

SECURE SHELL (SSH)

Secure Shell (SSH) is a Unix-based strong authentication method used to allow administrators to securely access and control remote systems. SSH is actually a suite of newer Unix protocols and utilities, including ssh, scp, and slogin that replace the older Unix rcp, rsh, and rlogin utilities. Unlike these older utilities, password encryption and digital certificates are used with SSH to ensure the entire communication channel is secure from the client to server and server to client. This makes it virtually impossible for attackers using spoofing and IP source redirecting techniques to interfere with a communication session.

HIGH LEVEL DATA LINK CONTROL (HDLC)

High Level Data Link Control (HDLC) is a transmission protocol that operates at the data link layer (Level 2) of the OSI model. HDLC and SDLC (Synchronous Data Link Control) were originally developed for IBM SNA (Systems Network Architecture).

HDLC today, is most commonly used in X.25 Frame Relay packet-switching networks that are used by the Internet. With HDLC, a session is established for communication where one node is designated as the primary node, and another node is designated as the secondary node. After this designation takes place, the following communication modes can be implemented:

Normal unbalanced mode: The secondary node responds only to the primary node's request.

Asynchronous mode: The secondary node can begin the communication by sending a message.

Asynchronous balanced mode: Both stations can send and receive messages by duplex transmission. Networks that implement X.25 packet switching most commonly use this mode.

SYNCHRONOUS DATA LINK CONTROL (SDLC)

SDLC is the original IBM-developed communications protocol on which HDLC is based. SDLC is based on a primary/secondary communications model where a secure connection is established between a mainframe (host) and a client. Multiple clients can be connected to a common point with SDLC. This connection technique is known as multipoint or multidrop. SDLC is an efficient protocol for private networks with dedicated lines of communication.

PASSWORD AUTHENTICATION PROTOCOL (PAP)

Password Authentication Protocol (PAP) is a basic type of authentication where a username and password are transmitted unencrypted across a network to an authenticating host. The host houses a security table or database that is typically encrypted. If the requesting username and password match those stored in the server's database, an acknowledgement is sent to the requester and authentication is granted. In a Windows client/server environment, the server's security database is called the SAM (Security Accounts Manager). PAP is an outdated authentication method. If CHAP (described next) is available on a server, it should be used in place of PAP.

CHALLENGE-HANDSHAKE AUTHENTICATION PROTOCOL (CHAP)

Challenge-Handshake Authentication Protocol (CHAP) is a much more secure method of authenticating communications between server or "agent" and requester than PAP. CHAP uses a secret one-way hash value that is generated by the requestor and sent to the server. The sever builds upon the hash value and generates a secret MD5 (algorithm used to create digital signatures) value that is only known to the requester and server. If the requester's value matches the server's hash value, the requester is authenticated. Only the hash value is transmitted during communication using CHAP. The CHAP authentication process is called a three-way handshake.

POINT-TO-POINT PROTOCOL (PPP)

Point-to-Point Protocol (PPP) is a full-duplex serial communication protocol that operates at the data link layer of the OSI reference model. Internet Service Providers (ISPs) often use PPP to link their customers to the Internet. PPP has replaced the older SLIP (described next) based on its error-checking capabilities and its capability to provided more stability.

SERIAL LINE INTERNET PROTOCOL (SLIP)

Serial Line Internet Protocol (SLIP) is an older TCP/IP communications protocol used to connect two computer systems together. SLIP was and sometimes is still used to connect systems to the Internet through a slow analog dial-up connection. SLIP does not handle error detection as PPP does, is considered outdated technology, and is not supported in newer operating systems such as Windows Vista.

SECURE REMOTE PROCEDURE CALL (RPC)

Secure Remote Procedure Call (RPC) is essentially a protocol that is used to allow a client-side application program to execute or request a service from a server computer without being concerned with network intricacies or server procedures. The RPC protocol operates at the transport and application layers of the OSI reference model. RPC allows for multiple programs to be easily distributed and executed across a network environment. For Example, RPC over HTTP allows for access to an Exchange server over an Internet connection.

BRIDGES, ROUTERS, SWITCHES, AND HUBS

Network devices such as routers, switches, bridges, and hubs connect computing systems and networks together. They are responsible for productive network functionality, backbone support, and the proper forwarding of information to other networks. In short, without them, there would be little or no network connectivity and minimal network security at best.

As the number of computers or nodes on a network increases, a network requires specialized equipment to expand its length, direct its flow of traffic, and provide a centralized location for troubleshooting and maintenance. Next, we will discuss the functionality of each of these devices.

BRIDGES

Bridges are hardware devices that operate at the MAC sublayer of the OSI reference model's data link layer. Bridges are used to segment or separate LANs. Separating a larger network into smaller, more manageable segments can improve network performance and provide a way to isolate network bottlenecks.

A bridge reads the MAC hardware address that is stored in the NIC of every computer or node installed on either side of the bridge. The bridge knows where all the computers are on the network and can forward information to a particular computer by the use of its NIC MAC address. Let's say you are sitting at a computer that resides on network segment number 1. You want to send Brian, whose computer is located on network segment number 2, a Word document. There is a bridge that separates you on network segment number 1 from Brian on network segment number 2. The bridge can identify both of your computers by their respective NIC MAC addresses. Therefore, when you send a Word document to Brian, it is forwarded to his network segment by the use of the bridge.

Bridges can provide the following services:

- Reduce network traffic that results from too many computers being attached to a network.
- Connect different types of media connections, such as coaxial cable and TP cable.
- Expand the length of a network segment.
- Connect different network typologies together, such as Token Ring and Ethernet.

Although bridges serve their primary purpose, they are limited in their capabilities. If a destination's MAC address is not found in a bridge's internal table, the bridge will proliferate, or broadcast (pass traffic) to all network segments. This can result in a broadcast storm that can slow or take down a network.

As networks grew larger, the demand increased for a more intelligent device that could handle an increasing number of attached computer nodes and direct network traffic in a more efficient manner. The router was technology's answer to this demand.

ROUTERS

A router is another device that connects different network segments; but unlike a bridge, a router does not use a computer's MAC address to forward information. Instead, a router operates at the network layer of the OSI reference model and has the ability to forward information based on a network or an individual computer's TCP/IP address. This allows a router to connect entirely separate networks and to filter information to the proper network or network segment. In other words, a router has the ability to send a request to a specific location without broadcasting to all the other computer nodes on a network or network segment.

Routers are very intelligent. They hold sophisticated routing tables and have the ability to remember previous connections that were used as pathways from one computer node to another. Routers can actually decide which path is most efficient for a packet of information to take to reach its final destination.

Routers are primarily used for the following tasks:

■ Provide filtering of packets and reduce broadcast storms.
■ Segment networks into smaller, more manageable pieces.
■ Provide a network security layer between separate networks (a firewall).

Routers use specialized protocols, such as Internet Control Message Protocol (ICMP), Open Shortest Path First (OSPF), and Routing Information Protocol (RIP), to communicate with each other and carry out their advanced functions.

Network Address Translation (NAT) is an Internet standard that is most often used with routers to provide firewall security by hiding the internal private network's range of IP addresses from outside networks. What NAT actually does is translate a given set of internal IP addresses to a separate set of IP addresses that can be seen and accessed outside of a LAN. The translation of internal to external and external to internal IPs provides security and a sort of authentication service to requests. Another benefit of using NAT is that many internal IP addresses can be translated to use one external address. This allows a company to conserve global IPs and use one address to connect outside of the network. For example, a company could combine or map the IP addresses of several ISDN connections into one connection to the Internet. It is possible for administrators to use NAT to map in the following fashions:

- Statically map a local network IP address to a single global IP address.
- Map a local network IP address to a pool of global IP addresses owned by a company.
- Map a single global IP address to a pool of local network IP addresses.
- Map a local network IP address and TCP port address to a global IP address or global pool if IP addresses.

SWITCHES

A switch is a network device similar to a router; it chooses certain paths or routes in a network on which to send data. A switch is not a router, although a switch can contain router functionality. Most modern switches can operate at both the data link and network layers of the OSI reference model. A switch that has the ability to operate at the network layer is known as a layer 3 or IP switch. Switches can connect networks and subnetworks comprised of the same or different cable types. They can send units of data (packets) faster than most routers based on digital packet-switching technology. Switches typically connect LAN segments that use the same protocol.

HUBS

A hub is a network device that acts as a central point used to connect computers together. In network terms, a hub is a simple connection device that sends all data packets to all connected systems. A basic hub operates at the physical layer of the OSI reference model. Generally speaking, in a basic networking setup, if the hub goes down or becomes dysfunctional, all systems connected to the hub will be unable to communicate with each other.

NETWORK INTERFACE CARDS

A NIC is a circuit board that is inserted into an available bus expansion slot on a computer system's motherboard. It allows a computer to connect to and communicate with other computers on a network or LAN.

ROM chips, such as EEPROM on an NIC, store vital information, such as the NIC's I/O address, IRQ, and MAC address.

On a 10BaseT Ethernet network, a TP wire with an RJ45 connector is plugged into the back of a typical 10/100 Mbps PCI-bus NIC. If the NIC has been properly attached to the network, the green and amber LEDs on the back of the NIC will flicker on and off.

NICs are fairly easy to install if you have purchased a popular brand name and are using a PnP operating system. Most newer operating systems have fully compliant software drivers built in that support newer NICs. However, if you are using an ancient, legacy NIC, or your operating system does not support PnP, it will be necessary to use the software driver that came with the NIC. If you do not have the installation software or drivers for the NIC, you should consult the NIC manufacturer's Web site for a possible free driver download.

There are several ways that settings on NICs can be configured. Older, legacy NICs were configured with the use of jumpers or DIP switches on the card itself. Today, most NIC settings are configured with the use of software provided by the manufacturer, or simply by letting PnP make the necessary settings automatically if your NIC card is PnP.

NICs and their connections are notorious for causing network-related trouble if they are malfunctioning or improperly connected. If you or a customer cannot connect to your network, first verify that the NIC and the patch cable connected to it are in working order. If all the hardware is intact, and you see flashing lights on the back of the NIC, you may want to try typing in the correct password to access your network resources.

THE INTERNET AND VIRUSES

The Internet is a huge network that connects millions of host computers with unique IP addresses, all over the world. It is the largest source of information available. The Internet offers a vast array of services. You can buy almost anything, see just about anywhere, and talk or chat with anyone who is connected.

Here are some important Internet-related terms that you should be familiar with for both of the A+ exams:

Uniform Resource Locator (URL): The URL is the line typically located at the top of the browser, such as *http://www.charlesrivermedia.com*. The first part of the line is the Internet protocol to be used—for example, http:. The second part of the URL line is used for the Internet address you are trying to access. It can be an IP address or a domain name, such as charlesrivermedia.com.

Hypertext Transfer Protocol (HTTP): Internet protocol used to transmit instructions to the Web from a Web browser.

Hypertext Markup Language (HTML): HTML allows Web pages to be formatted with graphics and symbols other than plain text. HTML provides the Web page with a set of instructions pertaining to how the page should be displayed to the end user.

Extensible Markup Language (XML): XML is similar to HTML, but XML offers developers and designers more flexibility in creating Web pages through the use of call tags. Call tags are responsible for calling methods inside the objects created in a program.

VIRUSES

A virus is a program or specific piece of code that is designed, when executed, to duplicate itself and/or spread itself to other areas of a system or other systems in a networked environment. In general terms, a virus will replicate itself until it uses up all available system resources, such as memory or hard drive space. An undetected virus that has infected a system and has been successful at achieving its goal results in a system that simply will not function. In most cases, this makes the system unavailable to other systems or results in a denial of service.

Never open an e-mail attachment if you are not sure of the identity of its sender. That "Incredibly Interesting and Free Offer" may lead to the death of your system.

The Internet also offers a vast array of threats to you and your computer. You can lose your good credit standing if certain personal information is obtained and used for illegal purposes. Computers are vulnerable to computer viruses, as well as full-scale marketing attacks.

The Internet is swarming with many unfriendly computer viruses. If you are interested in protecting the integrity of your stored data or the business you may be responsible for, it is very important to use a good virus protection program and update your antivirus .DAT files (definitions) on a regular basis. .DAT is the file extension used for a file or program that contains a list of the most current viruses. If you are running an enterprise network, you should incorporate a good enterprise antivirus solution. The top manufactures of antivirus software offer single-user or multi-user versions of their antivirus software programs. Remember that computer viruses are most commonly obtained from the Internet and floppy disks.

Worms

A worm is a type of virus that gets its name from its inherent ability to spread itself to other networked systems, remain resident in memory, and keep in contact with other segmented pieces of itself until triggered by a certain event to duplicate and spread itself.

Most worm viruses reside in memory, unattached to files, and when triggered, will reproduce themselves until available resources are exhausted. A worm is a self-contained unit or program that is typically spread through e-mail attachments and network connections, such as drive mappings.

A worm is a type of virus that can replicate itself; however, worms do not attach to other programs. In other words, worms are not carried by or attached to hosting files.

Trojan Horses

A Trojan horse is a program that appears on the outside to be harmless. It masquerades itself as an apparently nondestructive, harmless, and innocent application, program, or message. Trojan horses can carry very dangerous payloads that are highly destructive to networks and systems.

Most Trojan horses are hidden in Internet attachments that oftentimes are distributed with e-mail in the form of jokes, love letters, and misguiding advertisements. One of the most important facts to understand about Trojan horses is that they do not replicate or copy themselves. They require actions by the user to activate and deliver their dangerous contents, such as the opening of an attachment or the running of an application. Worms and viruses duplicate themselves. Trojans do not.

ANTIVIRUS PRACTICES

A combination of education, training, and management practices, along with the use of strong antivirus products, are essential to the survival and welfare of computer systems and networks.

Following are some basic guidelines that should be followed when using and managing antivirus software at home or in a business enterprise:

■ Install, update, and maintain reputable, quality antivirus software in servers and workstations. This includes setting up daily antivirus definition updates, enabling real-time protection, setting up scheduled scans of all system drives, and enabling e-mail and attachment scanning.

If you are unable to install new software programs or device drivers on your system, your virus protection software or firewall may be blocking your install abilities. You may have to disable real-time protection or disable your entire antivirus suite altogether before installing new software. You should consult your antivirus manufacturer's manual for protection and new installation instructions.

■ All users of computer systems (at home or in the workplace) should be educated/ alerted when virus attacks occur or are expected to occur. Symantec Corporation does a great job of updating their Web site when virus threats are anticipated. This information can prove invaluable to administrators who need to apply particular patches or make updates in preparation for new or anticipated variations of viruses.

■ Educate all users (at home or in the workplace) that opening e-mail attachments as well as instant messaging attachments may be detrimental to your system's life span.

■ In a business environment, ensure that your corporate antivirus business policy is up to date and accurate. Ensure that new and existing employees sign an addendum that states they are familiar with the company's policy regarding computer usage as well as virus policy and procedures.

CABLE, ISDN, DSL, AND SATELLITE

Most connections to the Internet are accessed through an Internet Service Provider (ISP). A local or national ISP provides an IP address that can be used to gain access to the Internet. Although many individuals and businesses still use a 56 Kbps analog dial-up connection to access the Internet, broadband services such as cable, ISDN, and DSL, are the most popular ways of connecting to the Internet. See Table 9.2 for a quick reference of Internet technology connection types and associated speeds.

TABLE 9.2 Internet Connection Types and Speeds

Connection Type	Average Connection Speed
Telephone modem	14.4–56 Kbps
Cable modem	1–2 Mbps
ISDN	128 Kbps
DSL	1.5 Mbps and higher
Satellite	400 Kbps
T1 line	1.544 Mbps

CABLE

Broadband cable modem connections seem to be the Internet connectivity tool of choice for today's home users. All you really need for this technology is a cable modem, a NIC, an RJ45 cable, a coaxial cable, and an ISP. This technology allows Internet access speeds of around 1.5 Mbps. It provides a connection similar to that of cable television. The signal is always at the end of the cable wire, waiting to be accessed; in other words, the connection is always available. There is no need to reconnect to the ISP every time you want to access the Internet.

A traditional cable modem uses two connections. It connects to a wall-mounted incoming cable connection with a coaxial cable and connects to a computer system, hub, or router using a standard 10BaseT Ethernet cable with an RJ45 connector.

The previously mentioned cable connection speed of approximately 1.5 Mbps is much faster than that of a 56 Kbps telephone modem. Cable is also faster than ISDN, which has a speed of approximately 128 Kbps, and cable currently competes with speeds by DSL.

INTEGRATED SERVICES DIGITAL NETWORK (ISDN)

ISDN is a baseband transmission technology that is well suited for the transmission of audio and video at rates of up to 128 Kbps. ISDN uses an adapter that is included with an ISDN router in place of a standard analog modem.

Two types of ISDN services are typically available from ISPs or local phone carriers: Basic Rate Interface (BRI) and Primary Rate Interface (PRI).

Basic Rate Interface (BRI): BRI is an ISDN technology made up of two 64 Kbps B channels that carry data and voice and a 16 Kbps D channel that is responsible for control information. BRI implementations are common for small-business and home use.

Primary Rate Interface (PRI): PRI is an ISDN technology that is used with larger businesses, such as ISPs and telecommunication companies. PRI is made up of 23 B channels and one D channel. PRI typically uses the bandwidth capabilities of a T1 connection.

ISDN has for the most part been replaced with DSL technology, which is described next.

DIGITAL SUBSCRIBER LINE (DSL)

DSL is a connection technology that uses regular copper wire telephone lines, or Plain Old Telephone Service (POTS), to bring access speeds of up to 6.1 Mbps to homes or businesses. In actuality, DSL offers upload speeds of up to 128 Kbps and download speeds of 1.5 Mbps for individual connections. DSL uses a modem for a highly sophisticated modulation process and is well suited for high-speed transmission of audio and video.

DSL has provided major competition to the cable modem and is commonly used in locations that cable service or access is not offered.

Unlike using less secure cable modem services, DSL is not a shared service connection. To be more specific, you do not share your DSL connection with your neighbors, as cable subscribers do.

DSL implements two types of speeds. An upload speed, or upstream speed, and a download speed, or downstream speed. The upload speed represents how fast you can transmit information to other locations or computers connected to the Internet. The download speed represents how fast you can download such things as files, programs, or music to your system from other systems on the Internet.

As well as these two types of speeds, there are two separate forms of DSL technology available that can offer different speeds. They are ADSL (Asymmetric DSL) and SDSL (Symmetric DSL), which are described next.

NOTE

DSL is a connection technology that uses existing POTS wires. It requires a special modem and typically requires that a signal splitter be installed in the home or office. DSL is a technology that can be remotely activated.

ADSL (Asymmetric DSL)

ADSL is by far the most commonly used form of DSL today. ADSL works simultaneously with voice over existing telephone lines. It works asymmetrically, meaning that the speed used for downstream receiving transmissions is far greater than the speed used for upstream sending. ADSL was developed with the home- and small-business user in mind. The ADSL conceptual theory is based on the fact that the typical end user will download far more information than they will be sending.

It supports receiving data rates (downstream rate) from 1.5–9.0 Mbps and sending data rates (upstream rates) from 16–640 Kbps.

Remember for the exam, asymmetric means that transmission rates are not the same in both directions.

SDSL (Symmetric DSL)

SDSL is well suited for business applications and programs that require and depend on the same speed for sending and receiving data. In other words, with SDSL, your upstream speed is identical to your downstream speed. SDSL can support data rates up to 3 Mbps.

SDSL operates on the same phone wires that are used for normal voice communication. But because SDSL technology works at higher frequencies than that of normal voice, it can exist on the same media without interfering.

Remember for the exam, symmetric means that transmission rates are the same in both directions.

SATELLITE

A satellite is a wireless communications device that orbits the earth, acting as a receiver/transmitter for such things as Internet connectivity and GPS (Global

Positioning Systems). A satellite Internet connection is similar to a satellite TV connection in that a satellite signal is transmitted to a receiver and the signal is decoded on the satellite subscriber's end. Most satellite Internet connections are considered asynchronous, with upstream speeds for a single system averaging 50–150 Kbps and up to 1,200 Kbps for downloads or downstreaming.

Satellite connections are ideal for those who are located out of the range of cable and DSL service providers. To use a satellite Internet connection, you will need a satellite dish antenna, a transceiver (for transmitting and receiving), and a two-way satellite ISP.

In general terms, here's how it works:

- The satellite dish antenna is mounted on or near your home or business.
- The satellite dish antenna is connected to a satellite modem (transceiver) with a coaxial cable.
- The satellite modem communicates with your PC through an Ethernet or USB connection.
- Information is transmitted to and received from a two-way geosynchronous satellite that orbits approximately 22,300 miles above the equator.
- The geosynchronous satellite communicates with a provider facility that is connected to the Internet.

Using an Internet satellite connection is not always perfect or guaranteed; solar interference and periods of rain fade (signal loss caused by inclement weather) sometimes cause signal degradation or loss of connection.

FIREWALLS

A firewall is an implementation of software, hardware, or a combination of both specifically designed to keep unauthorized users, programs, and other threats from entering a computer system or network. A typical firewall analyzes every packet of information that attempts to enter or exit a network or computer system. If the packet does not meet the specifications implemented by the firewall, the packet or connection is denied access. Several implementations of firewall techniques are provided through the use of a packet filter, a proxy server, an application, or a circuit gateway. For our test study focus, you should be aware that a software firewall is installed or located on a hard drive. For more protection from outside influences, you should also consider the use of data encryption.

There are many types of firewalls that can be implemented to protect inside information from outside sources. Some of the most common types of firewalls are listed here:

Dual Homed Host: A dual homed host, sometimes referred to as multihomed, is a system with two NIC cards. One NIC card supports access to a private network, and one supports access to a public network. This acts as a filter and is also known as a multihomed bastion host.

Packet Filter: Packet sniffing programs and network monitors can capture and analyze network packets coming into or going out of a network. A packet filtering firewall identifies good from bad packet information. The main downfall with most of the packet filtering programs available today is their inability to identify whether the packets were sent by a normal, innocent user or a threatening, vicious source. What most packet filters actually do is examine UDP and TCP ports and packet header information. Table 9.3 displays some of the most "well known" TCP and UDP ports and the upper layer protocols that use them.

Circuit Gateway: A circuit gateway operates at the session layer of the OSI reference model. It is essentially a packet filter that relays packets from one host to another based on the protocol and IP address. A circuit gateway forms a sort of tunnel through a firewall, allowing two specified hosts to interact.

Stateful Inspection Firewall: This type of firewall has the ability to remember detailed information about packets that have previously passed through. Then, they are able to compare and analyze this information and decide whether to let certain packets through the firewall. In other words, a stateful firewall can compare incoming requests to outbound messages and see if there is a relationship between the two. If not, the firewall can block the incoming request. Stateful firewalls provide better overall analysis than most other firewall types, such as packet filters.

NOTE

You should be very familiar with Table 9.3 for the exam.

TABLE 9.3 Important TCP/UDP Ports

Type	TCP/UDP	Port Number
FTP	TCP	20, 21
TELNET	TCP	23
SMTP	TCP	25
SMTP\Trap	UDP	161\162
DNS	UDP	53
HTTP	TCP	80
POP3	TCP	110
NETBIOS	UDP	137-139

The well-known ports are those in the range 0–1023. For a complete list of ports and port numbers, visit the Wikipedia Web site that has a fantastic list of ports and their values at http://en.wikipedia.org/wiki/List_of_TCP_and_UDP_port_numbers.

VIRTUAL PRIVATE NETWORK (VPN)

As soon as the efficiency and security of LANs became evident to administrators, it became clear that these secure networks needed a farther reach. Until the advent of VPN (virtual private networking), this involved the costly use of fiber optic or ISDN leased lines. Unfortunately, the expense of maintaining a private WAN grows with the distance from point A to point B. So, after the Internet proved itself as a reliable way to exchange data, businesses naturally turned to it to extend their networks. The Internet, however, is as wide open as the big skies of Montana. A process was needed to harness the global reach of this massive TCP/IP network while ensuring secure, reliable, and quick communications. Enter VPN.

In a nutshell, a VPN is a private network routed through public lines. VPNs use virtual connections established over the Internet as opposed to a dedicated, leased line approach. They are used to connect multiple LANs together (site-to-site) as well as to facilitate communications with users in the field. For instance, when a mobile user connects to the ISP from any location, the user can then be authenticated on the company network over a VPN. This type of remote access VPN is also called a VPDN (Virtual Private Dial-up Network). It's fast, secure, scalable, and best of all, the intricacies are transparent to the user.

So now that you have an idea of what VPN is and why it's used, let's talk about security. By nature, the study of security is a sensitive endeavor. If you have been hired to establish a secure network, you'd better be sure that's what your employer ends up with. So how does this VPN achieve such security through the vast gulf that is the Internet? There are actually several ways VPN keeps your data secure:

Firewall: The first step in implementing a VPN is having a solid firewall installed. Firewalls are used to prevent access to private networks from the Internet or other interconnected networks. A firewall can be programmed to block traffic based on the type of packet trying to get through, which protocol or port is being used for the transmission, or a host of other user-defined rules. A firewall is an implementation of software, hardware, or a combination of both specifically designed to keep unauthorized users, programs, and other threats from entering a computer system or network. A typical firewall analyzes every packet of information that attempts to enter or exit a network or computer system. If the packet does not meet the specifications implemented by the firewall, the packet or connection is denied access.

IPSec (Internet Protocol Security): Using a group of protocols developed by the IETF (Internet Engineering Task Force), this method enables the secure transfer of packets at the IP layer. IPSec employs two encryption modes: transport and tunnel. Using the transport mode, only the data portion (or payload) of a packet is encrypted, and the header remains unchanged. In tunnel mode, security is further enhanced because both the payload and header are encrypted. An IPSec-compliant device (router, firewall, etc.) is required on the receiving end to decrypt the packet. Sending and receiving devices must both obtain a common public key for this method to work, which is accomplished by using a protocol called Internet Security Association and Key Management Protocol/Oakley (ISAKMP/Oakley). ISAKMP/Oakley also enables the receiver to authenticate the sender using a digital certificate.

Encryption: This is a way of sending data in a form that only the intended receiving computer can decrypt. Most encryption systems use one of two standard ways of accomplishing this: symmetric-key encryption and public-key encryption.

- **Symmetric-key encryption** employs a single key to encode and decode messages. Although simpler than the public-key approach, this method requires the sending and receiving computers to first exchange the key securely. Think of this approach as a "secret code" that both parties must have to decrypt messages. Public-key encryption gets around this problem by transmitting the public key to anyone who wants it, and never transmitting the private key.

- **Public-key encryption** (also called asymmetric encryption) employs both a public key and a private key. Only your computer knows the private key, and the public key is handed to any computer that wants to engage in secure communications. To decipher an encrypted message, the receiving computer must use both the public key provided by you and its own private key. For instance, if Computer A wants to send a secure message to Computer B, it would use Computer B's public key to encode the message. Computer B then uses its own private key to decrypt it. Using this method, it's nearly impossible to discover the private key if all you have is the public key. This process was developed in 1976 by Whitfield Diffie and Martin Hellman and is sometimes referred to as Diffie-Hellman encryption. One public-key system, Pretty Good Privacy (PGP), is now widely used for secure transmissions over the Internet.

Another technology that enables VPNs to work is called tunneling. This process involves encapsulating a network protocol within a packet prior to transmission. To tunnel data, three types of protocols are used:

Carrier Protocol: The native protocol used by the network carrying the data.

Tunneling Protocol: The protocol (PPTP, IPSec, L2F, L2TP, GRE) that the original data is encapsulated in.

Passenger Protocol: The protocol (IPX, NetBeui, IP) native to the original data.

Tunneling enables the secure transmission of packets using protocols not supported by the Internet, to be sent inside IP packets. For instance, a remote user sends a message from his laptop over the VPN. The original message was in the form of a NetBeui packet, which is useless on the Internet. After this packet is encapsulated in an IP packet, it can make its way through the Internet via PPP, for example, and arrive at its destination back in its original form.

In a VPDN, PPP is usually used to tunnel packets. A few other protocols developed in the image of PPP are L2TP (Layer 2 Tunneling Protocol), L2F (Layer 2 Forwarding), and PPTP (Point-to-Point Tunneling Protocol). In a site-to-site VPN, GRE (Generic Routing Encapsulation) or IPSec in tunnel mode are most often the tunneling methods of choice.

TROUBLESHOOTING AND BASIC NETWORKING TEST TIPS

The troubleshooting and basic networking test tips that are provided next have been included to give you a taste of the various types of networking topics and questions that may come your way on the real exam.

Pay very close attention to the following test tips. They just might be what you need to secure a passing score on the networking portion of the exams.

- If you have a workstation physically connected to your network, but you cannot PING or communicate with other systems on your network, you should first verify the link status on your NIC to see if it is blinking.
- If you are connected to the Internet using a 56 Kbps modem, but your connection speed is only 28 Kbps, it is likely that there is noise on your phone line connection, or your ISP is only handing out 28 Kbps connections.
- The easiest way to connect two computers that both have NICs in a peer-to-peer style network fashion is to use a crossover cable.
- A device called a repeater can be used to extend the length of a 10Base2 network.

■ If you keep receiving the message "This page cannot be displayed" while attempting to access a particular Web site, it is very likely that the host computer that provides the resource you are trying to access is having issues or is down.

■ If you are using a dial-up connection and your mouse pointer freezes on your screen when you attempt to access the Internet, you are likely experiencing an IRQ conflict. Check this first, and then get cable or DSL!

■ ISDN (Integrated Service Digital Network) carries data and voice over traditional telephone networks.

■ DSL (Digital Subscriber Line) is considered a better and faster replacement for ISDN. DSL is a technology that can provide considerable bandwidth capabilities to small businesses and homeowners alike. DSL uses traditional existing TP telephone lines.

■ Cable modem is considered the most insecure technology based on the fact that a default installation does not provide a firewall or any other sort of packet filtering. With a default installation method, users share a single coax cable connection.

■ Wireless technology is the fastest growing area for connectivity.

■ Dial-up (asynchronous) is the traditional connection method that uses an ISP and an analog phone line to connect to the Internet.

■ When assessing a network-related or computer-related issue over the phone, you should only ask users or clients troubleshooting questions that are directly relate to gaining information that will assist with fixing the issue at hand. Questions such as, "When did this issue first start happening?" or "What were you specifically doing when the issue began?" are purposeful, structured questions that are directly focused on gaining helpful troubleshooting information. Questions such as "what color is your mom's computer?" or "What kind of system would you buy if you won the lottery?" are useless when attempting to gain information that will directly affect the time it takes to resolve a system or network related issue. Yes, you may actually experience customer service related questions like this on the real exam.

■ ICMP (Internet Control Message Protocol) enables systems on a TCP/IP network to share status and error information, for example, the use of PING and TRACERT utilities.

■ POP3 (Post Office Protocol) is a protocol used to receive e-mail. A POP3 mail server holds all mail until the requestor or user is ready to receive it.

■ TELNET provides a virtual terminal that allows remote login access across a network. The Telnet service must be running on the remote server for clients to connect.

■ HTTP (Hypertext Transfer Protocol) is a protocol used for exchanging files, messages, sound, and video on the Web.

- 127.x.x.x is reserved for loopback testing on a local computer system. IP address ranges 10.0.0.0–10.254.254.254, 172.16.0.0–172.31.254.254, and 192.168.0.0–192.168.254.254 are reserved for private networks.
- The HTTPS (Secure HTTP) protocol is used for accessing secure Web servers and pages on the Internet. When the protocol HTTPS is used, HTTPS appears in the URL, for example, *https://verysecuresite.com*.

CHAPTER SUMMARY

The primary focus of this chapter was to get you up to speed on the basic concepts of networking. At this point, you should be familiar with the basic network categories and topologies and the media access methods used for networks. You should also have a basic understanding of TCP/IP and be able to troubleshoot simple network connectivity issues.

This chapter was designed to help you handle just about any networking questions the A+ exams may ask. Once again, however, there is no substitute for hands-on training. As a final important note and warning regarding your A+ exam study, CompTIA seems to be putting more operating systems and setup-related questions into all of the exams. For example, the exam may ask you something like "Where is regedit.exe found or stored?" For this reason, it is highly recommended that you complete all sections of this book to better increase your chances of passing any of the four current exams.

REVIEW QUESTIONS

1. **A computer on your network is unable to communicate with other computers. What would you check first?**

   ○ A. That other computers are working
   ○ B. That your Internet connection is functional
   ○ C. The computer's IP address configuration
   ○ D. The IP address configuration of the network file server

   Correct Answer = C

   If a single computer on your network cannot communicate with other systems on the same network, the IP address is probably invalid or the system has not received an IP address from a DHCP server, which hands out IP addresses randomly on the network.

2. **For two computers to communicate with each other, they must have a common language. What is this common language called?**
   - A. Binary conversion
   - B. Data translation
   - C. IPCONFIG /ALL
   - D. Protocol

   Correct Answer = D

   For two computers to communicate, they must have a common language or set of rules known as a protocol. Binary conversion is a process used to convert binary numbers to decimal numbers to binary. IPCONFIG /ALL is a TCP/IP command used to display TCP/IP configuration settings.

3. **What are two tools you can use to test a modem? (Choose Two)**
   - A. A loopback plug
   - B. A digital multimeter
   - C. An analog loopback adapter
   - D. A small brush and compressed air

   Correct Answers = A and C

   A loopback plug or analog loopback adapter can be used to test the integrity of a modem. A digital multimeter is used to troubleshoot system power-related issues. A small brush and compressed air are used to clean a system unit.

4. **You want to connect a new computer to your Ethernet network. What device must you install to do so? To communicate with your Ethernet network, you would need to install and configure a NIC with associated software drivers. Keep in mind that most newer systems have Gb Ethernet cards built in.**
   - A. An internal modem
   - B. A switch
   - C. An IP converser
   - D. A NIC card

   Correct Answer = D

5. **Ten users on your network have all downloaded a fancy game from the same Internet site. Unfortunately, none of the computers will work anymore. What question would ask each of the 10 users?**

○ A. Is the game really worth it?

○ B. Did you do this on company time?

○ C. Did you virus scan the game's executable program before running?

○ D. What version of BIOS is installed on your computer?

Correct Answer = C

If you get this question wrong, please start reading this book from page one again. Always virus scan any programs you download from the Internet!

6. **Where do most computer viruses come from? (Choose Two)**

   □ A. A borrowed floppy disk

   □ B. A mosquito

   □ C. The Internet

   □ D. Software provided by the manufacturer

   □ E. A big wooden horse from Greek Mythology

Correct Answers = A and C

Most computer viruses arrive through a borrowed floppy or other removable media disk or the Internet.

7. **A customer cannot log in to the network. Others on the network segment can log in without an issue. You are logged in to the network using your computer and the customer's ID and password without an issue. What is most likely causing login issue at the customer's workstation? (Choose 3)**

   □ A. The customer is entering the wrong password at his workstation.

   □ B. The NIC in the customer's workstation is malfunctioning.

   □ C. The patch cable that attaches the customer's workstation to the network is bad.

   □ D. The entire network is experience RFI (Radio Frequency Interference).

   □ E. The switch that both you and the customer are attached to has been powered off.

Correct Answers = A, B, and C

If the entire network were affected by RFI, you would have problems with more than one user. A network hub or switch is used to connect several computers together on a network. If the hub or switches were powered off, all users on that particular network would be affected.

8. **What type of connections can be used with TCP/IP? (Choose 3)**

   ☐ A. Ethernet
   ☐ B. Token Ring
   ☐ C. RJ45 and RJ11
   ☐ D. Analog modem dial-up connection

   Correct Answers = A, B, and D

   Ethernet, Token Ring, and modem connections can all be configured to use TCP/IP. RJ45 and RJ11 are connector types. They are not actually configured to use TCP/IP.

9. **How can configuration settings on a NIC be changed? (Choose 3)**

   ☐ A. Jumpers
   ☐ B. Wire traces
   ☐ C. Configuration software
   ☐ D. Operating system's PnP features

   Correct Answers = A, C, and D

   You can configure your NIC settings with onboard jumpers or NIC configuration software usually provided by the manufacturer. If you are using a PnP operating system, your NIC setting can be configured automatically in most cases.

10. **Which of the following represent peer-to-peer networks? (Choose 2)**

    ☐ A. Centralized administration and security
    ☐ B. Limited number of computers (usually less than 10)
    ☐ C. One computer acting as a client and a server
    ☐ D. Requires a high-end server computer to provide login authentication and provide resources

    Correct Answers = B and C

    A peer-to-peer network is a small network, usually of 10 or fewer computer systems, connected without the use of a larger specialized server computer. In peer-to-peer networks, a workstation can function as both a client and a server computer.

11. **You have a NIC that doesn't have jumpers and is not PnP compliant. How will you configure it to be used with your system?**

    ○ A. Purchase add-on jumpers.
    ○ B. Install IPX/SPX.
    ○ C. The operating system will detect it.
    ○ D. Use manufacturer's configuration software.
    ○ E. None of the above.

    Correct Answer = D

    Legacy NICs were configured with the use of jumpers or DIP switches on the card itself. Today, most NIC settings are configured with the use of software provided by the manufacturer or simply by letting PnP make the necessary settings automatically.

12. **You are attempting to install a 64-bit video card driver for a newly purchase video card, but when you try to install the driver, nothing happens. What could be the problem?**

    ○ A. Most newer computer operating systems require P.A. (Parents Approval) before the installation of new video card drivers.
    ○ B. Your antiviral software or a firewall may be blocking your install abilities.
    ○ C. You forgot to enter the EULA (End User License Agreement) code for the video card software.
    ○ D. Your ISP does not allow 64-bit video cards to be used on connected systems.
    ○ E. All of the above.

    Correct Answer = B

    If you are unable to install new software programs or device drivers on your system, your virus protection software or firewall may be blocking your install abilities. You may have to disable real-time protection or disable your entire antivirus suite before installing new software.

13. **Which are considered to have the least amount of overhead and are meant for efficient communications in small networks or LANS?**

    ○ A. TCP/IP and IPX/SPX
    ○ B. TCP/IP and NetBIOS
    ○ C. NetBEUI and TCP/IP
    ○ D. NetBIOS and NetBEUI
    ○ E. None of the above

Correct Answer = D

NetBIOS is not routable. NetBIOS works well in LANs but not WANs. For WAN communication, you need TCP/P. NetBEUI is a nonroutable, small, efficient transport layer protocol meant for use in small networks with 1 to 200 workstations.

14. **With which type of DSL is the data rate considered the same in both directions?**
    - ○ A. ADSL (Asymmetric DSL)
    - ○ B. SDSL (Symmetric DSL)
    - ○ C. BiDSL (Bi-directional DSL)
    - ○ D. DDRDSL (Dual Data Rate DSL)
    - ○ E. All of the above transmit and receive data at the same data rate.

Correct Answer = B

SDSL (Symmetric DSL) is well suited for business applications and programs that require and depend on the same speed for sending and receiving data. With SDSL, your upstream speed is the same as your downstream speed.

15. **Which statement is not true regarding DSL?**
    - ○ A. DSL most often uses exiting POTS lines.
    - ○ B. ADSL and SDSL are DSL transmission types.
    - ○ C. DSL most often requires a special DSL modem and splitter.
    - ○ D. DSL is less secure than a cable modem Internet connection because a single DSL is shared.
    - ○ E. All of the above statements are true.

Correct Answer = D

Unlike using less secure cable modem services, DSL is not a shared service connection. To be more specific, you do not share your DSL connection with your neighbors as cable subscribers do.

16. **Which statement is not true regarding satellite Internet connectivity?**
    - ○ A. Satellite modems communicate with your PC through an Ethernet or USB connection.
    - ○ B. A two-way geosynchronous satellite is used.
    - ○ C. Satellite connections are ideal for those located outside the range of cable and DSL services.

○ D. To use a satellite Internet connection, you need a satellite dish antenna.

○ E. All of the above statements are true.

Correct Answer = E

All of the statements are true of satellite Internet connectivity.

17. **Which IEEE specification is concerned primarily with security?**

○ A. 802.3

○ B. 802.5

○ C. 802.10

○ D. 802.11

Correct Answer = C

802.3 is concerned with Carrier-Sense Multiple Access with Collision Detection (CSMA/CD) in local area Ethernet networks. The 802.5 specification is for Token Ring LANs. 802.11 is an IEEE specification for wireless communications.

18. **Which type of network cabling is the most difficult to tap into and considered the most secure?**

○ A. Shielded Twisted Pair

○ B. Twisted Pair

○ C. Coax

○ D. Fiber

Correct Answer = D

Fiber-optic cable is much more difficult to tap into than other types of network cable. Special equipment and skilled hands are required to carry out such a task. This is not the case with twisted pair, shielded twist pair, and coaxial types of cable.

19. **Which statement is true regarding firewalls?**

○ A. They will protect your internal network from a virus that resides on workstation on your internal network.

○ B. If properly configured, a firewall will protect an internal network from an external network.

○ C. Firewalls are used to protect your internal network from unauthorized external access through dial-up modem connections.

○ D. Firewalls are used to protect internal server room computers from external natural disasters.

Correct Answer = B

Properly configured firewalls will protect an internal network from an external network. An antivirus program and updated operating system service packs are used to protect your internal network from a virus that resides on a workstation on your internal network. Firewalls do not provide protection through dial-up modem connections, nor do they protect against natural disasters.

20. **Which of the following describe an FDDI ring? (Choose Three)**
    - ☐ A.   Offer up to 100 Mbps data transmission speeds
    - ☐ B.   Are composed of dual rings with data traveling in opposite directions
    - ☐ C.   Can serve as a network backbone
    - ☐ D.   The easiest topology to tap into
    - ☐ E.   Uses CSMA/CD technology

Correct Answers = A, B, and C

Answers A, B, and C are all true statements regarding FDDI rings. Option D is a sort of a trick. FDDI uses fiber cable, which as you are already aware is more difficult to tap into than most other cable types. FDDI uses token-passing technology not CSMA/CD (Carrier Sense Multiple Access with Collision Detection). CSMA/CD is used in Ethernet networks.

21. **Which of the following choices forms a sort of tunnel for two hosts to communicate?**
    - ○ A.   Packet filter
    - ○ B.   Circuit gateway
    - ○ C.   Application proxy
    - ○ D.   FDDI

Correct Answer = B

A circuit gateway forms a sort of tunnel through a firewall allowing two specified hosts to interact. Packet filters examine UDP, TCP ports, and packet header information. They can identify good from bad packet information. Application proxies (or gateways) are concerned more with specific applications and actual data. FDDI is a network topology standard that uses dual fiber-optic rings.

22. **Of the following protocols, which protocol uses a one-way hash function to assist with the authentication process?**

    ○ A.   Password Authentication Protocol (PAP)
    ○ B.   Challenge-Handshake Authentication Protocol (CHAP)
    ○ C.   Point-To-Point Protocol (PPP)
    ○ D.   Serial Line Internet Protocol (SLIP)

    Correct Answer = B

    CHAP uses a secret one-way hash value that is generated by the requestor and sent to the server. PAP is a basic type of authentication where a username and password are transmitted unencrypted across a network to an authenticating host. PPP is a full-duplex serial communication protocol that operates at the data link layers of the OSI reference model. SLIP is an older TCP/IP communications protocol used to connect two computer systems together.

23. **Which of the following protocols is used to map or "resolve" an IP address to a system's physical hardware address?**

    ○ A.   HTTPS
    ○ B.   SDLC
    ○ C.   HDLC
    ○ D.   ARP

    Correct Answer = D

    Address Resolution Protocol (ARP) is used to map an IP (Internet Protocol) address at the network layer of the OSI model to a physical hardware address at the MAC (Media Access Control) sublayer. Hypertext Transport Protocol Secure (HTTPS) is a secure protocol used to transmit messages over the Internet. Synchronous Data Link Control (SDLC) is based on a primary/secondary communications model where a secure connection is established between a mainframe (host) and a client. High Level Data Link Control (HDLC) is a transmission protocol that operates at the data link layer (Level 2) of the OSI model.

24. **Which of the following provides a type of firewall by hiding internal IP addresses from outside networks?**

    ○ A.   ARP
    ○ B.   NAT
    ○ C.   PAP
    ○ D.   RPC

Correct Answer = B

Network Address Translation (NAT) is an Internet standard most often used with routers to provide firewall security by hiding an internal private network's range of IP addresses from outside networks. Address Resolution Protocol (ARP) is used to map an IP (Internet Protocol) address at the network layer of the OSI model to a physical hardware address at the MAC (Media Access Control) sublayer. Password Authentication Protocol (PAP) is a basic type of authentication where a username and password are transmitted unencrypted across a network to an authenticating host. Secure Remote Procedure Call (RPC) is essentially a protocol that is used to allow a client-side application program to execute or request a service from a server computer without being concerned with network intricacies or server procedures.

25. **Which device does not forward all broadcast traffic and has the ability to forward data packets to other networks based on IP address information?**
    - ○ A. Bridge
    - ○ B. Router
    - ○ C. Hub
    - ○ D. Repeater

Correct Answer = B

A router operates at the network layer of the OSI reference model and has the ability to forward information based on a network's or individual computer's TCP/IP address. A router has the ability to filter out broadcast traffic. Bridges are limited in their capabilities. They forward packet information based on a MAC address. A bridge proliferates or broadcasts (pass traffic) to all network segments. This can often result in a broadcast storm that can slow or take down a network. A hub is a simple connection device that sends all data packets to all connected systems. A repeater is used to boost or regenerate the signals placed on a 10Base2 or bus network. Adding a repeater to your bus can extend the length of your entire bus network.

26. **Which TCP port is HTTP associated with?**
    - ○ A. 21
    - ○ B. 25
    - ○ C. 53
    - ○ D. 80

Correct Answer = D

HTTP traffic uses TCP port 80. FTP uses TCP port 21. SMTP uses TCP port 25. DNS uses UDP port 53. Please refer to Table 9.3.

27. How long are IPv6 addresses?

   ○ A.   16 bits
   ○ B.   32 bits
   ○ C.   64 bits
   ○ D.   128 bits

Correct Answer = D

IPv6 allows for IP addresses to be lengthened from the IPv4 limitation of 32 bits to 128 bits. IPv6 also allows for better authentication, privacy and improved data delivery assurance.

28. FTP uses which TCP ports?

   ○ A.   25
   ○ B.   20, 21
   ○ C.   23
   ○ D.   80

Correct Answer = B

FTP uses TCP ports 20 and 21, SMTP uses TCP port 25, TELNET uses TCP port 23, and HTTP uses TCP port 80. You better know this for any security exam!

29. You are configuring e-mail for one of your remote clients on your Microsoft Exchange e-mail server so they can send and receive e-mail. What two protocols allow the client to send and receive e-mail?

   ○ A.   SMTP and SNTP
   ○ B.   SMTP and POP3
   ○ C.   POP3 and SNTP
   ○ D.   None of the above

Correct Answer = B

Simple Mail Transport Protocol (SMTP) is a protocol that e-mail servers use to transmit messages. In other words, it is used to send e-mail. The Post Office Protocol (POP3) is a protocol that e-mail clients use to retrieve messages from an e-mail server. In other words, it receives e-mail. Simple Network Management Protocol (SNMP) is a protocol used to manage networks.

30. **Which Internet protocol is used to establish a secure connection?**

○ A.   ICMP
○ B.   POP3
○ C.   Telnet
○ D.   HTTP
○ E.   HTTPS
○ F.   None of the above

Correct Answer = E

ICMP (Internet Control Message Protocol) enables systems on a TCP/IP network to share status and error information. POP3 (Post Office Protocol) is an e-mail protocol used to receive e-mails. Telnet provides a virtual terminal that allows remote login access across a network. HTTP (Hypertext Transfer Protocol) is a protocol used for exchanging files, messages, sound, and video on the Web. It is not a secure protocol. HTTPS (Secure HTTP) protocol is used for accessing secure Web servers and pages on the Internet.

REFERENCES

www.ieee.org/portal/index.jsp. This site is the home of the IEEE standards, as well as updates to these standards.

http://en.wikipedia.org/wiki/Osi_model. This Wikipedia Web site has a great description of the OSI model.

http://en.wikipedia.org/wiki/List_of_TCP_and_UDP_port_numbers. This Wikipedia Website has a fantastic list of TAP/UDP ports and their corresponding functions.

2-9 Test Taker's Cumulative Practice Exam

The questions in this practice exam are based on topics that have been presented in Chapters 2 through 9 of this book. The answers to the following questions as well as the chapter headers they are taken from are provided at the end of the exam.

If you can answer all 80 questions in this practice exam correctly, as well as understand the theory behind each topic mentioned, you are halfway to passing any of the current four A+ examinations.

1. **Which of the following will work with Slot 1 architecture? (Choose Two)**
   - ☐ A. AMD AT
   - ☐ B. AMD K6
   - ☐ C. Pentium II
   - ☐ D. Pentium III

2. **What advantages does the ATX form factor have over AT? (Choose Two)**
   - ☐ A. Dual power supplies
   - ☐ B. PS/2 integration
   - ☐ C. Micro channel
   - ☐ D. "Soft Switch" Power support

3. **You are plugging the connectors from an AT power supply into the motherboard. What wire colors must match up?**
   - ○ A. Red and Red
   - ○ B. Orange and Orange
   - ○ C. Black and Red
   - ○ D. Black and Black

4. Where are the system settings stored when the computer is off?

   ○ A. CMOS
   ○ B. RAM
   ○ C. A permanent swap file
   ○ D. Disaster Recovery Site

5. You are planning to upgrade the CPU on your motherboard. What else must you consider?

   ○ A. SCSI chain priorities
   ○ B. Upgrading the CMOS chip
   ○ C. Upgrading the operating system
   ○ D. Adding an RS232c

6. Intel's Single Edge Connector (SEC) technology design incorporates a processor and?

   ○ A. CMOS
   ○ B. Level 2 cache
   ○ C. Centronics D-shell
   ○ D. Level 3 caches

7. A major difference between the original Pentium (I) and the Pentium II is?

   ○ A. IEEE 1394
   ○ B. LBA support
   ○ C. Pipeline cache size
   ○ D. File allocation table

8. The Pentium III is designed for what type of technology?

   ○ A. Slot A
   ○ B. Slot B
   ○ C. Slot 1
   ○ D. Slot III

9. There are three programs running in protected mode. One program fails. What happens to the other two programs?

   ○ A. Both programs fail.
   ○ B. One fails, and one does not.
   ○ C. Neither program fails.
   ○ D. Only the program in slot 1 fails.

10. Which of the following are valid types of video memory? (Choose Three)

☐ A. RWAM
☐ B. VRAM
☐ C. XRAM
☐ D. WRAM
☐ E. XGRAM
☐ F. SGRAM

11. **What is the memory bus width of a 30-pin SIMM?**

○ A. 8 its
○ B. 4 bits
○ C. 1 bit
○ D. 1,024 bits

12. **What is the memory bus width of a 72-pin SIMM?**

○ A. 8 bits
○ B. 4 bits
○ C. 32 bits
○ D. 64 bits

13. **IRQ 4 is reserved for?**

○ A. COM2 and COM4
○ B. COM3 and COM4
○ C. COM1 and COM4
○ D. COM1 and COM3

14. **You connect to the Internet with a 56 Kbps modem. At times, your access speed is faster than others. What can you do maximize your potential access speed? (Choose Two)**

☐ A. Get the most recent driver update for your modem.
☐ B. Use a crossover cable.
☐ C. Change your RJ11 connector to RJ45.
☐ D. Resolve your IRQ5 conflict.
☐ E. Have your telephone company clear the phone line.
☐ F. Grant full-access permissions to your 56 Kbps modem.

15. **You need to manually reset your modem. Which AT modem command would you use?**

    ○ A. ATA
    ○ B. ATH
    ○ C. ATZ
    ○ D. ATREST=ALL

16. **By default, which IRQ is reserved for the Real-Time Clock (RTC)?**

    ○ A. IRQ0
    ○ B. IRQ1
    ○ C. IRQ7
    ○ D. IRQ8

17. **There is no sound coming from your speakers as you play your favorite CD. What is most likely the problem?**

    ○ A. Your floppy drive cable is connected backwards.
    ○ B. You need to refresh your sound card RAM.
    ○ C. Your CD-ROM audio cable is disconnected.
    ○ D. Your sound card drivers have become corrupt.

18. **What is the default IRQ for COM2?**

    ○ A. 3
    ○ B. 4
    ○ C. 2
    ○ D. 5

19. **A customer is trying to print very large documents to a laser printer and consistently receives memory overflow error messages. How can you resolve this issue? (Choose Three)**

    ☐ A. Decrease the print resolution.
    ☐ B. Increase the size of the toner cartridge.
    ☐ C. Add more memory to the printer.
    ☐ D. Use a SCSI cable connector.
    ☐ E. Press Ctrl-Alt-Delete twice.
    ☐ F. Decrease the Resolution Enhancement Technology.

20. **What component of a dot matrix printer strikes a ribbon and leaves a character, number, or symbol on the paper?**

    ○ A. A print hammer
    ○ B. A toner impaction device
    ○ C. A pin
    ○ D. A ribbon presser

21. **A customer informs you that he keeps getting paper jam error messages on his printer. You observe that there isn't any paper in the paper feed tray. What would you observe next to fix this issue?**

    ○ A. The daisy wheel
    ○ B. The printer's I/O memory address
    ○ C. The printer's paper feed sensors
    ○ D. The printer rollers

22. **You have collected several used laser printer toner cartridges. What is a standard procedure for disposal of such items?**

    ○ A. Place them in the dumpster out back.
    ○ B. Send them back to the manufacturer.
    ○ C. Do not dispose. Shake the cartridges to free up loose toner. Toner is very expensive.
    ○ D. Empty toner into a half used cartridge. Place the empty toner cartridge into a recycle bin.

23. **How many pins does a dot matrix print head typically have?**

    ○ A. 9 or 24
    ○ B. 27 or 16
    ○ C. 14 or 7
    ○ D. 1 or 4

24. **What are the stages of the laser printing process collectively known as?**

    ○ A. Electric Photo Magnetic Process.
    ○ B. Electronic Laser Photographic Process.
    ○ C. Electro Photographic Process.
    ○ D. ELO Imaging Process.

25. Which of the following are considered to be valid parallel port standards? (Choose Three)

☐ A. Bidirectional
☐ B. ECP
☐ C. Encapsulated Postscript
☐ D. Reverse DNS lookup
☐ E. EPP
☐ F. Serial

26. At what stage of the laser printing process is image melted onto the paper?

○ A. Writing
○ B. Developing
○ C. Conditioning
○ D. Fusing

27. When working on the inside of a laser printer, what should you never touch based on its extremely high temperatures?

○ A. A toner cartridge
○ B. The print head
○ C. The fuser
○ D. The power supply

28. Your computer is plug and play. You install a second hard drive. What will determine its drive letter?

○ A. You
○ B. The ribbon cable position
○ C. The jumpers and dip switches
○ D. The PnP operating system

29. You need to terminate a SCSI bus that has an external CD-ROM and an internal hard drive. What devices would you terminate?

○ A. The SCSI controller and the motherboard.
○ B. The hard drive and the CD-ROM.
○ C. The motherboard, the SCSI controller, and the CD-ROM.
○ D. You do not have to terminate both ends of a SCSI chain.

30. **You want to install two new IDE drives on the same ATA controller and configure them as master/slave. You install drive 1 as master and drive 2 as slave. Your BIOS does not detect drive 2 on boot up. What would you do next to troubleshoot drive 2?**

    ○ A. Install an IDE add-on card.
    ○ B. Set up drive 2 to be the master. Remove drive 1, and reboot.
    ○ C. Configure both drives to be the master.
    ○ D. Set the BIOS hard drive detection method to cable select.

31. **What would you have to enable on a SCSI controller card to use a tape device?**

    ○ A. Direct Memory Access
    ○ B. Termination
    ○ C. C000-C7FFF
    ○ D. The INT 13h support

32. **You are trying to access your "A" drive. You keep getting an error message Drive not ready, abort, retry or fail. What is causing this problem? (Choose Two)**

    ☐ A. You need to change the jumpers on your floppy drive back to slave.
    ☐ B. You have bad media inserted in your floppy drive.
    ☐ C. The spindle motor needs adjustment.
    ☐ D. Your physical floppy drive needs cleaning. Use compressed air.

33. **Which of the following devices are compatible with SCSI technology? (Choose Three)**

    ☐ A. A tape drive unit
    ☐ B. A modulation device
    ☐ C. A NIC
    ☐ D. A hard drive
    ☐ E. A CD-ROM

34. **What is the highest ID assignment on a SCSI 1 device with a block of three jumpers?**

    ○ A. 0
    ○ B. 7
    ○ C. 1,024
    ○ D. 15

35. Name the minimum category cable type that can be used to support 100BaseTX?

   ○ A. Category6
   ○ B. Catagory43
   ○ C. Catagory4
   ○ D. Category5

36. Modems use which type of connector?

   ○ A. BNC
   ○ B. RJ45
   ○ C. RJ11
   ○ D. Kevlar

37. What technological communication method is most popular with PDAs today?

   ○ A. USB
   ○ B. 10BaseT
   ○ C. The fourth OSI layer
   ○ D. Infrared technology

38. What types of connectors are used with coaxial cable? (Choose Two)

   ☐ A. BNC
   ☐ B. RJ45
   ☐ C. RJ11
   ☐ D. BNC T

39. What type of connector is most commonly used with twisted-pair cabling?

   ○ A. RJ11
   ○ B. RJ45
   ○ C. BNC
   ○ D. STP

40. What is the best choice of cable used to connect two computers together in a peer-to-peer network without a hub?

   ○ A. Crossover cable
   ○ B. RJ45
   ○ C. BNC
   ○ D. STP

41. What IRQs by default are available for additional devices in a computer system? (Choose Three)

    ☐ A. IRQ9
    ☐ B. IRQ11
    ☐ C. IRQ15
    ☐ D. IRQ10
    ☐ E. IRQ4

42. If a device such as a NIC has an ST or SC connector, it will most likely be used with which type of cable?

    ○ A. Thicknet
    ○ B. 100BaseTX
    ○ C. Fiber optic
    ○ D. Shielded twisted pair (STP)

43. Name three characteristics of a peer-to-peer network. (Choose three)

    ☐ A. Password-protected shares.
    ☐ B. 10 or less workstations.
    ☐ C. Individual workstations can act as both client and server.
    ☐ D. A user must authenticate with a security accounts manager database.

44. What device would you use to extend the length of your 10Base2 bus segment?

    ○ A. A gateway
    ○ B. A bridge
    ○ C. A hub
    ○ D. A repeater

45. A star typology typically uses which type of cable to connect workstations?

    ○ A. Token Ring cable
    ○ B. FDDI cable
    ○ C. Twisted pair
    ○ D. Fiber optic

46. A 10Base2 would be implemented in which type of network typology?

    ○ A. Ring
    ○ B. Bus
    ○ C. Star
    ○ D. FDDI

47. **What type of network would be implemented if users must be authenticated before they could access resources?**

    ○ A. Peer-to-peer
    ○ B. Standalone
    ○ C. Server based
    ○ D. Share level permission

48. **What does 10/100 mean?**

    ○ A. 10 users for peer-to-peer; 100 for server based
    ○ B. 10 Mbps or 100 Mbps transmission
    ○ C. A processor that uses 10 threads and 100 processes
    ○ D. A Sonet technology term for high-speed access

49. **An EEPROM chip on a NIC is capable of storing certain settings. Name three of these settings. (Choose Three)**

    ☐ A. MAC address
    ☐ B. IRQ
    ☐ C. I/O
    ☐ D. IP Address

50. **A customer is trying to access a Novell network using a NIC with the IPX/SPX protocol bound to it. The customer cannot access the network. What is most likely the problem?**

    ○ A. Incorrect frame type setting.
    ○ B. Incorrect IP configuration.
    ○ C. The IPX/SPX protocol should be the first in the binding order.
    ○ D. IPX/SPX and TCP/IP cannot run together.

51. **Which is a specification for motherboard architecture that allows analog I/O functions to be separate from the motherboard by placing them on a riser?**

    ○ A. PnP
    ○ B. MCA
    ○ C. AMR
    ○ D. ISA
    ○ D. None of the above

52. **How does AGP differ from PCI?**
    - ○ A. AGP uses a point-to-point dedicated channel to directly access RAM.
    - ○ B. AGP offers faster NIC support.
    - ○ C. PCI specifications include 2x, 4x, and 8x.
    - ○ D. PCI offers faster video acceleration speeds

53. **How much memory can a PCI 32-bus access?**
    - ○ A. Up to 1 GB
    - ○ B. Up to 4 GB
    - ○ C. 512 KB
    - ○ D. Up to 17 billion GB
    - ○ E. All of the above

54. **Which of the following is used to translate drive information such as sectors, cylinders, and heads into BIOS understandable format?**
    - ○ A. POST
    - ○ B. ROM BIOS
    - ○ C. CMOS Checksum
    - ○ D. LBA (Logical Block Addressing)
    - ○ E. None of the above

55. **Which of the following is usually posted in a hazardous area?**
    - ○ A. ESD wrist strap
    - ○ B. APW Hose
    - ○ C. Uninterruptible Power Supply (UPS)
    - ○ D. Halon gas warning
    - ○ E. MSDS

56. **Recently, manufacturers such as Intel have developed technology that brings an additional 1 MB (512 KB) onto the CPU chip. This addition has dramatically increased the speed at which a processor can access stored information. What is the new addition being described as?**
    - ○ A. MICRODIMM
    - ○ B. L3 Cache
    - ○ C. SODIMM
    - ○ D. L5 Cache
    - ○ E. Direct Memory Address (DMA)

57. **What type of technology do all of the processors in the AMD Athlon XP line use?**

    ○ A. Pentium IV technology
    ○ B. Slot technology
    ○ C. Socket A technology
    ○ D. AMD Duron technology
    ○ E. None of the above

58. **What is used to fill the area between a CPU and a heat sink to transfer heat from the CPU to the heat sink?**

    ○ A. Liquid Nitrogen
    ○ B. CNR
    ○ C. L3 Cache
    ○ D. Thermal Compound
    ○ E. All of the above

59. **Which of the following is a motherboard-installable module that regulates the electrical voltage that is fed to the system's microprocessor?**

    ○ A. VRM
    ○ B. CNR
    ○ C. AMR
    ○ D. LCA (Liquid Cooling Apparatus)
    ○ E. None of the above

60. **There were two SODIMM memory module configurations mentioned in Table 4.3 of Chapter 4. What were the number of pins and memory bus widths associated with the SODIMMS? (Choose Two)**

    ☐ A. 72 pins and 32 bits
    ☐ B. 144 pins and 64 bits
    ☐ C. 184 pins and 16 bits
    ☐ D. 168 pins and 64 bits

61. **These memory modules are often used in subnotebook computers. They have 144 pins and provide a 64-bit data path. What are they?**

    ○ A. DIMMs
    ○ B. RIMMs
    ○ C. MicroDIMMs
    ○ D. L3 Cache SIMMs

62. **Of the following choices, which is a handheld pen-shaped device that is commonly used as a pointing or writing instrument to input text into a system such as a PDA?**
    - ○ A. Optomechanical pencil
    - ○ B. Stylus
    - ○ C. MIDI pen
    - ○ D. Joystick
    - ○ E. None of the above

63. **Which of the following choices is not a touch screen technology?**
    - ○ A. Surface Wave.
    - ○ B. Resistive.
    - ○ C. Capacitive.
    - ○ D. Foam element.
    - ○ E. All of the above represent touch screen technologies.

64. **What is DMA channel 2 assigned to?**
    - ○ A. Second DMA controller (cascades to DMA channels 0–3)
    - ○ B. Floppy drive (possible tape drive)
    - ○ C. Available
    - ○ D. Port 1024
    - ○ E. None of the above

65. **Where in Windows 2000 and Windows XP would you go to easily add or configure a digital camera or scanner?**
    - ○ A. Command prompt
    - ○ B. DOS prompt
    - ○ C. Control Panel > Scanners and Cameras
    - ○ D. Control Panel > Cameras and Scanners
    - ○ E. None of the above

66. **Which is considered the newest battery type that produces hydrogen converted from methanol or alcohol?**
    - ○ A. NiCAd (Nickel-cadmium)
    - ○ B. NiMH (Nickel Metal Hydride)
    - ○ C. Fuel Cell
    - ○ D. Lithium ion
    - ○ E. None of the above

67. **Using a video resolution of 800 x 600 is equivalent to using which video mode?**

    ○ A. Raster
    ○ B. Vector
    ○ C. VGA
    ○ D. SVGA
    ○ E. MCA
    ○ F. None of the above

68. **How many pins does a VGA connector have?**

    ○ A. 7
    ○ B. 9
    ○ C. 10
    ○ D. 15
    ○ E. None of the above

69. **Which of the following represent possible printer connections?**

    ○ A. Centronix
    ○ B. DB25
    ○ C. USB
    ○ D. All of the above

70. **What is a common name used to describe a single device that combines printing, scanning, copying, and faxing capabilities?**

    ○ A. PSCAF (Printing, Scan, Copy and fax)
    ○ B. MFD (Multifunction Device)
    ○ C. Hub
    ○ D. Sublimation device
    ○ E. None of the above

71. **What type of printing technology has become very popular based on the growth of digital camera use?**

    ○ A. Dye sublimation
    ○ B. CAD/CAM
    ○ C. Ink dispersion
    ○ D. Saddle stitch and fold
    ○ E. Ozone filtering

72. **Which of the following commands will remove MBR infector viruses and replace a system's boot loader with a generic boot loader?**

    ○ A. Erase MBR
    ○ B. FDISK /?
    ○ C. Format C:\MBR
    ○ D. Scandisk /MBR
    ○ E. FDISK /MBR
    ○ F. None of the above

73. **Which RAID level is known as disk mirroring?**

    ○ A. RAID Level 0
    ○ B. RAID Level 1
    ○ C. RAID Level 3
    ○ D. RAID Level 5
    ○ E. None of the above

74. **What should your first troubleshooting step be if you have installed a new CD-ROM, CD-RW, or DVD device into a computer, and it doesn't work?**

    ○ A. Insert a pin or paper clip into the tiny hole on the front of the unit.
    ○ B. Verify that the jumper settings on the device are correct.
    ○ C. Purchase a new device.
    ○ D. Verify that the CD, CD-RW, or DVD audio cable is connected to an installed sound card.
    ○ E. None of the above.

75. **How many USB devices will one system resource (IRQ) support?**

    ○ A. 1
    ○ B. 15
    ○ C. 2
    ○ D. 127
    ○ E. None of the above

76. **What is WEP?**

    ○ A. A wireless transceiver that transmits and receives RF signals.
    ○ B. WEP is a standard for Windows Enterprise Programming.
    ○ C. Wireless security protocol specified under the IEEE 802.11b.2.
    ○ D. Windows Standard for Encapsulated Post Script.
    ○ E. None of the above.

77. **What is considered the hub in a wireless network?**

   ○ A. Router
   ○ B. Server computer
   ○ C. Access point
   ○ D. Wireless NIC
   ○ E. WAP
   ○ F. None of the above

78. **Which of the following is a nonroutable, small, and efficient transport layer protocol meant for use in small networks with 1 to 200 workstations?**

   ○ A. NetBEUI
   ○ B. TCP/IP
   ○ C. IPX/SPX
   ○ D. LDAP
   ○ E. WEP
   ○ F. All of the above

79. **What does a DNS server do?**

   ○ A. Allows Web pages to be formatted with graphics and symbols other than plain text
   ○ B. Converts fully qualified domain names to IP addresses
   ○ C. Offers developers and designers more flexibility in creating Web pages through the use of call tags
   ○ D. Connects different network typologies together, such as Token Ring and Ethernet
   ○ F. None of the above

80. **At this point, what should you do before taking the CompTIA A+ Exams?**

   ○ A. Have the ability answer every question in this test correctly.
   ○ B. Read the first section of this book a second time.
   ○ C. Study the operating systems section of this book because CompTIA is going to ask operating systems questions on the exams.
   ○ D. All of the above.

TEST TAKER'S CUMULATIVE PRACTICE EXAM ANSWERS

Answer Key	Question taken from:
1. C and D	Chapter 2 "Slots and Sockets"
2. B and D	Chapter 2 "Motherboards and Form Factors"
3. D	Chapter 2 "Electricity and The Power Supply"
4. A	Chapter 2 "Complementary Metal Oxide Semiconductor (CMOS)"
5. B	Chapter 2 "Complementary Metal Oxide Semiconductor (CMOS)"
6. B	Chapter 3 "SEC and SEP"
7. C	Chapter 3 "Processors and Modes"
8. C	Chapter 3 "Processors and Modes"
9. C	Chapter 3 "Processors and Modes"
10. B, D, and F	Chapter 4 "Memory Types and Characteristics"
11. A	Chapter 4 "Memory Packaging"
12. C	Chapter 4 "Memory Packaging"
13. D	Chapter 5 "Interrupt Requests (IRQs)"
14. A and E	Chapter 5 "Modems"
15. C	Chapter 5 "Modems"
16. D	Chapter 5 "Interrupt Requests (IRQs)"
17. C	Chapter 5 "Sound Cards"
18. A	Chapter 5 "Interrupt Requests (IRQs)"
19. A, C, and F	Chapter 6 "Laser Printers"
20. C	Chapter 6 "Dot Matrix and Inkjet Printers"
21. C	Chapter 6 "Dot Matrix and Inkjet Printers
22. B	Chapter 6 "Laser Printers"
23. A	Chapter 6 "Dot Matrix and Inkjet Printers"
24. C	Chapter 6 "Laser Printers"
25. A, B, and E	Chapter 6 "Parallel Port Standards"
26. D	Chapter 6 "Laser Printers"
27. C	Chapter 6 "Laser Printers"
28. D	Chapter 7 "The Hard Drive"
29. B	Chapter 7 "Drive Controllers and Interfaces"

30. B	Chapter 7 "Drive Controllers and Interfaces"
31. D	Chapter 7 "Drive Controllers and Interfaces"
32. B and D	Chapter 7 "The Floppy Drive"
33. A, D, and E	Chapter 7 "Drive Controllers and Interfaces"
34. B	Chapter 7 "Drive Controllers and Interfaces"
35. D	Chapter 8 "Networking Connectors and Cables"
36. C	Chapter 8 "Networking Connectors and Cables"
37. D	Chapter 8 "Wireless Connections"
38. A and D	Chapter 8 "Networking Connectors and Cables"
39. B	Chapter 8 "Networking Connectors and Cables"
40. A	Chapter 8 "Networking Connectors and Cables"
41. B, C, and D	Chapter 5 "Interrupt Requests (IRQs)"
42. C	Chapter 8 "Networking Connectors and Cables"
43. A, B, and C	Chapter 9 "Network Categories"
44. D	Chapter 9 "Network Topology"
45. C	Chapter 9 "Network Topology"
46. B	Chapter 9 "Network Topology"
47. C	Chapter 9 "Network Categories"
48. B	Chapter 9 "Network Interface Cards"
49. A, B, and C	Chapter 9 "Network Interface Cards"
50. A	Chapter 9 "Protocols"
51. C	Chapter 2 "Expansion Bus Architecture"
52. A	Chapter 2 "Expansion Bus Architecture"
53. B	Chapter 2 "Expansion Bus Architecture"
54. D	Chapter 2 "Power-on Self-Test (POST) and Error Codes"
55. E	Chapter 2 "Preventive Maintenance and Safety"
56. B	Chapter 3 "Cache, Levels 1, 2, and 3 "
57. C	Chapter 3 "Processors and Modes"
58. D	Chapter 3 "Thermal Compounds"
59. A	Chapter 3 "VRM (Voltage Regulator Module)"
60. A and B	Chapter 4 "Memory Packaging"

61. C   Chapter 4 "Memory Packaging"
62. B   Chapter 5 "Mice and Pointing Devices"
63. D   Chapter 5 "Touch Screen"
64. B   Chapter 5 "Direct Memory Access Channels (DMAs)"
65. C   Chapter 5 "Digital Cameras"
66. C   Chapter 5 "Batteries and Power"
67. D   Chapter 6 "Liquid Crystal Display"
68. D   Chapter 6 "Liquid Crystal Display"
69. D   Chapter 6 "Laser Printers"
70. B   Chapter 6 "Laser Printers"
71. A   Chapter 6 "Laser Printers"
72. E   Chapter 7 "The Hard Drive"
73. B   Chapter 7 "RAID (Redundant Array of Independent Disks)"
74. B   Chapter 7 "Optical Storage Devices"
75. D   Chapter 8 "USB Connections"
76. C   Chapter 8 "Wireless Connectivity"
77. C   Chapter 8 "Wireless Connectivity"
78. A   Chapter 9 "Protocols"
79. B   Chapter 9 "The Internet and Viruses"
80. D   Chapter 9 "Chapter Summary"

10 Operating System Fundamentals and DOS

In This Chapter

- Operating System Fundamentals
- Introduction to DOS
- DOS System and Configuration Files
- DOS Filename Structure
- DOS Commands, Switches, and Wildcards
- DOS Windows Utilities
- Memory Management Utilities
- Windows Initialization Files
- Command-Line Tutorial: MS-DOS and 32-Bit Commands: A Practical Tutorial and Reference
- Operating System Fundamentals Test Tips

You may have noticed that the chapters in the latter portion of this book are titled by individual operating systems (OSs) as opposed to the CompTIA domain structure titles. In fact, this whole book's structure is in place to avoid the confusion of going back and forth between hardware devices and OSs within the same chapters, as many other books do. It is very important for you to learn and retain the concepts and functionality of each OS individually. We will refer to and compare some of the functions in different OSs within the same chapters, but the main intention is to keep your focus on the particular OS at hand.

CompTIA states that you should have at least six months of hands-on experience with the OSs you will be tested on. These include DOS, Windows 9.x/Me, Windows NT, Windows 2000, and Windows XP. Be forewarned, however, that two years of hands-on experience with these OSs is not enough to pass the tough CompTIA examination questions if you do not focus on the specific concepts and theory required to answer the test questions correctly.

The 2006 CompTIA Objectives also make mention of Unix, Linux, and MAC OS X. However, CompTIA focuses mainly on Windows OSs and so will this guide.

In fact, very little or no Unix, Linux, or MAC OS X questions have been identified on the most recent exams.

Keep in mind that this book is designed to prepare you to take and pass all of the CompTIA A+ exams. It is not a substitute for hands-on experience, nor does it explain the entire history and every detail of all the OSs covered.

The A+ exams will ensure that you are knowledgeable about the underlying command prompt (or line) functions associated with Windows 9.x, Windows Me (yes Me), Windows NT, Windows 2000, and Windows XP. Many of the DOS commands and command-line utilities you will learn about in this chapter can be used through the command prompt provided with newer OSs. It is therefore highly recommended that you pay close attention to the details and concepts in this chapter so that you are prepared for the command-line functions and utilities discussed in the chapters that follow.

In this chapter, we focus on DOS (Disk Operating System) commands, procedures, and utilities. We also address system configuration files and DOS memory management.

Before we begin our focus on DOS, it is important for you to understand the basic functions of an OS.

OPERATING SYSTEM FUNDAMENTALS

To run applications and interact with input and output devices, every functional computer system must have an OS. An OS is the core software platform of a computer system. It is the underlying program or set of programs on top of which applications reside.

Some of the more popular OSs in use today are DOS, Windows, Novell Netware, OS/2, Unix, Linux, and Mac OS.

An OS controls computer access and processing, and provides a user interface through which human beings interact with the computer system and its resources. Operating systems such as DOS and Unix provide a text-based user interface or environment. With a text-based interface, letters, numbers, and symbols are entered on a command line to communicate with the OS, whereas other OSs, such as Windows 9.x, Windows Me, Windows NT, Windows 2000, and Windows XP provide a GUI (Graphical User Interface) environment.

In a GUI environment, graphic representations of commands, such as icons and menu bars, are used to interact with the OS. What about Windows 3.x? For the record, Windows 3.x is a GUI that sits on top of DOS. It is not technically considered an OS. Windows 9.x is a true multitasking GUI OS that consists of three basic core files: GDI.EXE, KRL386.EXE, and USER.EXE.

An OS is primarily responsible for the following:

- Providing a user interface used to store and manage data and program
- Providing a platform on which applications and commands can be run
- Acting as a mediator for input and output devices
  The major Microsoft OSs are the following:
- MS-DOS
- Microsoft Windows 3.x
- Microsoft Windows 95 OEM Release, Win95A (OSR1), Win95B (OSR2), Win95C (OSR2) (Windows 9.x refers to all versions of Windows 95.)
- Microsoft Windows 98
- Microsoft Windows 98 Second Edition (SE)
- Microsoft Windows Millennium Edition (Me)
- Microsoft Windows NT 3.51
- Microsoft Windows NT 4.0 (Workstation and Server)
- Microsoft Windows 2000 (Professional and Server)
- Microsoft Windows XP (Home, Media Center, and Professional)
- Microsoft Windows 2003 (Server)
- Microsoft Windows Vista (Starter, Home Basic, Home Premium, Business, Enterprise, and Ultimate)

CompTIA has not identified Windows Vista as being tested in their 2006 Objectives. So, you have to wait for the third edition of this book for that.

Before we move forward, it is important for you to understand the level of detail involved with any OS-related test questions that come your way. The exam poses very specific questions that compare various OS concepts and technologies. A good example of the comparison between OS technologies is shown by the following sample question.

> **Q. You have one connection to the Internet that you want to share with other systems. Which OSs will allow you to do this? (Choose Four)**
>
> ☐ A.   Windows 2000
> ☐ B.   Windows NT 4.0
> ☐ C.   Windows 98
> ☐ D.   Windows 98 SE
> ☐ E.   Windows Me
> ☐ F.   Windows XP
> ☐ G.   Windows 95
>
> Answers: A, D, E, and F

The question refers to Internet Connection Sharing (ICS), which is available in Windows 98 SE, and Windows 2000/Me/XP. This type of detail is what makes OS-related test questions so tough. You may know one or two OSs inside and out, but you must remember the details of all the major systems to pass these tests.

Keep in mind the following concepts of each OS as we proceed:

- The filesystem structure of each OS
- The minimum hardware requirements needed to install the OS
- The boot or start-up file sequence for each OS
- The emergency repair operations and procedures for each OS (e.g., creating an emergency boot disk)
- The ability of an OS to support new applications and APIs (Application Programming Interfaces)
- The methods used by each OS to access, move, delete, copy, and rename files, as well as methods used to access certain hidden system files
- The methods used by each OS to change and configure display, printer, modem, and Internet connection options and settings

CHECKING THE OPERATING SYSTEM VERSION

Operating systems are packaged in different releases and versions, each of which has its own set of characteristics and updates. Our study of OSs focuses on the popular versions of MS-DOS, Windows 9.x, Windows Me, Windows NT 4.0, Windows 2000, and Windows XP.

The exams will most likely test your ability to display an OS's version by using the Control Panel in Windows or entering the VER (version) command at the command prompt.

To determine which OS version of Windows 95/98, Windows Me, Windows NT, Windows 2000, or Windows XP is currently running on a computer, follow these steps:

1. Click the Start button, select Settings > Control Panel.
2. Double-click the System icon in the Control Panel.
3. Verify that the General tab is selected.
4. Look under the System heading for the OS, version, and any service packs applied. You should also notice the total memory installed under the Computer heading. Figure 10.1 shows the Windows 2000 System Properties window of the installed OS, version, service pack, and memory.

To determine which OS version of DOS or Windows you are running from a command prompt, use the VER command. In a true DOS environment, type the

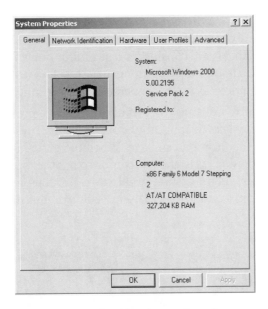

FIGURE 10.1 Checking the version of Windows in system properties.

"VER" command at the DOS command prompt (as follows) and press Enter. Later on in this chapter, we will cover all major DOS commands in detail. This is a great reference not only for the exams but for your career as well.

```
C:\VER
```

The version of DOS will be displayed.

In a Windows 2000 environment, navigate to the command prompt by selecting Start > Programs > Accessories > Command Prompt, and type "VER" on the command line. Press Enter, and the version of Windows will be displayed. Figure 10.2 displays the VER command and the version of Windows at a Windows 2000 command prompt.

MULTITASKING

Multitasking is defined as the ability of an OS to handle more than one function or carry out more than one task at the same time. Older OSs, such as DOS, were designed to handle only one task at a time. Newer OSs can handle many tasks at once. If you are using a relatively new OS, you can download MP3 files, run an application program, and take the A+ practice tests on the CD-ROM included with this book, all at once. There are two types of multitasking you should be familiar with:

Cooperative multitasking: With cooperative multitasking, the application or task is in control of the CPU until it is finished with processing. Cooperative multitasking is not considered true multitasking. Although more than one task at a time appears to be running, only one task actually gets the CPU cycle at a time. Windows 3.x uses cooperative multitasking techniques.

Preemptive multitasking: With preemptive multitasking, the OS hands out CPU time slices to applications or programs. The OS is in control of how much time the application can have. When the period allotted expires, the OS stops the processing cycle and allots time to another application. Newer versions of Windows, such as Windows 9.x/Me/NT/2000 and Windows XP, as well as Linux, Unix, and MAC OS use preemptive multitasking techniques.

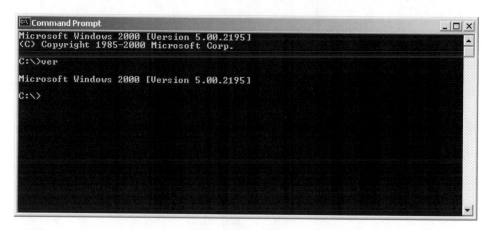

FIGURE 10.2   Checking the Windows Version at a Windows 2000 command prompt.

INTRODUCTION TO DOS

DOS is a 16-bit (FAT16), command-line driven, text-based OS. Microsoft's version of DOS is called MS-DOS. IBM's version of DOS is called PC-DOS. Our study and the current CompTIA exams focus on MS-DOS, which we refer to from now on simply as DOS. Microsoft has introduced 12 versions of pure DOS since the original 1.0 version. There is no need for you to study or memorize the fine details of each separate DOS version for this exam. However, it is important for you to understand how a "pure DOS" environment works to understand how and why we still use the command prompt in newer releases of Windows. It is also important to note that not all DOS commands and functions are interchangeable between DOS versions and OSs.

Windows 3.x and Windows 9.x require DOS and DOS system files to boot and function properly. These OSs are basically GUIs that sit on top of DOS. Windows 95 attempted to separate from 'pure DOS' with its implementation of DOS version 7.0. Windows Me/2000/NT 4.0, and Windows XP include specialized system files that allow them to boot and function without the necessity of DOS.

COMMAND INTERPRETER

All Windows OSs use a command interpreter. The *command interpreter*, also called a command processor, is a program built-in to an OS that has the ability to interpret entries and make decisions based on the data entered with a mouse, keyboard, or other input device.

DOS, Windows 3.x, Windows 9.x, and Windows Me use the DOS file COMMAND.COM as the *shell*, or command interpreter. COMMAND.COM basically waits for instructions to be entered at a command prompt. It then makes a decision on whether to pass the instructions on to a program or display, such as an error message to the screen.

Unlike the version of DOS used with Windows 3.x and Windows 9.x, a file named CMD.EXE actually carries out the instructions entered at the Windows NT/2000/XP command line. In other words, CMD is the command interpreter for Windows NT/2000/XP.

The DOS file COMMAND.COM is actually a utility program that contains internal DOS commands, such as the DIR and COPY commands.

CMD.EXE is a 32-bit command-line interpreter in Windows NT/2000/XP.

NOTE

DOS SYSTEM AND CONFIGURATION FILES

Three files make up the core of DOS: IO.SYS, MSDOS.SYS (both hidden system files), and COMMAND.COM (a visible file). All three of these files are located on the primary active boot partition and are stored at the root of drive C:. All three files are required to successfully boot a system into DOS. They are also the minimum files required for booting Windows 9.x to a DOS prompt. If one of these files is corrupt or missing, the message Missing or unknown operating system will be displayed.

Although these three system files meet the minimum requirements to boot to DOS on a Windows 9.x OS, the complete DOS boot order is as follows.

1. **IO.SYS:** Interacts with the BIOS to determine the hardware environment.
2. **MSDOS.SYS:** Houses the DOS kernel and interacts with programs and devices.

3. **CONFIG.SYS:** Primarily loads device drivers.
4. **COMMAND.COM:** Translates or interprets commands entered.
5. **AUTOEXEC.BAT:** Configures specific user settings.

*The exams may ask for the overall system starting order, regardless of what OS you are running. The overall system start order is **POST**, **BIOS**, **Boot Sector**, and **GUI**. See the "Windows 9.x Start-Up Process" in Chapter 11 for further details.*

The major functions of the DOS system and configurations files, as well as their relationships with newer OSs, are explained next.

IO.SYS

IO.SYS is a binary (uneditable) executable hidden file that is loaded first when a computer system is booted. IO.SYS works with the systems BIOS to determine what hardware is to be used by the OS. IO.SYS is like a scout that discovers the physical layout of a system by looking at the CONFIG.SYS file, which is used to load hardware drivers and control DOS memory. Keep in mind that Windows 9.x comes with a newer version of IO.SYS that replaces the old IO.SYS and MSDOS.SYS used in 'pure DOS.' The new version of IO.SYS eliminates the need for use of the AUTOEXEC.BAT and CONFIG.SYS files in newer OSs. Newer OSs still allow the use of AUTOEXEC.BAT and CONFIG.SYS to maintain backward compatibility with legacy programs and hardware.

Binary files consist of 0s and 1s, and are basically unreadable without being interpreted. Text files contain readable characters that can be understood by the average human being.

MSDOS.SYS

MSDOS.SYS is a hidden system text file that contains the DOS kernel. The kernel is the core software code of an OS that is retained in memory to control all processes.

The kernel that resides in the MSDOS.SYS file and the kernel used in newer OSs are two totally separate things.

MSDOS.SYS is loaded after IO.SYS and is responsible for the interaction of software applications and hardware settings. MSDOS.SYS controls whether the computer will be booted into a DOS, Windows 3.x, Windows 9.x, or Windows Me GUI environment. If you want to set up Windows 9.x or Windows Me for dual-booting purposes, you can modify the BootGUI=0 to BootGUI=1 entry under [Options] in the MSDOS.SYS file.

The BOOT.INI file is modified in Windows NT 4.0, Windows 2000, and Windows XP for dual-booting purposes.

CONFIG.SYS

The CONFIG.SYS file is the first editable DOS configuration text file that you can modify at system start-up. Its primary function is to load 16-bit real mode device and memory management drivers for a DOS environment. At system start-up, MSDOS.SYS loads the device drivers and instructions specified in the CONFIG.SYS file before continuing on to AUTOEXEC.BAT.

In DOS, typing "EDIT CONFIG.SYS" or "EDIT AUTOEXEC.BAT" and pressing Enter at the DOS command prompt opens the DOS utility editor known as EDIT. COM. You can use EDIT.COM to view and make changes to the CONFIG.SYS and AUTOEXEC.BAT files. This can be very useful for troubleshooting if you encounter errors on start-up with settings in either of these files.

The CONFIG.SYS is available in Windows 9.x and Windows Me for backward compatibility with legacy devices. It can be edited by running the SYSEDIT program at the Start > Run line in Windows 9.x. Simply click Start > Run, type "SYSEDIT", and press Enter. Windows NT 4.0, Windows 2000, and Windows XP have basically replaced the CONFIG.SYS file with the file CONFIG.NT. You can also edit either of these files by using any available text editor in Windows, such as Notepad.

Next, we look at a typical CONFIG.SYS file that is used to configure hardware- and memory-related settings for a DOS Windows environment. Each of the lines in the following CONFIG.SYS file are explained in the list that follows the code.

```
DEVICE=C:\WINDOWS\HIMEM.SYS
DEVICE=C:\WINDOWS\EMM386.EXE NOEMS
DEVICE=C:\DOS\SETVER.EXE
FILES=40
STACKS=9,256
BUFFERS=10
FCBS=16,0
DOS=HIGH,UMB
SHELL=C:\DOS\COMMAND.COM C:\DOS /P /E:1024
DEVICE=C:\WINDOWS\IFSHLP.SYS
DEVICEHIGH=C:\WINDOWS\COMMAND\ANSI.SYS
DEVICEHIGH=C:\MTMCDAI.SYS /D:MSCD0001
LASTDRIVE=Z
```

DEVICE=C:\WINDOWS\HIMEM.SYS: HIMEM.SYS is a memory device driver that allows device drivers to be loaded into the upper memory area. It is necessary for a Windows 3.x OS load.

DEVICE=C:\WINDOWS\EMM386.EXE NOEMS: This loads the EMM386 memory manager that manages the extended memory area.

DEVICE=C:\DOS\SETVER.EXE: This line loads the SETVER program that is used to instruct whichever DOS program is being run to recognize the MS-DOS version table that is currently loaded into system memory.

FILES=40: This sets the number of files that can be opened by DOS at one time. In this case, DOS can open or access 40 files.

STACKS=9,256: STACKS is a rarely used line-handled access to hardware interrupts. It was sometimes necessary to increase or decrease the STACKS value when receiving Stack overflow or Internal stack failure error messages.

BUFFERS=10: This line allows disk buffers to be loaded into memory for Windows to use.

FCBS=16,0: The number of File Control Blocks (FCB) that windows can have open and share at any one time is specified. FCBS can be set from 1 to 255. Today's programs rarely require the use of FCBS.

DOS=HIGH,UMB: This line should always be placed after the HIMEM.SYS line. It is used to load DOS into the upper memory block in the high memory area.

SHELL=C:\DOS\COMMAND.COM C:\DOS /P /E:1024: The SHELL command specifies the location and particular command interpreter that you want DOS to use. In this case, the SHELL command is telling the system to use the COMMAND.COM interpreter that is located in the C:\DOS directory.

DEVICE=C:\WINDOWS\IFSHLP.SYS: Otherwise known as the Installable Filesystem (IFS) manager, this is a driver that assists with the integration of 32-bit APIs.

DEVICEHIGH=C:\WINDOWS\COMMAND\ANSI.SYS: ANSI.SYS is a driver that configures color, cursor, and keystroke settings in a DOS environment.

DEVICEHIGH=C:\MTMCDAI.SYS /D:MSCD0001: This line is used to load the Real Mode CD-ROM driver that will be used for the OS. The CD-ROM driver in this statement must match the CD-ROM driver specified in AUTOEXEC.BAT.

LASTDRIVE=Z: The LASTDRIVE statement is used to specify the last drive letter that can be addressed by the system. If you are using this command, the letter assignment must be equal to at least the number of drives in your system. For example, if you have A, B, C, and D drives, the minimum setting for the LASTDRIVE= statement would be LASTDRIVE=D.

COMMAND.COM

As previously mentioned in this chapter, COMMAND.COM is responsible for translating what you input into the computer into information that the OS can understand. COMMAND.COM processes information entered and passes it back to MSDOS.SYS, where the OS's kernel resides.

In DOS, COMMAND.COM is responsible for providing a user interface, such as the DOSSHELL or command prompt. With a default installation of DOS, Windows 3.x, Windows 9.x, or Windows Me, COMMAND.COM is stored in the root directory of the C: drive. Windows 9.x and Windows Me also store a backup copy of COMMAND.COM in the C:\Windows directory. The AUTOEXEC.BAT file uses the SET COMSPEC= command to place COMMAND.COM in a location other than the root directory of C:. With Windows NT, Windows 2000, and Windows XP, COMMAND.COM is stored in the C:\WINNT\SYSTEM32 directory.

It is important to note that the DOS COMMAND.COM file should be from the same version of DOS installation as the IO.SYS and MSDOS.SYS files. If it is not, you may receive the error message Incorrect DOS version at system start-up.

AUTOEXEC.BAT

The AUTOEXEC.BAT (automatically executed batch) file is the second editable DOS batch file that is used at start-up to create an environment for the OS. The AUTOEXEC.BAT file sets the stage for programs to run. It holds terminate-and-stay-resident (TSR) programs, such as DOSKEY and MOUSE.COM, which are held in RAM, and can be quickly accessed and easily loaded by the system. The AUTOEXEC.BAT sets environment variables with the PATH= statement, which is used to tell the system where to look for files and executable programs. The AUTOEXEC.BAT file is the last program that is run in the DOS boot sequence. It is important to remember that any command that is in the AUTOEXEC.BAT file can be run from the command prompt.

Now we will look at a typical AUTOEXEC.BAT file that is used to configure user-related and environment settings for a DOS Windows environment.

Each of the lines in the following AUTOEXEC.BAT file is described following the file listing.

```
@ECHO OFF
SET COMSPEC=C:\DOS\COMMAND.COM
SET TEMP=C:\TEMP
PROMPT $P$G
PATH=C:\;C:\WINDOWS;C:\DOS
REM LH C:\WINDOWS\COMMAND\MSCDEX.EXE /D:MSCD0001
```

```
DOSKEY
CLS
LH C:\MOUSE\MOUSE.EXE
WIN
```

@ECHO OFF: This line instructs DOS to turn ECHO off, which disables the display of DOS batch file messages on the screen when a batch file is executed.

SET COMSPEC=C:\DOS\COMMAND.COM: The SET command is used to specify or set environmental variables each time the AUTOEXEC.BAT is run. This SET statement sets a variable for the command interpreter.

SET TEMP=C:\TEMP: This statement sets a variable for the location of temporary files.

PROMPT PG: This line configures how the DOS prompt will display on-screen. For example, PG displays C:\. You can change the prompt line to display the date, time, and DOS version, to name a just few possibilities.

PATH=C:\;C:\WINDOWS;C:\DOS: Remember for the exam that the PATH= statement, or "'line,'" is located in the AUTOEXEC.BAT file. This statement sets an environment variable that simply finds the location of a program. For example, if you are in the C:\Windows directory and want to run a program that is located in another directory, such as C:\DOS, that program can be executed from the C:\Windows directory as long as the C:\DOS directory is specified in the AUTOEXEC.BAT. You can tell the system where to look for a program on the fly by simply typing "PATH=(name of directory where file is located)" at a DOS prompt and pressing Enter.

REM LH C:\WINDOWS\COMMAND\MSCDEX.EXE /D:MSCD0001: Notice the REM statement at the beginning of this line; REM means remark. Any statements contained in the AUTOEXEC.BAT or CONFIG.SYS files that begin with the REM statement will not be processed when the file is loaded at system start-up. The statement that is being remarked out here contains the file MSCDEX.EXE. This file contains the driver necessary for DOS and Windows 3.x to recognize and run a CD-ROM device. Remember for the test that Windows 9.x has replaced the 16-bit MSCDEX.EXE with the 32-bit CD-ROM Filesystem (CDFS).

DOSKEY: DOSKEY is a TSR program used to remember commands that you have entered at the DOS command line. It keeps a history of what you have entered. If DOSKEY is loaded into memory, you can use the up-arrow or down-arrow keys on your keyboard to scroll through recently entered commands.

CLS: This is a DOS command used to clear the screen. Only the DOS command prompt is left on the screen after the cls command has been entered.

LH C:\MOUSE\MOUSE.EXE: This line loads the mouse executable program into upper memory, which will make more conventional memory available for other programs to run. Remember Chapter 4 and memory utilization? For the test, remember that lh statements are used in the AUTOEXEC.BAT file. DEVICEHIGH statements are used in the CONFIG.SYS file.

WIN: This command calls on the file WIN.COM. WIN.COM is used to configure the system automatically to boot directly into the Windows 3.x GUI. If the win statement is not in AUTOEXEC.BAT, the system will boot to a DOS prompt. Four switches can be added to the win command; each switch starts Windows 3.x in a different mode. The four switches used with the WIN command are /R, which starts Windows 3.x in Real Mode; /S, which starts the OS in Standard Mode; /3, which starts Windows 3.x in Enhanced Mode; and /B, which is used to keep a log file of Windows 3.x start-up problems.

WIN.COM is built into Windows 9.x.

DOS FILENAME STRUCTURE

DOS files are stored in directories or subdirectories. In today's Windows world, directories are called *folders*. In DOS, specific rules apply to creating and naming files and directories.

DOS uses what is called an 8.3 file-naming structure, otherwise known as *eight dot three*. This simply means that a filename can be up to 8 characters long and have a 3-character extension representing the file type. A period is used to separate the filename from the extension. The total length of the DOS filename plus the extension cannot exceed 11 characters. The file extension is not necessary unless the file is associated with a particular function. Table 10.1 displays a list of common DOS Windows file extensions with their associations.

Let's use the DOS filename AUTOEXEC.BAT as an example. The AUTOEXEC segment is the DOS filename. The .BAT extension specifies that the file is a batch file. The same is true for the CONFIG.SYS file. CONFIG is the name of the file, and the .SYS extension identifies the file as a system file.

Following are rules that apply to DOS file and directory name creation:

- A file or directory name can be no more than eight characters long.
- An extension can be no more than three characters long.

■ No spaces can be included in the filename, the extension, or the directory name.
■ Certain characters (? * , ; = + < > | [ ] / \) are illegal and cannot be used.

TABLE 10.1 DOS/Windows Common File Extensions

File Extension	Association
.BAK	DOS backup file
.BAT	DOS file housing a sequence of commands
.BMP	Windows bit-mapped graphics file
.CAB	Windows 9.x cabinet file
.COM	DOS command program file
.DLL	Windows dynamic link library file
.DOC	Text document file (usually Microsoft Word)
.EXE	DOS executable program
.GRP	Windows 3.x program group file
.HTM	Hypertext Markup Language file
.ICO	Windows 3.x icon file
.INI	DOS Windows initialization file
.SYS	DOS system driver/hardware configuration file
.TMP	Temporary file
.TXT	Text file created by DOS or the Windows text editor
.VXD	Virtual device driver file

LONG FILENAMES (LFNs)

Windows 9.x/NT/2000/Me and Windows XP support long filenames (LFNs). LFNs can be up to 255 characters in length. Although these newer OSs support LFNs, they still allow for backward compatibility with the 8.3 naming structure associated with DOS by creating an associated 8.3 filename for every new file created. LFNs are broken into 12-byte sections that allow the use of up to 255 characters, as in the following: LFN = BEST CERTIFICATIONBOOK.DOC. The 8.3 associated filename is BESTCE~1.DOC. Notice that the space after BEST is eliminated in the 8.3 associated filename. Windows automatically removes any spaces or invalid characters and truncates the filename.

It is important to note that the Windows 9.x root directory (C:\) can hold only 255 files. The truncation of LFNs to 8.3 names can quickly fill up this 255-file storage limitation and cause your system to halt. For this reason and others, it is good practice to avoid storing files in the root directory of any OS.

NOTE

The following PC Guide Web site has a great page that describes LFNs: www. pcguide.com/ref/hdd/file/fatLong-c.html.

FILE ATTRIBUTES

System files in DOS and Windows, such as IO.SYS and MSDOS.SYS, are hidden, read-only system files. This means that they cannot be viewed or deleted unless their file attributes are modified. Four major attributes can be assigned to DOS and Windows files: R (read-only), A (archive), H (hidden), and S (system).

In DOS, the ATTRIB command can be used to modify the attributes of a file at the command line. For example, to change the attributes for the system file MSDOS.SYS from a read-only/hidden file, enter the following command at a DOS prompt:

```
C:\ATTRIB –R –H MSDOS.SYS
```

This command removes the read-only and hidden attributes associated with the file. You will then be able to read and delete the file. Don't delete MSDOS.SYS until you are certified. You can add the attributes back to MSDOS.SYS by issuing the following command at the DOS prompt:

```
C:\ATTRIB +R +H MSDOS.SYS
```

In Windows 9.x/Me/NT/2000 and Windows XP, the attributes of a file can be viewed and changed (if the currently logged on user has permissions to do so) by simply right-clicking a file in Windows Explorer and either checking or unchecking the appropriate file attribute.

To locate the file MSDOS.SYS in Windows 9.x, right-click the Start button. Click Explore > View (located on the top menu bar). Then click Folder Options > View. Under the Files and Folders/Hidden Files section, click Show all files, click Apply, and then click OK. Close the Folder Options window. The MSDOS.SYS file, along with other system files, will now be visible on the right side of screen. Find the MSDOS.SYS file and right-click it. Click Properties. You should now see a window similar to the one shown in Figure 10.3. You can remove the selected file attributes by removing the check marks, or you can add desired attributes by adding check marks. Keep in mind that folders as well as files also have attributes.

Many important OS files are hidden with a typical default OS installation for the protection of the average user. You should always remember to choose Show all files or Show hidden files and folders under Folder Options before troubleshooting.

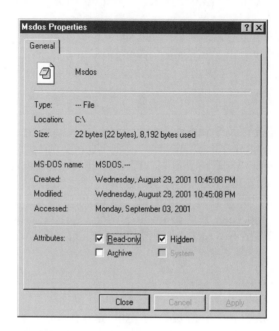

FIGURE 10.3 Windows 9.X display of file attributes.

DOS Commands, Switches, and Wildcards

DOS has its own set of commands that are entered at a DOS command prompt to instruct the OS to carry out specific instructions or tasks. DOS commands are defined as internal or external.

- Internal DOS commands reside in the DOS file COMMAND.COM. They are the most commonly used DOS commands implemented at the DOS command prompt. Some examples of internal DOS commands are COPY, DIR, DEL, RD, and CLS.
- External DOS commands are typically located in the C:\DOS directory. They are usually associated with running a program or a task. External DOS commands are most often associated with file extensions such as .COM, .BAT, and .EXE. External DOS commands are often implemented by more advanced users. Some examples of external DOS commands are DELTREE, ATTRIB, EDIT, and MEM.

You should be familiar with the important DOS commands and switches displayed in Table 10.2. Practice using these DOS commands.

TABLE 10.2   DOS Commands and Switches

Command	Function	Switches Used
ATTRIB	Displays or sets the attributes of a file	+R/-R, +A/-A, +S/-S, +H/-H
CD	Changes to another directory	\ Takes you to the root
CD..	Back up one directory level	
COPY	Copies the files and directories	
XCOPY	Copies file directories and subdirectories	/H Copies hidden files /S Copies subdirectories /V Verifies each file copied
DISKCOPY	Copies the entire disk	
DEL	Deletes a file	
DELTREE	Deletes the directory, subdirectory, and files	
TREE	Displays directory and subdirectory structure	| more View one screen
DIR	Displays all files in current directory	/P Pauses each screen /W Displays wide view
MEM	Displays memory used and available	/C Detail memory list
MD	Creates or makes a directory	
MOVE	Moves a file	
RD	Removes a directory or subdirectory	
REN	Renames a file	
SETVER	Updates the current DOS version table	
SYS	Makes a drive bootable by copying the three main system files to it; used to create bootable DOS disks	
VER	Displays the version of DOS installed	

Switches

Switches are symbols used in conjunction with DOS commands that instruct DOS to carry out specific functions, such as displaying a screen in wide view or pausing a screen after a certain number of lines have been displayed.

The most common switch is the forward slash (/). It is often used in conjunction with the DIR command. For example, if you enter the "DIR /P" switch at a DOS or Windows command prompt, 23 lines will be displayed at a time. You can then press Enter for the next 23 lines to display, and so on. This lets you read what is listed one page at a time instead of watching many pages scroll by. If you enter the "DIR /W" switch, a wide view of the files in the current directory will be displayed to the screen.

A very useful switch to use in a DOS or Windows environment is the forward slash question mark switch (/?). When this switch is entered in combination with a DOS command, you are presented with a screen that displays all the switches that can be used with that DOS command, as well as the function of each. Figure 10.4 displays the DIR /? switch and its results at a Windows 2000 command prompt.

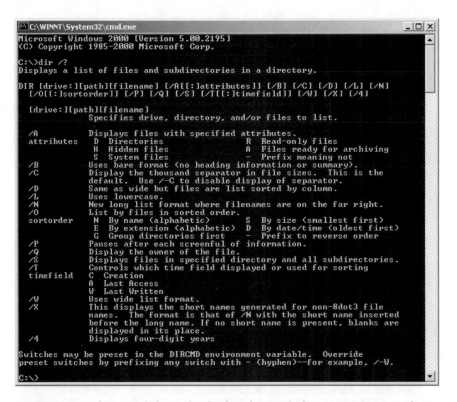

FIGURE 10.4   The /? switch results displayed at a Windows 2000 command prompt.

WILDCARDS

Two wildcards used in DOS and Windows allow you to find or display multiple occurrences of similar filename associations. In other words, wildcards are used to find or identify common directories and files. DOS reserves the question mark (?) and the asterisk (*) to be used as wildcards. These wildcards can also be used through a Windows GUI at the command prompt or in Windows 2000 by selecting Start > Search > For Files or Folders, and then entering the required criteria in the Search for files or folders named selection box.

Asterisk (*): The asterisk symbol replaces the characters to the right of itself and finds all instances of the specified criteria. For example, if you enter "DIR *.*" at the C: prompt in DOS, all the files in the ROOT directory of C:\ are displayed. If you are in the C:\Windows directory and enter "DIR *.INI", all the .INI files in the C:\Windows directory are displayed.

Question mark (?): The question mark wildcard is similar to the asterisk, except that the question mark can represent only one character at a time for each question mark specified. For example, if you wanted to find all of the .INI files stored in the C:\Windows directory from a command prompt, you would enter the following:

```
C:\WINDOWS\DIR *.INI
```

■ To display the .INI files with up to three characters in the filename, enter the following:

```
C:\WINDOWS\DIR ???.INI
```

DOS WINDOWS UTILITIES

Several DOS command prompt utilities can be very useful to a computer technician for memory configuration and hard drive or floppy disk preparation. A few of the more useful DOS utilities are described next, with an emphasis on how some of them are used through the GUIs of newer OSs.

FDISK AND FORMAT

The two DOS command-line utilities FDISK and FORMAT were described in detail in Chapter 7. It is important to remember that FDISK is a disk-partitioning utility used to separate a single physical hard drive into 24 logical partitions for more efficient use of storage. FDISK also makes it possible for you to install multiple OSs on a single physical drive.

Before you run FDISK, consider which OS or systems you are going to install and how much space you need to allocate for each partition. Keep in mind that different BIOS settings can affect the size of the partitions you can create, and that various filesystems require different cluster sizes.

DOS uses a FAT16 partition table. The maximum size of a FAT16 partition is 2.1GB. Windows 95 B/C and Windows 98 use a FAT32 partition table that allows for a single partition to reach 2TB (terabytes) in size.

Following are some important notes about FDISK.

■ You can use the FDISK command FDISK/MBR from a DOS prompt to construct a new Master Boot Record (MBR) if yours has become corrupt or infected by a virus.

■ You can partition a disk in Windows 2000 using disk management (this is discussed in Chapter 13).

■ FDISK is accessible from a bootable floppy disk, which can be useful for troubleshooting undetected hard drive issues. For example, suppose you have a desktop or laptop system that does not detect a hard drive when booted. You can boot to a bootable floppy disk and run the FDISK utility on the undetected hard drive to see if the drive is configured properly.

The FORMAT utility is used to prepare a hard disk or floppy for a filesystem. Remember, FORMAT.COM creates the FAT (File Allocation Table) and the root directory on a hard disk or floppy disk.

The syntax for formatting a floppy disk from a DOS or Windows command prompt is as follows.

```
C:\FORMAT A: /S
```

The /S option copies the three system files necessary to make the disk bootable.

To format a floppy disk in Windows 9.x or Windows 2000, simply insert a blank floppy disk into your 3.5-inch floppy drive, navigate to Windows Explorer, and right-click the 3.5-inch floppy (A:) icon (drive A:). Next, click Format. The Format A: window appears. Click Start to begin the formatting process.

SYS

As mentioned previously, SYS is really a DOS command. It is used to copy the three main DOS system files (IO.SYS, COMMAND.COM, and MSDOS.SYS) to a disk. The proper syntax for using the SYS command is C:\SYS A:. The message System transferred appears after the command has been entered.

This is an easy way to transfer the system files to a disk without going through the whole format routine. If you are missing the important system files on your hard drive, you can also use the SYS command to SYS C: from a floppy.

CHKDSK AND ScanDisk

CHKDSK is an old DOS utility that was used to search out bad clusters and lost allocation units on a hard drive. It was common to implement the CHKDSK /F command to attempt to repair bad clusters. The CHKDSK utility has been for the most part replaced by the ScanDisk utility. ScanDisk is a Microsoft disk analysis and repair utility that is used to recover and repair lost or bad clusters on a disk. Windows 9.x and Windows Me use a GUI version of ScanDisk that can be accessed and run by selecting Start > Programs > Accessories > System Tools > ScanDisk. You can use the GUI version of ScanDisk to scan your floppy or hard disk. You will have the option of running a standard scan, which checks files and folders for errors, or a thorough scan, which also scans the disk surface for errors. For best results, make sure that you select the thorough option and place a check mark in the Automatically Fix Errors box before you start the scan.

To check a disk for errors in Windows NT, Windows 2000, and Windows XP, open My Computer and right-click on the drive you want to check. Select Properties > Tools, and under Error-checking, select Check Now. A Check Disk message box will open, and you will have the options to Automatically fix file system errors and Scan for and attempt recovery of bad sectors. You should then select both options and click Start. If you are checking your system drive, you will receive a message stating that the disk check could not be performed because the check utility needs exclusive access to the drive. In the same message box, you are asked if you want to schedule the check on the next restart of your computer. If you select Yes, the check utility will run the next time your computer is restarted.

DEFRAG

Defrag is a DOS and Windows utility that improves system performance by placing files that are fragmented into a contiguous order on a hard or floppy disk. In the Windows world, the program is actually called Disk Defragmenter. This tool can be run from Windows 9.x/Me/2000 or Windows XP by selecting Start > Programs > Accessories > System Tools > Disk Defragmenter. Alternately, you can open My Computer, right-click the C: drive, and click Properties > Tools > Defragment now. Windows NT does not come with a built-in defrag utility.

Keep in mind that there are usually at least three ways to accomplish the same task in a typical Windows GUI. You must practice these concepts and explore others if you want to become a well-rounded technician. See if you can find a third way to use the defragmenter utility in Windows 9.x. Here is a hint: Start > Run >. . . .

SMARTDRV.EXE

SMARTDRV.EXE and SMARTDRV.SYS make up a 16-bit disk caching utility that is used to improve the access speed to data stored on a hard drive in a DOS or Windows 3.x environment. The SMARTDRV line is only used in the AUTOEXEC. BAT file. Windows 9.x uses a 32-bit program known as VCACHE in place of SMARTDRV. VCACHE can automatically adjust the hard drive's cache size based on the needs of the OS and programs.

MSD.EXE

MSD.EXE is a DOS-based utility that is executed at the command prompt. It is used to view information on the system configuration, including devices, memory, video display, mouse, disks, ports, and TSR programs. In the old DOS days, MSD was a very useful program that provided vital information for troubleshooting. Although MSD.EXE is included on the Windows 9.x installation CD-ROM, most people prefer to use the Device Manager in Windows 9.x for troubleshooting purposes.

POWER.EXE

POWER.EXE is an optional program that is loaded in CONFIG.SYS. If your computer supports Advanced Power Management (APM), the POWER.EXE driver can be loaded to reduce the amount of power a system uses when it is idle.

The syntax for loading the POWER.EXE device driver in the CONFIG.SYS file is as follows:

```
DEVICE=[drive:] [path] POWER.EXE
```

POWER.EXE has proven to be a very useful tool for conserving battery life in laptop computers.

LABEL.EXE

The LABEL.EXE utility is used to create, change, or remove the name of a disk. The LABEL command can be used in DOS, Windows 9.x/Me/NT/2000 or Windows XP to create a volume name of up to 11 characters, including spaces. Use the following syntax to label a floppy disk:

```
C:\LABEL A: [Enter a label name up to 11 characters in DOS.]
```

DEBUG.EXE

DEBUG.EXE is simply a DOS program that is used to debug or test programs. Changes made to programs using DEBUG.EXE cannot be undone; therefore, only advanced users should use it.

MEMORY MANAGEMENT UTILITIES

In Chapter 4, you were introduced to the basic DOS memory model and concepts. You should recall that conventional memory is used primarily for programs and applications. *Conventional memory* encompasses the first 640 KB of memory used in the DOS memory structure. *Expanded Memory Specification* (EMS) is extended or reserved memory that emulates conventional memory. It ranges from the top of the 640 KB barrier to 1024 KB. The High Memory Area (HMA) uses the top 384 KB of expanded memory in the DOS memory model. The *Extended Memory Specification* (XMS) is above the HMA. It includes all the memory addresses over 1088 KB. If you need more information about this structure, refer to Chapter 4 for a refresher.

Several DOS memory management utilities and software drivers organize and make better use of available memory.

- MEMMAKER is a DOS memory utility program that is run from a DOS command line. It loads device drivers and TSRs into Upper Memory Blocks (UMBs). This helps to free up conventional memory space for programs.
- HIMEM.SYS is a DOS device driver loaded in the CONFIG.SYS that allows applications to run in extended memory. HIMEM.SYS is also present in Windows 9.x. In fact, both Windows 3.x and Windows 9.x require HIMEM.SYS for booting up.
- EMM386.EXE is a DOS memory management utility that opens the door to UMBs so that software drivers and programs can be loaded. EMM386.EXE uses limulation. *Limulation* is a technique used to translate or change extended memory to expanded memory.

VIRTUAL MEMORY AND SWAP FILES

A portion of a hard disk that is set aside for a certain range of memory address is referred to as *virtual memory*. This space on the hard drive acts as a sort of overflow buffer for RAM, or "'real memory"' as more memory is needed. A process called *memory paging* is used to create and swap memory addresses in and out of the hard drive's allocated virtual memory space. The main purpose of virtual memory is to allow the CPU to use hard drive space as memory. The virtual memory manager controls virtual memory. If the virtual memory manager cannot allocate memory requested by a specific application in Windows 9.x, a page fault will occur.

Virtual memory space is allocated on a hard drive in two ways: as a temporary swap file and as a permanent swap file.

- A *temporary swap file* is hard drive space that is used temporarily for memory overflow. If the computer is powered off, all information in the temporary swap file is lost. In other words, a temporary swap file is considered volatile memory. The original temporary swap file was named WIN386.SWP in Windows 3.x.
- A *permanent swap file* doesn't go away when the computer system is turned off. It handles the memory paging process faster than a temporary swap file. The permanent swap file was called 386PART.PAR in Windows 3.x.

The procedures for changing virtual memory settings in Windows 9.x/Me, NT, 2000 and Windows XP are discussed in their respective chapters (i.e., Chapters 11, 12, 13, and 14).

THE VIRTUAL MACHINE

When you start a DOS session or go to the command prompt from within Windows, the OS actually creates a separate memory space for your session to run in. This is called a Virtual Machine (VM). It was evident in Windows 3.x that multitasking was occurring because the user could open several 'DOS windows' or VMs at once.

The most important thing to realize about VMs is that they run in their own protected memory space. This means that if one program running in its own VM fails, other programs running in separate VMs are not affected. In other words, you can open multiple DOS or command prompt sessions. If one of the sessions fails, the other sessions will not be affected. This explains why the core components of an OS, such as KERNEL.EXE, GDI.EXE, and USER.EXE, are designed to run in a protected memory space—so that they are protected from other programs that may fail.

In Windows 3.x, we used Program Information Files (PIFs) to allocate specific amounts of memory to our separate DOS VMs. In newer OSs, you can still create PIFs and assign properties to VMs.

To display the assigned properties of the MS-DOS prompt in Windows 95, click Start > Programs, right-click the MS-DOS prompt, and click Properties. You will see the following tabs: General, Program, Font, Memory, Screen, and Misc. If you click the Memory tab, you will see the conventional, expanded, and extended memory assigned to the DOS VM. If you click the Program tab and select Advanced, the window shown in Figure 10.5 will display. If you are trying to run a DOS application in a Windows 95 environment and receive the message This Program cannot be run in Windows, you should make sure that the Prevent MS-DOS-based programs from detecting Windows box (also shown in Figure 10.5) is checked for the advanced properties of the DOS prompt properties associated with the application. Click OK twice and run your DOS application again.

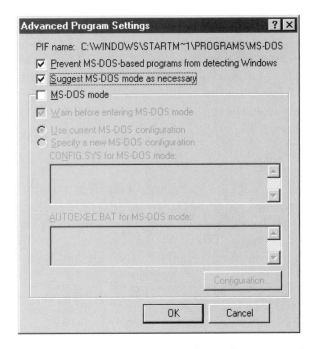

FIGURE 10.5   MS-DOS prompt advanced program settings.

WINDOWS INITIALIZATION FILES

Initialization files are Windows plain ASCII configuration text files that have an .INI extension. Windows 3.x used the SYSTEM.INI, WIN.INI, PROGRAM.INI, and PROTOCOL.INI files to configure almost all its settings and device drivers. Operating systems such as Windows 9.x/Me/2000 and Windows XP still make use of .INI files, such as the SYSTEM.INI, to load old 16-bit drivers for backward compatibility. However, the newer OSs do not need these files to boot up, as did Windows 3.x.

The main Windows initialization files and the text editors used to view and modify them are described next.

THE SYSTEM.INI

The SYSTEM.INI file got its start in Windows 3.x. It is a configuration file that is used to load 32-bit VxDs (Virtual Device Drivers) and 16-bit device drivers. It is often said that the SYSTEM.INI is the Windows version of the DOS file CONFIG.SYS because it deals mostly with device settings and drivers.

The SYSTEM.INI file in Windows 3.x is divided into two main sections: the [386Enh] section, where most 16-bit device drivers are loaded; and the [boot] section, which contains information on Windows 3.x start-up operations.

As mentioned previously, the SYSTEM.INI file in newer versions of Windows is maintained for backward compatibility with 16-bit drivers. Most of the device drives and environmental settings stored in the early OS initialization files are now stored and loaded by the registry in newer OSs. The registry is discussed in Chapters 11 through 14.

THE WIN.INI

The Windows WIN.INI file is often compared to the DOS file AUTOEXEC.BAT, based on its configuration of environment and user-related settings. The WIN.INI is also an ASCII readable text file. It is used to configure settings such as fonts, date, time, and language. When Windows is started, the system looks first at the SYSTEM.INI and then at the WIN.INI. The following lines are from a typical WIN.INI file found in Windows 2000.

```
; For 16-bit app support
[fonts]
[extensions]
[mci extensions]
[files]
[Mail]
MAPI=1
CMC=1
CMCDLLNAME=mapi.dll
CMCDLLNAME32=mapi32.dll
MAPIX=1
MAPIXVER=1.0.0.1
OLEMessaging=1
[MCI Extensions.BAK]
```

There are two items here that are important to note. Notice the first line of the WIN.INI file:

```
; For 16-bit app support
```

The semicolon (;) is used to remark out the line. This line is being used for informational purposes only. The semicolon can also be used in the SYSTEM.INI to exclude a line from being processed.

The semicolon is used in .INI files to remark out information. In AUTOEXEC. BAT and CONFIG.SYS files, the REM *statement is used to remark out information.*

TEXT EDITORS

Text editors such as SYSEDIT.EXE, Notepad, and WordPad can be used in Windows to view and edit the SYSTEM.INI, WIN.INI, CONFIG.SYS, and AUTOEXEC.BAT files. The SYSEDIT utility in particular can be used in any of the major OSs for this purpose. For example, in Windows 9.x/NT/2000, click Start > Run, enter "SYSEDIT" on the Open: line, and click OK. The SYSTEM.INI, WIN.INI, CONFIG.SYS, and AUTOEXEC.BAT files will open as displayed in Figure 10.6.

The SYSTEM.INI, WIN.INI, CONFIG.SYS, and AUTOEXEC.BAT files display different results on different systems. The display depends on which OS you are running and what else you have installed on your system.

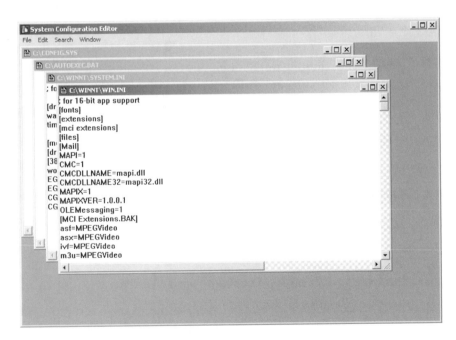

FIGURE 10.6   The results of SYSEDIT in Windows 2000.

COMMAND-LINE TUTORIAL

MS-DOS AND 32-BIT COMMANDS: A PRACTICAL TUTORIAL AND REFERENCE

This is a practical study focusing on the general practice of MS-DOS and 32-bit commands. Many of these commands have already been explained this book. Use this information as a quick study reference to ensure you are up to speed with basic commands before attempting the current A+ Exams.

The most basic information is how to access commands. Commands can be accessed from the following locations:

MS-DOS Prompt in 9x: Start > Programs > MS-DOS prompt in 95/98; Start > Programs > Accessories > MS-DOS Prompt in Me. Alternatively, you can type "command" in the Run dialog box (Start > Run).

Run dialog box (all versions): Start > Run. Many commands are accessible from here.

32-bit Command Prompt (2000/XP): Start > Programs (or All Programs) > Command Prompt or type "cmd" in the Run dialog box (Start > Run).

MS-DOS Command Prompt (all versions): Type "command" in the Run dialog box (Start > Run).

MS-DOS Prompt from Boot (95/98): After booting, you'll automatically get a prompt.

MS-DOS Prompt from Boot Floppy (all versions): After booting, you'll automatically get a prompt.

Safe Mode Command Prompt Only (Me/2000/XP): After powering on the computer, press <F8> and select Safe Mode Command Prompt Only from the boot menu.

USING COMMANDS

Before we get to actual commands, we will provide information that will make it easier to use them.

SELECTING AND COPYING TEXT FROM A COMMAND PROMPT WINDOW

1. Click the icon in the upper-left corner of the bar on top of the window, point to Edit in the menu that appears, and click Mark.
2. Click at the beginning of the text you want to copy.

3. Press and hold down the Shift key, and then click at the end of the text you want to copy.
4. Click the icon again, click Edit > Copy.
5. Paste the text into a document by holding the Ctrl key and pressing C, or by selecting Edit > Paste. If you want to paste the text back into the command prompt window, click the icon again, point to Edit, and click Paste.

USING WILDCARD CHARACTERS

Wildcard characters can be used when using Windows Search or Find, and to represent multiple files or folders when using a command prompt. Wildcard characters are as follows:

Asterisk (*): Acts as a substitute for zero or more characters. For example, to search for or make a change to any .txt file that starts with *G*, enter "G*.txt". If you want any file that has an extension starting with *.tif*, enter "*.tif". For all files in a particular folder, enter "*.*".

Question mark (?): Acts as a substitute for any single character. For example, to search for or make changes to all .doc files that start with *Karen* followed by a single character, enter "karen?.doc". This would find or change *karen1.doc*, *karen2.doc,* and so forth but would ignore *karen10.doc* because the number *10* has two characters.

COMMENT INDICATORS

When directly editing the MS-DOS configuration files AUTOEXEC.BAT and CONFIG.SYS, or their XP/2000 counterparts, CONFIG.NT and AUTOEXEC.NT, the safest way to stop a line of text from being implemented is to "comment it out." In these files, you do this by typing "REM" at the beginning of a line. This tells the system to ignore that line. The advantage to using these indicators as opposed to simply deleting the line is that it's very easy to reverse if you discover that you erroneously commented out an important line.

For .ini files such as WIN.INI and SYSTEM.INI, comment out lines using a semicolon.

COMMAND NOTES

- For information on commands not listed here, 2000's and XP's Help files have lists of all available prompts. Search 2000's Help for "Command Reference Main Page," or XP's for "Command-Line Reference." For 9x's commands, search the Internet. You can also search Windows' Help for individual commands.

- Not all commands are available in all versions. Additionally, certain MS-DOS commands won't be available in 2000 or XP if you access the 32-bit command prompt (Start > Programs or All Programs > Accessories > Command Prompt), or by typing "cmd" in the Run dialog box. However, if you type "command" in the Run dialog box, you'll be able to run some MS-DOS commands that would normally not be available in that version of Windows. Finally, not all commands work as described in Microsoft's documentation.

- For a description and syntax of each command, plus a complete list of switches and parameters, enter the command followed by a space and "/?". For example, for information about the CD command, type:

```
CD /?
```

- Because folders were originally called *directories*, Microsoft uses the term whenever writing about commands. The two terms (*folders* and *directories*) are interchangeable.

- Most of these commands can be used either by entering the full path of the file or folder being acted upon after the command name, or by navigating to that folder first. It is usually easier to navigate to the folder first, eliminating any chance of typos invalidating the command and requiring the command to be retyped. For instructions on navigating to the correct folder, see the description of the CD (CHDIR) command.

- In addition to the 8.3 limitation of file and folder names in MS-DOS, there cannot be spaces in MS-DOS file and folder names. When referring to file and folder names containing spaces when using an MS-DOS prompt on Windows, you might need to use quotation marks around the folder or filename. Otherwise, the system might interpret only the first word as the name and anything after that as invalid parameters or switches. This is however, by no means a universal rule, especially in 2000 and XP.

- Commands, parameters, and switches are not case sensitive.

- All switches must be preceded by a space character when typed as part of a single command line. The only time you would omit the space is when you are responding to a prompt, such as is possible in the CHKDSK command.

- Press Enter after each command to start it.

- A great trick that you can use with these commands is use of the < and > keys. The < key inputs the text from a text file into a command, and the > key sends the output from a command to a text file. For example, if you use the DIR command with the /p switch and want the output to go to a file in the current folder that you want to name OUTPUT.TXT, type "DIR /p > output.txt".

- If you want to import text from a file into a command, use the < key after the command and switches, followed by the name of the file.

■ If you find that commands you want to use are not available, running the PATH command might help. This tells the system where to find commands.

COMMAND LIST

The following commands are not all available in all versions and in all locations.

ATTRIB

In Windows, files and folders have certain properties (called *attributes)* that can be configured. If you right-click on the file or folder's icon, you'll see some check boxes that allow you to change these attributes. The ATTRIB command allows you to do this when the Windows GUI is not available. The possible attributes, which vary based on Windows version and other factors, are as follows:

Read only: When set, this allows the file to be opened and viewed but not changed or deleted.

Archive: This attribute affects whether the file will be backed up in certain backup schemes using a backup program, or whether running the XCOPY command will copy that particular file. For more information, see Windows Backup help files.

System: This indicates that the file is necessary for some Windows process.

Hidden: Windows hides certain files by default; however, any file can be hidden or displayed by changing this attribute. In 2000 and XP, when the user has enabled the showing of hidden files (in any Windows folder in Tools > Folder Options > View tab), icons for hidden folders and files appear translucent.

The most common repair use for the ATTRIB command is to replace corrupted registry files in Windows 9x. When run without switches, ATTRIB shows the attributes of each file in the current folder.

ATTRIB displays, sets, or removes the read-only, archive, system, and hidden attributes assigned to files or folders. Used without parameters, ATTRIB displays attributes of all files in the current folder.

Use

ATTRIB uses the plus sign (+) to turn on an attribute, and the minus sign (-) to turn off an attribute. To use ATTRIB, navigate to the folder where the desired file is located (see the CD command description later in this appendix), and type the command followed by the filename (with or without wildcards) and the desired parameters and switches.

Parameters

+r: Sets the read-only file attribute.

-r: Clears the read-only file attribute.

+a: Sets the archive file attribute.

-a: Clears the archive file attribute.

+s: Sets the system file attribute.

-s: Clears the system file attribute.

+h: Sets the hidden file attribute.

-h: Clears the hidden file attribute.

Switches

/s: Applies the command to matching files in the current folder and all its subfolders.

/d: Applies the command to the entire folder.

 When applying a change to a group of files using wildcard characters, files with their system and/or hidden attributes will not be affected unless you turn off the hidden and system attributes first.

Examples

To display the attributes of a file named CHAPTER07.DOC, navigate to the folder and enter:

```
ATTRIB chapter07.doc
```

To assign the read-only attribute to the file, enter:

```
ATTRIB +r chapter07.doc
```

To remove the read-only, hidden, and system attributes from all .REG files on the C: drive, including in all subfolders, navigate to the C: drive and enter:

```
ATTRIB -r -h -s *.reg /s
```

CD OR CHDIR

This refers to *Change Directory* and is used to change the current folder. When directions for another command say, "navigate to the xxx folder," this is the command that you would use to do that.

Use

When narrowing down to a subfolder within the current folder, type CD, followed by the subfolder name. For example, if the current folder is C:\WINDOWS, and you want to navigate to C:\WINDOWS\DESKTOP, type:

```
CD Desktop
```

To change the current folder to a root level (a drive letter without any additional folders) (e.g., C:\Documents and Settings to C:), make sure to enter the backslash (\) after the drive letter. For example, if the prompt says *C:\Documents and Settings>* and you want to navigate to the C drive, enter:

```
CD C:\.
```

Switch

The .. switch navigates to the higher level folder. For example, if the current folder is C:\Documents and Settings\All Users, running CD with this switch will take you to C:\Documents and Settings. Note that there is a space before the two periods.

CHKDSK (PRESENT IN ALL VERSIONS, USEFUL IN 2000 AND XP ONLY)

CHKDSK is a program used for checking the status of magnetic drives/disks, fixing certain errors, and even recovering readable data from bad disk sectors. It isn't particularly useful in 9x, except for obtaining a report on files on the disk. To correct any disk errors on 9x, run ScanDisk. In 2000 and XP, CHKDSK replaces 9x's ScanDisk. In 2000 and XP, it is easier to run CHKDSK from Windows, so you might as well save the command-line version for when the computer is booted into Safe Mode, Command prompt only. When invoked with the /f and/or /r switches to run on a disk in use, CHKDSK will prompt you to run at the next boot.

Use

Type "CHKDSK" followed by the drive letter and colon (:), followed by any switches (each switch must be preceded by a space character).

Switches

/c: Use with NTFS-formatted drives only. Skips folder structure cycle checking, resulting in a faster completion.

/f: Fixes filesystem errors on the disk. If run on a disk currently in use, /f causes CHKDSK to be run on the next boot.

/i: Use with NTFS-formatted drives only. Performs a less exhaustive check of index entries, resulting in a faster completion.

/r: Recovers readable information from bad disk sectors. If run on a disk currently in use, /r causes CHKDSK to be run on the next boot. See the listing for the RECOVER command for another tool that can recover lost data.

/v: Displays the name of each file in every folder as the disk is checked.

/x: Use with NTFS-formatted drives only. Makes all necessary changes to any network-mapped drives in order for CHKDSK to work on them. /x also includes the functionality of the /r switch.

Notes

- Running CHKDSK without the /f, /r, and/or /x switches is usually pointless and might report false disk errors.
- If you are prompted to convert lost chains (unidentified file fragments) to files, do so by pressing Y. You can then find the files in the root folder (C:\ in the C: drive). The files are named File****.chk (the asterisks stand for any character). If the files don't contain any data you need, you can delete them. If you press N (answer no) to the prompt, the fragments will be deleted automatically.
- If you use the /f or /x switch on a very large disk such as 80 GB, or one with huge numbers of files (e.g., millions of files), CHKDSK might take several days to complete. CHKDSK cannot be stopped while it is running, so the computer will not be available for this time.

CLS

CLS removes all text except the main heading and prompt from the command prompt window. CLS stands for *Clear Screen*.

Use

Type "CLS".

CMD (2000 AND XP ONLY)

Although this command can be used in a command prompt window, its most common use is to be entered in the Run dialog box for the purpose of opening a new 32-bit command prompt window in 2000 and XP.

Use

Type "CMD" in the Run dialog box and click OK or press Enter.

COMMAND

Although this command can be used in a command prompt window, its most common use is to be entered in the Run dialog box for opening an MS-DOS prompt window in all versions.

Use

Type "COMMAND" in the Run dialog box and press Enter.

COMP (2000 AND XP ONLY)

Compares the data in two files or sets of files byte by byte. The two files or sets can be on the same or different drives or folders.

Use

Type "COMP" and press Enter. You'll be prompted for the first file to compare. Enter the full path and press Enter. You'll then be prompted for the second file to compare. Enter the full path and press Enter. You'll then be prompted for any switches. If you want to use no switches, press Enter. If you do want to use a switch, enter the first desired switch with any applicable parameters, if any, and press Enter. Every time you enter a switch, you'll be prompted to enter another after you press Enter. After you press Enter after having entered no switches, COMP will proceed to make the comparison.

Alternatively, you can type "COMP" followed by the first file path, the second file path, and any switches and other parameters desired. For example, using the 32-bit command prompt in 2000 or XP, compare two files designating the output to be noted in characters:

```
COMP C:\Documents and Settings\Rojo\My Documents\Chapter05.doc D:\
Book Chapters\Chapter05KJI.doc /a
```

Switches

/**a:** Displays differences as characters.

/**c:** Performs a comparison that is not case sensitive.

/**d:** Displays differences in decimal format. (The default format is hexadecimal.)

/**l:** Displays the number of the line on which a difference occurs, instead of displaying the byte offset.

/**n=number:** Compares the first *number* of lines of both files, even if the files are different sizes.

Notes

- Use wildcard characters to compare groups of files.
- COMP displays the results in memory addresses, so it's useful only to indicate that the files are different, not to display the differences.
- Files must be the same size, or the only result will be that the files aren't the same size. The exception to this is if the /n=*number* switch is used. In place of the word *number*, enter the number of lines of data to be compared. If you enter, for example, 10, the first 10 lines of each file will be compared.
- This command is extraordinarily particular; even a change in case somewhere in the path might cause COMP to report that it cannot open the file. If you use it in an MS-DOS prompt, you might have to convert folder names or filenames to the 8.3 standard. Look up 8.3 filename standards on the Internet if you need help.

CONVERT (XP AND 2000 ONLY)

Converts hard drive partitions formatted as FAT and FAT32 to NTFS. CONVERT cannot convert a partition to any filesystem other than NTFS.

Use

Type "CONVERT" followed by the drive letter and colon, and then "/fs:ntfs" followed by any switches. If you were converting drive C to NTFS in the verbose mode (see the switch listings), you would type:

```
CONVERT C: /fs:ntfs /v
```

and then press Enter.

Switches

/fs:ntfs: CONVERT won't work without this switch following the drive letter. fs means *filesystem*.

f/nosecurity: Specifies that files and folders already on the drive are accessible to everyone who uses the computer.

/v: Verbose mode. All possible information will be displayed while the conversion is taking place.

/x: Performs all changes to network-mapped drives necessary for the conversion to take place.

Any drive in use will be converted at the next boot.

NOTE

COPY

Copies one or more files. XCOPY provides much more flexibility than does COPY.

Use

Type "COPY" followed by general switches, and then type the path of the file(s) to be copied followed by any switches that apply to the source files, then the path of the destination, if desired, followed by any switches that apply to the destination. The source can be a path to a drive, folder, or file. If it is a drive or folder, it will copy all the files in that folder to the destination, but it will not copy subfolders or any files within subfolders. Wildcards can be used in a source. Two or more files or folders can be specified in the source by using the plus sign (+) followed by a space character before each file after the first one listed, as in:

```
COPY /v D:\Backup\*.dll + D:\Backup\Example.txt C:\Windows\System32
```

This example would copy all .DLL files in the Backup folder on the D drive, but no files in subfolders of Backup, plus the file EXAMPLE.TXT to the C:\ Windows\System32 folder. The /v switch verifies that each file is copied properly.

The destination can also be a path to a drive, folder, or file. If the destination is a path to a drive or folder, the copy will keep the name of the original file. If the destination is a file with a name different from the original, the copy will have the new filename. If the destination is not specified, the copy will be placed in the current folder, as long as the current folder isn't the same as the source folder; in which case, no copying will occur.

If two or more source files are specified but only one destination file is specified, the files will be combined into a single file, assuming the file formats are compatible with each other and can handle such a change. Text files (.TXT), for example, can be combined.

Switches

/**d:** If any of the source files are encrypted, this switch removes the encryption attribute on the copies.

/**n:** Causes the filename to be converted to one that complies with the DOS 8.3 filename convention.

/**v:** Verifies that new files are copied correctly. It is advisable to use when copying critical files. It does cause the copying to take more time than without /v.

/**y:** By default, Windows prompts you to confirm that you want to overwrite an existing destination file of the same name in the same folder; /y stops these prompts.

/-y: Turns off the /y switch. Restores prompts to confirm that you want to overwrite an existing destination file of the same name in the same folder.

/z: In case copies are being made over a network and the network connection is lost, or one of the computers goes offline, /z sets the copy operation to automatically resume from where it left off after the connection is reestablished.

/a: Indicates an ASCII text file (see Windows' Help for more information).

/b: Indicates a binary file (see Windows' Help for more information).

You might have to surround folder names or filenames containing spaces with quotation marks or use the 8.3 standard filenames when using this command.

DEL OR ERASE

Deletes specified files.

Use

Navigate to the folder that contains the file, and type "DEL" or "ERASE" followed by the filename and by any desired switches. You can also enter the entire path at the prompt rather than navigating to the folder. Multiple filenames can be entered separated by spaces, commas, or semicolons, or wildcards can be used. If only a folder name is entered, DEL or ERASE will delete only the files in the root of the folder. Subfolders and files within subfolders will not be affected unless the /s switch is used.

Switches

/f: Normally, files with the read-only attribute will not be deleted. /f overrides this and forces deletion.

/p: Prompts you to confirm that you want the file to be deleted.

/q: Prevents Windows from prompting you to confirm that you want the file to be deleted.

/s: Deletes specified files from the current folder and all subfolders. Displays each filename as the file is deleted.

After you delete a file using the DEL or ERASE command, that file does not appear in the Recycle Bin and is considered irretrievable without some third-party recovery program.

DIR

Displays a list of the subfolders and files in a folder or drive with some information such as total file size, the last date and time each file was modified, and the amount of free disk space on the disk.

Use

Navigate to the desired folder and type "DIR" followed by any desired switches. This does not show hidden or system files unless you use the /a switch.

Switches

/**p:** Displays one screen at a time. To continue, press any key on the keyboard.

/**q:** Displays the owner of each file, if applicable.

/**a:** Displays all files, including files with the hidden and system attributes.

/**a followed by attribute codes:** Displays only files or other items with attributes you specify.

Attribute Codes

a: Files ready for archiving only.

d: Folders only.

h: Hidden files and folders only.

r: Read-only files only.

s: System files and folders only.

Each of these codes can be inversed by preceding it with a minus sign (-). For example, -r displays only files with the read-only attribute. In addition, using multiple attribute codes, Windows will display only files with all of the attributes indicated by the codes. Don't leave a space between codes when using multiple codes. For example, to display only files that are both read only and hidden, type:

```
DIR /arh
```

/**s:** Lists every occurrence, in the specified folder and all its subfolders, of the specified filename.

/**x:** Displays both long filenames and 8.3 filenames.

DIR has several more switches. Consult Windows' Help or run DIR *with the* /? *switch for more information.*

EDIT (Limited Use in 2000 and XP)

Starts the MS-DOS Editor, which creates and changes ASCII text files. EDIT is an antiquated text editor that works without benefit of a mouse. It can be essential to use if you boot into DOS and need to edit a text file such as AUTOEXEC.BAT or CONFIG.SYS. You access menu commands by pressing and holding the Alt key while typing the first letter of the menu and the highlighted letter of each command. After you have accessed a menu, the arrow keys can be used to navigate the menus. Another way to invoke a menu command is to highlight it by using the arrow keys, and then press Enter.

Use

Type "EDIT" followed by the full path to the file you want to open or create, followed by any desired switches.

EXIT

Closes a DOS prompt and many DOS programs. If you click the X to close the window in a DOS program, you'll get a message indicating that closing the program this way will cause any unsaved data to be lost. Although you'll rarely have any unsaved data, it is probably easier to use this command to avoid the prompt.

Use

Type "EXIT".

EXPAND (2000 and XP Only)

Expands one or more compressed files. This command is used to retrieve compressed files from distribution disks such as Windows installation disks, often designated with an underscore as the final character in the file extension, or found in 9x in the \Windows\Options\Cabs or \Windows\Options\Install folder.

Use

Type "EXPAND" followed by the path of the source file and the path of the destination file. If you are expanding a file within a cabinet file, navigate to the cab file's folder and type "EXPAND" followed by the cab filename and then the -f: switch, followed, without a space, by the individual files within the cab file. For example, navigate to C:\Windows\Options\Cabs (found in many Windows 9x installations) and type:

```
EXPAND net10.cab -f:snip.vxd C:\Windows
```

This will expand the SNIP.VXD file into the C:\Windows folder.

Switch

-f: -f followed, without a space, by filenames of files within cab files.

FDISK (DOS and 9x Only)

Opens a program that allows creation and deletion of partitions, and the viewing of partition information. After the program is open, it is no longer a command-line program but instead is menu based.

Use

While booted into DOS, type "FDISK" to open the program. Two switches will also perform functions without opening the menu-based program.

Switches

/mbr: This will replace the Master Boot Record (MBR). The MBR is the first sector on the hard disk. There is a small program in the MBR that tells the system which partition is bootable. You cannot boot without the MBR being intact. Use this switch to replace a damaged MBR. This can occur if there is a boot-sector virus, or for other reasons. Try using this if you can't boot and you can't determine another cause. Using this switch does not open the menu-based program.

/status: This will display information about the partition. Using this switch does not open the menu-based program.

/x: Ignores extended disk partition support. If you receive a disk access or stack overflow error, use this switch; /x can be used with /status, but if used by itself, the menu-based program does open.

FORMAT

Formats magnetic disks and partitions in specified file formats (FAT, FAT32, NTFS). Works with floppy and hard disks.

Use

Type "FORMAT" followed by the drive letter and a colon, a space, then /fs: and the name of the filesystem (FAT, FAT32, or NTFS). For example, to format drive E: as FAT32, you would type:

```
FORMAT E: /fs:FAT32
```

Floppy disks can be formatted only as FAT. FAT is the designation for FAT16. If you omit the /fs switch, the system will use the default.

Switches

/**fs:** followed by the desired filesystem: This switch determines the filesystem, but if you leave it out, Windows will use the default. For example, floppies will automatically be formatted as FAT.

/**q:** Quick format. Skips a sector-by-sector surface scan of the disk. Use only with a disk known not to have any bad sectors.

/**c:** Compress newly added files. Works only with NTFS partitions.

/**s:** (95, 98, and DOS only) Formats a floppy and copies the three DOS files (COMMAND.COM, IO.SYS, MSDOS.SYS) onto it. This switch will work in 95 and 98, and any time the computer is booted into MS-DOS.

NOTE

Formatting a disk erases all data on the disk, regardless of the method used to format.

MD or MKDIR

Stands for Make Directory. Creates a folder or subfolder.

Use

Type "MD" followed by the full path of the new folder, including the name of the new folder. Alternatively, you can navigate to the drive or folder one level above that of the new folder, and type "MD" followed only by the desired name of the new folder.

MMC (2000 AND XP ONLY)

Opens a Microsoft Management Console (MMC). It is normally run from the Run dialog box rather than the command prompt. If you have created or saved an MMC, this command is an easy way to open it. MMC is beyond the scope of this book, but you might be instructed to use it by a Microsoft support technician. For more information on MMCs, search Windows 2000's or XP's Help for MMC.

Use

Type "MMC" in the Run dialog box. If opening a saved console, navigate (browse) to the location of the saved console file, and then type "MMC" followed by a space and the filename.

Switch

/a: Opens a saved console in author mode. This switch is necessary to make changes to saved consoles.

MORE

Allows the viewing of files and the output of other commands one screen at a time. This command is commonly used to view long files. When the window is full, you will get the MORE prompt. There are several options for how you want to view the remaining output.

Use

To use MORE by itself, navigate to the folder that contains the files you want to view, type "MORE" followed by any desired switches, and then the path to the file. If you want to view multiple files, you can enter all the filenames separated by space characters. You can even view files in different folders by entering the full path for each. For example, to view files in 2000 or XP in the root folder of the C: drive, My Documents, and in a folder on a CD-ROM, clearing the screen before displaying the next page, navigate to My Documents, and type:

```
MORE /c test1.txt C:\test2.txt D:\"text files"\test3.txt
```

This will display one screen of TEST1.TXT and allow you to view the remainder of the file using commands that will be described later. After the entire TEST1 file has been displayed, TEST2 will be displayed, followed by TEST3.

To use MORE with another command, type the command followed by any desired switches for the command, a space, the pipe character (|) (see the note at the end of this listing), "MORE", and then the path to the file or files you want to view. For example, to use the MEM /P command with MORE, clearing the screen after each page, type:

```
MEM /p | MORE /c
```

Switches

/c: Clears each screen before you use a command to view the next screen.

/s: Reduces a series of blank lines to a single blank line.

Responses to the – More – ***Prompt***

<spacebar>: Displays next page.

Enter: Displays next line.

<F>: Skips to next file.

<Q>: Quits.

<?>: Displays available responses to – More – prompt.

<=>: Displays line number.

<P> followed by a space and a number: Displays the specified number of lines.

<S> followed by a space and a number: Skips the specified number of lines.

To type the pipe character, hold Shift and press the backslash (\\) key.

MOVE

Moves files or folders from one drive or folder to another. Similar to COPY, except that MOVE deletes the source file.

Use

Type "MOVE" followed by a switch, if desired, then the source folder or filename, and then the destination folder or filename. If moving more than one file, the destination must be a folder.

Switches

/y: Normally, you would be prompted to confirm if you want to overwrite an existing destination file or folder of the same name; /y turns off this prompt. It is not necessary to use unless there actually is such a destination file or folder and you want to suppress the prompt.

/-y: Turns on the prompt to confirm that you want to overwrite a destination file or folder of the same name, if present.

MOVE *will not move encrypted files or folders to a drive that doesn't support the Encrypting File System (EFS). EFS is supported on NTFS drives in 2000, XP, or Windows Server 2003 only. Nonupgraded NTFS drives on systems that were upgraded from Windows NT do not support EFS, but that scenario is rare. To move these files, decrypt them first.*

PATH

Although "path" has a more general meaning, "the path" refers to the path to all of these commands. In 9x, some of these are in the root folder of the boot drive (usually C:\), some are in the Windows folder (usually C:\Windows), and some are in the Command folder (usually C:\Windows\Command). In 2000 and XP, commands can be found in the Windows folder (usually C:\Windows or C:\Winnt), and in the System32 folder (usually C:\Windows\System32). There also might be a Command folder (usually C:\Windows\Command or C:\Winnt\Command). The PATH command sets the computer to recognize the locations of these commands. That is how Windows can find each command simply from the user entering commands at the command prompt or in the Run dialog box. Run by itself, PATH displays the current path.

Use

Type "PATH" followed by the path that contains commands. You can enter multiple command paths by separating them with semicolons (;).

Parameter

;: Separates the different paths that make up "the path." If you use this by itself, the existing command path will be deleted.

Example

In 9x, if you find you don't have access to all commands that should be available, type:

```
PATH C:\;C:\Windows;C:\Windows\Command
```

You can add any other paths you want, separated by semicolons. This can be especially useful if you boot a 9x machine with a startup (MS-DOS) floppy disk.

RECOVER

Recovers readable data from a damaged or defective disk.

Use

Type "RECOVER" followed by the path to the file you want to rescue. RECOVER requires that the disk not be in use, so it cannot be used on the Windows boot partition while the computer is booted to Windows.

RECOVER reads a file sector by sector and recovers data from the good sectors. Data in bad sectors is lost. It is common practice to open the file after recovery and attempt to reenter missing data manually.

REN or RENAME

Changes the name of a file or folder.

Use

Navigate to the folder that contains the file you want to rename, or to the parent folder of the subfolder you want to rename. Type "REN" followed by the existing file or folder name, a space, and then the new file or folder name. REN cannot be used to move files or folders, so you cannot enter a new path for the file.

You can use wildcards in either or both the existing and the new filenames, with the caveat that the wildcard characters will stand for the same real characters in both names. For example, let's say that the current folder has three files named TEST1.DOC, TEST2.DOC, and TEST3.DOC. You enter TEST*.DOC as the existing filename and SAMPLE*.DOC as the new filename. TEST1.DOC will become SAMPLE1.DOC, TEST2.DOC will become SAMPLE2.DOC, and so on.

If you try to rename a file to a filename in use in the same folder, you'll get an error message and the renaming operation will not proceed.

REPLACE

Replaces files in the destination folder with files in the source folder that have the same name. It also can be used to add files to the destination folder that don't already exist there. For example, if you need to make sure that all files on an optical disc have been copied to a folder on the hard drive, you could use another method to copy them again, and then get the prompt to overwrite existing files. Using REPLACE with the /a switch automatically copies only files that don't exist on the destination folder while ignoring those files that do exist there.

Use

To replace files or folders, type "REPLACE" followed by the path to the source files or folders, then the destination files or folders, followed by any appropriate switches. You can also navigate to the source folder before running the command. If you specify neither a source nor a destination folder, the current folder is used.

Switches

/a: Adds only files to the destination folder that aren't there already; /a cannot be used at the same time as the /s or /u switches.

/p: Prompts you for confirmation before replacing or adding a file or folder.

/r: Replaces read-only, hidden, or system files or folders. Files or folders in the destination folder with these attributes normally would cause the operation to stop.

/w: Waits for you to insert a disk before searching for source files or folders. Without this switch, REPLACE attempts to replace or add files immediately after the user presses Enter.

/s: Includes subfolders of the destination folder (not the source folder); /s cannot be used at the same time as the /a switch.

/u: Replaces only those files in the destination folder that are older than those with the same names in the source folder; /u cannot be used at the same time as the /a switch, nor can it be used to update hidden or system files. You'll have to remove these attributes first, using the ATTRIB command or the Windows interface.

RD OR RMDIR

Deletes a folder. RD stands for Remove Directory.

Use

Type "RD" followed by the path to the folder you want to delete, followed by any desired switches. Make sure to enter the full path, starting with the drive letter. Do not navigate first to the folder you want to delete; RD won't work if you do. Additionally, RD won't work if the folder to be deleted is a subfolder of the current folder.

Switches

/s: Includes all subfolders and their contents.

/q: Quiet mode. Normally, a confirmation is given after the deletion is complete; /q turns off this confirmation.

 You cannot delete a folder with hidden or system files without removing these attributes first. See DIR to locate these files and ATTRIB to remove these attributes.

SHUTDOWN (XP ONLY)

Allows you to shut down, restart, or log a user off the computer. Used without switches, SHUTDOWN will log off the current user.

Use

Type "SHUTDOWN" followed by any desired switches.

Switches

-**s:** Shuts down the computer.

-**r:** Reboots the computer.

-**f:** Forces any running programs to close.

-**t followed by a space and a number of seconds:** This sets the timer for system shutdown in the specified number of seconds. The default is 20 seconds.

-**a:** Aborts shutdown. If you run shutdown and then change your mind, during the timed interval before the machine shuts down, you can abort the shutdown by running SHUTDOWN -a.

SYS (DOS AND 9X ONLY)

Copies the DOS system files, COMMAND.COM, IO.SYS, and MS DOS.SYS, to a disk.

Use

Navigate to the drive and folder you want to copy the DOS system files to and type "SYS". *Never* run SYS on an NTFS drive.

SYSTEMINFO (XP ONLY)

Displays detailed configuration information about a computer and Windows, including OS configuration, security information, product ID, and hardware properties, such as memory, disk space, and network adapters.

Use

Type "SYSTEMINFO". If you want to configure the format of the output, use the /fo switch. SYSTEMINFO is an ideal command to be accompanied by the MORE command.

Switches

/**fo** **followed by one of the three possibilities:** TABLE, LIST, or CSV (Comma-Separated Values). LIST is the default.

You might get the error message indicating that a required file, FRAMEDYN.DLL, is missing. If this is the case, you'll need to find the file FRAMEDYN.DL_ on the XP installation disk in the I386 folder. Copy this file to Windows\System32. Then, use the EXPAND *command to expand it and then* REN *or the Windows interface to rename it FRAMEDYN.DLL.*

TASKKILL (XP ONLY)

Terminates one or more programs or processes. Processes can be called by their process ID or by their name. View running processes by using the TASKLIST command.

Use

Run TASKLIST or Windows' Task Manager (press Ctrl - Alt - Delete). After you've determined which processes to terminate, type "TASKKILL" followed by the appropriate switches and parameters.

Switches and Parameters

/**pid** **followed by the process ID:** Specifies the process ID of the process to be terminated.

/**im** **followed by the process name:** Specifies the process name (called *image name*) of the process to be terminated. TASKKILL will terminate all instances of a process.

/**f:** Terminates the process(es) by force, if necessary. Some processes will ordinarily not be terminated without this switch. Most of these are crucial to the operation of Windows, so don't be surprised if Windows shuts down if you end the wrong process.

/**t:** Terminates all "child processes" of the specified process.

TASKLIST (XP ONLY)

Displays a list of programs and processes with their Process ID (PID) for all tasks running on the computer. This is useful to compile data for the TASKKILL command.

Use

Type "TASKLIST" followed by any desired switches.

Switches and Parameters

/**fo followed by the type of output desired:** Possible output types are TABLE, LIST, and CSV. The default is TABLE.

/**m followed by the module name:** A module is a program that uses DLL (Dynamic Link Library) files. Files with this extension are used by programs, and are often used by more than one program. For example, different card games might all use the same CARDS.DLL file to provide a deck of cards. If you run TASKLIST with this switch and specify a module, the output will show all the DLL files that could be used for that module. If you use the /m switch without a module name, all modules will be listed. The /m switch is incompatible with the /svc and /v switches.

/**svc:** Lists complete service information for each process. This switch will work only if the output is set to TABLE, the default (see the /fo switch). /svc is incompatible with the /m and /v switches.

/**v:** Verbose mode. All information will be displayed. /v is incompatible with the /svc and /m switches.

TYPE

Displays the text in a text file.

Use

Navigate to the text file's folder and type "TYPE", or type "TYPE" followed by the path to the file or files to view. To view multiple files, separate them with spaces.

This is a command in which it is very helpful to use the MORE command.

VER

Displays the Windows version and number.

Use

Type "VER".

WINNT32 (2000 AND XP ONLY)

Performs an installation of or upgrade to Windows 2000 or XP. WINNT32 is not in the usual command path. It is available when the current folder is an installation source such as a Windows 2000 or XP CD.

Use

Insert the 2000 or XP installation disk or connect to another installation source. Close the installation program after it opens. Open a command prompt, and navigate to the installation folder, which will probably be I386. Type "WINNT32" followed by any desired switches.

Switches

/**checkupgradeonly:** Checks your current version of Windows to determine if it's eligible to be upgraded to the new version, and checks your hardware to make sure it's compatible with the new version. If you use this option with /unattend, you will not be prompted for any input. If you don't use /unattend, the output is displayed, and you are prompted to save it in a file. The default filename is UPGRADE.TXT, and its default location is in the System32 folder, usually C:\Windows\System32 or C:\Winnt\System32.

/**cmdcons:** Use this switch on a system that already has Windows 2000 or XP installed to install the Recovery Console as a startup option.

/**unattend:** Upgrades existing 98, Me, 2000, or XP in a mode that requires no user input. All information that is normally requested during setup is taken from the existing installation.

There are a great many other switches for WINNT32 that are beyond the scope of this book. They are of use primarily to network administrators and others responsible for installing Windows on many machines simultaneously.

XCOPY

Copies files, folders, and subfolders. XCOPY offers great flexibility over any other way to copy, whether by command line or using the Windows GUI.

Use

Type "XCOPY" followed by the path to the source file or folder, then the destination file or folder, and then any desired switches.

Switches

/**w:** Prompts you to press a key before copying commences.

/**p:** Prompts you to confirm that you want to create each destination file.

/**c:** Continues copying regardless of errors.

/**q:** Quiet mode. XCOPY messages are not displayed.

/f: Displays filenames while copying.

/l: Displays the names of all the files that are set to be copied.

/g: Specifies that destination files not be encrypted (2000 and XP only).

/d followed by a colon and the date in the mm-dd-yyyy format: Copies only those source files that had been modified on or after the specified date. If you do not include a date, all source files newer than the existing destination files of the same name are copied. The purpose of this command is to update files with newer versions. For example, to copy only .DOC files newer than March 5, 2006 from a CD to a folder, you would type:

```
XCOPY D:\*.doc c:\folder /d:03-05-2006
```

/u: Copies only those source files with the same names as those already in the destination folder.

/i: If you have specified a folder or a filename with wildcards as the source and the destination folder doesn't already exist, /i causes XCOPY to create the new folder. The default is for XCOPY to prompt you to specify whether the destination is a folder or file.

/s: Copies folders and subfolders as long as there are files inside them.

/e: Copies all subfolders, regardless of whether there are files inside them.

/t: Copies the entire folder tree but none of the files. Add the /e switch to copy empty folders.

/k: (2000 and XP) Causes the copied files to retain the read-only attribute if the source files had it. By default, copied files do not have the read-only attribute.

/k: (9x) Causes all attributes to be copied with the files.

/r: Copies files with the read-only attribute but is not supposed to copy the attribute. However, it might actually copy the attribute in some cases.

/h: Copies files with hidden and system attributes. The default is for system and hidden files not to be copied.

/a: Copies only files with the Archive attributes.

/m: Copies only files with the Archive attributes, but removes the Archive attribute from the *source* file.

/n: Applies 8.3 file and/or folder names to the copies. Necessary when copying files with long filenames to systems that can handle only 8.3 filenames.

/y: Normally, XCOPY prompts you to confirm that you want to overwrite a destination file of the same name as the one being copied; /y turns off this prompting.

/-y: Restores prompting to overwrite existing files of the same name as the one being copied.

/z: (2000 and XP only) If you are copying over a network, and the network connection is lost for whatever reason, if you used /z, copying can pick up where it left off when the connection is restored; /z saves you from having to start over again. /z also displays the copying progress for each file.

If you attempt to copy encrypted files onto a drive that doesn't support the EFS, there will be an error, and copying will not continue.

If you don't specify a destination, XCOPY *uses the current folder.*

By default, unless you use the /m *switch,* XCOPY's *file copies all have the Archive attribute set, regardless of whether it was set in the source files.*

RECOVERY CONSOLE COMMANDS (2000 AND XP ONLY)

The Recovery Console has a limited number of commands. Many of the commands are the same, but most of these have different switches and parameters. Additionally, there are other commands that are unique to the Recovery Console. Because the functions of the shared commands are very similar or the same as in the standard commands, only the differences, if any, will be noted. Moreover, only selected commands and switches will be presented here. For a complete list, search Windows' Help for "Recovery Console."

There are a few rules to be concerned with when using the Recovery Console:

- Except where indicated, wildcard characters don't work.
- Type quotation marks around folder and filenames containing spaces.
- Only certain folders can be accessed:
  - The root folder of any hard drive partition.
  - The Windows or Winnt folder and its subfolders.
  - The Cmdcons folder, which is the folder, usually in the root folder of the C:\ drive, that contains the Recovery Console. It is hidden by default.
  - Removable media but only to read and copy files. Files on removable media cannot be modified using the Recovery Console.
  - The Windows installation media.
- Attempts to access other folders will cause an Access Denied message.
- The /? switch for help works with all Recovery Console commands.

ATTRIB

Switches

+r: Sets the read-only attribute.

-r: Clears the read-only attribute.

+s: Sets the system attribute.

-s: Clears the system attribute.

+h: Sets the hidden attribute.

-h: Clears the hidden attribute.

+c: Sets the compressed attribute.

-c: Clears the compressed attribute.

CD OR CHDIR

This is the same as the command-prompt version, except that you always have to use quotation marks around folder names containing spaces.

CHKDSK

Switches

/p: Normally, a disk that doesn't indicate problems will not be checked exhaustively. Use /p to override this indication and run the exhaustive check anyway. CHKDSK does not make any changes to the drive when run only with /p.

/r: Locates bad sectors and recovers any readable data. /r automatically includes /p.

CHKDSK *requires the file AUTOCHK.EXE to work. If it cannot find it in the system folder (usually \Winnt\System32 or \Windows\System32), it will look for it on the Windows Installation CD.*

CLS

This command is the same as the command-prompt version.

COPY

Copies a single file only to another location. COPY will not copy a folder.

When copying a compressed file from the Windows installation CD, the file is automatically decompressed.

DEL or DELETE

Deletes a single file only. DEL will not delete a folder.

DIR

Lists the volume (drive) label, serial number, and contents, along with codes indicating what each item is and what attributes are set in each.

Parameter

/ followed by a folder name, filename, or group of filenames: DIR can limit itself to showing just those folder or filenames you select, along with everything within a folder. *Wildcard characters can be used with this parameter.* Multiple filenames can be used by using wildcards or separating filenames with spaces, commas, or semicolons.

NOTE

The /p switch is not available with DIR in the Recovery Console because the command runs as if used with the MORE command prompt command.

DIR's output includes the volume (drive) label, serial number, total number of files, the total size of all displayed items, and the amount of free disk space remaining (in bytes). Other information in the output includes time of last modification, file extension, individual file size, file attributes, and whether the item is a file or directory (folder). The last two items use the following codes:

d: Directory (folder).

h: Hidden.

s: System.

e: Encrypted.

r: Read-only.

a: Archive.

c: Compressed.

p: Reparse point.

DISABLE

Disables a device driver or service. The opposite command is ENABLE.

Use

Type "DISABLE" followed by the service or driver name. You can use the LISTSVC command for a list of services and drivers on the computer.

Parameters

Service name: Type "DISABLE" followed by a service name, as shown:

```
DISABLE Messenger
```

This causes the messenger service to be disabled the next time the computer is booted to Windows. The previous state of the service is displayed as well.

Device driver name: Type "DISABLE" followed by the driver name. The driver will be disabled for the next boot to Windows. The previous state of the service is displayed as well.

DISKPART

Allows management of disk partitions.

Use

Type "DISKPART" followed by the appropriate switches and parameters. Run without switches and parameters, DISKPART starts the Windows Setup partitioning program. You'll recognize the program if you have installed NT 4.0, 2000, or XP.

Switches and Parameters

/add followed by the device name and the desired size, in MB, of the partition: Creates a new partition. For example, to add a 10-MB partition, type:

```
DISKPART /add \Device\HardDisk0 10
```

Device name is defined after the /delete switch.

/delete followed by the drive letter, partition name, or device name: Deletes an existing partition. *Partition name* and *device name* are defined here:

Device name: An identifier for the hard drive that uses a direct naming convention. This precludes the confusion that can come about due to drive letters than can change. To get this, run the MAP Recovery Console command with no switch and ignore the partition portion of the output. A typical device name is \Device\Harddisk0. The device name is valid only with both the /add and /delete switches.

Partition name: This uses the same naming convention as the device name but has the added partition number at the end. A typical partition name is \Device\Harddisk0\Partition1. The partition name is valid only with the /delete switch.

Deletion Examples

```
DISKPART /delete \Device\HardDisk0\Partition2
DISKPART /delete E:
```

ENABLE

Enables a service or device driver.

Use

Type "ENABLE" followed by the service name or device driver name and the startup type. The possible startup types are SERVICE_BOOT_START, SERVICE_SYSTEM START, SERVICE_AUTO_START, SERVICE_DEMAND_START. For example, to enable the Messenger service to start automatically, type:

```
ENABLE Messenger SERVICE_AUTO_START
```

When ENABLE is run with a device driver name or service name but no start type, the current start type is displayed. Write this down if you need to keep a record of it.

You can use the LISTSVC command for a list of services and drivers on the computer.

Parameter

Startup type: The possible startup types are defined here:

Startup Type	Definition	Applies Primarily To
SERVICE_BOOT_START	Starts with Windows	Device drivers
SERVICE_SYSTEM_START	Starts with the computer	Device drivers
SERVICE_AUTO_START	Starts with Windows	Services
SERVICE_DEMAND_START	Starts manually by a program or user	Services

EXIT

Exits the Recovery Console and restarts the computer.

EXPAND

Use

Type "EXPAND" followed by the source file and then the destination folder. If you want to select an individual file to extract from a cab file, type "EXPAND" followed by the cab filename, /F: followed without a space by the name of the file within the cab file, the destination folder, and then the /y switch if desired. The source cannot use wildcards, but the name of a file within a cab file can use wildcards. If you do not specify a destination folder, the current folder is used.

For example, to expand the DRVSPACE.BIN file from within the C:\Windows\ Options\Cabs\Base4.cab file to the root directory (realizing that this file is from Windows 98 and wouldn't actually be expanded using the Recovery Console), from the C:\ prompt, type:

```
EXPAND \Windows\Options\Cabs\Base4.cab /F:drivespace.bin C:\
```

Entering the destination was optional because the command was run from the C:\ prompt. Recall that EXPAND uses the current folder if the destination folder isn't specified.

Switches and Parameters

/d: Lists the files within the cabinet file. /d performs no action on the file. It is not recommended for use on folders with large number of files.

/y: Normally, you are prompted to confirm that you want to overwrite files in the destination; /y turns off these prompts.

FIXBOOT

Creates a new boot sector on the system partition. It is useful if the boot sector has been damaged.

Use

Type "FIXBOOT". This will create a new boot sector on the partition that you are logged onto. If you want to create a boot sector on a different drive, enter the drive letter followed by a colon after "FIXBOOT" and a space. For example, to create a new boot sector on the E: drive, type:

```
FIXBOOT E:
```

FIXMBR

Creates a new MBR on a hard drive. The MBR is the first sector on a hard drive. A small program on the MBR contains information about the partitions, indicating which one is bootable in case there is more than one.

Use

Type "FIXMBR". This will create a new MBR on the existing boot disk drive. To select another drive, enter the device name after "FIXMBR". Run the MAP command to find the device name. For example, to replace the MBR on the first drive on the system, you can type:

```
FIXMBR \Device\HardDisk\0
```

Use FIXMBR *with caution. Never run* FIXMBR *unless you are having trouble accessing the drive or booting the computer, and you cannot determine another reason. In certain cases, you can damage your partition. It is recommended not to use* FIXMBR *unless directed to do so by Microsoft support personnel or unless you are well versed in its use.*

FORMAT

Use

Type "FORMAT" followed by the drive letter, fs:, the desired filesystem, and any desired switch. This version of FORMAT does not work with floppy disks, only hard drives.

Switches and Parameters

/q: Normally, FORMAT scans the disk for bad sectors. The /q switch causes FORMAT to skip this step, so it should be used only if the drive is known to be good and has been formatted before.

/fs: followed, without a space, by the name of the filesystem (NTFS, FAT, or FAT32): Specifies the filesystem. If you don't specify a filesystem, FORMAT uses the existing filesystem, if there is one.

LISTSVC

Lists the services and drivers available on the computer along with the start-up type and description for each. The output appears one page at a time as if the MORE command prompt command were used.

LOGON

Logs you onto a particular installation of Windows. Useful on dual- or multi-boot systems when each OS is compatible with Recovery Console (NT 4.0, 2000, XP, Windows Server 2003). You will be able to select from a list of all Windows installations the Recovery Console can find. You will be prompted for the administrator password. If you get the password wrong three times, the Recovery Console will quit, and the computer will automatically reboot.

MAP

Displays the assignment of drive letters to physical partitions. The output is useful if you want to run DISKPART, FIXBOOT, or FIXMBR.

Use

Type "MAP", followed by the arc switch, if desired.

Switch

> **arc:** Causes the output to use the ARC format rather than the device name format. The arc switch is preceded only by a space, not by a slash or any other punctuation mark, as shown:

```
MAP arc
```

The ARC *name looks like the following:* `multi(0)disk(0)rdisk(0)partition(1)`.

The device name for the same drive and partition is \Device\HardDisk0\ Partition1. For more information on device names and the ARC naming convention, search the Web.

MD OR MKDIR

Wildcard characters will not work.

MORE

Displays the text in a text file.

Use

Type "MORE" followed by the path to the text file you want to read. Use quotation marks or asterisks around filenames with spaces. MORE displays one page at a time and prompts for input on how to view the next part of the text file.

> *In the Recovery Console,* MORE *is identical to the* TYPE *command.*

REN OR RENAME

Renames a single file. Wildcards will not work.

RD OR RMDIR

RD will not delete a folder unless it is empty.

SYSTEMROOT

Makes the system root folder (almost always \Windows or \Winnt) the current folder.

OPERATING SYSTEM FUNDAMENTALS TEST TIPS

The following OS fundamentals test tips will assist you with your final test preparation. Although some of these tips are not explained in detail in this chapter, they are important facts that may prove valuable to you in the exam room. Remember them.

- A corrupt or very old version of the file COMMAND.COM can lead to the error message bad or missing command.com. To correct this issue, you can boot to an emergency repair disk and use SYS.COM to correct this error.
- In Windows 95, a duplicate copy of COMMAND.COM can be found in C:\WINDOWS.
- The OS Windows 3.X used a utility called File Manager to manage folders and files. Early versions of Windows 9.X used this File Manager instead of Explorer, which is found in newer versions of Windows. It should be noted that File Manager does not support long filename structures. File Manager will truncate long filenames to 8.3 names.
- If you are installing a program and it cannot make changes to files such as AUTOEXEC.BAT or CONFIG.SYS, you should verify that their attributes are not set to read only. From a DOS prompt, type "ATTRIB -R" and the filename. Or right-click the file, select Properties, and uncheck the Read-only box in Windows Explorer.
- To hide a file while at a DOS command prompt, enter "ATTRIB +H (FILE-NAME)".
- If you receive error messages that states there is not enough disk space while trying to install old DOS legacy programs (FAT16) on newer OSs (FAT32), it is likely that the old DOS programs do not recognize the FAT32 filesystem. The maximum size of a FAT16 logical drive is 2 GB. FAT32 has a 2 TB limit.
- In most Windows OSs, you can type "SYSEDIT" or "REGEDIT" in at the Start > Run command line to troubleshoot SYSTEM.INI, WIN.INI, AUTOEXEC.BAT, CONFIG.SYS, or Windows registry-related issues.

- If you ever receive the message `sector 0 bad, disk not usable` while formatting a hard drive, it is very likely that you have a bad or defective hard drive.
- The tool `EDIT.COM` can easily be used to edit text files from a command prompt.
- To easily display the current running OS in Windows, right-click on the My Computer icon, and select Properties.
- `FDISK/MBR` will repair a MBR.
- The proper syntax for formatting a floppy disk from a command prompt is `FORMAT A:`.
- If you want to edit MSDOS.SYS from a command prompt, you must first enter "ATTRIB –S –H -R MSDOS.SYS".
- With protected mode memory, the OS manages memory resources and controls application access to memory.
- Disk Defragmenter is used to improve hard disk access time, which results in faster data transfers.
- The command-line utility `SCANREG` can be used to restore a backed up copy of a registry if the registry has become damaged or corrupt.
- If your system's BIOS is set to boot to a floppy and you boot with an unformatted floppy disk inserted in your floppy drive, you will receive the error message `No OS found`.
- Using the `/?` switch after a particular DOS command will list the possible switches available for the DOS command as well as their functions.
- If you want to check your "C" drive for surface disk errors before Windows 9.X starts, you can enter "SCANDISK C:/SURFACE" from a command prompt. Also remember, `SCANDISK` fixes cross-linked files.
- To truly be considered PnP, an environment requires a PnP OS, BIOS, device drivers, and peripheral devices.

CHAPTER SUMMARY

This chapter has given you a solid foundation in OS basics, DOS, and command prompt functionality in Windows. It is meant to prepare you for the chapters that follow. In fact, this entire book has been preparing you for the study of Windows 9.x/Me, Windows NT 4.0, Windows 2000, and Windows XP OSs.

In this chapter, you should have gained an understanding of the underlying files and command-line utilities that were used to create and maintain the operation of early OSs. Although many DOS and Windows 3.x details were not covered in this chapter, the concepts needed to prepare you for the core OSs components of the test have been well defined.

REVIEW QUESTIONS

1. **The ability for an OS to control and delegate the processor's time to different tasks is called?**
   - ○ A.   Preemptive multitasking
   - ○ B.   Time slice
   - ○ C.   Cooperative multitasking
   - ○ D.   Multiprocess collaboration

   Correct Answer = A

   With preemptive multitasking, the OS hands out CPU time slices to applications or programs. The OS is in control of how much time the application can have. With cooperative multitasking, the application or task is in control of the CPU until it is finished with processing.

2. **Which entry is not found in the CONFIG.SYS?**
   - ○ A.   `Buffers=`
   - ○ B.   `Device=`
   - ○ C.   `Files=`
   - ○ D.   `C:\path`

   Correct Answer = D

   The C:\path entry is found in the AUTOEXEC.BAT file. All other entries listed can be located in the CONFIG.SYS file.

3. **The DIR and COPY commands are considered internal DOS commands. Where do internal DOS commands reside?**
   - ○ A.   C:\Windows\Command
   - ○ B.   C:\Winnt\System32\Drivers\ETC
   - ○ C.   C:\Windows\System\Command
   - ○ D.   COMMAND.COM

   Correct Answer = D

   Internal DOS commands are considered part of COMMAND.COM. External DOS commands are typically located in the C:\DOS directory although their location can be modified.

4. **What file should you change to set up your Windows 9.X OS to dual boot?**
   - ○ A. COMMAND.COM
   - ○ B. IO.SYS
   - ○ C. MSDOS.SYS
   - ○ D. BOOT.INI

   Correct Answer = C

   The file MSDOS.SYS in Windows 9.X can be modified for dual-booting purposes. The BOOT.INI file is used for similar purposes in Windows NT. COMMAND.COM is a utility program that contains internal DOS commands such as the DIR and COPY commands. IO.SYS interacts with the BIOS to determine the hardware environment.

5. **Your computer has Windows 9.X installed. You want to boot your computer to a DOS prompt. What are the three files necessary to do this? (Choose Three)**
   - ☐ A. IO.SYS
   - ☐ B. MSDOS.SYS
   - ☐ C. CONFIG.SYS
   - ☐ D. COMMAND.COM
   - ☐ E. AUTOEXEC.BAT

   Correct Answers = A, B, and D

   IO.SYS, MSDOS.SYS, and COMMAND.COM are all located on the primary active boot partition and are stored at the root of C:\. All three of these files are required to successfully boot a system into DOS. The files CONFIG.SYS and AUTOEXEC.BAT are not required.

6. **You have received a message on boot-up stating that a line in your CONFIG.SYS is incorrect. What DOS command-line tool can you use to correct this issue?**
   - ○ A. AUTOEXEC.BAT
   - ○ B. SYSEDIT
   - ○ C. EDIT.COM
   - ○ D. CONFIG.EDITOR

   Correct Answer = C

   You can use DOS utility EDIT.COM to view and make changes to the CONFIG.SYS and AUTOEXEC.BAT files. This can be very useful for troubleshooting if you encounter errors on boot up with settings in either of these files. SYSEDIT is a GUI text editor that can be used to edit these files from within an OS. CONFIG.EDITOR is invalid.

7. Which line can be found in the CONFIG.SYS file?

- ○ A.   `PATH=C:\WINDOWS`
- ○ B.   `PROMPT $P$G`
- ○ C.   `SET TEMP=C:\TEMP`
- ○ D.   `DEVICE=C:\WINDOWS\HIMEM.SYS`

Correct Answer = D

The `DEVICE=C:\WINDOWS\HIMEM.SYS` is used to load HIMEM.SYS from within the CONFIG.SYS file. All other choices are located in the AUTOEXEC.BAT file.

8. You have accidentally deleted COMMAND.COM while using Windows 95. Where can you get a backup copy of COMMAND.COM that will be compatible with your particular OS?

- ○ A.   C:\DOS
- ○ B.   C:\Windows
- ○ C.   C:\Winnt\System32
- ○ D.   Go to the COMMAND.COM Web site and download your version

Correct Answer = B

Windows 9.X stores a backup copy of COMMAND.COM in the C:\WINDOWS directory.

9. What file should you change to set up your Windows 2000 OS to dual boot?

- ○ A.   COMMAND.COM
- ○ B.   IO.SYS
- ○ C.   MSDOS.SYS
- ○ D.   BOOT.INI

Correct Answer = D

The BOOT.INI file is used in Windows NT, Windows 2000, and Windows XP to configure a system for dual booting. MSDOS.SYS is used for dual booting in Windows 9.X and Windows Me.

10. **DOS uses COMMAND.COM as its command-line interpreter. What does Windows 2000 use as a command-line interpreter?**

   ○ A. COMMAND.COM
   ○ B. A bilingual expert
   ○ C. CMD.EXE
   ○ D. The Windows 2000 HAL

   Correct Answer = C

   The command interpreter for Windows 2000, NT, and XP is CMD.EXE. The command interpreter for DOS, Windows 9.X, and Windows Me is COMMAND.COM.

11. **After a typical installation, what do you need to do to view an important OS file such as MSDOS.SYS?**

   ○ A. Modify the `BootGUI=0` to `BootGUI=1` entry under `[Options]` in the MSDOS.SYS file.
   ○ B. Show all files or Show Hidden files and folders.
   ○ C. Reinstall the operating system.
   ○ D. Reinstall a noncorrupt command interpreter.

   Correct Answer = B

   MSDOS.SYS is an important hidden system file by default. You should always remember to Show all files or Show Hidden files and folders under Folder Options before troubleshooting.

12. **Which of the following commands is used to clear the screen at a DOS prompt?**

   ○ A. `CMD/C`
   ○ B. `CLR`
   ○ C. `Clear`
   ○ D. `CLS`

   Correct Answer = D

   CLS is used to clear the screen at a DOS prompt.

13. **You are working at a command prompt and want to defrag a hard disk and want to know available switches for the DEFRAG command. How would you display the switches that are available with the DEFRAG command?**

○ A. `Defrag /Helpme`
○ B. `Defrag \?`
○ C. `Defrag /?`
○ D. `Defrag > help`
○ E. None of the above

Correct Answer = C

If you are at a command prompt and you want to view available switches for a command, entering /? after the command will display any available switches.

14. **You are working from a command prompt and want to create partitions on a hard a disk. Which utility can you use to partition the drive from the command prompt?**

○ A. `FDISK`
○ B. `FPART`
○ C. `SYS Dsk c:\`
○ D. `DISKPART`
○ E. None of the above

Correct Answer = A

Entering FDISK at the command prompt with start the partition utility required.

15. **You are attempting to find a hidden file on your boss's computer called MYRAISE.DOC. Which of the following commands could you use to reveal this file?**

○ A. `ATTRIB -s myraise.doc`
○ B. `ATTRIB +s myraise.doc`
○ C. `ATTRIB +h myraise.doc`
○ D. `ATTRIB -h myraise.doc`
○ E. None of the above

Correct Answer = D

The ATTRIB command can be used to change the attributes of a file or folder. -h can be used to remove the hidden file attribute from the file MYRAISE.DOC.

REFERENCES

www.pcguide.com/ref/hdd/file/fatLong-c.html. This PC Guide Web site describes LFNs in great detail.

11   Windows 9.x/Me

In This Chapter

- Overview of Windows 9.x
- Installation and Upgrading
- The Windows 9.x Start-Up Process
- The Windows 9.x Registry
- Utilities and Settings
- Printers
- Windows 9.x Networking
- Windows Me
- Windows Me Installation Process
- Windows Me Upgrade Procedures
- Windows Me Start-Up Process
- Windows Me Tools and Utilities
- Profiles
- Windows Me Networking and the Internet
- Diagnosing and Troubleshooting Test Tips

OVERVIEW OF WINDOWS 9.x

In this chapter, we will focus on the Windows 9.x family of operating systems (OSs). As stated in Chapter 10, by *Windows 9.x,* we generally mean Windows 95 and Windows 98. Windows 95 and Windows 98 are considered true 32-bit OSs that are backward compatible with Windows 3.x and DOS. Windows 95 had two major release versions: Windows 95A (OSR1) and Windows 95B (OSR2). Windows 98 also had two release versions: Windows 98 and Windows 98 Second Edition (SE).

Windows 95B (OSR2) and both versions of Windows 98 come packaged with the ability to provide hard drive partitions above the 2 GB barrier that was a limitation of Windows 95A (OSR1).

The Windows 9.x family as a whole has introduced many major improvements to the computing world, including the following:

- Plug and play (PnP) support
- Preemptive multitasking abilities
- Improved network capabilities and Internet sharing
- Better support for multimedia devices and applications
- Dynamic support for 32-bit applications and supporting devices
- Long filename (LFN) support (up to 255 characters)
- Support for Protected Mode versus Real Mode device drivers
- Installation and support wizards to assist with installation and OS administration
- The implementation of a Windows registry that is used to support environments and devices in place of initialization files

These are just a few of the important improvements that were introduced by the OS that changed the world. We will discuss these improvements as well as other OS characteristics specific to Windows 9.x throughout this chapter.

INSTALLATION AND UPGRADING

Manufacturers of OSs provide minimum and recommended hardware specifications that should be considered before installing or upgrading an OS.

The current A+ exams are not likely to focus on specific questions about the amount of memory or hard disk space required to install a particular OS. Instead, it will most likely focus on OS installation processes and the techniques used to troubleshoot or debug failed installations.

BEFORE YOU START

The following steps should be considered in preparation for a full Window 9.x installation or an upgrade from a previous version of DOS or Windows.

First, you should always check the manufacturer's recommended hardware requirements for a Windows OS installation. Do not count on study guides or books for this information. For some reason, all OSs seem to have their own special set of specifications.

Second, verify that you are using the correct CD-ROM for your choice of OS installation or upgrade. Windows 9.x is available in many versions, as stated in

Chapter 10. A full Windows 9.x installation can be performed on a blank hard drive without a previously installed OS, but an upgrade requires the presence of a previously installed Windows version. OEM OS releases, such as the Windows 95 OEM release, are designed for specific systems and do not work as a full installation on all systems.

The test may get tricky and ask you why a Windows 95 installation keeps failing for no apparent reason. Remember that using the nonbootable OEM Windows 95 release CD-ROM that is not intended for the system you are installing it on could cause this problem.

Next, consult the Microsoft Hardware Compatibility List (HCL) at *www. microsoft.com/whdc/hcl/search.mspx* to see if your hardware is supported by the Windows OS you want to install.

Finally, you should consider the type of file system that will be used to support the OS.

If you are going to do a full installation or an upgrade to Windows 95B or Windows 98, you should consider configuring your hard disk as FAT32 to take advantage of its many benefits. One of the benefits of FAT32 includes 4 KB cluster sizes that make better use of the hard disk's space. Smaller 4 KB cluster sizes increase the overall storage efficiency and file-access speed of the disk. FAT32 makes better use of system resources than FAT16, which in turn provides better use of storage. FAT32 also allows for the ability to support more than 65,535 files with fewer resources.

If you plan to install Windows 9.x, it is best to install Windows 98 SE. It has many advantages over its predecessors, Windows 95 and Windows 98. It can handle larger hard drives and support newer technologies, such as USB, FireWire, and Internet Connection Sharing (ICS).

If you need to maintain backward compatibility with older versions of DOS and Windows, you need to configure for dual-booting scenarios, or if you plan on installing the original version of Windows 95 that doesn't support FAT32, you should configure your system for FAT16. However, if you configure a partition using FAT16, you will not be able to take advantage of features such as encryption and disk quotas that are offered in newer OSs.

Windows 98 comes with a powerful FAT32 drive conversion utility program called Drive Converter, which has the ability to convert an already formatted FAT16 partition into a FAT32 or NTFS partition. The only caveat here is that it is said to be impossible to go back to FAT16 after the Drive Converter program has been run and the partition has been converted. (With a partitioning tool such as Power Quest Partition Magic 7.0, you can convert back to FAT16 if you like.) Keep in mind that the correct order of preparing a hard disk before a Windows 9.x installation is to partition with FDISK, format the drive, and finally reboot the system.

INSTALLATION OR UPGRADE PROCESS

The processes for installing Windows 9.x to a blank hard drive or upgrading from an earlier version of Windows 9.x are almost the same. The only exceptions are in the early stages of the installation or upgrade processes. Installing a full version of Windows 9.x requires you to first format and partition the drive. After you have prepared the hard drive for a new OS, all you have to do is run the SETUP.EXE program from the Windows 9.x installation CD-ROM. You may need a boot disk that contains your particular CD-ROM drivers to support the CD-ROM device. For the test, remember that the minimum files required on a boot disk to support a CD-ROM device are AUTOEXEC.BAT, COMMAND.COM, and MSCDEX.EXE. It is also recommended that you have the following files on a high-density 1.44 MB boot disk for troubleshooting and diagnostic purposes:

- IO.SYS
- MSDOS.SYS
- SYS.COM
- EDIT.COM
- ATTRIB.EXE
- REGEDIT.EXE
- CHKDSK.EXE
- SCANDISK.EXE
- UNINSTAL.EXE
- FDISK.EXE
- FORMAT.EXE
- EDB.SYS

If you are performing an upgrade of Windows, simply place the Windows 9.x upgrade CD-ROM into the CD-ROM drive under the current version of Windows. You will be presented with the Windows 9.x upgrade prompt. Here is where it all comes together. At this point, the install or upgrade processes are basically identical. Both methods check the system for the minimum set of requirements necessary for the installation or upgrade to continue. After a restart, you are presented with the Windows Setup Wizard Setup Options menu, which gives you the option of choosing a Typical, Portable, Compact, or Custom setup type. After you choose the setup type you want, you are prompted with the Windows Product Key screen. Enter the Product Key, excluding any dashes, and click the next radio button.

Next, you are prompted to select a directory in which Windows is to be installed. By default, the C:\WINDOWS directory is selected for you. If you are upgrading from Windows 95 to Windows 98, you must install Windows 98 to the same directory that contained your previous Windows 95 files; otherwise, Windows 98 installs itself without consideration of the existing settings and applications, leaving them useless. Now you are asked if you want to create a start-up disk. This step can be bypassed; a start-up disk can be created from the Add/Remove Software option in the Control Panel after the installation is complete.

From there, you go on to network options, starting with the option to configure the NIC. In practice, it is probably better to bypass this option and configure the NIC and network settings after the Windows 98 upgrade has been completed. At this point, a huge copying phase takes place, followed by the hardware detection phase. The Windows 98, PnP features make this phase quite painless. After all that, the point you will need to remember for the exam is that the upgrade from Windows 95 to Windows 98 is considered the easiest of all upgrades.

INSTALLATION LOG FILES

Windows 9.x keeps track of problems that may arise with the setup process in a group of log files stored in the root directory. These log files keep track of devices detected during the installation process, as well as successes and failures associated with the various stages of the installation process. The main installation log files are the following:

SETUPLOG.TXT: A log of the entire setup process, it tracks all successes and failures that occur during installation. It is a good tool for finding the last process that may have failed and caused the system to halt.

DETLOG.TXT: This log file keeps a record of all hardware detected. It is a viewable version of DETCRASH.LOG.

DETCRASH.LOG: This is an unreadable log file that is created if setup fails during the hardware-detection phase. If the entire setup process completes without error, this file is removed from the system.

BOOTLOG.TXT: This logs all device drivers and programs during the installation.

NETLOG.TXT: This log file is used to track the network portion of setup.

THE WINDOWS 9.x START-UP PROCESS

The overall system starting order for a typical system is covered in Chapter 10. As you may recall, the exam may look for POST, BIOS, boot sector, and GUI as the overall system starting order. To reveal what happens behind the scenes when a computer system is turned on and booted into Windows 9.x, we will break down the start order into the POST/BIOS, Real Mode load, Protected Mode load, and GUI load.

POST/BIOS

When the system is first powered up, the POST is loaded by the ROM BIOS. Next, the MBR is read by the Bootstrap loader, which determines the OS that is loaded into the system's memory.

REAL MODE LOAD

After the system BIOS has run, and the OS is loaded into memory, 16-bit Real Mode drivers are loaded. This is how Windows 9.x maintains backward compatibility with DOS and Windows 3.x. In this sequence of the start-up process, IO.SYS, MSDOS.SYS, CONFIG.SYS, COMMAND.COM, and AUTOEXEC.BAT are processed.

As mentioned in Chapter 10, Windows 9.x uses its 32-bit drivers in place of the AUTOEXEC.BAT and CONFIG.SYS files. These files are not needed by Windows 9.x; they are there simply to maintain backward compatibility.

PROTECTED MODE LOAD

In this phase of the Windows 9.x start-up process, WIN.COM is used to start up Windows 9.x. Next, VMM32.VXD, which contains an entire package of Windows 9.x 32-bit virtual device drivers, loads necessary drivers (VxDs) into memory.

The VMM that was used to load 16-bit and 32-bit device drivers for Windows 3.x is replaced in Windows 9.x with VMM32.VXD.

Finally, the SYSTEM.INI file is processed for any device drivers it may contain that need to be loaded.

GUI LOAD

In the final phase of the Windows 9.x start-up process, KERNEL32.DLL, KRNL386.EXE, GDI.EXE, GDI32.EXE, USER.EXE, and USER32.EXE are loaded, and the user is finally presented with the Windows interface screen known as Explorer.

STARTUP MENU AND OPTIONS

If the OS cannot boot into Windows 9.x successfully, the Windows 9.x Startup Menu will most likely appear. The Startup Menu interacts with MSDOS.SYS (which should have a minimum size of 1024 KB for a stable OS environment) and is used to isolate and troubleshoot problems related to system start-up. You can access the Startup Menu manually by pressing the F8 function key just before the Windows 9.x splash screen appears on your display. The Startup Menu offers eight configuration options for various diagnostic and configuration purposes:

Normal: This option is used to simply boot the system up normally. No special drivers are added or removed with this configuration.

Logged (BOOTLOG.TXT): This option is similar to the Normal option. The only exception is that the steps of the start-up process are written to the file BOOTLOG.TXT.

Safe Mode (Press F5): This is considered the most useful mode for trouble-shooting purposes. Safe Mode loads a generic VGA driver for basic video, a key-board driver, and HIMEM.SYS (which manages extended memory). Safe Mode does not load the configuration files AUTOEXEC.BAT and CONFIG.SYS. It does not load NIC, modem, and other specialized drivers. Safe Mode is an excellent tool for troubleshooting drivers that do not work properly with the OS. For example, if after installing a new advanced video driver, you can no longer view the screen, simply reboot the computer and enter Safe Mode. Safe Mode loads a basic set of drivers that allow you to remove the new video driver from the system and reboot normally.

You can also enter Safe Mode directly by pressing the F5 function key before the Windows 9.x splash screen is displayed.

Safe Mode with Network Support (Press F6): This option also allows you to enter Safe Mode and loads support for networking devices and connections. By pressing the F6 function key before the Windows 9.x splash screen is displayed, you can directly enter Safe Mode with network support.

Step-by-step configuration (Press Shift-F8): When this option is used, you are prompted as to which configuration files and file lines will be executed on start-up. For example, if you press the Shift-F8 keys before the Windows 9.x splash screen is displayed, you will be asked if you want to process such files as the CONFIG.SYS and AUTOEXE.BAT. If you enter "Y" for yes, you will be asked if you want to process each line of each of these files. This is an excellent way to troubleshoot individual devices and settings that are loaded by each file, one line at a time.

Command prompt only (Press Shift-F5): This option is used to start up the system in MS-DOS. It is often used for troubleshooting purposes if Safe Mode doesn't work.

Safe Mode command prompt only: This option is used to start DOS without network support. The major configuration files are bypassed, and you are directed to a command prompt.

Previous version of DOS (Press F4): This option is available if a previous version of DOS is installed on your system. Pressing the F4 function key before the Windows splash screen appears will get you there.

THE WINDOWS 9.X REGISTRY

The Windows 9.x registry, as well as the registries implemented in Windows NT and Windows 2000, is a hierarchical databases made up of special registry keys that hold most of the OS's software, hardware, and application settings. The Windows 9.x registry was developed with the intention of replacing the dependency on the WIN.INI, SYSTEM.INI, AUTOEXEC.BAT, and CONFIG.SYS files for loading system initialization, device, and user environment settings.

The Windows registry is a sort of common ground that is used to link applications, programs, objects, and settings. Windows 3.x used the Object Linking and Embedding (OLE) functionality of a binary file called REG.DAT. *Object linking* is a method whereby a program or application can use an object or part of a program that is created by another program.

The Windows 9.x registry is made up of two important files called USER.DAT and SYSTEM.DAT. These files are stored as hidden, read-only system files in the C:\WINDOWS directory. The USER.DAT file stores user-related registry settings, such as user preferences and desktop settings. The SYSTEM.DAT file is used to store device settings. Every time Windows 9.x is started, the system looks for USER.DAT and SYSTEM.DAT to create and load the OS's environment and related device settings. If these two files are not found, the system automatically looks for the files USER.DA0 and SYSTEM.DA0, which are backup copies of the two main registry files maintained by the OS.

It is very important to note that system files are purposefully hidden by default as a security precaution.

NOTE

VIEWING AND MODIFYING THE REGISTRY

Warning! Great care should be taken when entering or making changes to the Windows 9.x registry—or any registry, for that matter. Making improper changes to the binary values stored in the registry or installing certain software that can cause registry corruption may leave you with a system that is unstable at best. If your users or customers observe strange happenings, such as a missing taskbar, blank icons, or programs that won't load, they are most likely experiencing a corrupt registry or virus activity. You should always manually back up the registry before making any changes to it. Windows 98 comes with an excellent tool called Registry Checker that works well for this purpose. If your registry becomes corrupted, you can use the SCANREG utility from a DOS prompt to restore a backup copy of the registry. The command used for restoring a registry from a DOS prompt is SCANREG/RESTORE.

Using the Windows 9.x Device Manager and Control Panel options to change settings and devices is considered the safest way for most users to make edits to the registry. It is more common for advanced users to edit the registry in Windows 9.x with the REGEDIT.EXE program stored in C:\WINDOWS in Windows 9.x by default. To enter the Windows 95 registry, simply click Start > Run, and then type in "REGEDIT" on the Open command line. The window shown in Figure 11.1 will appear.

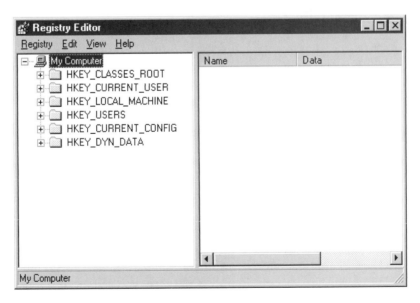

FIGURE 11.1   The Windows 9.x registry.

The six major registry keys are displayed in Figure 11.1. Each of these keys and their subkeys are responsible for holding system and device settings and information. The current A+ exams will expect you to be familiar with the techniques used to edit, back up, and restore the Windows 9.x registry. For the exam's purposes, you should know the functionality associated with HKEY_LOCAL_MACHINE.

The functions of each of the six major registry HKEYs are as follows:

HKEY_CLASSES_ROOT: Stores file extensions and OLE information.

HKEY_USERS: Stores all user preferences for each separate user with a profile located on the local system.

HKEY_CURRENT_USER: Stores all information as it pertains to the specific user who is currently logged into the local system.

HKEY_LOCAL_MACHINE: Stores all the software, hardware, and OS settings of all configurations used on the system.

HKEY_CURRENT_CONFIG: Stores the current hardware profile for peripheral devices, such as monitors and printers.

HKEY_DYN_DATA: Stores all current performance data, such as the results of running System Monitor.

UTILITIES AND SETTINGS

Windows 9.x has many useful utilities for managing and maintaining the integrity of the OS. This section is dedicated to the many utilities, configuration options, and settings that are available in Windows 9.x. Pay close attention to the details listed in this section—it is very likely that they will appear on the exam.

SYSTEM MONITOR AND SYSTEM RESOURCE METER

System Monitor is an excellent troubleshooting tool used to monitor the system's performance in a real-time graphics snapshot (see Figure 11.2). It can be used to view the system's CPU, virtual memory, and network client/server resources used (only on the local system), just to name a few. If System Monitor is not installed on your system, you can install it by navigating to Start > Settings > Control Panel > Add/Remove Programs > Windows Setup > System Tools > System Monitor. Select the OK button, and you will be prompted to insert the Windows installation CD-ROM. After System Monitor is installed, you can locate and run it from Start > Programs > Accessories > System Tools. Figure 11.2 displays a snapshot of System Monitor.

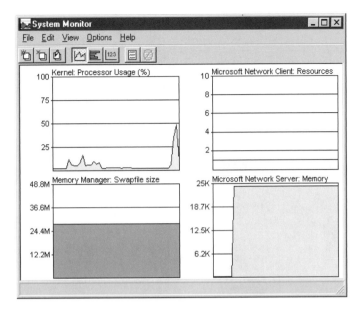

FIGURE 11.2   System Monitor.

Remember that System Monitor is not used to monitor the network use of other client and server computers.

Many other useful tools, including the Windows 9.x Resource Meter, which is used to monitor system, user, and GDI heap resources, are installed through the Add/Remove Program applet in the Control Panel.

TASK MANAGER

The Task Manager is by far one of the most useful tools available in most Microsoft OSs. Pressing Ctrl-Alt-Delete displays the Task Manager and programs that are currently running on the OS. If a process or program is stalled or not responding, you can select the program and click the End Task radio button to remove it. Pressing Ctrl-Alt-Delete twice restarts the system. Figure 11.3 displays some of the many system processes in the Task Manager of Windows 2000.

DR. WATSON

Dr. Watson™ is a program error debugger tool used in Windows 9.x/NT/2000 to detect and log critical error information pertaining to system halts. Dr. Watson also attempts to point you in the right direction by offering possible tips for problem

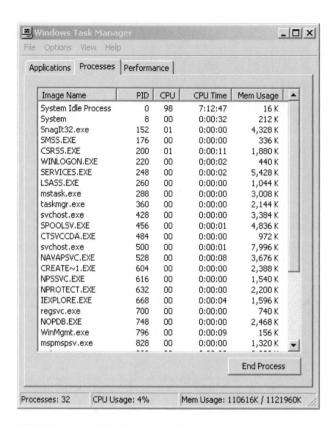

FIGURE 11.3 Windows Task Manager.

and error resolution. The question at hand does not seem to be "Dr. Watson, I presume?" Instead, the question seems to be, "Dr. Watson, where are you storing your log files?" The Dr. Watson tool stores its information in log files located in various places. In Windows 9.x, the Dr. Watson log file is called WATSONXXX.WLG and is stored in C:\WINDOWS\DRWATSON. In Windows NT, Dr. Watson creates two log files named DRWTSN32.LOG and USER.DMP that are stored in C:\WINNT. When Dr. Watson intercepts a program fault in Windows 2000, the file DRWTSN32.LOG is produced and is stored in the C:\DOCUMENTS AND SETTINGS\ALL USERS\DOCUMENTS\DRWATSON. Dr. Watson offers a standard view and an advanced view for diagnostic reporting purposes.

DEVICE MANAGER

The Device Manager is probably the most useful utility ever created for viewing, troubleshooting, and installing devices that are attached to a computer system. As mentioned earlier in this book, the Device Manager can be used to view or change system resources, such as IRQs, I/Os, and DMAs. The Device Manager is available in Windows 9.x and Windows 2000. It is not available in Windows NT.

There are two easy ways to navigate to the Device Manager utility in Windows 9.x. A quick way to access it is to right-click the Desktop icon My Computer, and select Properties > Device Manager. You can also access Device Manager by clicking Start > Settings > Control Panel, double-clicking the System icon, and choosing the Device Manager tab. The Device Manager opens, and you see a display similar to that shown in Figure 11.4.

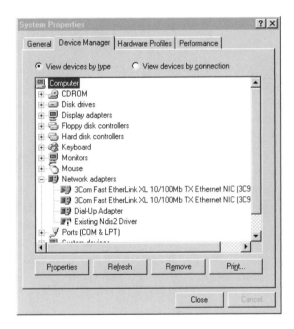

FIGURE 11.4   Windows 9.x Device Manager.

The Properties button depicted in Figure 11.4 allows you to view more information about the device that you select. If you click Computer and select Properties, you can view information regarding the IRQs, DMAs, I/Os, and memory of your particular system. The Refresh button forces the system to refresh the device through a process called enumeration. This means the system will simply start the PnP process for the device. The Remove button forces the device to be deleted from the OS's registry. The Print button prints out a report based on the devices listed in Device Manager. You can expand and view more information for a particular device by clicking on the plus (+) sign that is located to the right of it.

The Device Manager places specific symbols on its list of devices to notify you if a particular device is having a problem or has been disabled. The most common Device Manager symbols and their meanings are as follows:

- A black exclamation point (!) in a yellow circle represents a device in a problem state. The device in question may still be operational; the error may be related to the system's ability to detect the device, or it may be a device driver issue.
- A red "X" means that the device in question has been disabled by the system. A resource conflict or a damaged device usually causes this error.
- A blue "I" on a white background is used to show that a device's system resources have been manually configured. It is the least common symbol of the three and is used for informational purposes only.

What do you do if you are having trouble with devices in the Device Manager? Here are two important tips:

- It is important to understand that the Device Manager may not always be able to list a device's properties. If you have a device that seems to be running properly, but you cannot list its properties in the Device Manager, you are most likely using a CONFIG.SYS file to load older Real Mode drivers for the device. This often occurs when running older CD-ROM devices with Windows 9.x.
- If a device is displaying a black exclamation point (!) on a yellow circle, you should check the properties of the device and identify any resource conflicts. You may have to reassign an IRQ for the device in question before the system can use it. You can also troubleshoot this error by starting the Hardware Conflict Troubleshooter that is located in Windows Help. To practice using the Windows 98 troubleshooters, select Start > Help > Troubleshooting.

NOTE

The Device Manager should always be your first-choice utility to view and modify device resources.

The Windows 95 installation CD-ROM contains several useful hardware diagnostic tools, such as MSD.EXE and HWDIAG.EXE. MSD.EXE is based on the old DOS diagnostic reporting tool. HWDIAG.EXE is a more robust diagnostic tool that will provide detailed information about hardware devices. Neither of these tools loads by default; your best bet is to use the Device Manager.

WINDOWS UPDATE

All current versions of Windows OSs include the Windows update feature known as Windows Update Manager. This utility is used to keep your OS up to date with current patches, fixes, security updates, service releases, and other information offered by Microsoft. Simply select Start > Windows Update. You will be directed to *http://windowsupdate.microsoft.com/*. Follow the instructions on this site to bring your OS up to date.

Here are some important notes regarding Windows Update:

- It is recommended that you view the Web pages on the Windows Update site at an 800 × 600 or higher screen resolution.
- When you enter the Microsoft Windows update site, ActiveX controls are downloaded to your system. These controls are used to check your system for specific updates that your system may require. After checking your system, Windows update provides you with a list of updates, software, and drivers that are suggested to keep your system up to date.
- If you reinstall Windows or upgrade you system, it is recommended that you reinstall any components you had previously installed using Windows Update.

DISPLAY SETTINGS

When you experience display-related problems, start by navigating to the Windows 9.x Display Properties Window. Select Start > Settings > Control Panel, and double-click on the Display icon. The Display Properties Settings Window should appear by default (see Figure 11.5). You can also get to this window by right-clicking the Windows desktop, selecting Properties, and clicking the Settings tab.

Figure 11.5 shows the Display Properties Settings window for the second time in this book—and for good reason. The current as well as past A+ OS exams focus on your ability to resolve display-related issues with this graphic. For example, If you are running a 640 x 480-pixel display, as shown in Figure 11.5, and you are unable to view entire Web pages through your Internet browser, or you want to fit more icons on your desktop, simply use the mouse to move the Screen area bar to 800 x 600 pixels or more. If your video card supports a higher resolution, you will be able to fit more into the viewable screen area with this method. If you select the Advanced > Performance button, you will have the option of changing the Graphics Hardware acceleration settings.

The exam may try to confuse you here. Another way to navigate to the Graphics Hardware acceleration settings is Control Panel > System > Performance > Graphics.

Changing these settings can be useful if you are having trouble with how fast your system is handling graphics. If you select Advanced > Adapter, the system's video Adapter/Driver information will look like that shown in Figure 11.6. If you

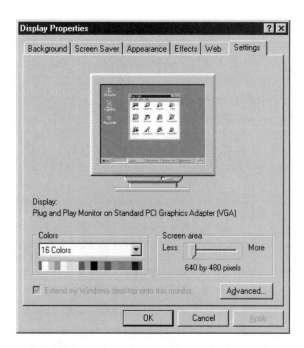

FIGURE 11.5 Windows 9.X Display Properties Settings Window.

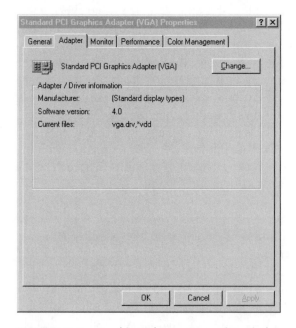

FIGURE 11.6 Graphics Adapter Properties window.

select the Change radio button on this screen, the Update Device Driver Wizard window will appear and lead you through the process of updating the video adapter driver. Remember, there are usually several ways to achieve a single goal in a Windows OS. You can update your video adapter driver, as well as many other device drivers, through Device Manager.

VIRTUAL MEMORY SETTINGS

In Chapter 10, we discussed virtual memory and swap files. You should recall that Windows 9.x has the ability to use a portion of free hard disk space as a temporary storage area or memory buffer area for programs that need more memory than is available in RAM. This temporary hard disk memory area is called virtual memory or swap file. The actual name for this memory in Windows 9.x is called WIN386.SWP.

To view or change your virtual memory settings in Windows 9.x, select Start > Settings > Control Panel > System > Performance > Virtual Memory. You will be presented with a window similar to that shown in Figure 11.7. As stated in the Virtual Memory window, you should be very cautious when changing your system's virtual memory settings. If you are not sure of what these settings should be, you should obviously let Windows manage your settings for you. If Windows is managing your virtual memory settings for you, it allocates around 12 MB above the amount of physical RAM installed in your system. For example, if you have 64 MB of RAM installed in your system, Windows will create and manage a swap file of around 76 MB of hard drive space.

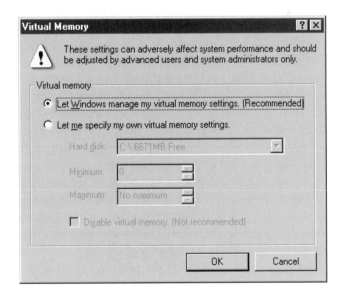

FIGURE 11.7   Windows 9.X Virtual Memory settings.

THE RECYCLE BIN

The Windows 9.x Recycle Bin is a desktop icon that represents a directory in which files are stored on a temporary basis. When you delete a file from a computer system's hard drive, it is moved to the Recycle Bin. To restore a file that has been deleted to its original location on the hard drive, right-click on the file in the Recycle Bin and select Restore, or select File > Restore. If you want to remove a file from the Recycle Bin to free up hard drive space, select File > Empty Recycle Bin. You can also delete entries in the Recycle Bin by selecting File > Delete. When you delete a file from the Recycle Bin, its associated entry in the hard drive's FAT is removed. It is still possible to recover the deleted file with many available third-party utility programs.

DISK CLEANUP UTILITIES AND MORE

Your hard drive can get bogged down after a while with unnecessary files. Applications and programs can leave temporary files scattered on your hard drive, temporary Internet files and cookies are left behind when you surf the Internet, and all those downloaded shareware programs that you haven't used in ages can take up precious hard drive space.

Windows 98 has an excellent tool known as Disk Cleanup. This built-in utility allows you to get rid of those unnecessary files and free up space. To access the Disk Cleanup in Windows 98, click Start > Programs > Accessories > System Tools > Disk Cleanup. A window appears that asks you to select the drive you want to clean up. The default is (C:). Select the OK button, and the window shown in Figure 11.8 will be displayed. You can select the options you want to have removed from your drive by inserting a check mark next to the appropriate selections. Always review your downloaded program files as well as files located in the Recycle Bin to verify that you no longer have a use for them before removing them. You can do this by selecting the View Files radio button on the Disk Cleanup window.

If you select the More Options tab in the Disk Cleanup window, you will have the options of removing optional Windows components and other programs that you do not often use. If you choose to remove Windows components from within this window, you will automatically be directed to the Add/Remove Programs Properties/Windows Setup Window shown in Figure 11.9. This window lets you add or remove a Windows component. Notice the Install/Uninstall tab. The Install/Uninstall window lets you install applications and programs from a floppy or CD-ROM, or uninstall registered software that you do not use. The Add/Remove Programs Properties window can also be accessed by clicking Start > Settings > Control Panel > Add/Remove Programs.

You should also take note of the Startup Disk tab in Figure 11.9. With the Startup Disk window, you can create a Windows 9.x bootable troubleshooting floppy disk that you can use later for diagnostic purposes.

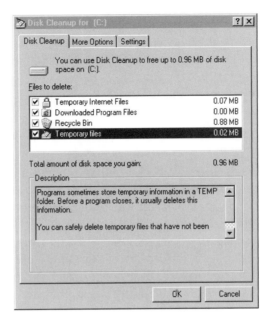

FIGURE 11.8   The Disk Cleanup window.

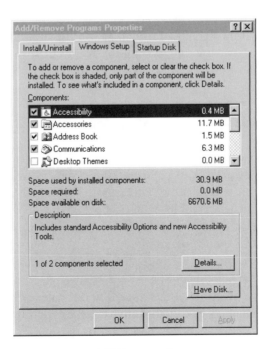

FIGURE 11.9   Add/Remove Programs
Properties window.

Windows 9.x allows you to schedule routine maintenance jobs easily through the use of the Maintenance Wizard. This utility is a handy tool that can be used to automatically run utilities such as Defrag, ScanDisk, or Disk Cleanup at times that are convenient for the computer user. In Windows 9.x, the Maintenance Wizard utility can be run by selecting Start > Programs > Accessories > System Tools > Maintenance Wizard.

BACKUP UTILITY

Windows OSs come with a Backup utility program that is used to back up information to a tape storage device for future restoration. It is of utmost importance that you back up your critical information in the event of an OS failure or accidental deletion of files.

A good backup program consists of a backup schedule that can be created using the Backup utility or a third-party backup utility program. In Windows 9.x, the Backup utility can be accessed by selecting Start > Programs > Accessories > System Tools > Backup. If the Backup utility is not installed, you can install it through the Add/Remove programs applet located in the Control Panel.

There are several backup types and strategies that you can implement. These backup types have already been discussed in this book. However, it never hurts to be overly familiar with them. You will see these on the exams!

The backup type and strategy that you use depends on the amount of storage capacity you have, the time it takes to back up files, and the time it takes to restore files. The following types of backups can be used to build your own personalized backup strategy.

- *Copy* backs up only selected files. The Copy backup turns the Backup archive bit off or resets it.
- *Full backup* backs up everything on your hard drive. If you have to restore an entire system, it is the best backup to have. During this backup, the backup archive bit is turned off. This simply means that every file will be backed up again whether or not its contents have changed. The disadvantages of this type of backup are that it takes longer, to run and it is often redundant because most system files do not change.
- *Incremental backup* backs up all the files that have changed or been created since the last backup job and have their archive bits set to on. This backup type uses less tape storage space and spreads the storage of files across several tapes. With an incremental backup, files are backed up much faster than with a differential backup, but they take much longer to restore. To do a proper incremental restore, you will need the last full backup tape and multiple incremental tapes.

■ *Differential backup* backs up all files that have been created or have changed since the last backup and does not reset the archive bit. The archive bit is left on. Differential backup takes much longer to do but is much faster to restore. To do a proper restore, you will need the last full backup tape and the last differential backup tape.

A Zip drive is a popular information storage device. The average Zip drive can hold about 100 MB of data, which can be very useful for the daily storage and backup of important files. Users of Windows can use a third-party utility, such as WinZip™, to store files in compressed form and then back them up. Windows stores compressed files in .ZIP format.

PRINTERS

The current A+ exams are likely to make sure that you are familiar with file and printer sharing, as well as methods used to create and rename printer shares and change printer properties.

In Windows 9.x, if you want to add a printer, rename a printer, share a printer, connect to or disconnect an already shared network printer, or change a currently installed printer's properties, you can select Start > Settings > Printers, or My Computer > Printers, or Control Panel > Printers. After you have navigated to the printer's applet, you can right-click an already installed printer and rename it, change its shared name, cancel current print jobs, or select Properties to change advanced features and settings for a printer. If you want to add a local or networked printer, simply select the Add Printer icon, select Next, and choose Local Printer or Network Printer. If you select Local Printer, you will be required to choose a printer manufacturer and printer, or choose the Have Disk option and insert your local printer's driver disk or CD-ROM. If you select Network Printer, you will need to specify the UNC name for the location of the shared network printer or browse to the printer on the network with the Browse radio button. Remember for the exam that the proper UNC syntax to browse to a shared network printer is \\Computername\Printername.

A shared printer can use spooling techniques. When spooling is implemented, print jobs are stored on a networked computer system's hard drive. The print jobs are sent to a printer when it is available to print. If you want to print directly to a printer without print jobs being spooled, you can change a printer's spool settings to Print directly to the printer. This can be accomplished by right-clicking a currently installed printer, selecting Properties > Advanced, and choosing the Print directly to the printer option.

So that others can access your locally installed printers and files, you must enable File and Print Sharing on your local system in the Network applet in the Control

Panel. The same is true if others in a Windows 9.x workgroup or network want to share their printers and files. Besides printers and files, you can also share CD-ROM devices and modems in Windows 9.x.

WINDOWS 9.X NETWORKING

Windows 9.x clients can be part of a workgroup or a domain. A workgroup is typically implemented when a network consists of 10 or fewer computers. A workgroup, otherwise known as a peer-to-peer network, uses share-level security (password-protected shares) and does not require the use of high-end server computers. Three components that must be present and properly configured for a computer to operate successfully in a peer-to-peer network are a NIC, a protocol, and the ability to share resources. A *domain* is implemented when the number of computers exceeds 10. A domain uses high-end server computers that hand out or serve resources to users who are authenticated through the use of user-level security.

Computers must have a common language or protocol to communicate with one another over a network. Windows 9.x provides built-in support for several commonly used protocols. These protocols and their descriptions follow:

■ TCP/IP is the most widely used protocol on the planet. Every computer using the Internet has a unique TCP/IP numeric address. This protocol can be used in a Windows 9.x network to share information. If you are currently connected to a network, you can view your own TCP/IP address information in Windows 9.x by selecting Start > Run, entering "WINIPCFG" on the Open line, and clicking OK. Your computer's IP configuration will appear, including the NICs MAC address, IP address, Subnet Mask, and Default Gateway.

To display your IP address information in Windows NT, enter "IPCONFIG" in place of "WINIPCFG".

■ IPX/SPX is a Novell protocol that allows Windows clients to communicate with resources on a Novell network. IPX/SPX and its Windows counterpart, NWLink, can be used to share information in a Windows 9.x network.
■ Don't be fooled on the exam—NetBIOS is not used to share printers and files on a network. It is actually an API program that allows computers within a LAN to communicate.
■ NetBEUI is a small, fast, efficient transport protocol that is well suited for small networks. NetBEUI can be used to share information in a Windows 9.x network.

Connecting a Windows 9.x system to a network is a fairly basic task. The first thing to do is navigate to the Network applet located in Control Panel or right-click the Network Neighborhood icon on the desktop and select Properties. A network configuration window will appear, similar to that shown in Figure 11.10.

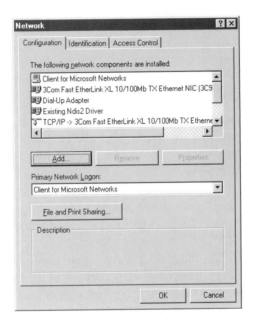

FIGURE 11.10   Network configuration window for Windows 9.X.

The second step is to install the Client for Microsoft Networks. You do this by clicking on the Add radio button and selecting Client from the type of network components you want to install. Click the Add button again, and select Microsoft and Client for Microsoft Networks from the list of manufacturers and network clients. After the client for Microsoft Networks is installed, highlight it in the network components configuration window, and click Properties. The Client for Microsoft Networks Properties General tab appears, from which you can choose to log on to a Windows NT domain.

Next, you must install any special protocols necessary to communicate and share information with other computers on the network. Remember, if you want to communicate with Novell systems, install IPX/SPX. TCP/IP and NetBEUI are installed by default if you chose to install networking during the Windows Install and Setup routine. These two protocols can be used to communicate with other Windows systems on a network. If you did not install networking when you installed the OS, select the Add button in the Network Configuration window. Highlight Protocol and click the Add button. Select a manufacturer and protocol, and then click OK.

Finally, if you want to share your resources with others, you will need to install the file and print sharing service, and make sure you give access to your resources by selecting the File and Print Sharing button in the Network configuration window.

WINDOWS ME

Windows Me you ask? Yes. You can learn a lot from this OS that is still among business workstations and home user environments. There are many utilities and descriptions in this section that will definitely be on the exams. Windows Millennium (Me) was originally introduced in the summer of 1999 and was released to the general public in September of 2000 as a follow up to the very successful Windows 98 SE.

Windows Me is based on the Windows 9.x kernel, with an updated frontend that makes it look more like Windows 2000. Although Windows Me may look a little different than Windows 98 SE, it is basically the same.

Windows Me was not a major release, and was mostly viewed as an incremental update to the Windows 9.x family. Upon installing Windows, the first thing you will notice is that there is no sign that AUTOEXEC.BAT or CONFIG.SYS files attempt to load; this was done to reduce start-up time. Another big difference that you may notice is the absence of DOS; though rest assured, it's still there. Microsoft decided to remove access to (Real Mode) DOS "to prevent customers [from] having trouble with the DOS features and to make the computer boot up and shutdown more quickly." True, you can no longer reboot into DOS (from the Start menu) or use F8 in the boot sequence to go directly to a DOS prompt, but it is still easy enough to make a boot disk to accomplish this task. There is only one version of Windows Me (with two different installation types: Full and Upgrade). New features included in Windows Me are listed here:

Auto-Update: This is a feature added to Me that basically tries to determine when your modem isn't being used to download content from the Internet and uses that time to find (and notify you) if any updates are available for your system.

System Restore: Available in Windows for the first time, System Restore will make a "save point," collecting all of your current system and registry settings (including drivers for your hardware), which you can choose to return to, should a newly installed feature be causing you grief.

MS Driver Signing: Notifies you when a driver you are attempting to install is Microsoft certified by WHQL (Windows Hardware Quality Labs).

Home Networking Wizard: Also added for ease of setting up home networking features, such as PC-to-PC connectivity and Internet sharing. The Home Network wizard takes much of the grief out of setting up a home-based network and installs the appropriate drivers for your networked components.

System File Protection: Also included with Windows Me, this feature works to ensure that new programs being installed cannot overwrite critical system files with their own, possibly incompatible files.

Expanded Multimedia Content: A newer version of Windows Media Player (version 7.0) was included with Windows Me. It includes better support for MP3 and DVD playback. Also included for the first time in this version of Windows is Windows Movie Maker, a great tool for editing digital video.

Scanner and Camera Wizard: This wizard was included to streamline the process of adding such devices without having to use the interface software included with the device.

Enhanced USB and FireWire Support: The growing demand for expansion devices and their ever-changing connectivity types brought better support for USB devices and finally brought FireWire (or IE 13394) support to Windows 9.x. FireWire is a high-performance serial bus that can connect upwards of 60 devices in a daisy chain configuration. FireWire supports connection speeds of up to 400 Mbps.

Most of the enhancements that Windows Me offers over Windows 98 SE revolve around digital media content. It came with an updated Windows Media player (version 7.0), and DVD playback software, as well as Windows Movie Maker. Included with Windows Me, is the Scanner and Camera Wizard, which makes adding such devices much easier, and generally a walk-through procedure (as opposed to having to use the interface software included with the device). Other enhancements included updates to USB and FireWire support for better functionality.

WINDOWS ME INSTALLATION PROCESS

Manufacturers of OSs provide minimum and recommended hardware specifications that should be considered before installing or upgrading an OS.

The basic system requirements are listed here:

- Pentium 150 MHz processor or better
- 32 MB of RAM
- Minimum 320 MB of hard drive space (formatted as FAT32)
- CD/DVD-ROM drive

These are the very basic system requirements. Different hardware is required for some of Windows Me features (e.g., Movie Maker requires more memory).

BEFORE YOU START

As always, you should always check the manufacturer's recommended hardware requirements for OS installation. Next, make sure that you have the correct version of the Windows Me installation CD-ROM that fits your needs. There are two versions of Windows Me available: the full version and the upgrade version. The upgrade version requires a previous version of Windows 95/98/98 SE installed on your hard drive for installation. (At the very least, you must have the CD-ROM with one of those OSs on it to verify that you are doing an upgrade.) Both the upgrade and the full version can be installed on a hard drive on a separate partition from a nonupgradeable OS (such as Windows NT); however, only the full version can be used to install on a completely blank hard drive, should you not own a copy of Windows 95/98/98 SE (more on that later). Remember, OEM disks were designed for specific systems and do not work as a full installation on all systems (which can subsequently cause problems with trying to use nonbootable OEM CD-ROMs in the installation process).

WINDOWS ME UPGRADE PROCESS

The full installation and upgrade processes aren't all that dissimilar from other Windows 9.x installations (e.g., Windows 98).

If you are performing an upgrade from an older version of Windows, simply place the Windows Me upgrade CD-ROM into the CD-ROM drive while in the current version of Windows. You will be presented with the Windows Me installation prompt: "This CD-ROM contains a newer version of Windows than the one you are presently using. Would you like to upgrade your computer to this new version of Windows Millennium now?"

If you are using a version of Windows 3.x or have Auto Insert Notification turned off, you will not be prompted with this query box. You can browse to the setup.exe using the File Manager; or if you are using Windows 9.x, you can go to Start > Run and then type (if D: is the correct drive letter for the CD-ROM that the upgrade CD-ROM is in) D:\win9x\setup.

After you choose to upgrade, your system will check to ensure that no programs are running (and if they are, prompt you to close them). After that, a routine check will run to determine if your disk has any errors and corrects them as necessary. You'll be greeted by the Windows Millennium Setup Wizard screen followed by the license agreement and finally the Product key entry screen. (Make sure to enter it excluding any dashes.) From here, Windows Me will determine what hardware you currently have installed and will initialize the system's registry file. A check will determine if you have enough disk space for the upgrade, and you will be prompted to save your system files. This is important, as should you choose not to save your system files, you will be unable to revert to your current OS should Windows Me not completely fit your needs. It is recommended that you always choose to back up system files at this point because you can always remove them later. (Should you run out of disk space, removing the files will free up 50 to 100 MB.)

If the installation determine that backing up your files would leave too little space, you will be alerted and prompted with the option of skipping the backup to free up disk space.

You will now be prompted to create an Emergency Startup Disk that can be used should the hard drive be damaged or system files are lost or corrupted. These things happen to the best of us, so it is highly recommended that you have Windows create this disk and have it handy—at all times. Also, should this installation fail, this disk is necessary to uninstall Windows Me. Click on Finish, and you'll go on to the meat of the installation, the file copy process. A status bar lets you know just how much progress has been made in copying files from the CD-ROM to your hard drive. After the copying is complete, your PC will need to reboot. Remove the floppy disk from the drive (you did make the Emergency Startup Disk, right?) and reboot. Once rebooted, your system will begin installing drivers for various devices and reboot as necessary. This process is completely automated; you should be ready to go in about 30 minutes.

If you want a little more control over what exactly Windows Me installs and where, you can choose to do the install from the command prompt. Using a boot disk (refer to the Windows 9.x installation section to review components necessary for boot disk), boot up your PC to the command prompt. Type "D:" (or whichever drive letter represents the CD-ROM where your Windows Me disk is being installed from), and then type "Setup" to start the Setup program.

If you have previously copied the Windows Me installation files to your hard drive, you enter the address of the folder to where you copied the files.

When the Startup program starts, an instance of ScanDisk checks out the hard drive for errors, and after a few moments, you are greeted by the familiar GUI mode (with mouse support). You are taken from the license agreement through the product key entry, just as in the upgrade. Next, you are prompted to enter the installation directory where you want Windows Me to be installed (the default is C:\Windows). Following this, provided that you are installing on a formatted hard drive, you are prompted to save existing system files. Moving through familiar paces, you are prompted for creation of a boot disk, which is highly recommended. If you are installing to a previously unused Windows folder (or if you changed the default installation directory), you are prompted to pick the type of installation: Typical, Portable, Component, or Custom.

You are then prompted for your Name/Company Name; select the components you want to install, followed by the various network options (IDs, workgroups, etc.). Much like the 9.x family, it is highly recommended that you wait until your computer is finished with the OS installation to configure network options (a choice made that much easier with the ease of Home Network Wizard). After choosing country, time, and date, you should be all but finished.

The installation process really doesn't differ too much between an upgrade and a full install. The same basic differences existed in Windows 9.x (e.g., making sure the hard drive is formatted for the particular OS you are trying to install, creation of a boot disk, etc.); so while the command prompt portion of the installation section focuses on a full installation, rest assured it is the same for the upgrade installation.

DUAL BOOTING

It is possible for Windows 9.x (as well as Windows Me) to be set up in a dual-boot situation with another OS from the Windows NT/2000 family on the same hard drive. There will be a few complications that you can expect, due to the fact that Windows 9.x wants to be the only OS and will often overwrite system files. If Windows NT/2000, for example, is installed on a FAT16-partitioned drive, you will receive an error when installing Windows Me that Windows NT system files are present. If Windows NT is installed on an NTFS partition, Windows Me will report that it is damaged and will not let you continue the installation (as interactive reparation is not allowed during Setup). Should you have a Windows NT/2000 installation on a FAT16-partitioned drive and choose to install Windows Me anyway, the Windows NT/2000 boot files will be overwritten with the Windows Me files. Windows NT and Windows 2000 do come with repair tools to correct the problem, though, so there's a solution to the problem. Before you get started, you should realize that you will need to make or have a copy of the boot disk for Windows Me (or Windows 95/98, should you be trying to dual-boot with those).

Do not attempt to use a boot disk for another OS; that is, if you are trying to set up Windows Me in a dual-boot situation, do not try and use a Windows 98 boot disk. Boot disks are fairly regimented in terms of revision control and their own particular internal files and utilities.

To install Windows Me (or any of the Windows 9.x family, for that matter), follow these steps:

1. Ensure that your Windows NT installation is up to date. Make sure that you have all the latest service packs and any hot fixes that are pertinent to your system. Windows 2000 comes ready out of the box to be able to see Windows 9.x. (Windows 95/98/Me), but you should be updated to at least Service Pack 1 for other reasons.
2. Create a Repair Disk for either Windows NT or Windows 2000. This disk contains copies of key registry entries, along with a description of the partition geometry of the disk.
3. To build a Repair Disk(s) in Windows NT, use the RDISK.EXE command line and follow the prompts.
4. To build a Repair Disk(s) in Windows 2000, run the Backup utility and click the Emergency Repair Disk option on the Welcome tab.
5. Create a FAT32 partition for the Windows Me installation. It does not have to be the boot partition, but it does have to be a DOS-accessible partition for the installation to succeed.

Windows NT can recognize FAT16 partitions but not FAT32 partitions. If no such partition exists, use a third-party tool such as Partition Magic to create one.

6. Using Windows NT/2000, insert your Windows Me CD-ROM and copy the SETUP folder to your FAT32 partition. You should use the same folder name to copy installation files, but if SETUP already exists, try using NEW SETUP or something similar.
7. Restart your computer and boot from your Windows Me boot disk. At the command prompt, type "SYS C:" to transfer the boot files. This should return the command line SYSTEM TRANSFERRED.
8. Switch to the folder where you installed the Setup files (remember the syntax: drive name:\folder name), and type "Setup.exe" to start the Setup process.

9. You will receive the aforementioned warning about Windows NT system files being present (or possibly files from another OS, depending on what else you have installed). In any event, ignore these messages for now. Otherwise, the installation process shouldn't be all that different from a normal Windows Me installation. The only difference is that the location of the Windows installation cannot be on the same partition as your Windows NT installation (which can cause inconsistencies in your Programs folder).

10. After the installation finishes, you need to ensure that your system boots to Windows Me normally. If it does not boot normally, unrepaired disk problems may have occurred during installation.

11. We are now ready to repair the NT boot files, which will allow you to use the NT boot loader so you can choose between Windows NT, Windows 2000, or Windows Me. Boot the computer using your Windows NT/2000 setup disks or CD-ROM (if you can boot from a CD-ROM), and choose R for Repair. Choose to Repair only the Windows NT boot sector, nothing else.

If your Windows NT/2000 installation is not found, you can use the Repair Disk made in step 2 to correct the problem.

12. After the Repair operation is finished, boot the computer, and you should see the Windows NT/2000 boot menu option menu with Windows Me at the bottom.

Should you not receive the boot option, you will have to edit your BOOT.INI (should be a read-only file in the root directory of your boot drive). You'll need to modify the permissions so that you can edit the file. Add the line "C:\Windows Me", and reboot. (Actually, you can add whatever you like in the description after C:\, as long as it is different from the other menu choices.)

USING DOS

As stated earlier, no real-mode DOS comes included with Windows Me. You can boot to a command prompt, though, and you may find it easy to troubleshoot and add/delete certain files from here. To boot into DOS, you will need a start-up disk. Here is how you can create a start-up disk:

1. Go to Start > Settings > Control Panel.
2. Double-click Add/Remove Programs.
3. Click the Start-Up Disk tab, and then choose to Create Disk (you will need a formatted floppy disk).

4. Restart your PC with the disk in the floppy drive. Make sure that your BIOS is set to boot from the floppy drive first, or you will just be taken back into Windows Me. If all goes well, you will be taken to the Microsoft Windows Millennium Startup Menu. From here, you can press Shift-F5 to go to the command prompt.

WINDOWS ME START-UP PROCESS

Windows Me is a member of the Windows 9.x family and as such uses the exact same start-up process, with the notable exclusion of AUTOEXEC.BAT and CONFIG.SYS. Windows Me finally did away with legacy support for these files. In previous iterations of Windows 9.x, Windows was actually using its own 32-bit versions instead of these files; they were only used for backward compatibility.

WINDOWS ME TOOLS AND UTILITIES

The tools used in Windows Me remain largely unchanged from the tools offered in the earlier versions of Windows 9.x. Windows Me does add some notable exceptions, though, such as PCHealth tools (including the very helpful System Restore utility). Let's take a look at some of the new tools as well as some of the best tools to help you troubleshoot errors.

DISPLAY SETTINGS

Display settings are accessed the same way across all of the Windows 9.x family of OSs by either right-clicking on the desktop and choosing Properties or by going through Start > Settings > Control Panel, and clicking the Display icon. From either of these avenues, you are taken to the Display Properties applet (see Figure 11.11). Click on the Settings tab to change the desktop resolution (which may be featured on the exam) and color depth. If you click the Advanced button, and then the Monitor tab, you can adjust your monitor's refresh rate, which by default is typically set to 60 Hz. Did you note the Hide modes that this monitor cannot display checkbox on the Monitor tab? It should stay checked (toggled on) because running your monitor at unsupported refresh rates can seriously affect the life span of a monitor. When changing the desktop resolution, Windows Me will automatically set the refresh rate for the lowest possible setting (equal to or greater than 60 Hz) that the monitor can handle at that particular resolution (i.e., it may be possible to run your monitor at 75 Hz at 1024 x 768, but Windows Me will typically default to

65 Hz at this resolution). Make sure that you are running the highest possible re-fresh rate for your monitor to avoid headaches, strained eyes, and other physical ailments that can be caused by prolonged use of a monitor with a low refresh rate.

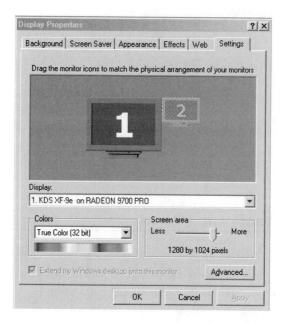

FIGURE 11.11   Windows Me Display Properties applet.

DXDIAG

DXDIAG is another useful command line that is run from the Run prompt in the Start menu to use the DirectX Diagnostic tool. The DirectX Diagnostic tool is another display applet relating specifically to DirectX, a 3D API that is directly supported by Microsoft. Most computers have some form of 3D processing unit in the video card, either on-board or as AGP/PCI, and Windows Me comes with a version of DirectX automatically installed. Direct Draw and DirectX capabilities can be tested from the DirectX Diagnostics applet, and general information can be found by clicking the General tab.

MSCONFIG

Windows Me, being a member of the Windows 9.x family, shares many of the quali-ties found in Windows 95 and Windows 98 SE. Unfortunately, it contains many of the same issues that plague its older siblings, as well. Boot times have been improved from those found in Windows 95/98, but booting can still be slowed by having too many services running at start-up. To check exactly what you have starting within the boot-up process, go to Start > Run, and type in "MSCONFIG" (not case sensitive) on the Open line. This will bring up the System Configuration Utility (see Figure 11.12), which contains several system tabs, including System.ini, Win.ini, and Startup. The one we're interested in is Startup. From here, you can choose what applications will start with Windows, with checkboxes to the left indicating if you want them to be toggled on or off. For optimal performance, only leave enabled what is absolutely necessary at start-up. Most programs, Microsoft Office included, have a tendency to leave start-up files as a part of the boot sequence, which (when compounded with several other start-up enabled programs) can seriously slow down the amount of time it takes to boot into Windows.

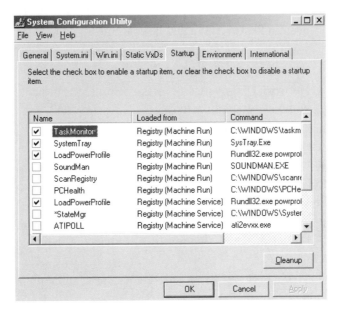

FIGURE 11.12   Windows Me System Configuration Utility.

DEVICE MANAGER

Although not specific to Windows Me, the Device Manager is one of the most useful tools you have at your disposal when trying to troubleshoot hardware difficulties. By right-clicking My Computer, which will bring up the System Properties applet, and choosing the Device Manager tab, you have access to your entire list of hardware. From here, you can uninstall, reinstall, and update drivers for all of your hardware. When in doubt, in dealing with malfunctioning devices, turn to the Device Manager first.

PCHEALTH TOOLS

Windows Me has a variety of PCHealth features that are used to monitor and correct problems with your system. All of the resources used by the 9.x family are carried over and can be found in the same locations. Some of the more useful tools that can be used are listed here:

Viewing System Information: This can be accessed through Start > Programs > Accessories > System Tools > System Information. From here, you will be given a folder tree on the left, with +/- boxes that let you expand/contract any particular category. When in the System Information applet, pay special attention to the Tools menu, which gives you access to the following:

System Restore: We will discuss this in the next section.

Fault Log: Fault Log provides a comprehensive error log for troubleshooting issues.

Network Diagnostics: This is a helpful little utility that diagnoses problems with network connectivity.

DirectX Diagnostics: Discussed earlier in this section, the DirectX Diagnostics utility contains tools for testing 3D system drawing capabilities, as well as DirectX sound functions.

Update Wizard Uninstall: This utility aids in uninstalling downloaded updates using the Windows Update feature.

Signature Verification Tool: This tool is useful in troubleshooting when you need to ensure that certain critical system files have not been modified since installation

Registry Checker: The Registry Checker scans your registry for errors that could be causing issues.

Automatic Skip Driver Agent: This is a wonderful tool if you are trying to diagnose problems with Windows' start-up. This utility identifies problems with drivers loaded at start-up that keep Windows Me from starting correctly, and it allows you to skip them.

Dr. Watson: Dr. Watson™ is a program error debugger tool used in Windows 9.x/NT/2000 to detect and log critical error information pertaining to system halts. Dr. Watson also attempts to point you in the right direction by offering possible tips for problem and error resolution.

System Configuration Utility: Gives you the ability to change start-up services and programs that load at start-up.

ScanDisk: Discussed in Chapter 10, ScanDisk is a Microsoft disk analysis and repair utility that is used to recover and repair lost or bad clusters on a disk. Windows 9.x and Windows Me use a GUI version of ScanDisk that can be accessed and run by selecting Start > Programs > Accessories > System Tools > ScanDisk.

WMI Control: WMI (Windows Management Implementation) Control lets you take control of remote PCs on a network for security and maintenance.

Resource Meter: The Resource Meter is a great tool for monitoring your GDI (Graphical Device Interface), system resources, and user resources. This tool can be found by navigating Start > Programs > Accessories > System Tools > Resource Meter.

System Monitor: A more complex version of the Resource Meter, the System Monitor can be used to graph kernel usage (by default), File System, Memory Manager, and Microsoft Network Client. To change the graph target, choose Edit > Add Item, and then choose another statistic to graph.

You can also remove items from the graph using the Edit menu.

NOTE

Windows Update: This utility automatically keeps your OS up to date with current patches, fixes, security updates, service releases, and other information offered by Microsoft (see Chapter 11 on Windows 9.x for an in-depth discussion).

Auto Update: This feature runs from the system tray. Auto Update uses downtime (time when you are using the Internet) and downloads what it deems to be appropriate updates, and then prompts you to install them. To disable this feature, go to the Control Panel and double-click the Automatic Updates icon. From here you can choose to:

- Automatically download updates and notify me when they are ready to be installed (on by default).
- Notify me before downloading any updates and notify me again when they are ready to be installed.
- Turn off automatic updating. I will update my computer manually.

System Restore: System restoration is accomplished in Windows Me using the new System Restore tool. It can be found by navigating to Start > Programs > Accessories > System Tools > System Restore. System Restore essentially takes a snapshot of your current system setup (e.g., current drivers, installed programs, etc.), which it can revert to previous settings at any point. System Restore compresses these files and saves them as CAB files in C:\Restore\Archive. It's a good tool to use prior to a major driver update for your hardware, before installing new software (or major updates to current software), or any other action that might cause your system to function incorrectly as a result of an upgrade. Using the System Restore tool before doing any such action allows you to capture a working image of your current setup, so that if something does go wrong in the process of upgrading, you can always revert back to a working setup.

Windows automatically captures an image of your machine once a day and holds it for a period of about two weeks. You can always choose from one of Windows' Restore Points, or choose to revert to one you've specifically made.

From the System Restore applet's initial screen, you are asked if you want to restore your computer to an earlier setup or create a new Restore Point. To create a Restore Point:

1. Go to Start > Programs > Accessories > System Tools > System Restore.
2. Choose Create Restore Point.
3. Click Next.
4. You are then prompted to enter a description of your Restore Point. You can enter anything you like (up to 64 characters). When you've entered your desired description, click Next to continue. Windows will create the Restore Point and indicate that it is complete. A time/date display is listed with your personalized description (as entered in the previous step).

To revert to an earlier Restore Point:

1. Go to Start > Programs > Accessories > System Tools > System Restore.
2. Choose Restore My Computer to an Earlier Time.
3. Click Next.
4. The next screen has a calendar on the left and an option box on the right. Choose from the dates displayed in bold to open the available Restore Points made on those given days/dates. The Restore Points available appear in the option box to the right. Choose the appropriate Restore Point, and click Next to continue (see Figure 11.13). You will be prompted with a cautionary message that reads, `Before restoring your computer, save and close all open files, and close all open programs. Do not alter, open, or delete any files or programs until the restoration is complete.` Click Next to continue.

5. The following screen will display the progress of the System Restore and restart the system. The System Restore screen will appear when the system restarts. Click Close to continue.

The system restoration tool is completely reversible. If for any reason you are displeased with the image you chose, you can always go back to where you were before you restored.

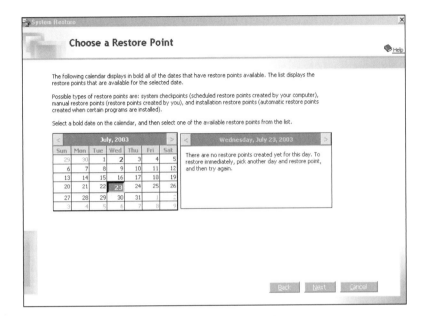

FIGURE 11.13   Windows Me System Restore: Restore Point selection applet.

It is also possible to start the System Restore tool from a command prompt. You would want to consider this when you cannot start Windows Me normally or in Safe Mode. To do this, follow these steps:

1. Boot your PC using a Windows Me start-up disk.
2. From the Startup menu, choose Minimum Boot.
3. At the command prompt, type "edit c:\windows\system.ini" (provided that this is your Windows directory), and press Enter.
4. Edit the shell = line so that it reads, "shell =program.exe".
5. Press ALT-F, and then "S" (to save changes made to the SYSTEM.INI).
6. Press ALT-F again, and then "X".

7. Remove the Windows Me start-up disk, and restart the computer.
8. The Program Task Manager should start. If it doesn't, repeat the previous steps, making sure you follow the instructions exactly.
9. Choose File > Run, type "MSCONFIG" (is not case sensitive) in the command line, and press Enter.
10. Click Launch System Restore to begin restoring you computer to a previous, functional Restore Point.

After you configure your computer to start Program Manager (progman.exe), you can also start the System Restore tool with the command line C:\windows\ system\restore\rstrui.exe.

PROFILES

Profiles in Windows Me can be broken down into two categories: Hardware and User.

Hardware Profiles are useful when you are using a machine under different circumstances, where it's beneficial to load different devices at different times. A perfect example would be a laptop because you are not always connected to a network. It takes several seconds for your network connection to time out when you start a laptop that is not connected to the network. By disallowing Windows to start up with network connectivity, boot times can be greatly increased. You can create several different hardware profiles, disabling certain devices on your system. When you set up these profiles, Windows will prompt you at start-up for which profile you want to use at that time. To set up a hardware profile:

1. Go to Start > Settings > Control Panel > System to open the System Properties applet. Click the Hardware Profiles tab (see Figure 11.14).
2. Select the profile that you want to use as the basis for the new profile you will be setting up. Click Copy to open the Copy Profile dialog box, and create a duplicate.
3. Enter a name for the copied profile, and click OK. (The new profile file appears in the Hardware Profiles list.)
4. Restart the PC, and when prompted, select your new profile.
5. Choose the individual hardware drivers for your new profile by going to Start > Settings > Control Panel > System, and select the Device Manager.
6. Click the + sign next to a device to expand the selection to all devices under it.

7. Double-click the device you want to edit (which will bring up a Properties box). Choose to Disable or leave that particular device enabled in this hardware profile.
8. Click OK.
9. Close the Device Manager tab to exit.

FIGURE 11.14   Windows Me System Properties
Hardware Profiles tab.

User Profiles are created if you want to allow different user accounts to customize their own desktop settings and passwords. By default, Windows Me is installed as a single-profile system, where all users get the same settings every time they log on, regardless of the username and password they use. To set up User Profiles:

1. Go to Start > Settings > Control Panel > Passwords. You will now be at the Password Properties dialog box.
2. Select the User Profiles tab, which prompts you with two options:
   ▪ **All users of this computer use the same preferences and desktop settings:** On by default, this is the option you use if you don't want to have customized User Profiles.

- **Users can customize their preferences and desktop settings. Windows switches to your personal settings when you log on:** This is the option you want to set up—customized desktop settings for multiple users (see Figure 11.15). When you select this option, you will be given two other options:

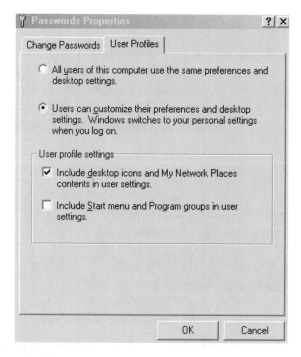

FIGURE 11.15 Windows Me Password Properties User Profiles tab.

3. **Include Desktop Icons and Network Neighborhood contents in User Settings:** Allows desktop icons and Network Neighborhood contents to be customized for the individual user (can include desktop colors, fonts, and passwords).

4. **Include Start Menu and Program Groups in User Settings:** Allows the contents of the Start menu and the options in the Program menu to be customized by the user.

5. After you have made your choices for permissions regarding Desktop icons, Network Neighborhood, the Start menu, and Program groups, you are ready to set up User Profiles through the Users icon in the Control Panel at Start > Settings > Control Panel > Users.

6. This screen will show you all existing users and the ability to add a new user, delete an existing user, or make a copy of an existing User Profile. To create a new user, click the New User button to the right.

7. You will be taken through the Add User Wizard, which will walk you through the process of adding a new user. First, you will be prompted to enter a new username and password. Next, you will be prompted with the Personal Items Settings dialog box, where you can choose to select the items you want to personalize for that account (which is also the same menu you would get if you had clicked Change Setting on the previous screen), and how you want them to be created. The options for personalization include Desktop folder and Documents menu, Start Menu, Favorites folder, Downloaded Web pages, and My Documents folder. A couple of important things to realize here are the following:

   ■ Should you choose to personalize these items, you must realize that the changes made to these items are only for this User Profile. If you enabled the Start Menu, for example, and the user changed the icons around or removed shortcuts, it would only be reflected there when the user logged on to their User Profile (not others).

   ■ When choosing to create copies of current items and their contents, or when creating new items to save disk space, you need to realize that if you choose to create new items to save disk space, users will not have access to what you already have installed. If you had Favorites created to save disk space, they would not see any favorites currently in other profiles; they would be starting from scratch.

8. Close the wizard, and you're done. You can log off or log on to that new account at any time.

Note that this is the most daunting method of setting up a new User Profile. In fact, you can just follow steps 1 to 3, and then choose to restart. When you log on, choose to log on with a different username (any name you choose) and password (again, any of your choosing), and you will be prompted with a Windows message that reads `You have not logged on at this computer before. Would you like this computer to retain your individual settings for use when you log on here in the future?` If you choose Yes, you have created a new User Profile, which can be edited in the Users menu from the Control Panel. Editing, deleting, and copying User Profiles can all be handled through the Control Panel > Users menu, as well.

NOTE

Creating User Profiles with different editable properties requires a lot of hard drive space for storage. If you are going to be creating separate profiles, each with their own settings (as in step 2 of the preceding User Profiles steps), make sure you have at least 500 MB of free hard drive space.

WINDOWS ME NETWORKING AND THE INTERNET

Windows Me offers the Home Networking Wizard to set up local connections and the Internet Connection Wizard to help you establish a connection to the Internet. In previous versions of the Windows 9.x family, you had to manually configure your network card and install necessary protocols and clients through the Network applet in the Control Panel. This can all still be done the same way, but the Home Networking and Internet Connection Wizards will accomplish all of this for you, including setting up and installing necessary protocols for features such as ICS. All of the protocols handled by Windows 9.x are supported in Windows Me (e.g., Net-BEUI, TCP/IP, etc.) and are handled the same. For information on these protocols, refer to Chapter 11 on Windows 9.x.

First, we will take a look at the steps necessary to create an Internet connection in Windows Me.

CREATE AN INTERNET CONNECTION

Creating an Internet connection can be started in several ways:

- Go to Start > Programs > Accessories > Communication > Internet Connection Wizard.
- Go to Start > Settings > Control Panel > Internet Options, open the Internet Properties applet, choose the Connections tab, and then click the Setup button.
- If you do not currently have an Internet connection set up, you can simply start an instance of Internet Explorer to start the Internet Connection Wizard.
- From Internet Explorer, go to Tools > Internet Options, and then select the Connections tab, followed by the Connect button. You will start the Internet Connection Wizard, which will guide you through the process of starting a new Internet connection. From here, you have three options:

    I want to sign up for a new Internet account (My telephone line is connected to my modem): This option dials you into Microsoft's Referral Service using your modem, and then gives you a list of recommended ISPs to set up a new account. You are led through several screens of data entry—everything from credit card information to address/ZIP code for local dial-up numbers. At the end, you will have an established Internet account.

    I want to transfer my existing Internet account to this computer. (My telephone line is connected to my computer.): This option is for those who already have an existing service or who are signing up with a service not listed on Microsoft's Referral Service page. To do this, you will need all of the information provided by the ISP for that particular account (e.g., dial-up phone numbers, usernames, passwords, POP and SMTP information for your mail account, etc.).

I want to set up my Internet connection manually, or I want to connect through a Local Area Network (LAN): Both this and the previous option are identical in nature in terms of the steps you will have to complete. Should you choose one of these last two options, the process will continue on as follows.

1. You will be prompted to choose if you connect through a phone line and a modem. Click Next.
2. The next screen asks you to enter the telephone number for your ISP. (Make sure you uncheck the box for Dial using the area code and country code if it is not necessary in your area.)

Most ISPs do not require you to enter static or specific DNS or IP addresses. However, if your ISP requires it, you can click on the Advanced tab to enter these numbers.

3. Click Next to continue.
4. Enter your username and password in the appropriate fields, and click Next.
5. Enter a name that you want to associate with this particular connection. This should be something that you can easily identify; it does not necessarily have to be the name of the ISP.
6. Click Next to continue.
7. You are now prompted to set up an e-mail account. Click Yes and Next to continue.
8. If Windows finds an existing e-mail account, you are prompted to either edit that account or set up a new one. Choose Create New Internet Account, and click Next to continue.
9. Enter your display name in the appropriate field (the name that will be attached to all outgoing e-mail that you send). Click Next to continue.
10. Enter the e-mail address for sending/receiving e-mail messages. Click Next to continue.
11. This screen will have you fill out your incoming mail server type (usually POP3), as well as enter your POP3 (IMAP or HTTP) server name and your SMTP server name. Click Next to continue.
12. You will be prompted for your username and password. Enter these, and then click Next to finish the process.

Essentially, you have used the ICW (Internet Connection Wizard) to avoid having to set your TCP/IP and dial-up networking settings manually (and installed Dial-Up Networking, had it not been installed previously). If you need to edit the settings or set up a new dial-up connection, you can do so from the Dial-Up Networking folder located at Start > Settings > Dial-Up Networking (which is possible if your ISP requires you to change settings due to a connection failure).

DIAL-UP NETWORKING

Dial-up networking is handled exactly in the same way as it is for the rest of the Windows 9.x family. Again, it can be found at Start > Settings > Dial-Up Networking. From there, you will have access to any previous connections or the ability to create a new one. If you are modifying an existing connection, right-click on it from the Dial-Up Networking folder, and click Properties. Dial-up networking handles standard modem connections, ISDN connections, and null-modem connections between serial ports. From the General tab, you can choose from the following:

General tab: You choose the phone number to dial, whether to use an area code and country code when dialing, or choose a different modem for the connection from the drop-down menu. (Click the Configure button to open the Properties for the selected modem, and edit them if necessary.)

Networking tab: TCP/IP, NetBEUI, and IPX/SPX compatible protocols can be easily selected/deselected, and you can choose to specify an IP or DNS address.

Security tab: Modify your username and password. Check the box if you want your Internet connection to connect automatically and log on to network options.

Dialing tab: Select/deselect the default Internet connection, retry settings (in case of a failed connection), and idle disconnect settings.

You can actually change the default Internet connection much more easily by going to Internet Explorer > Tools > Connections, and choosing which connection should be the default from there.

CREATING A PEER-TO-PEER NETWORK

Creating a peer-to-peer network in Windows Me is just as easy as setting up an Internet connection:

1. Go to Start > Programs > Accessories > Communications > Home Networking Wizard. At the introductory screen, click Next.
2. Choose if your computer is currently connected to the Internet and in what manner. Click Next to continue.

3. Depending how you answered in the previous step, you'll be asked if you want to share your connection with the Internet. If you do, then choose the Network Adapter to share (that is the NIC you have installed to connect your home network). Click Next to continue.

4. Enter a name that you want to be associated with this computer on your network. You will also be choosing the workgroup name. (You can leave it at the default or change it as you feel necessary but realize that all computers must use the same workgroup name.) Click Next to continue.

5. On the TCP/IP screen, you will be prompted to choose whether to share certain folders and printers associated with this PC. Choose which items you want to share, and click Next to continue.

6. You will be prompted to create a setup disk. Should you have any other Windows 9.x machines on your network, choose Yes. If the other computers are running Windows Me or Windows 2000/NT, you will not require the disk.

7. When you reach the Completing the Home Networking Wizard Screen, choose Finish, and the necessary files will be copied.

8. If you are prompted to restart your machine, do so. When you restart, you will be prompted for a username and password (just make them up if you don't have them already), and your computer is now networked.

Use the disk created in this process to set up networking on Windows 95/98 machines. (Run it from the My Computer menu in that OS.)

You can still manually install network drivers if you do not want to relinquish control to the Home Network Wizard, or if you find it necessary to use other protocols. Manual installation of network drivers starts with:

9. Go to Start > Settings > Control Panel, and then double-click Network.
10. Review the list of components on the Configuration tab.
11. If Client for Microsoft Networks does not appear there, click Add, click Client, and click Add again. A list of provided Microsoft Clients appears.
12. Choose Client for Microsoft Networks, and click OK.

You may be prompted to insert the Windows Me CD-ROM. Do so if necessary.

13. From here, choose your desired protocol (ATM, ATM LAN Emulation, IPX/SPX compatible, NetBEUI, PPP over ATM, or TCP/IP). Click the protocol to install, and click OK to continue.
14. Open the Network Logon drop-down list and choose the client for the network (e.g., Client for Microsoft Networks).

15. Click File and Print sharing to choose your file and print sharing permissions (make sure both boxes are checked to share both of them).

16. Click OK to finish. The system may require you to reboot; do so if necessary.

CONNECTING TO A WINDOWS NT/2000 SERVER

You can still connect to a Windows 2000/NT server using the Home Networking Wizard. However, you must take the following into consideration:

- If the Windows NT Server is a domain server, you need to create a user account on the NT server for every Windows Me user who will need to access resources on the NT server.
- If you are using Windows NT Workstation, make sure you have the same workgroup name entered as you do for each Windows Me station that will be in that workgroup.
- If you are using Windows NT Server, you must set the Windows Me PC to log on to the Windows NT domain and enter the correct domain in the domain entry field at each station. To do this:
  1. Go to the Control Panel > Network Properties > Client for Microsoft Windows Networks.
  2. Click the Domain checkbox, and enter the name of your Windows NT domain.

CREATING A FIREWIRE SUBNET

Users who have created an Ethernet or modem network and use a mobile device or laptop may want to consider setting up a subnet (or secondary network) using IEEE 1394 (FireWire) or a wireless connection so that they can move about freely with the mobile device while having access to all resources. If you are using an external DSL or cable modem, you will require two Ethernet cards on your primary ICS machine where the Internet is shared from. Otherwise, you will need only one to connect to the rest of your network. Make sure that you have ICS set up on your primary ICS server before you begin. To create this subnet:

1. Go to Start > Settings > Control Panel > Internet Options.
2. Click on the Connections tab.
3. On the LAN tab, click Sharing.
4. Choose the device that connects you to the secondary network from the list.

If sharing is not an option, you have not enabled ICS on your system. Follow the steps in the Home Networking Wizard to set up this feature.

5. Click OK, and you will be prompted to restart your computer.

COOKIES

A *cookie* is a message that is sent or "transmitted" to a Web server from a Web browser. It is important to note that a cookie can also be referred to as a state object or persistent cookie. The cookie is used to provide the Web server with unique information that is used to identify where the request to the server is coming from. In other words, the cookie provides information about you. When you access pages on the Internet and enter your personal information into Web forms, that information along with other prepared information is combined into a file called a cookie. Most often, server-side scripts known as CGI (Common Gateway Interface) scripts are used to control what happens with the cookie. The next time you happen upon the same Web site, your Internet browser will automatically forward the locally stored cookie to that Web site's server. If set up to do so, the server will provide you with a prepacked, customized page that targets you for specific advertisements. In other words, you will get "spammed."

Many Web servers use trusted cookies as their only form of authentication. This widespread misuse of cookies has spawned a major security threat to both Web servers and users alike. If an attacker, or "cookie hijacker," is able to infiltrate a user's session while the user is logged on to a server service, the attacker can steal the user's cookie and use it to access such things as account information. A common practice that attackers use to grab cookies during an active session is to execute a fake JavaScript routine on an unprotected server.

Although many servers are open to this cookie authentication exploitation, most servers that provide important financial information and extremely sensitive data have more secure authentication mechanisms and devices in place.

There are several good ways to protect your system from the threats to security provided so nicely by the use of cookies. You can set up your Internet browser to alert you when a cookie is present, you can direct your browser to only download cookies from trusted sites, or you can disable cookies altogether. Depending on your OS and Internet browser, this procedure will vary.

JAVASCRIPT

JavaScript is a programming script language that is supported by Internet browsers provided by Netscape and Microsoft. JavaScript is commonly used by Web developers to interact with Web pages, which are typically created using HTML or XML source codes. In simple terms, JavaScript allows developers to spruce up Web pages by adding features such as self-updating software packages, popup windows, link-to pages, and 3D interactive worlds to new or existing Internet Web pages. JavaScript is considered to be a portable, object-oriented, robust, and secure scripting language.

The productive tools that we manufacture to design and create a better, more intuitive Internet experience all seem to come with a heavy price tag concerning security. Java, JavaScript, and Java applets (little programs sent with Web pages that do not require user interaction) are no exception. They all provide transportation mechanisms that can allow attackers to insert code to infiltrate and destroy your system. JavaScript, applets, and Java are programs that actually run on your system.

Hijackers and attackers often create scripts and applets, which are oftentimes able to circumvent network security parameters. They can be used to manipulate files on users' computers.

SIGNED APPLETS

As mentioned earlier, applets are small programs that contain scripts that are sent with Web pages to users. Applets, such as Java applets, allow calculations, animations, and other functions to take place on a user's system without a need for communication to take place with the applet-providing server.

Applets can contain malicious code that can easily destroy a system if allowed to run. A popular technique known as sandboxing is often used to quarantine applets that appear suspicious or malicious.

Signed applets contain a digital signature to prove that the applet has come from a trusted location, author, or site. Signed applets receive permission to access local system resources. Plain applets only have access to the directories from which they originally run. Some books state that signed applets cannot be altered. This is simply not true. Anyone can create or forge a signed applet. This makes them very dangerous and provides a huge security vulnerability to local as well as networked systems.

Note that most applets on the Web are unsigned applets. These applets can be assigned various security levels, which include untrusted, high, medium, and low levels of security. Table 11.1 provides the various levels of unsigned applet security.

ACTIVEX

ActiveX is a set of object-oriented programs, technologies, and tools that are Microsoft's answer to Java technology, which by the way was created by Sun Microsystems. ActiveX is basically a combination, or "outgrowth" of the Microsoft

TABLE 11.1   Applet Security Levels

Applet Security Level	Action Taken
Untrusted	Untrusted applets do not have permission to run on a system at all. They only have the ability to start.
High	Applets with this security rating run under what are considered safe restrains and are only permitted certain functions. They are not permitted to carry out unsafe actions. They cannot access most browser settings. They cannot read, write, delete, or change files. They can only listen to network ports located above port 1024. They cannot access a system's printer queue or clipboard.
Medium	These applets can run under safe restraints. By default, if one of these applets attempts to read, write, change, or perform any of the other "High" restraints, you will prompted (warned) by your Internet browser. Next, you may grant the requested permission to the applet if you choose.
Low	This level carries the greatest security risk. Applets with Low security run under minimum restraint. Your browser will not warn you about the actions listed previously unless the applet attempts to start local applications.

technologies known as OLE (Object Linking and Embedding) and COM (Component Object Model). When this technology is used in a networked environment that provides directory support and other service, the COM technology becomes DCOM (Distributed Component Object Model).

The goal of this technology is to create a self-sufficient program, known as a component or ActiveX control, which can be run anywhere your ActiveX network exists.

ActiveX's controls, or components, can be compared to Java applets and can be reused by applications and other systems throughout your network.

ActiveX provides a power tool for developers and programmers. Unfortunately, ActiveX carries with it security risks, as JavaScript and applets do. But, the ActiveX security model is quite different from the security controls in place for Java and Java applets. As you may recall, Java applets are restricted based on a set of actions that are considered safe. The ActiveX security model does not limit an application package to a set of individual restrictive controls. Instead, its controls are based on digital signatures. These digital signatures are registered and certified with a trusted digital authority, such as VeriSign. When a person registers a software package or application with a trusted CA (Certificate Authority), they are agreeing that the package or ActiveX control is free of malicious code. From that point on, the risks involved with downloading the controls are totally the responsibility of the user.

In simple terms, the main weaknesses or problems associated with ActiveX controls are the following:

■ After the user has accepted the certificate, responsibility for the control's actions are placed completely on the user. If an uneducated user on your network happens to accept a certificate from an unknown or unofficial CA, you may not have many systems left operable by the end of the day.

■ Users can change browser settings to allow unsigned ActiveX controls to be downloaded with a warning.

■ There is no good logging or audit trail available to track down what an ActiveX control has done to your system.

If you need help troubleshooting problems associated with active content such as JavaScript and ActiveX using Internet Explorer, Microsoft provides an excellent white paper on the subject. You will also be shown how to disable dangerous active content altogether in this white paper: *http://support.microsoft.com/default.aspx?scid=KB;EN-US;Q154036.*

To access the ActiveX settings for Internet Explorer, navigate to Internet Explorer > Tools > Internet Options > Security Settings. Choose the network resource where you want to edit ActiveX settings (e.g., Internet, Local Intranet, Trusted Sites, Restricted Sites), and Reset custom settings. From here, you will be able to Disable/Enable/Prompt settings for:

■ Download signed ActiveX controls
■ Download unsigned ActiveX controls
■ Initialize and script ActiveX controls not marked as safe
■ Run ActiveX controls as plug-ins (this also has an option for Administrator approved)
■ Script ActiveX controls marked safe for scripting

CGI

The Common Gateway Interface is a language-independent interface or standard that Internet Web servers use to pass a user's request to an application program and forward a response back to the Web server, which in turn provides the results to the user. In English, when a user fills out an HTML form on a Web page, a CGI program is typically used to process the form's data behind the scenes and get the information back to the server. This allows Web servers to dynamically serve and interact with the users. The actual method of passing data between a server and an application is called the CGI.

CGI programs run on Web servers and are considered to be server-side applications. JavaScript, applets, and ActiveX controls are run on individual systems and are considered client-side programs. A disadvantage with using CGI programs is that they start a new service on a Web server every time a CGI program runs. This can result in a major decrease in the performance of a Web server.

The use of CGI programs allows the vulnerabilities associated with HTTP to be exploited. Also, for CGI programs to work, they are written to run on most OSs and have access to important server system files, as well as connected hosts.

Poorly executed CGI scripts and lack of or improper filesystem permissions can open the security hole doors and leave your system vulnerable to attack.

DIAGNOSING AND TROUBLESHOOTING TEST TIPS

The information provided in this section is intended to serve as a quick reference to assist you with diagnosing and troubleshooting many Windows 9.x/Me-related issues. Although some of the information mentioned in this section has not been discussed in detail, many of these tips and shortcuts are likely to show up on the exam. It is a good idea to read over the following information in final preparation for the Windows 9.x section of the test.

- If you install a hard drive larger than 2 GB, and your OS doesn't see beyond the 2 GB, your drive is not partitioned as FAT32. You may also need to get a BIOS upgrade from the manufacturer of your motherboard. Always remember, FAT16 has a 2 GB limit.
- The smallest unit of measure that Windows 9.X can work with on a hard drive is called a *cluster*.
- To create a folder in Windows Explorer, select File > New > Folder, or right-click the window and select New > Folder.
- To create a shortcut on your Windows desktop, right-click the desktop and select New > Shortcut.
- In Windows 9.X, the file MSDOS.SYS should be at least 1 KB.
- Installation files in Windows 95 are called cabinet or .CAB files. The proper name syntax used for Windows 95 .cab files is Win95_xx.cab (xx = a numeric value, such as 13).

- For a mapped network drive to retain its mapping on reboot, you must check the Reconnect at Logon box when establishing the mapping.
- The End key is used to access the interactive startup menu during the Windows 98 boot sequence.
- The Alt-Tab key sequence allows you to toggle between applications that are currently running on your system.
- The Shift-F8 key sequence can be used to refresh your desktop in Windows.
- Menus within Windows programs, such as Word or Windows Explorer, designate hot keys with an underscore (for example, Files, Edit, and View).
- You can get a system configuration printout from a Windows 9.X command prompt by entering "MSDN" and pressing the Print Screen key.
- If you want to access a printer by its UNC name, the proper syntax is \\computername\printername.
- If you have installed a new modem, and your previous dial-up networking configuration does not work, go to the dial-up networking properties of your original entry and configure them for the new modem.
- The DOSSTART.BAT file is automatically executed when you restart your system in MS-DOS mode.
- The correct starting order for Windows 9.X is IO.SYS, MS-DOS.SYS, CONFIG.SYS, COMMAND.COM, AUTOEXEC.BAT.
- SCANREG can be used to restore a registry from DOS. If you want to replace the registry with an older registry, use SCANREG/RESTORE. If you want to fix the current loaded registry, use SCANREG/FIX.
- If you have recently installed Client for Microsoft networks, IPX/SPX, and File and Print Sharing and are still unable to browse your network, verify that File and print sharing is checked. Without this setting enabled, you will not be able to see other workstations in Windows 9.X.
- To make a network dial-up connection to the Internet in Windows, you need two important network components: TCP/IP and a Dial-up Adapter.
- If you want to configure a dial-up connection to the Internet, you must have the network protocol TCP/IP bound to a dial-up adapter.
- If you are using a laptop computer with a NIC and the NetBEUI protocol, File and print sharing must be enabled on the NIC if you want to share information.
- If you are having difficulty moving a window between two monitors connected to the same computer system, you may already have the window maximized.
- To remove unneeded items from the Windows 98 Start menu, right-click the item in the Start menu and choose Delete, or right-click on the taskbar, select Properties, navigate to the Customize Start Menu Options, and use the Remove button to eliminate unwanted Start menu items. It should be noted that items in the Start folder are loaded in alphabetical order.

- Client, Adapter, Protocol, and Service are network components that can be added through the Windows 9.X Network applet.

- If you are having trouble detecting USB devices, you are most likely running the original version of Windows 95, which doesn't support USB without an update. Alternatively, you may not have USB support enabled in your BIOS settings. Again, Windows 95 does not support USB without additional software.

- If your system hangs at the Windows 9.X splash screen on boot up, hold down the Shift key on startup to stop possible corrupt Startup folder programs from loading.

- If items on your desktop look different from usual or are unidentifiable, the first step for resolving this problem is to refresh the desktop by right-clicking the desktop and selecting Refresh.

- If you are having trouble installing or updating Windows system files, you should try disabling any antivirus features in your systems BIOS as well as your antivirus real-time protection. Then attempt to reinstall the software.

- If you need to restore an OS file that has been deleted from your system, you can use the EXTRACT command to restore a file from the Windows 9.X Installation CD.

- Windows 98 comes with a powerful FAT32 drive conversion utility program called Drive Converter, which has the ability to convert an already formatted FAT16 partition into a FAT32 or NTFS partition.

- If you double-click a shortcut on your Windows desktop and nothing happens, it is likely that the application program that is tied to the shortcut has been moved, removed, or is corrupted.

- If you have two printers installed on your Windows 9.X system, and you delete your default printer, the remaining printer automatically becomes your default printer.

- If you have just completed a Windows 9.X OS installation, and you are having difficulties adjusting your screen resolution, the first thing you should do is update your Windows and video drivers.

- Windows 9.X is not compatible with NTFS.

- The root directory under Windows 9.X supports a maximum of 512 entries.

- Common protocols that are used to share printers in Windows 9.X are TCP/IP, IPX/SPX, and NetBEUI.

- The Windows 9.X registry is a hierarchical database made up of special key entries.

- If you do not want to have your print jobs spooled in Windows 9.X, you can choose to print directly to the printer in the Spool Settings dialog box.

- The undocumented Microsoft utility MKCOMPAT.EXE can be used to assist older Windows 3.1 applications to run in a Windows 9.X environment.

- The statements PROMPT PG and LH C:\Windows\COMMAND\MSCDEX are commonly found in the AUTOEXEC.BAT file.
- The navigation path to capture a printer port in Windows 9.X is My Computer > Control Panel > Printer applet > File > Properties > Details.
- A .CPL file is a (Control Panel Extension) file. If you ever receive an invalid page default (kernel32) error when opening Control Panel, you will need to determine which .CPL file is damaged or corrupt and replace it.
- To create a startup disk in Windows 9.X, navigate to Control Panel > Add/remove programs, and select Create Disk from the Startup Disk tab.
- The first thing you should do if you receive the out of memory error while using Windows 9.X is to check the System Resources in the system Control Panel for any applications or processes that are using up valuable system resources.
- If a memory manager cannot provide an application with requested memory, a memory page fault occurs.
- To increase graphics acceleration speed in Windows 9.X, navigate to Control Panel > System > Performance > Graphics.
- Windows 98 SE is the only version of Windows 9.X that offers ICS (Internet Connection Sharing) capabilities.
- Windows 9.X is fully capable of being upgraded to Windows 2000 Professional.
- The correct booting order for a system is POST, BIOS, BOOT SECTOR, GUI.
- The Windows 9.X System Monitor can be used to monitor virtual memory and networked client and server info.
- If Windows 9.X finds a damaged or corrupt registry upon booting, it will attempt to automatically repair the damaged registry.
- If you select N for large disk support while running FDISK, a FAT16 partition will be created.
- If the Starting Windows 98 logo screen is missing at startup, it is likely that the file LOGO.SYS is missing or corrupt.
- You should never share more that 300 folders in Windows 9.X. If you do, the folders may not appear to be shared when displayed in Explorer.
- To create a start-up disk in Windows Me, click Start > Settings > Control Panel > Add/Remove Programs > Startup Disk > Create Disk > OK.
- To disable ICS in Windows Me, click Start > Settings > Control Panel > Add/Remove Programs > Windows Setup > Communications > Details. Uncheck the Internet Connection Sharing checkbox, and click OK.
- To place encryption on a compressed folder in Windows Me, right-click on the Compressed folder and select Encrypt. Type a password in the Password box, and verify the password by entering it again in the Confirm Password box.
- System Monitor can be used in Windows Me to monitor dial-up networking connections and measure download and upload speeds.

- To maximize ISP/Internet and dial-up networking connection speeds, you should disable any unused or unnecessary protocols. To do so, navigate to Dial-Up Networking and right-click on your connection icon. Next, select Properties > Networking tab, and uncheck NetBEUI and IPX/SPX compatible. These protocols are not normally used for ISP connections.

- In Windows Me, you can print out your system configuration summary by clicking Start > Programs > Accessories > System Tools > System Information. Choose File > Print.

- To associate a file with a program in Explorer, right-click on the file, select Open With, and choose the program you want to open the file with. You can change the start order of items in the Windows Me Start menu by dragging them to a different location.

- To increase your capacity for temporary Internet page storage, simply navigate to Internet Explorer > Tools > Internet Options > General tab > Settings. You can then increase your storage space for temporary Internet pages by moving the slider to the right.

- To undo a previous system restoration or restoration point prior to your last system restoration in Windows Me, click Start > Programs > Accessories > System Tools > System Restore. For undoing your last system restoration, select Undo my last restoration, and select Next. For rolling back to a restoration point prior to your last system restoration, click Start the System Restore Wizard, and navigate through the wizard instructions.

- A default install of Windows Me does not have Direct Memory Access (DMA) enabled for CD-ROM devices and hard drives. Enabling DMA for these devices will improve the overall CPU access time to these devices. To enable DMA support in Windows Me, select Start > Settings > Control Panel > System. Next, select the Device Manager tab, and then double-click on your desired hard drive or CD-ROM device. Select the Settings tab and place a check mark in the DMA box. A message, Unsupported hardware alert, will be displayed. Select OK, and reboot your system.

- To turn off 32-bit PC card support in Windows Me, select Start > Settings > Control Panel > System. Next, select the Device Manager tab, and verify that View devices by type is selected. Select the plus sign (+) next to PCMCIA Socket, and select your PC card controller. Next, under Device Usage, place a check mark in the Disable in this hardware profile box, and select OK.

- To disable the Smart Start menu in Windows Me, select Start > Settings > Taskbar. Next, select Start Menu, and remove the check mark from the Use Personalized menus checkbox.

- To reset your Internet Explorer settings to their default installation settings, select Tools > Internet Options on the Internet Explorer menu. Next, select the Programs tab, and click the Reset Web Settings button.

- To add or modify a device driver in Windows Me, navigate to the System Properties icon in the Control Panel, select the Device Manager tab, select the plus sign (+) next to hardware type, and double-click on the hardware. Select the Driver tab, and click Update Driver. You will then need to follow the specific instructions displayed on the screen.

- In most cases, Windows Me will detect and repair a bad or corrupt registry. If you need to do a manual restore of the Windows Me registry, you should first boot to a start-up disk. Then, from a command prompt, type "cd\windows\command", and press Enter. Next, at the command prompt, type "scanreg / restore". You will then need to select the registry to be restored, and press Enter. You will be told whether or not you have restored a good, working registry. You will then need to reboot your system.

- Disk Defragmenter is still located in the same location: Start > Programs > Accessories > System Tools > Disk Defragmenter. Don't forget to use it if your programs are slow to load, and you haven't done it in a while.

- Shortcuts are handled exactly the same way they were in previous versions of the Windows 9.x family. Don't forget that special symbols (e.g., \ / < > | : " ? *) are not allowed.

- Programs being installed often like to create unnecessary shortcuts in your Start menu. Removing them is as easy as right-clicking the desired shortcut and selecting Delete. (This will not uninstall the program, only remove the shortcut to its destination file.)

- Should you lose mouse support, you can begin troubleshooting by bringing up the Start menu using CTRL-ESC.

- The Start menu Favorites contain the exact same Favorites found in Internet Explorer. If you want to disable them in the Start menu, go to Control Panel > Settings > Task Bar & Start Menu > Advanced, and disable them there.

- DCC (Direct Cable Connection) is still supported by Windows Me; however, the absolute fastest port supported is the parallel port (or the even slower serial port), so they are not a very attractive solution. However, if you are using a laptop and just want to quickly connect to zip a file, or if your need an external drive that is not available to you, it will do the trick. To set up a DCC connection, go to Start > Programs > Accessories > Communications to make sure DCC is installed. (If it is not installed, install it from the Add/Remove Programs section of the Control Panel; you will need the Windows Me CD-ROM.) To start the DCC applet, go to Start > Programs > Accessories > Communications > Direct Cable Connection. The DCC setup process will guide you through the rest of the setup.

CHAPTER SUMMARY

This chapter introduced many of the Windows 9.x/Me concepts, utilities, shortcuts, and filesystems that you will be required to know for the A+ exam. As a final note regarding Microsoft Windows Me, you should think of Windows Me as an extension of Windows 9.x. In other words, Windows Me is very similar to Windows 98, with the exception of a few new features and support for such technologies as USB and FireWire. It is not likely that you will have to know very minute details regarding Windows Me on the exam. However, you will need experience in Me when you go in the field. Many businesses and home users still use it!

Windows Me was intended to be the next supercharged version of Windows 98, with all new bells and whistles. But, as recent history has shown, the real supercharged OS of choice award belongs to Windows XP, and Windows Me stands as more of an incremental update from Windows 9.x. We will cover Window XP in Chapter 14.

It is impossible to identify every detail that the current exam will cover; therefore, it is very important that you practice with the tools mentioned in this chapter to back up your knowledge with hands-on experience and give you the best chance of passing the exam. There are many details of Windows 9.x that are beyond the scope of this book. Use all the resources you can get your hands on to pass this exam. Scan the Microsoft white pages at *www.microsoft.com*; they refer to all the Windows OSs mentioned in this book. The following review questions are a great preparation tool. If you do not understand the concepts behind one of the review questions, use your OS's Help utility or the Internet to give you more details.

REVIEW QUESTIONS

1. **You are interested in using the Windows 98 Drive Converter to convert your FAT16 partition to FAT32. What can you gain from this conversion? (Choose Three)**

   ☐ A. Your applications will load quicker.
   ☐ B. You will use fewer resources.
   ☐ C. You will gain file-level security.
   ☐ D. You will lose valuable storage space based on smaller 4 KB clusters.
   ☐ E. Your storage space overall will become more efficient.

   Correct Answers = A, B, and E

A, B, and E are all benefits that can be achieved when you convert to FAT32. File level security is a feature of NTFS (Net Technology File System), which is only available with Windows NT and Windows 2000. Choice D is incorrect because smaller 4 KB clusters will allow you to gain more storage space.

2. **You plan on using only the OEM Windows 95 CD to install Windows on a blank hard drive. Why won't this work?**
   - ○ A. The Windows 95 OEM Installation CD is not bootable.
   - ○ B. You do not have enough hard drive space.
   - ○ C. You are using a nonregistered OEM version.
   - ○ D. You must partition the drive as NTFS5 first.

Correct Answer = A

The Windows 95 OEM installation CD is not bootable. If you plan on using this CD with a hard drive that is not bootable (in this case blank), then you will need a bootable floppy disk with supporting CD-device drivers installed to successfully install this Windows version.

3. **What doesn't Windows 95A support?**
   - ○ A. COMMAND.COM
   - ○ B. Defragmenter
   - ○ C. FAT32
   - ○ D. FAT16

Correct Answer = C

Windows 95 release A does not support FAT32. It does use COMMAND. COM, come with a Defragmenter utility, and provide support for FAT16.

4. **Which is considered the easiest upgrade path?**
   - ○ A. Windows NT to Windows 98
   - ○ B. Windows 95 to Windows 98
   - ○ C. Windows NT to Windows 2000 Professional
   - ○ D. Windows 2000 Professional to Windows 3.X

Correct Answer = B

Windows NT cannot be upgraded to Windows 98. Choice D is out of the question. Although the transition from Windows NT to Windows 2000 Professional is fairly straightforward, upgrading from Windows 95 to Windows 98 is considered the easiest upgrade path.

5. **Which are considered the safest ways for common users to edit or make changes to the registry in Windows 95? (Choose Two)**
   - ☐ A. REGEDT32
   - ☐ B. REGEDIT
   - ☐ C. DEVICE MANAGER
   - ☐ D. CONTROL PANEL
   - ☐ E. REGEDT34

   Correct Answers = C and D

   Using the Windows 9.X Device Manager and Control Panel options to change settings and devices are considered the safest ways for common users to make edits to the registry. Common users should not have the ability to make direct edits to the registry using REGEDT32 or REGEDIT.

6. **The Windows 9.X registry is considered to be what?**
   - ○ A. A big spreadsheet
   - ○ B. A hierarchal database made up of keys
   - ○ C. A multitiered tree text file
   - ○ D. A national database

   Correct Answer = B

   The Windows 9.X registry, as well as the registries implemented in Windows NT and Windows 2000, are hierarchal databases made up of special registry keys that hold most of the OSs software, hardware, and application settings.

7. **You are currently running Windows 95A on a 2 GB hard drive. You install a new 10 GB drive and configure it as a slave drive. You can only see 2 GB of the new drive when running FDISK. What is the problem?**
   - ○ A. Windows 95A has a 2 GB limit.
   - ○ B. Windows 95A is only good for a one hard drive system.
   - ○ C. Windows 98 was previously installed.
   - ○ D. Hard drive manufacturers have been doing cost cuts and are keeping the other 8 GBs.

   Correct Answer = A

   Windows 95A only provides support for up to 2 GB partitions on a hard drive. If you want to use partitions greater than 2 GB, you should install Windows 95B or Windows 98.

8. **You want to empty all of the files in your Recycle Bin, but you are not quite sure what will happen to them. What happens to files located in the Recycle Bin when it is emptied?**

   ○ A.   They are converted from FAT to NTFS.
   ○ B.   They are bound to the IPX/SPX protocol.
   ○ C.   Only the entries in the FAT are removed.
   ○ D.   The hard drive sector is wiped out and marked bad.

   Correct Answer = C

   When you empty the Recycle Bin, only the entries in the FAT are removed. This gives you the ability to recover these files using third-party recovery tools.

9. **You are interested in renaming a printer in Windows 9.X. What paths could you take? (Choose Two)**

   ☐ A.   Star t> Settings > Printers
   ☐ B.   Start > Run > Printers > Rename
   ☐ C.   My Computer > Printers
   ☐ D.   Start > Control Panel > Label Printer

   Correct Answers = A and C

   A and C are valid paths to renaming a printer in Windows 9.X.

10. **You have installed a new program on your Windows system that is configured to start up automatically when your system starts. When you reboot, the systems hangs at the Windows logo screen. What should you do to get into Windows?**

    ○ A.   Turn the system off and back on. Hold the Shift key down after seeing the Windows logo screen.
    ○ B.   Reinstall Windows.
    ○ C.   Use Alt-Print Screen and present the error to a senior technician.
    ○ D.   After you see the logo screen, count to three and press the Esc Key.
    ○ E.   Boot to an antivirus disk, and run a full virus scan with updated virus definition files.
    ○ F.   All of the above.

    Correct Answer = A

    The Shift key is often used at boot up to bypass applications that start automatically. Reinstalling Windows will help you get into Windows; however, it is not the logical choice here. Choices C, D, and E are invalid selections that will not accomplish the goal of getting into Windows.

11. **When you access a Web page on the Internet, what can be placed in your system that is used as a sort of tracking device to uniquely identify you?**
    - ○ A. Acceptor
    - ○ B. Cookie
    - ○ C. A Multi-Purpose Internet Extension
    - ○ D. UNC

    Correct Answer = B

    A cookie is a unique identifier that Web servers place in your system to identify you. A UNC name is used to access a particular share on a particular workstation or server on a network.

12. **Which of the following are potentially harmful to the welfare of a system?**
    - ○ A. Cookies
    - ○ B. Signed Applets
    - ○ C. Java Scripts
    - ○ D. All of the above

    Correct Answer = D

    Many Web servers use trusted cookies as their only form of authentication. This is a major security risk. Hijackers and attackers often create scripts and applets, which at times are able to circumvent network security parameters. They can be used to manipulate files on users' computers.

13. **Select the choice that best represents the most restrictive to the least restrictive applet security level.**
    - ○ A. Low, Untrusted, Medium, High
    - ○ B. Untrusted, High, Medium, Low
    - ○ C. High, Medium, Low, Untrusted
    - ○ D. None of the above

    Correct Answer = B

    Applets can be assigned various security levels, which include untrusted, high, medium, and low levels of security. Refer to Table 11.1 for the various levels of unsigned applet security and their levels of restriction. All other choices are invalid.

14. **Which of the following would you consider using in the event of a failed software installation for new hardware?**

    ○ A. System Restore
    ○ B. Disk Defragmenter
    ○ C. ScanDisk
    ○ D. None of the above

    Correct Answers = A

    Disk Defragmenter would be used if you were experiencing unusually long load times for programs (hard drive thrashing), whereas ScanDisk should be used if you think you may have errors on your hard drive.

15. **If you were interested in setting up User Profiles that you wanted to be completely independent of each other (where all the Favorites, Start Menu, etc. were different), where would you go first to specify that you wanted such accounts created?**

    ○ A. Start > Settings > Control Panel > System
    ○ B. Start > Settings > Control Panel > Passwords
    ○ C. Command line DXDIAG
    ○ D. None of the above

    Correct Answer = B

    The first option takes you to the system applet, which is where you'd go to set up a Hardware Profile, not a User Profile. DXDIAG actually brings up the DirectX diagnostic tool.

16. **You can access a real DOS prompt using Windows Me (not a Windows applet); what is required to do so?**

    ○ A. A Windows Me startup disk
    ○ B. A version of Windows XP installed opposite your Windows Me installation
    ○ C. Install DOS from Add/Remove Programs list
    ○ D. None of the above

    Correct answer = A

    A version of XP installed on your machine won't help you access a DOS prompt. Unfortunately, DOS cannot be added or removed from within Windows Me.

17. **Which of the following does not come enabled with an installation of Windows Me? (Choose two)**

    ☐ A. System Restore
    ☐ B. DMA support for hard drives
    ☐ C. Remote Assistance
    ☐ D. Device Manager

    Correct Answers = B and C

    Both System Restore and Device Manager are set up and enabled after a Windows Me installation

18. **When using Windows Me to connect to an NT domain server, which of the following is true?**

    ○ A. Windows Me cannot connect to an NT domain server.
    ○ B. You will be unable to use System Restore while connected to the NT domain server.
    ○ C. A loss of performance will be felt when accessing NT network resources.
    ○ D. User accounts must be created on the NT server for every Windows Me user who will need to access resources on the NT server.

    Correct Answer = A

    It is possible to connect to an NT domain server as long as the user accounts are created for every Windows Me user. System Restore still works fine, and no performance loss is present when accessing networked resources.

19. **Which two files are noticeably absent from the Windows Me startup process?**

    ○ A. AUTOEXEC.BAT
    ○ B. CONFIG.SYS
    ○ C. All of the above
    ○ D. None of the above

    Correct answer = C

    In fact these two missing-in-action files are the only noticeable difference between Windows Me start up and other Windows 9.X applications.

20. **When setting up a subnet on a machine that is a client (or station that receives) ICS from another machine (server), how many network cards will you need?**

○ A. One.

○ B. Two.

○ C. You cannot setup a subnet from a machine that is not the server for ICS.

○ D. None of the above.

Correct Answer = C

You must set up the subnet on the machine that is the server for ICS when setting up a subnet

REFERENCES

www.microsoft.com/whdc/hcl/search.mspx. This site is the home of the Microsoft Windows HCL. This list can be used to see if your hardware is compatible with a specific Microsoft OS.

http://windowsupdate.microsoft.com/. You should use this site to keep your Windows OS up to date with the most recent Microsoft updates and security patches.

http://support.microsoft.com/default.aspx?scid=KB;EN-US;Q154036. This Microsoft Web site describes how to disable active content in Internet Explorer.

http://support.microsoft.com/search/preview.aspx?scid=kb;en-us;Q279736. This Microsoft Web site explains the process of starting System Restore from a command prompt in Windows Me.

www.Microsoft.com. Visit this site and sharpen up on as many OSs white pages as possible before taking the A+ exams.

12 Windows NT

In This Chapter

- Overview of Windows NT
- NT Server versus NT Workstation
- Installation and Upgrading
- The Windows NT Start-Up Process
- The Windows NT Registry
- Windows NT Networking and Administration
- Resource Sharing and Drive Mapping
- Utilities and Settings
- Printers
- Diagnosing and Troubleshooting Test Tips

OVERVIEW OF WINDOWS NT

Although CompTIA does not specify Windows NT in its 2006 Objectives, it is imperative that you understand some of the technology that was first presented to the world in this operating system (OS). The current exams are going to focus on NTFS (which you'll learn about shortly), file and folder permissions, and security. Understanding the technological concepts born from Windows NT will give you the tools you need to pass most of the OSs questions that are presented to you. This chapter is also jammed packed with exam-related TCP/IP information and concepts that you will see on the real exams.

In 1993, Microsoft introduced Windows NT to the world to meet the great demand for a true network OS business solution. The original implementation of NT came in the form of Windows NT Server 3.1. After several modifications, Windows NT Server 3.51 was released. In 1996, Windows NT Server 4.0 and NT Workstation 4.0 were released.

Windows NT was originally designed with the following concepts and features in mind:

Compatibility: It was imperative that Windows NT be able to support and communicate with other filesystems, such as FAT, OS/2 HPFS (High Performance File System), Mac OS, CDFS (Compact Disc File System), Unix, Novell Netware, and other NTFS (NT File System) OSs. To be compatible with such filesystems, NT was designed to provide support for networking protocols such as TCP/IP, IPX/SPX, NWLink, AppleTalk, DLC, and NetBEUI.

Reliability and stability: Windows NT was designed to protect the major components of the OS from other programs and applications that might fail. It was also designed to protect each program and application from all others by allowing each to run in its own Virtual Machine (VM). Windows NT is also considered the first truly fault-tolerant OS. It was designed to provide built-in support for redundant storage through the use of Redundant Array of Independent Disks (RAID).

Security: Unlike a peer-to-peer network that uses password-protected shares, Windows NT was designed to centralize the control of user access to network resources through the use of special domain controller computers that authenticate users. These controller computers are known as *primary* and *backup domain controllers.*

Performance: Windows NT was designed to provide support for the use of multiple processors and true multitasking abilities. It can support true 32-bit preemptive multitasking while maintaining backward support for 16-bit cooperative programs.

Internet Explorer and Web services support: Windows NT has built-in support for Internet Explorer and a personal Web server.

The current A+ exams will most likely focus on your ability to troubleshoot boot operations, emergency repair operations, and filesystem compatibility issues. Although the exams may not specifically say "Windows NT," the questions asked of you will focus on technology born from this OS, such as NTFS. To give you the best possible chance of passing the exam, it is highly recommended that you support the knowledge you will gain in this chapter with hands-on experience. In other words, follow along with the examples provided in this chapter on a real computer system running Windows NT Server or Workstation 4.0 if possible.

NT SERVER VERSUS NT WORKSTATION

Windows NT Server 4.0 and Windows NT Workstation 4.0 can simply be referred to as Windows NT or Windows NT 4.0. Many of the procedures for carrying out specific tasks are similar in both OSs. Remember, the exams are going to focus on the technologies and terms, many of which are carried on into Windows 2000 and Windows XP.

For example, a Windows NT technology question relating to the creation of an Emergency Repair Disk (ERD) may come in the following form:

1. **You want to create an Emergency Repair Disk in Windows NT 4.0. What command would you use to do this?**
   - ○ A. FDISK/ERD
   - ○ B. ERD/MAKE
   - ○ C. RDISK.EXE
   - ○ D. ERD/RDISK

Correct Answer = C

Notice that the question does not focus specifically on Windows NT Server or Windows NT Workstation; an ERD can be created using either OS. Although you should know the difference between a server computer and a client workstation, focus your studies on the capabilities of the OS technology as a whole.

WINDOWS NT SERVER

Windows NT was designed for client/server-based network environments. In a client/server environment, the client computer or workstation requests information from the server computer. For our purposes, the client computer can be Windows 9.x, Windows NT Workstation, Windows Me, Windows 2000 Professional, or Windows XP. The server computer can be Windows NT Server or Windows 2000 Server. This section focuses on Windows NT Server.

A Windows NT Server computer is used to provide access to network resources and provide print/file sharing, database, e-mail, and fax services. Windows NT Server can also act as a gateway to mainframe computing systems or act as an Internet gateway server for client computers.

Before a user can log on to a Windows NT domain, the user must be assigned a user ID, which allows the user to be authenticated on the Windows NT domain. The user ID is assigned specific rights to resources such as directories, files, and printers. This method of assignment provides centralized control of network access and serves as a way to control and secure network file and printer sharing. A *domain* is defined as a group of networked computer systems that share a common Security Accounts Manager (SAM) database that is used as a reference to grant users network access. When a new user is added to a Windows NT domain through the User Manager for Domains administrative tool, the user ID is stored in the Primary Domain Controller's (PDC's) SAM database. This database is replicated to all Backup Domain Controllers (BDCs) that exist in the same domain as the PDC. The purpose of a BDC is to improve network performance by load balancing the network authentication process and provide backup to the PDC in case of failure.

In other words, users or clients can be granted access to the network through a BDC or a PDC. The BDC stores an identical copy of the SAM database in case the PDC suffers a crash. There can only be one Windows NT PDC server in a single Windows NT domain. There can be several BDC servers in a single Windows NT domain. The amount of BDCs needed in a domain is directly tied to the amount of users requiring authentication. Microsoft recommends having one BDC for every 2,000 user accounts.

A well-trained network administrator or technician is usually assigned the duties of managing a Windows NT Server domain. The typical duties of a Windows NT network administrator include the following:

Managing network access and user permissions: This includes adding and removing user accounts from the SAM database, managing groups of users, and assigning permissions for users or groups of users to access network resources.

Installing and upgrading software: The administrator is usually responsible for installing and fine-tuning OS software, such as Windows NT Server or Windows NT Workstation. This may also require software service pack installations, patches, and upgrades. Depending on the business needs of a company, the administrator may also be required to support and integrate many forms of third-party software.

Backups and virus protection: It is the responsibility of the network administrator to provide backup and fault-tolerant systems in the event of an emergency or system failure. In some cases, federal law and business contracts require proof that regular backups and backup procedures are in place for business to be conducted or contracts to be maintained. The recent onslaught of damaging computer viruses has created the need for enterprisewide antivirus business solutions and skilled administrators that can maintain them properly. If you do not have a good backup plan and virus protection implemented, your entire business is at serious risk.

Network monitoring and use: It is important that a network be properly monitored for maximum use and possible problem areas that may decrease overall network performance. Several tools included with Window NT are used for network monitoring; these will be discussed later in this chapter.

WINDOWS NT WORKSTATION

The majority of clients or computer users never actually see server computers or domain controllers. They access resources on server computers from desktop workstations or laptops that are running client OSs, such as Windows 9.x, Windows Me, Windows NT Workstation, Windows 2000 Professional, or Windows XP.

Windows NT Workstation was developed to be the client-side workhorse of the Windows NT domain. It is designed to handle multitasking operations and support processor-intensive applications and programs. A Windows NT Workstation computer can act as a standalone OS in a peer-to-peer network or be joined to a Windows NT domain. Many of the administrative functions available in Windows NT Server are also available in Windows NT Workstation. Workstations are thought to have less functionality and are only useful at the local OS level.

INSTALLATION AND UPGRADING

Many factors must be considered as you prepare for a successful installation or upgrade of Windows NT. The installation processes for Windows NT Workstation and Windows NT Server are quite similar. Shortly, you will be guided through a full installation of Windows NT Server. Before the installation process is explained, there are several factors you need to consider, which are explained next.

BEFORE YOU START

Microsoft provides strict minimum hardware requirements for the installation of Windows NT Workstation and Windows NT Server. You should verify that your system meets or exceeds the minimum recommendations before installation. The minimum hardware requirements for a typical Windows NT Workstation installation are a 486 processor, 12 MB of RAM, a VGA display adapter, 110 MB of available hard drive space, a CD-ROM device, and 3.5-inch floppy drive. The recommended requirements for a Windows NT Workstation installation are a Pentium processor, 16 MB of RAM, SVGA support, 300 MB of available hard drive space, a CD-ROM device, a 3.5-inch drive, and a NIC.

As mentioned in Chapter 11, you should always consult the manufacturer's specifications before installing any software. Minimum and recommended hardware requirements for Windows NT Server as well as other Microsoft OSs can be found at the Microsoft Web site (*www.microsoft.com*). It is also important to verify that your installed hardware is supported by the OS you are installing. If you are installing a Windows OS, you should check your installed hardware against the HCL at *www.microsoft.com/whdc/hcl/default.mspx*.

Before installing Windows NT on a hard drive, you must also consider which type of filesystem the OS will use. Windows NT works with FAT16 and NTFS. It is not compatible with FAT32 partitions unless you use special third-party programs. If you are planning a clean install of Windows NT on a hard drive, you should use NTFS to take full advantage of its many benefits. The benefits of NTFS include its overall ability to recover from system failure; support for RAID mirroring, which enables data to be written to two hard drives simultaneously, resulting in a complete hard disk backup; smaller cluster size than FAT16, which enables NTFS to support larger partitioned drive volumes and make better overall use of disk space; and the ability to provide file-level security and auditing.

If you are installing Windows NT on the same hard drive as Windows 9.x or DOS, you will want to use FAT16. FAT16 gives you the ability to see files across OSs and partitions located on the same hard drive. You can always convert a FAT16 partition to NTFS later from a command prompt by entering the following command:

```
CONVERT C:/FS:NTFS
```

The Windows NT command prompt can be accessed by selecting Start > Run and entering "CMD" at the Open line. CMD.EXE is the actual command prompt in Windows NT, Windows 2000, and Windows XP. You can also navigate to the Windows NT command prompt by selecting Start > Programs > Command Prompt.

If you want to create a dual-boot scenario, which will allow you to boot into either the Windows 9.x or Windows NT OSs (assuming they are installed on the same hard drive), you must have a bootable FAT system partition.

If you have Windows NT installed on the same hard drive as Windows 9.x, and you cannot view files between the OSs' partitions, you most likely have Windows 9.x installed on a FAT32 partition. This is a perfect example of what you are likely to see on the real exams as they relate to OSs and technology.

Another important fact about NTFS and FAT32 partitions is that if you copy files from an NTFS partition or volume to a FAT32 partition or volume, the files will retain their file attributes and long filenames. They will also retain any information stored in the file. However, they will lose their compression status, file permissions assigned from within Windows NT, and any encryption status.

This may seem like a lot to consider before installation, but it is important to consider all these items to achieve your OS goals.

THE INSTALLATION PROCESS

The Windows NT Server installation process can be started in one of two ways.

To initiate an *over-the-network installation*, do the following:

1. Share a networked CD-ROM device, and place the Windows NT Server CD-ROM in the shared device. Alternatively, copy the I386 directory and its contents to a local or shared network drive.

2. If you are using Windows or DOS, use the `WINNT.EXE` command from the client computer to execute the start-up process. If you are upgrading from an older Windows NT version, use the `WINNT32.EXE` command from the client computer. You will be presented with the Windows NT Setup screen. From this point on, follow the instructions in the next section.

To initiate the installation process *using the three Windows NT installation floppy disks and the Windows NT Server CD-ROM*, do the following:

3. Assuming that your system is configured to boot first to a floppy drive, insert the installation floppy disk labeled "Setup Boot Disk" into the floppy drive, place the Windows NT Server installation CD-ROM into the CD-ROM device, and restart the system.

4. The Windows NT Setup screen appears. The installation will continue until you are prompted for the second installation floppy disk. While the information on the second disk is processed, you will see the Windows NT kernel loading the version and associated build number. The Welcome to Setup screen appears, which gives you the options to Continue, Repair, or Exit the installation process. In this case, choose the Continue option and proceed with installation. Next, the license agreement appears. Page down to the end and press the F8 key to acknowledge your acceptance.

5. You will be asked to insert the third installation floppy disk. The installation process continues searching your system for installed hardware devices. At this point, the installation process has gathered enough information to determine if an older Windows NT OS has been installed on the hard drive. If the process finds evidence of an earlier version, you will be prompted with the following options:
   - To upgrade, press Enter.
   - To cancel upgrade and install a fresh copy, press N.

6. Because we are doing a clean install, the second option is appropriate. The installation process continues, displaying the system type, video card, keyboard, and mouse information. The installation process continues until a list appears of the available partitions the program has found on your hard drive. If you have multiple partitions, you must select one on which to install Windows NT. Be careful not to install NT onto a partition that currently contains a filesystem with information you want to keep. If you have one partition, select it and press Enter.

7. Next, you are given two options, including a choice of filesystem to format the partition with.
   - Format the partition using the FAT filesystem.
   - Format the partition using the NTFS filesystem.

8. As explained previously, format with FAT if you want to maintain compatibility or dual boot with a DOS or Windows 9.x partition. Use NTFS if you are interested in performance, program protection, file-level security, and support for filenames of up to 254 characters in length. Choose the filesystem you want to format with, and press Enter.

9. After the partition has been formatted, you are asked for the location in which to install the Windows NT files. The default location provided for you is \WINNT. Accept the default by pressing Enter. You will then be prompted for permission to scan the hard drive for corruption. Press Enter to continue. The Setup program will continue to copy files to the hard drive, and you will eventually be asked to press Enter again to restart the system. As the system starts back up, you will notice the Last Known Good Menu pass by. This feature will be available every time you restart the OS in the future. It is used to assist you with restoring the last known good system configuration stored on your drive in case you make OS configuration mistakes.

10. You are asked for the type of installation you want, including Typical, Portable, Compact, or Custom. It is best at this point to choose the Typical installation, and click Next. You will then be asked to supply a name and company name. Enter the appropriate information and continue. Next, you are asked to provide a CD key, which is provided with the installation CD-ROM kit. Enter it and continue. Then you must enter the type of licensing you want to use. The two licensing options are per seat and per server.

    ■ **Per seat means per device:** If you have 300 per-seat licenses, 300 users can sign on to and legally use any of the Windows NT servers in your business.

    ■ **Per server:** If you purchase 50 per-server licenses, or CALS, as Microsoft calls them, any 50 devices can connect to the specific server simultaneously.

11. Enter the appropriate license type, select the number of licenses you have purchased, and continue. Next, you will be asked to specify a computer name of 15 characters or less for your server and to choose whether it will be a PDC, BDC, or standalone server. If this is the first server on your network, you should choose the PDC option. If it is the second domain controller installed, choose the BDC option. If the server is going to be used for exchange (e-mail), SQL (database), fax, or as a file and print server, you should choose the standalone server option. After you have chosen the type of server that will be created, the installation process will ask you to configure a password of 14 characters or less for the administrator account. Confirm the password by entering it a second time, and click Next.

12. You are now prompted to create an ERD. If you choose the Yes option, Setup will ask you to insert a blank floppy disk into the floppy drive, and the ERD is created. You can select the No option and create an ERD later by entering RDISK/S at the Start > Run > Open line in the Windows NT GUI. The ERD disk contains valuable system configuration information that can be used to restore your system if it fails. The /s switch used with the RDISK command is used to back up the SAM database.

13. After you have created an ERD, Setup offers you the opportunity to install additional components, such as accessories, communications options, games, multimedia, and Windows messaging. Select the components you want to add, and click Next.

14. Windows NT Setup then informs you that you are entering the Windows NT Networking portion of Setup. You are asked to choose how to connect the server from the following choices:
   ■ Do not connect this computer to a network at this time.
   ■ This computer will participate on a network. Then choose from either Wired to the network or Remote access to the network.

15. To connect to a network and allow the installation process to continue, select This computer will participate on a network: and choose Wired to the network. Setup then asks if you want the Internet Information Server (IIS) installed. Do not select this option unless you want the server to provide Web services.

16. You are prompted to allow Setup to automatically detect your NIC.

17. Assuming that Setup has found the NIC, and it has been configured properly, you are then asked which network protocols you want to install. By default, Windows NT Setup chooses TCP/IP, NetBEUI, and IPX/SPX for you. Accept the defaults, unless you require additional protocols. Setup then asks if you require special services. Accept the default unless you have special needs, and continue. Next, you will be asked if the system will be part of a workgroup or a domain. If this is the first server in a new domain, you will not be presented with this option. If you are joining this server to an existing domain, you can add it with a domain administrator's user ID and password.

18. Finally, you need to set your system's time zone and adjust the video display options. After this, the system will restart at least once, and you boot directly into the Windows NT GUI.

INSTALLATION NOTES

Windows NT can use a unique database file and an answer file to automate the setup of multiple Windows NT installations. If you use these two files to automate your installation, you will be required to include within these two files most of the responses to the installation questions described previously.

There are several important switches that you can use in combination with the Windows NT Setup commands. Some of these important switches and useful installation notes are described here:

- Windows NT can be installed on the same hard drive as Windows 9.x, but Windows 9.x cannot be upgraded to Windows NT. Windows NT uses a different registry and OS structure. If you are installing Windows NT on the same hard drive as Windows 9.x, you must specify a different location for Setup to install the necessary files to; otherwise, Setup will overwrite your previous Windows 9.x installation.
- If you want to create the three Windows NT installation floppy disks after Setup has completed, you can use the command WINNT32.EXE with the switch /OX from a Windows NT command prompt. You can install Windows NT without being prompted for the three installation floppy disks by entering the command WINNT/B2 from a command prompt. This assumes that you have the Windows NT CD-ROM inserted in a CD device.
- The /I:inf_file switch is used with the WINNT command to identify the name of the Setup information file to be used for an automated installation. The default filename is DOSNET.INF. The /udf switch is used during an unattended installation to specify unique settings for specific computers in the uniqueness database file.

THE WINDOWS NT START-UP PROCESS

To support and troubleshoot the Windows NT OS, it is very important to understand the Windows NT boot sequence and what really happens behind the scenes before the Windows NT GUI appears.

The following steps detail the Windows NT start-up process:

1. When you push the power button on your system unit or select Restart the computer? from the Shut Down Windows menu, the system BIOS executes the POST (power-on self-test).
2. The BIOS then looks to load the MBR (Master Boot Record), which is located on the hard disk. The MBR, which is actually a small program, is used to locate the active partition on the hard drive, which holds the OS's boot sector.
3. The MBR runs the OS program boot instructions, which are located in the boot sector.
4. The file NTLDR (NT Loader) that is stored in the root directory of the system partition (C:\) is executed. NTLDR is the first Windows NT OS file

loaded during the start-up process. It is the main file used to see that the OS boot process is carried out properly. It can be compared to the IO.SYS file that is used with Windows 9.x. NTLDR is used to boot Windows NT and Windows XP into their OSs.

5. NTLDR changes the OS processor mode from Real Mode to 32-bit mode. This allows a 32-bit filesystem to be loaded. Keep in mind that Windows NT is a 32-bit OS. For NTLDR to read both FAT and NTFS, the processor mode must be altered to run in 32-bit mode.

6. NTLDR reads the BOOT.INI file, which displays a choice of OS boot-up options to the screen. By default, the choices are the following:
   - Windows NT Workstation Version 4.00 (or Windows NT Server if installed)
   - Windows NT Workstation Version 4.00 [VGA mode]

7. These options display for a default of 25 seconds. If you do not choose an option, the system will boot to the option that is selected in the System Startup section of System Properties in the Windows NT Control Panel (see Figure 12.1). As shown in Figure 12.1, you can change the amount of time that the System Startup menu list is displayed. You can also change the location of where the MEMORY.DMP file is stored if a STOP error occurs during system startup. Note that the MEMORY.DMP file is stored in the system root by default.

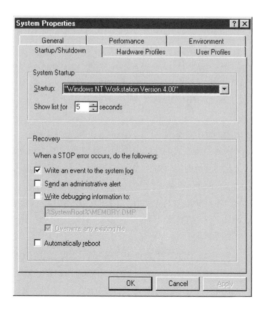

FIGURE 12.1 The Startup/Shutdown tab of the System Properties window.

8. If the option to boot into Windows NT Workstation (or Server) Version 4.00 was chosen in the previous step, NTLDR will call on the program Ntdetect.com to gather information on hardware that is connected to the OS. This information will later be loaded into the Windows NT registry. If another option was chosen in step 6, such as an option to boot into DOS or Windows 9.x (assuming that a dual-boot scenario was created), NTLDR will call on the file BOOTSECT.DOS to handle the responsibility of loading alternative OSs.

9. In this step, NTLDR reads the system archive that is located in the Windows NT registry for all hardware devices and associated drivers. NTLDR also loads the files NTOSKRNL.EXE and HAL.DLL. Ntoskrnl is known as the Windows NT kernel. It resides in main memory at all times after it is loaded. It is the core or central module of the Windows NT OS and is responsible for memory management and all tasks associated with the OS. The Windows NT Hardware Abstraction Layer (HAL) is a device-level layer of code that allows programs for the OS to be used without the overhead of APIs. The HAL is a required OS component that provides a seamless connection from the Windows NT kernel to hardware devices.

10. NTLDR hands complete control of the OS over to Ntoskrln, which completes the start-up process.

RESOLVING NT BOOT ISSUES

Many things can cause Windows NT Server or Windows NT Workstation to boot up improperly, including incorrectly configured IRQ and I/O settings, problems with NTLDR, and important system files being deleted or overwritten. Following are some of the most common boot issues and the proper methods of troubleshooting or resolving them:

■ If you can't boot into your Windows NT OS, you should always first attempt to use the Last Known Good Configuration option on start-up. You can initiate this option by pressing the space bar when you see the Last Known Good Configuration option displayed at start-up. As stated earlier, when you choose this option on start-up, the system attempts to restore the last good OS configuration load. This option is not useful if you have already booted into a configuration that is corrupt.

■ If you receive the error message `Boot could not find NTLDR. Please insert another disk.` on start-up, it is advisable to run the ERD process. The ERD process restores important system files. For Windows NT to boot properly, the files NTLDR, BOOT.INI, and NT DETECT.COM must be located in the root directory of the system partition.

NTLDR, BOOT.INI, and NT DETECT.COM are the same three files that must be on a Windows NT boot disk for it to be bootable.

NOTE

- If you receive an error message stating that Windows NT could not start because the file NTOSKRNL.EXE could not be found, you need to install a backup copy of this file from the ERD.

THE WINDOWS NT REGISTRY

The Windows NT registry is very similar to the registry used with Windows 9.x. The main difference is that the Windows NT registry is a 32-bit program. The Windows 9.x registry is a 16-bit program. Windows NT stores registry information in a file called REG.DAT. To maintain the ability to modify and communicate with older 16-bit programs, Windows NT supports the 16-bit registration database program editor REGEDIT.EXE that is used with Windows 9.x. REGEDT32.EXE is the Windows NT Registry Editor that displays the registry keys in the right pane of the display and the registry values in the left pane (see Figure 12.2).

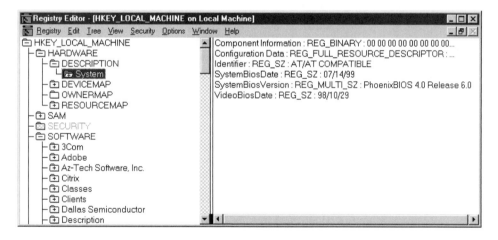

FIGURE 12.2   Windows NT Registry Editor displaying subkeys and values.

You can use either REGEDIT.EXE or REGEDT32.EXE to make changes to the registry in Windows NT. Make sure that you update your ERD disk using RDISK /S from a Windows NT command prompt before making any changes to the registry.

If you want more information about the differences between REGEDIT.EXE and REGEDT32.EXE, visit the Microsoft Product Support Web site at *http://support.microsoft.com/support/kb/articles/Q141/3/77.ASP.*

WINDOWS NT NETWORKING AND ADMINISTRATION

As mentioned earlier in this chapter, a Windows NT Workstation can participate in a workgroup or a domain environment. In a workgroup, each computer system houses its own SAM database. In a domain environment, the SAM database is located in a more central location, such as a PDC or BDC. This allows administrators to control user access to the network and provide for the sharing of network resources from a centralized location. A workgroup model mirrors a peer-to-peer network in which security and the sharing of resources is controlled at every machine. Imagine organizing a workgroup of 200 users—you would have to control user access to the workgroup and password-protected shares at every single system!

USER ACCOUNT CREATION AND MANAGEMENT

Windows NT comes with an administrator account that is used to manage and maintain the OS. You were asked to create a password for this account during the Windows NT installation process. Keep in mind that a Windows NT administrator account can be renamed, but it cannot be deleted. After you are logged on as the administrator, you can create user accounts (or user IDs) that grant users access to a Windows NT network.

User accounts are created in User Manager on Windows NT Workstation. User Manager can be accessed by selecting Start > Programs > Administrative Tools [Common] > User Manager. Selecting User Manager brings up the window shown in Figure 12.3. If you are using Windows NT Server, you will administer user accounts with User Manager for domains. User Manager for Windows NT Workstation is a scaled-down version of the more complex User Manager for Domains.

Username	Full Name	Description
Administrator		Built-in account for administering the computer/domain
Dr Vankman	Dr. Vankman	The PC Specialist
Guest		Built-in account for guest access to the computer/domain

Groups	Description
Administrators	Members can fully administer the computer/domain
Backup Operators	Members can bypass file security to back up files
Guests	Users granted guest access to the computer/domain
Power Users	Members can share directories and printers
Replicator	Supports file replication in a domain
Users	Ordinary users

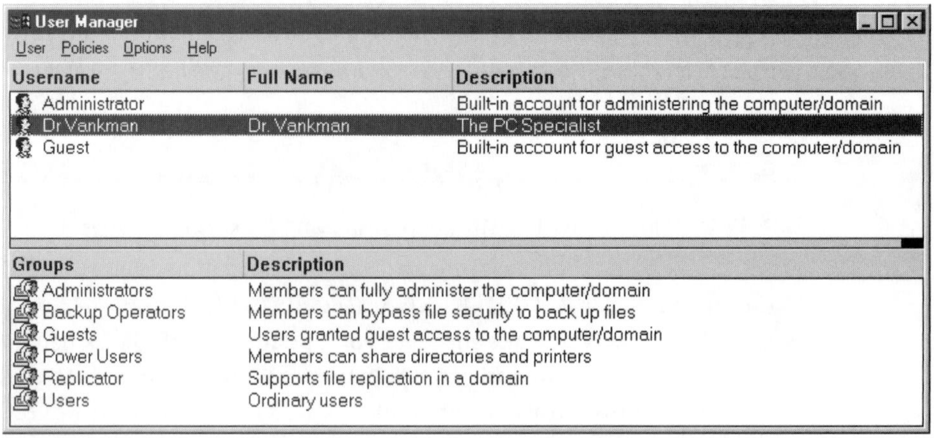

FIGURE 12.3 The Windows NT User Manager.

Following are guidelines for creating Windows NT User IDs and passwords:

- User IDs can be up to 20 characters long and are not case sensitive.
- User IDs can be made up of numbers, letters, and allowable characters.
- Passwords can be up to 14 characters long and are case sensitive.
- Passwords can be made up of numbers, letters, and allowable characters. The following characters can be used to make up a password: ` ~ ! @ # $ % ^ & * ( ) _ + - = { } | [ ] \ : " ; ' < > ? , . /.

As shown in Figure 12.3, User Manager has several built-in groups. These groups are designed for ease of administration. A Windows NT built-in group has preassigned user rights. Windows NT user rights allow users or groups of users to carry out specific tasks, including the right to back up the system, shut down the system, or change the system time. After a user ID has been created in User Manager, it can be placed in a group. When the user ID is placed in a group, the ID inherits all the rights associated with that group. For example, if the user ID BSAWYER were created and added to the Administrator Group, the user BSAWYER would inherit all the user rights associated with the Administrator Group.

Every Windows NT Workstation or Server has a set of built-in local groups. If a user has been placed into a local group, it is possible for the user to access resources and be granted rights on the local system. To ease domain-level administration efforts, Windows NT Server also makes use of global groups. Many users can be placed in a global group, and the global group can then be added to a local group located on a workstation or server. The end result is that it is possible for all users in the global group to access resources assigned to the local group on a particular workstation or server.

In addition to creating user IDs and assigning user rights, User Manager also has the ability to audit the success and failure of events that occur on the system. An administrator can audit access to files and objects, users who have logged on or logged off the system, and security policy changes, just to name a few. The results of the events that have been audited are displayed in the Windows NT Event Viewer. Event Viewer is described under "Utilities and Settings," later in this chapter.

LOGON

When Windows NT first boots up, a user ID and password are required to sign on to the local computer system or the network (domain) the system is connected to.

After a user ID and password have been created for a user, the user can proceed to sign on. When a user is signed on to the OS, the Windows NT Security and Logon Information box can be displayed by pressing the Ctrl-Alt-Del keys, all at once. The Logon Information box displays the computer name, currently signed-on user, logon date, and logon time. The following options are also displayed to the currently signed-on user:

Lock Workstation: This is a great built-in security feature that lets the user secure the computer while away. To unlock the workstation, the user presses Ctrl-Alt-Del again and enters the proper credentials to sign back on to the system.

Logoff: The option to end the current Windows NT session is available. Simply select the Logoff radio button. The message `This will end your Windows NT session` appears. Select the OK button, and you will be logged off the system.

Shut Down: If you select the Shut Down option, you are presented with the option to shut down the system or shut down and restart. These options are the same as the options offered by selecting Start > Shut Down from the Windows NT desktop display. The only exception is that you are also offered the ability to close all programs and log on as a different user if you use Start > Shut Down.

Change Password: If you have been granted the right to change your own password by a network administrator or network security person, you can select the Change Password radio button to change your sign-on password (user rights are discussed shortly).

Task Manager: Similar to Windows 9.x, Windows NT comes with a built-in Task Manager. (Task Manager is discussed in more detail later.) You can enter the Task Manager by selecting the Task Manager radio button. You can access Task Manager in Windows NT, 2000, or XP by pressing Ctrl-Alt-Del.

Cancel: The last option is the Cancel radio button. If Cancel is selected, you are directed back to the Windows NT desktop.

It is important to note that the same Windows Security and Information display can be accessed in Windows 2000 Professional and Windows NT Server by following the same procedures. The information and options available are identical.

LSA, SID, AND ACL

Security access to resources and the entire security sign-on process that takes place when a user logs on to Windows NT is very complicated and beyond the scope of this book. However, a basic explanation of the process is in order.

When a user logs on to Windows NT Workstation, the Local Security Authority (LSA) generates what is called a Security Access Token (SAT). This SAT is assigned a SID (Security ID for the user). The unique user SID contains access rights and privileges that have been assigned to the user's ID that was created in User Manager or User Manager for Domains (explained in the next section). Windows NT maintains an *Access Control List* (ACL) for all objects on the Windows NT domain. An object can be a file, a folder, or a printer share, just to name a few. For a user to be granted access to an object on the domain, the user's SAT must be accepted by the ACL. It is improbable that the A+ Operating System Technologies exam will address detailed questions on this subject.

USER PROFILES AND SYSTEM POLICIES

A Windows NT local User Profile is created when a user first logs on to a Windows NT system. The local User Profile is a configuration of the environmental settings and preferences that have been established by the user. In simple terms, a User Profile is a combination of desktop configuration settings the user sees every time he logs on. An administrator may implement a roaming User Profile for an individual if he wants to use the particular configuration settings assigned to the user at any other computer.

With a roaming User Profile, the user's profile information is stored on a server computer and is presented to the user wherever he logs on to the network.

Windows NT has a useful tool for controlling user environments called the System Policy Editor. With the System Policy Editor tool, an administrator can configure system policies for computers, users, or groups of users. For example, let's say you wanted all users who signed on to the network as the user ID GUEST to be restricted from changing the screen saver and wallpaper, and editing the registry. You can use the built-in settings within the System Policy Editor to create a policy for the user ID GUEST and apply the mentioned restrictions. You then need to copy the file NTCONFIG.POL (which is the policy you have saved in the System Policy Editor) to the NETLOGON share on the authentication server. When the user GUEST logs on to the network, the policy takes effect.

Profiles and system policies are basically tools used by administrators to control a Windows NT network.

DIAL-UP NETWORKING

Dial-up networking allows you to connect to remote networks using a modem or ISDN connection from within Windows NT. If you did not choose the Remote Access to the Network option during the Windows NT installation process, dial-up networking is not installed on your system. If this is the case, you can add dial-up networking by accessing the Network applet located in the Control Panel, selecting the Services tab, and clicking the Add radio button. A list of network services opens. Choose Remote Access Service, and click OK. Remote Access Service must be installed to use dial-up networking. You will be asked for the location of the I386 folder, which contains Windows NT installation .CAB files. Insert the Windows NT installation CD-ROM if you have not copied the I386 directory to the C:\ drive (which, by the way, is common practice among NT administrators; this avoids the need to use the installation CD-ROM to install services and drivers). Select Continue, and the Remote Access Service will attempt to find a modem connected to your system. Simply follow the instructions for the modem identification and associated COM port, and reboot the system when prompted. This process also installs a network dial-up adapter, which can be seen in the Network applet of the Control Panel after you have rebooted.

After you have rebooted your system, navigate to My Computer > Dial-Up Networking. You will be required to set up a phone book entry and configure the proper protocols and authentication methods used to communicate with the dial-up server. From here, it's as simple as clicking the phone book entry you have created to access a server remotely.

If you are using dial-up networking in Windows 9.x or Windows NT and cannot connect to a dial-up server—or an ISP, for that matter—you should first try to establish a new connection within dial-up networking. For Windows 9.x, select the New Modem option from the Dial-Up Networking Connection Properties. For Windows NT, attempt to create and configure a new phone book entry from within the Dial-Up Networking applet in My Computer.

To establish a dial-up connection with the Internet, you must have TCP/IP and a network dial-up adapter.

RESOURCE SHARING AND DRIVE MAPPING

The procedures for sharing folders, printers, and other resources in Windows 9.x, Windows NT, and Windows 2000 are all relatively similar.

To share a folder within the Windows NT OS, navigate to Windows NT Explorer by clicking Start > Programs > Windows NT Explorer, or right-click the Start button and select Explore. Once in Explorer, right-click on a folder to be shared with other users, and then select the Sharing tab. If the folder has been previously shared, the Share As button will be selected, and a Share Name will appear, as shown in Figure 12.4. You will also notice that in Windows Explorer, a previously shared folder is displayed with a hand holding it so as to share its contents. If a folder is not shared, the Not Shared button will be selected. Simply select the Share As button, and enter a Share Name. Select Apply and then OK, and the folder will be shared.

Notice the Permissions button shown in Figure 12.4. If you click Permissions from within the OS, you will see the users who have access to the newly created share. By default, the Everyone Group in Windows NT has access and full control of newly created folder shares and printer shares. You can choose the Add or Remove options in the Access Through Share Permissions box to grant or disallow specific users to access your share. You can also change the type of access a particular user or group of users has to your share. The types of access rights that can be assigned to folder-level shares in Windows NT are No Access, Read, Change, and Full Control.

So far, we have discussed folder sharing and permissions. If you look at Figure 12.4 once again, you will notice the Security tab. The presence of this Security tab indicates that the system has been configured with NTFS. We can use the Security tab to apply file-level permissions, implement auditing, or take ownership of selected items (see Figure 12.5). These features are available only with Windows NT and Windows 2000. File-level permissions and auditing are not available in Windows 9.x.

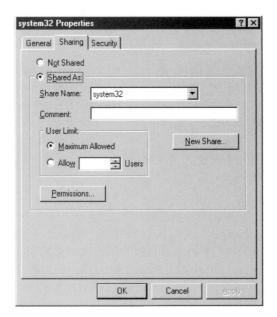

FIGURE 12.4   Sharing a folder in Windows NT.

FIGURE 12.5   Windows NT Security tab.

Establishing drive mappings in an OS allows you to connect to other computers, printers, and network resources. Having static drive mappings comes in very handy for displaying, moving, and copying information from one location to another.

To map a network drive in Windows NT, follow these instructions:

1. Right-click on the Network Neighborhood icon on the desktop.
2. Select Map Network Drive. The Map Network Drive dialog box appears.
3. From the Drive list, select the drive letter you want to map.
4. Enter a path for your mapping. You need to enter the UNC name for the location of the server and share you want to map to, for example, "\\Server-name\Sharename".

5. Select Reconnect at login to retain your mappings when you reboot the system.
6. Click OK.

Another way to access the Map Network Drive dialog box is to navigate to Windows NT Explorer and select Tools from the menu bar. You will have the option to Map Network Drive or Disconnect Network Drive.

After you have mapped to a resource on the network, your drive mappings can be located in Windows NT Explorer or My Computer.

UTILITIES AND SETTINGS

Windows NT offers utilities and tools for such tasks as formatting hard drives and assigning drive letters to volumes; monitoring and logging the performance of workstation or server computers; viewing system, security, and application event logs; and backing up critical information. Some of the more commonly used tools and their functions are described next. All the following tools are located in the Administrative Tools [Common] area, which can be accessed by selecting Start > Programs > Administrative Tools [Common].

BACKUP

Windows NT comes with a built-in backup tool known as Backup. Backup provides the ability to back up and restore important system files and data. When Backup is first run, it attempts to find a tape drive unit attached to the system. If Backup does not find a tape drive unit attached to the system, a Tape Drive Error Detected window appears that suggests you check to see that the proper cables are connected, power to an attached tape unit is turned on, and that you have properly configured a tape unit using the Tape Devices option in Control Panel.

After you enter the Backup main window, you can use the Operations dropdown menu to back up, restore, and perform general backup tape maintenance functions.

Most organizations today use third-party backup software that offers more functionality than the Windows NT Backup tool.

DISK ADMINISTRATOR

The Windows NT Disk Administrator is a very useful administrative tool that lets you format drive space, assign and change drive labels, and implement fault-tolerant systems by establishing disk mirror sets and disk stripe sets.

Disk Administrator is located in the Administrative Tools [Common] area. When you open the Disk Administrator, the window shown in Figure 12.6 appears.

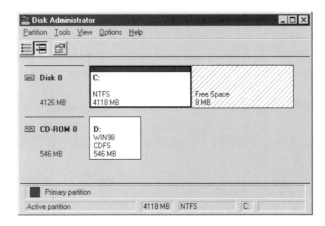

FIGURE 12.6   Windows NT Disk Administrator.

From the Partition drop-down menu, you can delete, create, or extend partitions, and create volume sets or stripe sets. From the Tools drop-down menu, you can format a displayed drive or volume, assign a drive letter to a disk or volume, or display the properties of a drive.

FAULT TOLERANCE AND RAID

Fault tolerance is the ability of a computer system to recover from a hardware or software failure or crash. There are several types of fault-tolerant hard disk configurations and specifications known as RAID levels.

Several levels of RAID are available today that provide fault-tolerant systems. It is important that you have a basic understanding of the following three levels of RAID.

RAID level 0, or disk striping without parity: With this level of RAID, data is spread or written over multiple hard disks. This technique provides better performance of read-and-write operations than other levels of RAID, but it is not considered fault tolerant.

RAID level 1, disk mirroring, or disk duplexing: To use RAID level 1 and establish what is called a disk mirror with the Windows NT Disk Administrator, you need two installed hard drives. After you have established a mirror within Windows NT Disk Administrator, all data written to your first hard drive is also written to the second hard drive. This provides true fault tolerance. If one of your hard drives fails, the other drive can be used to recover data. With disk mirroring, only one hard drive controller card is used to support both hard drives. *Disk duplexing* is the same as disk mirroring, with one exception: a second hard drive controller card is used; therefore, disk duplexing is more fault tolerant than disk mirroring.

RAID level 5, otherwise known as disk striping with parity: RAID level 5 is one of the most widely used fault-tolerant implementations. This RAID level requires a minimum of three hard drives installed in a single system and can support up to 32 hard drives. With RAID level 5, all information and parity data are spread across the disks. If one disk crashes, the information needed to implement a complete recovery by the system can be gathered from the other two disks.

If you encounter a question on the exams that asks which Windows built-in administrative tool can be used to format a drive, change a drive letter assignment, or establish a fault-tolerant recovery implementation, *Disk Administrator* should be your answer.

VOLUME SETS

A combination of hard disk space from different partitions that is used to form a single logical area is known as a *volume set*. A volume set can combine the free drive space from up to 32 separate partitions to form one logical drive. For example, if you have three hard drives with a combined free space of 4 GB, you can select each area of free space from each of the three drives displayed in the Windows NT Disk Administrator utility and combine the three areas to form one logical drive.

EVENT VIEWER

The Windows NT Event Viewer, also located in the Administrative Tools [Common] area, is used to monitor and evaluate significant events that occur within the OS. Event Viewer maintains three separate event logs, each of which has its own unique purpose for monitoring and troubleshooting important events: the System Log, the Security Log, and the Application Log.

System Log: This log maintains information pertaining to important system events, such as services that have been stopped or started within the OS. Some of these services may include the Event Log service, the computer browser service, DHCP service, or any other service run by the system. The System Log also maintains useful start-up information that can be used to troubleshoot components that are attached to the system.

Security Log: As mentioned earlier in the User Manager sections, enabled events in the Audit Policy are displayed in the Security Log. The Security Log can keep a record of successful and unsuccessful logon attempts to the domain or network. It can also track file and object access, as well as system restarts and shutdowns.

Application Log: The application log keeps track of important information about system-related applications. These applications may include Microsoft Office, antivirus software, and Windows Update.

Over time, the event logs that are maintained within the Event Viewer can use up important hard drive space and cause your system to run slowly or crash. A good practice is to change the default settings from Overwrite events older than 7 days to Overwrite events as needed.

PERFORMANCE MONITOR

Windows NT includes an important add-on utility that can be used to track and monitor the performance of system components and the overall performance of a workstation or server computer. This tool is called the Windows NT Performance Monitor. Some of the most useful information that can be gathered and logged by Performance Monitor includes processor use, memory use, memory page faults per second, percentage of free disk space, and real-time server counters to keep track of important server use.

WINDOWS NT DIAGNOSTICS

Yet another very useful tool included with Windows NT is the Windows NT Diagnostics utility. This utility can be used to view and troubleshoot system resources, such as IRQs, I/O ports, DMA channels, memory, and devices. All system services as well as environmental variables can also be viewed through Windows NT Diagnostics.

The Windows NT Diagnostics utility can be accessed through the Administrative Tools [Common] area or by selecting Start > Run and entering "WINMSD" on the Open line. The Windows NT Diagnostics utility is not meant to be used for updating or changing system or environmental settings; it is simply a representation of settings and information stored in the registry and used for diagnostics and troubleshooting.

TCP/IP UTILITIES

Several important utilities are part of the TCP/IP package and are installed with Windows NT Workstation and Windows NT Server by default. These utilities are used to troubleshoot and test network connectivity issues. Following are descriptions of the most commonly used TCP/IP utilities and their functions. Note that all these utilities work in a similar manner in Windows 2000.

PING

Short for Packet Internet Groper, PING is a utility used to test the connection between two computers. The following syntax is used to PING a computer by IP address or by name:

```
PING 209.15.176.206
PING CHARLESRIVER.COM
```

The PING utility works by sending a TCP/IP packet to a destination IP address and waiting for a reply. If the destination host receives the packet of information, four echo replies are received at the computer that initiated the PING command. PING is most commonly used to test connections to the Internet and ISPs. If you want to test a particular connection to a host IP address over a period of time (persistent), you can use the PING -t command. For example, to run a persistent PING to test your connection to the Charles River Media Web site, enter the following at a command prompt:

```
PING -t 209.15.176.206
```

To stop your connection test, press the Ctrl-C key combination.

IPCONFIG

You should recall from Chapter 11 that the WINIPCFG command is used at a Windows 9.x command prompt to display TCP/IP information, such as a system's IP address, subnet mask, and default gateway. Windows NT and Windows 2000 use the TCP/IP utility IPCONFIG to display the same information. You can display a system's IP address and additional information by navigating to a Windows NT or Windows 2000 command prompt and entering "IPCONFIG".

The following results are from entering the IPCONFIG command at a Windows 2000 command prompt:

```
Windows 2000 IP Configuration
Ethernet adapter Local Area Connection 3:
 Connection-specific DNS Suffix . : srst1.fl.home.com
  IP Address . . . . . . . . . . . . : 192.168.1.101
  Subnet Mask . . . . . . . . . . . : 255.255.255.0
  Default Gateway . . . . . . . . . : 192.168.1.1
```

Pay close attention to all of the TCP/IP utilities mentioned here. The IPCONFIG command mentioned previously shows up on just about every A+ exam!

TRACERT

The TCP/IP TRACERT utility is used to troubleshoot connections between routes that a packet will take before reaching its destination address. In other words, TRACERT measures the time it takes for a packet of information to move between routers in hops until it reaches its destination. You can view the results of TRACERT and the time it takes for the packet to move between routers to see where the slow response is located. To run a TRACERT to the Charles River Media Web site, enter the following command at a command prompt:

```
TRACERT CHARLESRIVER.COM
```

The results from a system running a TRACERT to the Charles River Media Web site are displayed next. The TRACERT results end when you see Trace complete.

```
Tracing route to CHARLESRIVER.COM [209.15.176.206]
over a maximum of 30 hops:
1  10 ms  10 ms  10 ms  10.101.0.1
2  20 ms  10 ms  20 ms  atm5-0-953.tampflerl-rtr2.tampabay.rr.com [65.32.11.146]
3  10 ms  10 ms  10 ms  srp8-0.tampflerl-rtr4.tampabay.rr.com [65.32.8.228]
4  10 ms  10 ms  10 ms  pop2-tby-P0-1.atdn.net [66.185.136.185]
5  10 ms  10 ms  20 ms  bb1-tby-P0-3.atdn.net [66.185.138.208]
6  30 ms  30 ms  30 ms  bb2-atm-P7-0.atdn.net [66.185.152.245]
7  30 ms  30 ms  30 ms  pop2-atm-P5-0.atdn.net [66.185.138.43]
8  30 ms  30 ms  30 ms  level3.atdn.net [66.185.138.34]
9  30 ms  30 ms  50 ms  so-4-1-0.bbr2.Atlanta1.level3.net [209.247.9.169]
10  40 ms  50 ms  50 ms  so-0-0-0.bbr1.Washington1.level3.net [64.159.1.2]
11  40 ms  51 ms  50 ms  so-6-0-0.edge1.Washington1.Level3.net [209.244.11.10]
12  40 ms  70 ms  60 ms  qwest-level3-oc48.Washington1.Level3.net [209.244.219.182]
13  40 ms  41 ms  50 ms  dca-core-03.inet.qwest.net [205.171.209.113]
14  40 ms  50 ms  41 ms  dca-core-02.inet.qwest.net [205.171.9.49]
15  60 ms  70 ms  60 ms  atl-core-02.inet.qwest.net [205.171.8.153]
16  60 ms  60 ms  60 ms  atl-core-01.inet.qwest.net [205.171.21.149]
17  51 ms  60 ms  80 ms  atx-edge-01.inet.qwest.net [205.171.221.18]
18  70 ms  61 ms  60 ms  genesis2net.net-gw.qwest.net [63.237.0.30]
19  50 ms  60 ms  60 ms  64.224.0.72
20  50 ms  61 ms  60 ms  charlesriver.com [209.15.176.206]
Trace complete.
```

The output, or results of using PING, IPCONFIG, or TRACERT can be directed to a text file for future reference, documentation, and further troubleshooting purposes. To direct the results of any of these utilities to a text file, simply add the greater than sign (>) followed by any name you choose to the end of the command.

For example, to direct the results of a persistent PING to Charlesriver.com to a text file named publisher, enter the following command at a command prompt:

```
PING -t CHARLESRIVER.COM >publisher
```

To view the results in the text file named publisher, navigate to C:\, and edit the file named publisher. You can also view these results by opening the text file "publisher" using Notepad in Windows.

NSLOOKUP

NSLOOKUP is used to query a DNS for a host name to IP address resolution. In simple terms, when the NSLOOKUP command is given, a request is issued to resolve a fully qualified domain name, such as CompTIA.com, to an IP address.

From a command prompt, enter "NSLOOKUP CompTIA.COM". The results of this command is shown here:

```
Name: Comptia.com
Address: 216.219.103.72
```

TELNET

Telnet is a TCP/IP terminal emulation program/protocol that allows a user to access another system by entering the command "telnet" at a command prompt followed by a valid host name. For example, if you wanted to access a program or directory on a computer named joeshmo.edu, you would enter the following command at a command prompt:

```
telnet joeshmo.edu
```

You would then be welcomed and challenged for a username and password. If you enter the proper credentials, you will be able to access information as a normal user of the system named joshmo.edu.

For an excellent and detailed description of how the Telnet protocol really works, visit the following www2.rad.com Web site: *www2.rad.com/networks/1997/telnet/proj.htm#INTRODUCTION*.

PRINTERS

The current A+ OS Technologies exam will most likely make sure that you can resolve basic Windows NT or Windows 2000 printing problems. Troubleshooting printing-related issues from within either of these two OSs is basically the same.

There are several questions that you should ask yourself and/or your customer who is having difficulty printing.

Is the printer you are sending a document to set as the default printer in the Printers applet of My Computer or Control Panel? If the desired printer is not set as the default printer, you can rectify this situation by right-clicking the installed printer icon located in the Printers applet and selecting Set as Default Printer. Print the document again. Another way to direct a print job to a specific printer is to select File > Print from within the document you want to print. From the Printer Name drop-down menu, select the installed printer to which you want to direct the print job.

Is there enough memory installed on the print server or user's workstation to handle the print job or jobs that have been submitted to print? It is very common to experience out of memory errors when attempting to print to a locally installed or networked printer. More often than not, there is simply not enough physical memory installed on the system to handle the transition of the print job from the system to the printer. This can be resolved by installing more memory in the system itself.

Is the printer spooler service stalled on the shared network printer? The printer spooler service manages print jobs sent to a Windows NT or Windows 2000 shared network printer. If a print job or multiple print jobs are stalled on a network print server running the spooler service, the simple solution is to stop and start the printer spooler service. In Windows NT, the Services applet is located in the Control Panel. In Windows 2000, the Services applet is located within the Control Panel/Administrative Tools applet.

Do you or the customer have rights to print to the shared printer? As discussed earlier in this chapter, under Resource Sharing and Drive Mapping, file, folder, and printer shares can all be assigned access rights within Windows NT and Windows 2000. If you or a customer cannot access a certain printer share on a network, you may not have been granted the proper rights.

DIAGNOSING AND TROUBLESHOOTING TEST TIPS

The following information is designed to assist you with last-minute study preparation for the current CompTIA A+ exams. Not all of these tips are described within this chapter. However, they are very relevant to the exam, and you should review these important Windows NT diagnosing and troubleshooting test tips before taking the test.

- In all OSs, including Windows Vista, NT, XP and 2000, files, folders and directories are managed using Windows Explorer.

- Windows NT is a multitasking, multithreaded OS that can run applications in their own NTVDMs or virtual memory spaces. NTVDMs (NT Virtual DOS Machines) are part of a built-in Windows NT subsystem that allow 16-bit applications to act as if they are running in their own memory-protected DOS environment. If you are running an application or program that interferes with another application or program, you should attempt to run the offending program in its own protected memory space.

- It is not possible to upgrade to Windows NT 4.0 from Windows 9.x. You can install Windows NT on the same hard drive but not in the same directory as Windows 9.x. However, you can upgrade to Windows 4.0 from Windows NT 3.1 or Windows NT 3.51 OSs.

- Dr. Watson is a Windows NT diagnostic tool that takes a picture, or "snapshot" of a system during an error state or fault. The Windows NT Workstation Dr. Watson log files are stored in C:\WINNT. The A+ exams love to ask questions concerning Doctor Watson!

- Programs and files with the extensions .EXE, .COM, and .BAT can be run from the Windows NT command prompt.

- Windows NT supports port replication through the use of hardware profiles. If you want to ensure that the port replicator works on your laptop while at the office but is ignored while out of the office, you will need to enable Hardware Profiles in the System applet of Control Panel.

- Windows NT supports FAT16 and NTFS partitions. It does not include support for FAT32.

- Windows NT does not have a native Disk Defragmenter utility.

- Windows NT does not have the Device Manager utility that was implemented with Windows 9.x.

- If you ever receive the message `Boot could not find NTLDR. Please insert another disk` while booting into Windows NT, you will need to run the emergency repair process.

- The best way to remove a virus from Windows NT, or any other Windows OS for that matter, is to boot to a virus-free floppy disk and run antivirus software with up-to-date virus definition files.

- You need the files NTLDR, NTDETECT.COM, and BOOT.INI on a boot disk for Windows NT, Windows 2000, and Windows XP.

- If you are using an Internet browser in Windows NT or any other Windows OS to access a secure Internet site, your URL line will most likely begin with HTTPS://.

- If you receive an error message stating that a service failed to start upon booting Windows NT, you can check to see what particular service didn't start in the System Event Log in Event Viewer.

- The file NTBOOTDD.SYS is used by the OSs Windows NT, Windows 2000, and Windows XP to support SCSI hard drives. It must be present at Windows boot-up for SCSI to be supported.
- The BOOT.INI is a required file used by Windows NT/2000/XP at start-up.
- If a user can't log on to the network in a Windows NT/2000 domain environment, the first thing you should check is the user's network credentials, such as their user ID and password.
- If there is no sound coming from your speakers, you should first check the Volume Control applet and verify that no devices are muted.
- There are three easy ways to set the system time: Control Panel > Date/Time; open the clock in the system tray; and from a command prompt, enter "Time".
- In Windows NT 4.0, the command-line utility RDISK.EXE can be used to create an ERD (Emergency Repair Disk).
- You can use the PING command to verify the presence of a remote system.
- Windows NT does not provide native support for USB, FireWire (IEEE 1394), or PnP.
- PING, TRACERT, and NSLOOKUP are TCP/IP utilities that can be used to determine the IP address of known Internet domain names.
- To change a computer name or join a workgroup or domain in Windows NT, right-click on Network Neighborhood, then select Properties > Identification tab > Change.
- After installing a new hard drive, you can prepare the drive for use by accessing the Windows NT utility Disk Administrator and format the drive.

CHAPTER SUMMARY

By reading this chapter, you should have gained enough understanding to install, upgrade, and troubleshoot the Windows NT OS. At this point, you should also have a basic understanding of the following:

- How to create an ERD from within Windows NT
- How the Windows NT domain model is structured
- How the Windows NT authentication process works
- How security and access rights are implemented and supported in Windows NT
- How to access and use some of the many important utilities associated with Windows NT, including User Manager, Task Manager, and Event Viewer, to name a few
- Sharing network resources and establishing drive mapping
- Diagnosing basic printing problems from within Windows NT and Windows 2000

Although it is beyond the scope of this book to cover every detail of this complex OS, you should now have enough knowledge to answer the following review questions, which are designed to fine-tune your skills in preparation for the real CompTIA exams. As always, if you do not understand a topic, or if you require more information, the Microsoft Web site is an invaluable resource.

REVIEW QUESTIONS

1. **You have installed Windows NT Workstation on a computer that is already running Windows 9.X. You cannot see Windows 9.X files from within Windows NT Workstation. What is most likely the problem?**
   ○ A. The Windows NT Workstation partition is FAT32.
   ○ B. The Windows NT Workstation partition is FAT16.
   ○ C. You need to select View > Show All Files in Explorer.
   ○ D. The Windows 9.X partition is FAT32.

   Correct Answer = D

   NTFS and FAT32 are incompatible filesystems. You cannot see across these two partitions when installed on the same hard drive. This question states that you cannot see the Windows 9.X files from within Windows NT Workstation. The obvious choice would be that the Windows 9.X partition is FAT32.

2. **You have just installed Windows NT. You attempt to boot into the OS and receive the message Boot could not find NTLDR. Please insert another disk. What should you do?**
   ○ A. Make a copy of NTLDR from another NT computer and use it in yours.
   ○ B. Run the Emergency Repair Process.
   ○ C. Restart and use the Last Known Good Configuration.
   ○ D. Insert a blank floppy and type "RDISK /S".

   Correct Answer = B

   If you receive the error message Boot could not find NTLDR. Please insert another disk. on boot up, it is advised that you run the Emergency Repair Process. The ERD process will restore your important system files.

3. **Which important files must be located in the root directory of the system partition for Windows NT to boot properly? (Choose Three)**

   ☐ A.   COMMAND.COM
   ☐ B.   NTLDR
   ☐ C.   MSDOS.SYS
   ☐ D.   BOOT.INI
   ☐ E.   NTDETECT.COM
   ☐ F.   IO.SYS

   Correct Answers = B, D, and E

   For NT to boot properly, the files NTLDR, BOOT.INI, and NT DETECT. COM must be located in the root directory of the system partition.

4. **What should you always try first if you can't boot into your Windows NT OS?**

   ○ A.   Reformat the boot partition with FAT16.
   ○ B.   Press F8 on boot up to enter Safe Mode.
   ○ C.   Reinstall from three set-up floppies and the installation CD.
   ○ D.   Use the Last Known Good Configuration option.

   Correct Answer = D

   If you can't boot into your NT OS, you should always first attempt to use the Last Known Good Configuration option on boot up. You can initiate this option by pressing the space bar when you see the Last Know Good Configuration option displayed on the screen at boot up.

5. **You are currently running Windows NT and want to convert your FAT16 partition to NTFS to provide for a more secure OS. What command would you enter at a DOS prompt to do this?**

   ○ A.   `FDISK /MBR`
   ○ B.   `CONVERT C:/FS>NTFS`
   ○ C.   `CONVERT C:/FS:NTFS`
   ○ D.   `FORMAT C:/ FAT16>NTFS`

   Correct Answer = C

   You can always convert a FAT16 partition to NTFS from a command prompt by entering the command `CONVERT C:/FS:NTFS`. `FDISK /MBR` will format your MBR.

6. **What command can you use to bring up the command prompt in Windows NT?**

   ○ A. CMD.EXE
   ○ B. COMMAND.COM
   ○ C. Ctrl-Alt-Del
   ○ D. SYSPOL.EXE

   Correct Answer = A

   The Windows NT command prompt can be accessed by selecting Start > Run and entering "CMD" at the Open line. CMD.EXE is the actual command prompt in Windows NT and Windows 2000.

7. **You want to transfer files from within a Windows NT Workstation volume that is formatted with NTFS, to a Windows 9.X volume that is formatted with FAT32. Which of the following will happen to your files? (Choose Three)**

   ☐ A. They will retain any information stored in the file.
   ☐ B. They will retain their long filenames.
   ☐ C. They will retain their file attributes.
   ☐ D. They will retain their compression status.
   ☐ E. They will retain their encryption status.
   ☐ F. They will retain file-level permissions.

   Correct Answers = A, B, and D

   If you transfer files from an NTFS volume to a FAT32 volume, You will retain information saved within the file, the files' LFN (Long Filename), and the file attributes. However, the files will not remained compressed, they will not remain encrypted, and they will lose file-level permissions.

8. **Which service must be installed to use dial-up networking with Windows NT?**

   ○ A. Dial-Up Networking Service
   ○ B. Dial-Up Networking Monitor Service
   ○ C. Remote Access Service
   ○ D. Windows Installer Service

   Correct Answer = C

   The Remote Access Service must be installed to use dial-up networking with Windows NT.

9. **You have a 20 GB hard drive with Windows NT installed. You are interested in formatting the free space available on the drive, labeling the newly formatted space with a drive letter, and exploring opportunities for a fault-tolerant implementation. Which Windows NT tool would you use?**

   ○ A.   Drive Converter
   ○ B.   Backup
   ○ C.   Disk Administrator
   ○ D.   Partition Administrator

   Correct Answer = C

   The Windows NT Disk Administrator is a very useful administrative tool that offers the abilities to format drive space, assign and change drive labels, and implement fault-tolerance systems by establishing Disk Mirror sets and Disk Stripe Sets.

10. **You believe that your customer is unable to print documents because the wrong printer is set as the Default Printer in the Printer applet of Control Panel. What suggestions do you have to assist with the customer's printing issue? (Choose Two)**

    ☐ A.   Ask the customer to print to a different networked printer.
    ☐ B.   Navigate to the proper printer and choose Set as Default Printer.
    ☐ C.   Tell the customer a reboot should take care of the problem.
    ☐ D.   Reinstall the printer drivers.
    ☐ E.   Have the customer use the Print option from the document File menu and choose a specific printer.

    Correct Answers = B and E

    If the wrong printer is set as the default printer, you will not be able to print documents. The simple solution is to set the desired printer as the default printer. Answers B and E are the proper procedures for setting a default printer or directing a print job to a specific printer.

11. **Which file must be present at Windows NT boot up for SCSI devices to be supported?**

    ○ A.   CMD.EXE
    ○ B.   NTBOOTDD.SYS
    ○ C.   NTVDM.VXD
    ○ D.   NTCONFIG.POL
    ○ E.   None of the above

    Correct Answer = B

The file NTBOOTDD.SYS is used by the OSs Windows NT, 2000, and XP to support SCSI hard drives. It must be present at Windows boot up for SCSI to be supported.

CMD.EXE is the 32-bit command interpreter for Windows NT, Windows 2000, and Windows XP. NTVDM.VXD is an invalid selection that is in place to fool you. NTCONFIG.POL is the name of the Windows NT policy that is created by using the System Policy Editor.

12. **Where does Dr. Watson store his log files in Windows NT?**
    - ○ A. C:\Windows
    - ○ B. C:\
    - ○ C. C:\WINNT
    - ○ D. On a highly fault-tolerant RAID 5 Array
    - ○ E. None of the above.

Correct Answer = C

Dr. Watson is a Windows NT diagnostic tool that takes a picture or "snapshot" of a system during an error state or fault. The Windows NT workstation Dr. Watson log files are stored in C:\WINNT.

13. **Which of the following is a graphical interface used in Windows to manage files, folders, and directories?**
    - ○ A. Event Viewer
    - ○ B. Windows Arrow
    - ○ C. Event Manager
    - ○ D. Explorer
    - ○ E. None of the above

Correct Answer = D

Windows Explorer is the graphical utility used to manage files, folders, and directories in most versions of Windows, including Windows NT, Me, 2000, XP, and Vista. Just right-click the Start button and choose the Explore option. The Event Viewer is used to display events that occur on a system. Windows Arrow is an invalid option, although Windows Aero is real and provides an intuitive interface in Windows Visa. Event Manager is used in Event Viewer to manage certain events and can be started from the Event Viewer icon in the Control Panel.

14. **Which of the following statements are true regarding the advantages of NTFS over FAT32? (Choose Two)**

    ☐ A.   NTFS offers disk compression.
    ☐ B.   NTFS is only available in 16-bit OSs.
    ☐ C.   NTFS provides file- and folder-level security.
    ☐ D.   NTFS offers the ability to get free unlimited Internet and cell phone usage.
    ☐ E.   If you buy an OS configured with NTFS, Microsoft will give you a second free.

    Correct Answers = A and C

    NTFS is more efficient than FAT32 in terms of security and data retrieval. It offers file and folder level security as well as disk compression and encryption abilities. Microsoft doesn't really offer anything for free accept TechNet magazine, and you have to get certified before you can get that.

15. **You are considering a backup strategy for a new client. Which of the following backup strategies backs up all of the files that have been changed or been created since the last full backup?**

    ○ A.   Internal
    ○ B.   Complete
    ○ C.   Incremental
    ○ D.   Differential
    ○ E.   Partial
    ○ F.   None of the above

    Correct Answer = D

    A differential backup backs up all files that have changed or been created since the last full backup. An incremental backs up files that have changed or created since the last incremental backup. Internal, complete, and partial are not valid types of backup strategies.

16. **You are having problems with currently running processes and applications on your system. Which combination of keystrokes will open the Task Manager so you can troubleshoot these issues?**

    ○ A.   Ctrl-Alt-Tab
    ○ B.   Ctrl-Alt-Del
    ○ C.   Q-W-E-R-T-Y
    ○ D.   Ctrl-Shift-Del
    ○ E.   Alt-Task Manager quick start key
    ○ F.   None of the above

Correct Answer = B

The Windows Task Manager displays programs, processes, and services currently running on your system. You can use Task Manager to monitor performance and or to close programs that are not responding. All other choices are invalid. However, they should have a quick start Task Manager key!

17. **You have loaded new device drivers for users running Windows NT, 2000, XP, and Vista. The systems are now experiencing problems. You want to log back in to all systems using the registry and drivers that previously worked. Which of the following Advanced Boot options would help you accomplish this?**

   ○ A. Last Known Good Configuration
   ○ B. Safe Mode
   ○ C. Safe Mode with Networking
   ○ D. Passenger Restore
   ○ E. Driver Restore
   ○ F. None of the above

Correct Answer = A

There are several Advanced Boot options offered in Windows NT, 2000, XP, and Vista. The option you choose depends on the system problems observed. Using the Last Known Good Configuration option starts Windows with the last registry and driver configuration that worked. Safe Mode is used to start a system with basic drivers and will not work here.

18. **You have a Windows NT and a Windows XP system. Neither system will boot into the OS during the boot processes. Which of the following files do you suspect is corrupt?**

   ○ A. BOOT.DAT
   ○ B. NTLDR
   ○ C. BOOTSECT.DOS
   ○ D. NTDETECT.COM
   ○ E. XPDETECT.COM
   ○ F. None of the above

Correct Answer = B

NTLDR is a boot process file responsible for loading the OS during boot operations. BOOTSECT.DOS stores boot sector information of other OSs loaded on a system. NTDETECT.COM detects the hardware in a system.

19. **For file and folder security purposes, you are converting all of your client's FAT partitions to NTFS. Which of the following choices would you consider using to achieve this goal?**

    ○ A. In Windows Explorer, right-click the FAT volume, and select Tools > Convert to NTFS.

    ○ B. In Windows Explorer, right-click the FAT volume you want to convert, and select Convert to NTFS.

    ○ C. From a command prompt, run convert c: /fr:ntfs.

    ○ D. None of the above.

    Correct Answer = D

    The correct answer here is D. None of the available options will work! To convert the FAT partitions to NTFS, you would run the `convert c: /fs:ntfs` command from the command line. Notice in choice C, the command is invalid. It is likely you will see a similar question on the real exams so pay close attention.

20. **You are having problems with TCP/IP addressing on several systems and need to view IP configurations from a command line. Which TCP/IP command would you use on these systems to view their IP configurations?**

    ○ A. `Ip/Config`

    ○ B. `Ipconfig`

    ○ C. `Config/IP`

    ○ D. `Config/all`

    ○ E. None of the above

    Correct Answer = B

    The `Ipconfig` command will display the current IP address, the subnet mask, DNS server, DHCP server, and more information. For troubleshooting IP configurations, this is the way to go.

REFERENCES

www.microsoft.com. The minimum and recommended hardware requirements for Windows NT Server as well as other Microsoft OSs can be found at this Microsoft Web site.

www.microsoft.com/whdc/hcl/default.mspx. This Microsoft Web page offers access to the HCL that can help you verify if your hardware is supported by Windows NT.

http://support.microsoft.com/support/kb/articles/Q141/3/77.ASP. This Microsoft site compares the differences between REGEDIT.EXE and REGEDT32.EXE.

www2.rad.com/networks/1997/telnet/proj.htm#INTRODUCTION. This www2.rad.com Web site has an excellent description of how the Telnet protocol really works.

13 Windows 2000

OVERVIEW OF WINDOWS 2000

In case you haven't heard, Windows 2000 was built on Windows NT technology. And you were wondering why there was a Windows NT chapter in this A+ Study Guide. There is your answer!

If you have used Windows 2000 Professional or Windows 2000 Server to any extent, you may have noticed that the Windows 2000 family of operating systems was built with a combination of the best Microsoft operating system technologies available, including Windows 9.x and Windows NT.

As you may recall, Windows 9.x is suitable for client workstation use and supports only FAT16 and FAT32 partitions. Unlike Windows NT, it does not support file-level security. Windows 9.x offers built-in Disk Defragmenter and Device Manager utilities, which are very useful tools for maintaining hard drives and troubleshooting hardware devices and drivers, respectively.

Windows NT was developed for a domain structure environment and offers better security and administration capabilities than Windows 9.x, but it only provides support for FAT16 and NTFS partitions. Windows NT does not have a native Disk Defragmenter utility and does not offer the Device Manager that was available in Windows 9.x.

Windows 2000 combines the functionality of Windows 9.x and Windows NT by including the following features:

- Support for FAT16, FAT32, NTFS, and CDFS file systems (Windows 2000 does not support HPFS)
- A built-in Disk Defragmenter utility
- A built-in Device Manager utility
- Safe Mode support similar to Windows 9.x
- File-level and folder-level security
- Full administrative support for a client/server environment

In addition to the combined features included from the previous operating systems, Windows 2000 offers many new technologies and improvements. We will discuss many important Windows 2000 advances in this chapter. Here are some of the most notable:

Improved security: Windows 2000 offers file- and folder-level encryption with Encrypting File System (EFS). EFS uses public and private encryption keys. To decrypt a file or folder, you must be the one who originally encrypted it or be a recovery agent.

Better support for hardware: Windows 2000 offers better overall support for PnP, USB, and infrared.

Better support for laptops: Windows 2000 assists with the overall performance of laptop computers by providing Advanced Configuration and Power Interface (ACPI) and smart battery.

Active Directory: Windows 2000 Server provides Active Directory, which gives administrators a single point to manage network objects and resources.

Better disk management capabilities: Windows 2000 makes use of disk quotas, which allow administrators to restrict the amount of hard drive space a particular user can use. Disk quotas can be applied to volumes or users.

Better support for the Internet: Windows 2000 supports Dynamic HTML (DHTML) as well as Extensible Markup Language (XML), which helps Web developers create better solutions for businesses.

Windows 2000 file system protection: Windows 2000 has a built-in backup feature called Windows File Protection that keeps a backup of important system files. If you write over important system files with programs or applications, Windows File Protection prompts you that it needs to restore the important system files you just replaced.

WINDOWS 2000 INSTALLATION PROCESS

Before installing Windows 2000 or any other Windows operating system, you must verify that your computer meets the minimum hardware requirements. The minimum hardware requirements for Windows 2000 Professional are as follows:

- 133 MHz Pentium processor
- 2 GB hard drive with 650 MB of free drive space
- 64 MB of RAM
- VGA monitor
- Keyboard
- Mouse
- 12x CD-ROM (not required for over-the-network installation)

The second pre-installation step is to verify that your hardware is in compliance with the Hardware Compatibility List (HCL) located at *www.microsoft.com/whdc/hcl/search.mspx.*

The Windows 2000 Professional installation CD-ROM contains a copy of the HCL, but this HCL is outdated. Your best bet is to visit the Web site to review the most recent hardware compatibility updates.

Next, you need to choose one of three Windows 2000 Professional installation methods. The three installation methods and their general descriptions are as follows.

CD-ROM INSTALLATION

Installing Windows 2000 Professional by CD-ROM is by far the easiest method. If your system BIOS supports the ability to boot to CD-ROM, all you have to do is place the installation CD-ROM in your CD drive and reboot. The installation process will begin by copying the installation files to your hard drive. Your system is then rebooted, and the GUI phase of the installation process begins.

Four Setup Disks

The Windows 2000 Professional CD-ROM can create four installation floppy disks to be used for installation if your system cannot boot from a CD-ROM.

If you are currently running DOS or Windows 3.x, open the Bootdisk folder located on the Windows 2000 Professional Installation CD-ROM and run the makeboot.exe program. If you are currently running Windows 9.x, Windows NT, or Windows 2000, run the makebt32.exe program, which is also located in the Bootdisk folder on the installation CD-ROM. After you have created all four floppy disks, place the first disk in the floppy drive and restart the system.

NETWORK INSTALLATION

To implement an over-the-network installation of Windows 2000 Professional, you need to copy the entire contents of the Windows 2000 Professional CD-ROM to a shared network folder. It is advisable to have this shared location on a server computer. In Windows 2000 lingo, this server is called a *distribution server*.

To begin an over-the-network installation from a Windows 9.x client or Windows NT Workstation, connect to the shared folder and execute the winnt32.exe program. To perform an over-the-network installation from a blank hard drive, boot the system from a bootable network floppy disk, and execute the winnt.exe program from the distribution server.

No matter which installation method you choose, the Windows 2000 installation process will progress through the following modes and steps:

Text mode setup:

1. A partition for Windows 2000 is created.
2. A file system is chosen.
3. The partition on which the file system will be installed may need to be formatted.
4. The installation files are copied to the hard drive.
5. Setup Wizard (GUI mode of setup) commences.
6. Choose your regional settings.
7. Enter the name and organization.
8. Enter the product key.
9. Enter a 15-character computer name.
10. Select and enter a local administrator account password.
11. Enter the date and time.
12. Network configuration commences.

13. Setup attempts to autodetect installed NICs and proceeds to install Windows networking protocols and services, including TCP/IP, file and print sharing, and the Client for Microsoft Networks.
14. You are prompted to join the computer to a workgroup or a domain.

Final phase of installation:

15. Startup menu shortcuts are created.
16. Installation configurations are saved to the hard drive.
17. Temporary installation files are removed.
18. The system restarts.

AUTOMATED INSTALLATION

Although you will not be tested on the fine details of carrying out an automated installation of Windows 2000, it is important that you have a basic understanding of the tools used to carry out this type of installation. Passing the A+ exam is an important step toward a career in the computer industry. Understanding and implementing the newest operating system tools is just as important.

Like Windows NT, Windows 2000 offers the ability to carry out automated, unattended installations. To configure and carry out these types of Windows 2000 Professional installations, you need to understand the following three important installation tools—Setup Manager, SYSPREP, and RIS—and you must do some planning.

SETUP MANAGER

The Windows 2000 installation CD-ROM comes with a utility called Setup Manager. Setup Manager can be used to create an unattended installation file called UNATTEND.TXT. UNATTEND.TXT is a file that Setup Manager uses to store and automate answers to installation questions that would normally have to be answered by a person sitting at a computer.

To install Setup Manager and implement the UNATTEND.TXT file, you must first extract Setup Manager from the Windows 2000 installation CD-ROM. To do this, navigate to the *Support\Tools* folder located on the CD-ROM, and double-click the file DEPLOY.CAB. Next, you extract the file's SETUPMGR.EXE and SETUPMGR.DLL to a common folder located on the hard drive. To do this, right-click each file (separately), and select the extract option. After this process is complete, executing the SETUPMGR.EXE file on the hard drive starts a wizard that allows you to create the UNATTEND.TXT file and asks you which options you want UNATTEND.TXT to perform. You can also use UNATTEND.TXT to create an automated installation of SYSPREP or RIS. SYSPREP and RIS will be mentioned shortly.

Here are some of the installation questions that can be answered by using UNATTEND.TXT.

■ Confirmation (agreement) to the End-User License (EULA)
■ Name and organization
■ Computer name
■ Password for the local administrator account
■ Display settings, such as monitor refresh rate and number of colors
■ Network settings, such as protocols, services, and IP address settings
■ Whether to join a workgroup or a domain
■ Time zone settings

If you recall the installation process mentioned earlier in the chapter, these bulleted items should look familiar to you.

System Preparation Tool (SYSPREP)

The System Preparation Tool (SYSPREP) is a Windows 2000 utility that allows you to prepare for the creation of a Windows 2000 disk image by making sure that the Security Identifiers (SIDs) are unique for all target systems that will have an image copied to them.

With the use of third-party disk-imaging software, such as Symantec Ghost, an exact duplicate or mirror image of a system can be made and distributed to multiple systems on a network. SYSPREP prepares a system for this image. Besides generating a unique computer SID (Sysprep's job is to *remove* the SID so that you won't ghost multiple systems with the same SID), SYSPREP contains a mini setup wizard that is used to specify settings such as computer name, regional settings, network settings, time zone, and workgroup or domain membership.

SYSPREP is a very useful tool for configuring many computers with the same operating system, configuration settings, and software. The process for installing SYSPREP as well as RIS was described under "Setup Manager" earlier in this chapter.

Remote Installation Service (RIS)

RIS is a Windows 2000 Server utility service that is used to deploy Windows 2000 Professional to connected client computers over a network. You can use RIS to deploy the images you have created with third-party software to connected systems, to generate images with the RIS Server software, or to repair bad or corrupted installations you have already deployed. For more information regarding RIS, visit the Microsoft TechNet site at *http://technet.microsoft.com/en-us/library/Bb742378.aspx.*

WINDOWS 2000 UPGRADE PROCEDURES

Windows 2000 offers several upgrade paths. The following operating systems can be upgraded to Windows 2000:

- Windows 95 (All Versions)
- Windows 98 (All Versions)
- Windows NT 3.51
- Windows NT 4.0

Before upgrading to a new operating system, your first consideration should always be to make a complete backup of the current operating system and data. This is crucial if you want to have a path back to your current operating system and information. Next, you should scan your current operating system with updated antivirus software so that any viruses are not transferred during the upgrade process. Finally, you should uncompress any compressed drives.

Upgrading from a previously installed operating system to Windows 2000 is a fairly simple task. The most important thing to keep in mind for a successful upgrade is that the Windows 2000 setup program must be run from within the operating system you want to upgrade for your settings and information to be transferred to Windows 2000. To upgrade from Windows 9.x or Windows NT using the Windows 2000 installation CD-ROM, do the following:

1. Boot your system into Windows 9.x or Windows NT.
2. Insert the Windows 2000 installation CD-ROM.
3. If your system autodetects the installation CD-ROM, your current operating system is detected, and you are asked if you want to upgrade to Windows 2000. Select Yes if you want to upgrade, and continue with the upgrade process. If the installation CD-ROM is not autodetected, select Start > Run, and type in the CD-ROM drive letter, followed by "\I386\WINNT32.EXE", and click OK.

To upgrade from Windows 9.x or Windows NT to Windows 2000 over a network, do the following:

4. From within the operating system you want to upgrade, connect to a network share that contains the Windows 2000 installation or setup files.
5. Navigate to and run *\I386\WINNT32.EXE* from the shared network location.
6. Answer Yes to perform the upgrade, and follow the installation instructions provided.

If you have trouble running a previously installed application after you have upgraded to a new operating system, you are advised to reinstall the application on the upgraded operating system.

WHAT ABOUT WINDOWS ME (MILLENNIUM EDITION)?

There is no recommended upgrade path provided by Microsoft to upgrade from Windows Me to Windows 2000. This is because Windows 2000 was actually released before Windows Me. That's right, Windows 2000 is not a supported upgrade from Windows Me.

If you attempt to upgrade to Windows 2000 Professional from within the Windows Me operating system, you will most likely encounter a message stating that the version of Windows you are attempting to install is newer, and you will be asked if you want to upgrade. If you select OK to the upgrade, you will most likely encounter the following error message:

```
Cannot load C:\windows\upgdlls\w95upg.dll\WIN9XUPG\W95UPG.DLL.
```

This is because Windows 2000 is looking for the upgrade path from Windows 9.x! Windows Me is described in much more detail in Chapter 11.

For more information regarding this unsupported Microsoft upgrade, visit the following Microsoft site: *http://support.microsoft.com/default.aspx?scid=kb; en-us;272627.*

WINDOWS 2000 START-UP PROCESS

The current A+ exam will most likely focus on your ability to use the Windows 2000 tools that are available during the start-up process or boot sequence to complete or troubleshoot a system that will not completely boot into the operating system. Pay special attention to such tools as the Last Known Good Configuration option in the Advanced Options menu (described immediately after the start-up process). It is more likely that the exam will target your ability to use these tools than expect you to have memorized the fine details of the Windows 2000 start-up process.

The steps in the Windows 2000 start-up process are as follows:

1. The POST (power-on self-test) is run.
2. The start-up process begins, and PnP devices are recognized.
3. The MBR (Master Boot Record) is located and processed.

4. NTLDR.COM (bootstrap loader) is loaded. The hardware detection phase begins.
5. The BOOT.INI is loaded, and the operating systems are detected. If multiple operating systems are located in the BOOT.INI, BOOTSECT.DOS is processed, allowing a system to boot with Windows 9.x, Windows Me, or DOS. Remember for the exam that multiple boot options are specified in the BOOT.INI file at system start-up.
6. NTDETECT.COM runs. Hardware and hardware profiles are detected.
7. The Windows 2000 kernel (NTOSKRNL.EXE) is loaded.
8. HAL.DLL is loaded, which creates the hardware abstraction layer.
9. The system reads the registry and loads all necessary device drivers.
10. The logon process begins with the execution of WINLOGON.EXE.

ADVANCED OPTIONS MENU

You should recall from Chapter 11 that Windows 9.x offers a start-up menu that provides several boot configuration options to be used for troubleshooting purposes. Windows 2000 offers a similar feature called the Advanced Options menu. When the Windows 2000 boot sequence is in its final phase, the Starting Windows screen appears. At this point, the option to press the F8 key and enter the Advanced Options menu is presented. If you press the F8 key, you will be offered the following options:

- Safe Mode
- Safe Mode with Networking
- Safe Mode with Command Prompt
- Enable Boot Logging
- Enable VGA Mode
- Last Known Good Configuration
- Directory Services Restore Mode (Windows 2000 domain controllers only)
- Debugging Mode
- Boot Normally

You should already be familiar with the functions of several of these options from our previous discussions of the Windows 9.x start-up menu. The most important point that can be made here is that you should not completely advance into the Windows 2000 operating system if you have experienced trouble at start-up. Instead, press the F8 key, and choose the Last Known Good Configuration option. This loads the last known good registry settings (HKEY_LOCAL_MACHINE\System\CurrentControlSet) and allows you to boot into the operating system successfully if you have not already logged on to the system with a bad configuration.

RECOVERY CONSOLE

The Windows 2000 installation CD-ROM comes with a utility called the Windows 2000 Recovery Console. The Recovery Console can be used to assist with the recovery of a computer system that is having problems starting or will not boot into an operating system at all.

The Windows 2000 Recovery Console can be installed so that it is available at system start-up by navigating to the i386 folder located on the installation CD-ROM and entering the command "WINNT32 /CMDCONS". This makes the Recovery Console option available when Windows 2000 boots up. The Recovery Console can also be used to copy system files to a hard drive and configure services that will be available when the system boots into the operating system.

DUAL BOOTING

With Windows 2000, you can set up your computer for several different dual-booting scenarios. Windows 2000 can be dual booted with DOS, Windows 3.x, Windows 9.x, Windows Me, and Windows NT. However, some very strict rules apply to dual booting with Windows 2000, depending on the booting scenario you want to create.

Here are some general rules to consider before installing multiple operating systems in a dual-boot scenario with Windows 2000:

- Each operating system you install must be installed and configured on a separate volume. Microsoft does not support multiple operating systems installed on the same volume with Windows 2000. This is mainly to ensure that each operating system can maintain separate configuration settings and file structures. Each operating system is considered separate. All programs and drivers installed on one particular operating system are considered separate from any other installed operating systems.
- The volume that the system is booted from must be formatted with the proper file system to support the dual-boot configuration. For example, if you are going to dual boot between Windows 2000 or Windows NT and Windows 9.x, the volume that the system boots to must be formatted as FAT.
- Windows 2000 should be installed after DOS, Windows 95, or Windows Me. If you install Windows 2000 first and then attempt to install DOS, Windows 95, or Windows Me, you will write over important system and boot files. The following section describes the proper order of operating system installations necessary to achieve specific dual booting goals.
- To dual boot between DOS Windows 95 or Windows 98 or Windows Me and Windows 2000, install DOS first, followed by Windows 95 or Windows 98 or Windows Me followed by the Windows 2000 installation.

■ To dual boot between Windows NT 4.0 and Windows 2000, install Windows NT 4.0 first, followed by Windows 2000. If you are using an NTFS partition with Windows NT 4.0, make sure that you have installed a minimum of NT Service Pack 4 so that your Windows NT 4.0 NTFS partition can access files on the Windows 2000 NTFS 5 partition.

After you have installed multiple operating systems on your hard drive, you can navigate to the Startup and Recovery Window and choose a default operating system. The default operating system displayed in Figure 13.1 is Windows 2000 Professional. The default operating system is the one that will be booted into when your system boots up. You can change the default operating system by selecting the Default Operating System drop-down menu, and selecting the installed operating system to be used as the default. You can also change the time limit for which the list of operating systems is displayed at system start-up. To access the system Startup and Recovery window, navigate to Control Panel > System > Advanced > Startup and Recovery.

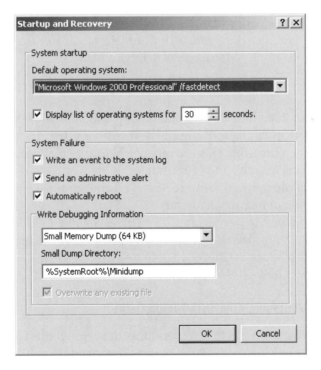

FIGURE 13.1   Choosing a default OS in the Startup and Recovery window.

WINDOWS 2000 TOOLS AND UTILITIES

Although Windows 2000 is similar to Windows NT and offers many of the same tools and utilities, such as Task Manager and Event Viewer, Windows 2000 is a much more robust operating system that offers many new useful utilities, tools, and newly designed wizards. In this section, we focus on the Windows 2000 tools and utilities you are most likely to be tested on in the current A+ exams.

DEVICE MANAGER

The Device Manager was discussed in detail in Chapter 11. As you may recall, Device Manager is available in Windows 9.x, Windows Me, and Windows XP but not with Windows NT. It is a useful utility that is a welcomed feature with Windows 2000.

Device Manager lists all the hardware devices that are attached to a system and ensures that the devices are operating properly. You can troubleshoot devices, view device resources, and update drivers for specific devices by double-clicking on a device listed in the Device Manager utility and selecting the appropriate option.

To access Device Manager in Windows 2000 Professional, navigate to Control Panel > System > Hardware > Device Manager, or Control Panel > Administrative Tools > Computer Management > Device Manager.

DRIVER SIGNING

Windows 2000 offers Driver Signing options that allow you to prevent or block users from installing software and device drivers that are not digitally signed or approved by Microsoft. This is a very useful feature that can save administrators and technicians from having to reconfigure systems that have been corrupted by unsigned or unapproved software or driver installations. To navigate to and block the installation of unassigned drivers, select Start > Settings > Control Panel > System > Hardware > Driver Signing. The Driver Signing Options window appears (see Figure 13.2). By default, the option to warn users when an unsigned driver or file is installed is selected. Choose the option to block the installation of unsigned files, and select OK.

ADMINISTRATIVE TOOLS AND COMPUTER MANAGEMENT

There are many ways to access administrative programs and carry out administrative tasks in Windows 2000. You can use individual utilities and programs, create your own administrative console with Microsoft Management Console (MMC) and snap-in programs, or use preconfigured tools, such as Computer Management,

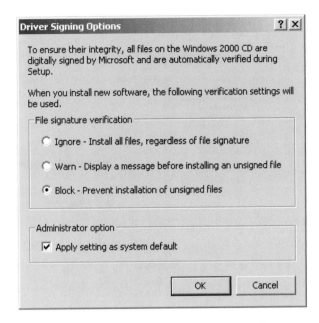

FIGURE 13.2   The Driver Signing Options window.

to carry out many administrative duties from one central location. The MMC will be discussed in more detail later in the chapter.

The Windows 2000 Control Panel is the Administrative Tools folder contains many useful tools that were present with Windows NT 4.0, such as Performance Monitor, Event Viewer, Services, and Local Security Policy. This folder also contains an icon for a very useful administrative tool known as Computer Management. Computer Management is a prepackaged group of administrative programs, otherwise known as *MMC snap-ins*, which can be administered from one central location. As shown in Figure 13.3, Computer Management provides quick access to system resources and tools such as Device Manager, Event Viewer, System Information, and Local Users and Groups. You can also manage disks and logical drives, and run Disk Defragmenter from the Storage section of the Computer Management tree. You can quickly access the Computer Management window by right-clicking on the My Computer Desktop icon and selecting Manage.

LOCAL USERS AND GROUPS

The Local Users and Groups snap-in (see Figure 13.3) is the Windows 2000 Professional replacement for the User Manager, which was available with Windows NT 4.0 Workstation. Using this tool, you can add and remove users, make new local

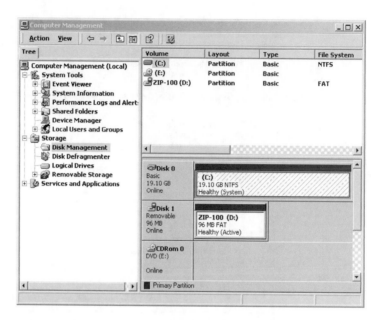

FIGURE 13.3   The Computer Management window.

groups, add users to groups, assign user profiles (profiles are discussed later in this chapter), set passwords, and disable or unlock user accounts.

Windows 2000 Professional comes with built-in accounts for Administrator and Guest. The built-in groups available with Windows 2000 Professional are Administrator, Power Users, Backup Operators, Replicator, Users, and Guests. Each of these groups has built-in, pre-assigned permissions that allow user accounts assigned to a particular group to have special rights. The most powerful group is the Administrator group. Administrators have the privileges to carry out all tasks. Power Users have some administrative privileges and can install legacy applications. Backup Operators can back up and restore files and folders. The Replicator group is used for replicating directories. The Users group has very basic privileges. All users of the system are automatically added to the Users group.

The Guest group is similar to the Users group and has very limited rights to the system.

BACKUP UTILITY

The Backup utility has been revamped and included with Windows 2000. The newly designed Backup utility provides useful backup and restore wizards that can be used to design a backup or restoration job for files on a local machine or over the network.

As displayed in Figure 13.4, the Backup utility also offers the ability to create an ERD (Emergency Repair Disk).

Windows 2000 does not offer the ability to create an ERD using the Windows NT 4.0 utility RDISK.EXE.

You can use the Windows 2000 Backup utility to back up information from one file system type and restore the information to another file system type. For example, you can back up files located on an NTFS partition and restore the files to a FAT32 partition, but you must keep in mind that NTFS and FAT32 are not compatible file systems. However, it is possible for a Windows 2000 machine to have one partition formatted with NTFS and another with FAT32. If you restore to FAT32 from NTFS, you will retain long file names and file attributes, but you will lose file properties such as compression, encryption, and permission values.

DISK MANAGEMENT AND VOLUME TYPES

As discussed in Chapter 12, Windows NT 4.0 uses the Disk Administrator tool to manage hard disks and logical drives. Windows 2000 has a similar tool called Disk Management, which offers the ability to manage hard disks, logical drives, and dynamic disks (discussed in the next section).

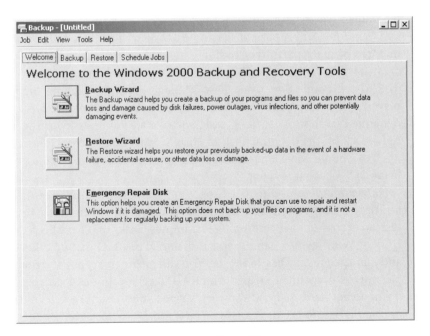

FIGURE 13.4   The Windows 2000 Backup utility.

To access the Windows 2000 Disk Management tool, open Control Panel > Administrative Tools > Computer Management > Storage > Disk Management. The Disk Management tool gathers information about local physical drives and displays information similar to that shown earlier in Figure 13.3.

With the Disk Management tool, you can change the drive letter and path for a disk or logical drive, format a drive, delete a logical drive, delete a partition, or mark a partition as active.

Similar to Disk Administrator in Windows NT 4.0, Windows 2000 Disk Management provides support for RAID levels 0, 1, and 5, which include striped volumes, mirrored volumes, and disk striping with parity. You should note that RAID levels 1 and 5 are only available in the Server versions of Windows NT 4.0 and Windows 2000. As you may recall, RAID levels were described in detail in Chapter 12.

The Disk Manager tool also supports simple and spanned volumes. Simple volumes are constructed from space on one physical disk drive. Spanned volumes are made up of areas of disk space located on different physical disks, which are combined to form one logical drive space.

Basic and Dynamic Disks

Windows 2000 supports two disk storage types known as basic and dynamic disks. A *basic disk* is one that has been configured or "partitioned" with the traditional techniques we are familiar with from our previous studies of DOS, Windows 9.x, and Windows NT. A basic disk can be configured to have four primary partitions or three primary partitions and an extended partition. By default, a basic disk is created when Windows 2000 is installed. After installation, you can convert a basic disk to a dynamic disk using Disk Manager by right-clicking the basic disk displayed in Disk Manager and selecting Upgrade to Dynamic Disk. To convert a dynamic disk back to a basic disk, remove all volumes from the dynamic disk, right-click on the dynamic disk in Disk Manager, and select Revert to Basic Disk.

You should leave a hard disk configured as basic if you want to access its data from DOS or Windows 9.x.

Dynamic disks are areas of space on a single disk, or areas combined from multiple disks, created and organized using volume techniques to organize areas instead of traditional partitioning techniques. Disks that have been configured with DOS or Windows 9.x cannot access dynamic disks. Dynamic disks can be created and managed using Disk Manager. You can create five types of dynamic disks: simple, mirrored, spanned, striped, and RAID level 5 volumes. According to Microsoft, if you do not need spanned volumes, striped volumes, mirrored volumes, or RAID-5 sets, it is best to use basic disks.

It is highly likely that you will be asked questions about dynamic disks on the exams. Windows 2000, Windows XP, and Windows Vista all support the use of dynamic disks. Older operating systems such as Windows 9.x and Me do not support dynamic disks.

Disk Quotas

Disk quotas can be implemented in Windows 2000 to track and control the amount of disk space used by a particular user or disk volume. To enable quota management, right-click on the disk from Windows Explorer or My Computer, select Properties, choose the Quota tab, and choose the appropriate options to suit your administrative needs. Disk quotas can be used only for volumes configured with NTFS.

With disk quotas, an administrator can do the following:

- Limit the amount of disk space used by a user, and create an event log message if this limit has been met.
- Create an event log message if a user or volume has met a warning level set for the amount of disk space specified.

The exams love to target disk quotas. You better know what disk quotas are and when to use them!

Compression and Encryption

If your Windows 2000 system is configured with NTFS, you can take advantage of compression and encryption. Compression allows the size of files and folders to be reduced so they do not use as much disk space as they would if they were uncompressed. To compress or uncompress a file or folder in Windows 2000, simply right-click on a file or folder from within Windows Explorer and select Properties. From the General tab, click the Advanced button. The Advanced Attributes window appears (see Figure 13.5). From this window you can compress a file or a folder in the Compress or Encrypt attributes section.

If files are compressed, they will be displayed in a different color in Windows Explorer. The default color for compressed files and folders is blue.

Files and folders created on NTFS partitions can be encrypted. *Encryption* is a feature of EFS that allows you to secure volumes, files, and folders. You can set the encryption attribute for a file or folder to secure its contents from the Compress or Encrypt attributes section (see Figure 13.5). To decrypt a file or folder, you must be the creator of the file or folder, or be an Encrypted Data Recovery Agent (EDRA).

FIGURE 13.5   Setting compression and encryption attributes.

 Heads up! Security is a primary concern in today's technical world. The exams will ask you questions regarding encryption.

LOCAL SECURITY POLICY

As mentioned at the beginning of this section, the Local Security Policy icon can be accessed from the Administrative Tools folder located in the Windows 2000 Control Panel. Policies are used in Windows 2000 to enforce certain rules and restrictions on user accounts to protect the integrity of the operating system and to provide administrators with the ability to audit important events.

If you open the Local Security Policy icon, you will see that you can make security policy and settings changes for the following policies:

Account Policies: You can use the Account Policies section to create and apply a Password Policy and an Account Lockout Policy. This allows you to apply policies that force the implementation of such items as minimum or maximum password age, password length, and account lockout after so many failed password attempts.

Local Policies: These policies include an Audit Policy, User Rights Assignment, and Security Options. This is where you enable the auditing of events, such as File and Object Access and System events in Windows 2000. You can also make changes to the rights that users and groups have on the local machine from this area.

Public Key Policies: This policy is part of the Windows 2000 EFS that allows the recovery of lost data by designated recovery agents. In this area, administrators can create and add EDRAs, which can be used to unlock or decrypt encrypted files and folders that have been encrypted by other users.

MICROSOFT MANAGEMENT CONSOLE

Windows 2000 offers Microsoft Management Console (MMC), which is used to provide a personalized central location for administration through the installation of snap-ins. Snap-ins are applications that represent the various utilities and tools available in Windows 2000, such as the Disk Defragmenter, Device Manager, Computer Policies, Event Viewer, Services, and Certificates, just to name a few. To navigate to and personalize your own Management Console, select Start > Run, and enter "MMC" in the Open line. Click OK. A somewhat empty-looking Management Console appears. To add or remove snap-in programs, select Console from the menu options bar. Next, select Add/Remove Snap-in, and from the Stand Alone tab, select Add. A list of available standalone snap-in programs is presented. Simply choose the programs you want to design your own console.

REGISTRY EDITORS

Like Windows NT 4.0, the Windows 2000 Registry holds system configuration and environmental settings that can be directly edited with utilities such as REGEDIT.EXE and REGEDT32.EXE. To edit the Windows 2000 Registry directly using either of these utilities, select Start > Run, enter either "REGEDIT" or "REGEDT32" on the Open line, and select OK. The REGEDIT utility is an easy tool to use if you need to locate a specific registry key. The REGEDT32 utility is more useful for editing specific registry keys.

Normal users should never have the ability to directly edit the registry.

SYSTEM CONFIGURATION UTILITY

The System Configuration utility, known as MSCONFIG.EXE in Windows 9.x, is also available in Windows 2000. It provides a graphical display of important system information, such as hardware resources, components, software, and Internet

Explorer settings and information. One of the most useful features of the System Configuration utility is the System Summary. The System Summary gives detailed information about the system, including the installed operating system, system name, BIOS version, time zone, total physical memory, physical memory available, and many other important system values.

The System Configuration utility also gives you the ability to quickly launch programs, such as Disk Cleanup, Dr. Watson, Hardware Wizard, and the Windows Backup utility.

To access the System Configuration Utility in Windows 2000, select Start > Programs > Accessories > System Tools > System Information, or select Start > Run, enter "WINMSD" at the Open line, and press Enter. The System Summary appears by default. If you want to launch any of the other tools, such as Disk Cleanup, from the menu bar, select Tools > Windows > Disk Cleanup or any of the other programs listed.

POWER MANAGEMENT AND OPTIONS

In the Windows 2000 Control Panel, you will notice an icon for Power Options. From within Power Options, you can configure power schemes that are designed to help reduce the amount of power consumed by devices attached to your system. The following are the built-in power schemes available from the drop-down menu in the Power Options Properties/Power Schemes window:

- Home/Office Desk
- Portable Laptop
- Presentation
- Always On
- Minimal Power Management
- Max Battery

You can change the default power settings for each of the power schemes displayed by selecting the appropriate power scheme and changing the settings listed in the Settings for section, below the Power Schemes section. The three built-in options that can be changed are Turn off monitor, Turn off hard disks, and System standby.

ACTIVE DIRECTORY

Windows 2000 Server offers a directory service known as Active Directory. Active Directory provides a hierarchical view of network objects and provides a central location from which all resources on a network can be managed. With Active

Directory, administrators can easily view and make changes to user IDs, permissions, rights, computer systems, printers, and any other objects listed in Active Directory. It is not likely that you will encounter many questions about Active Directory on the A+ exams because this robust Windows 2000 server component has its own exam.

PROFILES

Windows NT and Windows 2000 use user profiles to customize and provide desktop environments for computers and users. Specific settings for the network, printers, modems, and display options, as well as many other settings can be configured to provide special desktop atmospheres for users. Three types of user profiles can be implemented in Windows 2000: local profiles, roaming profiles, and mandatory profiles.

Local profiles: When a user first logs on to a Windows 2000 system, a local user profile is automatically created for that specific user. This profile is stored on the local machine on the system partition in the ROOT\Documents and Settings folder. For example, if Windows 2000 were installed on the C drive, and a user named JoeShmo logged on to the system, a local profile for JoeShmo would be created. The profile and its settings would be stored in *C:\Documents and Settings\JoeShmo*. A local user profile is created for any other user who logs on to the same system. Their profile will also be stored in the *C:\Documents and Settings* folder.

Roaming profiles: Roaming user profiles are created and stored on network servers to provide identical environments for users wherever they log on to the network. For example, an administrator could create a profile for a user named SteveShmo. The administrator would then copy the profile for SteveShmo to a profile server. The profile would then be automatically copied to any system that the user SteveShmo logs on to. Any settings or changes that have been made by the user SteveShmo will be copied back to the profile server and presented the next time the user logs on to the network.

Mandatory profiles: A mandatory profile is similar to a roaming user profile. The main difference is that changes to settings made by the user are not copied back to the profile server when the user logs off the system. Administrators provide a controlled environment for users by implementing mandatory user profiles. A user gets the same desktop (which was created by the administrator) wherever he logs on to the network.

HARDWARE PROFILES

When you install Windows 2000, a hardware profile named Profile 1 is automatically created. This profile is used to tell your operating system what hardware devices (and their settings) are to be used when your system is started.

Hardware profiles are commonly implemented with the use of laptop or portable computer systems. Laptops are often used with docking stations, which are typically configured with devices such as printers, modems, NICs, or CD-ROMs. A *docked hardware profile* can be created on a laptop system to automatically recognize all devices attached to a docking station when the laptop is inserted into the docking station. Docking stations are typically used at home or at the office. A more suitable hardware profile, called *undocked*, can be created for a laptop when the laptop is not being used with a docking station. This hardware profile loads only the devices, drivers, and settings needed when you are not connected to the docking station. Hardware profiles can be managed by selecting Control Panel > System > Hardware > Hardware > Hardware Profiles.

PRINTERS

Installing and managing printers in Windows 2000 is not difficult if you have already carried out similar tasks using Windows 9.x, Windows Me, or Windows NT.

Windows 2000 uses an Add Printer Wizard to assist with the installation of local or network printers. To add a new printer using the Add Printer Wizard, select Start > Settings > Printers, or open Control Panel > Printers. Next, double-click Add Printer. The Add Printer Wizard will start. After clicking Next, you will be asked if the printer is connected locally or on the network.

If the printer you want to install is connected directly to your system, select Local Printer, and click the radio button to automatically detect and install a PnP printer. If the printer and associated printer driver are detected, continue with the instructions to finish the installation. If the printer and associated printer driver are not detected, a message like the one in Figure 13.6 appears, and you will be asked to click Next to configure your printer manually. You will need to configure a printer port and provide the printer drivers from the printer manufacturer so that the operating system can recognize your printer.

If the printer you want to connect to is located on a network, select Network Printer from the Local or Network Printer window, and click Next. Then you will need to locate the network printer by entering the proper UNC name for the system to which the network printer is connected and the share name of the printer. Alternatively, you can click Next to browse for the printer on the network. The proper UNC for locating a printer share on a network is *Servername\Printername*.

If the printer you want to connect to is located on the Internet or your intranet, select the Connect to a printer on the Internet or your Intranet radio button, and enter the appropriate URL address to connect to the printer.

If you want to change the printer properties for installed printers in Windows 2000, right-click on a printer, and select Properties. You will be able to change printer port settings, sharing options, security, and color management settings, just to name a few options.

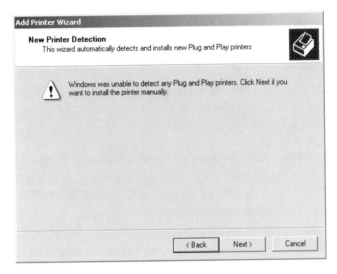

FIGURE 13.6   The Add Printer Wizard suggesting a Manual Mode printer installation.

WINDOWS 2000 NETWORKING AND THE INTERNET

The current A+ exams will most likely focus on your ability to configure network settings and protocols from within the Windows 2000 Professional operating system. The configurations of Windows 2000 Server and Advanced Server operating systems for network support are beyond the scope of this book. However, the exam will expect you to have a general understanding of network services such as WINS (Windows Internet Naming Service), DNS (Domain Name Service), DHCP (Dynamic Host Configuration Protocol), and FTP (File Transfer Protocol). In this section, we focus on Windows 2000 Professional network connectivity and define some of the important protocols and services used in networks, including the largest network of all—the Internet.

Important Network and Internet Protocols and Services

In the previous operating system chapters, we have discussed protocols in some detail. In Chapter 12, you learned how to install protocols and services from within the Network applet of Control Panel. In Windows 2000 Professional, protocols and services are installed in much the same way, with the exception that they are installed from a different location. To install protocols and services, right-click on My Network Places, right-click on Local Area Connection, and select Properties. You will be presented with the General tab from which you can configure NICs, protocols, and services.

Following are the most important protocols and services that you may have to identify on the A+ exams:

Critical note! All the information that follows concerning Internet protocols and services has been identified on the current A+ exams! Don't say you weren't forewarned!

Windows Internet Naming Service (WINS): WINS is used to determine the NetBIOS computer name associated with a particular IP address on a network. This process is known as *name resolution*. The WINS database resides on a server or servers on a network.

Domain Name Service (DNS): DNS is a name resolution service that resolves Internet or fully qualified network domain names to an IP address. You can change what is known as the DNS server search order on client computers by adding DNS server IP address entries on the client systems. To navigate to this section, right-click on My Network Places, select Properties, right-click on Local Area Connection, and select Properties. Select Internet Protocol (TCP/IP), click the Properties button, click the Advanced button, select the DNS tab, and select Add under the DNS Server addresses in the Order of use section. Enter the IP addresses of the DNS servers you want to use to resolve domain names. It's that simple! This tells the client computer in which order DNS servers should be used to resolve domain names. On another DNS note, domain names have extensions that identify an associated affiliation. .EDU is used for schools and colleges, .COM is for commercial use, .ORG is reserved for non-profit groups, .GOV is reserved for the U.S. government, and .NET is used for networking systems or as a replacement for .COM.

Dynamic Host Configuration Protocol (DHCP): DHCP is a protocol used to assign IP addresses automatically on a TCP/IP network. The DHCP server hands out IP addresses to client computers configured to use DHCP. The alternative to DHCP is configuring your system to use a static IP address. To use a static IP address, you will need an IP address, a default gateway, and a subnet mask. If you are using DHCP and need to renew your current dynamically assigned IP address, you should enter the following at a Windows 2000 command prompt: "IPCONFIG /RENEW".

Internet Connection Sharing (ICS): ICS is a feature of dial-up networking that allows all the computers in a home or small business to share one connection to the Internet. In Windows 2000 Professional, ICS can be configured by selecting Start > Settings > Network and Dial-up Connections, right-clicking on an icon configured for an Internet connection, selecting Properties, selecting the Sharing tab, and clicking Enable Internet Connection Sharing for This Connection. You will then be presented with settings that you can customize for your connection.

It is very important for you to remember that ICS is available in Windows 98 SE, Windows 2000, Windows Me, and Windows XP. ICS allows two or more connected computers to share one Internet connection, whether it be a dial-up, DSL, cable, ISDN, satellite, or T1 connection.

Automatic Private IP Addressing (APIPA): APIPA is a service used with Windows 98 and Windows 2000 Professional that allows client computers to configure themselves automatically with the IP address and subnet mask for network connectivity if a DHCP server fails or is not found. If a DHCP server fails, APIPA uses an IP address in the range of 169.254.0.0 through 169.254.255.254.

Hypertext Transfer Protocol (HTTP): HTTP is an Internet protocol used to define consistent connections.

Hypertext Transfer Protocol Secure (HTTPS): HTTPS is a secure protocol used to transmit information over the Internet. To access a secure Internet site, such as ChristopherCrayton.com, you would need a URL entry of *https://Christopher-Crayton.com*. HTTPS is concerned with the secure transmission of individual messages between client and host by using TCP port 443 as opposed to the port 80 that is normally used to transmit HTTP data. It is important to note that HTTPS and SSL (described shortly) complement each other for secure Internet connectivity. Once again, you will know that you are using HTTPS when you make a request through your Internet browser and the URL begins with https://.

SSL (Secure Sockets Layer): SSL is a protocol that uses public and private keys to secure data transmitted over the Internet. With SSL, a secured connection is established between a client and a server. SSL is a commonly used security protocol that provides transport security through Internet browsers provided by Netscape and Microsoft. SSL is a session-based X.509 digital certificate-supporting protocol that uses a public and private key exchange to encrypt the passing of data between client and server systems. The SSL protocol supports RSA, DES, IDEA, 3DES, and MD5. SSL can be used by services such as HTTP, FTP, SMTP, IMAP, POP, and Telnet. SSL uses a combination of the SSL Record protocol and the SSL Handshake protocol to provide security. The Handshake protocol provides authentication services, and the Record protocol provides for a secure connection. Many Internet Web sites use SSL as a secure means of obtaining confidential customer information, such as bank account and other personal information. It provides confidential Web sessions and authentication services for Web servers.

Simple Mail Transport Protocol (SMTP): SMTP is a protocol used for transferring e-mail between client computers and e-mail severs. For a client to send e-mail messages using SMTP successfully, a client computer should be configured with an IMAP (Internet Message Access Protocol) or POP (Post Office Protocol) server address. POP and IMAP accounts use SMTP to allow a person using a dial-up or Internet connection to gain access to mail on a mail server computer. In most cases, SMTP is used for sending mail only. This is based on its inability to handle message queuing properly at the mail-receiving end. To receive stored messages properly from a mail server, most client-side systems are set up for POP or IMAP. Figure 13.7 displays POP3 and SMTP server settings on a client system. Figure 13.8 displays SMTP and POP3 server port numbers on a client system.

You send mail with SMTP. You download or receive mail with POP or IMAP. Remember for the exams, SMTP uses server port 25, and POP3 uses port 110!

SMTP is most often used with TCP port 25. SMTP Relay is when an intermediary mail server (relay server) is used to accept any incoming mail and forward it to another mail server or final destination. This final destination is typically the e-mail server where the user's e-mail account is stored. There can be many relay servers involved with the relaying of e-mail. The problem here is that mail servers that implement SMTP Relay usually accept most mail received and deliver or relay outgoing mail without verifying or authenticating the sender or receiver. Spammers, spoofers, and unauthorized users can take advantage of this vulnerability by faking a sender's address and using just about any receiving address they want. This can cause a great proliferation of junk

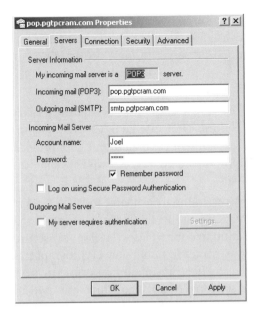

FIGURE 13.7   POP3 and SMTP server settings on a client system.

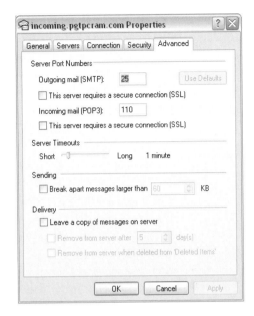

FIGURE 13.8   POP3 and SMTP server settings on a client system.

mail or spam, and it usually does. A common problem among companies that use improperly configured e-mail and SMTP Relay servers is that they are un-knowingly being used as hosts to spam other servers and hosts. This can result in a company's mail server being black holed—meaning they are banned or blocked from using e-mail services provided by ISPs. This can then result in major downtime and loss of productivity. SMTP Relay anyone?

NNTP (Network News Transfer Protocol): NNTP is a protocol included with Internet browsers such as Internet Explorer and Netscape, which allows clients and server systems to post and retrieve Usenet newsgroup messages. A program called a newsreader is often used on the client side for this purpose.

File Transfer Protocol (FTP): FTP is a protocol used to transfer data between computers on a TCP/IP network. Special file servers known as FTP servers are used to handle FTP functions. Users are typically authenticated anonymously on FTP file servers, which means that users can read and update information stored on the FTP server without being authenticated or authorized to access the server. The FTP server does care who the user is. Here are some good prac-tices when configuring and using FTP:

- Configure your FTP server to run FTP services only; do not run unneces-sary services that can be exploited.

- Do not store valuable data that cannot be recovered on your FTP server.
- Use a secure file transfer package, such as SSL, and encrypt all important data.
- Disallow unnecessary access to your FTP server; do not use a "blind" or anonymous FTP.
- Audit and log events on your FTP server.

TFTP (Trivial File Transfer Protocol): TFTP is a scaled down, simplistic version of FTP. Instead of using TCP like FTP does, TFTP use UDP (User Datagram Protocol). Unlike FTP, TFTP does not use authentication and does not provide any security features whatsoever. It is commonly used by servers as a mechanism to reboot diskless systems and X-terminals.

S/FTP (Secure/FTP): Many third-party programs are available today that assist in making your FTP server more secure. Many of these programs are Java based and allow for an SSL-encrypted connection to your FTP server. For very secure FTP, X.509 certificates and the use of asymmetric public-key cryptography is often used to encrypt public keys. For larger file transmissions, symmetric keys are used to encrypt and decrypt data sessions. Many algorithms are used in securing FTP, including DES, 3DES, and Blowfish. S/FTP is meant to provide strong authentication and encryption services and support for FTP.

Extensible Authentication Protocol (EAP): EAP is a protocol that allows the use of Transport Level Security (TLS), which is an encryption method for user-names and passwords.

Bandwidth Allocation Protocol (BAP): Allows multilink bandwidth capabilities. In other words, multiple lines of bandwidth can be set up for users to connect. If all the lines are not being used, certain lines can be dropped and allocated to other users.

Internet Protocol Security (IPSec): IPSec is essentially a suite of Internet security protocols that includes the ability to use encrypted keys. IPSec is widely used today and is considered one of the more secure Internet protocols.

Layer Two Tunneling Protocol (L2TP): This protocol creates a tunnel through a public network and provides a secure connection by providing authentication on both ends of the tunnel. The IPSec protocol is used with L2TP to provide data encryption as it passes through the tunnel.

WORKGROUP OR DOMAIN?

If you have installed Windows 2000 Professional and are not currently attached to a workgroup or domain, you can join your system to a workgroup or domain or change your system's name by right-clicking on the My Computer icon, selecting the Network Identification tab, and choosing the Properties button. You will then have the options of changing your computer name or becoming a member of a workgroup or a domain. To join your system to a workgroup or domain, you must have administrative privileges.

INTERNET CONNECTIVITY

Configuring your system to connect to the Internet is not difficult. You need a local area connection, TCP/IP, an Internet browser (such as Internet Explorer or Netscape Navigator), a modem, and an ISP.

You can use the Internet Connection Wizard to connect your system to the Internet. To do this, right-click on the Internet Explorer icon located on the desktop, select Properties, select the Connections tab, and click the Setup button. You will be offered several options for configuring and finally making your connection. Figure 13.9 displays the Internet Connection Wizard and the various options for connecting to the Internet. Choose your connection method, and follow the instructions presented by the wizard.

FIGURE 13.9 Internet connection options presented by the Internet Connection Wizard.

VIRUSES

Computer viruses are becoming more and more of a threat to the integrity of computer systems and computer data. If a virus has wiped out your important personal information or destroyed your business' data, then you are probably already aware of how critical it is to have a good antivirus package, updated antivirus DAT files, and a good backup plan.

Viruses are easily spread via the Internet, through e-mail attachments, infected floppy disks, and network shares. The most common types of viruses are the following:

Trojan: A virus that comes disguised as a useful file or program; the file or program is used to deliver the Trojan virus to the system.

Macro: Often spread through e-mail, a macro virus is one that infects programs, files, and templates associated with applications such as Microsoft Word or Excel. Macro viruses usually insert undesired objects or words into documents. They are usually programmed to be triggered by a specific action or event.

Boot sector: These viruses infect the MBR on hard disks. They can easily make the hard disk unbootable. Thus, it is always good practice to have a bootable floppy virus-scanning disk available to assist with recovery from this type of virus.

Polymorphic: This is a very popular type of virus that mutates so that it is virtually undetectable by antivirus software.

File infectors: These types of viruses typically attach to executable programs, such as files with a .COM or .EXE extensions.

Worm: A worm virus resides in computer memory and duplicates itself until it finally consumes enough system resources to render the system inoperative.

Stealth: A stealth virus can infect partition tables, boot sectors, and executable programs, and hides from antivirus detection software.

The recommended way to clean a virus from an infected computer is to boot the system to a virus-scanned boot disk that includes an updated DAT (virus definition) file, and which cleans the virus from the infected system by running the antivirus cleaning software program from the boot disk.

The current A+ exams are likely to test your knowledge regarding the types of media and software that can actually be infected by viruses. For the exams, note that floppies cannot be infected when they are write-protected, CD-ROMs cannot be infected, hard drive boot sectors can be infected, and system and network files can be infected.

DIAGNOSING AND TROUBLESHOOTING TEST TIPS

Windows 2000 introduced many changes to the operating system world. It is much more robust than its predecessors. For that reason, you will face a vast array of questions regarding Windows 2000 technology when you take the current A+ exams. This list provides diagnosing and troubleshooting test tips to prepare you for the tests:

- Windows 2000 components can be added to the operating system from the Windows 2000 Installation CD-ROM by using the Add/Remove Programs applet in the Control Panel.

- The System File Checker, which is available in Windows 98, 2000, XP, and Vista, allows you to quickly scan for and restore corrupted system files in Windows. It can be run from the command line using the syntax: `sfc /scannow`.

- If you are trying to connect to an ISP through a dial-up connection and receive the error message "Server cannot negotiate an appropriate protocol," this is most likely the result of an improperly configured or corrupt TCP/IP configuration.

- By default, files with the extensions .INI, .INF, and .DLL not are displayed in Windows 2000 Explorer. If you want hidden files and folders to be displayed, choose Tools > Folder Options > View, and select Show Hidden Files and Folders in the Advanced Settings box of the View section.

- To assign or map a drive letter to a network folder in Windows 2000, right-click My Network Places or My Computer, and select Map Network Drive.

- Windows 2000 provides network protocols for communication with other networked systems. Remember for the exams that Windows 2000 supports TCP/IP, NWLINK, and NetBEUI. TCP/IP is used for most networks, including the Internet. NWLINK is used for communication with Novell Networks. NetBEUI is a fast, efficient Microsoft network protocol. TCP/IP is the networking protocol of choice. TCP/IP is used to communicate with even Macintosh networks.

- If you have the ability to send e-mail and attachments over the Internet but cannot receive e-mail and attachments from others, you should verify that your SMTP settings and mail server settings are accurate.

- If you want to connect to a specific newsgroup on the Internet via an ISP, you will need to acquire the IP address associated with the Network News Transfer Protocol (NNTP) server for that ISP.

- In Windows 2000, a hidden Start menu can be displayed by pressing Ctrl+Esc.

- You can create a shortcut for a program from within Windows Explorer by right-clicking the program and selecting Create Shortcut. To create a shortcut that will be placed on the Windows desktop, right-click the program from within Windows Explorer, select Send to, and select Desktop (create shortcut).

- Entering "cmd" from the Run dialog box in Windows 2000, XP, or Vista will get you to a command prompt.

- You can use the Alt+Tab keyboard sequence to switch between applications running in Windows 2000.

- In Windows 2000, your NIC type can be displayed in Device Manager. Device Manager can be accessed through the System applet in the Windows 2000 Control Panel.

■ To set a default printer in Windows 2000, navigate to Start > Settings > Printers, right-click on the printer and, check Set as Default Printer.

■ You can prevent Windows 2000 users from installing unsigned device drivers by navigating to System Properties > Hardware > Driver Signing. You may then select from the Ignore, Warn, or Block options.

■ Virtual memory uses swap file space on a hard drive for storage.

■ If you are running out of memory while running multiple programs in Windows 2000, you can increase the size of your paging file by navigating to System Properties > Advanced > Performance Options > Change.

■ If you delete files that are stored on removable media such as a floppy disk, CD-RW, or removable hard drive, the files will be immediately deleted. They will not go into the Recycle Bin.

■ If you restore data to a FAT32 partition that was originally backed up from an NTFS partition, you will only retain file attributes and the long file names. You will lose any file-level permissions, compressions, or encryption. These are only supported under NTFS.

■ The Windows 2000 operating system provides support for FAT16, FAT32, NTFS, and CDFS file systems.

■ You can use the Disk Cleanup Wizard or navigate to Internet Explorer > Tools > Internet Options to clean up temporary Internet files.

■ In Windows 2000, user profiles are stored in *C:\Documents and Settings*.

■ Hypertext Transport Protocol Secure (HTTPS) is a very popular secure protocol used to transmit messages over the Internet.

■ FTP sessions by default are not encrypted. User names and passwords are transmitted in clear text. FTP user IDs and passwords can be easily grabbed with a network packet sniffer.

■ Adding a DNS server's IP address to a local system's DNS server search order will tell the local system where the DNS server is located.

■ If you have an application that ran just fine under Windows 95 but won't run after upgrading to Windows 2000, you should reinstall the application.

CHAPTER SUMMARY

On completion of this chapter, you should have gained the information and skills necessary to carry out the following tasks and understand the following concepts:

■ Install Windows 2000 Professional.

■ Upgrade to Windows 2000 Professional from Windows 9.x or Windows NT 4.0.

- Prepare for dual-boot scenarios with Windows 2000, Windows 9.x, Windows Me, and Windows NT 4.0.
- Understand the steps and progression of the Windows 2000 start-up process.
- Implement Windows 2000 tools and utilities to carry out specific tasks and maintain operating system integrity.
- Understand the different user profiles that can be implemented with Windows 2000.
- Configure general file and folder options.
- Install and configure printers in Windows 2000.
- Diagnose and troubleshoot basic operating system problems.
- Have a general understanding of networking protocols and Internet connectivity.
- It is very important that you have a solid understanding of the operating systems information provided to you thus far. Use the information you have learned as you progress on to the next chapter. But first, see if you can answer the following questions:

REVIEW QUESTIONS

1. **Windows 2000 provides support for which of the following file systems? (Choose Three)**
   - ☐ A. FAT32
   - ☐ B. OS/2
   - ☐ C. CDFS
   - ☐ D. CFDS
   - ☐ E. NTFS
   - ☐ F. HPFS

   Correct Answers = A, C, and E

   Windows 2000 provides support for FAT32, CDFS, and NTFS. The OS/2 operating system uses HPFS (High Performance File System), which Windows 2000 does not support.

2. **Which operating systems can you upgrade to Windows 2000 Professional? (Choose Three)**
   - ☐ A. Windows 95
   - ☐ B. Windows 98
   - ☐ C. OS/2
   - ☐ D. Windows 3.X
   - ☐ E. Windows NT 4.0

Correct Answers = A, B and E

From the choices listed, only Windows 95, Windows 98, and Windows NT can be upgraded to Windows 2000 professional.

3. **You just wrote over important Windows 2000 system files after installing a third-party application. Windows 2000 prompts you with the message "Files that are required for Windows to run properly have been replaced by unrecognized versions. To maintain system stability Windows must restore the original versions of these files." Where did this message come from?**

   ○ A.   System Protector 2000
   ○ B.   Windows 2000 File Protection
   ○ C.   Windows 2000 File Authentication
   ○ D.   Windows 2000 File and Object Auditor

Correct Answer = B

Windows 2000 has a built-in backup feature called Windows File Protection that keeps a backup of important system files. If you write over important system files with programs or applications, Windows File Protection will prompt you that it needs to restore the important system files you just replaced.

4. **What should you always consider first before upgrading to a new operating system?**

   ○ A.   Verify that you have the most current service pack
   ○ B.   Back up the system partition
   ○ C.   Back up your current operating system and data
   ○ D.   Back up only critical information

Correct Answer = C

Before upgrading to a new operating system, your first consideration should always be to make a complete backup of your current operating system and data. This is crucial if you want to have a path back to your current OS and information.

5. **If you want to upgrade Windows 9.X or Windows NT to Windows 2000 Professional, what must you do?**

  ○ A. Insert the Windows 2000 installation CD and reboot.
  ○ B. Insert the first Windows 2000 installation floppy disk and reboot.
  ○ C. Run the Windows 2000 setup program from within Windows 9.X or Windows NT.
  ○ D. Connect to a network share that has the Windows 2000 setup program and reboot.

  Correct Answer = C

  To perform an upgrade to Windows 2000 professional, you must run the setup program from within an existing operating system. Choices A and B are valid options for a full Windows 2000 installation. D will not perform an upgrade or a full installation.

6. **You want to install the Windows 2000 Recovery Console so that it is available at system startup. Assuming that your CD-ROM has a drive letter of D, what command would you use?**

  ○ A. D:\i386\INSTALL/CMDCONS
  ○ B. D:\i386\WINNT32 /CMDCONS
  ○ C. D:\i386\WINN/EXECMDCONS
  ○ D. D:\i386\WINDOWS/EXECMDCONS

  Correct Answer = B

  The Windows 2000 Recovery Console is a useful tool that can be used to troubleshoot a system that will not boot, copy system files to a hard drive, or configure services. To install the Recovery Console so that it is available at system startup, insert the Windows 2000 installation CD, and enter the command "WINNT32 /CMDCONS" from the i386 folder. You can then select the Recovery Console option when your system restarts.

7. **Windows 2000 provides support for dynamic volumes. Which of the following dynamic volume types does Windows 2000 support? (Choose Four)**

  ☐ A. Duplicated volumes
  ☐ B. Multihomed volumes
  ☐ C. Spanned volumes
  ☐ D. Raid level 5 volumes
  ☐ E. Mirrored volumes
  ☐ F. Striped volumes

Correct Answers = C, D, E, and F

Windows 2000 provides support for five different types of dynamic volumes. The five dynamic volumes supported are spanned, Raid-5, mirrored, striped, and simple.

8. **Which are valid paths to creating a network drive mapping in Windows 2000? (Choose Two)**
   - ☐ A. Open My Computer, right-click on System, and select Map Network Drive.
   - ☐ B. Open My Computer, right-click on C:, select Map Network Drive.
   - ☐ C. Right-click on My Computer, and select Map Network Drive.
   - ☐ D. Select Explorer > Tools > Folder Options > Map Network Drive.
   - ☐ E. Right-click on My Network Places, and select Map Network Drive.

Correct Answers = C and E

Only choices C and E will enable you to establish a drive mapping.

9. **Where in Windows 2000 can you verify that a recently installed device is functioning properly?**
   - ○ A. Control Panel > Add/Remove Hardware
   - ○ B. The Windows 2000 HCL
   - ○ C. Hardware Profiles
   - ○ D. Device Manager

Correct Answer = D

Similar to Windows 9.X, Windows 2000 provides the Device Manager utility. The Device Manager will place a yellow field containing a black exclamation point on devices that are having a problem or a red "X" on devices that are disabled. To troubleshoot a device, double-click on the device and use the Troubleshooter utility.

10. **Where in Windows 2000 are settings for local user profiles located?**
   - ○ A. C:\Documents and Settings
   - ○ B. C:\Winnt\System32\Repl\Import
   - ○ C. C:\Windows\Profiles\Settings
   - ○ D. C:\Documents and Settings\Profiles

Correct Answer = A

Local user profiles are stored in the *c:\Documents and Settings* folder by default in Windows 2000.

11. **Several Windows 2000 and Windows 98 computers on your network are configured with DHCP and TCP/IP. What will happen to these computers if they are unable to acquire IP addresses from a DHCP server?**

    ○ A.   The computers will not be able to communicate on the network.
    ○ B.   Automatic Private IP Addressing will assign IP addresses to the computers from the 169.254.0.0 range.
    ○ C.   The computers will acquire valid IP addresses from a local WINS server.
    ○ D.   The computers will acquire valid IP addresses from a remote DNS server.

    Correct Answer = B

    A built-in feature of the Windows 98 and Windows 2000 DHCP client is Automatic Private IP Addressing (APIPA). This feature will automatically assign an IP address from the Class B IP range 169.254.0.0.

12. **Which of the following operating systems cannot be upgraded to Windows 2000 Professional?**

    ○ A.   Windows 95
    ○ B.   Windows 98
    ○ C.   Windows Me
    ○ D.   Windows NT Workstation
    ○ E.   All of the above

    Correct Answer = C

    Windows 2000 is not a supported upgrade from Windows Me.

13. **What must you do to begin the upgrade procedure from Windows 9.X or Windows NT to Windows 2000?**

    ○ A.   Insert the Windows 2000 installation CD-ROM and reboot.
    ○ B.   Insert the Windows 2000 installation floppy disk and reboot.
    ○ C.   Boot your system into Windows 9.X or NT. Insert the Windows 2000 CD-ROM, and select Yes to upgrade.
    ○ D.   Insert the Windows 2000 installation recovery CD-ROM and reboot.
    ○ E.   All of the above will begin the upgrade procedure to Windows 2000.

    Correct Answer = C

To upgrade from Windows 9.X or Windows NT to Windows 2000, boot your system into Windows 9.X or Windows NT. Next, insert the Windows 2000 installation CD-ROM. Select Yes when asked if you want to upgrade. Inserting the Windows 2000 CD-ROM and rebooting would perform a fresh Windows 2000 installation making choice A incorrect.

14. **Which of the following is a protocol that uses public and private keys to secure data transmitted over the Internet?**

    ○ A. MMC
    ○ B. POP
    ○ C. IMAP
    ○ D. SSL
    ○ E. All of the above

    Correct Answer = D

    SSL (Secure Sockets Layer) is a session-based X.509 digital certificate-supporting protocol that uses a public and private key exchange to encrypt the passing of data between client and server systems. MMC (Microsoft Management Console) is used to provide a personalized central location for administration through the installation of snap-ins. POP (Post Office Protocol) and IMAP (Internet Message Access Protocol) accounts use SMTP to allow a person using a dial-up or Internet connection to gain access to mail on a mail server computer.

15. **What is used to resolve a domain name to an IP address?**

    ○ A. Forward DNS
    ○ B. DNS
    ○ C. WINS
    ○ D. SMTP
    ○ E. None of the above

    Correct Answer = B

    DNS (Domain Name Server or Service) is used to resolve fully qualified domain names to a node or IP address. Choice A is invalid. WINS (Windows Internet Naming Service) is used to determine the NetBIOS computer name associated with a particular IP address on a network. SMTP (Simple Mail Transport Protocol) is a protocol used for transferring e-mail between client computers and e-mail severs.

16. **Which of the following can be easily infected by a virus? (Choose Three)**
    - ☐ A.   Network files
    - ☐ B.   CD-ROMs
    - ☐ C.   Write-protected floppy disk
    - ☐ D.   Boot sectors
    - ☐ E.   System files
    - ☐ F.   Inkjet cartridge
    - ☐ G.   All of the above

    Correct Answers = A, D, and E

    Write-protected floppy disks, CD-ROMs, and cartridges (an other consumable printer items) cannot be infected. Hard drive boot sectors, system files, and network files can be infected.

17. **What type of server would you connect to through your ISP for news-group information?**
    - ○ A.   NNTP
    - ○ B.   DNS
    - ○ C.   HTTPS
    - ○ D.   Polymorphic
    - ○ E.   None of the above

    Correct Answer = A

    NNTP (Network News Transfer Protocol) is a protocol included with Internet browsers such as Internet Explorer and Netscape that allows clients and server systems to post and retrieve Usenet newsgroup messages. DNS (Domain Name Server or Service) is used to resolve fully qualified domain names to a node or IP address. HTTPS (Hypertext Transfer Protocol Secure) is a secure protocol used to transmit information over the Internet. A polymorphic virus is a very popular type of virus that mutates so that it is virtually undetectable by antivirus software.

18. **You can send e-mail messages without any problems. Unfortunately, you cannot receive e-mail. What settings should you check?**
    - ○ A.   SMTP
    - ○ B.   POP or IMAP
    - ○ C.   C:\WINNT\SYSTEM32\REPL\IMPORT
    - ○ D.   Local user account password
    - ○ E.   None of the above

Correct Answer = B

You send mail with SMTP. You download or receive mail with POP or IMAP. In this situation, you need to check your incoming mail settings for POP or IMAP. All other choices are invalid.

19. **What key would you press during the Windows 2000 startup process to display the menu shown in Figure 13.10?**

   ○ A. F2
   ○ B. Delete
   ○ C. F1
   ○ D. F12
   ○ E. F8
   ○ F. None of the above

Correct Answer = E

Windows 2000 offers a feature called the Advanced Options menu. When the Windows 2000 boot sequence is in its final phase, the Starting Windows screen appears. At this point, the option to press the F8 key and enter the Advanced Options menu is presented. If you press the F8 key, you will be offered the options displayed in Figure 13.10.

```
Windows 2000 Advanced Options Menu
Please select an option:

   Safe Mode
   Safe Mode with Networking
   Safe Mode with Command Prompt

   Enable Boot Logging
   Enable VGA Mode
   Last Known Good Configuration
   Directory Services Restore Mode (Windows 2000 domain controllers only)
   Debugging Mode

   Boot Normally
   Return to OS Choices Menu

Use ↑ and ↓ to move the highlight to your choice.
Press Enter to choose.
```

20. **Your bosses' wife wants to know if she can upgrade her system's hard disks to dynamic disks. Which of the following operating systems support dynamic disks? (Select Three)**

    ☐ A.   Windows XP

    ☐ B.   Windows 98 SE

    ☐ C.   Windows 98

    ☐ D.   Windows Vista

    ☐ E.   Windows Me

    ☐ F.   Windows 2000

    ☐ G.   All of the above

    Correct Answers = A, D, and F

    Windows XP, Windows 2000, and Windows Vista support the use of basic and dynamic disks. The other operating systems listed do not support the use of dynamic disks.

21. **You are a highly respected technician from the Gizmo Computer Corporation. You are working on a laptop for a client. The laptop is very slow and seems frozen. You think it may be a memory or processor issue. Which of the following utilities will allow you to research the laptop's memory and CPU use?**

    ○ A.   Device Manager

    ○ B.   Laptop Manager

    ○ C.   Recovery Console

    ○ D.   Memory and CPU

    ○ E.   Task Manager

    ○ F.   None of the above

    Correct Answer = E

    Pressing the Ctrl+Alt+Del key combination will get you to Task Manager in Windows 2000, XP, and Vista. From there you can view such things as processor and memory. All other choices will not allow you to research your memory or processor issue.

22. **From the Run dialog box, which command will get you to the command prompt in Windows 2000, XP, or Vista?**

    ○ A.   cmd
    ○ B.   Run
    ○ C.   prompt
    ○ D.   open
    ○ E.   dosopen
    ○ F.   None of the above

    Correct Answer = A

    Entering cmd from the Run dialog box in Windows 2000, XP, or Vista will get you to a command prompt.

23. **Which command can be used to check for and restore corrupted Windows system files?**

    ○ A.   cmd /Chk
    ○ B.   Chkdsk /sfc
    ○ C.   sfc /scannow
    ○ D.   Dsk /Fix
    ○ E.   syssfc /mbr
    ○ F.   None of the above

    Correct Answer = C

    SFC is the System File Checker utility in Windows 98, 2000, XP, and Vista. You can run sfc /scannow from a command prompt to check and restore important Windows system files.

REFERENCES

www.microsoft.com/whdc/hcl/search.mspx. The Microsoft Hardware Compatibility Web site provides the updated Hardware Compatibility List.

http://technet.microsoft.com/en-us/library/Bb742378.aspx. This Microsoft TechNet Web site describes RIS.

http://support.microsoft.com/default.aspx?scid=kb;en-us;272627. This Microsoft Web site describes why there is no supported upgrade path from Window Me to Windows 2000.

14 Windows XP

In This Chapter

- Overview of Windows XP
- Windows XP Installation Process
- Windows XP Upgrade Procedures
- Windows XP Start-Up Process
- Windows XP Tools and Utilities
- Profiles
- Printers
- Windows XP Networking and the Internet
- Diagnosing and Troubleshooting Test Tips
- Overview of Windows XP

On October 25, 2001, Microsoft finally accomplished what had been sought after for approximately six years; with the release of Windows XP, the consumer-oriented Windows 9.x and business-oriented Windows NT families had been successfully merged into one Windows platform based on Windows 2000.

Windows XP comes in three flavors: Home, Professional, and Media Center. Windows XP Home Edition is the replacement for Windows 98, Windows 98 Second Edition, and Windows Millennium Edition. Windows XP Professional serves as an upgrade for the same versions Windows Home Edition supports, as well as including Windows NT 4.0 Workstation and Windows 2000 Professional. The Professional edition offers extra networking capabilities and hardware/software options not found in the Home Edition. Windows XP Media Center (MCE) severs as a hub for home entertainment enthusiasts. Note that none of the versions of Windows XP will support an upgrade from Windows 95 or versions of Windows NT prior to 4.0.

Windows XP Home Edition includes the following, which expand on some of the existing Windows Me/2000 features:

System Restore: System Restore allows the OS to be turned back to a saved point in time, restoring lost or changed data and registry entries.

Remote Assistance: Windows XP Home provides software to grant an authorized technician or friend (using Windows XP Professional) to assist you with troubleshooting or to demonstrate procedures.

Network Setup Wizard: This wizard provides a step-by-step, end-user interface for installing or setting up networked printers, sharing files, adding network connections, and performing Internet Connection Sharing (ICS).

Quick Access: The new looks of the Start menu and Explorer allow the most frequently used programs and commands to be accessed quickly and consistently.

Windows File Protection (WFP): As mentioned in Chapter 13, WFP protects critical operating system files from being changed or deleted improperly.

Expanded Multimedia Support: Enhanced DVD playback, built-in CD writer, and audio CD ripping support all provide users with rich multimedia experiences.

Internet Explorer 6 (IE6): IE6 contains enhanced security and encryption, per-site third-party cookie blocking, and integrated multimedia capabilities using Windows Media Player 8.

Windows Firewall: This is the first integrated firewall included in a consumer version of Windows, guarding the computer from intrusion from the Internet.

Fast User Switching: User switching allows multiple local user accounts to be active and running software simultaneously on a single computer.

Roll Back Driver: In the event that a hardware driver causes a software or hardware problem, you now have the option of returning to the previous driver, or like previous versions of Windows, completely uninstalling the existing one.

Windows XP Professional also includes the following supplemental features for business or workstation use:

Encrypted File System (EFS): Windows XP Professional offers key encryption transparently for sensitive data and for multiple users, simultaneously.

Remote Desktop: Windows XP Professional can create a virtual machine of a remote computer on your local machine via a network or the Internet, allowing you to see and control it.

Hibernation and Fast Resume: Hibernation is a battery-saving mode similar to Standby, freezing the running processes and reducing energy usage until you are ready to quickly resume them again. However, with Hibernation, processes and system memory are dumped to the hard drive, and the computer is shut down. When you start the system again, Windows XP then loads the image from the hard drive.

IEEE 802.1x: This offers secure wireless networking through authentication and key management.

Enhanced Driver Signing and Verification: This version of driver signing is based on Windows 2000; however, it provides tougher stress-testing and more rigorous standards for device driver certification, such as WHQL (Windows Hardware Quality Labs).

IP Security (IPSec): IPSec provides enhanced data protection and security, which is especially vital to virtual private networks (VPNs).

Kerberos Support: Kerberos is an Internet industry-standard high-strength authentication for Windows 2000, Windows XP, and enterprise-level resources.

RAM: Windows XP also supports up to 4 GB of RAM and two Symmetric Multiprocessors (SMPs).

Offline Files: Windows XP Pro offers the use of offline files and the ability to join a domain.

Windows XP Media Center is based on Windows XP Pro, so it has the Windows XP Pro features and technology as well as the following features:

- A preinstalled full-blown Media Center application that offers remote and playback capabilities for TV, DVD, and music
- Windows Movie Maker, Media player, and Microsoft Plus!
- Free Microsoft Media Center TV Guide Service
- Media Center Extenders devices that allow you to view the same content available on an MCE computer, Xbox, or Xbox360 over a wired or wireless network

WINDOWS XP INSTALLATION PROCESS

To use Windows XP Professional or Windows XP Home, your system needs to meet or exceed the following requirements:

- 233 MHz Pentium-compatible processor
- Approximately 1.5 GB of free drive space (however, it depends on the features and software you choose to install)
- 64 MB of RAM (bare minimum; some features may be unavailable or limited)

- Super VGA monitor (800 x 600)
- Keyboard
- Mouse
- CD-ROM

As with all Windows NT-based operating systems, it is always wise to ensure that your hardware is in compliance with the Hardware Compatibility List (HCL). You may search for your specific hardware by visiting the HCL, available at *www.microsoft.com/whdc/hcl/search.mspx.*

Consider upgrading your BIOS. Windows XP, like Windows 2000, attempts to use ACPI (Advanced Configuration and Power Interface) compliance to its fullest. Windows XP more strictly follows ACPI standards, so it is a good idea to look to your motherboard manufacturer's Web site for an upgrade. An old BIOS with buggy ACPI support is likely to cause Windows XP to behave erratically (e.g., you choose Standby and your system reboots instead).

CD-ROM INSTALLATION

If your BIOS supports CD-ROM booting, then you may insert the CD-ROM and reboot your system. After a delay while set-up inspects your hardware, the typical blue text-mode installation screen is shown. If you have any RAID devices or third-party SCSI adapters, you must press F6 when you see a message at the bottom of the screen requesting this in black-on-gray text. After this, you may press F2 to begin Automated System Recovery (ASR), which will allow you to recover an existing, nonbooting Windows XP system. ASR is not included in Windows XP Home. Otherwise, you are presented with options for installing or repairing an existing the Windows XP system using Recovery Console. After you choose to install and accept the licensing agreement, set-up will display the current partition(s) of your hard disk drive(s). You are able to create or delete partitions as necessary. Select either an existing partition or unpartitioned space, and the options for formatting to either an NTFS or FAT file system will appear. If you selected an existing partition, you may have extra options; you can choose not to format it or to convert a FAT file system to NTFS. After this step has been completed and Windows copies files to the partition you selected, your system will restart into GUI mode to continue set-up.

NOTE

If a system will not boot, and you cannot get to the Advanced Boot options menu, the next step in recovering from such a situation is to insert the Windows XP CD, restart the system, and begin the ASR restoration process.

Six Set-Up Disks

Unfortunately, Microsoft has taken away the last crutch from rapidly dying legacy systems. You are no longer able to create any set-up floppy disks from the CD-ROM. However, due to the demand for the disks, Microsoft has released two utility downloads on the Internet. They are both self-extracting compressed files that will generate six floppy disks, rather than four, for either Windows XP Home or Windows XP Professional. The Windows XP Professional disk creation utility will not allow Windows XP Home to boot, and vice versa. Microsoft has now made it clear that floppy disk support will be entirely absent from the future Windows product lines.

The Windows XP Home disk creation utility can be downloaded from:

www.microsoft.com/downloads/details.aspx?FamilyID=E8FE6868-6E4F-471C-B455-BD5AFEE126D8

The Windows XP Professional disk utility can be obtained at:

www.microsoft.com/downloads/details.aspx?FamilyID=55820edb-5039-4955-bcb7-4fed408ea73f

You cannot perform an upgrade to Windows XP from start-up disks.

Windows XP Upgrade Procedures

Although it is recommended to perform a clean install of any operating system, if you have an existing upgradeable version of Windows, such as Windows 98/98/SE or Windows Me, then you may choose to insert the CD-ROM for Windows XP Home at your Windows desktop. If you have Windows 2000 or Windows NT 4.0, then you must upgrade to Windows XP Professional. Windows 98, Windows 98 SE, and Windows Me may also be upgraded to Windows XP Professional.

After you insert either CD-ROM, autorun launches a menu allowing you to choose from several options. It is advisable to start with Check System Compatibility. This executes the Windows XP Upgrade Advisor, which scans your current hardware and software for known conflicts or bugs that have cropped up during Microsoft's initial testing of the operating system (see Figure 14.1). The first step of the Advisor (if a network connection is detected) is to prompt you for permission to download the updated set-up files, which is a great way to expand the list of incompatible software and hardware the Advisor searches for. The final report from the Upgrade Advisor may seem daunting or disappointing at first, but it is really not as critical as it sounds. Most of your hardware will obviously require drivers built for Windows XP (or Windows 2000 drivers that are compatible with Windows XP), and your incompatible software will most likely be superseded by software that either ships with Windows XP already, or the software manufacturer may have created a newer version that supports Windows XP directly. If you decide to install a Windows 2000 driver that is compatible with Windows XP, you must understand that there is a potential to cause system instability. Some drivers may work, but they are not guaranteed as a signed driver would be. The Advisor saves its report in the C:\WINDOWS directory by default.

Note that while the networking protocol NetBEUI is technically not supported and will show up in the Advisor's report, NetBEUI for Windows XP is actually available as an extra from the CD-ROM.

If you are interested in upgrading to Windows XP from another version of Windows, consult Table 14.1 to find the proper upgrade path.

TABLE 14.1 Microsoft Windows XP Upgrade Chart

Previous Windows Version	Windows XP Home	Windows XP Professional
Evaluation (any versions)	No	No
Server (any versions)	No	No
Windows 3.x	No	No
Windows 95	No	No
Windows 98/98 SE	Yes	Yes
Windows Me	Yes	Yes
Windows NT Workstation 4.0	No	Yes
Windows NT Workstation prior to 4.0	No	No
Windows 2000 Professional	No	Yes
Windows XP Home	N/A	Yes
Windows XP Professional	No	N/A

As you can see, the options for upgrading to Windows XP Home are somewhat limited. However, Microsoft currently offers a special price plan for consumer power users seeking an upgrade from Windows XP Home to Windows XP Professional.

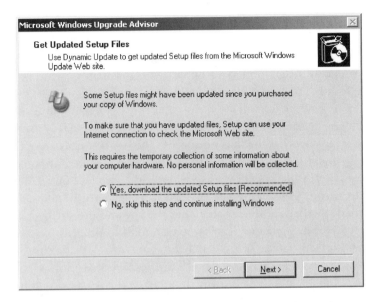

FIGURE 14.1   The Windows XP Upgrade Advisor updating the set-up files.

AUTOMATED AND NETWORK INSTALLATIONS

There are several ways to deploy Windows XP over a network or to multiple computers:

- Unattended, answer file-based installation
- Unattended, cloned image installation (Sysprep)
- Systems Management Server (SMS)

If you plan to install Windows XP on multiple computers with differing hardware and software configurations, then an unattended answer file installation will probably be most beneficial. You or your users will not have to answer the typical questions during set-up, saving time and money. It is possible, however, to create a cloned image of an existing installation that will be deployed to all computers, which is useful if all of the client computers will have the same hardware and software configurations. Windows XP can be automatically installed using a variety of methods. The first we will discuss is the unattended answer file method.

An answer file automates the set-up procedure by providing the answers to the typical prompts you would receive during a manual installation of Windows XP. The i386 folder on your Windows XP installation media comes with a sample answer file named Unattend.txt. The actual name of the file does not matter, as long as it is in plain text format and spelled correctly when used in conjunction with the set-up command (e.g., winnt.exe or winnt32.exe). For instance, `winnt.exe /u:mysetup.txt` or `winnt32.exe /unattend:computer.txt` are both valid commands to start an unattended installation. This allows you to possibly create multiple answer files, one for each section of your organization.

An answer file is made up of sections, keys, and values. A section is a word enclosed in square brackets, such as [GuiUnattended]. A key is a string of text following a section that has no spaces. The key is simply an option for the installation. A typical key could be "TimeZone." It is followed by an equals sign (=), then the answer, which is known as a value. So a line just under the [GuiUnattended] section could read `TimeZone=5`, specifying Eastern Standard Time for the unattended installation. If the value after the key and the equal sign is longer than one word, you must enclose it in quotation marks, for example, `OrgName="This is my organization"`. Some sections may not contain key/value combinations, but rather just a list of files, such as in the [OEMBootFiles] section. Comments start with a semicolon (;), and these lines are ignored by the set-up program. They are for your personal information or explanation purposes only.

To get started, simply insert the Windows XP installation CD-ROM in a computer that is already running Windows XP and choose Perform Additional Tasks. Then choose Browse this CD. You should now see the contents of the media. Open the Support folder, and then the Tools folder. Now make a new folder on your desktop or in a place that you can access easily. In the Tools folder you are browsing, find and double-click the file DEPLOY.CAB. Choose Edit > Select All. Click Edit > Copy, and then navigate to the new folder you created. Finally, choose Edit > Paste, and you will now have the Setup Manager and everything you need to create an answer file with ease.

Microsoft offers deployment utilities on its Web site. It is considered part of Windows XP Service Pack 1. You can find the newer DEPLOY.CAB here: www.microsoft.com/downloads/details.aspx?familyid=7a83123d-507b-4095-9d9d-0a195f7b5f69.

NOTE

Ref.chm and deploy.chm in your folder contain instructions and help on the answer file process. When you launch setupmgr.exe, a wizard will begin that will walk you through the creation or modification of an answer file. This wizard will help you create an answer file for an unattended installation, a Sysprep installation, or an RIS installation. Sysprep is a utility that prepares an existing Windows XP installation for cloning. If your computer systems are identical in hardware and software, you can create an "image" or "clone" of an existing Windows XP installation and install it on multiple systems using Sysprep. Remote Installation Services (RIS) allows you to deploy the operating system over a network to multiple clients from one or more remote locations.

The Setup Manager can help you create an answer file for Windows XP Home, Windows XP Professional, Windows 2002 Server, Windows 2002 Advanced Server, and Windows 2002 Data Center Edition. The next step in the Setup Manager requests the amount of interaction to be used during an answer file installation. There are currently five types:

Provide defaults: This option will fill in any info you have supplied in your answer file but allows interaction to change any and all information if necessary. This is not an unattended method.

Fully automated: There are no prompts for information and no chances to review or change any information.

Hide pages: This is similar to fully automated, except that it will prompt for information not supplied in the answer file. Any pages and information supplied by an answer file are not shown at all.

Read only: Pages and information provided by an answer file can be reviewed, but they cannot be changed.

GUI attended: The text mode portion of the installation is automated, but the graphical portion of the installation is not.

After choosing an interaction type, you are given a choice as to the medium of installation. You may choose a CD-ROM installation or a distribution folder installation. A distribution folder has advantages over a CD-ROM installation in that you are able to add files, such as drivers, that are not normally part of the installation. You are also able to store the distribution folder locally on the computer or on a network share.

After you have chosen a medium, Setup Manager prompts for all of the information that will be provided by the answer file. These are typical questions asked during an attended installation; however, the answers will be saved and used for all of your unattended installations. After the initial questions about time zone, display settings, and product key, the network settings are next.

The network settings portion of the answer file wizard first prompts you for computer names. You have the option of making Setup Manager create computer names based on the organization name. If you do not choose autogenerated names, and you enter more than one computer name, Setup Manager creates a Uniqueness Database (UDF) file. A UDF is simply an answer file that modifies the main answer file by overriding values according to the parameters with which you began the installation. For example, if you launch Windows XP Setup with the switch `/udf:1,myfile.udf`, then Setup will look inside the file myfile.udf for ID #1 and use that particular ID's answers, overriding your answer file's defaults. You can create an ID for each instance that you need to override answers in your answer file, and then use them on a case-by-case basis.

The next important step is to include the local Administrator account's password. If you choose a fully automated install, obviously it will not be able to prompt the user for one. You will have to specify a password here. It is recommended that you choose the option to encrypt the password in the answer file so that the password will not be in plain text inside the answer file. There is a limit of 127 characters to a password. You can also choose to have the Administrator account log on automatically each time the computer is started.

Next, you may add or remove networking components, such as Client for Microsoft Networks, File and Printer Sharing, and networking protocols. The final page of the network settings section is the Workgroup or Domain page. If you choose to include this computer in a domain, you may also have Setup create the account on the domain server if one has not already been created for it.

The final phase of the Setup Manager questions allows you to choose telephony settings, regional settings, languages, browser and shell settings, the folder in which Windows will be installed, network printers, "run once", and additional commands. Run once is a list of commands that will only be executed during the first logon of a newly installed Windows XP system. "Additional commands" allow you to specify commands that will be run after the end of an unattended set-up. You may only specify commands that do not require you to log on.

After you have completed all of the questions, Setup Manager will prompt you to create a .txt file in the directory you extracted Setup Manager to. You may change the location and file name. Again, if multiple computer names were specified, Setup Manager also creates a UDF. Depending on the type of answer file created, Setup Manager may also create a sample batch file (.bat) script. The batch file will automatically launch setup with the proper parameters to use your new answer file.

WINDOWS XP START-UP PROCESS

Aside from the standard POST performed during the initial start-up of a PC, Windows XP has a much more complicated boot process than its sister operating system family, Windows 9.x. Ntldr, located in the root of the C: drive, performs several tasks critical to start-up:

1. The x86-based processors always start out in Real Mode. Real Mode disables certain processor features to enable backward compatibility with software designed for 8-bit and 16-bit processors. Ntldr switches the processor to 32-bit Protected Mode, enabling access to large amounts of RAM and all extended processor functions.

2. Ntldr also contains code to enable read and write access to file systems such as NTFS or FAT16/FAT32. After this is parsed and loaded, Ntldr reads the BOOT.INI, also located in the root of the C: drive, to determine the location of the operating system.

3. For dual-booting systems, your old Master Boot Record (MBR) sector was saved to a file in the root of the C: drive during initial installation of Windows XP, and that file is called BOOTSECT.DOS. When BOOT.INI detects multiple operating systems, you are prompted with a menu that will enable you to choose your operating system. If you choose an operating system other than Windows XP/2000/NT, then Ntldr executes BOOTSECT.DOS as if it were read from the actual MBR sector, loading that operating system. The hidden file C:\BOOTSECT.DOS contains the boot sector to your old operating system, which was backed up during the Windows XP installation. The file system boot sector is the first sector of a logical volume or partition and is not to be confused with the MBR, which begins with the first physical sector on the hard drive.

4. If your system is single-booting, or you chose Windows XP/2000/NT through a multiboot menu, then Ntdetect.com loads and performs basic device detection. Ntdetect.com detects hardware profile information, as well as Advanced Configuration and Power Interface (ACPI) tables. After that has completed, Ntldr passes BOOT.INI, registry information, and hardware detection information obtained from Ntdetect.com on to Ntoskrnl.exe.

5. For non-ACPI systems, your hardware's firmware and your BIOS provide the resources such as interrupt requests (IRQs) to Windows XP. For ACPI-compliant systems, Windows XP is able to assign and manage all necessary resources. After Ntldr launches Ntoskrnl.exe, the Hardware Abstraction Layer (HAL) is loaded into memory, providing secured access to hardware and their associated resources. HAL catches all requests to hardware made by software and ensures security by preventing unauthorized direct access to hardware. All hardware interaction must be done via kernel-level system calls and APIs. Depending on your type of computer, Windows XP set-up installs a custom HAL. To see which HAL your system will have, consult Table 14.2.

TABLE 14.2   The Different HAL Files

Computer's Description in Device Manager	HAL File Copied
ACPI Multiprocessor PC	Halmacpi.dll
ACPI Uniprocessor PC	Halaacpi.dll
Advanced Configuration and Power Interface (ACPI) PC	Halacpi.dll
MPS Multiprocessor PC	Halmps.dll
MPS Uniprocessor PC	Halapic.dll
Standard PC	Hal.dll
Compaq SystemPro Multiprocessor or 100% Compatible	Halsp.dll

6. The kernel and HAL initiate a group of software components known as the Windows Executive. The Executive processes registry configuration data and starts services and hardware drivers. The registry information parsed by the Executive contains the common control sets, such as the Last Known Good control set. The CurrentControlSet entry in the registry is a clone of the control set created upon every boot of Windows XP. Ntldr searches the Services subkey of the registry to find drivers and services with a Start key value of 0, such as hard disk controllers. Ntoskrnl.exe searches for and starts drivers with a Start key value of 1, such as network protocols. After all of the drivers and services have been loaded in memory, started, or both, the kernel starts Session Manager (known as Smss.exe).

7. Smss.exe performs the following functions, in this order:
   - Creates system environment variables
   - Starts Win2k.sys, the kernel-mode portion of Windows, which switches Windows XP from text to graphics mode
   - Starts the user-mode portion, Csrss.exe
   - Starts the Logon Manager (Winlogon.exe)
   - Creates virtual memory swap files
   - Replaces pending files that were in use during the last boot (such as when you are requested to restart Windows after installing a driver)

8. After Winlogon.exe executes, it launches several subsystems that provide security and functionality for services. The first thing that Winlogon launches is Services.exe, also known as the Service Control Manager (SCM). Next, the Local Security Authority (LSA, or Lsass.exe) is executed. Finally, Winlogon waits for and parses the Ctrl-Alt-Del key combination at the logon prompt.

The LSA is responsible for validating local credentials, such as the username and password, using the appropriate security protocol (e.g., Kerberos V5).

9. The control sets mentioned in step 5, are updated during the next phase of Winlogon.exe. Group Policy settings take effect after logging on, and then the user's local start-up items, login scripts, and services are executed.

PnP detection runs asynchronously with the logon phases, and Windows XP extracts necessary drivers for new hardware from Driver.cab. If the drivers are not found, Windows XP prompts you to provide them. The logon and PnP processes are the final steps in the start-up process.

WINDOWS XP TOOLS AND UTILITIES

Windows XP has taken Windows 2000's Microsoft Management Console (MMC) a step further. Some of the Windows 2000 utilities have been redesigned to be only available through the MMC as a snap-in. The Services control panel applet, Disk Management, and Device Manager have now been integrated into the MMC. Even when launched as a separate entity, they still load MMC first. The MMC is a fully customizable utility for organizing commonly used administrative functions. Computer Management, as discussed in Chapter 13, is a preconfigured MMC with the most common utilities already snapped in. With only two clicks of the mouse, you are able to access the Device Manager, Services, Disk Management, or many other common administrative tools. Simply right-click My Computer, choose Manage, and Computer Management appears. It is always important that you know the Microsoft way to access utilities, as it is more likely to appear on the test than the aforementioned shortcut method. You navigate to Start (or Settings, for Classic Start Menu users) > Control Panel > Administrative Tools > Computer Management.

In this chapter, we will discuss the new, as well as improved, Windows system utilities.

DEVICE MANAGER

Device Manager has always been an invaluable tool for troubleshooting Windows systems. Windows XP includes a similar version of Windows 2000's Device Manager; and just like in Windows 2000, it is only available as a MMM snap-in. It features a new utility called Roll Back Driver. If you install an upgraded or alternate driver over an existing one, Windows XP will back up the old driver in case there is a problem. At any time, you may access a device's driver Properties pane and choose to revert to the older driver (see Figure 14.2). Obviously, this is a worthwhile addition to existing troubleshooting methods. To access Device Manager, navigate to Control Panel > System > Hardware tab > Device Manager button, or use Computer Management under Accessories > Administrative Tools, or Control Panel > Administrative Tools.

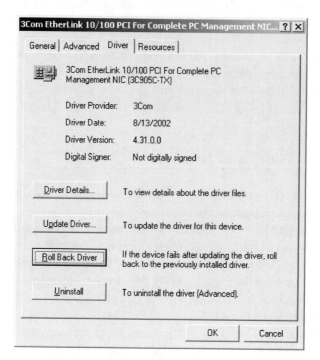

FIGURE 14.2 The enhanced Driver tab featuring the new Roll Back Driver.

DRIVER SIGNING

As with Windows 2000, Windows XP offers advanced Driver Signing options that will prevent unapproved device drivers from being loaded by unauthorized users. The Microsoft Driver Signing (also known as Windows Logo Testing) standards are much more rigorous and stress testing than ever before. This is to ensure compatibility and stability regardless of computer configuration. You may choose to ignore, warn, or completely disable unsigned driver installations. The default setting is Warn, which displays a dialog box requesting action when an unsigned driver installation is attempted. You may then choose the system default through this Properties pane. To access the Driver Signing Properties page, go to System Properties either through the Control Panel or by right-clicking on My Computer and choosing Properties. In System Properties, choose the Hardware tab to access the Driver Signing button.

MICROSOFT MANAGEMENT CONSOLE (MMC)

As discussed in Chapter 13, the MMC is a handy way to centralize your administrative tasks. Windows XP has modified several existing standalone applications to be only accessible as a snap-in. Event Viewer, Disk Defragmenter, Disk Management, Device Manager, Local Users and Groups, Performance Logs and Counters, and Services are only available in Windows XP through the MMC. You can open a blank MMC window by choosing Start > Run, typing "MMC" in the Open box, and then clicking OK. You may add the aforementioned tools or several other advanced administrative programs by selecting File > Add/Remove Snap-in.

BACKUP

Windows XP Home Edition does not include Backup by default. You can install it by delving deep into the installation CD-ROM. Navigate to X:\Valueadd\msft\nt-backup\ (where X is the drive letter for the CD-ROM drive you are using), and launch NTBACKUP.MSI. It may be listed as just NTBACKUP if file extensions are not enabled. The Windows XP Professional Backup has a Start Menu shortcut in the System Tools folder under Accessories.

After you have launched Backup, you will see that the opening interface is very simplistic, even in Advanced Mode. There are three wizards on the main dialog page that will allow you to perform a backup, perform a restore, or create an ASR image. After the wizard, Advanced Mode has a lot of options for customizing your backup or restore routine, including scheduling automatic backups. The test is most likely going to focus on the different backup types rather than the Backup application itself. The first two of the following backup types are specific to certain software (in this case, Windows XP Backup), but it is important to understand these as well as the last two, which are industry-standard types:

Normal: This type of backup has no special criteria other than the selection of specific files; and after each file is archived, the Archive attribute bit for each file is set to an unchecked state. All attributes for a file or folder are viewed by right-clicking on a file and selecting Properties > then Advanced (if necessary).

Copy: This type of backup is exactly the same as Normal, except that it does not clear the Archive attribute for each file once complete.

Incremental: Incremental is an industry-standard term for files that have been created or modified since the last backup. When you create a file or modify an existing one that has been backed up previously (which clears its Archive attribute), Windows automatically turns on the Archive bit for that file, telling the backup software that it needs to be backed up again. After each file is backed up using Incremental, the Archive bit is cleared again.

Differential: Differential is also an industry-standard term, and it performs the same as Incremental, except that the Archive bit is not cleared, much like Copy.

It is very important to remember from Chapter 13 that NTFS and FAT are not compatible file systems. NTFS contains extended features, such as compression, encryption, and security permissions. All of these extended attributes will be lost during the copy from NTFS to FAT. Long file names and regular attributes such as Read-Only and Archive will be retained, however.

SYSTEM RESTORE

System Restore, first introduced in Windows Me, is a valuable tool for "turning back the clock." Think of System Restore as an expanded Last Known Good configuration. Windows Me and Windows XP keep track of certain milestones; for example, if you install a new driver or use Windows Update to upgrade system software, Windows will create a Restore Point that allows you to revert back to a previous date's registry configuration (including replaced files) in case of a problem. You may also create a Restore Point at any time you wish. It is found in the Start menu under Accessories > System Tools. You are presented with a calendar that contains system Restore Points for each milestone.

You can disable or reenable System Restore by visiting System Properties, either in Control Panel > System, or by right-clicking on My Computer and selecting Properties. You will see a System Restore tab that allows you to disable it completely or adjust the amount of hard drive space (for each drive letter) that will be used to back up files during each milestone. The more hard drive space you allocate, the more fault tolerance your system will have. If there is not enough allocated hard drive space, certain files may be excluded from backup; System Restore becomes much less effective in this situation.

WINDOWS IMAGING ARCHITECTURE

Windows Imaging Architecture (WIA) is a new standard set forth by Microsoft for imaging devices (e.g., scanners or digital cameras) to communicate directly with the operating system. It was first introduced in Windows Me, and it offers internal support for many popular cameras and scanners. It provides a much more simplified interface for scanning or downloading digital images than TWAIN. According to the TWAIN group, TWAIN is not actually an acronym, but rather a take-off on the Kipling quote, "never the twain shall meet." It implies that the hardware and the imaging software will never directly communicate, but a device driver acting as a middleman will relay information and messages. TWAIN is the standard driver type for the majority of imaging devices prior to Windows Me. WIA is Microsoft's replacement for TWAIN.

EVENT VIEWER

As with all Windows NT-based operating systems, Event Viewer is a vital tool for troubleshooting software, hardware drivers, and services failure. You can find the Event Viewer in Administrative Tools in the Control Panel.

All events are logged to disk and time-stamped for organization. There are three main categories of events: Application, Security, and System. Under Application, you will find errors and warnings having to do with set-up programs (such as with InstallShield or the installer service for Microsoft, MSI) and regular applications (e.g., crashes, missing data, etc.). If you double-click on an entry, data useful for troubleshooting will appear, usually followed by a Web site address to Microsoft.com that will either attempt to explain the event in more detail or lead you to a fix or solution for a particular known issue. If you are looking for a particular log in any of the three sections, you should choose View > Filter.

In the Security section of the Event Viewer, you will find successful and unsuccessful logins, as well as items chosen by the administrator to be audited. By default, security logging is turned off. You can use Group Policy to enable security logging. To do this, navigate to Administrative Tools in the Control Panel and choose Local

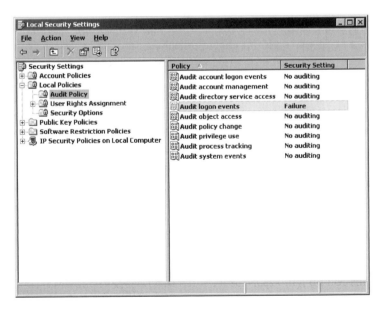

FIGURE 14.3   Enabling auditing with local security policies.

Security Settings (see Figure 14.3). The main two items of importance to the Security log are listed under Local Policies, and they are called Audit Policy and Security Options. For example, if you enable Failure auditing for the Audit logon events in the Audit Policy subcategory, Security logs will be created in the Event Viewer when a logon error occurs.

Last, but not least, under the System section, there will be events pertaining to information or errors from device drivers, services problems, and other Windows XP system components.

For computers configured as a domain controller, there will be two additional logs: Directory Service and File Replication. They will probably not be important for the test. Domain name system (DNS) computers will also record a DNS server log.

MSCONFIG (MICROSOFT CONFIGURATION UTILITY)

Since Windows 98, MSCONFIG has been an advantage to all technicians due to its compact interface and optimized layout. The first thing you will notice about it is that you are able to quickly select the type of start-up from the very first tab (General). This has always been helpful because it is the first step to narrowing the spectrum of possibilities for a given issue. If there is a software problem in the system, the first step is usually to disable third-party or background software to ensure that user software is not causing the particular problem. You can do so by choosing Selective Startup on the General tab and then fully unchecking the Load Startup Items box. This is a three state checkbox. If you have used MSCONFIG before, and you previously visited the Startup tab and disabled specific items, then your Load Startup Items checkbox will be checked but grayed out. It is not disabled; however, it means that there are specific items that are loading and specific ones that are not. If you were to completely uncheck this field, MSCONFIG would forget which particular items you had chosen to load, and it would completely unload all items. If you see a grayed checkbox, you should visit the Startup tab and write down the items that are not checked. That way, if you have to clear the Load Startup Items checkbox, you will be able to restore your old configuration when you have solved your problem. The General tab also has a button called Expand File that will extract files from Windows XP installation media or any location on your hard drive.

Diagnostic Startup causes Windows XP to interactively load device drivers and software when you restart the system. All Microsoft Services (e.g., networking, PnP, Event Logging, etc.) are temporarily disabled in this mode.

Diagnostic start-up permanently deletes all System Restore points.

NOTE

On the SYSTEM.INI and WIN.INI tabs, you are able to specifically disable, enable, or rearrange lines from those particular files. SYSTEM.INI commonly contains 386-Enhanced virtual device and legacy device driver entries, such as text mode fonts, keyboard and display drivers, and password lists (PWL files). WIN.INI contains Windows and software settings that have not yet migrated to the Windows registry. These files are mainly used for backward compatibility with 16-bit and old Windows programs.

The BOOT.INI tab contains options for starting the operating system, such as the paths to each Windows operating system you may have. You are also able to enable special options such as a safe VGA video driver (/BASEVIDEO) or specify the type of Safe Mode launch (/SAFEBOOT). You may change the amount of time Windows XP gives you to make an operating system selection by modifying the Timeout value.

The Services tab contains individual checkboxes for all services, including third party. Unchecking a service is the same as selecting Disabled for a service's properties in the Services section of Computer Management. There is a handy checkbox available for hiding all Microsoft services. This way, you can easily see third-party services. During troubleshooting, it is often wise to disable third-party services that are not required for your computer to function.

The last tab, Startup, contains the items from the registry that are going to launch whenever Windows XP boots. You may specifically disable or enable start-up items here. If there is a start-up item that has been removed during an upgrade from a previous version of Windows, you will be able to use the button marked Restore Startup Programs to bring them back. Windows XP Setup commonly disables start-up items that it knows have been replaced with newer software, such as an entry for Windows 9.x power management or video driver utility software (not to be confused with the actual driver).

REMOTE DESKTOP

Windows XP includes an interesting tool called Remote Desktop for troubleshooting a remote computer. Other common uses for it are accessing your data or controlling a machine from a remote location, such as an office computer while you are out of the office. The computer you are going to control is known as the host computer. The computer you will connect from is called the client. Your client computer can have Windows 9.x or Windows NT 4.0 and higher installed, provided that it has the Remote Desktop Connection client software installed. The host computer you will be controlling must have Windows XP Professional installed. Obviously, an Internet or network connection is required.

For a remote computer to connect for a Remote Desktop session, the Administrator or a user from the Administrator group must have enabled it. Right-click on My Computer, select Properties, and choose the Remote tab. Figure 14.4 displays the Remote tab under System Properties for setting up the remote connection options. You must check the Allow users to connect remotely to this computer checkbox under the Remote Desktop section. After that, it is advisable to select the remote users that will be connecting to the machine, unless you are the Administrator or part of the Administrator group.

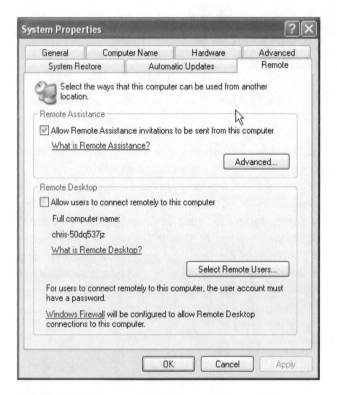

FIGURE 14.4 Remote Desktop connection options.

Both Windows XP Home and Windows XP Professional install the Remote Desktop client software by default. If you are running a previous version of Windows, such as Windows 98, then you will have to insert the Windows XP Home or Windows XP Professional CD-ROM into the drive and select Perform Additional Tasks from the autorun menu. Then you will choose Set up Remote Desktop Connection. Follow the on-screen directions, and the client will be installed.

After you have enabled Remote Desktop on the host and installed client software on a Windows-based client machine, you are ready to set up a VPN connection or remote access service connection to the host machine. Navigate to Start > Programs (or All Programs) > Accessories > Communications > Remote Desktop Connection. At the prompt screen, you will enter either the Universal Naming Convention (UNC) name (e.g., \\CRAYTON; the \\ is optional) or an IP address. You may either choose to connect or refine your parameters by choosing Options. Options will show you many new settings, including display settings, audio settings, and username, password, and domain settings. Choose Connect, and the Log On to Windows dialog pane should appear to request your username, password, and optional domain (if you have not specified them already in the Advanced Options area). You now have control over the host computer. The remote host computer will be locked so that no passersby can see what you are doing to it. Local users will still be able to log on if they have a proper username and password.

If you are taking exam 220-603 (Remote Support Technician), or if you need more information regarding Remote Desktop, refer to the following Microsoft Web site:

www.microsoft.com/windowsxp/using/mobility/getstarted/remoteintro.mspx.

REMOTE ASSISTANCE

Remote Assistance is similar to Remote Desktop but with a few exceptions. It is an interactive connection in which the host computer will display what the client computer is controlling. Remote Assistance also requires that there be someone at the host computer to send an invitation for a connection. To use Remote Assistance, both computers must either be running Windows XP Home or Windows XP Professional. Remote Assistance can happen in one of three ways.

- If both machines have Windows Messenger installed, you can navigate to the Tools menu of Windows Messenger and choose Ask for Remote Assistance. All online contacts will be displayed with their e-mail addresses. If your friend accepts the invitation, you will be prompted for confirmation. Although the remote computer will have temporary control over your machine, you will still be able to end the session by clicking on the Stop Control button or by pressing the escape (Esc) key. The person you chose to control your machine will receive a password confirmation dialog box to initiate the Remote Assistance session. After that, the user can either watch your display or chat with you, or click on Take Control to begin controlling your computer.
- Remote Assistance can also begin via e-mail. Click Start > Help and Support. When the Help and Support Center opens, you will choose the Invite a friend to connect to your computer with Remote Assistance option under the Ask for

assistance heading. Click Invite someone to help you, and then enter the e-mail address of the person you are inviting. Choose Continue, and enter your name and a brief summary of the issue. For security reasons, you are able to set an expiration date for this session, which will disallow Remote Assistance connections after that date. You must also specify a password, which you will have to give to the person in a separate communication. Choose Send Invitation. Your friend will receive an e-mail with an attachment. Your friend must open the attachment, enter the password in the dialog box, and choose Yes.

■ If you use Web-based e-mail or prefer not to send the request over the Internet, you may save the request to a file. During the e-mail type of Remote Assistance (in the previous list item), you can opt to Save Invitation as a file instead of Send Invitation. This way, you can transport the request via another means than e-mail, if you have to. You can also use Web-based e-mail and attach it as a file, avoiding the necessity for Outlook Express (or similar e-mail clients).

RECOVERY CONSOLE

Recovery Console is a tool used to repair a damaged system, such as a boot problem. Windows 2000 and Windows XP both have the Recovery Console on their installation CD-ROMs. To use the Recovery Console for Windows XP, simply insert the installation CD-ROM and boot it as you normally would to install Windows XP. Press R at the blue screen to repair a Windows XP installation using Recovery Console. You will be prompted to select which installation to repair. Although there is usually just one, this gives you the option to access other Windows 2000 or Windows XP installations. You will then be prompted for the Administrator password. After logging on, you will be at a screen similar to an MS-DOS prompt, but it is actually a CMD.EXE-style prompt. If you type "HELP" at the prompt, you will be presented with a list of all possible commands. If you type a command followed by a slash and a question mark (e.g., "ATTRIB /?") you will be presented with the syntax and options specific to that command.

Although you are logged on as an Administrator, it is a more secure environment than an MS-DOS or command prompt. You are able to do the following:

■ View the root directory of all disk drives.
■ View the Windows directory and all subdirectories.
■ Access removable media, such as floppy disks and CD-ROM drives.
■ Copy files from a floppy or CD-ROM to the accessible directories.
■ Extract files from cabinet (.CAB) files.
■ Write a new boot sector or write a new MBR using FIXBOOT and FIXMBR, respectively.
■ Manage disk partitions using DISKPART.

- List, enable, or disable services using LISTSVC, ENABLE, and DISABLE, respectively.
  You are not able to do the following:
- View any directory or access files in any place other than the root of any drive and the Windows directory.
- Copy files to a floppy disk or CD-ROM from the accessible directories.

There are eight different attributes possible for files and folders when in the console. Here is a quick run-down of those attributes:

- D is for directory. Files will show a dash (-).
- A is for a file or directory that has its Archive bit turned on (see the previous section on Backup).
- R is for files and directories that are set to read-only.
- H means the file or directory is hidden.
- S on a file or directory means it has its System attribute on.
- E is for encrypted files or directories.
- C stands for compressed files or directories.
- P means reparse point. Reparse points are special NTFS file stubs that contain user-controlled data. The format of this data is understood only by the program, which stores the data as well as a file system filter that you install to interpret the data and process the file. The test is not likely to ask any questions about reparse points.

PROFILES

Profiles are separate collections of user settings. Windows XP profiles are stored in a centralized location on the system drive. Profiles specify shortcuts, settings, retain "most recently used" information, and store My Documents and other common folders. By default, local user profiles are stored in C:\Documents and Settings\. Each folder under that folder is a user's name, such as Administrator. In addition to your documents and settings, Internet Explorer history, cache, cookies, and Favorites are also stored here. There is a folder under your username called Desktop that stores all of the shortcuts that will appear on your desktop.

The All Users profile provides systemwide settings and shortcuts that all users will receive. It can only be modified by the system Administrator. In contrast, the Default User profile only specifies default settings given to each newly created user. When a user is created, the contents of the Default User profile are copied to the new user's profile folder to provide a template. Only the Administrator may edit the Default User profile.

The hidden folders, Application Data and Local Settings, under your username folder are commonly where all Microsoft Internet programs store their information. Outlook and Outlook Express, Internet Explorer, and MSN/Windows Messenger all store data here, except for cookies and Favorites, which are found directly under your username folder. Application Data stores credentials and certificates, whereas Local Settings stores a copy of the credentials, an icon cache, a Temp folder, your history, and Internet Explorer's temporary Internet files. Desktop.ini, which you will find nearly everywhere, is a file that specifies the current look and settings of the given folder in Explorer, whether icons are shown as simply Icons, Details, or Thumbnails; whether to show hidden files or system folders; and so forth. If a special icon is chosen for a folder, or if there is wallpaper applied, then it is stored in Desktop.ini as well.

When you log on to a domain controller with your username, a roaming profile is copied from your network profile's home directory to the local hard drive, and it is combined with the All Users' profile. When you are done working, any changes made to your profile are saved back to the network profile's home directory so that you may access your changes from any workstation. You can see or modify a list of profiles by right-clicking on My Computer, choosing Properties, navigating to the Advanced tab, and clicking the Settings button in the User Profiles section. You will be able to change a roaming profile to a local profile (provided that there is a roaming profile for you), or copy and delete profiles from this screen. It will also list how large the profile is in megabytes, which is helpful if you are in a network environment with space limitations.

A "mandatory" user profile is a roaming profile that is not updated when the user logs off. The system Administrator sets up a profile of specific settings and shortcuts that is delivered to a user or group of users. Only members of the Administrator group may change the mandatory profile because it is designed to provide consistent or job-specific functionality to your profile.

PRINTERS

Microsoft has yet again expanded the ease of use and installation of peripherals in Windows XP. For those already familiar with Windows 2000 printer procedures, there will be little differences other than slight wording changes or merged dialog boxes and buttons.

There are two main types of printer installations: hot-pluggable and standard. Hot-pluggable refers to newer technologies, such as infrared, IEEE 1394 (FireWire), and Universal Serial Bus (USB). Standard usually refers to serial, parallel, or Centronics connectors. Hot-pluggable printers are the easiest to install.

To ensure accurate detection of hot-pluggable devices, connect them directly to your computer's main ports, rather than through an external USB or FireWire hub, which is designed to expand the amount of ports available. If your printer came with a CD-ROM that supports Windows XP, it is a good idea to attempt to install the driver prior to connecting and powering on the printer for the first time. An even better idea is to download the latest Windows XP driver from the printer manufacturer's Web site and install it.

After your printer is connected and powered on, Windows should automatically detect the brand and model of printer, and begin searching for drivers. If Windows does not have a driver in its database, and you have not already installed one, Windows will prompt you for it. You may insert the CD-ROM at the first Found New Hardware screen, and Windows will automatically begin searching the entire CD-ROM for it. If the hardware wizard is cancelled midway through, or if there is an error, your printer will no longer be detected as a brand new device from then on. It will be listed in Device Manager with a black exclamation point on a yellow field. You should right-click on it, and choose Uninstall. This usually allows Windows to start over when you detach and reconnect the printer. There are some instances where this will not work; and in those cases, you should refer to the printer's documentation and the manufacturer's technical support channels.

Parallel printers are not usually PnP (though on very rare occasions, it has been possible). After you connect one and power it up, you have to manually install the driver and hope that Windows can communicate with it. If your printer is very old, then you may have to use the Add Printer Wizard. Navigate to the Start menu > Printers and Faxes > Add Printer. A wizard will appear that will walk you step by step through the installation of your printer. You may choose to install a local printer (connected directly to your machine) or a network printer (set up as a network share). You have the option to disable PnP detection for your printer, and it is a good idea to do so if your printer is not new. After you choose Local printer, you will have to select a port that the printer is connected to. If your printer is on a special port (such as infrared), then you will be able to select it here (although most of the time, infrared printers are detected as PnP). Standard parallel printers on standard PCs will most likely communicate on LPT1 (short for Line Printer 1, a now archaic term). There are ways to print to communications (COM) ports (such as fax drivers and serial connection printers) or even straight to a file. In many other instances, there can be a special port to print to, such as an Adobe Acrobat Portable Document Format (PDF) Writer; or if a USB printer driver has been installed but not added to the Printers folder, then you may see a special USB port here.

If your serial, parallel, or Centronics printer is fairly new, then it probably came with a CD-ROM or disks that you can install from, which will add the printer to the Printers folder (and the Add Printer Wizard list), as well as installing informative printer monitor software and other miscellaneous tools. Again, it is always recommended to download the latest drivers from a manufacturer's Web site instead of using the included driver disks.

WINDOWS XP NETWORKING AND THE INTERNET

Windows XP includes expanded networking technologies not found in any other previous version of Windows. We will discuss the new and upgraded features of Windows XP networking in this section.

The first thing to know is how to view your IP configuration. There are two main ways. If you are familiar with or prefer the command prompt, you can launch CMD (Start > Run > CMD.EXE) and type "ipconfig". This will give you an overview of your network adapter(s) and IP configurations. Instructions about the advanced options for ipconfig are available if you type "ipconfig /? | more". If you prefer to see your statistics inside Windows, then you may double-click on an active connection's lights in the notification area (near the clock). You may also visit Network Connections in the Control Panel and double-click on an active connection icon. If you double-click on a disabled connection, Windows will attempt to enable it.

NETWORK SETUP WIZARD AND NEW CONNECTION WIZARD

As with most common tasks in Windows XP, Microsoft has created wizards to guide users through the set-up of a small home or office network, or through the management of Internet connections. The first wizard we will discuss guides you through setting up Internet Connection Sharing (ICS) using the included Internet Connection Firewall, and sharing files, folders, and printers. The Network Setup Wizard is located in Network Connections, which can be found in the Control Panel. The wizard is quite self-explanatory, and there are included diagrams that will try to describe your current or desired network set-up so that you can easily configure it (see Figure 14.5).

The New Connection Wizard, which is also available in Network Connections, gives you more flexibility and also allows you to perform Internet connectivity tasks not available in the Network Setup Wizard, such as selecting PPP over Ethernet (PPPoE). PPPoE is a technology used to encapsulate Point-to-Point Protocol (PPP) frames in an Ethernet packet. This is the networking frame type most commonly used with Asymmetric Digital Subscriber Line (ADSL) connections. In the previous versions of Windows, third-party software had to be deployed for Windows to support the PPPoE frame type, allowing your system to connect using ADSL. Windows XP now includes a built-in implementation of PPPoE that is more stable, compatible, and easier to use than most third-party PPPoE software. The

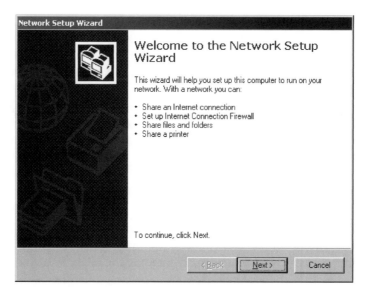

FIGURE 14.5   The Network Setup Wizard.

New Connection Wizard is the best method for connecting a new computer to the Internet because it has the most options available. If you choose the manual set-up of an Internet connection in the New Connection Wizard, you can select from three types of connections. You may connect via a dial-up modem, using a broadband connection that requires a username and password (most commonly used in ADSL or PPPoE), or using a simple broadband connection that is always on (such as a high-speed cable modem). The New Connection Wizard also allows you to easily set up a VPN or business-oriented dial-up connection. Finally, if you choose to set up an advanced connection to another computer, you have direct connection options such as serial, parallel, and infrared, or you may configure your computer to be a host for incoming direct cable connections.

BRIDGING AND INTERNET CONNECTION FIREWALL

In the Network Connections folder, your current connections and their statuses are listed. If a connection is present and enabled, but the actual cable is unplugged, you will see an icon of two computers with a red "X" over them. If a connection is present and plugged in but disabled, you will see an icon with gray computer screens. Finally, if a connection is present, plugged in, and working properly, the icon for the connection will have light blue screens on the computers. You can change the status of the connections by right-clicking on their respective icons, or selecting the icon and using the File menu. You have the options to repair, bridge, disable, or enable connections. The bridge option is unavailable via the File menu.

A Windows XP network bridge is a software solution for combining two or more local networks into one logical network. Computers on each of the two (or more) networks will be able to communicate with each other, share files and printers, and even share an Internet connection as though a hardware router or gateway were present. To create a network bridge, select two or more local networks by clicking on each network icon while holding down the Control key, and right-click on one of the icons. Choose Bridge Connections, and a new local area connection icon is created. When a local network is added to a bridge, it loses its normal properties, such as IP address, client software, protocols, and so forth. The bridged connection will keep track of all IP settings, clients, protocols, and the list of local area connections that are included in the bridge in its Properties.

Windows XP includes a new feature that no other version of Windows has included before. There is a built-in Internet Connection Firewall (ICF) that can protect your network from unwanted incoming connections and traffic (see Figure 14.6). It cannot protect you from unwanted outgoing connections, such as those coming from spyware, malware, Trojan horse virus programs, and other hacker tools, and it is not designed for use on computers that are not directly connected to the Internet. Only users of the Administrator group can enable or disable ICF. You must also understand that if ICF is enabled on a LAN connection with other computers, it will prohibit file and printer sharing.

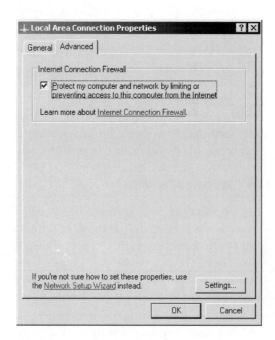

FIGURE 14.6 Enabling ICF.

To manually enable ICF, navigate to Network Connections, right-click on an Internet connection, and choose Properties. On the Advanced tab of the connection's properties, there will be a checkbox to enable ICF; and once enabled, the Settings button allows you to configure ICF further. On the Services tab of Advanced Settings, you can enable access from the Internet to certain services on your firewalled machine. This basically prevents these services from being firewalled (blocked). The next tab, Security Logging, allows you to choose whether to log dropped packets and successful connections, or change the location and size of the log file. The log file is called PFIREWALL.LOG, and it is stored in C:\WINNT or C:\WINDOWS (depending on your installation) by default. The last tab, ICMP, contains options for enabling or disabling incoming Internet Control Message Protocol (ICMP) packets. ICMP is a special error message, status, and diagnostics protocol; in contrast to TCP, ICMP is connectionless. The common ICMP messages listed here, such as echo, are used to relay error and diagnostics information. ICMP echo, also known as PING (for use with the PING program), is used to determine whether a remote computer is responding, and to check the latency and integrity between your computer and the destination. Any ICMP echo data sent to a remote computer will be returned unmodified as soon as possible. The PING program will also report how long it took to relay the information and will even glean how many route hops a given packet had to take. The Time-To-Live (TTL) value reported by the PING program refers to how long the packet will route around the Internet before it is discarded (see Figure 14.7). If there were no TTL, packets would float aimlessly on the Internet for eternity. An example of a practical use for the PING TTL is as follows: If your PING packet's TTL value is 255, and a PING response comes back with a TTL of 240, then you will know it took 15 hops through routers and other computers on the Internet before your packet reached its destination. Most TTL values are

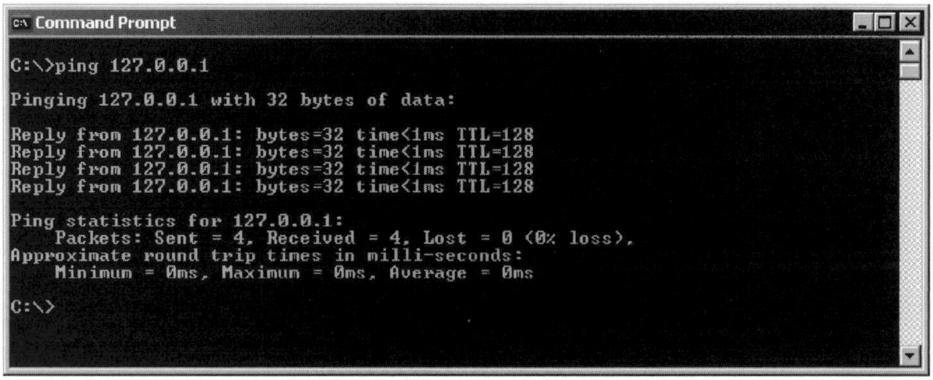

```
Command Prompt                                                    _ □ ×

C:\>ping 127.0.0.1

Pinging 127.0.0.1 with 32 bytes of data:

Reply from 127.0.0.1: bytes=32 time<1ms TTL=128
Reply from 127.0.0.1: bytes=32 time<1ms TTL=128
Reply from 127.0.0.1: bytes=32 time<1ms TTL=128
Reply from 127.0.0.1: bytes=32 time<1ms TTL=128

Ping statistics for 127.0.0.1:
    Packets: Sent = 4, Received = 4, Lost = 0 (0% loss),
Approximate round trip times in milli-seconds:
    Minimum = 0ms, Maximum = 0ms, Average = 0ms

C:\>
```

FIGURE 14.7   Pinging localhost (127.0.0.1).

based on powers of two, with the exception of 255. Common TTLs include 32, 64, 128, and 255. If a TTL value is too small, the packet will not reach its destination and will be discarded prematurely.

If an ICMP echo does not return at all, it does not necessarily mean the machine is down. It may be that there is a firewall, such as ICF, on the destination machine that is blocking ICMP echo (PING) requests. This tab is where you would specify whether you want to block such messages. Other ICMP messages you can block deliver routing, status, and troubleshooting data, such as "destination unreachable," and "parameter problem." The practical uses for the other ICMP types listed here are beyond the scope of the test. At the most, you will only need to understand ICMP echo and the use of the PING program.

FILE AND PRINTER SHARING

Like previous versions of Windows, Windows XP includes a peer-to-peer file and printer sharing client. It uses a packet protocol called Server Message Block (SMB). NetBIOS relies heavily on SMB packets to access network shares, access networked printers, and send network messages. You can install File and Printer Sharing as a client via the Properties of any connection icon in the Network Connections folder.

Windows XP Home contains only simple file sharing, but Windows XP Professional has two levels of detail for file and printer sharing. When you first enable File and Printer Sharing in Windows XP Professional, it is in simple mode. In simple mode, you do not specify which users and permissions will go to which files, folders, and printers. All users have access to all shares. Windows XP prefers that you use the Network Setup Wizard to safely share files and printers. To share files locally, you simply drag files or folders into the Documents folder for the All Users profile (located in C:\Documents and Settings\). If you want to share files or printers remotely, Microsoft recommends you use the Network Setup Wizard.

For more power and flexibility in sharing files, folders, and printers, you can enable Advanced File Sharing (in Windows XP Professional only). To do this, open any folder (or My Computer), and choose Tools > Folder Options. Under the View tab, there is a list of checkboxes for folder options. The very last item is usually Use simple file sharing (Recommended). If you uncheck this checkbox, you enable Advanced mode. In Advanced mode, you must right-click on a folder or printer and choose Sharing and Security. Then you will be able to change all the typical settings for shared folders, such as the name of the share, the users, groups, and permissions for each object you are sharing, and even shared files caching (for offline use). The test is not likely to go into shared files caching. This type of sharing uses an Access Control List (ACL), just like all of the other secured objects in a Windows NT family operating system.

DIAGNOSING AND TROUBLESHOOTING TEST TIPS

Behind the scenes, Windows XP is quite a complicated operating system. Merging the best of all Windows worlds into a single platform creates a mammoth burden of information you will have to study and remember for the new A+ exams. The following refresher tips, as well as the review questions and practice exams on the CD-ROM, are designed to give you an edge in the exam room.

■ Windows XP merges the Windows 9.x and Windows NT families into a set of two operating systems, mostly based on Windows 2000: Windows XP Home Edition and Windows XP Professional.

■ Windows XP Home can upgrade the following Windows operating systems: Windows 98/98 SE and Windows Me.

■ Windows XP Professional can upgrade the same ones as Windows XP Home, as well as Windows NT 4.0 Workstation, Windows 2000 Professional, and Windows XP Home.

■ You cannot upgrade any evaluation version or server version of Windows to Windows XP.

■ Automated System Recovery (ASR) requires Microsoft Backup, and ASR is only present in Windows XP Professional. Microsoft Backup for Windows XP Home is installable separately from the installation CD-ROM. Still, ASR is not available for Windows XP Home, even if you install Backup for Windows XP Home from the CD-ROM.

■ Windows XP includes the hibernate feature, which saves your work to your disk, turns off your monitor and hard disk, and then turns off your computer. After you restart your system, your desktop is restored to the way it was when your system went into hibernation. The hibernation feature in Windows XP is configured using the Screen Saver dialog box.

■ You cannot create installation floppy disks from a Windows XP installation CD-ROM; you must download them from Microsoft.

■ Windows XP Upgrade Advisor saves its reports to the WINDOWS directory by default.

■ Windows XP includes the Driver Rollback feature. You can use Driver Rollback to replace a corrupt or newly installed device driver that is not working properly. For example, if you install or update a video driver, and it causes your system display to flicker or freeze intermittently, you can use Driver Rollback to restore the video driver that previously worked.

■ The protocol NetBEUI is no longer supported. It can be installed separately via the CD-ROM, however, but it is still officially unsupported by Microsoft.

- ACPI is an industry standard for controlling power management features, such as Standby and Hibernate, as well as assigning resources such as IRQs, DMAs, and I/O addresses to PnP operating systems.
- WDM refers to a driver model supported in Windows Me and Windows XP. VxD files (virtual device drivers) are not supported in any Windows NT platform, including Windows XP. WHQL is the name of the Microsoft lab that performs driver testing and driver signing.
- WIA, developed by Microsoft, is a replacement technology for TWAIN, a driver model for scanners, cameras, and other imaging input devices.
- MSCONFIG's Diagnostic Startup permanently deletes all System Restore points.
- Point-to-Point Protocol over Ethernet (PPPoE), used for most ADSL or DSL installations, is supported internally by Windows XP.
- Microsoft recommends using the Network Setup Wizard to share files, folders, and printers, but you can enable advanced file sharing by opening a folder window, choosing Tools > Folder Options > View tab, and removing the check from Use simple file sharing.
- Internet Connection Firewall (ICF) will block file and printer sharing if used on a local network connection. ICF logs are stored in C:\WINDOWS (or C:\WINNT) as PFIREWALL.LOG, by default.

Chapter Summary

Although Windows XP combines the best features of every version of the entire Windows family, it is by no means an easy task to apply and understand all of the available technologies. And wait until you try to master Microsoft's latest OS release Windows Vista! With the help of this chapter, you should now be well versed in the intricate utilities and networking technologies present in Windows XP. You should now have a good understanding of the following concepts:

- The Windows XP installation and upgrade processes, specifically, which versions can be upgraded and which cannot
- The Windows XP start-up process, including HAL and its functions
- The basics of Remote Installation Service (RIS), unattended, and answer file based installations
- Windows XP administration utilities, such as MMC, Backup, System Restore, Event Viewer, Device Manager, Remote Desktop, Remote Assistance, Recovery Console, and MSCONFIG.
- Profiles: local, roaming, and mandatory
- Printer installation and troubleshooting

- How to use the Network Setup Wizard to configure networking components
- How to use the New Connection Wizard to connect to the Internet, especially with broadband adapters
- How to install ICF and understand what it can and cannot do

The best way to assert your skills is to ensure that you understand not only which answer is the correct answer but why a particular answer is correct and others are not. The following review questions will give you an opportunity to test your comprehension of this chapter, as well as help prepare you for the exam.

REVIEW QUESTIONS

1. **While installed on a local area connection, an Internet Connection Firewall (ICF) will do which of the following (choose two)?**
   - ☐ A. Block unwanted outgoing traffic
   - ☐ B. Block unwanted incoming traffic
   - ☐ C. Block File and Printer sharing traffic
   - ☐ D. Block unwanted cookies

   Correct answers = B and C

   ICF cannot block outgoing traffic. Cookies are documents created by Web pages that want to store information about your visit to a particular site, and therefore are not blocked by ICF. File and Printer sharing traffic is blocked only if you install ICF on a local area connection (instead of an Internet connection).

2. **PPPoE is a technology used for which of the following connection types?**
   - ○ A. Broadband
   - ○ B. Cable
   - ○ C. Dial-up
   - ○ D. ADSL

   Correct answer = D

   Broadband is a general term that refers to carrying several data channels across a common wire. Cable TV, cable Internet, and DSL are all broadband technologies. The specific connection type that uses PPPoE is typically ADSL. PPPoE allows the user to experience the same traditional login that they were used to on dial-up, as well as keeping ISP costs down. PPPoE is very easy to implement on both the ISP and the end-user side.

3. **To create a new user account, you must navigate to:**

   ○ A. Control Panel—User Accounts
   ○ B. User Manager—User Accounts
   ○ C. Control Panel—Users
   ○ D. Settings—Users

   Correct answer = A

   Users are located in User Accounts in the Control Panel.

4. **The acronym for the central administration utility is:**

   ○ A. MCA
   ○ B. MCC
   ○ C. MMC
   ○ D. MAC

   Correct answer = C

   MMC stands for Microsoft Management Console.

5. **Time-to-Live (TTL) references which of the following?**

   ○ A. Amount of route hops before a packet is discarded
   ○ B. The time available to activate a Windows Evaluation product
   ○ C. Amount of latency between source and destination
   ○ D. The contrast of Time to Die

   Correct Answer = A

   Without TTL, packets could float around the Internet for eternity. You can see a TTL value when you PING a remote computer. Latency is a value in milliseconds, also reported by the PING program.

6. **The BOOT.INI tab of MSCONFIG shows you which of the following?**

   ○ A. The boot paths of each Windows operating system installed
   ○ B. Boot options for troubleshooting, such as /SAFEBOOT, /SOS, and /BASEVIDEO
   ○ C. All of the above
   ○ D. None of the above

   Correct answer = C

   The BOOT.INI tab of MSCONFIG can show you the menu delay time-out, the default operating system, the settings for each operating system, and a button to diagnose and repair invalid BOOT.INI boot paths as well.

7. **Which folder on a Windows XP machine commonly stores local profiles (e.g., Application Data)?**

   ○ A.   C:\My Documents\
   ○ B.   C:\Profiles and Settings\
   ○ C.   C:\Documents and Settings\
   ○ D.   C:\Documents and Profiles\

   Correct answer = C

   Documents and Settings is the name of the folder that houses each user's My Documents, Application Data, Temporary Internet Files, cookies, and more. My Documents has been moved to Documents and Settings under your username.

8. **Which version of Windows cannot be upgraded to Windows XP Professional?**

   ○ A.   Windows 98
   ○ B.   Windows NT 4.0
   ○ C.   Windows 2000 Professional
   ○ D.   Windows 3.1

   Correct answer = D

   The only version of Windows listed here that cannot be upgraded to Windows XP Professional is Windows 3.1.

9. **Which file allows you to extract Setup Manager for creating answer files?**

   ○ A.   EMPLOY.CAB
   ○ B.   SETUPMGR.CAB
   ○ C.   ANSWER.CAB
   ○ D.   DEPLOY.CAB
   ○ E.   None of the above

   Correct answer = D

   An updated DEPLOY.CAB is available on Microsoft's Web site, but the original file on the installation CD-ROM (Support > Tools) also allows you to install Setup Manager. The other answers are fictitious.

10. **BOOTSECT.DOS is:**
    - ○ A. A backed up copy of your old operating system's MBR
    - ○ B. A backed up copy of your old operating system's file system boot sector
    - ○ C. A backed up copy of your old autoexec.bat
    - ○ D. A backed up copy of MS-DOS 6.22
    - ○ E. None of the above

Correct answer = B

Not to be confused with the MBR, a file system boot sector is an operating system partition's program that loads the operating system into RAM. MBR is your hard drive's overall table of contents, including partitions, and a program that actually loads the desired operating system partition's boot sector to launch the operating system. MBR is the first physical sector on a drive, and a file system boot sector is the first sector in any given logical volume or partition.

11. **You are running Windows XP on a laptop and want it configured to hibernate when the lid is closed. Where do you set this feature set in Windows XP?**
    - ○ A. From the Screen Saver dialog box
    - ○ B. Control Panel > Power Options > Hibernate Lid
    - ○ C. In the BIOS
    - ○ D. In the CMOS
    - ○ E. None of the above

Correct answer = A

Windows XP includes the hibernate feature that saves your work to your disk, turns off your monitor and hard disk, and then turns off your computer. After you restart your system, your desktop is restored to the way it was when your system went into hibernation. The hibernation feature in Windows XP is configured using the Screen Saver dialog box.

12. **You work for the Gizmo Computer Corporation. You have a client who has recently attempted to update a video driver on his Windows XP system. After rebooting the system, the client states that the display freezes intermittently. What should do to assist this client with this issue?**
    - ○ A. Replace the video card.
    - ○ B. Reboot the system, go to Safe Mode, and use Driver Rollback.

○ C. Reboot the system. right-click on the desktop, select Properties, and lower the display resolution.

○ D. None of the above.

Correct answer = B

If you install or update a video driver, and it causes your system display to flicker or freeze intermittently, you can use Driver Rollback to restore the video driver that previously worked.

13. **You need to do some routine maintenance on some customer Windows XP systems. You have recently run the Disk Cleanup utility and emptied and removed Temporary Internet and Offline files. What utility should you use now that will better organize your files and allow your system to perform more efficiently?**

○ A. Checker.sys

○ B. Defrag.exe

○ C. File Manager

○ D. None of the above

Correct answer = B

Defrag.exe puts the files on your hard drive in contiguous order. This allows your system to access the files in a more organized fashion, which in turn provides better overall performance.

14. **You are installing Windows XP on a system. You put the Windows XP Installation CD into the CD-ROM and reboot the system. The computer boots straight into the currently installed OS and does not read your CD. What is most likely the problem?**

○ A. Windows XP Installation CDs are not bootable.

○ B. You need to configure the first OS in the Boot.ini file to use Windows XP.

○ C. You need to configure the CD-ROM as the first boot device in the BIOS.

○ D. None of the above.

Correct answer = C

By default, most BIOS settings are configured to use the hard drive as the first boot device in the boot order. In this situation, it is likely that you need to configure the CD-ROM as the first boot device in the BIOS.

15. **A colleague calls you and says his Windows XP system will not boot. He can't even get to the Advanced Boot options to troubleshoot. Which of the following could you suggest to your colleague to help get his system up?**

○ A. Insert the Windows XP CD-ROM, restart the system, and begin the ASR restoration process.

○ B. Configure the first OS in the Boot.ini file to use Windows XP.

○ C. Your colleague's system is now a boat anchor. Reformat and reinstall everything.

○ D. None of the above.

Correct answer = A

If a system will not boot, and you cannot get to the Advanced Boot options menu, the next step to recovering from such a traumatic event is to insert the Windows XP CD-ROM, restart the system, and begin the ASR restoration process.

16. **You have a new customer with a laptop configured using FAT. The customer uses one folder with many personal documents and is concerned with security. What two things should you do for this customer to better secure the data on his laptop?**

☐ A. Convert the file system on the laptop to NTFS.

☐ B. Tell the customer to install Linux on the laptop.

☐ C. Encrypt the folder that contains the customer's personal data.

☐ D. Suggest to the customer that he should get a new biometrically secured laptop if he is that concerned with security.

Correct answers = A and C

An NTFS is much more secure than FAT. NTFS offers the ability to encrypt files and folders. The best practice would be to encrypt the folder where the customer's data is stored and suggest that the customer store all future personal documents in that folder. Installing Linux is not a bad idea for those who are very computer literate. However, it is not the answer here. A biometrically secured laptop is a great idea if the customer has money to burn. The answers in this situation are A and C. At this point, if you missed this question, save your money, you are not ready for the exams.

17. **You have the daunting task of upgrading 10 systems from Windows 95 to Windows XP for a frugal customer. How should you go about this upgrade?**
    - ○ A.   To save time and money, upgrade all 10 systems directly to Windows XP.
    - ○ B.   Upgrade the 10 systems to Windows NT Server, and then upgrade to Windows XP.
    - ○ C.   Upgrade all 10 systems to Windows 98 and then to Windows XP.
    - ○ D.   None of the above.

    Correct answer = C

    When upgrading Windows versions, it is important to verify that the upgrade you want to do is a valid option. In this case, Windows 95 cannot be directly upgraded to Windows XP; it must first be upgraded to another operating system such as Windows 98 or Me and then to XP. However, it may be better to perform a clean install and avoid such cumbersome upgrade paths.

18. **To increase security, you want to disable some unnecessary services when your system starts up. How in Windows XP can you stop services from starting up automatically?**
    - ○ A.   Click Start > Run > Services.
    - ○ B.   From Administrative Tools, choose the Services applet.
    - ○ C.   Go to Control Panel > System > Services.
    - ○ D.   None of the above.

    Correct answer = B

    You can configure services to start automatically, start them manually, or prevent them from running all together from the Administrative Tools Services applet.

19. **Which tool is used to configure the Windows XP start-up environment?**
    - ○ A.   Msconfig
    - ○ B.   Config.dat
    - ○ C.   Startup.conf
    - ○ D.   None of the above

    Correct answer = A

    The System Configuration (msconfig) is a Windows tool used to isolate and fix system problems. It can be used to configure which programs start when Windows boots. This can be helpful in the diagnostic process. To start msconfig, type "msconfig" in the Run dialog box, and click OK.

20. **Your boss's Windows XP laptop running Windows XP is very low on virtual memory. Which of the following options should you consider? (Choose Two)**

    ☐ A.   Format the hard drive.
    ☐ B.   Increase the size of the paging file.
    ☐ C.   Add more physical memory to the system.
    ☐ D.   Suggest to your boss that he should get a new laptop. His resources are almost gone on this one.

    Correct answers = B and C.

    Adding more memory and/or increasing the size of your paging file will allow you to have more memory for programs and applications on your system. It is very likely that this question will appear in some form on the real exams!

REFERENCES

http://microsoft.com/whdc/hcl/search.mspx. The latest HCL is available from Microsoft.

http://microsoft.com/downloads/details.aspx?FamilyID=E8FE6868-6E4F-471C-B455-BD5AFEE126D8. The Windows XP Home floppy disk creation utility is available for download here.

http://microsoft.com/downloads/details.aspx?FamilyID=55820edb-5039-4955-bcb7-4fed408ea73f. The Windows XP Professional floppy disk creation utility is available for download here.

http://microsoft.com/downloads/details.aspx?familyid=7a83123d-507b-4095-9d9d-0a195f7b5f69. Get the updated Setup Manager to create answer files.

www.microsoft.com/windowsxp/using/mobility/getstarted/remoteintro.mspx. The Microsoft Web site that shows you how to set up and use Remote Desktop.

10-14 Test Taker's Cumulative Practice Exam

The questions in this practice exam are based on topics that have been presented in Chapters 10 through 14 of this book. The answers to the following questions as well as the chapter headers they are taken from are provided at the end of the exam.

If you can answer all of the questions in this practice exam correctly as well as the questions provided in the Chapters 2-9 cumulative Test Taker's exam, there is a good possibility that you may pass any of the four CompTIA A+ certification examinations.

1. **What is the overall system starting order?**

   ○ A. POST, BIOS, Boot Sector, GUI
   ○ B. Boot Sector, POST, BIOS, GUI
   ○ C. POST, GUI, MBR, BIOS
   ○ D. Push the button, hope the magic happens

2. **What is the command used to make a bootable floppy system disk?**

   ○ A. `FORMAT A: /S`
   ○ B. `FORMAT /S A:`
   ○ C. `SYS A: /FORMAT`
   ○ D. `MAKEFLOPPYBOOTABLE.BAT`

3. **How can you start the Disk Defragmenter utility in Windows 9.X? (Choose Three)**

   ☐ A. Start > Programs > Accessories > System Tools > Disk Defragmenter
   ☐ B. Control Panel > System > Performance > Virtual Memory
   ☐ C. My Computer > right-click on drive > Properties > Tools > Defragment Now
   ☐ D. Start > Run > type in "defrag" > click OK > click OK again
   ☐ E. Start > Programs > Accessories > System > Device Manager

4. **SCANDISK is a utility that scans and fixes problems with which? (Choose Two)**

☐ A. Hard drives
☐ B. Tape drives
☐ C. CD-ROM drives
☐ D. Floppy drives

5. **In Windows 9.X, what files can you edit by using the text editor SYSEDIT? (Choose Two)**

☐ A. MSDOS.SYS
☐ B. WIN.INI
☐ C. IO.SYS
☐ D. AUTOEXEC.BAT

6. **You want to make changes to the AUTOEXEC.BAT and WIN.INI files. What Windows text editors can be used? (Choose Two)**

☐ A. SYSEDIT
☐ B. REGEDIT
☐ C. EDITPAD
☐ D. NOTEPAD

7. **You attempt to run a 16-bit DOS program in Windows 95 and receive the error** This program cannot be run in Windows. **What action should you take?**

○ A. Reformat the drive, and install DOS 5.5.
○ B. Reboot in MS-DOS mode, and rerun the program.
○ C. Increase your virtual memory settings.
○ D. Change the Advanced Properties for the program to Prevent MS-DOS-based programs from detecting Windows.

8. **If you use the command** XCOPY /s **from a DOS prompt in Windows 9.X, what will happen?**

○ A. All of the directories and subdirectories will be copied.
○ B. Only hidden and archived files will be copied.
○ C. Only the system files will be copied.
○ D. Nothing. The /s switch is invalid with XCOPY.

9. **If the Memory Manager in Windows 9.X cannot provide memory to an application, what will occur?**

○ A. A Book fault
○ B. A hard drive crash
○ C. A Page fault
○ D. A blue screen of death

10. **In Device Manager, your NIC has a yellow circle with a black exclamation point on it. Why?**

○ A. It is not working properly and is in a problem state.
○ B. It has been disabled.
○ C. It is not recognized by the system at all.
○ D. Windows doesn't support cards from NIC anymore.

11. **You are running Windows 9.X. How can you direct a print job straight to the printer instead of the print spooler?**

○ A. Select Start > Settings > Control Panel > Disable Spooler
○ B. In the Spool Settings dialog box, select Print directly to the printer.
○ C. In the Spool Settings dialog box, select Disable printer spooling.
○ D. Specify Full-Duplex printing.

12. **What command can you use to get an important system file or executable file from the Windows 9.X installation CD?**

○ A. EXTRACT
○ B. COPY D:\FILENAME C:\WINDOWS\SYSTEM
○ C. RESTORE
○ D. IMPORT

13. **You are experiencing strange things in Windows 9.X. Your taskbar is missing, and you cannot load certain programs. What is most likely the cause?**

○ A. The AUTOEXEC.BAT file is corrupt.
○ B. You have experienced a total hard drive crash.
○ C. The Windows 9.X registry is corrupt.
○ D. The WIN.INI and SYSTEM.INI files are corrupt.

14. **Which file executes when you restart your computer in MS-DOS mode?**

○ A. DOSSTART.BAT
○ B. DEFRAG.EXE
○ C. WINSTART.BAT
○ D. DOSBOOT.EXE

15. **System Monitor in Windows 9.X can be used to monitor which information? (Choose Three)**

    ☐ A. RAID configurations
    ☐ B. Virtual memory
    ☐ C. Network client resources (on local computer)
    ☐ D. Network server memory (on local computer)
    ☐ E. Differential backup scenarios
    ☐ F. Windows NT audit trails

16. **You are having trouble displaying entire Web pages in your Web browser. You want to view entire pages without having to use the left to right scrollbars. What should you modify?**

    ○ A. Use the screen size buttons on your monitor.
    ○ B. Select the Advanced tab under Display Properties Settings and change the Font Size.
    ○ C. With your mouse, move the Screen Area Bar from 640 x 480 to 800 x 600 or more.
    ○ D. Select the Advanced tab under Display Properties Settings and select big screen.

17. **In what order should you prepare a hard drive before a Windows 9.X installation?**

    ○ A. FDISK, FORMAT, reboot the system.
    ○ B. Reboot the system, FDISK, FORMAT.
    ○ C. FORMAT, FDISK, reboot the system.
    ○ D. Simply run the DOS program PREPARE.BAT before installation.

18. **The Dr. Watson utility offers two ways to view information that it has logged. What are they?**

    ○ A. Diagnostic View and Report View
    ○ B. Standard View and Advanced View
    ○ C. Standard View and Graphics View
    ○ D. Text View and GUI View

19. **You need more hard drive space to install a really big game in Windows 9.X. You notice a large amount of unnecessary Temporary Internet files. How do you get rid of them? (Choose Three)**

    ☐ A. `C:\DELTREE`.
    ☐ B. The Disk Cleanup tool.
    ☐ C. Internet Explorer Tools > Internet Options > Delete Files.
    ☐ D. Control Panel > Internet Options > Delete Files.
    ☐ E. Internet Explorer Tools > Advanced > Restore Defaults.
    ☐ F. Drag the Internet Explorer icon to the Recycle Bin.

20. **Which backup type is the fastest and requires the least amount of tape storage space?**

    ○ A. Full backup
    ○ B. Incremental backup
    ○ C. Differential backup
    ○ D. Full/Copy backup

21. **What is characteristic of an incremental backup?**

    ○ A. Will only back files up to a ZIP drive
    ○ B. Backs up all files no matter what
    ○ C. Backs up all files with the archive bit set to off
    ○ D. Backs up all files with the archive bit set to on

22. **Which devices can be shared on a network using Windows 98? (Choose Three)**

    ☐ A. Monitor
    ☐ B. Printer
    ☐ C. Modem
    ☐ D. CD-ROM
    ☐ E. Mouse
    ☐ F. Keyboard

23. **Which protocols can be used to share printers in Windows 9.X? (Choose Three)**

    ☐ A. NETBEUI
    ☐ B. TCP/IP
    ☐ C. IPX/SPX
    ☐ D. NETBIOS
    ☐ E. TCP/IPRINT
    ☐ F. PTPTPC

24. **What action should you first attempt if print jobs are hung up or stalled in Windows NT or Windows 2000?**

    ○ A. Change the parallel printer cable
    ○ B. Stop and start the spooler service
    ○ C. Restart the file and print server
    ○ D. Reinstall the printer driver

25. **Which TCP/IP utility command would you use from a Windows NT command prompt to see your workstations IP address, subnet mask, and default gateway?**

    ○ A. IPCONFIG
    ○ B. WINIPCFG
    ○ C. PING
    ○ D. TRACERT

26. **Which TCP/IP utility command would you use from a Windows NT command prompt to test a connection that includes several computers and routers between you and a destination computer?**

    ○ A. NETSTAT
    ○ B. WINIPCFG
    ○ C. PING
    ○ D. TRACERT

27. **What does Dr. Watson do?**

    ○ A. Provides access to the blue screen of death
    ○ B. Takes a picture or "snapshot" of a system during an error state or fault
    ○ C. Automatically resets the Event Log files when run from a command prompt
    ○ D. Does a full system and registry scan for spyware

28. **Which utilities can be used to determine the IP address of known Internet domain names? (Choose Three)**

    ☐ A. NETBEUI
    ☐ B. PING
    ☐ C. TRACERT
    ☐ D. NETBIOS
    ☐ E. NSLOOKUP
    ☐ F. PONG
    ☐ G. All of the above

29. Where in Windows NT would you go to join a workgroup or a domain?

○ A. Control Panel > System > Network > Change

○ B. Right-click on Network Neighborhood > select Properties > select Change under the Identification tab

○ C. Start > Run > Command > Join

○ D. Right-click on My Computer > select Properties > Advanced > Environment

30. What will you often see when a Windows operating system suddenly halts or terminates?

○ A. A Red white and blue screen

○ B. A Unix or Linux replacement

○ C. The infamous BSOD

○ D. The message `Boot could not find NTLDR. Please insert another disk.`

31. If you are trying to connect to an ISP through a dial-up connection and you keep getting the error message `Server cannot negotiate an appropriate protocol`. What is most likely the problem?

○ A. You have IPX/SPX bound to your NIC.

○ B. Your ISP has run out of available connections.

○ C. Your modem driver is corrupt.

○ D. You have an improperly configured or corrupt TCP/IP configuration.

32. What protocol is used to communicate with Macintosh systems?

○ A. TCP/IP

○ B. AppleJacks

○ C. IPX/SPX

○ D. SMTP

○ E. None of the Above

33. You can receive e-mail messages without any problems. Unfortunately, you cannot send e-mail. What settings should you check?

○ A. IMAP

○ B. MAPI

○ C. POP

○ D. SMTP

○ E. None of the Above

34. **Which of the following are built-in power schemes available from the drop-down menu in the Power Options Properties/Power Schemes window in Windows 2000? (Choose Six)**

    ☐ A. Home/Office Desk
    ☐ B. Portable/Laptop
    ☐ C. Presentation
    ☐ D. Always On
    ☐ E. Minimal Power Management
    ☐ F. Max Battery
    ☐ G. Always Off
    ☐ H. Golf Course/Heath Club

35. **Which operating systems have Device Manager? (Choose Four)**

    ☐ A. Windows 9.X
    ☐ B. Windows Me
    ☐ C. Windows 2000
    ☐ D. Windows NT
    ☐ E. Windows XP

36. **How many set-up floppy disks can be created from the Windows XP (Home or Professional) CD-ROM?**

    ○ A. Three
    ○ B. Four
    ○ C. Six
    ○ D. None of the above

37. **Which of the following versions of Windows can be upgraded to Windows XP Professional (Choose Two)?**

    ☐ A. Windows 95
    ☐ B. Windows 98/SE
    ☐ C. Windows 3.1
    ☐ D. Windows XP Home

38. **Which of the following Windows XP utilities would you first use in troubleshooting hardware-related issues?**

    ○ A. Automated System Recovery (ASR)
    ○ B. CMD.EXE
    ○ C. SYSPREP.EXE
    ○ D. Computer Management

39. **Your USB printer has been detected, but Windows XP will not install the printer driver. What should you do?**
    - ○ A. Check the Device Manager for your printer, and perform an Uninstall on it.
    - ○ B. Check Peripheral Management for your printer, and perform a Reinstall on it.
    - ○ C. Disconnect and reconnect the printer.
    - ○ D. Roll-back the driver.

40. **Which version of Windows does not include NT Backup by default?**
    - ○ A. Windows XP Professional
    - ○ B. Windows XP Home
    - ○ C. Windows NT 4.0
    - ○ D. Windows 98

41. **An unattended installation of Windows XP requires which kind of file?**
    - ○ A. Question
    - ○ B. INI
    - ○ C. UDF
    - ○ D. Answer

42. **Which kind of file do you use to override specific settings created for an unattended installation?**
    - ○ A. Question
    - ○ B. INI
    - ○ C. UDF
    - ○ D. Answer

43. **Automated System Recovery (ASR) is available in which Windows NT-based operating system?**
    - ○ A. Windows XP Home
    - ○ B. Windows XP Professional
    - ○ C. Windows NT 4.0
    - ○ D. All of the above

44. **Which key must you press during text-mode setup of Windows XP to load RAID or SCSI drivers from a floppy?**
    - ○ A. F3
    - ○ B. F4
    - ○ C. F5
    - ○ D. F6

45. **A hardware abstraction layer (HAL) provides secured, restrictive access to which of the following (choose two)?**
   - ☐ A. The Registry
   - ☐ B. Software
   - ☐ C. IRQ
   - ☐ D. I/O addresses

46. **Driver signing and testing in Windows XP is also known as?**
   - ○ A. Windows Logo Testing
   - ○ B. Windows Hardware Quality Labs (WHQL)
   - ○ C. Windows Logo Compatible
   - ○ D. Windows Driver Testing

47. **Which of the following versions of Windows was the first to feature System Restore?**
   - ○ A. Windows 95
   - ○ B. Windows 98SE
   - ○ C. Windows Me
   - ○ D. Windows XP

48. **When upgrading to Windows Me, you are prompted to save your system files. Should you not choose to save these files, you will be unable to:**
   - ○ A. Revert back to your previous operating system after Windows Me is installed.
   - ○ B. Continue the upgrade installation.
   - ○ C. Use programs associated with the older operating system you are installing over.
   - ○ D. Use REGEDIT to update your registry after Windows Me has been installed.

49. **Which of the following operating systems could be upgraded to Windows Me (Choose two)?**
   - ☐ A. Windows 98SE
   - ☐ B. Windows XP
   - ☐ C. Windows 2000
   - ☐ D. Windows 98

50. Which of the following operating systems are considered a part of the Windows 9.x family (Choose Two)?
    - ☐ A. Windows 98SE
    - ☐ B. Windows CE
    - ☐ C. Windows XP
    - ☐ D. Windows Me

TEST TAKER'S CUMULATIVE PRACTICE EXAM ANSWERS

Answer Key	Question taken from
1. A	Chapter 10 "DOS System and Configuration Files"
2. A	Chapter 10 "DOS\Windows Utilities"
3. A, C, and D	Chapter 10 "DOS\Windows Utilities"
4. A and D	Chapter 10 "DOS\Windows Utilities"
5. B and D	Chapter 10 "Windows Initialization Files"
6. A and D	Chapter 10 "Windows Initialization Files"
7. D	Chapter 10 "Memory Management Utilities"
8. A	Chapter 10 "DOS Commands, Switches, and Wildcards"
9. C	Chapter 10 "Memory Management Utilities"
10. A	Chapter 11 "Utilities and Settings"
11. B	Chapter 11 "Printers"
12. A	Chapter 11 "Diagnosing and Troubleshooting Test Tips"
13. C	Chapter 11 "The Windows 9.X Registry"
14. A	Chapter 11 "Diagnosing and Troubleshooting Test Tips"
15. B, C, and D	Chapter 11 "Utilities and Settings"
16. C	Chapter 11 "Utilities and Settings"
17. A	Chapter 11 "Installation and Upgrading"
18. B	Chapter 11 "Utilities and Settings"
19. B, C, and D	Chapter 11 "Utilities and Settings"
20. B	Chapter 11 "Utilities and Settings"
21. D	Chapter 11 "Utilities and Settings"
22. B, C, and D	Chapter 11 "Printers"

23. A, B, and C	Chapter 11 "Windows 9.X Networking"
24. B	Chapter 12 "Printers"
25. A	Chapter 12 "Utilities and Settings"
26. D	Chapter 12 "Utilities and Settings"
27. B	Chapter 12 "Diagnosing and Troubleshooting Test Tips"
28. B, C, and E	Chapter 12 "Diagnosing and Troubleshooting Test Tips"
29. B	Chapter 12 "Diagnosing and Troubleshooting Test Tips"
30. C	Chapter 12 "Diagnosing and Troubleshooting Test Tips"
31. D	Chapter 13 "Diagnosing and Troubleshooting Test Tips"
32. A	Chapter 13 "Diagnosing and Troubleshooting Test Tips"
33. D	Chapter 13 "Windows 2000 Networking and the Internet"
34. A, B, C, D, E, and F	Chapter 13 "Windows 2000 Tools and Utilities"
35. A, B, C, and E	Chapter 13 "Windows 2000 Tools and Utilities"
36. D	Chapter 14 "Windows XP Installation Process"
37. B and D	Chapter 14 "Windows XP Upgrade Procedures"
38. D	Chapter 14 "Windows XP Tools and Utilities"
39. A	Chapter 14 "Printers"
40. B	Chapter 14 "Windows XP Tools and Utilities"
41. D	Chapter 14 "Windows XP Installation Process"
42. C	Chapter 14 "Windows XP Installation Process"
43. B	Chapter 14 "Windows XP Installation Process"
44. D	Chapter 14 "Windows XP Installation Process"
45. C and D	Chapter 14 "Windows XP Startup Process"
46. A	Chapter 14 "Windows XP Tools and Utilities"
47. C	Chapter 11 "Windows Me System Restore"
48. A	Chapter 11 "Windows Me Installation Process"
49. A and D	Chapter 11 "Windows Me Installation Process"
50. A and D	Chapter 11 "Windows Me"

15 Final A+ Exam Preparation

In This Chapter

- Final A+ Exam Preparation Tips
- Domain 1.0 Personal Computer Components
- Domain 2.0 Laptops and Portable Devices
- Domain 3.0 Operating Systems
- Domain 4.0 Printers and Scanners
- Domain 5.0 Networks
- Domain 6.0 Security
- Domain 7.0 Safety and Environmental Issues
- Domain 8.0 Communication and Professionalism

FINAL A+ EXAM PREPARATION TIPS

Welcome to Chapter 15! You are looking at the best available cram sheet for the new A+ Exam available on this planet. This is also like a book within a book. The good news is this is the only chapter you need to pass all four A+ exams. That's right. This chapter is a culmination of the very best A+ exams test tips available. In fact, 15 students were recently given the tips in this chapter alone to prepare for and take the four exams. All 15 students passed the various combinations of the four exams and became A+ certified the first time around.

You should go over this chapter directly before taking your exams. It includes very pertinent exam-related tips for all eight CompTIA A+ domains. There is not a lot of fluff or unnecessary information here. You will not find a lot or pretty screen-shots here. The fact is the exams do not show you a lot of screenshots and I don't either. These very direct tips that cut straight to the chase and give you what you need to pass. The short topics included in this chapter change very quickly. Just like the real questions on the exams. Going through these tips several times is the best brain stretch practice you can get before attempting the exams. Take your time here and focus.

DOMAIN 1.0 PERSONAL COMPUTER COMPONENTS

The exams require you to understand the names, purposes, and characteristics of PC components. The exams also want to know that you know how to install, update, and troubleshoot many hardware-related components and issues. Our goal here is to narrow the playing field a little. There are literally millions of questions you could be asked regarding hardware! Fortunately, we have some idea what they might be and how they might be worded. So pay close attention. These tips may be very close to what you see on the exams as they relate to computer hardware and technical procedures.

- SIMMs (Single Inline Memory Module), DIMMs (Dual Inline Memory Module), and SODIMMs (Small Outline DIMMs) are types of memory sticks. SIMMs were used in older computer systems and came in 30- and 72-pin memory modules. DIMMs are currently the most common types of memory modules and come in modules of 168-, 184-, and 240-pins. DIMMs have a 64-bit data transfer rate. SODIMMs are memory modules used in laptop computers. They are packaged in 72-, 100-, 144-, or 200-pin memory modules.
- If you are asked a question relating to the proper way to remove hardware from a system, for example, an external hard drive, you need to remember that it is recommended to use the Safely Remove Hardware icon located in the systems taskbar. Using the Safely Remove Hardware icon will cause the device to stop and allow you to safely remove it without causing damage to the system.
- The exams are going to ask you the most important consideration before installing, upgrading, or in fact making any changes to workstation or server systems. You will be presented with options such as document the whole procedure or make sure you follow the proper instructions. These are included to lead you astray. Before making any changes ever, you should make backups of the data on the workstation or server. Don't miss the easy ones!
- The A+ exams love to ask questions regarding wireless connectivity. You should remember for the exams that an IrDA connection is an ad-hoc point-to-point wireless standard used in most small wireless networks today. It transmits at speeds of 9600 to 16 Mbps and has a distance range of 0 to 1 meter. It is likely that you will see a question that states something to the effect that a customer has moved their wireless laptop or printer in their office. Why can't they

print anymore? The simple answer will be that they are using IrDA, and their wireless laptop and printer are too far apart.

■ Another wireless technology that is sure to appear on the exams is Bluetooth. Bluetooth is a short-range radio wireless technology standard that is often used to connect peripherals devices to a system. Bluetooth operates from the 2.4 GHz to 2.48 GHz range. And as long as we are on the subject, you should memorize the 802.11 wireless standard speeds and radio frequencies. 802.11a offers speeds up to 54 Mbps and uses a frequency of 5 GHz. 802.11b offers speeds up to 11 Mbps and operates at 2.4 GHz. And 802.11g offers speeds of 54 Mbps and uses a 2.4-GHz radio frequency.

■ The exams are going to ask you hardware questions that require basic common sense. For example, you have a client that used a monitor fine yesterday. Today, the customer turns the monitor on, and it is black. What is the first thing you should do in this situation? The simple answer is to check and ensure that the power cord to the monitor is plugged in! Don't over think the questions. You will over think your way to failure. Here is another example, the exams may ask you: A client calls and states that the fan in his main server's power supply has failed. What part of the power supply should you attempt to replace? This is a no-brainer that shows up on the exams all the time. You should replace the whole power supply. It is safer, faster, and more cost effective to do so.

■ When working with or troubleshooting SCSI devices, the biggest considerations are the SCSI device IDs, host adapter compatibility, and termination. Remember, a SCSI bus must be terminated at both ends.

■ When it comes to computer components, ESD is a major concern. You will see questions regarding ESD on the exams. The best precautions to take to avoid ESD are to implement ESD floor mats (especially in carpeted areas) and use antistatic wrist straps and antistatic spray.

■ You must remember for the exams that RAID 0 is not fault tolerant. If you implement a RAID 0 solution, and one disk fails, all data is lost. You must also remember that RAID 5 is the most fault-tolerant of the RAID implementations mentioned. RAID 5 uses a minimum of three disks and distributes the party among all three. If one disk fails, you can recover from the failure. It is likely the exams will expect you to know these two forms or RAID.

■ You will likely see a question on the exams that states something like you have just installed an IDE hard drive, and it is not recognized by the system after installation. What should you check? There is only one answer to this question. There is a red line on an IDE cable that should match up with pin#1 on the hard disk and pin#1 on the motherboard. On most new systems, the cable is keyed on the motherboard so you can't connect the cable incorrectly. However, this is not the case on many older systems.

■ Peculiar questions have been recently identified on the current A+ exams. One of these can be seen in the form of the following question. You hear a noise coming from a system. What is most likely the cause of the noise? This is a very general open-ended question. In reality, the answer to this question could be just about anything. What the exams are looking for is a worn out or broken CPU, power supply, or video card fan. When cooling fans that support these devices fail, they make noise. A very popular question regarding CPUs can also be seen in this form: You have recently installed a new CPU, heat sink, and fan in a system. You put the box together and turn the system on. Within minutes, the CPU overheats. What did you forget? Answer: You forgot to use thermal paste or grease between the heat sink and the CPU.

■ When a system boots, the POST runs. If the POST detects errors, it will produce a numeric POST error on the screen. Remember these POST error codes: 100 to 199=motherboard, 200 to 299=memory, 300 to 399=keyboard, and 600 to 699=floppy drive.

■ You should remember that a UPS is designed to hold power just long enough to a system to save your data and safely shut the system down. A good UPS should provide protection against power spikes, surges, and sags. It is not recommended that you count on a UPS for long-term power outages. It also not recommended to use UPSs for laser printers, scanners, and other higher powered peripheral devices. And a real-world tip, do not let users plug those little desk fans into the same circuit that is being used for computer devices. Big big no no!

■ If you continuously need to reenter the system time every time you reboot a system or you receive a CMOS Checksum error, you more than likely need to replace the CMOS battery. This battery is used to keep just enough power to the CMOS to store hardware, date, and time settings.

■ You will be asked to identify the proper video card specification for a given situation. For example, you are upgrading or replacing an AGP video card for a client who plays a lot of high-end games at work. What is the speed of AGP 8x? You need to remember the important AGP specifications that were previously detailed in this book for the exams:
  ■ AGP 1x (66 MHz with a maximum data rate of 266 MBps)
  ■ AGP 2x (133 MHz and a maximum data rate of 533 MBps)
  ■ AGP 4x (266 MHz with a maximum data rate of 1066 MBps)
  ■ AGP 8x (533 MHz and a maximum data rate of 2133 MBps)

DOMAIN 2.0 LAPTOPS AND PORTABLE DEVICES

Laptops and their peripherals have taken the world by storm. All four A+ Exams are going to bombard examinees with questions related to configuring and maintaining laptops, portable devices, and wireless connectivity. Remember what you see in this study guide regarding these technologies. Once again, this is as close to the real exams as it gets so focus!

You will see questions on the exams regarding the proper way to clean LCD screens. In a nutshell, the best way to clean an LCD screen is by spraying water on a lint free cloth and gently wipe the face of the LCD screen or monitor. Do not use Window cleaner or soapy water!

Laptop computers can overheat easily. They have vents that allow cool air to enter and exit the system. However, much too often these vents get obstructed. It is a very good practice to use laptop systems on hard flat surfaces and ensure that the air vents are unobstructed.

The current A+ Exams are huge on Bluetooth. There is no doubt you will be asked several questions regarding this technology, which is why you keep seeing it over and over again in this book. Yes, you are being programmed by repetition! Here is a similar example of a recently identified laptop/Bluetooth question on the current exams. You have a customer who doesn't want all the wires associated with a typical Ethernet network for their laptop and peripherals. You are looking for a low-cost 2.4 GHz to 2.48 GHz wireless solution. What do you recommend? Answer=Bluetooth. If the exams ask you what two technologies are the most popular concerning wireless networks yours answers would be Bluetooth and IrDA (Infrared).

There are three types of PCMCIA cards that you must remember for the exams: Type I, Type II, and Type III. Type I cards are 3.3 mm thick and support a 16-bit interface. Type I cards are used for memory. Type II cards are primarily used for NICs and modems. They are 5.0 mm thick and have a 16-bit or 32-bit interface. Type III cards are 10.5 mm thick. They have a 16-bit or 32-bit interface and are used primarily for hard drives.

ACPI-compliant systems include ACPI power setting specifications. You must remember these power settings for the exams:

- G0 (Normal operational state of the computer system)
- G1 (Sleeping states)
    1. S1 (Sleep state where controlled power to the CPU and memory is handled.)
    2. S2 (Deeper sleep than S1; CPU is powered down.)
    3. S3 (Standby Mode. Power to memory is maintained, but almost all other components are powered down.)
    4. S4 (Hibernation mode. All information in memory is saved to hard drive, including the status of the OS, programs, and open applications.)
- G2 (Soft off)
- G3 (Mechanical off)

- You should be familiar with the active matrix display for the exams, especially with the popularity of laptop computer systems at an all time high. If you are considering a new laptop or recommending one, you should get or recommend a laptop with a screen resolution of at the very least 1280 x 800. For the exams, remember that XGA supports a resolution of 1024 x 768, VGA 640 x 480, WXGA 1280 x 800, SVGA 800 x 600, WXGA+ 1440 x 900, SXGA+ 1400 x 1050, and UXGA ,which has the highest resolution of 1600 x 1200. Got all those?

- You will defiantly need to know laptop battery types for exams. In a nutshell, battery specifications for laptop computer systems include the following:
  - Nickel-cadmium cell (NiCd) is an old battery technology that only holds a charge for approximately 1 hour. These types of batteries suffer from memory effect and care should be taken care when disposing of them. They contain very toxic chemicals.
  - Nickel-metal-hydride batteries (NiMH) are better than NiCd. They hold approximately 40% more power than NiCd. However, they cannot be charged as many times as NiCd.
  - Li-Ion (Lithium Ion) is the battery of choice today. They last longer and are much lighter than their predecessors. Li-Ion batteries do not suffer from memory effect and are much better for the environment. You will likely see a question that asks: Which of the following battery types is the most common in use today and doesn't suffer from memory effect? Answer=Li-Ion (Lithium Ion).

- SODIMMs (Small Outline DIMMs) are the memory form factor used in laptops. They come in packaging of 72, 100, 144, or 200 pins. At this point, if you don't know what a SODIMM is, do not take the A+ Exams!

- For any questions you see on the exams that depict a group of users in an office environment who have been moving wireless equipment around on their own and cannot connect anymore, you will answer: They have moved the peripherals too far away from their systems.

- Many remote users of laptops and desktops use Remote Desktop on a daily basis to connect to file servers for various reasons. Many times, this is to upload information or update records such as accounting databases or the like. You should specifically remember for the exam that if newly configured Remote Desktop users cannot connect via Remote Desktop, TCP port 3389 is likely being blocked by a firewall or router. TCP port 3389 is required to be open for Remote Desktop to work. For security reasons, most administrators have this port blocked by default. Technicians often configure Remote Desktop and scratch their heads wondering why they cannot connect users to servers or other systems. Most often, port 3389 needs to be open. CompTIA will likely go after this one if you are taking the Remote Desktop Support Technician Exam.

DOMAIN 3.0 OPERATING SYSTEMS

The current A+ Exams focus on the specific technologies included with the most popular OSs in the business world today: primarily Windows 2000 and Windows XP. However, after reading this book, you should be well versed enough to understand and answer conceptual questions relating to most OSs in general. In other words, there will be many questions relating to the underlying technologies that make up these OSs, such as DOS, and the filesystems that control them such as FAT, FAT32, and NTFS. We have done the best job possible in this book to educate you on the many OSs that you will find in business today. Now, let's focus directly on the concepts you are almost guaranteed to see on the exams concerning the Operating Systems Domain.

- The Safe Mode Advanced Boot option is an excellent tool to use if you have loaded certain drivers, rebooted, and are having problems. The exams will most likely go after a bad video driver here. For example: You have updated your supersonic video card driver and now you are having problems. What is the best way to troubleshoot or correct this issue? You would boot into Safe Mode, which uses a standard VGA driver, and begin the troubleshooting process. Another target for the exams is Safe Mode with Networking. Common sense here! You need to boot into a system with minimal drivers and use the Internet for troubleshooting. Which Safe Mode would you use? Answer=Safe Mode with Networking. The exams are going to try to throw you off with Safe Mode. Remember that Safe Mode is entered by pressing F8 at boot up and is accessible through the Advanced Boot Options menu. Safe Mode is primarily used to recover from the bad loading of hardware device drivers. You can access Device Manager in Safe Mode to manage device drivers as well as enable or disable hardware. You can also access System Restore in Safe Mode.
- Most hardware is detected automatically by most modern day OSs and BIOSs. However, you may need to manually install certain network, video, or other expansion card supporting drivers. In these cases, you should always follow the manufacturer's instructions and specifications. Speaking of drivers, the exam is likely to focus on the Driver Rollback feature in Windows. Be alert for questions that state: You have updated a device driver for a device, and the system is behaving erratically. What should you do? Answer=Reboot the system. Go into Safe Mode, and use Driver Rollback to restore the previously working driver. Then search for a good working driver, preferably from the manufacturer's Web site.
- The easiest way to restore basic desktop icons for those pesky users who keep deleting them is to right-click on the taskbar, select Properties > Desktop tab > Customize Desktop button.

- Your local network administrator guru who is an old DOS pro has tasked you with copying many folders and subfolders from one location on a server to another location. He wants you to carry out this task without using Windows Explorer. What command would you use to carry out this daunting task from a command line? Answer=XCOPY /s. The XCOPY command used with the /s switch will copy a directory and all subdirectories of that directory to a specified location. Also remember that RD followed by the directory name will remove that directory, MD followed by a directory name will create that directory, and CD followed by a directory name will change your current location to that specified directory.

- The ATTRIB command is a very popular target for the exams. They figure if you can hide and unhide files on a system, you have some idea what you are doing. Remember that ATTRIB +h *filename* adds the hidden attribute to the file. In simple terms, it hides the file. The ATTRIB –h *filename* removes the hidden file attribute and makes it viewable.

- Your main client has informed you that they want all of their systems hardware upgraded. Where would you go to view the currently installed hardware on these systems? Answer=Device Manager.

- To block unsigned drivers from being installed on the system go to: Control Panel > System applet > Hardware tab > Driver Signing button > Block option.

- Make sure you are familiar with ASR (Automated System Recovery) for the exams. ASR is the last chance to restore a system. It should be used only as a last resort. If your system is corrupt, and you have exhausted all other restoration possibilities, you should then use ASR. ASR is composed of ASR backup and ASR restore. To use ASR to back up the system state and all other important supporting files, go to and run the Automated System Recovery Preparation Wizard located in the Backup utility.

- To use ASR to restore the system back to a "good state," you will need to boot the system using a Windows XP bootable CD-ROM and begin the ASR process from the CD.

- The exams want you to know that Windows Explorer is the organizational utility used to manage files and folders in an OS. The most common practice for creating folders in Windows Explorer is to right-click anywhere in an open space in Windows explorer and click the New Folder option.

- Windows XP and Windows 2000 both support NTFS and FAT32. NTFS is the filesystem of choice today because it is much more secure than FAT32. Don't let the exam throw you off with off the wall acronyms concerning incorrect filesystem names. You want NTFS, and if you see it as a possible answer, it is most likely the correct choice. NTFS includes the Encrypted File System (EFS) and offers the ability to use disk quotas, which limits the amount of hard drive space users of the system can take up with files and folders. Remember for the exams, the command `convert c: /fs:ntfs` can be used to convert a filesystem to NTFS from a command prompt. This convert command is used to convert FAT and FAT32 to NTFS. It cannot be used to go from NTFS back to FAT or FAT32. You can't go back. If the exams ask you: You have recently converted a FAT32 system to NTFS. How do you convert back to FAT32? Answer=You can't. Reformat and reinstall!

■ The Task Manager utility displays tabs for Applications, Processes, Performance, Networking, and Users. If a system is frozen in the OS, you can press Ctrl-Alt-Delete to open the Task Manager and stop any running processes or applications that may not be responding or hanging the system.

■ Before you install an OS on a hard disk, there are two very important considerations to remember for the exams. The disk must be partitioned and formatted. Yes, the exams actually may ask you this. Another gimme.

■ There are two main reasons for receiving the error message `Non-system disk or Disk error`. The BIOS does not have a hard disk set as a boot device, or you have a corrupt OS. Remember this! It is an old question that pops up a lot on the new exams.

■ The System Configuration utility MSCONFIG can be run by entering MSCONFIG from the Start > Run box. You will see MSCONFIG on your exams. MSCONFIG is used to configure which services and programs are started when the OS starts. It is an excellent troubleshooting tool and is another gimme on the exams

■ The exams may ask you questions that state: File NTUSER.DAT is corrupt or missing. What is the file NTUSER.DAT used for? Answer=NTUSER.DAT holds user-specific information and settings. It is important to note that NTUSER.DAT is stored in the registry under HKEY_Current_User.

■ NTLDR is the file responsible for loading the OS at boot up. If an OS will not boot up, it is very likely that the NTLDR file is corrupt. Also remember that the file NTDETECT.COM builds a hardware list and detects all hardware at boot up. NTBOOTDD.SYS is used for booting from SCSI devices, and BOOT-SECT.DOS contains information regarding other OSs that may exist on the system.

■ System Restore is used to restore a system to a previously working state using restore points. This is very useful if you install a program or application that causes your system to become unstable or act erratically. To turn System Restore on or off and apply how much disk space is allocated for creating restore points, go to Control Panel > System > System Restore. By default, System Restore is on. If the exams asks you: You have recently installed a new program, and your system is now acting strange, and performance has decreased. What should you do to rectify this problem? Answer=Restore your system to a good state using restore points.

■ The exams are going to ask you backup questions, such as: You are the best technician on the planet and are responsible for backing up 40 million dollars worth of accounting data daily using a differential backup scheme. This morning you lost all of the data. How many tapes will it take to restore all the data? Answer=Two. You need the last full backup tape and the most recent differential. In reality, this can vary. However, for the A+ Exams, two tapes will be your answer period! And at this point, if you don't remember what the GFS (Grandfather, Father, Son) backup scheme is you better go back in this book and find out.

■ Virtual memory is hard drive space reserved for memory. If your system runs low on physical memory (RAM), your system will use a paging file to temporarily store data in until the physical memory is free to use. If your system is continuously running low on memory, you should try increasing the size pf the paging file, and if you can afford it, add more physical memory.

■ The Windows Disk Cleanup Utility can be used to rid your system of such things as downloaded program files and temporary Internet files. It can also be used to empty the Recycle Bin and compress old files. If you notice that a customer's system is bogged down and low on hard drive space, this is the first place to go. Just go to Start > Programs > Accessories > System Tools > Disk Cleanup. Select everything, and click OK.

■ NTFS provides encryption capabilities for security, but, it also allows administrators to control access to files and folders through permissions. You should be familiar with the following NTFS permissions for your exams:

Full Control: Allows a user to do anything to a file or folder. They can modify it or delete it.

Modify: Allows a user to change, delete, or create files.

Read and Execute: Allows a user to view a file and execute it.

List Folder Contents: Allows viewing a file, but a user cannot open files. This is the one the exams will most likely go after.

Read: Allows viewing of files, but a user cannot change files.

Write: Enables a user to create files and to change files but not to delete files.

■ It is not likely that you will see many Linux or MAC OS questions on the A+ exams. However, it is highly recommended that you visit the following sites for the very basics concerning Linux and MAC OSX:

  ■ *www.comptechdoc.org/os/linux/usersguide/linux_ugbasics.html:* This Comptechdoc Web site is a great place to brush up on basic Linux commands.

  ■ *www.ss64.com/osx:* This Web site has a fantastic A-Z Index of the command-line commands for MAC OSX.

DOMAIN 4.0 PRINTERS AND SCANNERS

Over the years, the A+ Exams have become so big on printers that CompTIA had to create an entire Domain dedicated to them. You can bet your laser printer cartridges that the exams are going to hit you big with printer and scanner questions. There are literally hundreds of printer and scanner questions contained in the A+ the exam test databases. The Domain tips that follow are short and quick and designed to cover as many possible printer and scanner possibilities you may be asked.

- A laser printer uses a fuser to melt toner onto printer paper. The fuse heats up to a very high temperature to melt the toner. If you are asked: Which component of a laser printer is most likely to hurt a technician? Answer= Fuser. You need to be careful here and know the difference between the fuser and the transfer corona. The fuser permanently melts the toner onto the paper. The transfer corona places a positive charge on to the paper and forces the negatively charged drum to transfer the image to the paper.
- You may see printer-related questions that state: Several pieces of paper are being fed through a laser printer at once. This is causing jamming and customer conniptions. What are possible reasons for this? Answers=Wrong type or worn out paper is being used and/or the laser printer separation pad is worn out.
- If your text is printing out garbled, you need to install the correct printer driver.
- If you are asked any questions regarding scanner drivers, the answer is TWAIN! Most scanners use a common driver called TWAIN.
- If you are trying to print to a printer and receive buffer overflow or out of memory errors displayed on the printer, it is likely that you need to add more memory to the printer.
- The laser printing process was covered in great detail in Chapter 6. If you need to refresh yourself with the intricate details of this process please go back and read it again. The laser printing process includes the following stages: cleaning, charging, writing, developing, transferring, and fusing.
- The flatbed scanner is the most common type of scanner, which binds documents together and are often seen in business environments. With a flatbed scanner, a document or image is placed on a flat glass surface. A light source and an array of sensors (CCDs) pass below the document.
- Smaller, single-feed flatbed scanners can be purchased at reasonable prices for home use. This type of scanner uses a set of rollers to feed the image to be scanned past the light source and sensors. This is not a useful scanner for large amounts of information to be scanned.

■ A handheld scanner is a flexible device that allows you to scan stationary objects or images. It is also a useful tool for gathering inventory information; for example, a bar code scanner can be used to gather stock information at a grocery store or warehouse.

■ Commands can be entered from a command line to control manage and control printing. Two useful commands that you may see on the exams are the Net start spooler and the Net print commands. The Net start spooler command starts the printer spooler service, and the Net print command is used to manage or display a print queue. It is also possible to print from a command line. To print directly from a command line, you would enter the following syntax: net print *computername**sharename*.

■ You must be familiar with printer connection methods for the A+ exams. The most common ways for users to connect to printers are shared network printer connections, infrared and Bluetooth wireless connections, serial connections, and yes parallel connections are still being used. The questions that come your way concerning printer connections will most likely throw false port numbers at you. For example: Which are the most common ways to connect to a printer? Your choices will be similar to Serial Port, Infrared, Shared Network, Parallel and some off the wall technology or incorrect port number. Study these tips and use common sense here.

■ If a printer is producing light text on printed output, the toner cartridge is most likely running low on toner.

■ If you are experiencing "ghost images" on laser printer output, the laser printer drum is likely not being properly cleaned during the cleaning stage of the laser printing process.

■ The simplest and easiest way for multiple users to use a single printer is through a shared network printer connection.

■ A scratched or damaged laser printer drum will produce consistent markings and spotted patterns on printed output.

■ Parallel printing modes are set in the system BIOS. Parallel printer modes include unidirectional, bidirectional, Enhanced Parallel Port (EPP), and Enhanced Capability Port (ECP). For the exams, it is important to remember that EPP and ECP are the fastest parallel transmission modes.

■ The good old print spooler question: You have customers who are submitting multiple print jobs, and none of the jobs are printing. What is most likely the problem here, and how do you correct it? Answer=You have a stalled print spooler that needs to restarted.

■ Solid ink printers use CMYK colored solid ink sticks. They are also known as thermal transfer printers.

■ Laser jet and bubble jet print quality is measured in DPI (dots per inch). Printer speeds are measured in PPM (pages per minute).

- Inkjet printers propel tiny drops of ink onto paper.
- If you install a new network or local printer for users and their print jobs continue to print to their old printer, you have probably not set the new printer as the default printer.
- Inkjet printers discharge ink drops using electrically charged plates. The ink is heated to a boil, and the print head nozzles are used to disperse the ink drops.
- When installing printers, scanners, or any other peripherals for customers, you should always remember to do two important things when the job is complete: Always test the newly installed equipment, and document the procedure.
- Here is a real gimme question that you may be asked on the exams concerning printers: You have recently installed a brand new wing-ding multipurpose printer for a customer. Where would you find information regarding a routine maintenance schedule? Answers=The manufacturer's manual or Web site.
- USB 2.0 provides the greatest throughput for the printers in use today.

DOMAIN 5.0 NETWORKS

This is the Domain where many possibilities exist. In other words, you will be given ample opportunity to fail your exams right here. There are many networking technologies available that CompTIA can target. They seem to have recently combined their Network+ exam with A+. And as you will see next in Domain 6, CompTIA also seems to have combined many Security+ technologies and questions in all four of the current A+ Exams. The retired A+ exams used to ask questions like: What is the most redundant type of network topology? Answer=Mesh. Not that simple anymore! You need to know many protocols and versions of TCP/IP, including IP addressing. Network cabling, connectors, devices, and topologies were explained in great detail earlier in this book. If you need to go back and refresh on those subjects, you should do so now. We are going to turn up the heat here and get a little more advanced concerning networks. We are going to prepare you well quickly here!

Let's get right to the meat shall we? It is almost a guarantee that you will see Figure 15.1 on one of you're A+ exams. What is wrong in Figure 15.1? Why can't I get an IP address and connect to the Internet? What is the MAC address of my NIC card? You should be able to answer these questions before taking the exams.

It is also very likely that you sill see an example similar to Figure 15.2 on your A+ Exams. In fact, count on it! Figure 15.2 displays the results of the IPCONFIG /ALL command issued on my system. (Yes, you now have enough information to hack me. Go for it. But you have been warned: I have surprises waiting!)

```
C:\WINDOWS\system32\command.com                                    _□×
Microsoft(R) Windows DOS
(C)Copyright Microsoft Corp 1990-2001.

C:\DOCUME~1\CHRIS>ipconfig /all

Windows IP Configuration

        Host Name . . . . . . . . . . . . : chris-50dq537jz
        Primary Dns Suffix  . . . . . . . :
        Node Type . . . . . . . . . . . . : Unknown
        IP Routing Enabled. . . . . . . . : No
        WINS Proxy Enabled. . . . . . . . : No

Ethernet adapter Local Area Connection:

        Media State . . . . . . . . . . . : Media disconnected
        Description . . . . . . . . . . . : Intel(R) PRO/100 VE Network Connecti
on
        Physical Address. . . . . . . . . : 00-0C-F1-83-E3-E3

C:\DOCUME~1\CHRIS>
```

FIGURE 15.1   Answers=My network cable is not plugged in, and my MAC address is 00-0C-F1-83-E3-E3.

Looking at Figure 15.2, you should quickly be able to spot my IP address, subnet mask, and default gateway. You should also be able to figure out that I am leasing my IP address from a DHCP server. Notice when my lease expires. Also notice that I am using tampabay.rr.com for DNS. The exams will likely ask you to identify similar items in their example.

```
C:\WINDOWS\system32\command.com                                    _□×
        Node Type . . . . . . . . . . . . : Unknown
        IP Routing Enabled. . . . . . . . : No
        WINS Proxy Enabled. . . . . . . . : No
        DNS Suffix Search List. . . . . . : tampabay.rr.com

Ethernet adapter Local Area Connection:

        Connection-specific DNS Suffix  . : tampabay.rr.com
        Description . . . . . . . . . . . : Intel(R) PRO/100 VE Network Connecti
on
        Physical Address. . . . . . . . . : 00-0C-F1-83-E3-E3
        Dhcp Enabled. . . . . . . . . . . : Yes
        Autoconfiguration Enabled . . . . : Yes
        IP Address. . . . . . . . . . . . : 70.126.154.196
        Subnet Mask . . . . . . . . . . . : 255.255.254.0
        Default Gateway . . . . . . . . . : 70.126.154.1
        DHCP Server . . . . . . . . . . . : 10.96.128.1
        DNS Servers . . . . . . . . . . . : 65.32.5.74
                                            65.32.5.75
        Lease Obtained. . . . . . . . . . : Monday, September 10, 2007 1:55:45 P
M
        Lease Expires . . . . . . . . . . : Tuesday, September 11, 2007 7:54:27
AM
C:\DOCUME~1\CHRIS>
```

FIGURE 15.2

- TCP/IP is the protocol responsible for host and network addressing on the Internet and in most networks.
- Dynamic Host Configuration Protocol (DHCP) is used for the automatic assignment of IP addresses to computers in a TCP/IP network.
- DNS is used for host name resolution. In other words, it resolves computer host names to IP addresses. For example, DNS would resolve comptia.org to an IP address. A computer must be configured with a DNS server's IP address to resolve computers on other networks by name. By default, TCP/IP uses DNS to resolve computer host names to their proper IP addresses. WINS is used for NetBIOS name resolution. In other words, it is used to resolve NetBIOS computer names to IP addresses. If you don't have a DNS server available on a network, name resolution can be accomplished by configuring a local HOSTS file on each machine. If you do not have a WINS server available, NetBIOS names can be resolved on a network by manually configuring a LMHOSTS on every machine. It is important here to note that the NSLOOKUP command can be used for DNS name resolution.
- The default gateway is the most common IP address located on a local network routers interface. The default gateway must be configured on every computer within a network for it to communicate with other computers on other networks or subnetworks. If the default gateway address is missing or not properly configured, computers will only be able to communicate with other computers on the same network. The exams may ask you why computer A cannot communicate with computer B. They may show you a diagram of computer A and B with a router in between and ask you why computer A cannot reach computer B. The answer will be that the default gateway IP address on the router is incorrect. Remember this one!
- The subnet mask is used to distinguish the network ID from the host ID in an IP address. If a network uses a default subnet mask, this means that the network is not segmented into subnetworks. The default subnet mask used for class A IP addresses is 255.0.0.0. Class B addresses use a 255.255.0.0 subnet mask range, and the default subnet mask for class C IP addresses is 255.255.255.0.
- The IP addresses reserved for private class A networks range from 10.0.0.0 to 10.255.255.255.
- B networks range from 172.16.0.0 to 172.31.255.255. Class C private addresses range from 192.168.0.0 to 192.168.255.255. The IP address range 169.254.0.1 to 169.254.255.254 is used for APIPA. With this said, if the exams ask you questions about configuring, for example, a class C private network, your correct answer should include configuring workstations to use IP addresses in the private addresses range from 192.168.0.0 to 192.168.255.255. Got that?

- IPv6 IP addresses are made of 128 bits. IPv4 IP addresses consist of 32 bits. IPv6 uses DHCPv6 to automatically assign IP addresses. IPv4 uses DHCP to automatically assign IP addresses. IPv6 is more secure than IPv4, provides for more IP addresses, and offers more efficient routing capabilities than IPv4.

- Wireless ad hoc networks are very common. They are also called computer-to-computer wireless networks. Infrastructure wireless networks require that a wireless router be present.

- When conducting a site survey to measure proper distance and appropriate areas for a wireless network and its components, you should consider such things as trees, microwave ovens, mirrors, walls, and other obstacles that will interfere with the wireless transmissions.

- The protocols AppleTalk, IPX/SPX, and NetBEUI are not installed by default. They can be installed if needed. AppleTalk is a protocol used for communication in a MAC or Apple network. IPX/SPX is used for communication in a Novell network, and NetBEUI is a nonroutable protocol used in small Microsoft networks.

- The wireless networking standard 802.11n currently offers transmission rates up to 240 Mbps and distances up to 450 feet. 802.11n is totally compatible with the 802.11b and 802.11g wireless standards. However, it is not compatible with 802.11a. Note that 802.11a is also not compatible with 802.11b or 802.11g as well.

- Remote Assistance is a feature included with Windows 2000, Windows XP, and Windows Vista. It is an awesome tool that allows techs and admins to remotely assist and troubleshoot computer-related issues for customers.

- Remote Assistance was explained previously in the book in great detail. However, the exams will likely hit you hard with questions on this topic. So here's how it works: To establish a session, an invitation is sent from a user to a helper. For security purposes, the user can set a time limit of expiration for the invitation. The helper then accepts or rejects the invitation. When the invitation is accepted, the helper sends the user a connection request, and if accepted by the user, the remote session is established. Here are some tips you must remember regarding remote assistance:
    - Invitation can be sent by users in the form of e-mail attachments or as files over a network using an instant messaging program.
    - A helper can start a Remote Assistance connection by double-clicking the invitation file or by using the Offer to Help Someone link in Windows Help and Support.
    - You can protect Remote Assistance invitations with a password and keep the invitation validity time to a minimum time frame.

■ If an invitation has been sent to the wrong person or system, the user can still cancel the connection by not accepting the connection request from the helper.

■ A Remote Assistance session can be canceled at any time by the user selecting the Disconnect button.

■ The Send File button can be used during a remote session at any time to send a file to a helper.

■ A user can stop a helper from helping by selecting the Stop Sharing button.

■ The Pause button can be used to temporarily pause a session.

■ For Remote Assistance sessions to be established, TCP port 3389 must be open on a router or firewall! If you are asked: Which TCP port does Remote Assistance use? Answer=TCP port 3389.

■ Only one Remote Assistance session can be active at a time on a system.

■ The IP address 127.0.0.1 is used for loopback testing. If you ping 127.0.0.1 on your system and receive a successful response, TCP/IP is configured properly on your system.

■ Network Address Translation (NAT) is used in private networks within a firewall (router) to provide a shared single connection to the Internet or another network for multiple private IP addresses. NAT hides the private IP addresses from the public network. NAT, or NATING is commonly used in companies to allow users to gain Internet access without compromising the internal network or networks.

■ Link Layer Topology Discovery (LLTD) is a protocol that may show the exams. LLTD is a protocol used in Windows Vista to discover other network devices on a network. The exams may just pop out with a question stating: You are trying to view other computers on a network from your machine (Windows Vista) and you cannot see them. What is most likely the reason for this? Answer=The LLTD protocol may not be installed on the other computers, or it may be blocked by a firewall. Note: LLTP is installed on Windows Vista systems when a network adapter is present. It must be manually installed on Windows XP systems for the XP systems to see the Windows Vista systems. By the way, the current A+ Exams Objectives make absolutely no references to the OS Windows Vista!

■ Automatic Private IP Addressing (APIPA) assigns IP addresses automatically to client stations when a DHCP server is not available. And you better remember that if a client workstation is using an IP address from 169.254.0.1 to 169.254.255.254, the DHCP server is most likely down. By default, APIPA uses a subnet mask of 255.255.0.0. DHCP clients using APIPA will continue to look for the DHCP server using broadcasts called DHCP Discover messages *every*

5 minutes! When a DHCP server comes back up or goes online, it will automatically assign its IP addresses to the clients who have been temporarily using the APIPA addresses. You have been warned! You will see this on your exams.

- A Service Set Identifier (SSID) is a 1 to 32-character pass phrase used as a security precaution that can be configured on a wireless router (access point). The SSID on the client systems must match the SSID on the wireless AP for the clients to connect to the network.

- A computer with two NICs installed is known as a multihomed system. You should note that the ROUTE command is used to create a static routing table on a multihomed system.

- To test the availability of a DNS server on a network, you use the NSLOOKUP command.

- Use the TRACERT command to trace the path packets taken from a computer or network to a destination computer or network.

- To renew an IP address on a computer, you use the IPCONFIG /RENEW command.

- To display NetBIOS over TCP/IP statistics on a computer system, you use the NBTSTAT command.

- The File Transfer Protocol (FTP) is used to transfer files in a local network or over the Internet. For example, an FTP program, an FTP server, and an FTP protocol were used in this book's creation process to send chapters back and forth between the author and the publisher.

- If the exams ask you for the strongest or highest level of security offered for wireless networks and wireless devices, your answer better be Wi-Fi Protected Access version 2 (WPA2).

Domain 6.0 Security

The A+ exams are going to ask you very basic computer- and network-related questions. The Security Domain test tips that follow will prepare you well. If fact, you will learn enough in these test tips to lay a groundwork for the current CompTIA Security+ exam. So put your thinking cap on and remember these tips because they will also help you in the real hands-on world.

- An electronic device known as a key fob provides one part of a three way match to log in over a connection to a secure network. There are various kinds of key fobs. One may use a keypad on which the user must enter a PIN number to get an access code or VPN token such as RSA's popular SecurID token.

- A virus will replicate itself until it uses up all available system resources such as memory or hard drive space.

- Remember for the exams that .BAT files represent files that are executable. If you download a file or attachment from the Internet or from a network with a .BAT extension, you are taking a risk of being infected with a virus.

- Spyware is a program or piece of software that resides hidden on a system and monitors and logs the system's or another system's activities.

- A worm is a type of virus that can replicate itself, but worms do not attach to other programs.

- Worms and viruses duplicate themselves; Trojans do not.

- Malware is an acronym for malicious code. It is something that produces unwanted and unexpected results. It is a virus, Trojan horse, or worm.

- System or boot infectors are older viruses that damage system files such as a hard drive's MBR or the boot sector on a floppy disk.

- Variants are new viruses or "virus strains" that take code and sometimes modify the code of existing well-known viruses.

- Most macro-type viruses are designed to insert numbers, characters, words, or phrases into documents or spreadsheets.

- Viruses that are "in the wild" exist outside of controller virus research labs. Viruses that exist in these labs are known to be zoo viruses.

- The actual action that a virus carries out is called the virus's payload.

- A virus threat or "risk" rating is a calculated value that represents the possible level of severity or threat of a specific virus.

- Most Trojan horses are hidden in Internet attachments that are often distributed with e-mail in the form of jokes, love letters, and misguiding advertisements.

- A logic bomb can be a computer virus or Trojan horse that activates when certain conditions are met.

- Blended threats will typically spread automatically by continuously scanning the Internet for Web servers with open or vulnerable TCP/IP ports. They also plant Trojans and logic bombs, change permissions, and use internal network mapped drives to spread.

- A virus with stealth characteristics will hide itself and send bogus responses back to an antiviral software package's scan request to avoid detection.

- A polymorphic virus possesses the ability to change its own internal code and byte structure as it is being duplicated.

- *Root* is also the name of the administrative user account in Unix and Linux.

- Hypertext Transport Protocol Secure (HTTPS) is a very popular secure protocol used to transmit messages over the Internet.

- Always configure your e-mail server to block or remove e-mail that contains file attachments that are commonly used to spread viruses, such as .VBS, .BAT, .EXE, .PIF, and .SCR files. If you must use any of these extensions, make it a point to have your e-mail antivirus program scan these attachments before delivery.

- Instant messaging vulnerabilities have become a popular target for modern day hackers.
- A UNC name always follows the format: \\Servername\sharename.
- A cookie can also be referred to as a state object or persistent cookie.
- You can set up your Internet browser to alert you when a cookie is present, you can direct your browser to only download cookies from trusted sites, or you can disable cookies.
- JavaScript is commonly used by Web developers to interact with Web pages that are typically created using HTML or XML source codes.
- Hijackers and attackers often create or intercept Java scripts and applets, which are often able to circumvent network security perimeters, and use them to manipulate files on users' computers.
- A popular technique known as sandboxing is often used to quarantine applets that appear suspicious or malicious.
- The ActiveX security model does not limit an application package to a set of individual restrictive controls. Instead, its controls are based on digital signatures.
- With a Man-in-the-Middle attack, an intruder will typically place a packet-gathering program between a sender and receiver to capture or intercept data packets as they are transmitted. This type of attack is very difficult to detect and is not usually realized until after the information has been compromised.
- S/MIME (Secure Multi-Purpose Internet Mail Extensions) is a method/protocol used to secure the sending of messages between various e-mail clients.
- SSL and TLS are session-based X.509 digital certificate supporting protocols that use a public and private key exchange to encrypt the passing of data between client and server systems. Both protocols support RSA, DES, IDEA, 3DES, and MD5.
- You send with mail SMTP. You download or receive mail with POP3 or IMAP. SMTP is most often used with TCP port 25.
- FTP sessions by default are not encrypted. Usernames and passwords are transmitted in clear text. FTP user IDs and passwords can be easily grabbed with a sniffer.
- Known vulnerabilities exist with certain versions of LDAP that have lead to buffer overflow attacks, unauthorized access conditions, and denial of service attacks.
- An OS can use an Access Control List (ACL) as an authentication method to see what rights a user has to a certain object such as a file, folder, or network share.
- With discretionary access control, user access to an object (i.e., a file or folder) is controlled by the owner of the object. The owner of an object is usually the creator of the object unless ownership rights have been taken by an administrator or supervisor (Ultimate rights) and granted to another user. The Bell-Lapadula model is based on this access control.

- The principle of least privilege is a theory that says every user should be granted the very minimal level of permission required to perform his job properly.
- In a nutshell, centralized access control means that control over rights, permissions, user IDs, and system policies are maintained in one company location on one computer system.
- With decentralized access control, control of rights, permissions, user IDs, and system policies can be managed from several company locations using many computer systems. The Windows NT domain models are based on this concept.
- Mandatory access control is a nondiscretionary access control technique. This technique assigns hierarchical, multi-level sensitivity *labels* to users and data (as in the Military: unclassified, confidential, secret, top-secret). In this labeling system, user labels are referred to as security clearances, whereas object labels are referred to as security classifications.
- Role-based access control (RBAC) is essentially a type of MAC. Applications employing RBAC provide a mechanism of formulating the system's structure to complement the existing structure of an organization.
- Devices such as tokens and smart cards are used for authentication purposes.
- RADIUS and TACACS are considered a centralized access control methodology.
- Passwords are considered knowledge-based authentication mechanisms.
- Sniffers are software programs or devices that listen to and gather network traffic. They can be used to monitor network traffic and weaknesses or can be used to steal passwords, user IDs, or credit card information. Most network sniffers work well in networks that use broadcast techniques. They do not operate well in networks that use collision techniques.
- Password crackers are programs that figure out easy-to-guess passwords in encrypted password lists or databases.
- Remote penetration programs are software programs that use the Internet or networks as a vehicle to gain unauthorized and illegal control of a computer system or network resource.
- Local penetration programs gain unauthorized illegal access to systems on which they are run.
- Local denial of service programs shut down the computers on which they are run.
- Remote denial of service programs are used on the Internet or networks as vehicles to shut down other services or computers.
- Vulnerability scanners are programs that are sent out on the Internet to search for computers that may have a weakness or certain vulnerability for a specific type of attack.
- Network scanners are programs that are run on networks to map out where the particular network weaknesses are.

■ Multifactor authentication is the combined use of a password as well as a key-exchange system to provide strong authentication. This type of authentication scheme should be implemented when the use of a single user sign and password or an encrypted key system alone will not be enough security. Multifactor authentication is considered a very strong security practice. It is likely that the exam will expect you to know this concept.

■ With mutual authentication, a trust relationship is first established between a host and its intended recipients or clients. Second, digitally signed certificates are typically implemented to allow the host or server system to authenticate to the client system. Then, the recipient or client system is authenticated with the host or server.

■ You should always configure computer OSs to automatically update patches and service packs.

■ Weak key attacks in encryption lingo are attacks that occur on secret encrypted keys that exhibit a poor level of encryption.

■ Multiplexing is the combining of data channels over a single transmission line.

■ DNS (Domain Name Servers) resolve fully qualified domain names (or host names) to IP addresses. For example, Microsoft.com is a domain name. A properly configured DNS server could resolve Microsoft.com to the IP address 207.46.129.180.

■ A bastion host is a gateway or firewall that protects an internal network from external networks. Simply put, a bastion host is a system set up on an internal network that screens for possible attacks aimed at a particular internal network.

■ ATM (Asynchronous Transfer Mode) is a dedicated switching technology that transmits data in fixed length 53-byte units called cells. ATM is well suited for the transmission of audio and video and is said to be the answer to the low bandwidth problems that face Internet users.

■ A Demilitarized Zone (DMZ) is a neutral area between an internal network and the Internet that typically contains one host system or a small network of systems.

■ Network Address Translation (NAT) is an Internet standard most often used with routers to provide firewall security by hiding an internal private network's range of IP addresses from outside networks.

■ An FDDI ring is typically composed of two fiber-optic Token Rings: an outside ring that is used for the primary transport of data and an inside ring that acts as a backup if the primary ring fails. An FDDI ring is redundant and somewhat more secure than star, bus, or traditional ring topologies.

■ The seven layers of the OSI reference model from layer one to layer seven are physical, data link, network, transport, session, presentation, and application. Just remember "Programmers Do Not Throw Sausage Pizza Away."

■ Secure Remote Procedure Call (RPC) is a protocol that is used to allow a client-side application program to execute or request a service from a server computer without being concerned with network intricacies or server procedures

■ IPSec employs two encryption modes: transport and tunnel. Using the transport mode, only the data portion (or *payload*) of a packet is encrypted while the header remains unchanged. In tunnel mode, security is further enhanced because both the payload and header are encrypted. IPSec offers security services such as connectionless integrity, data origin authentication, and confidentiality.

■ A circuit gateway is a packet filter that relays packets from one host to another based on protocol and IP address. A circuit gateway forms a sort of tunnel through a firewall allowing two specified hosts to interact.

■ The term "transparency" is used in network security lingo to describe how intrusive a network countermeasure such as a firewall is to a user. For example, a packet filter is more transparent to a user than an application proxy. In other words, users will typically not be aware that a router is filtering their data packets. But, if an application gateway is used, users will have to authenticate with the firewall or configure their applications to authenticate through the firewall.

■ Point-to-Point Tunneling protocol (PPTP) allows a Virtual Private Network (VPN) to be created using the Internet. PPTP is essentially a set of communication rules that allows the boundaries of private networks to be extended. PPTP has in many cases eliminated the need for companies to use expensive dedicated leased lines to expand the privacy of their networks.

■ Leased line speeds:

DS-0 (Digital Signal Level 0): One channel transmits 64 KBps on a T1 line.

DS-1 (Digital Signal Level 1): Transmits 1.544 MBps on a T1 line.

DS-3 (Digital Signal Level 3): Transmits 44.736 MBps on a T3 line.

■ CAT5 UTP is also referred to as 100BaseT or 100BaseTX. It carries a data signal 100 meters or approximately 328 feet. It is the most popular UTP cable in use today.

■ Application proxies (or gateways) are concerned more with specific applications and actual data. The application proxy offers much more control than packet filters and circuit gateways by controlling or limiting user access from within the protocol itself. In other words, with an application proxy, administrators can actually control what information can be sent out of or pulled into a network.

■ CHAP uses a secret one-way hash value that is generated by the requestor and sent to the server.

■ SMTP (Simple Mail Transfer Protocol) is an unsafe protocol used to send e-mail messages between mail servers. SMTP was not originally developed to protect against e-mail and e-mail server attacks. The best way to protect your e-mail server and e-mail in general is to scan and filter all messages and secure each e-mail message with encryption.

- SNMP (Simple Network Management Protocol) is an unsafe network management protocol that allows the use of clear-text passwords. SNMP traffic should be filtered at the firewall.

- A multihomed server (system with two NICs) can be configured as a firewall by enabling IP forwarding and building a Routing Information Table (RIT).

- Devices such as routers, hubs, and switches are single points of failure. Each of these devices should be protected with a UPS (Uninterruptible Power Supply) in the event of power surges, spikes, and brownouts.

- There are four primary types of firewall architectures:

  Packet Filter: A packet filter router uses an ACL. It is the oldest of the mentioned architectures. It separates a private network from a public network.

  Screened Host: This firewall architecture combines a bastion host and a packet filter firewall, which requires the intruder to get by two separate systems to reach an internal network. This is more secure than a traditional Packet Filtering firewall.

  Dual Homed Host: Straight to the point, this is a system with two NICs. One NIC supports access to a private network, and one supports access to a public network. This acts as a filter and is also known as a multihomed bastion host.

  Screened Subnet: This firewall architecture combines the security of two packet filters and a bastion host. This is the most secure of the firewall architectures and requires high overhead. This overhead is realized in high maintenance requirements.

- VoIP (Voice over IP) technology is essentially the delivery of voice in digital packets over IP networks. This technology is generally less expensive than traditional circuit switching of voice using PSTN (Public Switched Telephone Network). VoIP is a rapidly growing technology that offers security and quality of service.

- Security services are a combination of security techniques, files, policies, and procedures. The following six security services are defined by OSI communication standards to provide secure communications:
  - Authentication
  - Access Control
  - Data Confidentiality
  - Data Integrity
  - Nonrepudiation
  - Monitoring and Logging

■ For packet-switching networks to work properly, packets must contain the sending system's as well as the destination system's network address.

■ When the functionality of devices such as a network bridge and a network router are combined, the result is a device known as a brouter.

■ Most communication takes place at the data link layer of the OSI reference model.

■ An extranet is part of a private network (intranet) that is extended to customers, vendors, suppliers, and possibly other remote users. Most extranets use tunneling to connect multiple intranetwork connections to an extranet.

■ Penetration testing is used to see how vulnerable a current environment is to risk and vulnerability. This testing is often done with an attacker's perspective in mind.

■ In operational security management terms, the protection of confidentiality, integrity, and availability make up what is known as the CIA triad.

■ Two-factor authentication strategies are implemented to better safeguard against security threats. Obviously, two factors are a combination of multiple safeguards. There are usually combinations of the following:
  ■ Something you have (key fob, pass card, or USB device)
  ■ Something you know (password, access code, or PIN number)
  ■ Something you are (retina scan, fingerprint, or DNA)

■ CCTVs (closed-circuit televisions) are often used in combination with surveillance cameras as physical security monitoring devices. CCTV signals use private channel to provide a signal from the TV to the camera. They do not broadcast signals to public areas.

■ The best way to protect the information stored on portable systems such as laptop computers, PDAs, and cell phones is to use encryption if possible.

■ Secured doors should be resistant to forcible entry and should unlock automatically in the case of an emergency. It is very important that you know this for the exam.

■ The goal of a solid disaster recovery plan is to provide proper policies, procedures, and documentation for backup and restoration of facilities and data in the event of an emergency. A GFS (Grandfather, Father, Son) backup strategy provides the "fastest" and "easiest" restore.

■ Many modern-day OSs such as certain versions of Microsoft Windows and Linux offer the ability, through software, to implement server or resource clustering.

■ SLAs (Service Level Agreements) are agreements or contracts between vendors of services or products that specify what the service agreement will provide.

■ A Disaster Recovery Plan (DRP) focuses on the implementation of procedures that should be followed during and after a disaster. A Business Continuity Plan (BCP) focuses on prevention and how a disaster affects the overall business plan of an enterprise.

- Building and network access should be granted to new employees based on their specific roles. The principle of least privilege should be considered with new as well as existing employees. When an employee is terminated or leaves a company, all physical and logical access should be denied for the individual.

- Two-factor SSO is often a better way to provide better security in single sign-on environment. With two-factor SSO, a user provides an ID and a password combination and is also required to authenticate with a token or biometric device.

- Social engineering is a technique used to gather or steal personal information. With social engineering, an unsuspecting user is tricked or deceived into giving up information such as passwords, security codes, company secrets, pin numbers, or credit card numbers. The biggest protection against social engineering is promoting awareness and educating the user environment concerning this type of attack.

- Change documentation is needed to preserve integrity to a program, network, system, or business when changes are needed and made to the configurations, policies, or documentation in general.

- A chain of custody must be in place to ensure that it is always known where the evidence is physically located and who has possession of it. If potential evidence is corrupted, damaged, or not handled with due care, the evidence may not be admissible in a court of law.

- With Qualitative Risk Analysis, threats and vulnerabilities are analyzed and defined, and then controls are put into place to reduce or offset possible risks.

- With Quantitative Risk Analysis, risks are guessed and money and/or insurance are appropriated as a means to offset the risk.

- Proper notification documentation should include emergency contact information for all company managers, security personnel, HR personnel, Network and Disaster Recovery team members (both local site and enterprisewide if necessary), and building maintenance staff.

- Biometrics is a computerized analysis of physical characteristics used to provide authentication or access, for example, fingerprint or retina scanning. Both are characteristic-based authentication methods. Character based authentication methods allow or disallow access to systems, resources, or physical locations based on physical characteristics. Biometrics is a combination of science and technology that is used to gather and measure human characteristic information from a subject and use that information as a means to allow or disallow access. Some of the most popular characteristics that can be measured and used with scanning devices through the use of biometric technology are handwriting, hand imprints, fingerprints, retina, iris, and voice patterns. A retina scanner is currently the most secure biometric device available. Fingerprint devices and signature scanner devices are the most widely accepted forms of biometric implementation.

- Event Viewer is a utility used to log such events as unsuccessful and successful logon attempts to a system. It contains such logs as Application, System, and Security.

- Dumpster diving is especially popular today. This is the act of jumping in the garbage with the intent of retrieving valuable secrets and prizes. To protect against those pesky dumpster drivers, users should be properly educated in the art of shredding. There are also professional shredding and disposal service providers for companies and institutions with bulk shredding and disposal needs.

- One of the biggest security threats and attacks on personal information in today's electronic world is known as phishing. Phishing is a technique used by people, Web sites, e-mails, popups, and other sources to gather information such as credit card numbers, pin numbers, social security information, and pass codes. The target (fish) is usually offered something free (worm) from a perpetrator disguised to be a valid source.

DOMAIN 7.0 SAFETY AND ENVIRONMENTAL ISSUES

The exams are going to focus on concepts that include proper cleaning methods, basic maintenance, disposal procedures, and general safety and environmental concerns. It you have read this entire book and use a little common sense, you should have no problem answering questions pertaining to the objectives in this Domain.

- Compressed canned air, soft brushes, and antistatic vacuums should be used to clean dust from electronic devices and computer-related devices. Lint-free swabs and isopropyl or denatured alcohol should be used to properly clean internal components.

- Electrostatic discharge (ESD) has been mentioned in this book many times. You should note the following points regarding ESD precautions before taking any of the A+ exams:
  - Use antistatic mats.
  - Humidifiers should be used to keep humidity above 50%.
  - Never wear an ESD wrist strap while working with high-voltage monitors.
  - Computer components should be transported in an antistatic or foam bag.
  - Never wear jewelry when working with computer components.
  - Touch the computer chassis while plugging the system into an outlet.

- Uninterruptible Power Supplies (UPSs) supply power to systems and devices in the event of power outages. However, you must remember these devices are only meant to be used long enough to provide enough time to save data and properly power systems down until power is restored.

- It is important that inkjet and toner cartridges, batteries, and old CRT monitors are properly recycled or disposed of. Material Safety Data Sheets (MSDS) are used to explain the proper handling of hazardous materials and are typically displayed as warnings in hazardous areas.
- What should you do if you are at a site to do computer repairs, it is apparent that ESD is everywhere, and, you have forgotten your trusty prevention bags and tools? Answer=You should reschedule the repairs for when you have ESD prevention equipment with you.
- Missing covers such as expansion slot covers are known culprits for overheating problems with computer systems. Always replace missing covers.
- What should you do if you are at a customer site working on a system and it starts on fire? Answer=You should put the fire out with a Class C fire extinguisher. The confusing part about most fire extinguishers is that they are marked with multiple ratings such as AB, BC, or ABC. Here are the fire extinguisher ratings (purposes):

  Class A: User for paper, wood, and normal combustibles (Green warning label).

  Class B: Used for greases or flammable liquids (Red warning label).

  Class C: Used for electrical fires (Blue warning label).

  Class D: Used for flammable metals (Yellow warning label).

- Full data backups should be performed on a regular basis and placed in fireproof safes. A copy should be kept onsite as well as offsite. In the real world, soft and hard copies of both disaster recovery and contingency planning procedures are also stored with backups.
- To clean metal contacts on computer components, use an emery cloth and denatured alcohol.
- Older CRT monitors and power supplies present the most danger to computer technicians. Take care when working with these items and remember this tip for the exam. It is likely you will see it!
- Clean mice X and Y rollers with a lint-free swab.
- Spikes and surges are fluctuations in electrical power that cause damage to computers and their components. Surge suppressors are used to provide power stability to computers and handle the fluctuations.
- If customers complain that their mouse balls are dirty, you should clean their mouse balls with a damp, soapy cloth.

DOMAIN 8.0 COMMUNICATION AND PROFESSIONALISM

Okay, you can breathe now. This is the easy, commonsense Domain. The A+ Exams are going to ask you many customer-related questions. When you answer these questions, you should take your time and use common sense. Ask yourself "how would I like to be treated as a customer?" These are basically gimme questions on the tests. You should take your time with these and answer them correctly. You should study the following customer-related tips before taking the exam. It is likely you will see them again!

- Whenever you arrive at a customer site to install, repair, or upgrade anything, the first thing you should always do is notify the customer that you have arrived and are ready to begin working. This is a courtesy to the customer, and you may also receive additional information from the customer that may be helpful to you.
- When talking and dealing with customers, you need to know certain customer protocols. For example, you should refrain from using jargon, and avoid abbreviations and acronyms. You should use clarifying questions (ask pertinent questions) and maintain an open posture. Plus, you should never interrupt the customer, and you should always listen with an open mind. You will see these proper protocols on the exams!
- Use job-related behavior that is professional, and always consider the customer's privacy and confidentiality, and respect the customer's property at all times.
- Use a positive tone of voice, and avoid arguing or becoming defensive. Never be judgmental or insulting to the customer. Never minimize the customer's problems.
- Always avoid distractions or interruptions when talking with customers about their issues.
- Customers love to blame technicians for issues unrelated to the work that was done. If you are pursuing a technical career as a computer or help desk technician or network administrator, it is likely that you will run across customers that blame you for things that happen if you don't touch anything. Always remain calm in these situations, and inform the customers of the actual actions you have taken while onsite.
- Because of possible theft or allegations thereof, or any emergency for that matter, you should always make sure there is at least one adult on the premises wherever and whenever you do work. Also, if you are ever working at a customer's home and there are distracting children around you, kindly ask the customer to take the children out of the work area.
- Always focus on the task at hand. If you receive multiple trouble or service calls while you are currently working on an issue with a customer, always be attentive to them, and never make them feel less important than any other situation that may arise. If the problem calls you receive while working with a customer are critical, inform the person that you will be there as soon as possible.

■ Sometimes customers have problems explaining issues they are having. If you experience a customer that is getting frustrated trying to explain something to you, restate to the customer what you think the problem may actually be.

■ Being a good technician often requires you to handle multiple problems and customers at a time with discretion, tact, and honesty. You may find yourself working on a particular problem at a customer site, and another customer at that site asks you for help, plus you already have a complete schedule ahead of you. What do you do in this situation? Inform the customer that you have scheduled work and would be more than happy to come back another time to attend to their issues.

REFERENCES

www.comptechdoc.org/os/linux/usersguide/linux_ugbasics.html. This Comptechdoc Web site is a great place to brush up on basic Linux commands.

www.ss64.com/osx. This Web site has a fantastic A-Z Index of the command-line commands for MAC OSX.

Appendix

A About the CD-ROM

The CD-ROM included with this book contains hundreds of CertBlaster A+ practice questions for all four of the current A+ Exams. It is worth its weight in gold and in fact is as close as you can get to the real exam simulations and questions. The CD-ROM included with this book is brought to you by CertBlaster. CertBlaster is a powerful and feature-laden testing engine. It provides you with a consistent, intuitive interface that allows you test yourself in the following modes, ensuring your knowledge of the subject matter.

Assessment. In this mode you take one of the sample exams, and based on your answers CertBlaster will determine where you need to focus. In this mode you cannot change the timer, the number of questions, or receive any help or hints. CertBlaster uses this mode to create your Personal Test preparation Plan (PTP).

Certification. This mode simulates an actual exam environment. You cannot change the timer or the number of questions. At the end of the exam, CertBlaster will determine your score. Your PTP will not be updated based on the results of this exam.

Study. In this mode you work with a sample exam. You can change the timer and the number of questions asked. These settings are available by clicking the Options menu. Answer each question to the best of your ability. At the end of the exam CertBlaster will update your PTP.

Flash. In this mode you can quickly work through an exam. Clicking the spacebar highlights the correct answer to the question. You cannot change the timer or the number of questions asked.

Minimum System Requirements

- Windows 98/2000/XP
- 5 MB Hard Drive install space
- 32 MB RAM
- 32 MHZ Processor

Appendix

B Acronym Glossary

AC (alternating current) Current that changes from a positive voltage to a negative voltage during one cycle. An example is household electricity in the United States, which is 110 volts at 60 Hertz.

ACPI (Advanced Configuration and Power Interface) A power management specification that makes better use of power by letting the operating system control the power provided to peripheral devices.

ADC or A/D (Analog-to-Digital Converter) A component on a sound card that converts analog sound to a digital bit stream.

ADSL (Asymmetric Digital Subscriber Line) A newer transmission technology in the global broadband access market. ADSL supports data rates from 1.5 to 9 Mbps when receiving data (known as the downstream rate) and from 16 to 640 Kbps when sending data (known as the upstream rate). Not only is ADSL winning devout followers with its impressive speed, but also such increased data flow occurs over existing copper telephone lines (POTS). With more than half the world's broadband subscribers now using one variation of the technology or another, the long term potential for this market is basically every phone line in the world.

AGP (Accelerated Graphics Port) A 32/64-bit expansion interface available on newer PCs that supports fast 3D graphics and provides the video controller card with a dedicated path to the CPU.

AMR (Audio Modem Riser) A new architectural design for motherboards developed by Intel. This new design places the analog I/O audio functions along with a codec chip on a small board, or "riser." Separating the analog functions from the motherboard means higher audio quality and more flexibility for manufacturers in further design advancements, thus allowing them a way to sidestep the lengthy certification process of new motherboard designs.

ANSI (American National Standards Institute) A nonprofit organization whose primary purpose is to develop standards for the information technology industry.

API (Application Program Interface) A set of uniform routines or rules that allow programmers and developers to write applications that can be used to interact with various operating system platforms. APIs define system calls for service. APIs are the building blocks and tools used by programmers in building software applications.

APM (Advanced Power Management) User-level program found in all modern laptop computers and most modern desktops. Its features, which can be disabled, include system Standby and Hibernate. For best results, Microsoft recommends that you disable Advanced Power Management in the BIOS because BIOS may have settings that Windows cannot override.

ARP (Address Resolution Protocol) A TCP/IP protocol used to determine the hardware MAC address for a NIC.

ASCII (American Standard Code for Information Interchange) Specifies a 7-bit pattern that assigns numeric values to letters, numbers, punctuation marks, and certain other characters by standardizing the values used. ASCII enables communication between computers and peripherals by using numbers in place of characters.

ASR (Automated System Recovery) Backup tool in Windows XP that creates an image of your boot partition for restoration in case of failure or replacement of boot hard drive.

AT (Advanced Technology) IBM's name for its 80286 PC that was introduced in 1984. The AT Form Factor refers to the layout of the components on a motherboard.

ATA (Advanced Technology Attachment) The American National Standards Institute standard for IDE drives.

ATAPI (Advanced Technology Attachment Packet Interface) Interface standards that allow devices such as CD-ROM drives, Iomega Zip drives, and tape backup drives to use IDE/ATA controllers.

ATX (Advanced Technology Extensions) A more recent motherboard form factor that has replaced the AT form factor.

BAP (Bandwidth Allocation Protocol) Allows Multilink bandwidth capabilities. In other words, multiple lines of bandwidth can be set up for users to connect. If all the lines are not being used, certain lines can be dropped and allocated to other users.

BIOS (basic input/output system) The BIOS is software built-in to a ROM BIOS or flash BIOS chip that is used to control hardware devices such as hard drives, keyboards, monitors, and other low-level devices before a computer system boots into an operating system.

BNC (bayonet nut connector, bayonet Neil-Concelman, or British Naval Connector) A connector used to connect a computer to a coaxial cable in a 10Base2 Ethernet network.

bps (bits per second) A standard measurement of the speed at which data is transmitted; for example, a 56 Kbps modem has the ability to transmit at a rate of 56,000 bps.

BTX (Balanced Technology Extended) A form factor created by Intel to alleviate some of the heat-related problems and restraints caused by newer graphics card, processors, heat sinks, and other components.

CAD/CAM (Computer-Aided Design/Computer-Aided Manufacturing) Software designed with dual functionality not only as a designing system but also for controlling manufacturing processes.

CAT (Computerized Adaptive Testing) An efficient testing process in which a test taker's selections of subsequent questions are based on the correctness or incorrectness of the previously answered questions. Therefore, adapting the test to the test taker's ability and eliminating the possibility of too many items that are either too easy or too hard for them.

CCD (charge-coupled device) A light-sensitive circuit in a device, such as a digital camera or optical scanner, which stores and displays the color representation of a pixel in electronic format. CCD arrays are made up of CCDs whose semiconductors connect.

CD (compact disc) A round metallic disc that stores information such as text, video, and audio in digital format.

CD-R (compact disc-recordable) A type of compact disc that can be written or recorded to once but read many times.

CD-RW (compact disc read/write) A type of compact disc that can be written to several times.

CGA (Color Graphics Adapter) The first color graphics adapter for IBM PCs. CGA can only produce a resolution of 640 x 480 and two colors. CGA has been replaced by VGA for the most part.

CHAP (Challenge-Handshake Authentication Protocol) A secure method of authenticating communications between server or "agent" and a requester. CHAP uses a secret one-way hash value that is generated by the requestor and sent to the server.

CMOS (Complementary Metal-Oxide Semiconductor) Nonvolatile RAM that is used to hold hard drive, DRAM, and other necessary startup information to boot a computer system. Modern CMOS is typically stored in flash RAM.

CNR (Communication and Network Riser) A new riser card developed by Intel to meet open industry specifications. Besides its original purpose to reduce the cost of implementing LAN and modem and audio subsystems, it also has the ability to keep electrical noise interference to a minimum.

CPU (central processing unit) Also referred to as the processor, the CPU is the brain or central element of a computing system where all main calculations occur.

CRT (cathode ray tube) A vacuum tube located inside a monitor that houses beams of electrons used to illuminate phosphors and produce graphic images.

CSMA/CD (Carrier Sense Multiple Access with Collision Detection) A contention-based protocol used to detect collisions of packets in Ethernet networks. If a collision occurs, the information is retransmitted.

DAC (Digital-to-Analog Converter) A device used to convert digital information to analog signals. A DAC is typically used by a modem to prepare information for analog phone line transmission.

DAT (Digital Audio Tape) Standard medium for recording audio. DAT tape and DAT units provide a simple and easy-to-use archival system. They are portable and compact.

DC (direct current) DC is the unidirectional movement or flow of electrons. DC is necessary for most electronic computer components.

DHCP (Dynamic Host Configuration Protocol) A protocol used to dynamically assign IP addresses to computer systems in a TCP/IP network. DCHP eases administrative overhead by reducing the need to assign individual static IP addresses.

DHTML (Dynamic Hypertext Markup Language) A new form of HTML programming code that allows developers to create more interactive or responsive Web pages for users.

DIMM (Dual Inline Memory Module) A 64-bit data path memory module. In Pentium computers, one DIMM can be installed in a memory bank.

DLT (Digital Linear Tape) Used to store large amount of data at very high data-transfer rates.

DMA (Direct Memory Access) A technique used by computer devices to access and move data in and out of memory without interrupting the CPU.

DNS (domain name system) An Internet service that translates fully qualified domain names to computer IP addresses.

DOS (disk operating system) A 16-bit operating system developed by Microsoft that does not support true multitasking capabilities.

dpi (dots per inch) A measurement of image resolution. The number of dots per horizontal inch is used to calculate the dpi that a device such as a printer is able to produce.

DRAM (Dynamic Random Access Memory) A popular type of memory used to store information in a computer system. DRAM chips must be electronically refreshed continuously to hold their data.

DSL (Digital Subscriber Line) A popular high-speed technology that uses phone lines for Internet connectivity. The two most widely used forms of DSL are ADSL (Asymmetric Digital Subscriber Line) and SDSL (Symmetric Digital Subscriber Line).

DVD (Digital Versatile Disk, or Digital Video Disk) A type of CD technology developed for full-length motion pictures that can hold 4.7 GB to 17 GB of information.

DVI (Digital Visual Interface) An interface technology that maximizes the visual quality of digital displays.

EAP (Extensible Authentication Protocol) A protocol that allows the use of transport-level security; this is an encryption method for usernames and passwords.

ECC (error correction code or Error Checking and Correction) A technique used to test data for errors as it passes out of memory. If errors are found, ECC attempts to make the necessary corrections.

ECP (extended capabilities port) An IEEE 1284 bidirectional parallel port standard that offers faster transfer rates than traditional parallel port standards. ECP is most often used for communication between computer systems and printers or scanners.

EDO (Extended Data Output) A type of DRAM that has the ability to read more information before needing to be refreshed. EDO is much faster than its predecessor FPM DRAM.

EEPROM (Electrical Erasable Programmable Read-Only Memory) A type of PROM chip whose information can be changed or erased with an electronic charge. EEPROM chips were very popular before the introduction of flash ROM chips.

EFS (Encrypting File System) A feature first fully implemented with Windows 2000 that enables any file or folder to be stored in an encrypted format by making the encryption an attribute of that file or folder. Only an individual user or an authorized recovery agent can decrypt the file or folder. This feature is extremely useful for storing highly sensitive data.

EGA (Enhanced Graphics Adapter) IBM introduced EGA in 1984. The EGA standard for video adapters offers a resolution of up to 640 x 350 and supports up to 16 colors. EGA has been replaced by VGA and is for the most part obsolete.

EIDE (Enhanced IDE) An enhancement to the IDE hard drive standard that offers access to hard drives larger than 528 MB through the use of LBA support. The EIDE standard also offers support for DMA; support for up to four attached devices, including tape drives and CD devices; and support for faster hard drive access time.

EMI (electromagnetic interference) An electronic phenomenon that occurs when the signal from two or more electronic devices interferes with each other. EMI can occur when one data cable is placed too close to a second cable. If the electrical signals cross, the integrity of the information passing along the data cable may be affected.

EMS (Expanded Memory Specification) A memory management tool used to gain access to memory above the 640-KB memory limitation in an MS-DOS-based environment. Advances in the ways that Windows manages access to memory have for the most part eliminated the need for EMS.

EPP (Enhanced Parallel Port) An IEEE parallel port interface standard; also known as IEEE 1284. EPP supports bidirectional or half-duplex data transmission methods.

EPROM (Erasable Programmable Read-Only Memory) A ROM chip whose contents can be erased by shining an ultraviolet light through a hole in the top of the chip.

ESD (electrostatic discharge) The movement or transfer of electrons from one location to another. Static electricity can be transferred from the human body to an electronic component, causing damage to the components. ESD can be avoided by wearing an ESD-protective wrist strap when working with components.

FAT (file allocation table) A table consisting of clusters that are logical units of information located on a hard drive and used by the operating system to identify the location of stored entries or files.

FIFO (First-In, First-Out) A data storage method in which the oldest information is read or used first.

FPM (Fast Page Mode) A DRAM memory type that makes use of memory paging, which increases overall memory performance. Most DRAM memory types are FPM.

FPU (Floating-Point Unit) A math coprocessor that is built-in to the CPU. An FPU is designed to handle higher-end mathematical equations that assist with today's complex formulas and graphical calculations.

FRU (Field-Replaceable Unit) An interchangeable or replaceable computer part or component that can be installed at a customer site or remote business location by a computer technician.

FTP (File Transport Protocol) A transfer protocol primarily used on the Internet to transfer files from one location to another.

GB (gigabyte) A measurement of computer system data storage space; 1 GB is equal to 1024 MB, or approximately 1 million KB.

GPS (Global Positioning System) A worldwide satellite navigational system that was designed originally for the U.S. military under the name NAVSTAR (Navigation System with Timing and Ranging). Even though its utility has crossed over into the civilian sector, it is still operated by the U.S. Department of Defense. Twenty-four GPS satellites continuously transmit digital radio signals of data, such as the satellite's location and the exact time, to their corresponding earth-bound receivers. By knowing how far away a satellite is from its receiver and its location on an imaginary sphere, GPS can be used to calculate longitude, latitude, and even altitude.

GUI (Graphical User Interface) A graphical means by which a person communicates with a computer system. In the early days of computing, operating systems such as DOS used text-based interfaces. Today, operating systems such as Windows allow the user to interact with the system by means of icons, pictures, and graphical toolbars.

HAL (Hardware Abstraction Layer) Allows an operating system to interact with hardware devices at a more general, or abstract level.

HCL (Hardware Compatibility List) A document that contains a listing of all hardware compatible with a specific OS.

HDLC (High Level Data Link Control) A transmission protocol that operates at the data link layer (Level 2) of the OSI model. HDLC and SDLC (Synchronous Data Link Control) were originally developed for IBM SNA.

HDMI (High-Definition Multimedia Interface) A digital audio/video interface capable of transmitting totally uncompressed streams.

HMA (high memory area) The memory location consisting of the first 64 KB of the extended memory area. The HMA is controlled by the software driver HIMEM.SYS.

HTML (Hypertext Markup Language) A programming language that is used to create pages or hypertext documents on the World Wide Web. HTML is a scripting language that uses tags to define the way Web pages are displayed.

HTTP (Hypertext Transport Protocol) A fast Internet application protocol used for transferring data.

HTTPS (Secure HTTP) A protocol used for accessing secure Web servers and pages on the Internet. When the HTTPS protocol is used, HTTPS appears in the URL–for example, HTTPS://verysecuresite.com.

HVD (high voltage differential) A now obsolete form of "Differential" signaling that is commonly used for long runs in noisy areas. LVD (low voltage differential) is the new technology replacing HVD.

ICMP (Internet Control Message Protocol) enables systems on a TCP/IP network to share status and error information–for example, the use of PING and TRACERT utilities.

IDC (insulation displacement connector) A type of connector that displaces the insulation on a cable allowing an electrical contact between the terminal and conductor. Insulation displacement occurs as the cable is pressed into a terminal slot smaller than the conductor diameter. Insulation displacement technology has become a highly effective alternative to stripping and soldering wire in thousands of applications, with its greatest benefit being placement spread.

IDE (Intelligent or Integrated Drive Electronics) A specification for hard disk and CD-ROM drive interfaces whose drive controllers are integrated onto the drive itself. IDE provides support for up to two drives per system, whereas EIDE supports up to four drives per system. Today, the more common reference used for this technology is ATA.

IEEE (Institute of Electrical and Electronics Engineers) The world's leading international standards organization whose primary purposes are the development of information technology standards and the welfare of its members.

I/O (input/output) A term used to describe devices and programs that transfer information into and out of a computer system. Input devices can include keyboards, mice, and touch screens. Output devices can include printers, monitors, and plotters.

IP (Internet Protocol) A TCP/IP protocol used primarily to allow computers to be connected in a local area network or to the Internet.

IPSec (Internet Protocol Security) Essentially a suite of Internet security protocols that includes the ability to use encrypted keys. IPSec is widely used today and is considered one of the more secure Internet protocols.

IPX/SPX (Internetwork Packet Exchange/Sequence Packet Exchange) A Novell networking protocol used primarily with Novell Netware.

IRQ (interrupt request) A communication link to a CPU that a device uses to notify the CPU that the device needs its attention. If two devices attempt to use the same IRQ to communicate with the CPU, an IRQ conflict will most likely occur.

ISA (Industry Standard Architecture) An industry standard that describes the expansion bus architecture for the IBM AT and XT PCs. ISA expansion slots can still be found in most systems today, although they are steadily being replaced by PCI and AGP technology.

ISDN (Integrated Services Digital Network) A digital communications standard that allows data and voice to be used on the same phone line connection. ISDN provides support for up to 128 Kbps transfer rates and is intended to replace traditional analog technology.

ISP (Internet Service Provider) A company whose primary business is to provide access to the Internet for other companies and individuals.

Kbps (kilobits per second) A measurement of data transfer rate, in which 1 Kbps is equivalent to 1000 bits per second.

KB (kilobyte) 1,024 bytes.

LAN (local area network) A network of computers that are typically connected in a central location, such as a building. In a LAN, computers are connected by wires or other media and share common resources such as printers, files, and modems.

LSA (Local Security Authority) The LSA is a key component of the logon process in both Windows NT and Windows 2000. For example, in Windows 2000, the LSA validates users for both local and remote logons.

LBA (Logical Block Addressing) An enhanced BIOS translation method used for IDE and SCSI disk drives that allows accessibility beyond the 504 MB limit imposed by traditional IDE. LBA is a way of addressing hard drives by assigning numbers to each sector on the drive. These numbers run sequentially with 0 representing the first sector. Originally used with SCSI drives, IDE drives began to support LBA with the advent of larger (over 504 MB) IDE drives. Basically, it is a translation of the cylinder, head, and sector specifications of a drive into addresses that can be used by a "translating" BIOS.

LCD (liquid crystal display) A technology for flat screen displays that uses polarized sheets and liquid crystals to produce images. LCD technology was originally used for laptop computers and watches but is becoming very popular for desktop computers.

LED (Light-Emitting Diode) A highly efficient, long-lasting light that illuminates when electrical current passes through it. Most LEDs are usually a monochromatic red. Benefits of LEDs include ability to display images, low power requirements, long life, and high efficiency. However, they require more power than LCDs.

L2TP (Layer Two Tunneling Protocol) A protocol that creates a tunnel through a public network and provides a secure connection by providing authentication on both ends of the tunnel. The IPSec protocol is used with L2TP to provide data encryption as it passes through the tunnel.

LVD (low voltage differential) An Ultra2 subset of the SCSI-3 standard. LVD increases the maximum burst transfer rates to 80 MBps, which is a requirement for multiple drive applications. Such increases in bandwidth means optimal performance for server environments where rapid response is required. Uses less power (3.3V DC) than high voltage differentials (5.0V DC).

MAN (Metropolitan Area Network) A network that is smaller than a WAN but larger than a LAN. It is usually confined to a city block or a college campus.

MAPI (Messaging Application Programming Interface) A Microsoft API that provides the ability to send e-mail and attachments from within programs such as Word, Excel, PowerPoint, and Access.

MAU (Multistation Access Unit) A special hub used in a Token Ring network that is used to connect computers for a star topology network while maintaining Token Ring capabilities. Also known as MSAU.

MB (megabyte) 1,024 kilobytes or 1,048,576 bytes.

MBR (Master Boot Record) A small program that is executed when a system first boots up. The MBR is located on the first sector of a hard drive.

MCA (Micro Channel Architecture) A proprietary 32-bit expansion bus developed by IBM for its PS/2 computers.

MDA (Monochrome Display Adapter) A standard for monochrome adapters introduced by IBM. Monochrome is only capable of displaying text.

MDDR (Mobile DDR SDRAM) Memory used in mobile devices such as PDAs, cell phones, and music players.

MicroDIMM (Micro Dual Inline Memory Module) Commonly used in subnotebook computers. Each 144-pin MicroDIMM provides a 64-bit data path, so they are installed singly in 64-bit systems.

MIDI (Musical Instrument Digital Interface) A standard or protocol used for the interface between a musical instrument or device and a computer system. Used for digital synthesizers for playing and manipulating sound.

MMC (Microsoft Management Console) Management application that draws upon a GUI and a programming framework to allow the creation and saving of consoles. MMC is particularly important because consoles are used to manage Windows-based software and hardware.

MMX (Multimedia Extensions) A multimedia technology developed by Intel to improve the performance of its Pentium microprocessor. MMX technology included 57 new processor instructions and is said to improve multimedia application performance up to 60%.

Modem (modulator-demodulator) A communication device used to convert signals so they can be transmitted over conventional telephone lines. A modem converts incoming analog signals to digital format and outgoing digital signals to analog format.

MPEG (Motion Picture Experts Group) A standards group that works with the ISO to establish rules and standards for audio and video compression. MPEG technology is used to make high-quality compressed files.

MSDS (Material Safety Data Sheet) Designed to provide employers, employees, and EMS personnel with the proper procedures for various substances and chemicals. The data sheet is broken down into 10 sections: General Information; Ingredients; Physical Data; Fire and Explosion Data; Health Hazard Data; Reactivity Data; Spill, Leak, and Special Disposal Features; Special Protection Information; Special Precautions; and Transportation Data. Access to MSDSs include work place laboratories, universities, the product's distributor, and online.

MSCDEX (Microsoft CD-ROM Extensions) A software driver used in Windows 3.x and DOS to allow the operating systems to communicate with CD-ROM devices. The actual file that contains the driver is called MSCDEX.EXE. More efficient 32-bit CD-ROM drivers, such as CDFS, have replaced MSCDEX.EXE.

MFD (Multifunction Device) Any device that is capable of multiple functions. For example, with printers, you can have a laser (or inkjet) printer capable of all the following: print/copy/scan/fax.

NetBEUI (NetBIOS Extended User Interface) An extended, or enhanced, version of the NetBIOS protocol.

NetBIOS (Network Basic Input Output System) An API protocol that expands the utility of the DOS BIOS by adding special functions for LANs. The message format (SMB) provides the foundation for NetBIOS.

NIC (network interface card) An electronic circuit board that attaches a computer to a network. A NIC is installed inside a computer system. It connects to a wire that typically leads to a networked hub, router, or bridge.

NLX (InteLex Form Factor) A computer motherboard form factor designed to provide more room for components than the LPX form factor.

NNTP (Network News Transfer Protocol) A protocol used to mange messages that are posted to Usenet newsgroups.

NTFS (NT File System) A Windows NT hard drive filesystem that offers file- and object-level security features, file compression, encryption, and long filename (LFN) support. A new version of the NTFS filesystem called NTFS5 is offered with the Windows 2000 operating system.

OEM (original equipment manufacturer) An OEM version of software, such as Windows 95, that is designed to be packaged and distributed by a specific manufacturer on specific computers.

OLE (object linking and embedding) A specification created by Microsoft that allows objects created in one program or application to be embedded or linked to other applications. With OLE, if a change is made to an application, the change is also made to the second application.

OSI (Open Systems Interconnect) The OSI reference model is a networking model developed to provide network designers and developers with a model that describes how network communication takes place.

PAP (Password Authentication Protocol) A basic type of authentication where a username and password are transmitted unencrypted across a network to an authenticating host.

PCI (peripheral component interconnect) A 32- to 64-bit expansion bus created by Intel and used in most modern computers. Today, most NICs, sound cards, and modems are connected to a motherboard through a PCI expansion bus.

PCI-e (PCI-Express) A serial computer expansion card interface that is a much faster technology intended to replace slower PCI, PCI-X, and AGP interfaces. PCI-e uses serial links called lanes.

PCI special interest group (SIG) Originally formed as the Peripheral Component Interconnect Special Interest Group, PCI SIG is the industry organization chartered with the development and management of the PCI bus specification, the industry standard for a high-performance I/O interconnect to transfer data between a CPU and its peripherals. Founded in 1992, PCI SIG stands at the forefront of its field and can tout an active membership base of 850 industry-leading companies. To reach PCI SIG, visit them online at *www.pcisig.com*.

PCMCIA (Personal Computer Memory Card Industry Association) A group of companies that are responsible for the specifications that apply to small expansion cards used in laptop computers. There are three main types of PCMCIA cards. Type I is used mainly for RAM, Type II is used for modems, and Type III is used for hard disks.

PDA (personal data assistant) A small handheld mobile computing device that provides functions similar to a desktop or laptop computer. Most PDAs today use a pen or stylus in place of a keyboard to input data.

PDF (Portable Document Format) A file format developed by Adobe Systems. PDF captures all the formatted elements of a printed document from a multitude of desktop publishing applications into an electronic image. Therefore, making it easier and possible to view, print, and send the formatted document to others. To create, view, and use the files, you need the free Acrobat Reader. PDF files are most beneficial when needing to maintain the on-line graphic appearance, quality, and clarity of documents, such as brochures, maps, and magazines.

PIF (Program Information File) A file that is used to provide settings for 16-bit DOS applications. A PIF file has a .PIF extension and stores information such as window size and memory that should be allocated to an application or program.

PnP (plug and play) A technology introduced in Windows 95 that has the ability to autodetect devices that are attached to a computer system. For a system to be fully PnP compliant, there must be a PnP operating system, a PnP BIOS, and PnP devices.

POP3 (Post Office Protocol) A protocol used to receive e-mails. A mail server holds all mail until the requestor or user is ready to receive it.

POST (power-on self-test) A program that tests computer components, such as RAM, disk drives, and peripherals, at system startup. If the POST finds a problem during its diagnostic testing, it usually reports a numeric error to the screen or sounds a series of beep error codes.

POTS (Plain Old Telephone Service) Also known as the public-switched telephone network (PSTN). Most homes have this telephone service. This standard service is in comparison to high-speed, digital services such as ISDN. Speed and bandwidth are the criteria that differentiate between POTS and non-POTS services. Generally, the standard speed for POTS is limited to about 52 Kbps.

PPP (Point-to-Point Protocol) A full-duplex serial communication protocol that operates at the data link layers of the OSI reference model.

PROM (programmable read-only memory) A ROM chip that can be written to once.

RAID (Redundant Array of Independent [or Inexpensive] Disks) A way of storing the same data in different places on a category of disk drives that employ two or more drives. This allows for a combination of increased fault tolerance and improved performance. RAID disk drives are more frequently used on servers rather than PCs. There are a number of different RAID levels, with the three most common being RAID-0, RAID-3, and RAID-5.

RAM (random access memory) A computer system's main memory storage location. Information held in RAM can be quickly accessed by the computer's CPU without the need to read the data preceding the required information.

RAMDAC (random access memory digital-to-analog converter) A chip on a video card that converts binary digital data into analog information that can be output to a computer monitor.

RDRAM (Rambus dynamic random access memory) A type of fast DRAM memory developed for today's Pentium computers by Rambus, Inc..

RGB (red, green, and blue) The three primary colors of light that are used in PC monitors. A color monitor has three electron guns. Each of the electron guns represents one of the three primary colors of light to produce a final color image to the computer screen.

ROM (read-only memory) A computer chip whose information cannot be deleted or erased but can be read by the system many times. ROM is nonvolatile memory that holds the system BIOS.

SAM (Security Accounts Manager) A built-in Windows NT and 2000 component that is used to manage the security of user accounts.

SAT (security access token) A security token that allows users access to resources in a Windows environment. A token carries access rights that are associated with a user's account.

SCSI (Small Computer System Interface) A standard that applies to fast electronic hardware interfaces in computer systems. SCSI technology can be used to allow up to 15 devices to be daisy-chained together. SCSI is most commonly used to connect hard drives, CD-ROM devices, scanners, and printers to computer systems.

SDLC (Synchronous Data Link Control) The original IBM-developed communications protocol from which HDLC is based. SDLC is based on a primary/secondary communications model where a secure connection is established between a mainframe (host) and a client.

SDRAM (Synchronous Dynamic Random Access Memory) A type of DRAM that synchronizes itself with the internal clock speed of the computer's processor.

SE (Single Ended) One of two kinds of parallel SCSI technology, the second kind being differential ended. Single-ended SCSI was the original technology used and has shorter distances than its counterpart. They are incompatible, although converters can bridge single-ended to differential. Can also be used to refer to the physical signal circuitry used on the SCSI bus.

SEC (single edge connector) Intel's chip package design that uses a circuit board with a single edge connector. A processor and memory cache are integrated onto the circuit board and inserted into the computer system's motherboard.

SEP (single edge processor) A processor chip package design similar to SEC.

Serial ATA (SATA) A completely new standard based on serial signaling technology, which will eventually make PCs even smaller and more efficient. Serial ATA only requires 7 wires per device (as compared to 40 wires for IDE ribbon cables), and its cables are capable of lengths of 1 meter (as compared to 40 cm. for IDE). SATA will eventually render the old IDE ribbon cables obsolete, resulting in an industry-wide move over to new hard drives, controllers, and connectors.

SGRAM (Synchronous Graphic Random Access Memory) A single-ported type of video RAM that is synchronized with the CPU's clock to achieve high speeds.

SID (security identifier) A unique security number that is associated with users, groups, and accounts in Windows NT or Windows 2000 networks. Access to processes that run in Windows NT or Windows 2000 require this unique SID and a token.

SIMM (Single Inline Memory Module) A type of circuit board on which DRAM chips are mounted. The circuit board is inserted into the motherboard. A SIMM module has a 32-bit-wide data bus.

SLIP (Serial Line Internet Protocol) An older TCP/IP communications protocol used to connect two computer systems together. SLIP was and sometimes is still used to connect systems to the Internet through a slow analog dial-up connection.

SMART (Self Monitoring Analysis and Report Technology) An example of a computer's start-up program or BIOS and the computer's hard disk proactively working together. If enabled during computer set-up, it has the ability to automatically monitor a disk drive's health and report potential problems. The BIOS receives analytical information from the hard drive and determines whether to send the user a warning message about possible future failure of the hard drive.

SMB (Server Message Block) A protocol used by DOS and Windows for sharing files, directories, serial ports, printers, and other devices. SMB works in a client/server, request-response format. Such servers make file systems and other resources available to clients over a network. SMB can be used over TCP/IP, NetBEUI, and IPX/SPX.

SODIMM (Small-Outline Dual Inline Memory Module) Commonly used in laptop computers because of their thinner profiles than DIMMS.

SQL (Structured Query Language) A programming language used to gather or query information from various computer databases. IBM developed SQL in 1974.

SRAM (Synchronous Random Access Memory) A fast type of memory that does not have to be refreshed over and over to maintain its contents. SRAM is faster than DRAM and is used mostly for cache memory in computer systems. Also referred to as *static RAM*.

RPC (Secure Remote Procedure Call) A protocol that is used to allow a client-side application program to execute or request a service from a server computer without being concerned with network intricacies or server procedures.

SSH (Secure Shell) A Unix-based strong authentication method used to allow administrators to securely access and control remote systems. SSH is actually a suite of newer Unix protocols and utilities, including ssh, scp, and slogin that replace the older Unix rcp, rsh, and rlogin utilities.

SSID (service set identifier) A code used in Wi-Fi wireless networks that is attached to all packets on the network identifying each packet as part of that wireless network.

STP (Shielded Twisted Pair) A type of copper cabling used in networks in which pairs of wires are twisted around one another to extend the length that a signal can travel on the cable and reduce the interference of signals traveling on the cable.

SVGA (Super Video Graphics Array) A video display standard that applies to any resolution or color depth higher than the VGA standard of 640 x 480 and 16 colors.

TB (terabyte) 1024 gigabytes, approximately 1 million megabytes, or 1,099,551,627,776 bytes.

TCP/IP (Transmission Control Protocol/Internet Protocol) The primary set of protocols used by the Internet and most networks. TCP/IP allows different networks and computers to communicate with one another.

TSR (terminate-and-stay-resident program) A program that remains resident in computer memory and can be run repeatedly without having to be reloaded into memory. Most TSR programs are loaded into memory by the DOS file AUTOEXEC.BAT. DOSKEY is a TSR program.

UART (Universal Asynchronous Receiver/Transmitter) A chip that converts data from serial information to parallel information and vice versa. UARTs are used for equipment or devices that are attached to serial ports.

UMA (upper memory area) The first 640 KB to 1024 KB of memory addresses reserved for device drivers and system use.

UMB (upper memory block) A reserved memory block in the UMA used to load device drivers and TSR programs.

UPS (uninterruptible power supply) Provides a continuous supply of power to a computer system when a primary power source fails. A UPS can also protect a system from power sags.

URL (uniform resource locator) A URL is an address that points to a resource or another URL located on the World Wide Web. An example of a URL is *http://www.charlesriver. com.*

USB (universal serial bus) An interface standard that supports up to 127 devices using one system resource (IRQ). With USB, PnP peripheral devices can be attached to a computer system while the power is on and the operating system is up and running.

UTP (Unshielded Twisted Pair) A common type of twisted-pair cable used in most networks. There are five categories of UTP that support different data transmission speeds. Unlike STP, UTP does not have a protective shielding.

VGA (Video Graphics Array) A display standard for video adapters developed by IBM. VGA replaced CGA and EGA standards and supports a resolution of 640 x 480 at 16 colors.

VL-Bus (VESA local bus) A 32-bit expansion bus that has been replaced by PCI expansion bus technology.

VoIP (Voice over Internet Protocol) A technology that uses special protocols and IP-based networks to route voice conversations over the Internet.

VPN (virtual private network) A way to provide secure network access to the individual users and remote offices of an organization without the excessive expenses associated with owning or leasing the lines. This is done, via the Internet, by using a shared public infrastructure and tunneling. Additional security features can be used to enhance privacy.

VRAM (Video Random Access Memory) A special type of dual-ported memory that is used in video adapters to produce graphic images to a computer monitor.

VRM (Voltage Regulator Module) A small, replaceable module that is installed on the motherboard to sense the microprocessor's voltage requirements and regulate the voltage fed to the microprocessor. Nearly all motherboards have either a built-in voltage regulator or VRM. Therefore, if the computer's microprocessor is changed, a VRM may need to be added to the existing voltage regulator to keep consistent with the voltage requirements of the new microprocessor.

VxD (Virtual Device Driver) A 32-bit device driver used in Windows. Virtual device drivers have a .VXD extension.

WAN (wide area network) A WAN is typically made up of two or more LANs linked together to form a larger network. WANs are usually spread over large areas. The Internet is a WAN.

WHQL (Windows Hardware Quality Labs) Refers to driver qualification with regards to the Windows Hardware Assurance team.

Wi-Fi A wireless technology based on the IEEE 802.11 standards that is used for Internet and VoIP phones, games, and connectivity for televisions, DVD players, and digital cameras.

WINS (Windows Internet Naming Service) A Windows networking service that provides a computer NetBIOS name to IP address resolution.

WLAN (wireless local area network) A type of LAN that allows a user to connect/communicate between nodes by using high-frequency radio waves (wireless connection). WLAN adapter cards have been created for use with laptop computers.

WPAN (Wireless Personal Area Network) is a computer network used mainly for one or a small number of people to communicate using wireless technology, computers, telephones, and PDAs.

WRAM (Windows Random Access Memory) A very fast type of dual-ported video memory that has the ability to read and write larger sections of memory than VRAM.

WUXGA (Widescreen Ultra eXtended Graphics Array) This has a display resolution of 1920 × 1200 pixels with a 16:10 screen aspect ratio. WUXGA is a widescreen version of UXGA. It is compatible with HDTV, which uses a 1920 × 1080 image at a 16:9 ratio.

XGA (eXtended Graphics Array) A video display standard developed by IBM that has the ability to support a resolution of 1024 × 768. XGA can also support up to 65,536 colors.

XMS (eXtended Memory Specification) The first 64 KB of memory located above 1 MB.

ZIF (zero insertion force) A lever-socket combination used to pull a CPU away or up from the motherboard's data bus. ZIF sockets were used for the early Pentium processors.

Index